FORECASTING
METHODS AND APPLICATIONS

THE WILEY/HAMILTON SERIES IN MANAGEMENT AND ADMINISTRATION
Elwood S. Buffa, Advisory Editor   University of California, Los Angeles

FORECASTING
METHODS AND APPLICATIONS

SPYROS MAKRIDAKIS

European Institute of Business Administration (INSEAD)

STEVEN C. WHEELWRIGHT

Harvard Business School

JOHN WILEY & SONS
New York • Chichester • Brisbane • Toronto

This book was copyedited by Carolyn Geiger,
designed by Bruce Kortebein and set in 10 point
Times Roman by Typesetting Services, Ltd. The
illustrations were prepared by Etc. Graphics and
printing and binding were done by Fairfield
Graphics. Jean Varven supervised production.

Library of Congress Cataloging in Publication Data

Makridakis, Spyros G.
    Forecasting.

    (The Wiley/Hamilton series in management and
administration)
    "A Wiley/Hamilton publication."
    Includes bibliographies.
    1. Forecasting   I. Wheelwright, Steven C.,
1943–   joint author   II. Title.
HD30.27.M34   338.5'442   77-18806
ISBN 0-471-93770-3

Printed in the United States of America

10 9 8 7 6 5 4 3

DEDICATED TO OUR FATHERS

TM

AND

MW

About The Authors

SPYROS MAKRIDAKIS

Spyros Makridakis is currently Professor of Management Science at INSEAD, the European Institute of Business Administration. He received his MBA and Ph.D degrees from New York University Graduate School of Business Administration. He has been a consultant to many organizations and has held teaching or research positions with several European and American institutions. He was an ICAME fellow at Stanford and a visiting scholar at Massachusetts Institute of Technology and Harvard University. He regularly contributes articles to professional journals and his work has appeared in several books on forecasting.

STEVEN C. WHEELWRIGHT

Steven C. Wheelwright received his degree in Mathematics from the University of Utah (*magna cum laude*) and an MBA and Ph.D from the Graduate School of Business, Stanford University. As part of his current assignment at the Harvard Business School he has responsibility for the required first-year MBA course in Production and Operations Management and for a two-week Summer Executive Program, Manufacturing in Corporate Strategy.

He has taught in executive programs for U.S. Steel, Western Electronics Manufacturing Association, Boise Cascade, and Corn Products. He is active in consultant work with particular emphasis on the application of computers and management science techniques to business strategy and operating problems.

He has written numerous cases and articles dealing with corporate strategy, forecasting, and production planning. He is also the co-author with Spyros Makridakis of *Computer-aided Modeling for Managers. Forecasting Methods for Management, and Interactive Forecasting*.

PREFACE

The past four decades have witnessed a number of developments in estimation and prediction that have direct relevance and applicability in organizational forecasting. These advances in both theory and practice have been necessitated by the increasing complexity, competitiveness, and rates of change in the environment. Organizations of all sizes find it essential to make future forecasts aimed at reducing the uncertainty of the environment and taking full advantage of the opportunities available to the organization. As with the development of most management science techniques, the *application* of forecasting methodologies has lagged behind their theoretical formulation and verification. Although many managers and students are aware of the need for improved forecasting, few are familiar with the full range of existing techniques and their characteristics and few have the knowledge required to select and successfully apply the most appropriate methods in a specific situation.

The forecasting literature is only now beginning to focus on translating what is theoretically possible and computationally feasible into a form that can be easily understood and applied. There are several excellent books and a plethora of research articles on forecasting, but these have generally been written by the specialists who have performed the theoretical formulation and verification of specific techniques and who are seeking to convey state-of-the-art knowledge to a group of specialists. For example, the works of Brown and of Box and Jenkins do a superb job in developing and proving the statistical properties of specific classes of forecasting methods but provide little information on the full range of techniques and the selection of an appropriate forecasting method in practice. Consequently, the person seeking to understand the alternatives available must first be a mathematical expert and, second, read not a single book but several books, each describing only a single method or a narrow class of methods for forecasting. In addition, the literature describing these individual methods is generally more concerned with their theoretical development and verification than with their practical application. Most users of forecasting are not directly concerned with these theoretical aspects (there are experts in the academic world who can examine each method's validity), and they do not have the time or inclination to study in depth the theoretical development of each alternative forecasting method.

We have found that what is needed is a book that covers the full range of forecasting methods, is accurate and complete in describing their essential characteristics and the steps for their application in practice, and does not get bogged down in theoretical questions underlying their development. The aim of this book is to begin to fill this gap by presenting in terms that are easily understandable (but that accurately and rigorously describe the techniques) a wide range of forecasting methods useful to students and practitioners of management, economics, engineering, and other disciplines requiring forecasting. This material has proved to be very effective when we have used it in seminars for middle management, in classes taught for both graduate and undergraduate levels of business education, and in specialist courses for statisticians, economists, and management scientists. It is our hope that in book form this material will be of much more general use to the management and educational communities.

Four objectives have motivated the structuring and development of sections of this book:

1. To describe the *essential aspects* of a wide range of forecasting methods with sufficient detail and clarity that they can be easily applied.
2. To make the presentation of alternative forecasting methods in such a form that a *minimum of technical background* is required to understand each technique, but to include the essential concepts of the theoretical basis of each methodology.
3. To provide information concerning the *cost and performance characteristics* associated with each of the major forecasting methodologies so that criteria for selecting the most appropriate method can be developed and applied.
4. To examine the important factors relating to the application of forecasting and planning and the effective *use of forecasting resources in an ongoing organization.*

It should be emphasized that while the body of each chapter is geared to the reader with only a basic background in algebra, the aim has still been to present a complete description of each technique and those factors that are relevant in deciding where and how to use it. Because we have sought to be complete in our coverage of the basic forecasting methodologies and their most commonly used variations, the reader may want to concentrate on the first few sections of some of the chapters on methodologies, then skim the final sections that deal with variations in those methodologies. The segments on variations can serve as a reference for specific applications at a later date or as material for additional study, once the basic methodologies have been examined and applied.

The book is divided into six parts. Part One contains two introductory chapters, the first providing a conceptual framework for existing methodologies and the tasks for which they can be used. Chapter 2 gives an overview of the quantitative computations and measures commonly used in forecasting and provides a basic quantitative foundation for the remainder of the book.

Parts Two, Three, and Four focus on quantitative techniques of forecasting. In Chapters 3 and 4, those methods commonly referred to as smoothing and decomposition approaches to time-series analysis are examined. The causal regression methods—simple regression, multiple regression, and econometric models—are discussed in Chapters 5 through 7. Next, the general purpose, autoregressive/moving average (ARMA) time-series methods are described in Chapters 8 through 11. These ARMA methods include generalized adaptive filtering, the Box-Jenkins methodology, and multivariate time-series analysis (transfer functions).

Part Five describes several more qualitative approaches to forecasting. Chapters 12 and 13 deal with predicting cycles (turning points) and obtaining subjective forecasts. Chapter 14 presents a summary of the most commonly used exploratory and normative approaches of technological forecasting.

Finally, Part Six deals with the organizational and management tasks of integrating forecasting and planning. Chapter 15 describes elements of a conceptual framework that can be used to integrate the forecasting function into existing planning and staff functions. Examples illustrate the use of that framework. In Chapter 16 the approaches most commonly suggested for comparing and evaluating forecasting methods are described, and a framework that we have found to be particularly useful is summarized. Chapter 17 deals with acquiring data and handling many of the "housekeeping" tasks associated with an effective forecasting organization. Finally, Chapter 18 describes empirical work on the implementation of forecasting in organizations during the 1970s and suggests approaches that can overcome many of the organizational and behavioral problems commonly surrounding forecasting applications.

Three appendices present additional material of use to more managers and forecasters. Appendix I contains statistical tables for the various tests of significance used in evaluating those quantitative forecasting methodologies for which statistics have been developed. Appendix II is a glossary of forecasting terms covering the techniques, concepts, and tools that are the essential components of forecasting. This glossary can serve as a dictionary and reference for terms that may be new to the reader or whose meaning is unclear. Appendix III provides a list of data sources that are often helpful in obtaining information on an organization's external environment. That is frequently a required preliminary step in forecasting.

As an additional aid to both the teaching and practice of forecasting, we have developed an interactive forecasting system for use on a time-shared computer. This system is referred to as SIBYL/RUNNER. This comprehensive set of computer programs covers the full range of quantitative forecasting methods described in Chapters 3 through 11 and facilitates their application in a timely and straightforward manner in a given situation. The programs are available on nationwide time-sharing services or can be obtained for commercial or educational use in either FORTRAN or BASIC from Applied Decision Systems, 15 Walnut Street, Wellesley Hills, Massachusetts 02181.

SPYROS MAKRIDAKIS
Fontainbleau, France

STEVEN C. WHEELWRIGHT
Boston, Massachusetts

January, 1978

CONTENTS

FORECASTING
METHODS AND APPLICATIONS

PART ONE
BACKGROUND AND PERSPECTIVE

Part One has two main purposes: first, to relate forecasting theory and technical knowledge to the practical problems of planning and decision making. Thus, in Chapter 1, a number of the basic concepts about the practice of forecasting and its value to managers and administrators are reviewed. While many of these topics will be picked up in later chapters in more detail, the aim in Chapter 1 is to provide an overview and rationale of elements the practical user of forecasting must understand and some of the considerations that are situation-specific rather than methodology-specific.

The second purpose of Part One is to present an overview of those concepts that will be used as building blocks in examining and presenting several different forecasting methodologies. Thus, Chapter 2 is somewhat technique oriented and strives to identify those concepts that relate to many different forecasting methodologies and that provide the vocabulary and basis for understanding a wide range of forecasting techniques.

1 INTRODUCTION

1/1 Needs and Uses of Forecasting

FREQUENTLY THERE IS a time lag between awareness of an impending event or need and occurrence of that event. This lead time is the main reason for planning and forecasting. If the lead time is zero or very small, there is no need for planning. If the lead time is long, and the outcome of the final event conditional upon identifiable factors, planning can perform an important role. In such situations forecasting is needed to determine when an event will occur or a need arise, so that appropriate actions can be taken.

In management and administrative situations the need for planning is great because the lead time for decision making ranges from several years (for the case of capital investments) to a few days or even a few hours (for transportation or production schedules). Forecasting is an important aid in effective and efficient planning.

The layman often questions the validity and efficacy of a discipline aimed at predicting the future because he fails to recognize the progress that has been made in forecasting over the past several centuries. There are a large number of phenomena whose outcomes can now be predicted easily. The sunrise can be predicted, as can the speed of a falling object, the onset of hunger, thirst or fatigue, rainy weather, and a myriad of other events. However, that was not always the case.

The evolution of science has increased the understanding of various aspects of the environment and consequently the predictability of many events. For example when the Ptolemaic system of astronomy was developed almost nineteen hundred years ago, it could predict the movement of any star with an accuracy unheard of before that time. Even then, however, systematic errors were common. Then came the emergence of Copernican astronomy, which was much more accurate than its Ptolemaic predecessor and could predict the movement of the stars to within hundredths of a second. Today, modern astronomy is far more accurate than Copernican astronomy. The same increase in accuracy is shown in the theory of motion, which Aristotle, Galileo, Newton, and Einstein each improved.

The ability to predict many types of events seems as natural today as will the accurate forecasting of weather conditions in a few decades. The trend in being able to accurately predict more events, particularly those of an economic nature, will continue providing a better base from which to plan. Formal forecasting methods are the means by which this improvement will occur.

A large number of forecasting methods are available to management today (Chambers et al. 1971; Wheelwright and Makridakis 1977). These range from the most naive methods such as use of the most recent observation as a forecast to highly complex approaches such as econometric systems of simultaneous equations. The widespread introduction of computers has made programs readily available for all quantitative forecasting techniques. Complementing such software and hardware achievements has been the development of data describing the state of economic events (GNP, consumption, etc.) and natural phenomena (temperature, rainfall, etc.). These data in conjunction with organizational statistics (sales, prices, advertising, etc.) and technological know-how provide the base of past information needed for quantitative and technological methods of forecasting.

Forecasting is an integral part of the decision-making activities of management. An organization establishes goals and objectives, seeks to predict environmental factors, then selects actions that it hopes will result in attainment of the goals and objectives. The need for forecasting is increasing as management attempts to decrease its dependence on chance and becomes more scientific in dealing with its environment. Since each area of an organization is related to all others, a good or bad forecast can affect the entire organization. Some of the areas in which forecasting currently plays an important role are:

1. *Scheduling existing resources.* In order to make efficient use of resources, scheduling of production, transportation, cash, personnel, and so on, must be done before the actual level of demand for product, material, financing, or services is known.
2. *Acquiring additional resources.* The lead time for acquiring raw materials, hiring new personnel, or buying machinery and equipment can vary from a few days to several years. Forecasting is required to determine what future resource requirements will be.
3. *Determining what resources are desired.* All organizations must determine what resource they want to have in the long term. Such decisions depend on market opportunities, environmental factors, and the internal development of financial, human, product, and technological resources. These determinations all require good forecasts and managers who can interpret the predictions and make appropriate decisions.

Although there are many different areas requiring forecasts, the above three categories are typical of the short-, medium-, and long-term forecasting requirements of today's organizations. This range of needs requires that a company develop multiple approaches to predicting uncertain events and build up a system for forecasting.

A forecasting system must establish a mutual relationship among forecasts made by different management areas. There is a high degree of interdependence among the forecasts of various divisions or departments, which cannot be ignored if forecasting is to be successful. For example, errors in sales projections can trigger a series of reactions affecting budget forecasts, operating expenses, cash flows, inventory levels, pricing, etc. Similarly, budgeting errors in projecting the amount of money available to each division will affect product development, modernization of equipment, hiring of personnel, and advertising expenditures. This, in turn, will influence, if not determine, the level of sales, operating costs, and cash flows. Clearly there is a strong interdependence among the different forecasting areas in an organization.

In simplified terms, the interrelationships of sales and other forecasting areas in a business can be summarized schematically as shown in Figure 1-1.

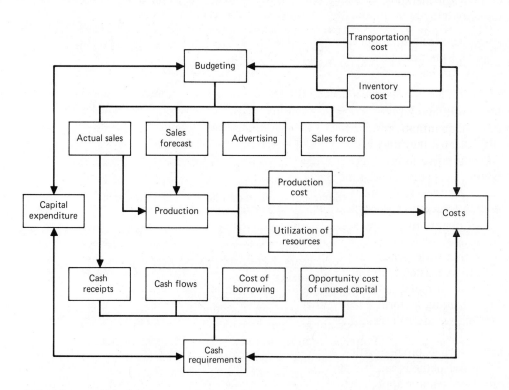

FIGURE 1-1 RELATED ELEMENTS IN AN ORGANIZATION'S FORECASTING SYSTEM

A major aim of this book is not only to examine the techniques available for meeting an organization's forecasting requirements but to consider the inter-dependence of needs in areas such as purchasing, production, marketing, finance, and general management. The final chapters focus on these interdependencies and the organizational steps that are most likely to lead to the development of a successful forecasting system.

1/2 Current Status of Quantitative and Technological Forecasting

The range of situations in which forecasts are required vary widely in time horizons, factors determining actual outcomes, types of data patterns and many other respects. To deal with such diverse applications, several techniques have been developed. These fall into two major categories—quantitative, and qualitative or technological methods. Quantitative forecasting can be applied when three conditions exist:

1. There is information about the past.
2. This information can be quantified in the form of data.
3. It can be assumed that the pattern of the past will continue into the future.

This last condition is known as the *assumption of constancy* and it is an underlying premise of all quantitative and many technological forecasting methods, no matter how sophisticated they may be.

Quantitative forecasting techniques vary considerably, having been de-veloped by diverse disciplines for different purposes. Each has its own properties, accuracies, and costs that must be considered in choosing a specific method. Quantitative forecasting procedures fall into two types: naive or intuitive methods, and formal quantitative methods based on statistical principles. The first type uses horizontal, seasonal, or trend extrapolation and is based on empirical experience that varies widely from business to business, product to product, and forecaster to forecaster. Naive methods are simple and easy to use but not always as accurate as formal quantitative methods. Because of this limitation their use has been declining as formal methods have gained in popularity. Nevertheless, many businesses are still using them, either because they are not aware of other simpler methods, or because they prefer to use more subjective approaches to forecasting such as predicting this year's sales as last year's plus, say 6%.

Formal methods can also involve extrapolation, but it is done in a standard way using a systematic approach that attempts to minimize the forecasting errors. There are several formal methods that are inexpensive and easy to use that can be applied in a mechanical manner. These methods are useful when forecasts are needed for a large number of items and when forecasting errors on a single item will not be extremely costly.

Persons unfamiliar with quantitative forecasting methods often think that the past cannot describe the future accurately because everything is constantly changing. After some familiarity with data and forecasting techniques, however, it becomes clear that although nothing remains the same, history does repeat itself in a sense. Application of the right method can often identify the relationship between the factor to be forecasted and time itself (or several other factors), thus making accurate forecasting possible.

An alternative scheme for classifying quantitative forecasting methods is to consider the underlying model involved rather than the level of statistical theory supporting each method. There are two major types of forecasting models: time-series and regression (causal) models. In the first type, prediction of the future is based on past values of a variable and/or past errors. The objective of such time-series forecasting methods is to discover the pattern in the historical data series and extrapolate that pattern into the future.

Causal models on the other hand assume that the factor to be forecasted exhibits a cause-effect relationship with one or more independent variables. For example, sales $= f$ (income, prices, advertising, competition, etc.). The purpose of the causal model is to discover the form of that relationship and use it to forecast future values of the dependent variable.

Both time-series and causal models have advantages in certain situations. Time-series models can often be used more easily to forecast, whereas causal models can be used with greater success for policy and decision making. Whenever the necessary data are available, a forecasting relationship can be hypothesized, either as a function of time or as a function of independent variables, and tested.

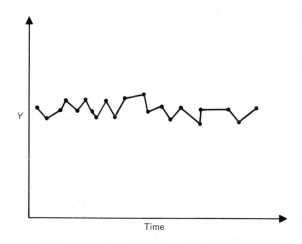

FIGURE 1-2 HORIZONTAL DATA PATTERN

An important step in selecting an appropriate time-series method is to consider the types of data patterns, so that the methods most appropriate to those patterns can be tested. Four types of data patterns can be distinguished: horizontal (or stationary), seasonal, cyclical, and trend.

1. A *horizontal* (H) pattern exists when data values fluctuate around a constant mean. (Such a series is "stationary" in its mean.) A product whose sales do not increase or decrease over time would be of this type. Similarly, a quality control situation involving sampling from a continuous production process that theoretically does not change would also be of this type. Figure 1-2 shows a typical pattern of such horizontal or stationary data.

2. A *seasonal* (S) pattern exists when a series is influenced by seasonal factors (e.g., the quarter of the year, the month, or day of the week). Sales of products such as soft drinks, ice creams, and heating oil all exhibit this type of pattern. For a quarterly seasonal pattern the data might be similar to Figure 1-3.

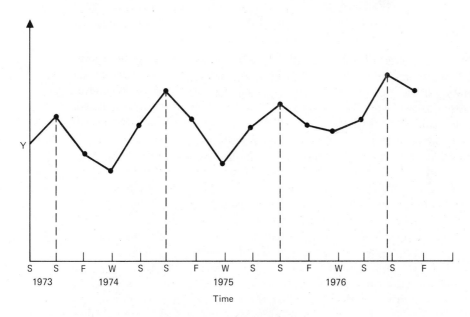

FIGURE 1-3 SEASONAL DATA PATTERN

3. *A cyclical* (C) pattern exists when the data are influenced by longer-term economic fluctuations such as those associated with the business cycle. The sales of products such as automobiles, steel, and major

appliances exhibit this type of pattern as shown in Figure 1-4. The major distinction between a seasonal and a cyclical pattern is that the former is of a constant length and recurs on a regular periodic basis, while the latter varies in length and magnitude.

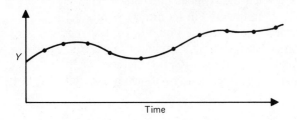

FIGURE 1-4 CYCLICAL DATA PATTERN

4. A *trend* (T) pattern exists when there is a long-term secular increase or decrease in the data. The sales of many companies, the gross national product (GNP), and many other business or economic indicators follow a trend pattern in their movement over time. Figure 1-5 shows one such trend pattern.

Many data series include combinations of the above patterns. Forecasting methods that are capable of distinguishing each of the patterns must be employed if a separation of the component patterns is needed. Similarly, alternative methods of forecasting can be used to identify the pattern and to best fit the data so that future values can be forecasted.

Qualitative or technological forecasting methods, on the other hand, do not require data in the same manner as quantitative forecasting methods. The inputs required depend on the specific method and are mainly the product of intuitive thinking, judgment, and accumulated knowledge. Technological approaches often require inputs from a number of specially trained people. Technological methods fall into the two general categories of exploratory and normative character. Exploratory methods (such as Delphi, S-curves, analogies, and morphological research) begin with the past and present as their starting point and move towards the future in a heuristic manner, often by looking at all available possibilities. Normative methods (such as decision matrices, relevance trees, and system analysis) start with the future by determining future goals and objectives, then work backwards to see if these can be achieved, given the constraints, resources, and technologies available.

As with their quantitative counterparts, technological techniques vary widely in cost, complexity, and value. They can be used separately but are more often used in combination with each other or in conjunction with quantitative methods.

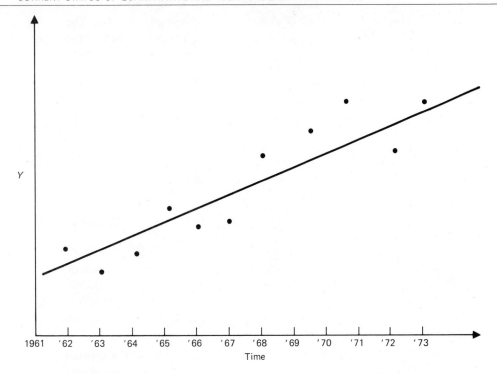

FIGURE 1-5 TREND DATA PATTERN

It is difficult to measure the accuracy of technological forecasts. They are used mainly to provide hints, to aid the planner, and to supplement quantitative forecasts, rather than to provide a specific numerical forecast. Because of their nature and cost, they are used almost exclusively for medium- and long-range situations such as formulating strategy, developing new products and technologies, and developing long-range plans. Although doubts are often expressed about the value of technological forecasting, it frequently provides very useful information for managers. It is a premise of the authors that technological methods can be used successfully in conjunction with quantitative methods in such areas as product development, capital expenditures, goal and strategy formulation, and mergers, by even medium and small organizations. Whatever the shortcomings of technological methods, frequently the only alternative is no forecast at all.

The forecaster has a wide range of methods available that vary in accuracy, scope, time horizon, and cost. Key tasks are deciding which method to apply in each situation, how much reliance to place on the method itself, and how much modification is required to incorporate personal judgment before predictions are used as a basis for planning future actions.

REFERENCES AND SELECTED BIBLIOGRAPHY

Ayers, R. U. 1969. *Technological Forecasting and Long Range Planning.* New York: McGraw-Hill.

Centrom, M. 1971. *Industrial Applications of Technological Forecasting.* New York: John Wiley & Sons.

Chambers, J. C., S. K. Mullick, and D. D. Smith. "How to Choose the Right Forecasting Technique," *Harvard Business Review,* July–August, 1971.

Clarke, A. C. 1971. *Profiles of the Future.* Bantam Books, U.S.A., 1971.

Hussey, D. E. 1971. *Introducing Corporate Planning.* Oxford: Pergamon Press.

Jantsch, E. 1969. *Technological Forecasting in Perspective.* Paris: Organization for Economic and Cultural Development.

Makridakis, S., A. Hodgsdon, and S. C. Wheelwright. "An Interactive Forecasting System," *The American Statistician,* November 1974.

Makridakis, S., and S. Wheelwright. 1977. "Generalized Adaptive Filtering," *Operational Research Quarterly,* Winter.

Miller, E. C. 1971. *Advanced Techniques for Strategic Planning.* New York: AMA Research Study, 104.

Reichard, R. S. 1966. *Practical Techniques of Sales Forecasting.* New York: McGraw-Hill.

Steiner, G. A. 1969. *Top Management Planning.* London: Macmillan.

Wheelwright, S., and S. Makridakis. 1977. *Forecasting Methods for Management,* 2nd ed. New York: John Wiley & Sons.

2 FUNDAMENTALS OF QUANTITATIVE FORECASTING

2/1 Explanatory versus Time-Series Forecasting

IN THE PREVIOUS chapter two major approaches to forecasting were identified: explanatory and time series. These approaches are complementary to each other and are intended for different types of applications. They are also founded on different philosophical premises.

Explanatory forecasting assumes a *cause and effect relationship* between the inputs to the system and its output, as shown in Figure 2-1.

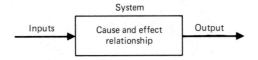

FIGURE 2-1 CAUSAL RELATIONSHIP

The *system* can be anything—a national economy, a company's market, or a household. According to explanatory forecasting, any change in inputs will affect the output of the system in a predictable way, assuming the cause and effect relationship is constant. The first task of forecasting is to find the cause and effect relationship by observing the output of the system (either through time or by studying a cross section of similar systems) and relating that to the corresponding inputs. For example, one might seek to determine the cause and effect relationships in a system in order to predict outputs such as GNP, company sales, or household expenses. Such a process, if carried out correctly, will allow

---

This chapter is intended for those with little or no background in statistics. Others can skim this material without losing continuity with the other chapters.

estimation of the type and extent of the relationship between the inputs and output. This relationship can then be used to predict future states of the system, provided the inputs are known for those future states.

The determination and application of cause and effect relationships can be illustrated by using a well-known physical relationship, Boyle's law. This law states:

$$P = \Theta \frac{N}{V},$$
(2-1)

where P is pressure,

N is the number of molecules,

V is the volume,

and Θ is a proportionality factor.

Assuming for a moment that (2-1) is known, it can be viewed as an example of Figure 2-1. For each value of the inputs N and V, and a value for Θ, there will be a corresponding output value P, pressure. Equation (2-1) is of forecasting value because with known inputs, the output can be predicted. Needless to say, there are almost infinite causal or explanatory relationships in the real world. A question of extreme importance to the forecaster, however, is whether or not specific relationships can be estimated. The best procedures for doing so will be discussed later in this chapter.

Unlike explanatory forecasting, time-series forecasting treats the *system* as a black box and makes no attempt to discover the factors affecting its behavior. As shown in Figure 2-2, the system is simply viewed as an unknown generating process.

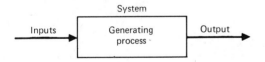

FIGURE 2-2 TIME-SERIES RELATIONSHIP

There are two main reasons for wanting to treat a system as a black box. One is that often it is not understood how the system operates, which makes it extremely difficult to discover the relationship governing its behavior. Even when the system is understood, it may be extremely difficult to measure, because a quantification process is not available. The second reason for treating the system as a black box is that the concern may be only in observing and predicting what will happen and not in knowing why it happens. During the eighteenth, nineteenth, and twentieth centuries, for example, there were several people concerned with the magnitude of sunspots. There was little known at that time as to the reasons for the sunspots or the sources of energy of the sun. This lack of knowledge, however, did not hinder many investigators who collected and analyzed the frequency of sunspots. Schuster (1906) found that there was a regular pattern in the magnitude of sunspots, and he and several others were able to predict their continuation through time-series analysis.

Quite often it is possible to forecast by using either causal or time-series approaches. Economic activity, for example, can be forecasted by discovering and measuring the relationship of GNP (gross national product) to several factors that influence it, such as monetary and fiscal policies, inflation, capital spending, and imports and exports. This will require that the form and parameters of the relationship be specified:

$$GNP = f(\text{monetary and fiscal policies, inflation, capital spending, imports, exports}) \qquad (2\text{-}2)$$

The procedure for selecting an appropriate functional form of equation (2-2) and estimating its parameters will be discussed in detail later on. At this point it should be emphasized that according to (2-2), GNP depends upon, or is determined by, the factors on the right-hand side of the equation. As these factors change, GNP will vary in the manner specified by (2-2).

If the only purpose is to forecast future values of GNP without concern as to why a certain level of GNP will be realized, a time-series approach would be appropriate. It is known that the magnitude of GNP does not change drastically from one month to another, or even from one year to another. Thus the GNP of next month will depend upon the GNP of the previous month and possibly that of the months before. Based on this observation, GNP might be expressed as follows:

$$GNP_{t+1} = f(GNP_t, GNP_{t-1}, GNP_{t-2}, GNP_{t-3}\ldots), \qquad (2\text{-}3)$$

where t is the present month,

     $t + 1$ is the next month,

     $t - 1$ is the last month,

     $t - 2$ is two months ago,

     etc.

Equation (2-3) is similar to (2-2) except that the factors on the right-hand side are previous values of the left-hand side. This makes the job of forecasting easier once (2-3) is known, since it requires no special input values as (2-2) does. However, one major problem with both equations (2-2) and (2-3) is that the relationship between the left- and right-hand sides of the equations must be discovered and measured.

2/2 Least Squares Estimates

Because physical and natural science relationships are usually exact, they are often called laws. For example, equation (2-1) will always hold under certain conditions. The same is true for Kepler's first two laws of planetary motion, which can specify precisely the position of planets as a function of time. However, high levels of precision disappear when one moves from physical or natural systems to social systems. The GNP relationship of equations (2-2) or (2-3) will never be exact. There will always be changes in GNP that will not be accounted for by variations in the right-hand side of (2-2) or (2-3), and thus some part of GNP changes will remain unpredictable. Therefore, to be exact, Figures 2-1 and 2-2 must be modified to include random causes that affect the GNP figures. These can be represented as shown in Figures 2-3 and 2-4. Equations (2-2) and

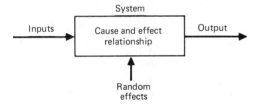

FIGURE 2-3 CAUSAL RELATIONSHIP WITH RANDOM NOISE

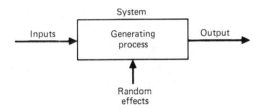

FIGURE 2-4 TIME-SERIES RELATIONSHIP WITH RANDOM NOISE

(2-3) should be modified also to include a random term, usually denoted by u, accounting for that part of the system's behavior that cannot be explained through the causal or time-series relationship.

$$GNP = \text{(monetary and fiscal policies, inflation, capital spending, imports, exports, } u), \tag{2-4}$$

where $\quad GNP_{t+1} = (GNP_t, GNP_{t-1}, GNP_{t-2}, GNP_{t-3}, \ldots, u_t).$ (2-5)

What is observed as the output of the system is dependent on two things: the functional relationship governing the system (or the pattern, as it will be called from now on) and randomness (or error). That is,

$$\text{data} = \text{pattern} + \text{randomness}. \tag{2-6}$$

The critical task in forecasting is to separate the pattern from the error component so that the former can be used for forecasting.

The general procedure for estimating the pattern of a relationship, whether causal or time series, is through fitting some functional form in such a way as to minimize the error component of equation (2-6). One form of this estimation is least squares. This approach is very old (developed first by Gauss in the 1800s) and is the one most widely used in classical statistics.* The name *least squares* is based on the fact that this estimation procedure seeks to minimize the sum of the squared errors in equation (2-6). The example shown below illustrates the basis of the least squares method. Its application to all types of functional forms (i.e., linear or nonlinear) is analogous to that shown here.

Suppose that the manager of a supermarket wants to know how much a typical customer spends in the store. The manager might start by taking a sample of say 12 clients, at random, obtaining the results shown in Table 2-1.

From Table 2-1, it is clear that not all customers spend the same amount. Some of the variation might be explained through factors such as time of the

TABLE 2-1 SAMPLE EXPENDITURES FOR SUPERMARKET CLIENTS

Client	Amount Spent
1	$9
2	8
3	9
4	12
5	9
6	12
7	11
8	7
9	13
10	9
11	11
12	10

* Many Bayesian statisticians view least squares estimation as a special case of a quadratic loss function which, while used extensively, is one of many procedures available.

day, day of the week, discounts offered, maximum or minimum amount of checks cashed, etc., while part of the variation may be random or unexplainable. For purposes of this illustration, it will be assumed that no variation can be explained through causal or time-series relationships. In such a case, the store manager faced with finding an appropriate estimator to describe the data may take a fixed value as an estimate. Having made this decision, the manager might decide to select an estimate in a way to minimize the mean (average) squared error. This could be done by trial and error. Suppose he chooses an estimate of 7, and then tries estimates of 9, 10, and 12. The resulting mean squared errors are shown in Table 2-2 below.

TABLE 2-2 MEAN SQUARED ERRORS FOR ESTIMATES OF CLIENT EXPENDITURES

Client	Amount Spent	Estimate of Value: 7		Estimate of Value: 9		Estimate of Value: 10		Estimate of Value: 12	
		Error*	Error Squared	Error	Error Squared	Error	Error Squared	Error	Error Squared
1	9	2	4	0	0	−1	1	−3	9
2	8	1	1	−1	1	−2	4	−4	16
3	9	2	4	0	0	−1	1	−3	9
4	12	5	25	3	9	2	4	0	0
5	9	2	4	0	0	−1	1	−3	9
6	12	5	25	3	9	2	4	0	0
7	11	4	16	2	4	1	1	−1	1
8	7	0	0	−2	4	−3	9	−5	25
9	13	6	36	4	16	3	9	1	1
10	9	2	4	0	0	−1	1	−3	9
11	11	4	16	2	4	1	1	−1	1
12	10	3	9	1	1	0	0	−2	4
Sum of squared errors			144		48		36		84
MSE† (mean squared error)			12		4		3		7

* Error = amount spent − estimated value.
† MSE = sum of squared errors/12.

From Table 2-2, it is apparent that the squared error will be minimized if the manager chooses 10 as the estimate. However, before drawing this conclusion, he may want to try additional values as possible estimates. Figure 2-5 summarizes the resulting MSEs for all estimate values of 0 through 20. It can be seen that the MSEs form a parabola. Furthermore, the lowest point of this parabola is the value of 10. Thus, the criterion of minimizing MSE will be achieved when the value of the estimate is 10.

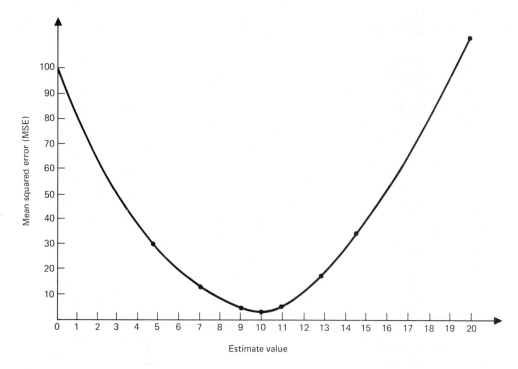

FIGURE 2-5 RELATING MSE TO ESTIMATE VALUE

Because Figure 2-5 is a mathematical function whose properties can be found exactly, it is not necessary to use trial and error to find the estimator that minimizes the MSE. Rather, this value can be found mathematically with the help of differentiation. The first step is to rewrite equation (2-6) so as to isolate the error on the left-hand side.

Error = data − pattern.   (2-7)

For convenience, the error will be denoted by e, the data by X and the pattern by $\bar{X}$. In addition, the subscript i ($i = 1, 2, 3, \ldots, 12$) will be added to denote the ith customer. Using this notation, equation (2-7) becomes:

$$e_i = X_i - \bar{X}. \tag{2-8}$$

To examine the squared error, both sides of (2-8) must be squared, giving:

$$e_i^2 = (X_i - \bar{X})^2. \tag{2-9}$$

Summing these values for all 12 customers and dividing by 12 gives the MSE:

$$\sum_{i=1}^{12} e_i^2 = \sum_{i=1}^{12} (X_i - \bar{X})^2. \tag{2-10}$$

Initially, the store manager does not know what value the estimate of the pattern, $\bar{X}$, will have. However, he knows he wants the one that will minimize the mean squared error. This value can be found by taking the derivative, setting it equal to 0, and solving for $\bar{X}$, the estimate value.

$$\frac{d \sum_{i=1}^{12} e_i^2}{d\bar{X}} = -2 \sum_{i=1}^{12} (X_i - \bar{X}) = 0,$$

$$\text{or} \quad \sum_{i=1}^{12} (X_i - \bar{X}) = 0,$$

$$\text{then} \quad 12\bar{X} = \sum_{i=1}^{12} X_i,$$

$$\text{and} \quad \bar{X} = \frac{\sum_{i=1}^{12} X_i}{12}. \tag{2-11}$$

Formula (2-11) is an easily recognized formula that gives the average of 12 numbers. This simple formula, as has been shown, gives a value that minimizes the mean squared error. Applying (2-11) to the store manager's data of Table 2-1 gives

$$\bar{X} = \frac{\sum_{i=1}^{12} X_i}{12} = \frac{120}{12} = 10.$$

This value is the minimum point of Figure 2-5. As a single point estimate of the pattern of the data, the mean fits the data as closely as possible, given the criterion of minimizing the MSE. While the mean is a somewhat simple estimate of the data in most situations, the procedure of least squares that was used to determine a MSE estimate can be applied no matter how complex or sophisticated the estimation situation is.

It is of course possible to minimize Σe_i, Σe_i^3, or Σe_i^4 instead of minimizing the MSE. However, minimizing the MSE is the most popular for several reasons. For one, attempting to minimize Σe_i will involve extra complications because some e_i values will be positive and some will be negative. To avoid having errors cancelling each other, one might minimize the absolute errors, $\Sigma |e_i|$. Computationally, this is not as easy as minimizing the Σe_i^2. Choosing to minimize Σe_i^4 or Σe_i^6 is unattractive because they have more than one minimum, which again adds to the computational and practical problems. Increasing the error power gives more weight to values that are further away from the mean. This result is attractive because a few large errors are less desirable than several small ones. However, it should not be overdone. Additionally, many cost relationships are quadratic in nature, suggesting the appropriateness of squaring. The use of Σe_i^2 is a compromise between giving too much weight to extreme errors and giving the same weight to all values (using $\Sigma |e_i|$).

TABLE 2-3   THE MEAN AS AN ESTIMATE OF FRENCH POPULATION

Year	Population of France (in millions)	Mean Value	Error
1961	46.163	48.776	−2.61
1962	46.998	48.776	−1.78
1963	47.816	48.776	−.96
1964	48.311	48.776	−.46
1965	48.758	48.776	.02
1966	49.164	48.776	.38
1967	49.548	48.776	.77
1968	49.915	48.776	1.14
1969	50.315	48.776	1.54
1970	50.768	48.776	1.99

$$\sum_{i=1}^{10} X_i = 487.756.$$

$$\overline{X} = \frac{\sum\limits_{i=1}^{10} X_i}{10} = \frac{487.756}{10} = 48.776.$$

2/3 Discovering and Describing Existing Relationships

If the measurable output of a system is viewed as data that include a pattern and some error, a major consideration in forecasting, whether causal or time series, is to identify the most appropriate pattern, then fit the functional form of that so as to minimize the MSE. The basic procedure for this process is illustrated in the next two sections.

2/3/1 Time-Series Pattern

Table 2-3 gives the population of France (in millions) for the years 1961 to 1970 and the resulting errors when the mean is used as the estimate for the pattern. If the mean is used to fit the population data following the approach outlined in the last section, the MSE will be minimized. The result is shown in Figure 2-6.

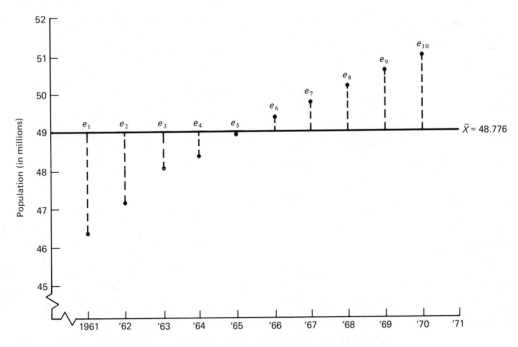

FIGURE 2-6 RESULTING ERRORS USING THE MEAN AS THE ESTIMATE OF POPULATION

Even a rough examination of Table 2-3 or Figure 2-6 indicates that there is something wrong with using the mean as the estimate of the pattern. What is labeled as the error is not random, but exhibits some systematic variation. This systematic variation could perhaps be included as part of the pattern. Since the errors go from negative to positive, an estimate of the pattern in the form of a trend line as shown in Figure 2-7 will give much smaller errors than using the mean as an estimate.

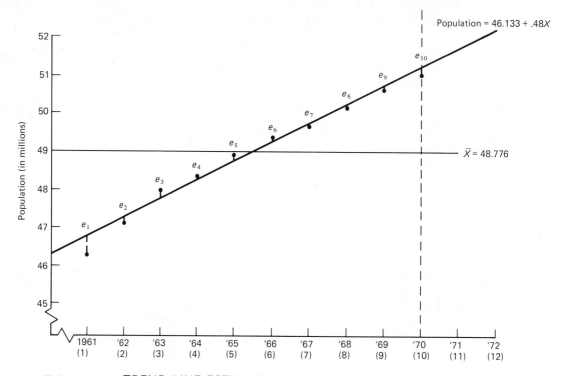

FIGURE 2-7 TREND LINE ESTIMATE OF FRENCH POPULATION

One possible trend line is of the form

Population $= 46.133 + .48X$,   (2-12)

where X is the number of the year.

The mechanics of how equation (2-12) was found are not important at this point. (They will be examined in detail in Chapter 5.) However, this particular trend line was determined in such a way that the MSE is minimized. As can be seen in Figure 2-7, a trend line does describe the data better than using the mean as an estimate as was done in Figure 2-6.

There is no way that a statistical method can determine the best pattern to describe a given set of data. Rather, this decision must be based on judgment; then a statistical method can be used to fit the specified pattern in such a way as to minimize the MSE. There are, however, several guidelines that can be applied to determine whether the selected pattern is appropriate. One of these is that the errors must be random. If they are not, as is the case in Figure 2-6, an alternative pattern should be considered.

For forecasting purposes, either Figure 2-6 or 2-7 can be used to predict the population for the year 1971. In terms of Figure 2-6, the forecast is 48.776 million. From Figure 2.7, the forecast is 51.4 million. From historical data, one would expect the actual population value to be closer to 51.4 million than to 48.776. (The actual 1971 population was 51.25 million.) Thus in practice it is clear that Figure 2-7 will be chosen, since it fits the pattern of the data much better than Figure 2-6.

The use of Figure 2-7 for forecasting is an example of a time-series approach using a trend pattern. This time-series approach is not concerned with the factors determining future population levels. Its purpose is simply to provide forecasts that are as accurate as possible, which in this case seems to have been achieved.

2/3/2 Causal Pattern

Time-series forecasting requires data on only one variable, the output of the system. The forecast is then based on past values of that variable as described above. Functionally, this can be represented as

$$P_{1971} = f(P_{1970}, P_{1969}, \ldots, P_{1961}, u), \tag{2-13}$$

where P is population and u is a random variable that represents the combined effect of influences other than past values of population on the population of 1971. The decision was then made to use as a specific linear form of this function,

$$P_{1971} = 46.133 + .48(11) = 51.4 \text{ million},$$

where 11 refers to the eleventh year (1971) (see Figure 2-7).

In this section we will attempt to determine the pattern of an output variable using a causal relationship involving at least one other variable. The annual gross national product of France will be used as the output variable in this example. Table 2-4 and Figure 2-8 shows the GNP of France (in billions of francs) during the years 1961 through 1970. This is the same time span shown in Table 2-3 for population in France. Like population, GNP is not accurately estimated using the mean value, as illustrated in Table 2-4. Rather, a trend line is required to best describe the pattern as a function of time. As shown in Figure 2-8, a trend line gives a time-series forecast for the year 1971 of 817.2 billion francs.

TABLE 2-4   FORECASTING FRENCH GNP—MEAN ESTIMATE

Year	GNP of France (billions of francs)	Mean GNP Value	Error
1961	328.327	534.54	−206.21
1962	367.172	534.54	−167.37
1963	411.989	534.54	−122.55
1964	456.669	534.54	−77.87
1965	489.834	534.54	−44.71
1966	532.529	534.54	−2.01
1967	574.77	534.54	40.23
1968	630.012	534.54	95.47
1969	733.959	534.54	199.42
1970	820.15	534.54	285.61

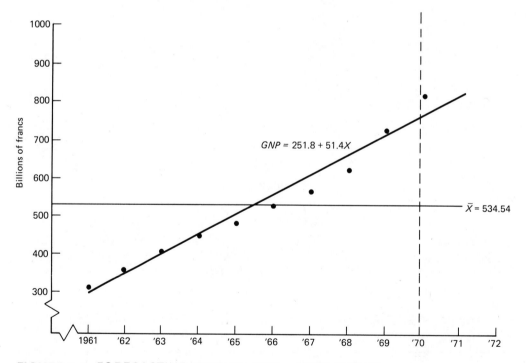

$GNP = 251.8 + 51.4X$

$\bar{X} = 534.54$

FIGURE 2-8   FORECASTING FRENCH GNP—TIME-SERIES TREND ESTIMATE

In order to obtain an even better estimate of French GNP, the factors that affect GNP might be considered explicitly. One such determining variable would be the number of people in the population. Functionally, this relationship can be stated as follows:

$$GNP = f(\text{population}) \tag{2-14}$$

To determine the appropriateness of this relationship, the pattern needs to be specified and the parameters measured. As in the previous illustrations, the objective is to decide on some pattern, then fit a functional form of that to the data in such a way as to minimize the MSE. If the errors that result from this approach are random and reasonably small, it is generally assumed that the pattern is adequate.

In order to proceed, GNP and population can be plotted on the same graph in order to represent the pair of values that occurred for each of the available ten years. This eliminates time as a determining factor of the output variable, GNP, replacing it with population. The results are shown in Figure 2-9.

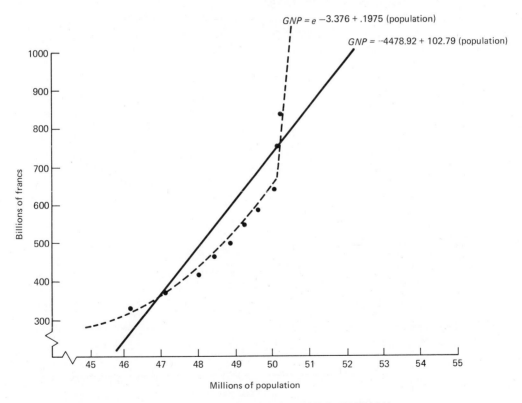

FIGURE 2-9 FORECASTING FRENCH GNP USING FRENCH POPULATION

Two different patterns have been fitted to the data in Figure 2-9. One is linear (a straight line) of the form

$$GNP = -4478.92 + 102.79P,$$

where P is population.

The second is a nonlinear one called an exponential pattern (see dotted line on Figure 2-9), and is of the form

$$GNP = e^{-3.376 + .1972P} \qquad (2\text{-}16)$$

The details concerning the fitting of the two patterns, (2-15) and (2-16), and the determination of their parameters will be covered in Chapters 5 and 6. It should be clear that the two quantities GNP and population, can be related by deciding on some pattern of relationship between them, then fitting this pattern to the available data (the pairs of values for GNP and population for the years 1961 through 1970) in such a way as to minimize the MSE.

An examination of Figure 2-9 shows that the dotted line representing equation (2-16) describes the relationship between the output (GNP) and the input (population) better than the straight line representing equation (2-15). Thus for forecasting purposes, (2-16) would provide better estimates of GNP, assuming population values are available. For example, the GNP forecast for 1971 would be

$$GNP_{1971} = 2.718^{-3.376 + .1972(P_{1971})}$$

$$= 862.7.$$

This is based on the estimated value of the population for 1971 of 51.4 million that was obtained from Figure 2-7. The actual GNP value for 1971 was 904.16, which means the percentage error of this forecast was 4.8%.

The forecast from the linear relationship (2-15) would have been

$$GNP_{1971} = -4478.92 + 102.79(P_{1971})$$

$$= 804.486.$$

This represents a forecast error of 11%, much worse than 4.8%. Since the number of data points used was only 10, the conclusions that can be drawn are limited. However, this restriction can be overcome by using more data.

2/4 Variances and Covariances

One of the things that makes equation (2-1) different from the other relationships examined in this chapter is that (2-1) can perfectly explain the system it describes. That physical relationship is deterministic—there are no errors or random variations. In such instances the job of prediction is straightforward. Unfortunately, in economic and behavioral systems there is always randomness. When randomness is present, the best that can be done is to attempt to isolate it and make it as small as possible. The fact that errors do exist means that methods for measuring them and assessing their magnitude are most useful. Usually these assessments are made by statistical measures of dispersion, the most common of which is called the variance.

The sample variance is defined as

$$S^2 = \frac{\Sigma(X_i - \overline{X})^2}{n - 1},$$
(2-17)

where S^2 is the variance,

X_i is the ith observation,

$\overline{X}$ is the mean of the data, i.e., $\overline{X} = \dfrac{\Sigma X_i}{n}$,

and n is the number of observations or data values.*

Equation (2-17) expresses the variance in terms of deviations or errors between each of the X_i values and the mean. Each deviation is squared, and they are added together to obtain the sum. The sum of the squared deviations is then divided by $n - 1$. It can be seen that the variance is very similar to the mean squared error defined earlier. The only difference is that in (2-17) the divisor is $n - 1$ rather than n, the divisor in the MSE calculation. The $n - 1$ term is referred to as the degrees of freedom, or d.f. for short, and is used frequently in statistics. The value of the degrees of freedom is $n - 1$ in this case because one degree of freedom is lost in using $\overline{X}$ in formula (2-17).

The variance, S^2, is a single number or statistic, which indicates the dispersion of the data, X_i, around the mean of the data. The variance is particularly important because when the distribution is "normal," the variance together with the mean specifies it uniquely and completely. In the majority of cases, forecasting assumes normality. This is so because the sampling distribution of estimators can be approximated by a normal distribution whenever n is sufficiently large, which in most cases occurs when n is greater than 30. The *central limit theorem* of statistics allows this approximation and makes it possible to use the normal curve to assess the extent of dispersion of a set of data around a specified pattern. Thus by knowing the mean value of the pattern and by calculating the variance using formula (2-17), the extent of possible errors for both past and future values can be assessed using the summary measure of variance.

---

* These symbols are routinely used in most statistical books and will not be defined from here on. All summations will be taken from 1 to n unless otherwise specified.

Although 30 observations are required to use the variance with confidence, only 4 will be used below to illustrate the calculations involved and to discuss the concept of variance. Table 2-5 shows the weights of four persons (50, 60, 40, and 70 kilos) and the mean of those values, 55. The calculations for the variance are also shown in Table 2-5.

TABLE 2-5   MEAN AND VARIANCE CALCULATIONS FOR WEIGHT DATA

Person (observation)	Data Value (kilos)	Mean Value	Deviation or Error	Squared Deviation or Squared Error
1	50	55	−5	25
2	60	55	5	25
3	40	55	−15	225
4	70	55	15	225
	$\displaystyle\sum_{i=1}^{4} = 220$		$\displaystyle\sum_{i=1}^{4} e_i = 0$	$\displaystyle\sum_{i=1}^{4} e_i^2 = 500$
	$\bar{X} = \dfrac{\Sigma X_i}{n}$		$e_i = X_i - \bar{X}.$	$S^2 = \dfrac{\Sigma(X_i - \bar{X})^2}{n-1}$
	$= \dfrac{220}{4}$			$= \dfrac{500}{3}$
	$= 55$			$= 166.67$

The square root of the variance is a statistic called the standard deviation and is denoted by S. Thus, the standard deviation of the four weight values is

$$S = \sqrt{166.67} = 12.91.$$

Figure 2-10 gives a graphic representation of these data and their dispersion from the mean value.

In addition to the weights of the four persons shown in Table 2-5, one might also have an interest in their heights. Suppose these are measured and found to be 1.50, 1.60, 1.20, and 1.70 meters. The variance of the heights would be

$$\bar{X} = \frac{\displaystyle\sum_{i=1}^{4} X_i}{4} = 1.50$$

$$\text{and} \quad S^2 = \frac{\Sigma(X_i - \bar{X})}{3} = .0467,$$

$$S = \sqrt{S^2} = .216.$$

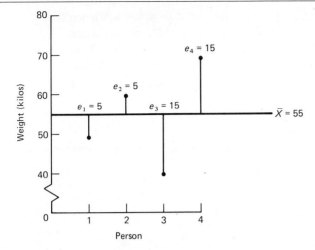

FIGURE 2-10 DISPERSION FROM THE MEAN OF THE WEIGHT DATA

These statistics tell a great deal about the data even without Figure 2-11, which graphically illustrates their dispersion around the mean.

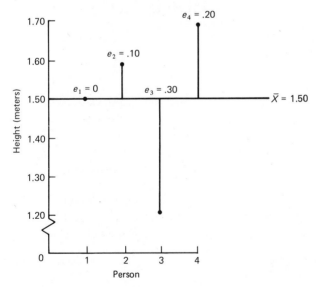

FIGURE 2-11 DISPERSION FROM THE MEAN OF THE HEIGHT DATA

One may be content to examine Figures 2-10 and 2-11 individually and consider their respective means and variances. However, since both figures reflect data on the same persons, one may want to go a step further and determine whether there is a relationship between the weight and the height of these four persons. Table 2-6 gives the relevant data.

TABLE 2-6   RELATING WEIGHT AND HEIGHT DATA

Person	Weight (Y_i)	Mean Weight $(\bar{Y})$	Weight Deviation	(X_i) Height	Mean Height $(\bar{X})$	Height Deviation	Weight Deviation × Height Deviation
1	50	55	− 5	1.50	1.50	0	0
2	60	55	5	1.60	1.50	.10	+ .5
3	40	55	−15	1.20	1.50	−.30	+4.5
4	70	55	15	1.70	1.50	.20	+3.0
						$\Sigma(Y_i-\bar{Y})(X_i-\bar{X}) =$	8.0

In Table 2-6 the weight is denoted by Y_i to distinguish it from the height, which is denoted by X_i. As in the previous calculations, the mean of each variable and each value's deviation from the mean is computed. However, it is now of interest to determine the relationship between these two variables. If there is a relationship between the weights and heights of individuals, one would expect that if the weight of a person is below the mean weight, the person's height would be below the mean height. Similarly, one would expect a heavier than average person to be proportionally taller than average. To capture the relationship of the dispersion of these two variables, the weight deviation and height deviation for each individual can be multiplied and summed as shown in the right-hand column of Table 2-6. The individual products should be positive if there is a positive relationship, zero if there is no relationship, and negative if there is a negative relationship.

The statistical measure that describes how two variables vary in relation to each other is called *covariance*, often abbreviated as *cov*. Its mathematical formula is given by equation (2-18).

$$\text{cov} = \frac{\Sigma(Y_i - \bar{Y})(X_i - \bar{X})}{n - 1}.$$

(2-18)

The larger the joint variation between two variables, the stronger the relationship will be, since they will move in the same direction. Thus, the covariance is a measure of the strength of the relationship between two variables: the bigger the covariance (in absolute value), the stronger the relationship.

In our example given in Table 2-6, the covariance is

$$\text{cov} = \frac{8}{3} = 2.667, \text{ since } \Sigma(Y_i - \bar{Y})(X_i - \bar{X}) = 8.$$

Graphically the covariance can be represented as in Figure 2-12. This graph is constructed by rotating Figure 2-11 90 degrees and overlaying it on Figure 2-10. Thus, Figure 2-12 illustrates the deviations of each observation from the means, $\bar{X}$ and $\bar{Y}$, as well as their joint variation, i.e., the product of the variations from each of the two means.

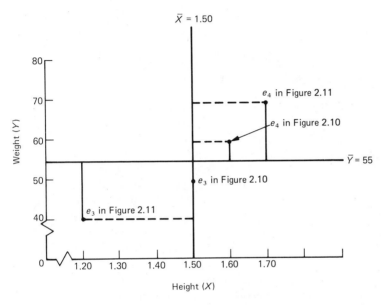

FIGURE 2-12 COMBINED HEIGHT AND WEIGHT DEVIATIONS

The value of 2.667 for the covariance indicates that the two variables, weight and height, are related. However, in this form, it is hard to know how strong the relationship is. To overcome this problem, the covariance can be standardized. This technique is often used in statistics because it provides measures that are independent of the scale of measurement. The standardized measure of covariance is called correlation, and it is found by dividing the covariance by the product of the standard deviations of the variables. This relationship is written mathematically as

$$\text{correlation} = r = \frac{\text{cov}}{S_Y S_X}. \tag{2-19}$$

In the height and weight example of Table 2-6

$$r = \frac{2.667}{12.667(.216)} = \frac{2.667}{2.736} = .975.$$

This value of the correlation coefficient indicates that the two variables, weight and height, are highly related, since a correlation of $+1$ would represent a perfect positive relation. (A value of 0 would indicate no relation and a value of -1 would be a perfect negative relation.) The correlation coefficient, therefore, is a relative measure of the joint variation of two variables and as such indicates the extent of the relationship of the two variables.

2/5 Autocovariance and Autocorrelation

The covariance and correlation coefficient are statistics (statistical measures) that measure the extent of the relationship between two variables. As such, they are used to discover and measure *causal relationships*. Autocovariance and autocorrelation are comparable measures that serve the same purpose for *time-series relationships*. As an illustration of these two statistics, the French GNP data of Table 2-7 can be analyzed. The question to be answered is to what extent the GNP figures for successive years are related to each other. In other words, is the GNP of last year correlated with the GNP of this year? Is the GNP of this year correlated with that of next year? And so on. To answer this

TABLE 2-7   FRENCH GNP (1961–1970)

(1) Year	(2) GNP_t	(3) Year	(4) GNP_{t-1}
1961	328.327	1962	367.172
1962	367.172	1963	411.989
1963	411.989	1964	456.669
1964	456.669	1965	489.834
1965	489.834	1966	532.529
1966	532.529	1967	574.77
1967	574.77	1968	630.012
1968	630.012	1969	733.959
1969	733.959	1970	820.15
1970	820.15	—	—

question, a first step is finding the correlation coefficient between the columns 2 and 4 of Table 2-7. These two columns are very similar except that in column 4 the GNP is listed for the year following the GNP listed in column 2 of that line. Essentially column 4 defines a second variable whose values are the same as those listed for the variable shown in column 2, but displaced by one time period. Thus to find the correlation between columns 2 and 4 is completely analogous to what was done in Table 2-6 for height and weight. Using formula (2-19) and dropping the last row of Table 2-7, since there is no value in column 4, the correlation coefficient is computed as

$$r = \frac{\text{cov}}{S_Y S_X} = \frac{19308.47}{129.93(149.35)} = .995.$$

This value indicates a very strong relationship between successive values of GNP. This correlation between successive values is called autocorrelation because both variables come from the same data but refer to different time periods. Thus, in Table 2-7, column 2 is current GNP figures, while column 4 refers to figures of one year later, or what is commonly called a time lag of one year. If the autocorrelation is close to $+1$ or -1, the relationship is a strong one. If it is close to 0, it indicates there is little relationship between GNP this year and GNP next year. The statistics of autocovariance and its standardized relative measure, autocorrelation, play a very important role in time-series forecasting. With them the extent of relationship between different time periods can be discovered, measured, and subsequently used as a basis for time-series analysis.

APPENDIX

Chapter 2

1. NOTATION FOR QUANTITATIVE FORECASTING

Quantitative forecasts are based on data, or observations, that describe some factor of interest. In this book a single observed value will be represented by X_i. This variable can be the actual number of units sold, the cost of production, the advertising budget, price per unit, gross national product, or any other event of interest, as long as it can be quantified. The objective of forecasting is to predict future values of X. The individual forecasts will be denoted by F_i, or $\hat{X}_i$, and the error by e_i, where the error is the difference between the actual value and the forecast value for observation i:

$$e_i = X_i - \hat{X}_i \quad \text{or} \quad e_i = X_i - F_i.$$

In time-series forecasting and in causal forecasting when the data are taken at equal time intervals, t will denote the present time period, $t - 1$ last period, $t - 2$ two periods ago, etc. A period can be a day, a week, a month, quarter, year, etc. The forecasts usually will be for future time periods such as $t + 1$.

TABLE 2-8 NOTATION USED IN TIME-SERIES FORECASTING

										Forecasted Values			
Observed values	X_1	X_2	X_3	X_4	$\ldots$	X_{t-2}	X_{t-1}	X_t	F_{t+1}	F_{t+2}	F_{t+3}	$\ldots$	F_{t+m}
Period i	1	2	3	4	$\ldots$	$t-2$	$t-1$	t	$t+1$	$t+2$	$t+3$	$\ldots$	$t+m$
Forecast values	$\hat{X}_1$	$\hat{X}_2$	$\hat{X}_3$	$\hat{X}_4$	$\ldots$	$\hat{X}_{t-2}$	$\hat{X}_{t-1}$	$\hat{X}_t$					
or	F_1	F_2	F_3	F_4	$\ldots$	F_{t-2}	F_{t-1}	F_t					
Error	e_1	e_2	e_3	e_4	$\ldots$	e_{t-2}	e_{t-1}	e_t					

Present

2. SUMMATION SIGN Σ

In order to simplify the manipulation of expressions involving the adding of many numbers, it is convenient to use a summation sign, Σ. The use of this sign and the elements of notation mentioned previously can be demonstrated using the data in Table 2-9.

TABLE 2-9 USE OF QUANTITATIVE FORECASTING NOTATION

Year	Period i	No. of Units Sold Actual	No. of Units Sold Forecasted	Error	Year	Period i	No. of Units Sold Actual	No. of Units Sold Forecasted	Error
1950	1	123	120	3	1961	12	175	173	2
1951	2	125	128	−3	1962	13	176	177	−1
1952	3	133	135	−2	1963	14	192	188	−4
1953	4	140	138	2	1964	15	199	195	−4
1954	5	144	148	−4	1965	16	210	215	5
1955	6	158	157	3	1966	17	225	230	5
1956	7	161	155	6	1967	18	230	236	−6
1957	8	160	168	−6	1968	19	238	242	−4
1958	9	163	168	−5	1969	20	251	248	3
1959	10	171	171	0	1970	21	259	255	4
1960	11	175	176	−1	1971	22	275	263	12
					1972	23	283	290	−7

Based on Table 2-9,

X_i is the actual sales,

$\hat{X}_i$ or F_i is the forecast values for sales,

and e_i is the error, or the difference between actual (X_i) and forecast value of sales ($\hat{X}_i$).

If one wants the sum of the errors, it can be obtained from

$$e_1 + e_2 + e_3 \cdots + e_{23} = \sum_{i=1}^{23} e_i,$$

or $3 - 3 - 2 \cdots - 7 = -2.$

The cumulative sales for the years 1960 through 1969 can be obtained from

$$\sum_{i=11}^{20} X_i = X_{11} + X_{12} + X_{13} + \cdots + X_{20}$$

$$= 175 + 175 + 176 + \cdots + 251$$

$$= 2{,}071.$$

The following rules apply to the use of summation signs:

1. $\displaystyle\sum_{i=1}^{n} \bar{X} X_i = \bar{X} \sum_{i=1}^{n} X_i,$

   where $\bar{X}$ is the sampling mean (therefore a constant) of the variable X_i.

2. $\displaystyle\sum_{i=1}^{n} \bar{X} = n\bar{X}.$

   For example suppose $\bar{X} = 10$ and $n = 5$, then

   $$\sum_{i=1}^{n} 10 = 10 + 10 + 10 + 10 + 10 = 50$$

   $$\text{or } 5(10) = 50.$$

3. $\displaystyle\sum_{i=1}^{n} (X_i - \hat{X}_i) = \sum_{i=1}^{n} X_i - \sum_{i=1}^{n} \hat{X}_i.$

4. $\displaystyle\sum_{i=1}^{n} (X_i - \bar{X}) = \sum_{i=1}^{n} X_i - \sum_{i=1}^{n} \bar{X}$

   $$= \sum_{i=1}^{n} X_i - n\bar{X}.$$

5. $\displaystyle\sum_{i=1}^{n} (X_i - \bar{X})^2 = \sum_{i=1}^{n} (X_i^2 - 2\bar{X}X_i + \bar{X}^2)$

   $$= \sum_{i=1}^{n} X_i^2 - 2\bar{X}\Sigma X_i + n\bar{X}^2.$$

REFERENCES AND SELECTED BIBLIOGRAPHY

Freund, J. E. 1962. *Mathematical Statistics.* Englewood Cliffs, N.J.: Prentice-Hall.

Koosis, D. J. 1972. *Business Statistics.* New York: John Wiley & Sons.

Locke, F. M. 1972. *Business Mathematics.* New York: John Wiley & Sons.

Schuster, R. 1906. "On the Periodicity of Sunspots." *Philosophical Transactions,* Series A, 206, pp. 69–100.

Spurr, W. A., and C. P. Bonini. 1959. *Statistical Analysis for Business Decisions.* Homewood, Ill.: Irwin.

EXERCISES

1. The following data are the median reading scores of grades 2 and 5 in different public schools in the areas of Brooklyn and Queens, New York (*New York Times,* January 12, 1976, p. 20).

	BROOKLYN District 13 (Brooklyn Heights, Bedford-Stuyvesant)			QUEENS District 24 (Maspeth, Middle Village)		
P.S.	Grade 2 Median Score	Grade 5 Median Score	P.S.	Grade 2 Median Score	Grade 5 Median Score	
3	2.5	5.3	12	3.2	6.7	
8	3.0	5.7	13	3.7	7.1	
9	3.3	5.7	14	3.3	6.3	
11	2.4	4.4	19	2.8	6.3	
20	2.9	5.5	49	3.5	7.6	
44	3.0	5.8	68	2.5	6.3	
46	2.5	5.0	71	2.9	6.3	
54	2.9	5.0	81	3.3	5.7	
56	2.9	4.9	87	4.1	5.9	
67	2.5	5.0	88	4.5	6.8	
93	3.1	4.9	89	3.7	7.0	
133	3.2	5.1	91	4.5	5.8	
256	2.3	5.7	102	4.0	6.9	
270	3.3	5.8	113	4.0	7.6	
282	2.7	5.7	128	3.6	6.8	
287	3.2	5.2	143	3.0	5.4	
305	2.6	5.0	153	3.5	7.0	
307	3.1	5.0	199	4.0	6.8	

a. Is there a relationship between the reading scores of grades 2 and 5 in the Brooklyn schools?
b. Is there a relationship between the reading scores of grades 2 and 5 in the Queens schools?
c. Is there a relationship between the grade 2 reading scores of the Brooklyn and Queens schools?
d. Is there a relationship between the grade 5 reading scores of the Brooklyn and Queens schools?

2. Table 2-10 gives average monthly temperatures in Paris.
   a. What is your best estimate of the average temperature in June 1975?
   b. Is there any time pattern in the temperature readings?

TABLE 2-10 AVERAGE MONTHLY TEMPERATURE IN PARIS (CENTIGRADE)

1974	Jan.	7.6	1974	Oct.	8.9
	Feb.	7.1		Nov.	8.5
	Mar.	8.3		Dec.	8.5
	Apr.	11.5	1975	Jan.	7.7
	May	13.7		Feb.	6.9
	June	17.2		Mar.	6.1
	July	18.5		Apr.	10.5
	Aug.	19.7		May	12.9
	Sept.	15.1			

3. Several approaches have been suggested by those attempting to predict stock market movements. Three of them are described briefly below. How does each relate to the different approaches to forecasting described in this chapter?
   a. Dow Theory: There are support and resistance levels for stock prices both for the overall market and for individual stocks. These levels can be found by plotting prices of the market or stock over time.
   b. Random Walk Theory: There is no way to predict future movements in the stock market or individual stocks, since all available information is quickly assimilated by the investors and moves market prices in the appropriate direction.
   c. The prices of individual stocks or of the market in general are largely determined by earnings.

PART TWO
SMOOTHING AND DECOMPOSITION TIME-SERIES METHODS

In Part Two, smoothing and decomposition time-series methods are described. These are frequently the most intuitively appealing techniques and are the most empirically based methodologies of forecasting being used today. Although both methods are somewhat weak in their statistical underpinnings and lack mathematical rigor in their theoretical development, they have been accepted very well by practitioners who find them easy to use and fairly accurate for the costs involved.

The basis of the smoothing methods described in Chapter 3 is the simple weighting or smoothing of past observations in a time series in order to obtain a forecast for the future. In smoothing these historical values, random errors are averaged and such methods result in a "smooth" forecast that seems to work well in certain situations. The major advantages of smoothing methods are their low cost, the ease with which they can be applied, and the speed with which they can be adopted. These characteristics make them particularly attractive when a large number of items are to be forecasted, such as would be the case in many inventory situations.

The decomposition methods described in Chapter 4 apply many of the concepts of smoothing, but use a somewhat different structural framework in doing so. Decompositional approaches seek to decompose or break a time series into its major subcomponents. Thus rather than trying to predict a single pattern, a separate effort is made at predicting the seasonal pattern, the trend pattern, and the cycle pattern, and at smoothing randomness. Forecasting using such methods involves extrapolating each of these component patterns separately and recombining them into a final forecast. Decomposition methods are often useful not only in providing forecasts but in providing information regarding the components of a time series and the effect of various factors, such as seasonality and cyclicality. Generally, these methods are devoid of statistical jargon and have been developed empirically, rather than based on theoretical constructs.

In both chapters the aim is to present the fundamental concepts involved in each class of methodologies, to then focus on what the authors have found to be perhaps the most commonly used method in that class, and to thoroughly describe its application. Next, some of the variations in the methodologies are presented, and finally some of the practical considerations as to when specific variations should be used and how that selection can be made are discussed.

3 SMOOTHING METHODS

3/1 Introduction

IN THE PREVIOUS chapter, the use of the simple average or mean as an estimator that minimizes the mean squared error of actual minus forecast values was illustrated. It could have also been shown (as is done in most statistics books) that the mean is an unbiased estimator and the best one available when certain conditions hold true. However, under many conditions the mean cannot be used as an accurate forecasting method. For example, to forecast the tenth value of the simple series $1, 2, 3, \ldots, 9$, the mean of the first nine values is 5, which is definitely a poor estimate. Using the mean as an estimate for this series gives a systematic pattern of errors that are clearly not random. Similarly, the mean of the harmonic series 1, 2, 3, 4, 3, 2, 1, 2, 3, 4, $\ldots$, 3, 4, 3, 2, is 2.5, which could be used as an estimator, but would not be the best one available. Again the errors would exhibit a systematic pattern that could be identified to make the forecasts more accurate.

As with all forecasting methods, optimal use of the mean requires a knowledge of the conditions that determine its appropriateness. For the mean, these conditions are that the data must be stationary (horizontal) and randomly distributed. The need for the first condition is obvious: for any nonstationary series, such as $1, 2, 3, \ldots, 9$, the mean will systematically overestimate the first half of the series and underestimate the last half. If the second condition is not met, some pattern in the data is implied. If such a pattern exists, other forecasting methods that could predict that pattern would be more accurate than the mean. Thus the mean should only be employed for stationary random series, or when no other forecasting method can be employed. The mean can therefore be used as a basis for comparison for other methods rather than as a method of its own.

A disadvantage of using the mean as a forecasting tool, particularly where time-series data are concerned, is the large number of data points required. This number continuously increases with time as new data become available and must be included in calculating the value of the mean. This proliferation of data can create storage problems and considerable computational requirements when forecasts for a large number of items are needed. In addition, such a mean for a time series is not responsive to changes in the mean value over time as can be seen from Figure 3-1. One approach frequently used for minimizing these problems is to keep constant the number of data points used in calculating the mean. This procedure provides a series of means (or moving averages), which can be computed by averaging the most recent N values.

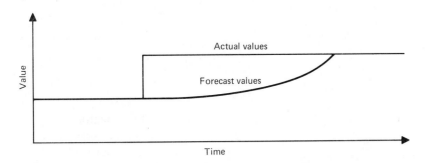

FIGURE 3-1 ACCURACY OF THE MEAN WHEN A STEP CHANGE OCCURS IN THE DATA (NO RANDOMNESS)

3/2 Single Moving Averages

The time-series technique of moving averages consists of taking a set of observed values, finding the average of those values, then using that average as the forecast for the next period. The actual number of past observations included in the average must be specified at the outset. The term *moving average* is used because as each new observation becomes available a new average can be computed by dropping the oldest observation from the average and including the newest one. The new average is then used as the forecast for the next period. Thus, the number of the data points from the series used in the average is always constant and includes the most recent observations.

Table 3-1 and Figure 3-2 illustrate the application of the technique of moving averages to the series of values for electric can opener shipments with both a five-month and a three-month moving average.

In Table 3-1, the three-month moving averages in column 4 are based on the values for the current month and the two previous months. For example, in time period 3, the value 176.7 is the average for periods 1, 2, and 3, i.e., $(200 + 135 + 195)/3$. This moving average could be used as a forecast for month 4.

TABLE 3-1   FORECASTING ELECTRIC CAN OPENER SHIPMENTS USING
MOVING AVERAGES

(1) Month	(2) Time Period	(3) Observed Values (shipments)	(4) Three-Month Moving Average	(5) Five-Month Moving Average
Jan.	1	200.0	—	—
Feb.	2	135.0	—	—
Mar.	3	195.0	—	—
Apr.	4	197.5	176.7	—
May	5	310.0	175.8	—
June	6	175.0	234.2	207.5
July	7	155.0	227.5	202.5
Aug.	8	130.0	213.3	206.5
Sept.	9	220.0	153.3	193.5
Oct.	10	277.0	168.3	198.0
Nov.	11	235.0	209.2	191.4
Dec.	12	—	244.2	203.5

The last figure in column 4, 244.2 is the average for periods 9, 10, and 11, and it could be used as the forecast for period 12 (December 1975). Similarly, in column 5, the value 207.5 is the average of the observed values in periods 1, 2, 3, 4, and 5. This value could serve as a forecast for month 6. The last entry in column 5, 203.5, is the average for periods 7, 8, 9, 10, and 11, and it could serve as a forecast for month 12. It should be clear that as new values for shipments become known, the moving average can be easily recomputed.

From Figure 3-2, it can be seen that the more observations included in the moving average, the greater the smoothing effect on the data. The two extreme cases of moving averages are when $N = 1$, in which case the most recent observation is used as the forecast for the next period, and $N = n$, in which case the mean is used as the forecast. Since the mean is the best estimator when the data are random, a large N should be used when there is a lot of randomness in the data. The effect of a large N will be to use an almost horizontal line as the estimator, which smooths the fluctuations caused by random variations. A small value for N should be used when there is a pattern but little random fluctuation in the data. Use of a small n allows the moving average to follow the pattern. With a small N, the forecasts will trail the pattern, lagging behind it by a few periods.

Algebraically, the techniques of forecasting with moving averages can be represented as follows:

$$F_{t+1} = (X_t + X_{t-1} + \cdots + X_{t-N+1})/N \qquad (3\text{-}1)$$

$$= \frac{1}{N} \sum_{i=t-N+1}^{t} X_i,$$

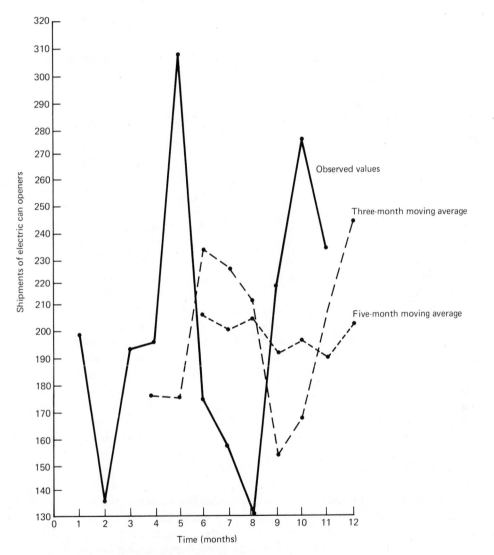

FIGURE 3-2 SHIPMENTS OF ELECTRIC CAN OPENERS—
ACTUAL AND MOVING AVERAGE VALUES

where t is the most recent value, and $t + 1$ is the next period, for which a forecast is desired.

It can be seen from this equation that in order to compute the moving average one must have the values of the past N observations. A somewhat shorter and easier way to state this equation for calculating the moving average is

$$F_{t+1} = \frac{X_t}{N} - \frac{X_{t-N+1}}{N} + F_t. \tag{3-2}$$

It can be seen from (3-2) that each new forecast based on a moving average is simply an adjustment of the previous moving average forecast (F_t). This adjustment includes the adding of the most recent observations (X_t) and the dropping of the least recent value (X_{t-N+1}). It is also easy to see that as N becomes larger the smoothing effect increases, because a much smaller adjustment is being made for each new time period, an attractive characteristic when randomness is substantial.

In order to apply moving averages, only a limited amount of historical data, N, is needed. Then either (3-1) or (3-2) can be used to compute the forecasts for future periods. Thus, both the data requirements and the computational requirements for applying moving averages to a single time series are minimal. However, the accuracy of the forecasts obtained through the moving averages method is usually low. In practice, the technique of moving averages is not used extensively because the method of exponential smoothing, which we will examine next, has all the advantages of moving averages plus a few additional ones that make it more attractive in those situations where moving averages would be suitable.

In summary, the method of moving averages can be used as a forecasting tool when the data is stationary. This method has, statistically, properties similar to those of the mean, since it is a special case of the mean. The advantage of the method of moving averages over the mean, however, is that it allows flexibility, since N can vary from 1 to n. This flexibility is attractive in time-series forecasting because N can be varied to respond to the pattern of the data.

3/3 Single Exponential Smoothing

There are two major limitations to the use of moving averages. First, to compute a moving average the past N observed values must be available. These data can take up considerable storage space if forecasts for a large number of items are required. Second, equal weight is given to each of the past N observations (i.e., the estimation is linear) and no weight is given to observations prior to period $(t - N + 1)$. A good argument can be made that in many cases the most recent observations contain more information than do older ones about what will happen in the future. Thus, recent values should be given relatively more weight in forecasting than the older observations. (This implies a form of nonlinear estimation that will be explored in more detail in Chapters 9 and 10.) Exponential smoothing satisfies this argument and in addition requires only two data points to forecast a future value.

The technique of exponential smoothing can be easily developed starting from equation (3-2) for moving averages. Suppose that X_{t-N+1} is not available. In such a situation, equation (3-2) might be modified so that in place of the observed value for period $(t - N + 1)$, an approximate value is used. One possible replacement would be the forecast value of the previous period, F_t. Making this substitution, equation (3-2) becomes equation (3-3). If the data are stationary, this is a fairly good approximation. Thus,

$$F_{t+1} = \frac{X_t}{N} - \frac{X_{t-N+1}}{N} + F_t \qquad (3\text{-}2)$$

becomes $\quad F_{t+1} = \dfrac{X_t}{N} - \dfrac{F_t}{N} + F_t \qquad (3\text{-}3)$

if the substitution $F_t = X_{t-N+1}$ is made.
Equation (3-3) can then be rewritten as

$$F_{t+1} = \left(\frac{1}{N}\right)X_t + \left(1 - \frac{1}{N}\right)F_t. \qquad (3\text{-}4)$$

From equation (3-4) it can be seen that this forecast is based on weighting the most recent observation with a weight of value $1/N$ and weighting the most recent forecast with a weight of value $[1 - (1/N)]$. Since N is a positive number greater than zero, $1/N$ will have to be a constant between zero (if $N = \infty$) and 1 (if $N = 1$). Substituting α for $1/N$, equation (3-4) becomes:

$$F_{t+1} = \alpha X_t + (1 - \alpha)F_t. \qquad (3\text{-}5)$$

This equation is the general form used in computing a forecast with the method of exponential smoothing. It substantially reduces any storage problem, since it is no longer necessary to store all of the historical data (as in the case of the mean) or a subset of them (as in the case of the moving average). Rather, only the most recent observation, the most recent forecast, and a value for α must be stored.

The implications of exponential smoothing can be better seen if equation (3-5) is expanded by replacing F_t with its components as follows:

$$\begin{aligned} F_{t+1} &= \alpha X_t + (1 - \alpha)[\alpha X_{t-1} + (1 - \alpha)F_{t-1}] \\ &= \alpha X_t + \alpha(1 - \alpha)X_{t-1} + (1 - \alpha)^2 F_{t-1}. \end{aligned} \qquad (3\text{-}6)$$

If this substitution process is repeated by replacing F_{t-1} by its components, F_{t-2} by its components, etc., the result is equation (3-7):

$$F_{t+1} = \alpha X_t + \alpha(1 - \alpha)X_{t-1} + \alpha(1 - \alpha)^2 X_{t-2} + \alpha(1 - \alpha)^3 X_{t-3}$$
$$+ \alpha(1 - \alpha)^4 X_{t-4} + \alpha(1 - \alpha)^5 X_{t-5} + \cdots + \alpha(1 - \alpha)^{N-1} X_{t-(N-1)} \tag{3-7}$$

From equation (3-7) it can be seen that the weights applied to each of the past values decrease exponentially, thus the name exponential smoothing. It should be pointed out that even though the objective may still be to minimize the MSE, the estimation involved in exponential smoothing is nonlinear.

An alternative way of writing (3-5) is to rearrange the terms in the following manner:

$$F_{t+1} = F_t + \alpha(X_t - F_t). \tag{3-8}$$

This is simply

$$F_{t+1} = F_t + \alpha e_t,$$

since the error for period t is just the actual minus forecast.

From equation (3-8) it can be seen that the forecast provided by exponential smoothing is simply the old forecast plus an adjustment for the error that occurred in the last forecast. In this form it is evident that when α has a value close to 1, the new forecast will include a substantial adjustment for the error in the previous forecast. Conversely, when α is close to 0, the new forecast will include very little adjustment. Thus, the effect of a large and small α is completely analogous (in an opposite direction) to the effect of including a small or a large number of observations when computing a moving average. It should also be observed that a single exponential smoothing will always trail any trend in the actual data, since the most it can do is adjust the next forecast for some percentage of the most recent error.

Equation (3-8) involves a basic principle of negative feedback, since it works much like the control process employed by automatic devices such as thermostats, automatic pilots, etc. The past forecast error is used to correct the next forecast in a direction opposite to that of the error. There will be an adjustment until the error is corrected. It is the same principle that directs an automatic pilot device to an equilibrium course once a deviation (error) has taken place. This principle, simple as it may appear, plays an extremely important role in forecasting. If properly applied, it can be used to develop a self-adjusting process that corrects for forecasting error automatically.

The application of single exponential smoothing can be illustrated by using the example given in Section 3-2. Table 3-2 shows the exponential smoothing results from electric can opener shipments using α values of .1, .5, and .9.

One can forecast with single exponential smoothing by using either equation (3-5) or (3-8). (In practice the former is most often used.) For example, in Table 3-2 the forecast for period 12 (December) when $\alpha = .1$ is computed as

$$F_{12} = \alpha X_{11} + (1 - \alpha)F_{11}$$

$$= .1(235) + .9(202.3)$$

$$= 205.6.$$

Similarly, when $\alpha = .9$ equation (3-5) gives for period 12

$$F_{12} = .9(235) + .1(270.9) = 238.6.$$

Single exponential smoothing requires only a minimal amount of data and number of computations. It is therefore attractive when a large number of items require forecasting. One point of concern, however, can be the first period when no previous forecast is available (F_t is unknown). This problem can be resolved by using the first observed value as the first forecast. In Table 3-2, the forecast of 193.5 in the $\alpha = .1$ column was obtained by taking 200.0 as the previous forecast value and adding to that, $\alpha(200.0 - 135.0)$. The resulting value of 193.5 was then used as the forecast for period 3.

An alternative solution to this starting problem is to use the first four or five values to calculate a forecast and then to use that value as the forecast initial value. There are still more complicated methods available that use least

TABLE 3-2 FORECASTING ELECTRIC CAN OPENER SHIPMENTS USING EXPONENTIAL SMOOTHING

Month	Time Period	Observed Values (shipments)	Exponentially Smoothed Values		
			$\alpha = .1$	$\alpha = .5$	$\alpha = .9$
Jan.	1	200.0	—	—	—
Feb.	2	135.0	200.0	200.0	200.0
Mar.	3	195.0	193.5	167.5	141.5
Apr.	4	197.5	193.7	181.3	189.7
May	5	310.0	194.0	189.4	196.7
June	6	175.0	205.6	249.7	298.7
July	7	155.0	202.6	212.3	187.4
Aug.	8	130.0	197.8	183.7	158.2
Sept.	9	220.0	191.0	156.8	132.8
Oct.	10	277.5	193.9	188.4	211.3
Nov.	11	235.0	202.3	233.0	270.9
Dec.	12	—	205.6	234.0	238.6

squares estimation procedures. However, it is the authors' opinion that these are of little importance, since the problem only arises at the outset. The forecasting accuracy is less important, at this early stage, since the goal is to develop the system and make it accurate over several periods.

The effect that the value of α has on the amount of smoothing done can be seen from Figure 3-3. A large value of α (.9) gives very little smoothing in the

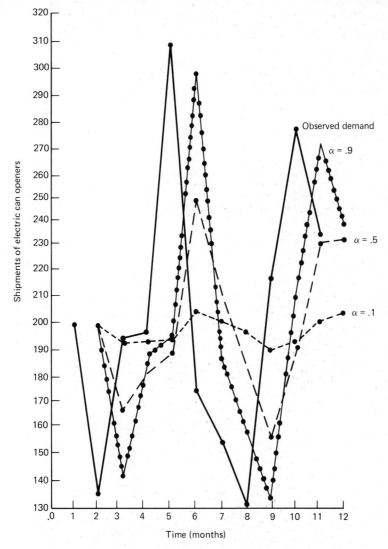

FIGURE 3-3 SHIPMENTS OF ELECTRIC CAN OPENERS— ACTUAL AND EXPONENTIAL SMOOTHING VALUES

forecast, whereas a small value of α (.1) gives considerable smoothing. The reason for this can be seen from equation (3-8) or by recalling the method of moving averages and the fact that the larger the value of α the smaller the corresponding value of N.*

Simple as single exponential smoothing is, it does have its problems. One of these arises in trying to find the best value for α in such a way as to minimize the MSE. Unlike the mean, where this minimization occurs any time the average of a set of numbers is calculated, for exponential smoothing the minimum MSE must be determined through trial and error. A value for α is applied, the MSE computed, then another α value is tried. The MSEs are then compared to find the α value that gives the minimum MSE. In the example of Table 3-2 the

MSE $= 3438.3$ when $\alpha = .1$,

MSE $= 4347.2$ when $\alpha = .5$, and

MSE $= 5039.4$ when $\alpha = .9$.

This wide range of MSE values indicates the important role of α in determining the resulting errors. Finding an α value that is close to the best possible generally requires only a few trials, since its value can be approximated by simply comparing a few MSE and α values. For the series in Table 3-2 it can be seen that the MSE decreases as α approaches 0. In fact,

$\alpha = .05$ gives MSE $= 3300.9$ and

$\alpha = .01$ gives MSE $= 3184.1$.

The reason for this is that the data are almost random, so the smaller the value of α, the smaller the MSE.

3/4 Adaptive-Response-Rate Single Exponential Smoothing

Adaptive-response-rate single exponential smoothing (ARRSES) has an advantage over single exponential smoothing—it does not require specification of a value for α. This characteristic is particularly attractive when several hundreds of even thousands of items require forecasting. Additionally, this method can change the value of α, on an on going basis when changes in the pattern of the data have made the initial α value no longer appropriate. ARRSES is adaptive

---

* It can be shown that $\alpha = 2/(N + 1)$ is the best equivalence relationship between single exponential smoothing and moving averages. Thus a moving average with $N = 12$ and exponential smoothing with $\alpha = 2/13 = .154$ give comparable results.

TABLE 3-3 FORECASTING ELECTRIC CAN OPENER SHIPMENTS USING ADAPTIVE-RESPONSE-RATE SINGLE EXPONENTIAL SMOOTHING

Period	Observed Value (shipments) (X)	Forecast (F)	Error (e_t)	Smoothed Error (E_t)	Absolute Smoothed Error (M_t)	α_t Value
1	200	—	—	—	—	—
2	135	200.0	−65.0	−13.0	13.0	.200
3	195	187.0	8.0	−8.8	12.0	.200
4	197.5	188.6	8.9	−5.3	11.4	.200
5	310	190.4	119.6	19.7	33.0	.462
6	175	245.7	−70.7	1.6	40.6	.597
7	155	203.5	−48.5	−8.4	42.1	.040
8	130	201.5	−71.5	−21.0	48.0	.199
9	220	187.3	32.7	−10.3	45.0	.438
10	277.5	201.6	75.9	7.0	51.1	.228
11	235	218.9	16.1	8.8	44.1	.136
12	—	221.1	—	—	—	.199

in the sense that the value for α will change automatically when there is a change in the basic pattern requiring a different α.

The basic equation for forecasting with the method of ARRSES is similar to equation (3-5) except that α is replaced by α_t.

$$F_{t+1} = \alpha_t X_t + (1 - \alpha_t)F_t \tag{3-9}$$

where
$$\alpha_{t+1} = \left| \frac{E_t}{M_t} \right|, \tag{3-10}*$$

$$E_t = \beta e_t + (1 - \beta)E_{t-1}, \tag{3-11}$$

$$M_t = \beta |e_t| + (1 - \beta)M_{t-1}, \tag{3-12}$$

$$e_t = X_t - F_t, \tag{3-13}$$

$$\beta = .2,$$

and | | denotes absolute values.

---

* Instead of α_{t+1} we could have used α_t in equation (3-10). We prefer α_{t+1} because ARRSES is often too responsive to changes, thus using α_t we introduce a small lag of one period, which allows the system to "settle" a little and forecast in a more conservative manner.

Table 3-3 illustrates the calculations required to forecast electric can opener shipments using the method of ARRSES.

The forecast for period 10, for example, is

$$F_{10} = \alpha_9 X_9 + (1 - \alpha_9)F_9$$

$$= .438(220) + .562(187.3) = 201.6.$$

Once the actual value for period 10 becomes known, α can be updated and used for the next period's calculations. This entails computing e_{10}, E_{10}, and M_{10} as follows:

$$e_{10} = 277.5 - 201.6 = 75.9,$$ [using (3-13)]

$$E_{10} = .2(75.9) + .8(-10.3) = 7,$$ [using (3-11)]

$$M_{10} = .2|(75.9)| + .8(45) = 51.1,$$ [using (3-12)]

and $$\alpha_{11} = \left|\frac{7}{51.1}\right| = .136.$$ [using (3-10)]

Similarly, the forecast for period 11 is:

$$F_{11} = \alpha_{10}X_{10} + (1 - \alpha_{10})F_{10}$$

$$= .228(277.5) + .772(201.6) = 218.9.$$

This forecast value can then be used to update the value of α_{t+1}.

$$e_{11} = 235 - 218.9 = 16.1,$$

$$E_{11} = .2(16.1) + .8(7) = 8.8,$$

$$M_{11} = .2|(16.1)| + .8(51.1) = 44.1,$$

$$\alpha_{12} = \left|\frac{8.8}{44.1}\right| = .199.$$

Finally, the forecast for period 12 can be computed using equation (3-9)

$$F_{12} = .136(235) + .864(218.9) = 221.1.$$

3/5 Linear Moving Averages

As indicated in Section 3-2, applying the method of moving averages to a set of data containing a trend gives forecasts that continually underestimate the actual values. This underestimation can be easily seen in the example shown in Table 3-4. The series used in this example contains no randomness but a perfect linear trend pattern. (The same problem of lagging behind actual values exists when randomness is present.)

TABLE 3-4   FORECASTING A SERIES WITH TREND USING A MOVING
AVERAGE ($N = 3$)

Period	Observed Value	Forecast ($N = 3$)	Error
1	2	—	—
2	4	—	—
3	6	—	—
4	8	4	4
5	10	6	4
6	12	8	4
7	14	10	4
8	16	12	4
9	18	14	4
—	—	16	4

To avoid the systematic error that occurs if moving averages are applied
to data with trend, the method of linear moving averages has been developed.
The basis of this method is to calculate a second moving average. This "double"
moving average is a moving average of the moving averages based on the actual
data. The double moving averages are going to lag behind the single moving
averages by the same amount that the single moving averages lag behind the
actual data. Thus the differences between the actual and the single moving averages
will be the same as the differences between the single and double moving averages
(see Table 3-5).

In order to forecast with no systematic error, the single moving average
(column 3 in Table 3-5) can have added to it the difference between the single
and double moving average (column 6 in Table 3-5). This will bring the forecast
to the level of the actual data as shown in columns 7 and 8 of Table 3-5. In
this example, N equaled 3, but in general, this same principle of linear moving
averages can be applied using the following formulas:

$$S_t' = \frac{X_t + X_{t-1} + X_{t-2} + \cdots + X_{t-N+1}}{N}, \tag{3-14}$$

$$S_t'' = \frac{S_t' + S_{t-1}' + S_{t-2}' + \cdots + S_{t-N+1}'}{N}, \tag{3-15}$$

$$a_t = S_t' + (S_t' - S_t'') = 2S_t' - S_t'', \tag{3-16}$$

$$b_t = \frac{2}{N-1} (S_t' - S_t'') \qquad (3\text{-}17)$$

$$F_{t+m} = a_t + b_t m \qquad (3\text{-}18)$$

where m is the number of periods ahead to be forecast.

Equation (3-14) is completely analogous to calculating the single moving averages. Equation (3-15) then computes the double moving averages and equation (3-16) provides a base adjustment to the starting point for a forecast (the most recent value), so that it will not lag behind the actual data. This basic adjustment is made by adding to the single moving average the difference between the single and the double moving average. However, this brings the forecast just to the point of the most recent period. (Notice that S_t' and S_t'' were used and not S_{t+1}', and S_{t+1}''.)

To forecast, the trend in the data must be found using (3-17). In equation (3-17) division is by $2/(N-1)$ because the moving averages are the average of N points, which need to be centered in the middle of the N points, or at $(N-1)/2$. If single moving average were used for forecasting, it would lag behind the actual value by $(N-1)/2b$ (where b is the amount of trend change in each period).

TABLE 3-5   FORECASTING A SERIES WITH TREND USING A LINEAR MOVING AVERAGE ($N = 3$)

(1) Period	(2) Actual Value	(3) Forecast Single Moving Average ($N = 3$)	(4) Error Difference $(2) - (4)$	(5) Forecast Double Moving Average ($N = 3$)	(6) Error Difference $(3) - (5)$	(7) Overall Forecast $(3) + (6)$	(8) Error Difference $(2) - (7)$
1	2	—	—	—	—	—	—
2	4	—	—	—	—	—	—
3	6	—	—	—	—	—	—
4	8	4	4	—	—	—	—
5	10	6	4	—	—	—	—
6	12	8	4	—	—	—	—
7	14	10	4	6	4	14	0
8	16	12	4	8	4	16	0
9	18	14	4	10	4	18	0
—	—	16	—	12	4	20	0
—	—	—	—	14	—	—	—

But since $(N - 1)/2b$ is equal to $S_t' - S_t''$, b can be found by simply solving this equation to obtain (3-17).

$$\frac{N - 1}{2} b_t = S_t' - S_t''$$

and

$$b_t = \frac{2}{N - 1} (S_t' - S_t'').$$

(3-17)

TABLE 3-6 APPLICATION OF LINEAR MOVING AVERAGES

Period	(1) Inventory Balance of Product E12	(2) Four-Month Moving Average of (1)	(3) Four-Month Moving Average of (2)	(4) Value of a	(5) Value of b	(6) Value of $a + b_m$ When $m = 1$ (lagged 1 mo.)
1	140	—	—	—	—	—
2	159	—	—	—	—	—
3	136	—	—	—	—	—
4	157	148.0	—	—	—	—
5	173	156.2	—	—	—	—
6	131	149.2	—	—	—	—
7	177	159.5	153.25	165.75	4.167	—
8	188	167.2	158.06	176.44	6.125	170
9	154	162.5	159.62	165.37	1.917	182
10	179	174.5	165.94	183.06	5.708	167
11	180	175.2	169.87	180.62	3.583	189
12	160	168.2	170.12	166.37	−1.250	184
13	182	175.2	173.31	177.18	−1.292	165
14	192	178.5	174.31	182.69	−2.792	176
15	224	189.5	177.87	201.12	7.750	180
16	188	196.5	184.94	208.06	7.708	209
17	198	200.5	191.25	209.75	6.167	216
18	206	204.0	197.62	210.37	4.250	216
19	203	198.7	199.94	197.56	−0.917	215
20	238	211.2	203.62	218.87	5.083	197
21	228	218.7	208.19	229.31	7.042	224
22	231	225.0	213.44	236.56	7.708	236
23	221	229.5	221.12	237.87	5.583	244
24	259	234.7	227.00	242.50	5.167	243
25	273	246.0	233.81	258.19	8.125	248
						266

In the example of Table 3-5, N equaled 3 and thus (3-17) reduced to

$$b_t = (S_t' - S_t'').$$

As an illustration of the method of the linear moving averages, Table 3-6 presents data on a series of 25 inventory values. Using a value of $N = 4$, columns 2 through 6 show the results obtained. Figure 3-4 illustrates these same results in graphic form. The computational steps are:

Column 2: the four-period moving averages   [using (3-14)]

Column 3: the double moving averages (frequently called 4×4 moving averages)   [using (5-15)]

Column 4: the values of a [using (3-16)]

Column 5: the values of b [using (3-17)]

Column 6: the forecasts for one period ahead ($M = 1$)   [using (3-18)]

As an example of the calculations required for Table 3-6 consider the forecast for period 24 that would be made in period 23.

$$F_{24} = a_{23} + b_{23}(1) = 237.875 + 5.583(1) = 243.5,$$

where $a_{23} = 2S'_{23} - S''_{23} = 2(229.5) - 221.125 = 237.875,$

$$b_{23} = \frac{2}{4-1}(S'_{23} - S''_{23}) = \frac{2}{3}(229.5 - 221.125) = 5.583.$$

$$S'_{23} = \frac{X_{23} + X_{22} + X_{21} + X_{20}}{4} = \frac{221 + 231 + 218.75 + 211.25}{4} = 229.5,$$

and $S''_{23} = \dfrac{S'_{23} + S'_{22} + S'_{21} + S'_{20}}{4} = \dfrac{229.5 + 225 + 218.75 + 211.25}{4} = 221.125.$

Similarly, the forecast for period 25 is:

$$F_{25} = a_{24} + b_{24}(1) = 242.5 + 5.1667(1) = 247.667,$$

since $a_{24} = 242.5$ and $b_{24} = 5.1667.$

The forecast for period 26 is:

$$F_{26} = a_{25} = b_{25}(1) = 258.187 + 8.125(1) = 266.31,$$

while for periods 27 and 28, the forecasts use the most recent values of a and b (period 25) as follows:

$$F_{27} = a_{25} + b_{25}(2) = 258.187 + 8.125(2) = 274.437,$$

$$F_{28} = a_{25} + b_{25}(3) = 258.187 + 8.125(3) = 282.562.$$

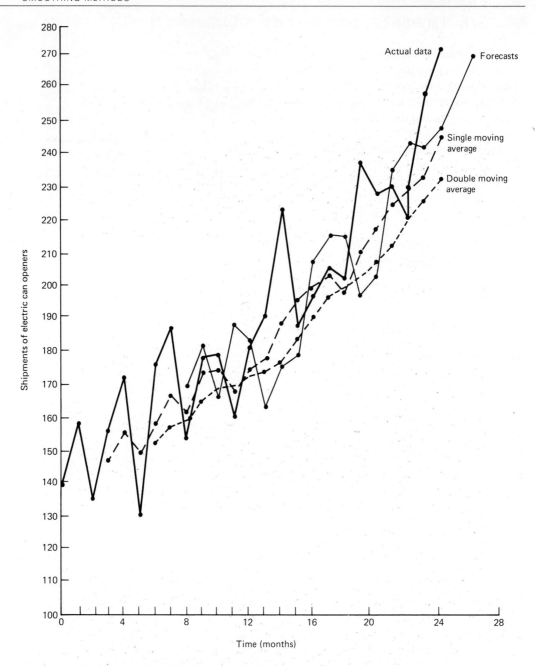

FIGURE 3-4 APPLICATION OF LINEAR MOVING AVERAGES TO
DATA IN TABLE 3-6

3/6 Linear Exponential Smoothing

In a manner completely analogous to that used in going from single moving averages to single exponential smoothing (see Section 3-3) it is possible to go from linear moving averages to linear exponential smoothing. Such a move may be attractive because the two limitations of single moving averages—the need to save the last N values and the application of equal weights to the last N observations— still exist with linear moving averages except that the number of data points required is now $2N$. Linear exponential smoothing can be computed with only three data values and a value for α. This approach also gives decreasing weights to past observations. For these reasons it is preferred to linear moving averages as a method of forecasting in the great majority of cases.

3/6/1 Brown's One-Parameter Linear Exponential Smoothing

The underlying rationale of Brown's linear exponential smoothing is similar to that of linear moving averages: since both the single and double smoothed values lag the actual data when a trend exists (as shown in Figure 3-5), the difference between the single and double smoothed values can be added to the single smoothed value and adjusted for trend. The equations used in implementing Brown's one-parameter linear exponential smoothing are shown below as (3-19) through (3-23) and their application is illustrated in Table 3-7.

Column 2 $\quad S_t' = \alpha X_t + (1 - \alpha)S_{t-1}',$ $\hfill$ (3-19)

Column 3 $\quad S_t'' = \alpha S_t' + (1 - \alpha)S_{t-1}'',$ $\hfill$ (3-20)

where $\qquad\quad S_t'$ is the single exponential smoothed value

and $\qquad\qquad S_t''$ is the double exponential smoothed value.

Column 4 $\quad a_t = S_t' + (S_t' - S_t'') = 2S_t' - S_t'',$ $\hfill$ (3-21)

Column 5 $\quad b_t = \dfrac{\alpha}{1 - \alpha}(S_t' - S_t''),$ $\hfill$ (3-22)*

Column 6 $\;F_{t+m} = a_t + b_t m,$ $\hfill$ (3-23)

where $\qquad\quad m$ is the number of periods ahead to be forecast.

---

* Equation (3-22) is multiplied by $\alpha/(1 - \alpha)$ for the same reason that (3-17) is multiplied by $2/(N - 1)$. This can be seen by recalling that the weights of exponential smoothing decrease exponentially in a manner given by (3-7). That is the weights are α, $\alpha(1 - \alpha)^2$, $\alpha(1 - \alpha)^3$, $\alpha(1 - \alpha)^4, \ldots, \alpha(1 - \alpha)^{n-1}$. The sum of this series is $(1 - \alpha)/\alpha$. Thus $(S_t' - S_t'') = b_t[(1 - \alpha)/\alpha]$, which when solved for b_t gives (3-22).

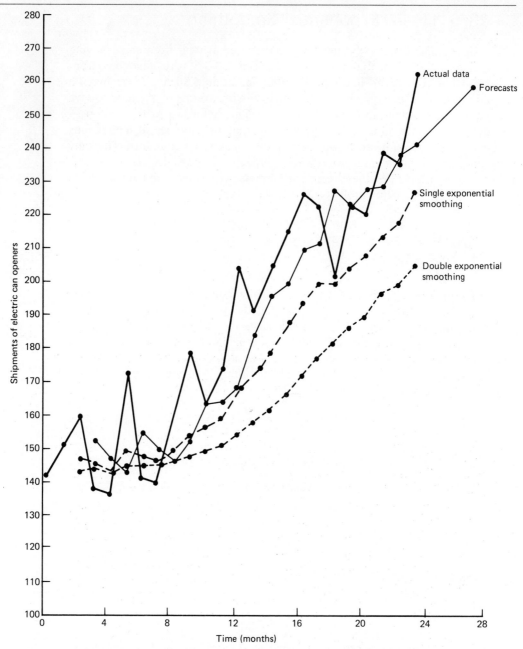

FIGURE 3-5 APPLICATION OF BROWN'S ONE-PARAMETER
LINEAR EXPONENTIAL SMOOTHING TO DATA IN
TABLE 3-7

TABLE 3-7 APPLICATION OF BROWN'S ONE-PARAMETER LINEAR EXPONENTIAL SMOOTHING

Period	(1) Inventory Demand for Product E15	(2) Single Exponential Smoothing	(3) Double Exponential Smoothing	(4) Value of a $[2(2) - (3)]$	(5) Value of b [see (3-22)]	(6) Value of $a+b$ $[(4) + (5)]$ (lagged 1 mo.)
1	143	143.000	143.000	—	—	—
2	152	144.800	143.360	146.24	.36000	—
3	161	148.040	144.296	151.784	.93600	147
4	139	146.232	144.683	147.781	.38720	153
5	137	144.386	144.624	144.147	.00595	148
6	174	150.308	145.761	154.856	1.13696	144
7	142	148.647	146.338	150.956	.57724	156
8	141	147.117	146.494	147.741	.15592	151
9	162	150.094	147.214	152.974	.72004	148
10	180	156.075	148.986	163.164	1.77228	154
11	164	157.660	150.721	164.599	1.73482	165
12	171	160.328	152.642	168.014	1.92145	166
13	206	169.462	156.006	182.919	3.36404	170
14	193	174.170	159.639	188.701	3.63274	186
15	207	180.736	163.858	197.613	4.21938	193
16	218	188.189	168.724	207.653	4.86607	202
17	229	196.351	174.250	218.452	5.52531	212
18	225	202.081	179.816	224.346	5.56621	214
19	204	202.465	184.346	220.584	4.52973	230
20	227	207.372	188.951	225.792	4.60519	225
21	223	210.497	193.260	227.735	4.30930	231
22	242	216.798	197.968	235.628	4.70754	232
23	239	221.238	202.622	239.855	4.65411	241
24	266	230.191	208.136	252.246	5.51377	245
25	—	—	—	—	—	258

The calculations in Table 3-7 are based on an $\alpha = .2$ and a forecast for one period ahead. For example, in period 23 the forecast for period 24 is as follows:

$$F_{24} = a_{23} + b_{23}(1) = 239.855 + 4.654(1) = 244.51,$$

where $a_{23} = 2S'_{23} - S''_{23} = 239.855,$

$$b_{23} = \frac{.2}{.8}(S'_{23} - S''_{23}) = \frac{1}{4}(18.616) = 4.654,$$

$$S'_{23} = .2X_{23} + .8S_{22} = .2(239) + .8(216.798) = 221.238,$$

$$S''_{23} = .2S'_{23} + .8S''_{22} = .2(221.238) + .8(197.968) = 202.622.$$

The forecast for period 25 is:

$$F_{25} = a_{24} + b_{24}(1) = 252.246 + 5.514(1) = 257.76,$$

where a_{24} and b_{24} are calculated as before.

The forecast for period 26 is

$$F_{26} = a_{24} + b_{24}(2) = 252.246 + 5.514(2) = 263.274,$$

while the forecast for period 30 will be

$$F_{30} = a_{24} + b_{24}(6) = 252.246 + 5.514(6) = 285.33,$$

since the most recent values available for a and b are from period 24.

In order to apply formulas (3-19) and (3-20), values of S'_{t-1} and S''_{t-1} must be available. However, when $t = 1$ no such values exist. Thus, these values will have to be specified at the outset of this method. This can be done by simply letting S_t' and S_t'' be equal to X_t or by using some average of the first few values as a starting point. This problem exists in all exponential smoothing methods. However, it is critical only in the starting phase.

3/6/2   Holt's Two-Parameter Linear Exponential Smoothing

Holt's linear smoothing is similar in principle to Brown's except that it does not apply the double smoothing formula. Instead it smooths the trend values directly. This provides greater flexibility, since it allows the trend to be smoothed with a different parameter than that used on the original series. The forecast for Holt's linear exponential smoothing is found using two smoothing constants (with values between 0 and 1) and three equations:

$$S_t = \alpha X_t + (1 - \alpha)(S_{t-1} + b_{t-1}), \tag{3-24}$$

$$b_t = \gamma(S_t - S_{t-1}) + (1 - \gamma)b_{t-1}, \tag{3-25}$$

$$F_{t+m} = S_t + b_t m. \tag{3-26}$$

Equation (3-24) adjusts S_t directly for the trend of the previous period, b_{t-1}, by adding it to the last smoothed value, S_{t-1}. This eliminates the lag and brings S_t to the approximate base of the current data value. Equation (3-25) then updates the trend, which is expressed as the difference between the last two smoothed values. This is appropriate because if there is a trend in the data, new values should be higher or lower than the previous ones. Since there may be some randomness remaining, it is eliminated by smoothing with γ (gamma) the trend in the last period $(S_t - S_{t-1})$, and adding that to the previous estimate of the trend multiplied by $(1 - \gamma)$. Thus, (3-25) is similar to the basic forms of single

TABLE 3-8 APPLICATION OF HOLT'S TWO-PARAMETER LINEAR EXPONENTIAL SMOOTHING

Period	(1) Inventory Demand for Product E15	(4) Smoothing of Data (3-24)	(5) Smoothing of Trend (3-25)	(6) Forecast When $m = 1$ (3-26) (lagged 1 mo.)
1	143.00	—	—	—
2	152.00	139.60	−5.57	—
3	161.00	139.42	−3.95	134.03
4	139.00	136.18	−3.74	135.47
5	137.00	133.35	−3.47	132.44
6	174.00	138.71	−0.82	129.88
7	142.00	138.71	−0.57	137.89
8	141.00	138.71	−0.40	138.14
9	162.00	143.05	1.02	138.31
10	180.00	151.25	3.18	144.07
11	164.00	156.34	3.75	154.43
12	171.00	162.28	4.40	160.10
13	206.00	174.54	6.76	166.68
14	193.00	183.65	7.47	181.31
15	207.00	194.29	8.42	191.11
16	218.00	205.77	9.34	202.71
17	229.00	217.88	10.17	215.10
18	225.00	227.44	9.99	228.05
19	204.00	230.74	7.98	237.43
20	227.00	236.38	7.28	238.72
21	223.00	239.53	6.04	243.66
22	242.00	244.85	5.82	245.56
23	239.00	248.34	5.12	250.68
24	266.00	255.97	5.88	253.46
25	—	—	—	261.85

smoothing given by (3-5) and (3-8) but applies to the updating of the trend. Finally, equation (3-26) is used to forecast by adding to the base value, the trend, b_t, times the number of periods ahead to be forecast.

Using the data shown in Table 3-7, Table 3-8 shows the application of Holt's linear smoothing to a series with trend. The calculations involved can be illustrated by first looking at a forecast for period 23, using $\alpha = .2$ and $\gamma = .3$:

$$F_{23} = S_{22} + b_{22}(1), \qquad \text{[using (3-26)]}$$

$$\text{where} \quad S_{22} = .2X_{22} + .8(S_{21} + b_{21}) \qquad \text{[using (3-24)]}$$

$$= .2(242) + .8(239.53 + 6.04) = 244.85,$$

$$\text{and} \quad b_{22} = .3(S_{22} - S_{21}) + .7b_{21} \qquad \text{[using (3-25)]}$$

$$= .3(244.85 - 239.53) + .7(6.04) = 5.82.$$

$$\text{Thus,} \quad F_{23} = 244.85 + 5.82(1) = 250.68.$$

Similarly the forecast for period 24 is

$$F_{24} = 248.34 + 5.12(1) = 253.46,$$

$$\text{since} \quad S_{23} = .2(239) + .8(244.85 + 5.82) = 248.34,$$

$$\text{and} \quad b_{23} = .3(248.34 - 244.85) + .7(5.82) = 5.12.$$

Finally, the forecasts for periods 25, 26, and 30 can be computed as

$$F_{25} = 248.34 + 5.12(1) = 253.46,$$

$$F_{26} = 248.34 + 5.12(2) = 258.58,$$

$$F_{30} = 248.34 + 5.12(6) = 279.06.$$

3/7 Brown's Quadratic Exponential Smoothing

Just as linear exponential smoothing can be used to predict data with a basic trend pattern, higher forms of smoothing can be used when the basic underlying pattern of the data is quadratic, cubic, or higher order. To go from linear to quadratic smoothing, the basic approach is to incorporate an additional level of smoothing (triple smoothing) and to estimate an additional parameter to deal with the quadratic equation. (Similarly, one could go from quadratic to cubic and so on for higher orders of smoothing.)

The equations for quadratic smoothing are

$$S_t' = \alpha X_t + (1 - \alpha)S_{t-1}', \qquad (3\text{-}27)$$

$$S_t'' = \alpha S_t' + (1 - \alpha)S_{t-1}'', \qquad (3\text{-}28)$$

$$S_t''' = \alpha S_t'' + (1 - \alpha)S_{t-1}''', \tag{3-29}$$

$$a_t = 3S_t' - 3S_t'' + S_t''', \tag{3-30}$$

$$b_t = \frac{\alpha}{2(1 - \alpha)^2}[(6 - 5\alpha)S_t' - (10 - 8\alpha)S_t'' + (4 - 3\alpha)S_t'''], \tag{3-31}$$

$$c_t = \frac{\alpha^2}{(1 - \alpha)^2}(S_t' - 2S_t'' + S_t'''), \tag{3-32}$$

and $$F_{t+m} = a_t + b_t m + \frac{1}{2}c_t m^2. \tag{3-33}$$

The equations required for quadratic smoothing are considerably more complicated than those for single and linear smoothing. However, the approach is the same in seeking to adjust the forecast values so they will follow changes in quadratic trends. The detailed derivation of equations (3-27) through (3-33) are given in Brown (1963, pp. 140–42).

As an application of quadratic smoothing the same data used in Tables 3-7 and 3-8 is presented in Table 3-9. The calculations required to develop Table 3-9 can be illustrated through preparation of a forecast for period 24. The first step is to compute a_{23}, b_{23} and c_{23}, which requires values for S_{23}', S_{23}'', and S_{23}'''. Assuming $\alpha = .15$, these are computed as

$$S_{23}' = .15(239) + .85(209.3) = 213.8,$$

$$S_{23}'' = .15(213.8) + .85(185.6) = 189.8,$$

$$S_{23}''' = .15(189.8) + .85(167.5) = 170.8,$$

and a_t, b_t and c_t are computed as

$$a_{23} = 3(213.8) - 3(189.8) + 170.8 = 242.8,$$

$$b_{23} = \frac{.15}{2(.85)^2}([6 - 5(.15)]213.8 - [10 - 8(.15)]189.8 + [4 - 3(.15)]170.8)$$

$$= .1038[(6 - .75)213.8 - (10 - 1.2)189.8 + (4 - .45)170.8]$$

$$= .1038(1122.45 - 1670.24 + 606.34) = 6.07,$$

$$c_{23} = \frac{.15^2}{.85^2}(213.8 - 2(189.8) + 170.8) = .1557.$$

Thus $$F_{24} = 242.8 + 6.07(1) + \frac{1}{2}(.1557)(1^2) = 248.95.$$

Similarly, the forecast for period 25 is computed as

$$F_{25} = 255.6 + 7.3(1) + \frac{1}{2}(.2)(1^2) = 262.97,$$

since $a_{24} = 255.6$, $b_{24} = 7.3$ and $c_{24} = 2$ (from Table 3-9).

Finally, forecasts for periods 27 and 30 can be computed as

$$F_{27} = 255.6 + 7.3(2) + \frac{1}{2}(.2)(2^2) = 270.60,$$

$$F_{30} = 255.6 + 7.3(6) + \frac{1}{2}(.2)(6^2) = 303.26.$$

TABLE 3-9   APPLICATION OF BROWN'S QUADRATIC EXPONENTIAL SMOOTHING

Period	Inventory Demand Product E15	Single Smoothing (3-27)	Double Smoothing (3-28)	Triple Smoothing (3-29)	Value of a (3-30)	Value of b (3-31)	Value of c (3-32)	Forecast (3-33)
1	143	—	—	—	—	—	—	—
2	152	144.4	143.2	143.0	146.5	.6	.0	—
3	161	146.8	143.7	143.1	152.4	1.5	.1	147.1
4	139	145.7	144.0	143.3	148.2	.6	.0	153.9
5	137	144.4	144.1	143.4	144.2	−.1	.0	148.8
6	174	148.8	144.8	143.6	155.7	1.8	.1	144.1
7	142	147.8	145.2	143.9	151.5	.9	.0	157.5
8	141	146.8	145.5	144.1	148.0	.2	.0	152.4
9	162	149.1	146.0	144.4	153.5	1.1	.0	148.2
10	180	153.7	147.2	144.8	164.4	2.7	.1	154.6
11	164	155.2	148.4	145.3	165.9	2.6	.1	167.2
12	171	157.6	149.8	146.0	169.5	2.9	.1	168.6
13	206	164.9	152.0	146.9	185.4	5.1	.2	172.5
14	193	169.1	154.6	148.1	191.6	5.5	.2	190.7
15	207	174.8	157.6	149.5	201.0	6.4	.3	197.2
16	218	181.3	161.2	151.2	211.5	7.3	.3	207.5
17	229	188.4	165.2	153.3	222.9	8.2	.4	219.0
18	225	193.9	169.5	155.8	228.8	8.2	.3	231.3
19	204	195.4	173.4	158.4	224.4	6.5	.2	237.2
20	227	200.2	177.4	161.3	229.4	6.4	.2	231.0
21	223	203.6	181.4	164.3	231.0	5.8	.2	236.0
22	242	209.3	185.6	167.5	238.8	6.3	.2	236.9
23	239	213.8	189.8	170.8	242.8	6.1	.2	245.2
24	266	221.6	194.6	174.4	255.6	7.3	.2	249.0
25	—	—	—	—	—	—	—	263.0

3/8 Selecting the Appropriate Smoothing Method for the Data Pattern

The set of moving average and exponential smoothing methods examined thus far in this chapter can deal with almost any type of stationary or non-stationary data as long as the data are nonseasonal. When seasonality does exist, these methods will do a poor job of forecasting, since there will be some systematic pattern (the seasonality) remaining in the errors that could be forecast to improve the accuracy.

As an illustration of the inadequacies of the smoothing methods examined thus far in dealing with seasonal patterns the methods of single and linear exponential smoothing can be applied to the seasonal data of Table 3-10. These data are for quarterly exports of a French company from 1970 through 1976. Figure 3-6 is a graph of these data.

Table 3-11 shows the forecasts and errors (actual versus forecast) that result when the methods of single and linear exponential smoothing are applied to the data of Table 3-10. From Table 3-11 it is easy to see the systematic pattern that exists: first the errors are all positive except for negative values that occur every fourth period. There is another negative error at period 21, probably due to randomness. Clearly such a seasonal series requires the use of a seasonal method

TABLE 3-10 QUARTERLY SALES DATA

	Quarter	Period	Sales (thousands of francs)		Quarter	Period	Sales (thousands of francs)
1970	1	1	362	1973	1	13	544
	2	2	385		2	14	582
	3	3	432		3	15	681
	4	4	341		4	16	557
1971	1	5	382	1974	1	17	628
	2	6	409		2	18	707
	3	7	498		3	19	773
	4	8	387		4	20	592
1972	1	9	473	1975	1	21	627
	2	10	513		2	22	725
	3	11	582		3	23	854
	4	12	474		4	24	661

if the systematic pattern in the errors is to be eliminated. Winters' linear and seasonal smoothing is such a method.

The example given in Table 3-11 raises the important concern of selecting the best smoothing method for a given data series. From the material covered thus far in this chapter, it can be seen that if the data are stationary, single or adaptive-response-rate exponential smoothing is appropriate. If the data exhibit a linear trend, either Brown's or Holt's linear models are appropriate, while if the trend is quadratic, Brown's quadratic model is appropriate. Finally, if the data are seasonal, Winters' method is suitable.

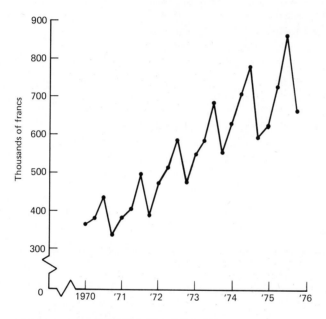

FIGURE 3-6 GRAPH OF QUARTERLY SALES DATA

To determine the basic pattern in the data, a number of steps may be taken. One is to plot the data as was done in Figure 3-6. This approach may take considerable time and requires that the data be studied carefully to identify seasonality and other patterns. A better approach for determining the type of pattern in the data is the study of the autocorrelations. This approach will be examined in detail in Chapter 8. Until that point it will continue to be assumed that the basic pattern of the data can be identified, even if only by looking at the errors generated by the application of simple exponential smoothing.

The importance of identifying the underlying pattern in order to select the appropriate method cannot be overemphasized. Even finding the parameters of a given method that minimize MSE for that method will not give nearly as good a result as selecting the most appropriate method. For example, for the data given in Table 3-10, the best form of single exponential smoothing method gives a MSE of 6925.64. The best form of Brown's one-parameter linear exponential smoothing gives a MSE of 6866.86, Holt's two parameters give a MSE of 7181.23, Brown's quadratic gives a MSE of 5855.35, and Winters' method gives a MSE of 619.41. Clearly the choice of the right smoothing method results in a substantial reduction of the MSE.

TABLE 3-11   APPLICATION OF SINGLE AND LINEAR SMOOTHING TO SEASONAL DATA

Period	Actual	Single Smoothing		Linear Smoothing	
		Forecast	Error	Forecast	Error
1	362	—	—	—	—
2	385	362	23	328	57
3	432	373.5	58.5	375.8	56.2
4	341	402.75	−61.75	411.59	−70.59
5	382	371.875	10.125	376.364	5.63599
6	409	376.937	32.0625	380.521	28.4794
7	498	392.969	105.031	398.89	99.1096
8	387	445.484	−58.4844	462.201	−75.2015
9	473	416.242	56.7578	429.846	43.1542
10	513	444.621	68.3789	461.735	51.2647
11	582	478.811	103.189	502.375	79.625
12	474	530.405	−56.4053	564.645	−90.6448
13	544	502.203	41.7974	531.919	12.0811
14	582	523.101	58.8987	552.671	29.3295
15	681	552.551	128.449	584.858	96.1416
16	557	616.775	−59.7754	659.773	−102.773
17	628	586.888	41.1123	623.992	4.00818
18	707	607.444	99.5562	643.03	63.9703
19	773	657.222	115.778	698.406	74.5945
20	592	715.111	−123.111	765.913	−173.913
21	627	653.556	−26.5555	691.03	−64.0297
22	725	640.278	84.7222	666.424	58.5759
23	854	682.639	171.361	709.619	144.381
24	661	768.319	−107.319	809.569	−148.569

3/9 Winters' Linear and Seasonal Exponential Smoothing

Winters' linear and seasonal exponential smoothing is based on three equations, each of which smooths a parameter associated with one of three components of the pattern—stationary, linear, and seasonal. In this respect it is very similar to Holt's method represented by equations (3-24) and (3-25), but includes three smoothing constants (with values between 0 and 1) and an additional equation to deal with seasonality. The basic equations for Winters' method are as follows:

$$S_t = \alpha \frac{X_t}{I_{t-L}} + (1 - \alpha)(S_{t-1} + b_{t-1}), \qquad (3\text{-}34)$$

$$b_t = \gamma(S_t - S_{t-1}) + (1 - \gamma)b_{t-1}, \qquad (3\text{-}35)$$

$$I_t = \beta \frac{X_t}{S_t} + (1 - \beta)I_{t-L}, \qquad (3\text{-}36)$$

where L is the length of seasonality (e.g., number of months or quarters in a year),

and I is the seasonal adjustment factor.

Equation (3-36) is comparable to a seasonal index that is found as the ratio of the current value of the series, X_t, divided by the current single smoothed value for the series, S_t. If X_t is larger than S_t, the ratio will be greater than 1, while if it is smaller than S_t, the ratio will be less than 1. Important to understanding this method is realizing that S_t is a smoothed (average) value of the series that does not include seasonality. The data values X_t, on the other hand, do contain seasonality. It must also be remembered that X_t includes any randomness in the series. In order to smooth this randomness, equation (3-36) weights the newly computed seasonal factor with β and the most recent seasonal number corresponding to the same season with $(1 - \beta)$. (This prior seasonal factor was computed in period $t - L$, since L is the length of seasonality.)

Equation (3-35) is exactly as Holt's equation (3-25) for smoothing the trend. Equation (3-34) differs slightly from Holt's equation (3-24) in that the first term is divided by the seasonal number, I_{t-L}. This is done to deseasonalize (eliminate seasonal fluctuations from) X_t. This adjustment can be illustrated by considering the case when I_{t-L} is greater than 1, which occurs when the value in period $t - L$ is greater than average in its seasonality. Dividing X_t by this number greater than 1 gives a value that is smaller than the original value by a percentage just equal to the amount that the seasonality of period $t - L$ was higher than average. The opposite adjustment occurs when the seasonality number is less than 1. The value I_{t-L} is used in these calculations because I_t cannot be calculated until S_t is known from (3-34).

The forecast based on Winters' method is computed as

$$F_{t+m} = (S_t + b_t m)I_{t-L+m}. \tag{3-37}$$

The data of Table 3-10 can be used to illustrate the application of Winters' method. With parameter values of $\alpha = .2$, $\beta = .05$ and $\gamma = .1$, forecasts and related smoothed values are as shown in Table 3-12.

TABLE 3-12 APPLICATION OF WINTERS' LINEAR AND SEASONAL EXPONENTIAL SMOOTHING TO SEASONAL DATA

Period	Actual	Single Smoothing (3-34)	Seasonal Smoothing (3-36)	Trend Smoothing (3-35)	Forecast when $m = 1$ (3-37) (lagged 1 mo.)
1	362.00	—	—	—	—
2	385.00	—	—	—	—
3	432.00	—	—	—	—
4	341.00	—	—	—	—
5	382.00	—	—	—	—
6	409.00	394.05	1.07	14.70	424.79
7	498.00	411.62	1.18	14.99	481.10
8	387.00	427.39	.90	15.07	383.53
9	473.00	448.17	1.01	15.64	444.32
10	513.00	467.08	1.07	15.97	495.53
11	582.00	485.20	1.18	16.18	569.34
12	474.00	506.52	.90	16.70	450.90
13	544.00	526.64	1.01	17.04	526.75
14	582.00	543.74	1.07	17.04	581.68
15	681.00	564.08	1.18	17.37	661.55
16	557.00	588.78	.90	18.11	523.98
17	628.00	610.11	1.01	18.43	611.79
18	707.00	634.99	1.07	19.07	672.48
19	773.00	654.15	1.18	19.08	772.49
20	592.00	669.65	.90	18.72	608.19
21	627.00	674.96	1.01	17.38	694.66
22	725.00	689.13	1.07	17.06	742.26
23	854.00	709.56	1.18	17.40	834.08
24	661.00	728.06	.90	17.51	656.03
25	—	—	—	—	749.39

The computations involved in this method can be illustrated for period 24 as follows:

$$F_{24} = [S_{23} + b_{23}(1)]I_{20} \qquad \text{[using (3-37)]}$$

$$= (709.56 + 17.4).9024 = 654.03,$$

$$S_{24} = .2\frac{X_{24}}{I_{20}} + .8(S_{23} + b_{23}) \qquad \text{[using (3-34)]}$$

$$= .2\frac{661}{.9024} + .8(709.56 + 17.40) = 728.06,$$

$$b_{24} = .1(S_{24} - S_{23}) + .9b_{23} \qquad \text{[using (3-35)]}$$

$$= .1(728.06 - 709.56) + .9(17.40) = 17.51,$$

$$\text{and} \quad I_{24} = .05\frac{X_{24}}{S_{24}} + .95I_{20} \qquad \text{[using (3-36)]}$$

$$= .05\frac{661}{728.06} + .95(.9024) = .9027.$$

Forecasts for periods 25, 26, 27, and 28, would then be:

$$F_{25} = [728.06 + 17.51(1)](1.01) = 753.0,$$

$$F_{26} = [728.06 + 17.51(2)](1.07) = 816.5,$$

$$F_{27} = [728.06 + 17.51(3)](1.18) = 921.1,$$

$$F_{28} = [728.06 + 17.51(4)](.90) = 718.3.$$

One of the problems in using Winters' method is determining the values for α, β, and γ that will minimize MSE. The only approach for determining these values is trial and error, even though there are some approaches that use nonlinear optimization algorithms to give optimal parameter values.

3/10 Other Smoothing Methods

In addition to the smoothing methods discussed in Sections 3-2 through 3-9, many others have been proposed. Most of these remaining methods require extensive computations, are often complicated, or simply have not been widely adopted in practice. The remainder of this section will discuss briefly several of these smoothing methods.

3/10/1 Chow's Adaptive Control Method

Chow's method is similar in philosophy to the ARRSES described in Section 3-4 but has the additional feature that it can be used for nonstationary data. However, the way that α_t is adjusted in Chow's method is not at all similar to that used in the ARRSES equation (3-10). Rather, α_t is "adapted" by small increments (usually .05) so as to minimize the MSE. The equations of Chow's adaptive smoothing are

$$S_t = \alpha_t X_t + (1 - \alpha_t)S_{t-1}, \tag{3-38}$$

$$b_t = \alpha_t(S_t - S_{t-1}) + (1 - \alpha_t)b_{t-1}, \tag{3-39}$$

and $$F_{t+1} = S_t + \frac{(1 - \alpha_t)}{\alpha_t} b_t. \tag{3-40}$$

3/10/2 Brown's One-Parameter Adaptive Method

Brown's one-parameter adaptive method involving a single smoothing constant (with a value between 0 and 1) is very general and has given satisfactory performance in practical situations. The computations used in this method are as follows:

$$S_t = S_{t-1} + b_{t-1} + (1 - \delta^2)e_t, \tag{3-41}$$

$$b_t = b_{t-1} + (1 - \delta)^2 e_t, \tag{3-42}$$

where $e_t = X_t - F_t,$

δ is the smoothing constant,

and $$F_{t+m} = S_t + b_t m. \tag{3-43}$$

Equation (3-41) differs from the computations used by many other methods in that it does not smooth previous values of S_t, but rather it smooths the current value of the errors. This approach is a different way of formulating the forecasts, which can be combined with that of formulating the forecast based on previous values of the series. As will be shown in Part Four, the combination of these two approaches provides a complete range of possible methodologies.

3/10/3 Box-Jenkins Three-Parameter Smoothing

This smoothing method developed by Box and Jenkins is based on the principle of smoothing errors—both present and past—as is Brown's adaptive method. Values of three parameters—θ_{-1}, θ_0 and θ_1—are determined so as to minimize the MSE. The Box and Jenkins three-parameter model is optimal, in the linear least square sense, and can be used for either stationary or nonstationary data. However, its main weakness is that it requires considerable computing for forecasting. The single equation needed is

$$F_{t+m} = F_t + \theta_{-1}(e_t - e_{t-1}) + \theta_0 e_t + \theta_1 \sum_{t=1}^{n} e_t. \tag{3-44}$$

3/10/4   Multiplicative Winters' Model

As can be seen from equation (3-34), Winters' method is an additive one in that the trend is added to a smoothed value. This can be a problem when the increase in the trend is not a constant amount, but is a constant percentage of the current actual data. When this is the case, a modification can be introduced that expresses the trend as a ratio shown in (3-46) and thus adjusts the smoothed value to take into consideration constant percentage increases or declines. The equations for this form of Winters' method are

$$S_t = \alpha \frac{X_t}{I_{t-L}} + (1 - \alpha)(1 - b_{t-1})S_{t-1}, \tag{3-45}$$

$$b_t = \gamma \frac{(S_t - S_{t-1})}{S_{t-1}} + (1 - \gamma)b_{t-1}, \tag{3-46}$$

$$I_t = \beta \frac{X_t}{S_t} + (1 - \beta)I_{t-1}. \tag{3-47}$$

The forecasts are computed as they were in Winters' additive model using equation (3-37).

3/10/5   Harrison's Harmonic Smoothing Method

Harrison's harmonic smoothing (HHS) method is an attempt to introduce additional mathematical sophistication into the smoothing field while maintaining most of the conceptual simplicity of smoothing methods. HHS is based on the use of Fourier transformations,* a methodology used by many early statisticians in their attempts to forecast. Harrison's method avoids the original shortcomings of using Fourier transformations by averaging several of them and using this average for forecasting purposes.

---

* Fourier transformations are a technique for expressing a series of numbers in a different notation or form. These transformations can be used in forecasting because they can express any series as a linear combination of transformed Fourier terms.

The HHS method requires considerable computation at the outset and requires a knowledge of Fourier transformations to be understood. However, once the original computations are done, their updating is fairly easy. An advantage of the method is that it optimizes the parameters automatically, and thus can be used with no outside interference. Its disadvantage is that the computational costs are considerable and its data requirements significant. Additional background information can be found in Harrison (1967) and completed examples are shown in Makridakis and Wheelwright (1977).

3/10/6 Trigg's Monitoring System (Tracking Signal)

A final smoothing method that should be mentioned is Trigg's monitoring system (tracking signal). While not a forecasting method by itself, it has considerable value as a means to monitor forecasting errors and determine when the errors are no longer random. Trigg's method is based on three equations very similar to those for calculating α_t in the ARRSES approach (Section 3-4). These equations are

$$E_t = \beta e_t + (1 - \beta)E_{t-1}, \tag{3-48}$$

$$M_t = \beta|e_t| + (1 - \beta)M_{t-1}, \tag{3-49}$$

and $$T_t = \frac{E_t}{M_t}, \tag{3-50}$$

where $e_t = X_t - F_t$,

and T_t is the tracking signal at period t.

The tracking signal indicates nonrandom errors (with a 95% confidence) when the value of T_t exceeds .51 for a β of .1 or .74 for a β of .2. These values were developed by Trigg (1964); Batty (1969) subsequently developed somewhat different values.

The major characteristic of Trigg's monitor is that when used in conjunction with a forecasting method in a routine manner, it can indicate when something has gone wrong. When forecasts of a great number of items are required, this is a considerable advantage, since the calculations of equations (3-48), (3-49), and (3-50) are easily performed with only three stored values.

3/11 General Aspects of Smoothing Methods

The major advantages of widely used smoothing methods are their simplicity and low cost. There is little doubt that better accuracy can usually be obtained using the more sophisticated methods of autoregressive/moving average schemes examined in Part Four or the intuitively appealing decomposition methods discussed in Chapter 4. However, when forecasts are needed for thousands of items, as is the case in many inventory systems, smoothing methods are often the only acceptable methods.

In instances of large forecasting requirements, even small things count. For example, having to store four values instead of three for each item can mean a great deal in terms of total storage requirements when forecasts for 30,000 items are required on a monthly basis. Furthermore, the computer time needed to make the necessary calculations must be kept at a reasonable level, and the method must run with a minimum of outside interference. For these reasons, exponential smoothing methods are preferable to moving average methods, and methods with fewer parameters are preferable to those with more.

If the data series is stationary, the adaptive-response-rate single exponential smoothing is often preferred to single exponential smoothing, because the latter method requires specification of α in such a way as to minimize the MSE. This takes extra computer and management time. More importantly, the optimal α will change when there is a basic change in the pattern of the data. Thus, an additional system such as the one proposed by Trigg (see Section 3/10/6) to monitor for possible changes in the pattern of data would be required. Otherwise there would be a risk of serious forecasting errors.

Adaptive-response-rate exponential smoothing, on the other hand, adjusts itself by changing the value of α to follow basic changes in the data. Although it may take one or two periods for α to catch up with changes in the data pattern, it will eventually do so. Thus, even if the forecasts from this method are somewhat inferior to those of single exponential smoothing with an optimal α, it is often preferable because it reduces the risk of serious errors and provides a system with minimal administrative worries. The fact that adaptive-response-rate exponential smoothing is completely automatic, in addition to having the other advantages of single exponential smoothing, makes it a favored method for practical use when the data are stationary and nonseasonal.

Brown's one-parameter linear exponential smoothing (Section 3/6/1) is the method preferred for nonstationary, nonseasonal data, largely because the method has only one parameter (versus Holt's two). In addition this parameter in practice takes on only a restricted range of values, even though theoretically α can assume any value between 0 and 1. Experience suggests that the optimal value lies in the range of .1 to .2. (See Brown 1963, pp. 106–22, 145–57.) An α of .1 makes the forecasts conservative, while an α of .2 gives a more responsive system. Given this narrowed set of choices for α, this method is usually viewed as being easier to apply.

Chow's adaptive control method (Section 3/10/1) is often described as performing the same role for linear exponential smoothing as the ARRSES (Section 3/4) performs for single exponential smoothing. However, this is not strictly the case because 1) Chow's method is more difficult to use and 2) α, in Brown's linear smoothing method, can be almost fixed in value.

Brown's quadratic smoothing (Section 3/7) is easy to use, too. It has only one parameter whose value is usually close to .1. In addition, it can predict turning points better than the linear smoothing method because it is quadratic. A weakness of quadratic smoothing is that it can overreact to random changes by assuming that they represent quadratic trends. This disadvantage can be reduced by setting α equal to a value below .1.

For seasonal data series, Winters' method is the only smoothing approach that is widely used. There are other seasonal smoothing approaches available (for example, see Groff 1973), but there is little evidence of their use in practice.

A major weakness of Winters' method that inhibits its wider applicability is that it requires three smoothing parameters. Since each of these parameters can take on any value between 0 and 1, many combinations must be tried before the optimal values for α, β, and γ can be determined. There are alternative methods (see Roberts and Reed 1969) that can identify the optimal parameter values, but they require considerable computations. Furthermore, once the optimal values have been found, there is no easy way to modify them when a basic change in the data has taken place. An alternative to worrying about optimal values is to find good initial estimates for equations (3-34), (3-35) and (3-36), then specify small values for α, β and γ (around .1 to .2). The forecasting system will then react slowly but steadily to changes in the data. The disadvantage of this strategy is that it gives a low response system. However, this price is often worth paying to achieve long-term stability and to provide a general, low-cost method for forecasting all types of data.

In summary, there are many different smoothing methods, and at least one of these is usually capable of dealing with any given data pattern when that basic pattern is known. If the pattern is not known, a general method such as Winters, which can deal with a range of patterns, is required.

3/12 Development of the Mathematical Basis of Smoothing Methods

Smoothing methods were first developed in the late 1950s by operations researchers. It is unclear whether Holt (1957) or Brown (1956) was the first to introduce exponential smoothing (see Cox 1961, p. 414), or if perhaps it was Magee (see Muth 1960, pp. 299). Most of the important development work on exponential smoothing was completed in the late 1950s and published by the early 1960s. This work included that done by Brown (1956) and Holt (1957) and subsequent work by Magee (1958), Brown (1959), Holt et al. (1960), Winters (1960), Brown and Meyer (1961), and Brown (1963). Since that time, the concept of exponential smoothing has grown and become a practical method with wide application, mainly in the forecasting of inventories.

The basic work on exponential smoothing had two purposes: first to introduce the method to a wide audience of academicians and practitioners and persuade them of its usefulness, and second to show the theoretical soundness of the method. Support for this latter purpose was launched by Brown and Meyer (1961) and continued through the work of Nerlove and Wage (1964), Theil and Wage (1964), and several others.

The fundamental theorem of exponential smoothing was proved by Brown and Meyer (1961). It states that for any time series, X_t, $(t = 0, 1, \ldots, n)$, there exists at time t a unique polynomial representing the time series:

$$F_{t+m} = a_t + b_t m + \frac{C_t}{2} m^2 + \cdots + \frac{g_t}{K'} m^K. \tag{3-51}$$

Furthermore, the coefficients of equation (3-51) can be estimated as linear combinations of the values resulting from the first $K + 1$ degrees (i.e., single, double, triple, etc.) of smoothing applied to the X_t values. The detailed proof of this theorem can be found in Brown and Meyer (1961, pp. 683–85) and Brown (1963, pp. 132–34). Estimating the values of a_t, b_t, C_t, $\ldots$, g_t requires expressing F_{t+m} as a Taylor series expansion around t and taking K derivatives to obtain K simultaneous equations, each expressing one degree of smoothing. All smoothing methods can be derived from this fundamental theorem as special cases of multiple exponential smoothing.

An additional property of multiple exponential smoothing identified by D'Esopo (1961) is that it provides an "exponentially discounted least squares" best fit to the observed series. In Part Four it will be shown that exponential smoothing is a special case of the general class of autoregressive/moving average methods.

REFERENCES AND SELECTED BIBLIOGRAPHY

Batty, M. 1969. "Monitoring an Exponential Smoothing Forecasting System." *Operational Research Quarterly*, Vol. 20, No. 3, pp. 319–23.

Box, G. E. P., and G. M. Jenkins. 1962. "Some Statistical Aspects of Adaptive Optimization and Control." *Journal of the Royal Statistical Society*, Series B, Vol. 24, pp. 297–343.

Brown, R. G. 1956. "Exponential Smoothing for Predicting Demand." Presented at the Tenth National Meeting of the Operations Research Society of America, San Francisco, November 16, 1956.

———. 1959. *Statistical Forecasting For Inventory Control*. New York: McGraw-Hill.

———. 1963. *Smoothing, Forecasting and Prediction*. Englewood Cliffs, N.J.: Prentice-Hall.

———, and R. F. Meyer. 1961. "The Fundamental Theorem of Exponential Smoothing." *Operations Research*, Vol. 9, No. 5, pp. 673–85.

Cox, D. R. 1961. "Prediction by Exponentially Weighted Moving Averages and Related Methods." *Journal of the Royal Statistical Society*, Series B, Vol. 23, No. 2, pp. 414–22.

D'Esopo, D. A. 1961. "A Note of Forecasting by the Exponential Smoothing Operator." *Operations Research*, Vol. 9, No. 5, pp. 667–86.

Geurts, M. D., and I. B. Ibrahim. 1975. "Comparing the Box-Jenkins Approach with the Exponentially Smoothed Forecasting Model Application to Hawaii Tourists." *Journal of Marketing Research*, Vol. 12, pp. 182–88.

Groff, G. K. 1973. "Empirical Comparison of Models for Short-Range Forecasting." *Management Science*, Vol. 20, No. 1, pp. 22–31.

Harrison, P. J. 1965. "Short-Term Sales Forecasting." *Applied Statistics*, Vol. 14, pp. 102–39.

———. 1967. "Exponential Smoothing and Short-Term Sales Forecasting." *Management Science*, Vol. 13, No. 11, pp. 821–42.

Holt, C. C. 1957. "Forecasting Seasonal and Trends by Exponentially Weighted Moving Averages." Office of Naval Research, Research Memorandum No. 52.

Holt, C. C., F. Modigliani, J. F. Muth, and H. A. Simon. 1960. *Planning Production Inventories and Work Force*. Englewood Cliffs, N.J.: Prentice-Hall.

Lewis, C. D. 1970. "Abbreviated Notes on Short-Term Forecasting." Birmingham, England. The University of Aston Management Centre.

———. 1975. *Demand Analysis and Inventory Control*. Lexington, Mass.: D.C. Heath & Co.

Magee, J. F. 1958. *Production Planning and Inventory Control*. New York: McGraw-Hill.

Makridakis, S., and S. Wheelwright. 1977. *Interactive Forecasting*. Second ed. San Francisco: Holden-Day.

Mathieu, A. 1970. "Technique de Controle de Prevision a Court Terme." *Revue Francaise d'Automatique, Informatique et Recherche Opérationnelle*, V-1, pp. 29–47.

Muth, J. F. 1960. "Optimal Properties of Exponentially Weighted Forecasts," *Journal of American Statistical Association*, Vol. 55, No. 290, pp. 299–306.

Nerlove, M., and S. Wage. 1964. "On the Optimality of Adaptive Forecasting." *Management Science*, Vol. 10, No. 2, pp. 207–24.

Roberts, S. D., and R. Reed. 1969. "The Development of a Self-Adaptive Forecasting Technique." In *AIIE Transactions*, Vol. 1, No. 4, pp. 314–22.

Thiel, H., and S. Wage. 1964. "Some Observations on Adaptive Filtering." *Management Science*, Vol. 10, No. 2, pp. 198–224.

Trigg, D. W. 1964. "Monitoring a Forecasting System." *Operational Research Quarterly*, Vol. 15, pp. 271–74.

Trigg, D. W., and D. H. Leach. 1967. "Exponential Smoothing with an Adaptive Response Rate." *Operational Research Quarterly*, Vol. 18, pp. 53–59.

Winters, P. R. 1960. "Forecasting Sales by Exponentially Weighted Moving Averages." *Management Science*, Vol. 6, pp. 324–42.

EXERCISES

1. The Canadian unemployment rate as a percentage of the civilian labor force (seasonably adjusted) between 1974 and the third quarter of 1975 is shown below.

	Quarter	Unemployment Rate
1974	1	5.4
	2	5.3
	3	5.3
	4	5.6
1975	1	6.9
	2	7.2
	3	7.2

   What is your estimate for unemployment in the fourth quarter of 1975? (Prepare an estimate using a single moving average with $N = 3$ and single exponential smoothing with $\alpha = .7$.)

2. Tables 3-13 and 3-14 show the sales of electric knives. Management wants to use both moving averages and exponential smoothing as methods for forecasting sales. Given the data in these tables, answer the following questions:

   a. What will the forecasts be for May 1976 using a 3-, 5-, 7-, 9-, and 11-month moving average?

b. What will the forecasts be for May 1976 for exponential smoothing with α values of .1, .3, .5, .7, and .9?

c. Assuming that the past pattern will continue into the future, what N and α values should management select in order to minimize the errors?

3. How do the α values of .1, .3, .5, .7, and .9 weight the past observations in forecasting with single exponential smoothing? How do they do it in Brown's linear exponential smoothing? What conclusions can you make by comparing the weights of single and linear exponential smoothings?

4. Using the single randomless series 2, 4, 6, 8, 10, 12, 14, 16, 18, and 20, compute a forecast for period 11 using:

a. the method of single exponential smoothing

b. Brown's method of linear exponential smoothing

TABLE 3-13   SINGLE MOVING AVERAGES—ELECTRIC KNIVES (1000s OF UNITS)

	Sales of Electric Knives	3-Month Moving Average	5-Month Moving Average	7-Month Moving Average	9-Month Moving Average	11-Month Moving Average
1975						
Jan.	19.0	—	—	—	—	—
Feb.	15.0	—	—	—	—	—
Mar.	39.0	—	—	—	—	—
Apr.	102.0	24.3	—	—	—	—
May	90.0	52.0	—	—	—	—
June	29.0	77.0	53.0	—	—	—
July	90.0	73.7	55.0	—	—	—
Aug.	46.0	69.7	70.0	54.9	—	—
Sept.	30.0	55.0	71.4	58.7	—	—
Oct.	66.0	55.3	57.0	60.9	51.1	—
Nov.	80.0	47.3	52.2	64.7	56.3	—
Dec.	89.0	58.7	62.4	61.6	63.6	55.1
1976						
Jan.	82.0	78.3	62.2	61.4	69.1	61.4
Feb.	17.0	83.7	69.4	69.0	66.9	67.5
Mar.	26.0	62.7	66.8	58.6	58.8	65.5
Apr.	29.0	41.7	58.8	55.7	58.4	58.6
May	—	—	—	—	—	—
Mean squared error (MSE)		1799.40	1172.29	874.30	1049.40	1557.52

TABLE 3-14   SINGLE EXPONENTIAL SMOOTHING—ELECTRIC KNIVES
(1000s OF UNITS)

	Sales of Electric Knives	$\alpha = .1$	$\alpha = .3$	$\alpha = .5$	$\alpha = .7$	$\alpha = .9$
1975						
Jan.	19.0	—	—	—	—	—
Feb.	15.0	19.00	19.00	19.00	19.00	19.00
Mar.	39.0	18.60	17.80	17.00	16.20	15.40
Apr.	102.0	20.64	24.16	28.00	32.16	36.64
May	90.0	28.78	47.51	65.00	81.05	95.46
June	29.0	34.90	60.26	77.50	87.31	90.55
July	90.0	34.31	50.88	53.25	46.49	35.15
Aug.	46.0	39.88	62.62	71.62	76.95	84.52
Sept.	30.0	40.49	57.63	58.81	55.28	49.85
Oct.	66.0	39.44	49.34	44.41	37.59	31.99
Nov.	80.0	42.10	54.34	55.20	57.48	62.60
Dec.	89.0	45.89	62.04	67.60	73.24	78.26
1976						
Jan.	82.0	50.20	70.13	78.30	84.27	87.93
Feb.	17.0	53.38	73.69	80.15	82.68	82.59
Mar.	26.0	49.74	56.68	48.58	36.70	23.56
Apr.	29.0	47.37	47.48	37.29	29.21	25.76
May	—	45.53	41.93	33.14	29.06	28.68
Mean square error (MSE)		1421.40	1211.80	1193.90	1225.40	1298.50

c. Holt's method of linear exponential smoothing

Which of the three methods is more appropriate? Why?

What value of α would you use in (a) above? How can you explain it in light of equation (3-8)?

What value of α and γ do you use in (b) and (c) above? Why?

5. Apply single exponential smoothing to the simple randomless series 3, 6, 9, 12, 3, 6, 9, 12, 3, 6, 9, 12. From this application, what can you conclude about the performance of single exponential smoothing?

6. Using the data series of exercise 5, apply Brown's quadratic exponential smoothing. Does this method do better than single exponential smoothing? Explain.

7. The Paris Chamber of Commerce and Industry has been asked by several of its members to prepare a forecast of the French index of industrial production for its monthly newsletter. Using the monthly data given below:

   a. Compute a forecast using the methods of single and linear moving averages with 12 observations in each average.

   b. Compute the error in each forecast. How accurate would you say these forecasts are?

   c. Which is better, the single or linear moving averages?

   d. Now compute a new series of single and linear moving averages using 6 observations in each average. Compute the errors as well.

   e. Which is better, the single or linear moving averages?

   f. How do these four moving average forecasts compare? Which seems most accurate? Why?

Period	French Index of Industrial Production	Period	French Index of Industrial Production
1	108	15	98
2	108	16	97
3	110	17	101
4	106	18	104
5	108	19	101
6	108	20	99
7	105	21	95
8	100	22	95
9	97	23	96
10	95	24	96
11	95	25	97
12	92	26	98
13	95	27	94
14	95	28	92

8. Given a bookstore's daily sales of paperback books (column 1), forecast sales for the next four periods using the method of linear moving averages.

9. Given a bookstore's daily sales of hard cover books (column 1, Table 3-15), use linear exponential smoothing with an α of .5 to forecast the next four periods.

10. Apply linear moving averages to the data of Table 3-16 using $N = 8$. Which N is better, 4 or 8?

11.   Apply linear exponential smoothing to the data of exercise 11 with an α of .1. Compare the results and decide which α is better.

TABLE 3-15 MOVING AVERAGES—SALES OF PAPERBACK BOOKS

(1)	(2)	(3)	(4)	(5)
		4-Period		
	4-Period	Double		
	Moving	Moving	Value of a	Value of b
Sales	Average	Average	$[2(2) - (3)]$	$[(2/4 - 1)(2) - (3)]$
199	—	—	—	—
172	—	—	—	—
111	—	—	—	—
209	172.75	—	—	—
161	163.25	—	—	—
119	150.00	—	—	—
195	171.00	164.250	177.750	4.50000
195	167.50	162.937	172.062	3.04167
131	160.00	162.125	157.875	−1.41667
183	176.00	168.625	183.375	4.91667
143	163.00	166.625	159.375	−2.41667
141	149.50	162.125	136.875	−8.4667
168	158.75	161.812	155.687	−2.04167
201	163.25	158.625	167.875	3.08333
155	166.25	159.437	173.062	4.54167
243	191.75	170.000	213.500	14.50000
225	206.00	181.812	230.187	16.12500
167	197.50	190.375	204.625	4.75000
237	218.00	203.312	232.687	9.79167
202	207.75	207.312	208.187	.291667
186	198.00	205.312	190.687	−4.87500
176	200.25	206.000	194.500	−3.83333
232	199.00	201.250	196.750	−1.50000
195	197.25	198.625	195.875	−.916667
190	198.25	198.687	197.812	−2.91667
182	199.75	198.562	200.937	.791667
222	197.25	198.125	196.375	−.583333
217	202.75	199.500	206.000	2.16667
188	202.25	200.500	204.000	1.16667
247	218.50	205.187	231.812	8.87500

TABLE 3-16 EXPONENTIAL SMOOTHING—SALES OF HARDBACK BOOKS

(1) Sales	(2) Single Exponential Smoothing	(3) Double Exponential Smoothing	(4) 2(2) − (3)	(5) $b = (\alpha/1\alpha)(S_t' - S_t'')$ where $\alpha = .5$
139	139	139	—	—
128	136.8	138.56	135.04	−.440002
172	143.84	139.616	148.064	1.056
139	142.872	140.267	145.477	.651199
191	152.498	142.713	162.282	2.44608
168	155.598	145.29	165.906	2.57697
170	158.478	147.928	169.029	2.63766
145	155.783	149.499	162.067	1.57099
184	161.426	151.884	170.968	2.38548
135	156.141	152.736	159.546	.851341
218	168.513	155.891	181.134	3.15543
198	174.41	159.595	189.226	3.70384
230	185.528	164.781	206.275	5.18667
222	192.823	170.39	215.255	5.6082
206	195.458	175.403	215.513	5.01366
240	204.366	181.196	227.537	5.7926
189	201.293	185.215	217.371	4.01942
222	205.434	189.259	221.61	4.04382
158	195.948	190.597	201.298	1.33767
178	192.358	190.949	193.767	.352234
217	197.286	192.217	202.356	1.26746
261	210.029	195.779	224.279	3.56252
238	215.623	199.748	231.499	3.96885
240	220.499	203.898	237.099	4.15015
214	219.199	206.958	231.44	3.06017
200	215.359	208.638	222.08	1.68019
201	212.487	209.408	215.566	.769791
283	226.59	212.844	240.335	3.43634
220	225.272	215.33	235.214	2.48548
259	232.017	218.667	245.367	3.33751

4 DECOMPOSITION METHODS

4/1 Introduction

The forecasting methods outlined in the previous chapter are based on the concept that when an underlying pattern exists in a data series, that pattern can be distinguished from randomness by smoothing (averaging) past values. The effect of this smoothing is to eliminate randomness so the pattern can be projected into the future and used as the forecast. Smoothing methods make no attempt to identify individual components of the basic underlying pattern. In many instances the pattern can be broken down (decomposed) into subpatterns that identify each component of the time series separately. Such a breakdown can frequently facilitate improved accuracy in forecasting and aid in better understanding the behavior of the series.

Decomposition methods usually try to identify three separate components of the basic underlying pattern that tend to characterize economic and business series. These are the trend, the cycle, and the seasonal factors. The trend represents the long-run behavior of the data, and can be increasing, decreasing, or unchanged. The cyclical factor represents the ups and downs of the economy or of a specific industry and is common to series such as Gross National Product (GNP), index of industrial production, demand for housing, sales of industrial goods such as automobiles, stock prices, bond rates, money supply, and interest rates. The seasonal factor relates to periodic fluctuations of constant length that are caused by such things as temperature, rainfall, month of the year, timing of holidays, and corporate policies. The distinction between seasonality and cyclicality is that seasonality repeats itself at fixed intervals such as a year, month, or week, while cyclical factors have a longer duration that varies from cycle to cycle.

Decomposition assumes that the data is made up as follows:

data = pattern + error

$$= f(\text{trend, cycle, seasonality}) + \text{error}.$$

Thus in addition to the components of the pattern, an element of error or randomness is also assumed to be present. This error is assumed to be the difference between the combined effect of the three subpatterns of the series and the actual data.

Decomposition methods are one of the oldest forecasting approaches. They were used in the beginning of this century by economists attempting to identify and control the business cycle. The basis of current decomposition methods was established in the 1920s when the concept of ratio-to-trend was introduced. Since that time decomposition approaches have been used widely by both economists and businessmen.

There are several alternative approaches to decomposing a time series, all of which aim at isolating each component of the series as accurately as possible. The basic concept in such separation is empirical and consists of first removing seasonality, then trend, and finally cycle. Any residual is assumed to be randomness which, while it cannot be predicted, can be identified. From a statistical point of view there are a number of theoretical weaknesses in the decomposition approach. Practitioners, however, have largely ignored these weaknesses and have used the approach with considerable success.

The general mathematical representation of the decomposition approach is:

$$X_t = f(I_t, T_t, C_t, E_t),\tag{4-1}$$

where X_t is the time series value (actual data) at period t,

   I_t is the seasonal component (or Index) at period t,

   T_t is the trend component at period t,

   C_t is the cyclical component at period t,

and E_t is the error or random component at period t.

The exact functional form of (4-1) depends on the decomposition method actually used. Several of these methods will be examined in this chapter. For all such methods the process of decomposition is similar and consists of the following steps:

1. For the actual series, X_t, compute a moving average whose length, N, is equal to the length of seasonality. The purpose of this moving average is to eliminate seasonality and randomness. Averaging as many periods as the length of the seasonal pattern (e.g., 12 months, 4 quarters, or 7 days) will eliminate seasonality by averaging seasonally high periods with seasonally low periods. Since random errors have no systematic pattern, this averaging reduces randomness as well.

2. Separate the outcome of (1), the N period moving average, from the original data series, obtaining trend and cyclicality.

3. Isolate the seasonal factors by averaging them for each of the periods making up the complete length of seasonality.
4. Identify the appropriate form of the trend (linear, exponential, S-curve, etc.) and calculate its value at each period, T_t.
5. Separate the outcome of (4) from (2) (the combined value of trend and cycle) to obtain the cyclical factor.
6. Separate the seasonality, trend, and cycle from the original data series to isolate the remaining randomness, E_t.

These steps in the decomposition procedure can be illustrated using the simple series shown in Table 4-1. This series contains trend, seasonality, and randomness. It can be seen from the last column of Table 4-1 that the observed values for the series represent the three components combined in an additive form. Thus the six steps outlined above will perform best if equation (4-1) is assumed to have the form:

$$X_t = I_t + T_t + C_t + E_t. \tag{4-2}$$

Since no cyclical component exists in these data, C_t has a value of zero.

In applying step 1 of the above procedure, the initial task is to determine the length of seasonality of the data so that number of periods can be used in

TABLE 4-1   DECOMPOSITION PROCEDURE FOR SERIES WITH TREND, SEASONALITY, AND RANDOMNESS

Period	T_t Trend	I_t Seasonality	E_t Randomness	$X_t = T_t + I_t + E_t$ Time Series
1	2	3	$-.3$	4.7
2	4	5	0	9.0
3	6	7	0	13.0
4	8	3	.3	11.3
5	10	5	.9	15.9
6	12	7	.6	19.6
7	14	3	$-.3$	16.7
8	16	5	$-.3$	20.7
9	18	7	0	25.0
10	20	3	.6	23.6
11	22	5	0	27.0
12	24	7	.3	31.3

the moving average. From Table 4-1, it is clear that the seasonal pattern is 3, since the same values (3, 5, and 7) repeat themselves every 3 periods. Thus a moving average of 3 periods, $N = 3$, should be computed and centered in the middle of the 3 numbers being averaged. The centering is appropriate because the concern at this point is not forecasting, as it was in Section 3/2, but rather finding the average of the 3 values surrounding each period's value. Table 4-2 shows the resulting moving average values.

TABLE 4-2 DECOMPOSITION COMPUTATIONS FOR MOVING AVERAGES

(1)	(2)	(3) $X_t = I_t + T_t + C_t + E_t$ X_t (time series)	(4) $M_t = T_t + C_t$ M_t (moving average)	(5) $I_t + T_t + C_t + E_t - (T_t + C_t) = I_t + E_t$ $I_t + E_t = X_t - M_t$
Period	Season			
1	I	4.7	—	—
2	II	9.0	8.9	.1
3	III	13.0	11.1	1.9
4	I	11.3	13.4	−2.1
5	II	15.9	15.6	.3
6	III	19.6	17.4	2.2
7	I	16.7	19.0	−2.3
8	II	20.7	20.8	−.1
9	III	25.0	23.1	1.9
10	I	23.6	25.2	−1.6
11	II	27.0	27.3	−.3
12	III	31.3	—	—

The 3-period moving average values represent trend and cycle only, since randomness and seasonality have been eliminated. Step 2 is then to subtract the moving average values from the time series values (column 3). The resulting difference (column 5) is seasonality and randomness. Table 4-2 has therefore separated the original time series, X_t, into two parts—one including the trend-cycle components and the other the seasonal-random components. Step 3 separates the randomness from the seasonality by averaging all available values referring to the same season (i.e., I, II, and III). Using this procedure, one finds that the random elements will cancel each other, since some values will be positive and some negative. This averaging is done in Table 4-3, where the basic data are the seasonal-random components found in column 5 of Table 4-2.

TABLE 4-3 DECOMPOSITION PROCEDURE FOR SEASONAL INDICES

	Seasons	
I	II	III
—	.1	1.9
−2.1	.3	2.2
−2.3	−.1	1.9
−1.6	−.3	—

	Sums of Seasonal Factors	
−6	0	6

	Average Seasonal Factor	
−2	0	2

The averaged seasonal factors, -2, 0, and $+2$, indicate that if season II (i.e., periods 2, 5, 8, and 11) is considered the base point for seasonality, then season I (periods 1, 4, 7, and 10) is 2 units below the base, and season III (periods 3, 6, 9, and 12) is 2 units above the base. That is in fact the case as can be seen in the third column of Table 4-1.

Steps 4 and 5 in the decomposition process are to separate the trend and the cycle. In this example this separation is not necessary because the cycle is zero and therefore the trend-cycle component is all trend. In general, however, some type of trend curve would be assumed, its value found for each period, and that value subtracted from the trend-cycle value (the moving average values).

The final step (6) isolates the randomness in the series by simply subtracting from the original time series the component values found above for trend, cycle, and seasonal factors.

Before discussing the range of variations available for applying the decomposition approach to forecasting, the topic of trend fitting will be discussed briefly. Although it is a basic method of forecasting in its own right, trend fitting will not be discussed in detail until Chapter 5. Section 4/5 of this chapter will examine the most widely used decomposition method. Census II, and Section 4/6 will briefly outline the Foran System.

4/2 Trend Fitting

Several alternative data patterns (stationary, nonstationary, seasonal, non-seasonal) and different methods and models for dealing with them were discussed in Chapter 3. The simplest of these patterns are referred to as stationary and nonseasonal. Basically, these are horizontal patterns that can be described by a one-parameter method. The mean is one such method, as are single moving averages and single exponential smoothing. Another common pattern is that of a linear trend that can be described by a two-parameter method. In general, as the complexity of the pattern increases, more parameters are required to represent it. It is also the case that the more difficult the estimation process, the more data required for that. Fortunately, it is frequently the case that simple patterns (or variations of them) are adequate to describe practical situations. One such extremely useful pattern is that of a linear trend line. This trend is used as a basic element in the decomposition procedures discussed in Sections 4/3 through 4/6 and therefore merits some attention at this point.

Section 2/2 demonstrated that fitting a straight line to stationary (horizontal) data could be done in a way to minimize the MSE using:

$$\bar{X} = \frac{\sum_{i=1}^{n} X_i}{n}. \tag{4-3}$$

In graphic terms, equation (4-3) represents a horizontal straight line and is specified by one parameter, $\bar{X}$. A trend line requires two parameters, a and b, for specification. The values of a and b can be found in a manner similar to that used for $\bar{X}$. Values for a and b can be found by minimizing the MSE where the errors are the differences between the data values of the time series and the corresponding trend line values. This procedure is known as simple regression and will be examined in detail in Chapter 5. However, at this point two things need to be made clear:

1. A trend line such as that shown in Figure 4-1 can be described by two parameters, a and b, in the form

$$X_t = a + bt. \tag{4-4}$$

2. The values of a and b that minimize the MSE can be found using (4-5) and (4-6):

$$b = \frac{n\Sigma tX - \Sigma t \Sigma X}{nt^2 - (\Sigma t)^2}, \tag{4-5}$$

$$a = \frac{\Sigma X}{n} - b\frac{\Sigma t}{n}. \tag{4-6}$$

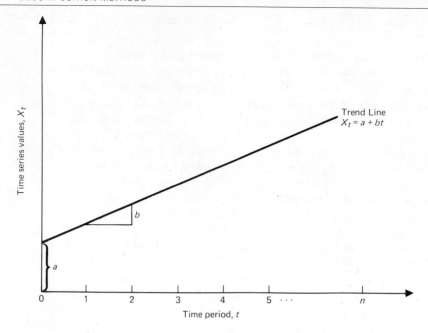

FIGURE 4-1 LINEAR TREND LINE FOR TIME-SERIES DATA

There are several alternative trend curves that are nonlinear that can be fit to a data series (e.g., exponential, S-curve, quadratic, logarithmic). For purposes of this chapter only a linear trend will be considered, although alternative forms could be used as part of a decomposition method wherever appropriate.

4/3 The Ratio-to-Moving Averages Classical Decomposition Method

Decomposition methods can assume an additive or multiplicative model and can be of varying forms. For example, the decomposition method of simple averages assumes the additive model:

$$X_t = I_t + T_t + E_t. \tag{4-7}$$

The ratio-to-trend method uses a multiplicative model of the form:

$$X_t = I_t \times T_t \times E_t. \tag{4-8}$$

The decomposition methods of simple averages and ratio-to-trend were used in the past mainly because of their computational simplicity. However, they have lost most of their appeal with the widespread introduction of computers, which has made application of variations of the ratio-to-moving averages method a much preferable approach.

Developed in the 1920s, the ratio-to-moving averages method was for many years the most commonly used decomposition procedure. This approach formed the basis for Census II decomposition, which is examined in Section 4/5. This method assumes a multiplicative model of the form:

$$X_t = I_t \times T_t \times C_t \times E_t. \tag{4-9}$$

The ratio-to-moving averages method first isolates the trend-cycle of the data by calculating a moving average whose number of terms is equal to the length of seasonality. A moving average of this length contains no seasonal effects and little or no randomness. The resulting moving averages, M_t, represent

$$M_t = T_t \times C_t. \tag{4-10}$$

Equation (4-10) includes only the trend and cyclical factors, since seasonality and randomness are eliminated with the appropriate averaging. Equation (4-9) can be divided by (4-10) to obtain

$$\frac{X_t}{M_t} = \frac{I_t \times T_t \times C_t \times E_t}{T_t \times C_t} = I_t \times E_t. \tag{4-11}$$

Equation (4-11) is the ratio of actual-to-moving averages (thus the name of the method) and isolates the additional two components of the time series. Table 4-4 shows the actual time series data, X_t, given by equation (4-9), the moving average values, M_t, given by equation (4-10), and the ratio of the two, given by equation (4-11). The ratio values range around 100, indicating the effects of seasonality on the average deseasonalized values.

The next step in this method is to eliminate the randomness from the values given by (4-11) by using some form of averaging of the same months. That is similar to the approach used in the decomposition methods discussed previously. Classical ratio-to-moving averages decomposition uses an approach called the method of medial average at this point.

To compute the medial average the ratios of actual-to-moving averages (last column of Table 4-4) are arranged by month for all years in Table 4-5. The medial average is the mean value for each month after the largest and smallest values have been excluded. The January medial average, for example, is 82.36. This value is found by excluding January 1975 (the highest of all Januaries) and January 1976 (the lowest of all Januaries). The remaining 3 January values are summed, $87.4 + 77.7 + 82.0 = 247.1$, and divided by 3 to obtain the medial average of 82.36. Seasonal indices can be obtained from the medial averages by multiplying each medial average by .99627 (1200/1204.492), which adjusts them so their average value is 100.

The final step in this method is to separate the trend from the cycle using (4-10). The linear trend line for these data was previously identified as

$$T_t = 975.37 + 6.035(t). \tag{4-12}$$

TABLE 4-4 MOTORCYCLE REGISTRATIONS: RATIO-TO-MOVING
AVERAGES DECOMPOSITION

Year		Data	Moving Averages	Ratio of Actual-to-Moving Averages
1971	Jan.	894.00	—	—
	Feb.	667.00	—	—
	Mar.	858.00	—	—
	Apr.	865.00	—	—
	May	989.00	—	—
	June	1093.00	—	—
	July	1191.00	1023.083	116.413
	Aug.	1159.00	1026.167	112.945
	Sept.	1046.00	1043.417	100.248
	Oct.	1191.00	1050.000	113.429
	Nov.	1203.00	1057.250	113.786
	Dec.	1121.00	1057.917	105.963
1972	Jan.	931.00	1065.000	87.418
	Feb.	874.00	1082.750	80.720
	Mar.	937.00	1096.750	85.434
	Apr.	952.00	1113.500	85.496
	May	997.00	1122.750	88.800
	June	1178.00	1122.917	104.905
	July	1404.00	1132.333	123.992
	Aug.	1327.00	1129.750	117.460
	Sept.	1247.00	1128.500	110.501
	Oct.	1302.00	1127.667	115.460
	Nov.	1205.00	1134.833	106.183
	Dec.	1234.00	1139.917	108.254
1973	Jan.	900.00	1158.167	77.709
	Feb.	859.00	1164.167	73.787
	Mar.	927.00	1169.667	79.253
	Apr.	1038.00	1175.417	88.309
	May	1058.00	1179.667	89.686
	June	1397.00	1184.833	117.907
	July	1476.00	1190.333	123.999
	Aug.	1393.00	1197.250	116.350
	Sept.	1316.00	1188.750	110.705
	Oct.	1353.00	1190.667	113.634
	Nov.	1267.00	1192.167	106.277
	Dec.	1300.00	1205.083	107.876

TABLE 4-4 *Continued*

Year		Data	Moving Averages	Ratio of Actual-to-Moving Averages
1974	Jan.	983.00	1199.417	81.957
	Feb.	757.00	1199.417	63.114
	Mar.	950.00	1206.083	78.767
	Apr.	1056.00	1210.417	87.243
	May	1213.00	1215.917	99.760
	June	1329.00	1234.750	107.633
	July	1476.00	1220.000	120.984
	Aug.	1473.00	1230.167	119.740
	Sept.	1368.00	1244.667	109.909
	Oct.	1419.00	1251.583	113.376
	Nov.	1493.00	1239.583	120.444
	Dec.	1123.00	1234.667	90.956
1975	Jan.	1105.00	1229.833	89.850
	Feb.	931.00	1235.083	75.380
	Mar.	1033.00	1243.583	83.066
	Apr.	912.00	1240.000	73.548
	May	1154.00	1240.333	93.040
	June	1271.00	1240.250	102.479
	July	1539.00	1257.250	122.410
	Aug.	1575.00	1245.167	126.489
	Sept.	1325.00	1247.083	106.248
	Oct.	1423.00	1244.000	114.389
	Nov.	1492.00	1267.500	117.712
	Dec.	1327.00	1288.083	103.021
1976	Jan.	960.00	1292.833	74.256
	Feb.	954.00	1311.250	72.755
	Mar.	996.00	1312.333	75.895
	Apr.	1194.00	1323.667	90.204
	May	1401.00	1341.750	104.416
	June	1328.00	1337.333	99.302
	July	1760.00	1351.000	130.274
	Aug.	1588.00	—	—
	Sept.	1461.00	—	—
	Oct.	1640.00	—	—
	Nov.	1439.00	—	—
	Dec.	1491.00	—	—

If equation (4-10) is divided by (4-12), the result is

$$\frac{M_t}{T_t} = \frac{T_t \times C_t}{975.37 + 6.035(t)} = C_t. \tag{4-13}$$

The resulting values are shown in the last column of Table 4-6. These ratio values fluctuate around 100, indicating cyclical factors higher than average (greater than 100) or lower than average (less than 100).

TABLE 4-5 SEASONAL INDICES FOR RATIO-TO-MOVING AVERAGES DECOMPOSITION METHOD

Year	Jan.	Feb.	Mar.	Apr.	May	June	July	Aug.	Sept.	Oct.	Nov.	Dec.	Total
1971	—	—	—	—	—	—	116.4	112.9	100.2	113.4	113.8	106.0	
1972	87.4	80.7	85.4	85.5	88.8	104.9	124.0	117.5	110.5	115.5	106.2	108.3	
1973	77.7	73.8	79.3	88.3	89.7	117.9	124.0	116.4	110.7	113.6	106.3	107.9	
1974	82.0	63.1	78.8	87.2	99.8	107.6	121.0	119.7	109.9	113.4	120.4	91.0	
1975	89.9	75.4	83.1	73.5	93.0	102.5	122.4	126.5	106.2	114.4	117.7	103.0	
1976	74.3	72.8	75.9	90.2	104.4	99.3	130.3	—	—	—	—	—	
Medial[a] average	82.36	73.97	80.36	87.02	93.16	105.00	122.85	117.85	108.89	113.82	112.59	105.62	1204.49
Seasonal index[b]	82.05	73.70	80.06	86.69	93.81	104.61	122.39	117.41	108.48	113.39	112.17	105.23	1200.00

[a] The column average excluding the highest and lowest values.
[b] An adjustment of the medial average so that the total is equal to 1200. The adjustment factor is 1200/1204.492 = .99627.

To prepare a forecast, the trend value for the period to be forecast is multiplied by the appropriate seasonal index and by the appropriate cyclical factor. Calculating the trend and identifying the appropriate seasonal factor are straightforward matters, but estimating the cyclical factor may not be. (Chapter 12 discusses this problem in detail.) Estimating the cyclical factor requires some knowledge of the level of economic or industry activity during the period to be forecast and such knowledge can frequently be based only on judgment.

If the cyclical values for January and February 1977 are assumed to be 98.2 and 98.6 respectively, the forecasts for these months will be

$$F_{J1977} = [975.37 + 6.035(73)](82.05)(98.2) = 1140.85$$

and $\quad F_{F1977} = [975.37 + 6.035(74)](73.70)(98.6) = 1033.31.$

These forecasts are based on the fact that January 1977 is month 73 and February is month 74, and the seasonal factor for January is 82.05 and for February is 73.70.

TABLE 4-6 CYCLICAL FACTORS FOR RATIO-TO-MOVING AVERAGES DECOMPOSITION METHOD

Year		Data	12-Month Moving Averages	Trend	Cyclical Factor (moving average/trend)
1971	Jan.	894.00	—	—	—
	Feb.	667.00	—	—	—
	Mar.	858.00	—	—	—
	Apr.	865.00	—	—	—
	May	989.00	—	—	—
	June	1093.00	—	—	—
	July	1191.00	1023.083	1017.61	100.54
	Aug.	1159.00	1026.167	1023.65	100.25
	Sept.	1046.00	1043.417	1029.69	101.33
	Oct.	1191.00	1050.000	1035.72	101.38
	Nov.	1203.00	1057.250	1041.75	101.49
	Dec.	1121.00	1057.917	1047.79	100.97
1972	Jan.	931.00	1065.000	1053.82	101.06
	Feb.	874.00	1082.750	1059.86	102.16
	Mar.	937.00	1096.750	1065.90	102.89
	Apr.	952.00	1113.500	1071.93	103.88
	May	997.00	1122.750	1077.97	104.15
	June	1178.00	1122.917	1084.00	103.59
	July	1404.00	1132.333	1090.03	103.88
	Aug.	1327.00	1129.750	1096.07	103.07
	Sept.	1247.00	1128.500	1102.10	102.39
	Oct.	1302.00	1127.667	1108.14	101.76
	Nov.	1205.00	1134.833	1114.18	101.85
	Dec.	1234.00	1139.917	1120.21	101.76
1973	Jan.	900.00	1158.167	1126.25	102.83
	Feb.	859.00	1164.167	1132.28	102.81
	Mar.	927.00	1169.667	1138.31	102.75
	Apr.	1038.00	1175.417	1144.35	102.71
	May	1058.00	1179.667	1150.38	102.54
	June	1397.00	1184.833	1156.42	102.46
	July	1476.00	1190.333	1162.46	102.40
	Aug.	1393.00	1197.250	1168.49	102.46
	Sept.	1316.00	1188.750	1174.52	101.21
	Oct.	1353.00	1190.667	1180.56	100.85
	Nov.	1267.00	1192.167	1186.59	100.47
	Dec.	1300.00	1205.083	1192.63	101.04

TABLE 4-6 *Continued*

Year		Data	12-Month Moving Averages	Trend	Cyclical Factor (moving average/trend)
1974	Jan.	983.00	1199.417	1198.67	100.06
	Feb.	757.00	1199.417	1204.7	99.56
	Mar.	950.00	1206.083	1210.74	99.61
	Apr.	1056.00	1210.417	1216.77	99.48
	May	1213.00	1215.917	1222.8	99.43
	June	1329.00	1234.750	1228.84	100.48
	July	1476.00	1220.000	1234.87	98.79
	Aug.	1473.00	1230.167	1240.91	99.13
	Sept.	1368.00	1244.667	1246.95	99.82
	Oct.	1419.00	1251.583	1252.98	99.89
	Nov.	1493.00	1239.583	1259.02	98.45
	Dec.	1123.00	1234.667	1265.05	97.60
1975	Jan.	1105.00	1229.833	1271.08	96.75
	Feb.	931.00	1235.083	1277.12	96.71
	Mar.	1033.00	1243.583	1283.16	96.91
	Apr.	912.00	1240.000	1289.19	96.18
	May	1154.00	1240.333	1295.23	95.76
	June	1271.00	1240.250	1301.26	95.31
	July	1539.00	1257.250	1307.29	96.17
	Aug.	1575.00	1245.167	1313.33	94.81
	Sept.	1325.00	1247.083	1319.36	94.52
	Oct.	1423.00	1244.000	1325.4	93.86
	Nov.	1492.00	1267.500	1331.44	95.20
	Dec.	1327.00	1288.083	1337.47	96.31
1976	Jan.	960.00	1292.833	1343.51	96.23
	Feb.	954.00	1311.250	1349.54	97.16
	Mar.	996.00	1312.333	1355.57	96.81
	Apr.	1194.00	1323.667	1361.61	97.21
	May	1401.00	1341.750	1367.65	98.10
	June	1328.00	1337.333	1373.68	97.35
	July	1760.00	1351.000	1379.72	97.92
	Aug.	1588.00	—	—	—
	Sept.	1461.00	—	—	—
	Oct.	1640.00	—	—	—
	Nov.	1439.00	—	—	—
	Dec.	1491.00	—	—	—

4/4 Different Types of Moving Averages

As illustrated in the previous sections, moving averages are used to eliminate seasonality and randomness from data series. In this sense moving averages are the backbone of decomposition methods. In the methods described thus far the single moving average equal to the length of seasonality was used. Census II, a much more sophisticated decomposition method uses more elaborate moving averages of different lengths and high orders (double, triple, etc.). The purpose of this section is to review the different types of moving averages in general and those used in Census II and to discuss the advantages and shortcomings of each of them. The Census II decomposition method will then be described in the next section.

4/4/1 Centered Moving Averages

To obtain more accurate results, a moving average (MA) should be centered to the middle of the data values averaged. That presents no problem when the number of averaged terms is odd, since the middle value will be $(N + 1)/2$. Thus, the 3-term moving averages (denoted 3 MA) of the 8 values shown in Table 4-7, will be those given in column 3. To calculate a 4-term moving average (4 MA) the

---

TABLE 4-7 CENTERED MOVING AVERAGES—3- AND 4-TERM

(1) Period	(2) Value	(3) 3 MA	(4) Ratio of (2)/(3)	(5) 4 MA	(6) Ratio of (2)/(5)
1	3	—	—	—	—
2	5	5	1	—	—
3	7	7	1	6	1.167
4	9	9	1	8	1.125
5	11	11	1	10	1.1
6	13	13	1	12	1.083
7	15	15	1	14	1.071
8	17	—	—	—	—

---

question arises as to whether to place the MA at period 2 or at period 3, since $(4 + 1)/2 = 2.5$. Placing it at period 2 makes it half a period late and placing it at period 3 makes it half a period early. In Table 4-7 the 4 MA is placed opposite to period 3 (column 5) and the ratios of actual to 4 MA are shown in column 6.

Given the linear trend, it would be desirable to have these ratios equal to one. The fact that the MA is not centered in this case can create problems of accuracy. Such problems are usually overcome by taking an additional 2-period MA of the 4-period moving average. This double moving average is denoted as $2 \times N$. Since $N = 4$ in the example given in Table 4-7, the result of this procedure is a 2×4. The results of following this centering procedure are shown in Table 4-8,

TABLE 4-8 CENTERED MOVING AVERAGES—2×4 MA

(1) Period	(2) Value	(3) 4 MA	(4) 2×4 MA	(5) Ratio of (2)/(4)
1	3	—	—	—
2	5	—	—	—
3	7	6	7	1
4	9	8	9	1
5	11	10	11	1
6	13	12	13	1
7	15	14	—	—
8	17	—	—	—

where column 4 is simply the average of 2 successive values of the 4 MA of column 3. Since the center of the 4 MA is at periods 2.5, 3.5, 4.5, 5.5, and 6.5, the center of the additional 2 MA is at periods 3, 4, 5, and 6. Thus the 2×4 MA overcomes the centering problem.

A double moving average like the one described above can be expressed as a single but weighted moving average, where the weights for each period are unequal. A 2-month MA of a 12-month moving average, for example, is equivalent to a 13-month weighted moving average (often called a 12-months centered moving average). This type of centered moving average is used in Census II rather than a single moving average of 12 periods.

The following notation is useful in discussing weighted and centered moving averages:

$$M_{6.5} = (X_1 + X_2 + \cdots + X_{12})/12, \tag{4-14}$$

$$M_{7.5} = (X_2 + X_3 + \cdots + X_{13})/12. \tag{4-15}$$

Equations (4-14) and (4-15) are not centered because 12 is an even number. However, centering can be achieved by averaging (4-14) and (4-15), which involves simply taking an additional 2-month MA of (4-14) and (4-15). The result is a centered moving average:

$$M''_7 = \frac{M_{6.5} + M_{7.5}}{2}. \tag{4-16}$$

Substituting (4-14) and (4-15) into this equation gives

$$M''_7 = \left(\frac{X_1 + X_2 + \cdots + X_{12}}{12} + \frac{X_2 + X_3 + \cdots + X_{13}}{12}\right)\Big/ 2, \tag{4-17}$$

$$(X_1 + 2X_2 + 2X_3 + \cdots + 2X_{11} + 2X_{12} + X_{13})/24. \tag{4-18}$$

From (4-18), it can be seen that the first and last terms in the average have weights of $1/24 = .04167$, and all other terms have weights of double that value, .0833.

4/4/2 A 3 × 3 Moving Average

A 3 × 3 moving average is a 3 MA of a 3 MA. It is equivalent to a 5-period weighted moving average as shown by equations (4-19) through (4-24).

$$M_2 = (X_1 + X_2 + X_3)/3, \qquad \text{[A 3-months moving average of months} \tag{4-19}$$
$$\text{1, 2, and 3 (centered at period 2)]}$$

$$M_3 = (X_2 + X_3 + X_4)/3, \qquad (\text{like } M_2 \text{ but for months 2, 3, and 4}) \tag{4-20}$$

$$M_4 = (X_3 + X_4 + X_5)/3, \tag{4-21}$$

$$M_5 = (X_4 + X_5 + X_6)/3, \tag{4-22}$$

etc.

$$M''_3 = (M_2 + M_3 + M_4)/3. \qquad \text{[a 3-months moving average of the moving} \tag{4-23}$$
$$\text{averages (centered at period 3)]}$$

Substituting (4-19), (4-20) and (4-21) into (4-23) gives

$$M''_3 = \left(\frac{X_1 + X_2 + X_3}{3} + \frac{X_2 + X_3 + X_4}{3} + \frac{X_3 + X_4 + X_5}{3}\right)\Big/ 3$$

$$= (X_1 + 2X_2 + 3X_3 + 2X_4 + X_5)/9$$

$$\text{or} \quad M''_3 = \frac{1}{9}(X_1 + 2X_2 + 3X_3 + 2X_4 + X_5) \tag{4-24}$$

Equation (4-24) is a 5-month weighted MA with weights of .1111, .2222, .3333, .2222, .1111 for the first, second, third, fourth, and fifth terms respectively.

4/4/3 A 3 × 5 Moving Average

A 3 × 5 MA is similar to the 3 × 3 MA except that the number of terms averaged the second time is 5 and then 3. This results in a 7-term weighted moving average with weights of .067, .133, .200, .200, .200, .133, .067.

4/4/4 Spencer and Henderson Moving Averages

Spencer and Henderson moving averages are of still higher order than those examined above. Spencer's MA is a 5 × 5 × 4 × 4, or quadruple, MA. Or equivalently, it is a 15-point weighted moving average as shown by equations (4-25) through (4-35).

$$M_{2.5} = (X_1 + X_2 + X_3 + X_4)/4 \tag{4-25}$$

$$M_{3.5} = (X_2 + X_3 + X_4 + X_5)/4 \tag{4-26}$$

$$\text{(4-month moving averages of the original data)}$$

$$M_{4.5} = (X_3 + X_4 + X_5 + X_6)/4 \tag{4-27}$$

$$M_{5.5} = (X_4 + X_5 + X_6 + X_7)/4 \tag{4-28}$$

$$M_4' = (M_{2.5} + M_{3.5} + M_{4.5} + M_{5.5})/4 \quad \text{(a 4 MA of the 4 MA)} \tag{4-29}$$

Substituting (4-25), (4-26), (4-27) and (4-28) into (4-29) gives

$$M_4'' = (X_1 + 2X_2 + 3X_3 + 4X_4 + 3X_5 + 2X_6 + X_7)/16 \quad \text{(a 7-month weighted moving average)} \tag{4-30}$$

Using these 7-month weighted MA, a 5-month moving average can be computed.

$$M_6'' = (M_4'' + M_5'' + M_6'' + M_7'' + M_8'')/5. \quad \text{(a 5-month MA of the 7-month weighted MA)} \tag{4-31}$$

Substituting (4-30) into (4-31) gives

$$M_6''' = (X_1 + 3X_2 + 6X_3 + 10X_4 + 13X_5 + 14X_6 + 13X_7 + 10X_8 + 6X_9 + 3X_{10} + X_{11})/80.$$

$$\text{(an 11-month weighted MA)} \tag{4-32}$$

The final moving average applied to the 11-month moving average of (4-32) is a 5-term moving average, which is weighted as follows:

$$M_8''' = \frac{-3}{4}M_6'' + \frac{3}{4}M_7'' + M_8'' + \frac{3}{4}M_9'' - \frac{3}{4}M_{10}'' \quad \text{(the final averaging)} \tag{4-33}$$

Substituting (4-32) into (4-33) gives (after considerable algebra)

$$M_8'''' = (-3X_1 - 6X_2 - 5X_3 + 3X_4 + 21X_5 + 46X_6 + 67X_7 + 74X_8 + 67X_9$$

$$+ 46X_{10} + 21X_{11} + 3X_{12} - 5X_{13} - 6X_{13} - 3X_{15})/360. \tag{4-34}$$

Of course the data values will be different for moving averages centered on different periods. For example, M_9'''' will include the periods:

$$M_9'''' = (-3X_2 - 6X_3 - 5X_4 + \cdots - 6X_{15} - 3X_{16})/360. \tag{4-35}$$

For a data series with n observations, M_t'''' can be computed for periods 8 to $n - 7$. Each average will include 15 terms whose weights will be $-.009$, $-.009$, $-.016$, $.009$, $.066$, $.144$, $.209$, $.231$, $.209$, $.144$, $.066$, $.009$, $-.016$, $-.009$, $-.009$.

Another Spencer's MA that is commonly used is the 21-point weighted moving average. Its weights can be derived in the manner shown above for Spencer's 15-point formula.

In addition to Spencer's moving averages, the newest versions of Census II also use Henderson's 5-, 9-, 13-, and 23-point weighted moving averages. The selection of a specific moving average is based upon the randomness present in the series—the greater the randomness, the larger the number of terms in the average.

4/4/5 Selecting the Appropriate Length Moving Average

Determining the appropriate length of a moving average is an important task in decomposition methods. As a rule, a larger number of terms in the moving average increase the likelihood that randomness will be eliminated. That argues for using as long a length as possible. However, the longer the length of the moving average, the more terms (and information) are lost in the process of averaging, since N data values are required for an N-term average.

The $[(N - 1)/2]$ terms lost in the beginning of the data are usually of little consequence, but those $[(N - 1)/2]$ lost in the end are critical, since they are the starting point for forecasting the cycle. Not only must the cyclical values for periods $t + 1$, $t + 2$, etc., be estimated, but the values for periods t, $t - 1$, $t - 2, \ldots, t - (N - 1 + 1)/2$ must also be estimated. To overcome the problem of missing values at the end of the data series, a shorter length moving average can be used. This may not completely eliminate randomness however. Clearly a trade-off must be made in selecting the appropriate length moving average.

The latest versions of Census II, notably X-11, use various length moving averages depending upon the amount of randomness in the data—the more randomness, the longer the moving average. This method is practical with Census II because it goes through several iterations of decomposition, each one further refining the component estimates. It is thus possible to obtain preliminary estimates of randomness to be used in subsequent decomposition steps to select the appropriate length moving average.

Another innovation in Census II is that rather than applying the final moving averages to the original data, they are applied to the seasonally adjusted data. Since the fluctuations in the seasonally adjusted data are small, a shorter moving average can be used. Furthermore, since the seasonally adjusted data include trend-cycle and randomness, determining the importance of the trend-cycle relative to the randomness allows the moving average to be chosen that results in the trend-cycle just dominating the randomness. This is done in Census II by calculating what is called the *months for cyclical dominance*—or MCD. The MCD is then used to set the length of the moving average applied to the seasonally adjusted data. In most cases, the final moving average is of length 3, 4, or 5, which means that only one or two values are lost at the end of the data. (Even for those few values, there are ways to estimate their magnitude as will be seen in Chapter 12.)

4/5 The Census II Decomposition Method

The Census II method has been developed by the Bureau of the Census of the U.S. Department of Commerce. Julius Shiskin is considered the main contributor in the development of this method. Census II has been used widely by the bureau, other government agencies in the United States and elsewhere, and by an ever increasing number of businesses. Census II has gone through several variations since 1955 when the first version was developed. The method is based in part on the ratio-to-moving average classical decomposition method. However, Census II is much more elaborate, providing additional information through several empirical tests designed to check the adequacy of decomposition and through calculation of many useful statistics. Census II takes full advantage of the computational power of today's computers to provide the user with as much information as possible. (Some have argued that too much output is provided, and that this excess reduces the usefulness of the method.)

The Census II method consists of four different phases. In the first phase an attempt is made to adjust the data for trading day variations. The second phase is the preliminary estimation of seasonal factors and the preliminary adjustment of the series for seasonality. The third phase refines the adjustments so that more accurate seasonal factors can be calculated. In addition, an estimation of the trend-cycle and random or irregular component is made. The final phase prepares summary statistics that can be used to determine how successful the adjustments for seasonality have been and provides information needed to estimate the trend-cycle in the data for purposes of forecasting.

To illustrate the application of Census II, eight years of monthly data representing international airline passenger travel (in thousands) from 1949 through 1956 will be used. The actual values for this data series are shown in Table 4-9.

4/5/1 Trading Days Adjustments

Trading days adjustments are often necessary because a given month may not have the same number of working, or trading, days in different years. In some industries such as retail sales and banks, this factor becomes very important, since it can have a significant influence on the level of sales. In the airline data of Table 4-9, trading days are not an important factor because their effects on airline schedules are largely random, owing to the fact that holidays vary from country to country. However, to illustrate the procedure for making trading day adjustments, the process will be applied below.

The first step is to determine the number of trading days for each of the months of the years of interest. Next, the average number of working days in each month are calculated. Table 4-10 shows the number of trading days for the United States for 1949 through 1956. It can be seen that any given month can have a substantially different number of trading days over such an eight-year span. Once the number of trading days for each month is known, a set of monthly averages is calculated. The appropriate average is then used to divide the actual values of the corresponding month.

An example of the trading days adjustment for the month of April is given in Table 4-11. The average number of trading days for April, 21.25, is divided

TABLE 4-9 ACTUAL DATA FOR INTERNATIONAL AIRLINE PASSENGER TRAVEL

Year	Jan.	Feb.	Mar.	Apr.	May	June	July	Aug.	Sept.	Oct.	Nov.	Dec.
1949	112	118	132	129	121	135	148	148	136	119	104	118
1950	115	126	141	135	125	149	170	170	158	133	114	140
1951	145	150	178	163	172	178	199	199	184	162	146	166
1952	171	180	193	181	183	218	230	242	209	191	172	194
1953	196	196	236	235	229	243	264	272	237	211	180	201
1954	204	188	235	227	234	264	302	293	259	229	203	229
1955	242	233	267	269	270	315	364	347	312	274	237	278
1956	284	277	317	313	318	374	413	405	355	306	271	306

into each one of the actual number of trading days for April for the eight years. The resulting coefficient of adjustment is then divided into the original data to obtain a set of data adjusted for trading days. This same procedure would then be applied for the other 11 months of the year. The complete set of data adjusted for trading days is shown in Table 4-12. These data would then normally be used as the input for Census II and would be referred to as the original data adjusted for trading days. In the example that follows the adjusted data of Table 4-12 will not be used because the adjustment does not improve the results of decomposition in this case.

TABLE 4-10   NUMBER OF U.S. TRADING DAYS

Year	Jan.	Feb.	Mar.	Apr.	May	June	July	Aug.	Sept.	Oct.	Nov.	Dec.
1949	20	20	23	21	21	22	20	23	21	21	21	21
1950	21	20	23	20	22	22	20	23	20	22	21	20
1951	22	20	22	21	22	21	21	23	19	23	21	20
1952	22	21	21	22	21	21	22	21	21	23	19	22
1953	21	20	22	22	20	22	22	21	21	22	20	22
1954	20	20	23	22	20	22	21	22	21	21	21	22
1955	20	20	23	21	21	22	20	23	21	21	21	21
1956	21	21	22	21	22	21	21	23	19	23	21	20
Average	20.875	20.25	22.375	21.25	21.125	21.625	20.875	22.375	20.375	22.0	20.625	21.0

TABLE 4-11   CALCULATION OF TRADING DAYS ADJUSTMENT FOR APRIL

Year	Trading Days	Trading Days Coefficient of Adjustment	Data (April)	Data Adjustment for Trading Days[a]
1949	21	21/21.25 = .9882	129	129/.9882 = 130.54
1950	20	20/21.25 = .9412	135	135/.9412 = 143.44
1951	21	21/21.25 = .9882	163	163/.9882 = 164.95
1952	22	22/21.25 = 1.0353	181	181/1.0353 = 174.83
1953	22	22/21.25 = 1.0353	235	235/1.0353 = 226.99
1954	22	22/21.25 = 1.0353	227	227/1.0353 = 219.26
1955	21	21/21.25 = .9882	269	269/.9882 = 272.21
1956	21	21/21.25 = .9882	313	313/.9882 = 316.74
	170/8 = 21.25			

[a] See Table 4-12 for a complete set of adjusted data.

TABLE 4-12 AIRLINE DATA ADJUSTED FOR TRADING DAYS

Year	Jan.	Feb.	Mar.	Apr.	May	June	July	Aug.	Sept.	Oct.	Nov.	Dec.
1949	116.9	119.5	128.4	130.5	121.7	132.7	154.5	144.0	132.0	124.7	102.1	118.0
1950	114.3	127.6	137.2	143.4	120.0	146.5	177.4	165.4	161.0	133.0	112.0	147.0
1951	137.6	151.9	181.0	164.9	165.2	183.3	197.8	193.6	197.3	155.0	143.4	174.3
1952	162.3	173.6	205.6	174.8	184.1	224.5	218.2	257.8	202.8	182.7	186.7	185.2
1953	194.8	198.5	240.0	227.0	241.9	238.9	250.5	289.8	229.9	211.0	185.6	191.9
1954	212.9	190.4	228.6	219.3	247.2	259.5	300.2	298.0	251.3	239.9	199.4	218.6
1955	252.6	235.9	259.7	272.2	271.6	309.6	379.9	337.6	302.7	287.0	232.8	278.0
1956	282.3	267.1	322.4	316.7	305.4	385.1	410.5	394.0	380.7	292.7	266.2	321.3

4/5/2 Preliminary Seasonal Adjustment

The second phase of Census II is aimed at making a preliminary separation of the seasonality from the trend-cycle and then isolating the randomness. Using the monthly airline passenger data of Table 4-9 as an example, the steps in this phase are as outlined below.

Calculation of a 12-month centered moving average

A 12-month moving average applied to the original data will eliminate most of the seasonality and randomness that is in the series. The problem of centering a 12-month moving average is avoided by averaging the moving averages of 2 successive months and placing that value opposite the 7th month in the data being averaged (see Section 4/4/1).

The calculations necessary to obtain a 12-month MA are shown in columns 2 and 3 of Table 4-13. The ratios of these MA values to the original data are shown at the bottom of Table 4-13. Mathematically, these computations accomplish the following:

$$X_t = I_t T_t C_t E_t, \tag{4-36}$$

$$M_t = T_t C_t, \tag{4-37}$$

$$\frac{X_t}{M_t} = R_t = \frac{I_t T_t C_t E_t}{T_t C_t} = I_t E_t. \tag{4-38}$$

The values for R_t that contain seasonality and randomness are those shown at the bottom of Table 4-13. It should be pointed out that there are 6 values missing at the beginning and 6 at the end because of the averaging procedure used.

TABLE 4-13 PRELIMINARY SEASONALITY COMPUTATIONS FOR CENSUS II

			(1) Original Data	(2) 12-Month Uncentered Moving Average (MA)	(3) 2-Month MA of the 12-Month MA (13-month weighted MA or 12-month centered MA)	(4) $\dfrac{(1)}{(3)} = $ 12-Month Centered Ratios
1949	Jan.	112	—	—	☐
	Feb.	118	—	—	☐
	Mar.	132	—	—	☐
	Apr.	129	—	—	☐
	May	125	—	—	☐
	June	135	—	—	☐
	July	148	126.667	126.792	116.727
	Aug.	148	126.916	127.252	116.305
	Sept.	136	127.587	127.960	106.283
	Oct.	119	128.333	128.583	92.547
	Nov.	104	128.833	—	(see values in
	Dec.	118	—	—	bottom portion
1950	Jan.	115	—	—	of this table)
	Feb.	126	—	—	
	Mar.	141	—	—	
	Apr.	135	—	—	
	May	125	—	—	

Centered 12-Month Ratios (original/moving average)

Year	Jan.	Feb.	Mar.	Apr.	May	June	July	Aug.	Sept.	Oct.	Nov.	Dec.
1949	0	0	0	0	0	0	116.7	116.3	106.3	92.5	80.6	90.9
1950	87.6	94.7	104.5	99.0	91.0	107.4	120.6	118.7	108.4	89.6	75.2	90.5
1951	92.3	94.0	110.0	99.3	103.2	105.3	116.2	114.6	104.9	91.6	82.0	92.1
1952	93.4	96.7	102.1	94.6	94.5	111.3	116.1	121.2	103.4	92.6	81.7	90.9
1953	90.8	89.7	106.8	105.4	102.2	108.1	117.2	120.7	105.4	94.0	80.2	89.1
1954	89.5	81.6	101.2	97.0	99.3	111.0	125.6	120.1	104.8	91.5	80.1	89.1
1955	92.4	87.4	98.5	97.7	96.9	111.7	127.4	119.9	106.4	92.2	78.7	91.0
1956	91.6	88.1	99.5	97.3	98.0	114.3	0	0	0	0	0	0

Replacement of extreme values

The ratios of Table 4-13 include such random or unusual events as strikes and wars. The next task in Census II is to exclude such extreme values before eliminating the randomness. This process has two stages.

1. Calculate a 3 × 3 month moving average. A 3 × 3 MA is applied to the centered ratios of Table 4-13. (This double moving average is the equivalent to a 5-month weighted moving average. See Section 4/4/3.) The purpose of this step is to eliminate as much of the randomness as possible. However, calculating a 3 × 3 moving average results in the loss of 2 values at the beginning of the data and 2 at the end. To avoid this loss, Census II estimates values for the beginning 2 months and the ending 2 months. Table 4-14 illustrates this procedure for the month of April. The two missing values are set equal to the average of the 2 following values. (The last 2 values are averaged to fill in the 2 months at the end of the series.) This gives 4 more values, so that after taking the 3 × 3 moving average, there are still as many values as there were before doing so.

TABLE 4-14   CALCULATION OF A 3 × 3 MOVING AVERAGE (APRIL)

	Centered Ratios (from bottom of Table 4-13, column 4)	Introduction of 2 Extra Values in Beginning and 2 Extra Values at End	3 × 3 Moving Average	
			3 MA	3 × 3 MA
1949		$\dfrac{99 + 99.3}{2} = \begin{cases} 99.15 \\ 99.15 \end{cases}$	— 99.1	—
1950	99	99	99.15	98.63
1951	99.3	99.3	97.63	98.85
1952	94.6	94.6	99.77	98.8
1953	105.4	105.4	99	99.68
1954	97.0	97.0	100.27	98.95
1955	97.7	97.7	97.57	98.45
1956	97.3	97.3	97.5	97.5
		$\dfrac{97.7 + 97.3}{2} = 97.5$	97.43	—
		97.5	—	—

2. Calculate the standard deviation. After the 3×3 moving averages are calculated, their differences from the centered ratios shown in Table 4-13 are found for each one of the months as illustrated in Table 4-15. The deviations are squared and summed and then divided by the number of terms used in the summation, i.e., the number of years. This calculation gives the variance of each month's values. The square root of the variance is the standard deviation. The standard deviation can be used to construct control limits that identify extreme values. For the month of April, the limits can be set at the 3×3 MA plus or minus 2 standard deviations. There is only 1 value (1953) that is outside these control limits. The value for this month of April 1953 is then replaced by taking the average of the preceding and the following period. If the values to be replaced are the first or last, the average of the 3 preceding or the 3 following months is taken. Table 4-16 indicates the values replaced for the airline data assuming that the control limits are the 3×3 MA ± 2 standard deviation. If the limit is raised to the 3×3 MA ± 2.5 standard deviation, then none of the values needs replacing.

TABLE 4-15 CALCULATION OF STANDARD DEVIATION AND REPLACEMENT VALUES (APRIL)

	(1) Centered Ratios (Table 4-13)	(2) 3×3 MA (Table 4-14)	(3) (1) − (2) Deviations	(4) Deviations Squared
1949	—	—	—	—
1950	99	98.63	.37	.1369
1951	99.3	98.85	.45	.2025
1952	94.6	98.8	−4.2	17.64
1953	105.4	99.68	5.72	32.72
1954	97.0	98.95	−1.95	3.80
1955	97.7	98.45	−.75	.56
1956	97.3	97.5	−.2	.04

$$55.1$$

$$Var = \frac{55.1}{7} = 7.871$$

$$SD = \sqrt{7.871} = 2.81$$

TABLE 4-16 REPLACEMENT OF EXTREME VALUES (APRIL)

	3 × 3 MA (Table 4-14)	Plus or Minus 2 * SD	Greater or Smaller Than Corresponding Ratio (Table 4-13)		Substitute in Table 4-13
1949	—	—	—	—	—
1950	98.63	±5.62	99	No	—
1951	98.85	±5.62	99.3	No	—
1952	98.8	±5.62	94.6	No	—
1953	99.68	±5.62	105.4	Greater	(94.6 + 97.0)/2 = 95.8
1954	98.95	±5.62	97.0	No	—
1955	98.45	±5.62	97.7	No	—
1956	97.5	±5.62	97.3	No	—

Replaced Extreme Values

Year	Month	Value
1954	Feb.	88.5386
1953	Apr.	95.8314
1951	Aug.	119.947
1950	Nov.	81.3118

Preliminary seasonal factors

After the extreme values have been replaced, the ratios of Table 4-13 are adjusted and used to calculate the preliminary seasonal factors. The adjustments to be performed are the following:

1. The 6 months at the beginning of the ratios (see Table 4-13) and the 6 months at the end are lost because of the 12-month centered moving average. These observations are replaced with the corresponding values of the following or preceding year as shown in Table 4-17.

2. The ratios of each year are adjusted so they add to 1200 by summing up the values of each of the years separately and dividing the sum by 12. The value obtained is the average of all months for each year. This value is divided into each month for the appropriate year, giving an average monthly figure of 100. This procedure is illustrated in Table 4-18.

TABLE 4-17 ESTIMATING VALUES FOR THE FIRST AND LAST 6 OBSERVATIONS

1949	87.6	94.7	104.5	99.0	91.0	107.4	116.7	116.3	106.3	92.5	80.6	90.9
1950	87.6	94.7	104.5	99.0	91.0	107.4	120.6	118.7	108.4	89.6	75.2	90.5
1951	·	·										
1952	·	·										
1953	·	·										
1954	·	·										
1955	92.4	87.4	98.5	97.7	96.9	117.7	127.4	119.9	106.4	92.2	78.7	91.0
1956	91.6	88.1	99.5	97.3	98.0	114.3	127.4	119.9	106.4	92.2	78.7	91.0

Several adjustments have now been made to the centered ratios of Table 4-13 as part of this preliminary stage. First, the extreme values were replaced. Second, values for the missing first and last 6 observations were estimated and filled in. And third, the ratios were adjusted to sum to 1200. The objective has been to eliminate the effect of unusual events and to adjust the series for effects caused by computational procedures. The next step is to eliminate randomness by taking a 3 × 3 MA of each month of the year individually. This moving average is analogous to the one

TABLE 4-18

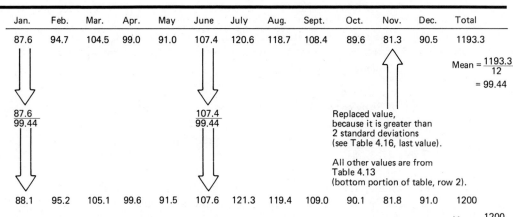

Jan.	Feb.	Mar.	Apr.	May	June	July	Aug.	Sept.	Oct.	Nov.	Dec.	Total
87.6	94.7	104.5	99.0	91.0	107.4	120.6	118.7	108.4	89.6	81.3	90.5	1193.3

$$\text{Mean} = \frac{1193.3}{12} = 99.44$$

87.6 / 99.44   107.4 / 99.44

Replaced value, because it is greater than 2 standard deviations (see Table 4.16, last value).

All other values are from Table 4.13 (bottom portion of table, row 2).

Jan.	Feb.	Mar.	Apr.	May	June	July	Aug.	Sept.	Oct.	Nov.	Dec.	Total
88.1	95.2	105.1	99.6	91.5	107.6	121.3	119.4	109.0	90.1	81.8	91.0	1200

$$\text{Mean} = \frac{1200}{12} = 100$$

TABLE 4-19 PRELIMINARY SEASONAL ADJUSTMENT FACTOR

Year	Jan.	Feb.	Mar.	Apr.	May	June	July	Aug.	Sept.	Oct.	Nov.	Dec.
1949	89.0	95.0	106.2	99.5	94.1	107.4	118.4	118.4	107.2	91.8	81.5	91.5
1950	89.7	95.0	105.9	98.8	94.7	107.5	118.3	119.0	106.7	91.5	81.6	91.3
1951	90.8	94.3	106.0	97.7	97.0	107.6	117.3	119.6	105.5	91.7	81.4	91.0
1952	91.4	93.3	105.0	96.6	98.2	108.7	117.8	120.3	104.8	92.2	81.2	90.5
1953	91.4	91.2	103.9	96.4	99.3	109.5	119.8	120.5	104.8	92.6	80.5	90.0
1954	91.1	89.4	101.8	96.7	98.8	111.0	123.3	120.3	105.3	92.4	79.9	89.9
1955	91.2	88.1	100.3	97.2	98.3	111.7	125.7	120.0	105.8	92.2	79.2	90.2
1956	91.3	87.8	99.4	97.2	97.8	112.6	126.8	119.8	105.9	91.9	78.9	90.4

described in Table 4-14 except that the modified data with replaced extreme values, estimates for missing values, and adjusted ratios is used. Table 4-19 shows the results, the preliminary seasonal adjustment factors.

The last step of this preliminary phase is to divide the preliminary seasonal factors of Table 4-19 into the original data to obtain the preliminary seasonally adjusted series of Table 4-20. This series constitutes the basis for further refining the estimates of seasonality, trend-cycle, and randomness performed as the third stage of Census II.

Table 4-13 gives values equivalent to equation (4-38) and these include seasonality and randomness. Since randomness was eliminated by replacing

TABLE 4-20 PRELIMINARY SEASONALLY ADJUSTED SERIES [ACTUAL DATA (TABLE 4-9)/PRELIMINARY SEASONAL ADJUSTMENT FACTORS (TABLE 4-19)]

Year	Jan.	Feb.	Mar.	Apr.	May	June	July	Aug.	Sept.	Oct.	Nov.	Dec.
1949	126	124	124	130	129	126	125	125	127	130	128	129
1950	128	133	133	137	132	139	144	143	148	145	140	153
1951	160	159	168	167	177	165	170	166	174	177	179	182
1952	187	193	184	187	186	201	195	201	199	207	212	214
1953	214	215	227	244	231	222	220	226	226	228	224	223
1954	224	210	231	235	237	238	245	244	246	248	254	255
1955	265	265	266	277	275	282	290	289	295	297	299	308
1956	311	315	319	322	325	332	326	338	335	333	343	338

extreme values and smoothing (4-38) through a 3×3 moving average, what remains is only the seasonal component. If this seasonal component is divided into the original data, only the trend-cycle and the irregular fluctuations in the data remain. These are the values shown in Table 4-20, and they can be written mathematically as:

$$PI_t = \frac{X_t}{I_t} = \frac{I_t T_t C_t E_t}{I_t} = T_t C_t E_t, \tag{4-39}$$

where the PI_t are the preliminary seasonally adjusted values.

4/5/3 Final Seasonal Adjustments

In this stage of Census II the preliminary seasonally adjusted series is processed further by using moving averages to eliminate any seasonal and irregular effects not detected previously. This result is achieved through a sequence of steps similar to those applied in the preliminary phase described in the last section.

Isolating the trend-cycle

Using the seasonally adjusted data as a starting point, one removes the randomness by applying Spencer's 15-month weighted moving average. The rationale for applying this average is that the data given by equation (4-39) includes trend-cycle and randomness. This moving average eliminates the randomness, providing a smooth curve that highlights the existence of a trend-cycle in the data. Table 4-21 illustrates this, showing the results obtained with equation (4-40). When the original data are divided by the Spencer 15-point moving averages only the seasonal and random factors remain. This result is called the final seasonal-irregular ratios and is given mathematically by equation (4-41):

$$M_t' = T_t C_t, \tag{4-40}$$

$$FIE_t = \frac{X_t}{M_t'} = \frac{I_t T_t C_t E_t}{T_t C_t} = I_t E_t, \tag{4-41}$$

where M_t' is Spencer's 15-point MA and FIE_t is the final seasonal irregular ratio.

Applying the Spencer 15-point formula would normally cause the loss of 7 values at the beginning of the series and 7 at the end. To avoid this loss, each of the missing values is replaced by an estimated value. The first 7 values are set equal to the average of the 4 following observations and the last 7 are set equal to the average of the 4 preceding observations. An illustration of this adjustment and computation of the Spencer 15-month moving average is given in Table 4-21.

TABLE 4-21 CALCULATING SPENCER'S 15-MONTH WEIGHTED MOVING AVERAGE

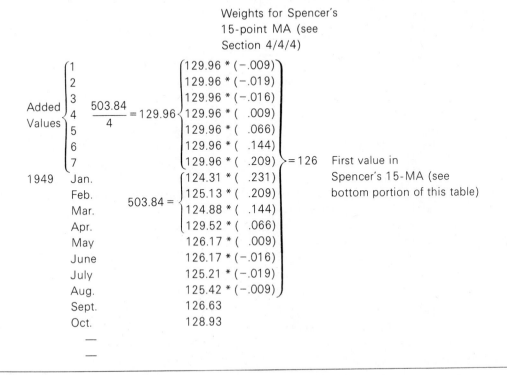

Weights for Spencer's 15-point MA (see Section 4/4/4)

$$\text{Added Values} \begin{cases} 1 \\ 2 \\ 3 \\ 4 \\ 5 \\ 6 \\ 7 \end{cases} \frac{503.84}{4} = 129.96 \begin{cases} 129.96 * (-.009) \\ 129.96 * (-.019) \\ 129.96 * (-.016) \\ 129.96 * (.009) \\ 129.96 * (.066) \\ 129.96 * (.144) \\ 129.96 * (.209) \end{cases} = 126$$

First value in Spencer's 15-MA (see bottom portion of this table)

1949	Jan.		124.31 * (.231)
	Feb.	$503.84 =$	125.13 * (.209)
	Mar.		124.88 * (.144)
	Apr.		129.52 * (.066)
	May		126.17 * (.009)
	June		126.17 * (−.016)
	July		125.21 * (−.019)
	Aug.		125.42 * (−.009)
	Sept.		126.63
	Oct.		128.93

Spencer's 15-Month Weighted Moving Averages (preliminary seasonally adjusted series)

Year	Jan.	Feb.	Mar.	Apr.	May	June	July	Aug.	Sept.	Oct.	Nov.	Dec.
1949	126	126	126	126	127	126	126	126	127	127	128	129
1950	130	131	133	134	137	139	141	143	144	146	148	152
1951	156	161	165	168	169	170	170	171	173	176	180	183
1952	185	187	188	189	191	193	196	200	203	206	209	213
1953	218	222	226	228	229	228	226	225	224	224	223	222
1954	222	224	227	231	235	239	242	244	247	249	253	257
1955	261	265	269	273	277	282	286	290	294	298	302	306
1956	310	315	319	322	325	328	331	333	335	337	338	338

Final seasonal-irregular ratios

The final seasonal-irregular ratios are calculated by dividing the values given by Spencer's 15-point formula into the original data. The result is the series of values represented by (4-41). (See Table 4-22). These values serve as the starting point for replacing extreme values and adjusting the ratios so they sum to 1200. These steps are identical to those applied in Tables 4-14, 4-15, 4-16, and 4-18. In summary, the four steps are as follows:

1. *Replace the extreme values.* The extreme values are replaced by calculating a 3×3 moving average for each of the months separately as in Table 4-14, then calculating the standard deviations for each of the months as in Table 4-15 and finally replacing the extreme values (those outside of the control limits) as in Table 4-16. The process is exactly the same as that applied in the preliminary phase of Census II except that the data to which it is applied is the ratio of the original data to the Spencer 15-point formula as shown in Table 4-21.

2. *Estimate missing values.* There is no need to fill in the first 6 values and the last 6 values as was done in Table 4-17, because values for these observations were estimated before applying the Spencer 15-point formula.

3. *Adjust ratios.* The ratios must be adjusted to sum to 1200 by exactly the same process as that shown in Table 4-18.

The outcome of this process is the set of final seasonal-irregular ratios presented in Table 4-22. The bottom portion of Table 4-22 gives the *stable factors*. These factors are the averages for each month and show the extent of the seasonality existing in the original airline data. They are the equivalent of equation (4-41) without randomness. These stable factors are equivalent to the seasonal indices calculated in the classical decomposition method. The only difference is that they have been found through two decomposition iterations. For example, April's stable factor is

$$(100.4 + 99.4 + 98.6 + 98.3 + 99. + 98.9 + 98.5 + 97.8)/8 = 98.9.$$

Final seasonal factors

The final seasonal factors are derived by applying a 3×3 moving average (or a 5×5 moving average if significant randomness is present) to the data of Table 4-22. The 3×3 moving average is computed as shown in Table 4-14. The 2 observations at the beginning and the 2 observations at the end that would normally be lost are estimated before the moving average is calculated. (When a 5×5 moving average is used, the 4 observations at each end are estimated.) The result is the set of final seasonal adjustment factors shown in Table 4-23. These factor values are projected

TABLE 4-22 FINAL SEASONAL-IRREGULAR RATIOS

Year	Jan.	Feb.	Mar.	Apr.	May	June	July	Aug.	Sept.	Oct.	Nov.	Dec.
				Centered Ratios (original/15 months moving average)								
1949	89.7	94.3	105.8	100.4	95.6	106.6	118.4	117.7	107.9	92.4	79.8	91.5
1950	90.1	94.7	105.8	99.4	95.6	107.1	118.4	118.1	107.4	92.1	79.7	91.5
1951	90.9	93.9	105.5	98.6	97.2	107.5	117.8	118.6	106.3	92.3	80.4	91.1
1952	91.3	92.3	104.6	98.3	97.9	108.7	118.1	119.6	105.2	92.5	80.8	90.7
1953	91.5	89.5	103.6	99.0	98.8	109.1	119.7	120.0	105.0	92.8	80.7	90.3
1954	91.6	87.6	102.2	98.9	98.5	110.5	122.6	120.3	105.2	92.3	80.1	90.1
1955	91.8	86.9	101.0	98.5	98.2	111.3	124.7	120.2	105.6	91.8	79.6	90.2
1956	91.9	87.1	100.3	97.8	97.9	112.3	125.5	120.4	105.7	91.4	79.6	90.2
				Stable Factors — Seasonal Indices								
	91.1	90.8	103.6	98.9	97.4	109.1	120.7	119.4	106.0	92.2	80.1	90.7

TABLE 4-23 FINAL SEASONAL ADJUSTMENT FACTORS

Year	Jan.	Feb.	Mar.	Apr.	May	June	July	Aug.	Sept.	Oct.	Nov.	Dec.
				Final Seasonal Adjustment Factors								
1949	90.1	94.3	105.7	99.6	95.9	107.0	118.2	118.0	107.4	92.3	79.9	91.4
1950	90.3	94.1	105.6	99.3	96.3	107.2	118.2	118.3	107.0	92.3	80.0	91.3
1951	90.7	93.3	105.2	98.9	97.0	107.8	118.3	118.7	106.3	92.4	80.3	91.0
1952	91.2	91.8	104.4	98.7	97.7	108.5	118.9	119.4	105.6	92.5	80.5	90.7
1953	91.5	89.9	103.4	98.7	98.2	109.4	120.3	119.8	105.3	92.5	80.4	90.4
1954	91.6	88.3	102.3	98.6	98.3	110.4	122.3	120.1	105.3	92.2	80.1	90.2
1955	91.8	87.4	101.4	98.5	98.2	111.1	123.8	120.3	105.5	91.9	79.9	90.2
1956	91.8	87.1	100.9	98.3	98.1	111.6	124.6	120.3	105.6	91.7	79.7	90.2
				One-Year-Ahead Forecasted Seasonal Factors								
	91.9	87.0	100.7	98.1	98.0	111.8	125.0	120.4	105.6	91.6	79.6	90.2

out one year by multiplying the factor in the last row by 3, subtracting the factors of the preceding row and dividing the result by 2. For example, the one-year-ahead forecast for April of 98.1 is calculated as

$$[(98.3 \times 3) - 98.5]/2 = 98.1.$$

Mathematically, this step is equivalent to computing the expected values in order to remove any randomness that is still present.

$$FA_t' = \varepsilon(I_t E_t) = I_t, \tag{4-42}$$

where FA_t' is the final seasonal adjustment factor for period t and ε denotes expected value.

Final seasonally adjusted series

The final seasonally adjusted series is found by dividing the final seasonal adjustment factors of Table 4-23 into the original data. The results for the international airline data are shown in Table 4-24. If the adjustment has been complete, fluctuations in the original data caused by seasonality will have been completely removed, and only the trend-cycle and randomness will remain. Mathematically, that is given by (4-43). Since seasonal adjustments tend to smooth the series, the result is a clearer and more refined estimate of the trend-cycle pattern mixed with randomness.

$$FA_t = \frac{X_t}{\varepsilon(I_t E_t)} = \frac{I_t T_t C_t E_t}{I_t} = T_t C_t E_t. \tag{4-43}$$

TABLE 4-24   FINAL SEASONALLY ADJUSTED SERIES

Year	Jan.	Feb.	Mar.	Apr.	May	June	July	Aug.	Sept.	Oct.	Nov.	Dec.
1949	124	125	125	129	126	126	125	125	127	129	130	129
1950	127	134	134	136	130	139	144	144	148	144	143	153
1951	160	161	169	165	177	165	168	168	173	175	182	182
1952	188	196	185	183	187	201	193	203	198	207	214	214
1953	214	218	228	238	233	222	219	227	225	228	224	222
1954	223	213	230	230	238	239	247	244	246	248	253	254
1955	264	267	263	273	275	284	294	289	296	298	297	308
1956	309	318	314	319	324	335	331	337	336	334	340	339

The preparation of the final seasonally adjusted series completes this major phase of Census II. An important characteristic of this phase is that the task of isolating randomness and seasonal factors is not done simultaneously as it is in most decomposition methods. The division of this task enlarges the computational requirements, but it also generally improves the accuracy.

Before proceeding with the final phase of Census II, two additional sets of values for the time series are needed—a final estimate of trend-cycle values and a final estimate of the random component. The first of these is calculated by applying a 15-month weighted moving average to the final seasonally adjusted data of Table 4-24. The results are as shown in Table 4-25. Mathematically, this calculation is equivalent to computing the expected value of equation (4-43).

$$(FA_t) = \varepsilon(T_tC_tE_t), \tag{4-44}$$

$$FA_t' = T_tC_t. \tag{4-45}$$

TABLE 4-25 FINAL ESTIMATE OF TREND-CYCLE COMPONENT

Spencer's 15-Point Weighted Average (seasonally adjusted series)

Year	Jan.	Feb.	Mar.	Apr.	May	June	July	Aug.	Sept.	Oct.	Nov.	Dec.
1949	125	126	126	126	126	126	126	126	127	128	129	129
1950	130	131	132	134	136	138	141	142	144	146	149	153
1951	157	162	166	168	169	169	169	170	173	176	180	184
1952	186	187	188	189	191	193	196	199	203	206	210	214
1953	218	223	226	228	229	228	226	225	224	224	223	222
1954	222	223	226	230	235	239	243	245	247	249	253	256
1955	260	264	268	272	277	283	287	291	295	298	301	305
1956	309	313	317	321	325	329	332	335	336	337	337	338

TABLE 4-26 FINAL ESTIMATE OF IRREGULAR (RANDOM) COMPONENT

Random Component (seasonally adjusted series/Spencer's 15-point formula)

Year	Jan.	Feb.	Mar.	Apr.	May	June	July	Aug.	Sept.	Oct.	Nov.	Dec.
1949	99.2	99.6	99.2	102.7	100.0	100.1	99.3	99.3	99.8	101.0	101.3	99.7
1950	97.6	102.0	100.9	101.4	95.4	100.4	102.3	100.9	102.4	98.6	95.7	100.5
1951	101.7	99.4	102.2	98.1	105.0	97.7	99.4	98.4	100.2	99.5	101.0	99.3
1952	100.8	104.7	98.2	97.0	98.3	104.1	98.7	101.7	97.6	100.3	102.0	100.1
1953	98.2	97.9	100.9	104.3	102.0	97.6	97.0	100.8	100.3	101.9	100.4	100.2
1954	100.5	95.5	101.7	99.9	101.2	99.9	101.9	99.6	99.6	99.5	100.3	99.1
1955	101.6	101.1	98.3	100.3	99.1	100.3	102.4	99.1	100.4	100.0	98.5	101.0
1956	100.1	101.5	99.0	99.2	99.6	101.8	99.7	100.6	100.1	99.0	100.8	100.5

Equation (4-45) is a much better estimate of the trend-cycle than either (4-37) or (4-40) because it is derived using (4-43) which is applied to the seasonally adjusted series.

Finally, equation (4-45) can be divided into (4-43) to obtain:

$$RC_t = \frac{FA_t}{FA_t'} = \frac{T_t C_t E_t}{T_t C_t} = E_t. \tag{4-46}$$

Equation (4-46) provides the estimate of the random component. The results of this step applied to the international airline passenger series are shown in Table 4-26.

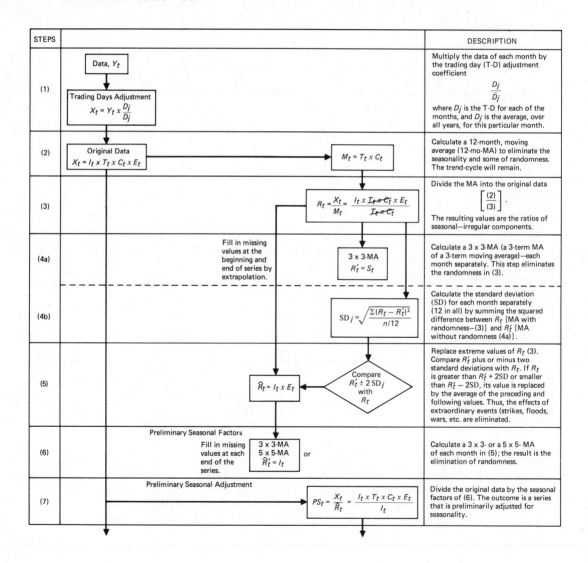

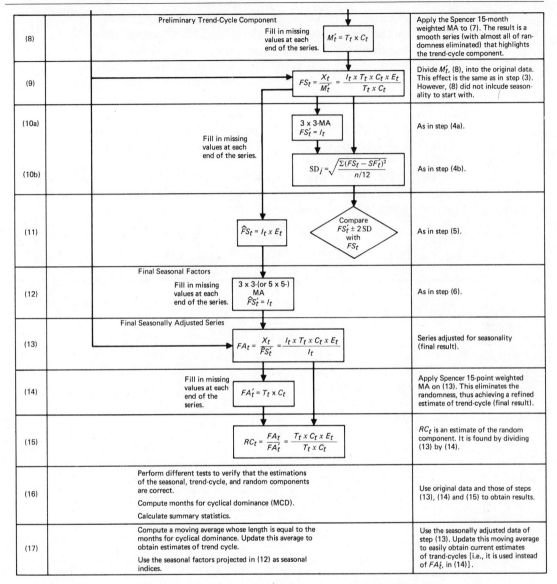

(8)	Preliminary Trend-Cycle Component Fill in missing values at each end of the series. $M'_t = T_t \times C_t$	Apply the Spencer 15-month weighted MA to (7). The result is a smooth series (with almost all of randomness eliminated) that highlights the trend-cycle component.
(9)	$FS_t = \dfrac{X_t}{M'_t} = \dfrac{I_t \times T_t \times C_t \times E_t}{T_t \times C_t}$	Divide M'_t, (8), into the original data. This effect is the same as in step (3). However, (8) did not inlcude seasonality to start with.
(10a)	Fill in missing values at each end of the series. $3 \times 3\text{-MA}$ $FS'_t = I_t$	As in step (4a).
(10b)	$SD_j = \sqrt{\dfrac{\Sigma(FS_t - SF'_t)^2}{n/12}}$	As in step (4b).
(11)	$\widehat{FS}_t = I_t \times E_t$ Compare $FS'_t \pm 2\,SD$ with FS_t	As in step (5).
(12)	Final Seasonal Factors Fill in missing values at each end of the series. $3 \times 3\text{-(or } 5 \times 5\text{-)}$ MA $\widehat{FS}'_t = I_t$	As in step (6).
(13)	Final Seasonally Adjusted Series $FA_t = \dfrac{X_t}{\widehat{FS}_t} = \dfrac{I_t \times T_t \times C_t \times E_t}{I_t}$	Series adjusted for seasonality (final result).
(14)	Fill in missing values at each end of the series. $FA'_t = T_t \times C_t$	Apply Spencer 15-point weighted MA on (13). This eliminates the randomness, thus achieving a refined estimate of trend-cycle (final result).
(15)	$RC_t = \dfrac{FA_t}{FA'_t} = \dfrac{T_t \times C_t \times E_t}{T_t \times C_t}$	RC_t is an estimate of the random component. It is found by dividing (13) by (14).
(16)	Perform different tests to verify that the estimations of the seasonal, trend-cycle, and random components are correct. Compute months for cyclical dominance (MCD). Calculate summary statistics.	Use original data and those of steps (13), (14) and (15) to obtain results.
(17)	Compute a moving average whose length is equal to the months for cyclical dominance. Update this average to obtain estimates of trend cycle. Use the seasonal factors projected in (12) as seasonal indices.	Use the seasonally adjusted data of step (13). Update this moving average to easily obtain current estimates of trand-cycles [i.e., it is used instead of FA'_t, in (14)].

FIGURE 4-2   MAJOR STEPS IN CENSUS II DECOMPOSITION METHOD

It may well seem that the Census II method is very complicated because of the number of steps involved up to this point. However, the basic idea is really quite straightforward—to isolate the seasonal, trend-cycle, and irregular components one by one. This process has two major phases. First, a preliminary estimate of the seasonality is made so that the seasonal component can be removed from the data. The remaining two components (trend-cycle and irregular) are therefore easier to identify and isolate. Second, refined estimates of seasonality, trend-cycle, and randomness are prepared. A summary diagram of the steps followed is given in Figure 4-2.

4/5/4 Tests and Summary Statistics

After phase III has been completed and the basic components of time series have been estimated, in phase IV a series of tests are used to determine whether or not the decomposition has been successful. These tests are not statistical

TABLE 4-27 ADJACENT MONTH TEST (ORIGINAL DATA)

	Ratios of Preceding and Following Month[a]											
Year	Jan.	Feb.	Mar.	Apr.	May	June	July	Aug.	Sept.	Oct.	Nov.	Dec.
1949	0	96.7	106.9	102.0	91.7	100.4	104.6	104.2	101.9	99.2	87.8	107.8
1950	94.3	98.4	108.0	101.5	88.0	101.0	106.6	103.7	104.3	97.8	83.5	108.1
1951	100.0	92.9	113.7	93.1	100.9	96.0	105.6	103.9	101.9	98.2	89.0	104.7
1952	98.8	98.9	106.9	96.3	91.7	105.6	100.0	110.3	96.5	100.3	89.4	105.4
1953	100.5	90.7	109.5	101.1	95.8	98.6	102.5	108.6	98.1	101.2	87.4	104.7
1954	104.9	85.6	113.3	96.8	95.3	98.5	108.4	104.5	99.2	99.1	88.6	102.9
1955	104.8	91.6	106.4	100.2	92.5	99.4	110.0	102.7	100.5	99.8	85.9	106.7
1956	102.3	92.2	107.5	98.6	92.6	102.3	106.0	105.5	99.9	97.8	88.6	0
	Averages											
	100.8	93.4	109.0	98.7	93.6	100.2	105.5	105.4	100.3	99.2	87.5	105.8

[a] *Sample computations* (values taken from Table 4-9):

The first ratio is 0 because there is no preceding month's value for month 1;

the second ratio is $\dfrac{118}{(112 + 132)/2} = 96.7$;

the third ratio is $\dfrac{132}{(118 + 129)/2} = 106.9$;

etc.

in the rigorous mathematical sense, but are based on intuitive considerations. The four types of tests most commonly used are described below.

Adjacent month test

Calculating the ratio of a given month to the average of the preceding and following months gives an indication of how that particular month varies from the preceding and following months. If the data is nonseasonal, such variations should be small. However, when strong seasonality exists, the variations will be considerable, reflecting the pattern that exists between successive months. If the ratios of all the years are averaged for each of the individual months, the results will give an even better indication of the variability of the series. Table 4-27 shows the ratios of the preceding and following months of the original airline passenger data. These ratios vary

TABLE 4-28 ADJACENT MONTH TEST (FINAL SEASONALLY ADJUSTED DATA)

					Ratios of Preceding and Following Month[a]							
Year	Jan.	Feb.	Mar.	Apr.	May	June	July	Aug.	Sept.	Oct.	Nov.	Dec.
1949	0	100.4	98.1	103.2	98.6	100.5	99.5	99.6	99.6	100.4	100.9	100.3
1950	96.8	102.7	99.0	103.2	94.5	101.5	101.8	98.6	102.6	99.3	95.8	101.5
1951	101.7	97.7	104.0	95.1	107.5	95.6	101.1	98.2	100.9	98.8	101.7	98.7
1952	99.1	105.3	97.4	98.6	97.5	105.5	95.8	103.6	96.7	100.3	101.7	99.9
1953	99.3	98.5	100.1	103.2	101.3	98.2	97.7	102.1	98.9	101.6	99.4	99.6
1954	102.3	94.1	103.8	98.4	101.4	98.6	102.3	98.9	100.0	99.5	100.9	98.2
1955	101.4	101.1	97.6	101.5	98.7	99.7	102.8	97.8	100.9	100.6	97.9	101.7
1956	98.8	102.0	98.7	99.8	99.2	102.3	98.7	100.8	100.4	98.6	101.1	0

					Averages							
	99.9	100.2	99.8	100.4	99.8	100.2	100.0	100.0	100.0	99.9	99.9	100.0

[a] *Sample computations* (values taken from Table 4-24):

The first ratio is 0 because there is no preceding month's value for month 1;

the second ratio is $\dfrac{125.1}{(124.3 + 124.9)/2} = 100.4$;

the third ratio is $\dfrac{124.9}{(125.1 + 129.5)/2} = 98.1$.

considerably from month to month, suggesting that the original series is strongly seasonal.

If the same calculations are performed on the seasonally adjusted data the resulting ratios should be much smaller if the seasonal adjustment has been successful. The seasonal adjustment which gives these ratios for data shows that the seasonality has been removed. If some values of the average ratios in Table 4-28 had been below 95 or above 105, it would indicate that the seasonal adjustment process had not been adequate in removing the seasonal variation. Since the adjacent month ratios in Table 4-28 are all close to 100, one would conclude in this case that the deseasonalizing had been successful.

The January test

Dividing the final seasonally adjusted series by the corresponding values of each preceding January gives a set of standardized values with January as the base. Examining these values of the standardized ratios could identify any constant pattern of longer than one month's duration. If such patterns exist, it suggests that seasonality has not been properly removed from the data. The January test reveals any intrayear seasonality that might remain, while the adjacent month test reveals any interyear seasonality that might remain. The adjacent month and January tests should be used in combination to be sure that the removal of seasonality has been successful. Table 4-29 illustrates the January test for the final seasonably adjusted airline data. The only apparent pattern in the ratios is trend, indicating that seasonality has been effectively removed.

Equality test

In applying a decomposition method such as Census II, over-adjustment is a concern just as under-adjustment is. One test to determine whether over-adjustment has taken place is obtained by dividing the 12-month moving average of the original data into the 12-month moving average of the seasonally adjusted data. The 12-month moving average of the original data should have eliminated the seasonality without altering the volume of the data. The 12-month moving average of the final seasonally adjusted data should also have eliminated seasonality, but in addition should make other adjustments such as the elimination of randomness, replacement of extremes, etc. As a result, the final seasonally adjusted data may have included some of the irregular components as part of the seasonality. The ratios between these two averages can be used to identify any over-adjustment for seasonality that may have taken place. If the ratios are close to 100, it indicates there is no over-adjustment. However, if the ratios are below 90 or above 110, it indicates that the seasonal adjustment

TABLE 4-29 JANUARY TEST

| | Standardized Ratios to Preceding January (seasonally adjusted series)[a] | | | | | | | | | | | |
Year	Jan.	Feb.	Mar.	Apr.	May	June	July	Aug.	Sept.	Oct.	Nov.	Dec.
1949	100.0	100.6	100.4	104.2	101.5	101.5	100.7	100.9	101.9	103.7	104.8	103.9
1950	100.0	105.2	104.9	106.8	102.0	109.1	113.0	112.9	116.0	113.2	112.0	120.5
1951	100.0	100.7	105.9	103.1	111.0	103.4	105.3	104.9	108.3	109.7	113.8	114.1
1952	100.0	104.6	98.5	97.8	99.8	107.1	103.1	108.1	105.5	110.1	114.0	114.0
1953	100.0	101.7	106.5	111.1	108.8	103.7	102.4	105.9	105.0	106.5	104.4	103.7
1954	100.0	95.6	103.2	103.4	106.9	107.5	111.0	109.6	110.5	111.5	113.8	114.0
1955	100.0	101.1	99.9	103.6	104.2	107.5	111.5	109.4	112.2	113.0	112.5	116.9
1956	100.0	102.8	101.6	103.0	104.8	108.4	107.2	108.8	108.7	107.9	109.9	109.7

[a] *Sample computations* (values taken from Table 4-24):

The first ratio is $\dfrac{124.3}{124.3} = 100$;

the second ratio is $\dfrac{125.1}{124.3} = 100.6$;

the third ratio is $\dfrac{124.9}{124.3} = 100.4$;

the thirteenth ratio is $\dfrac{127.3}{127.3} = 100$;

the fourteenth ratio is $\dfrac{133.9}{127.3} = 105.2$.

may have been overzealous in eliminating fluctuations in the data. Table 4-30 illustrates the calculations of the equality test for the passenger airline data. For these data there does not appear to have been any over-adjustment.

Percentage change tests

There are several percentage change tests each of which involves finding the percentage of change of each value from that of the previous month. Four percentage change tests are commonly used—one for the original data and one for each of the major components of the time series (seasonality, trend-cycle, and randomness).

TABLE 4-30   EQUALITY TEST

	Ratios (12-month MA seasonally adjusted data/12-month MA original data)[a]											
1949	101.9	100.1	98.5	97.7	98.1	99.6	99.5	99.8	100.8	100.3	100.0	100.9
1950	101.8	101.5	100.4	99.2	98.3	99.3	99.4	99.8	100.9	100.3	100.1	101.0
1951	101.7	101.4	100.3	99.1	98.4	99.5	99.6	99.9	101.1	100.6	100.5	101.3
1952	101.9	101.7	100.3	99.2	98.3	99.5	99.6	99.7	101.0	100.5	100.5	101.3
1953	102.0	101.7	100.4	99.3	98.4	99.3	99.4	99.3	100.5	100.2	100.2	101.1
1954	101.9	101.5	100.1	99.0	98.1	99.1	99.4	99.3	100.6	100.4	100.4	101.4
1955	102.2	101.5	99.9	98.8	98.0	99.1	99.4	99.2	100.5	100.3	100.3	101.4
1956	102.3	101.6	100.1	98.9	98.1	99.1	99.4	99.0	99.8	100.4	101.0	102.8

[a] *Sample computations:*

	(1)	(2) Final Seasonally Adjusted Data		(3) Original Data		(4)
	Period	Data	12-Month MA	Data	12-Month MA	Ratio (2)/(3)
	1	125.95		122.75		
	2	125.95		122.75		
	3	125.95		122.75		
	4	125.95		122.75		
	5	125.95		122.75		
	6	125.95	126.0	122.75	123.6	101.9
1949	Jan.	124.3	125.9	112	125.7	
	Feb.	125.1		118	127.8	100.1
	Mar.	124.9		132		98.5
	Apr.	129.5	Average = 125.95	129	Average = 122.75	(See upper
	May	126.1		121		portion of
	June	126.2		135		this table.)
	July	125.2		148		
	Aug.	125.4		148		
	Sept.	126.7		136		
	Oct.	128.9		119		
	Nov.	130.2		104		
	etc.					
		(from Table 4-24)		(from Table 4-9)		

Original data

The percentage change test for the original data is used as a comparison guide for evaluating the other percentage change tests. The values for the airline data are shown in Table 4-31. The values of the percentage change tests for these original data should be larger than those obtained from the other three percentage change tests.

TABLE 4-31   PERCENTAGE CHANGE TEST (ORIGINAL DATA)

Year	Jan.	Feb.	Mar.	Apr.	May	June	July	Aug.	Sept.	Oct.	Nov.	Dec.
					Percentage Change from Previous Month[a]							
1949	0	5.4	11.9	−2.3	−6.2	11.6	9.6	0	−8.1	−12.5	−12.6	13.5
1950	−2.5	9.6	11.9	−4.3	−7.4	19.2	14.1	0	−7.1	−15.8	−14.3	22.8
1951	3.6	3.4	18.7	−8.4	5.5	3.5	11.8	0	−7.5	−12.0	−9.9	13.7
1952	3.0	5.3	7.2	−6.2	1.1	19.1	5.5	5.2	−13.6	−8.6	−9.9	12.8
1953	1.0	0	20.4	−.4	−2.6	6.1	8.6	3.0	−12.9	−11.0	−14.7	11.7
1954	1.5	−7.8	25.0	−3.4	3.1	12.8	14.4	−3.0	−11.6	−11.6	−11.4	12.8
1955	5.7	−3.7	14.6	.7	.4	16.7	15.6	−4.7	−10.1	−12.2	−13.5	17.3
1956	2.2	−2.5	14.4	−1.3	1.6	17.6	10.4	−1.9	−12.3	−13.8	−11.4	12.9
					Overall average = 8.90942.							

[a] *Sample computations* (values taken from Table 4-9)

The first percentage is 0, because there is no preceding month's value for month 1;

the second percentage is $\dfrac{118 - 112}{112} = 5.4$;

the third percentage is $\dfrac{132 - 118}{118} = 11.9$;

etc.

The overall average of all the percentage changes in Table 4-31 is computed as

$$\frac{\sum\limits_{t=2}^{n} |PC_t|}{n-1} = \frac{846.40}{95} = 8.909\%.$$

Final seasonally adjusted series

The seasonally adjusted series does not include seasonal effects. Applying the percentage change test to this series and comparing it to the percentage change of the original data can reveal the amount of variation in the original data caused by seasonality (see Table 4-32).

TABLE 4-32   PERCENTAGE CHANGE TEST (FINAL SEASONALLY ADJUSTED DATA)

Percentage Change from Previous Month[a]

Year	Jan.	Feb.	Mar.	Apr.	May	June	July	Aug.	Sept.	Oct.	Nov.	Dec.
1949	0	.6	−.2	3.7	−2.6	.1	−.8	.2	1.0	1.8	1.0	−.9
1950	−1.4	5.2	−.2	1.8	−4.5	7.0	3.5	−.1	2.7	−2.4	−1.1	7.6
1951	4.2	.7	5.3	−2.7	7.7	−6.9	1.9	−.4	3.3	1.3	3.7	.2
1952	2.9	4.6	−5.7	−.8	2.1	7.3	−3.7	4.8	−2.4	4.4	3.5	0
1953	.2	1.7	4.7	4.3	−2.1	−4.7	−1.3	3.5	−.8	1.4	−1.9	−.7
1954	.1	−4.4	8.0	.1	3.4	.5	3.3	−1.3	.9	.9	2.0	.2
1955	3.9	1.1	−1.2	3.7	.6	3.1	3.7	−1.9	2.5	.7	−.4	3.9
1956	.3	2.8	−1.2	1.4	1.8	3.4	−1.1	1.5	−0.1	−.8	1.9	−.2

Overall average = 2.38334.

[a] *Sample computations* (values taken from Table 4-24):

The first percentage is 0 because there is no preceding month's value for month 1;

the second percentage is $\dfrac{125.1 - 124.3}{125.1} = .6$;

the third percentage is $\dfrac{124.9 - 125.1}{125.1} = -.2$.

The overall average of the absolute values of the percentage changes is 2.383%. The difference between 8.909 and 2.383, i.e., 6.526%, is the amount of variation in the original series attributable to seasonality.

Random component

The irregular component of the series is used as the basis for computing the percentage change of the random component. Thus for the airline passenger series, the data of Table 4-26 is used as illustrated in Table 4-33. The overall average of the random component is particularly useful as a guide to the minimum amount of forecasting error that can be expected.

   The overall average of 2.1% indicates that the maximum accuracy that can be expected in forecasting is 2.1%, the amount of randomness from month to month. Since the seasonal variation accounted for 6.526% of the 8.909% variation in the original data, and the random component accounts for 2.110%, the balance of 0.273% (8.909 − 2.110 − 6.526) must be accounted for by trend-cycle variation. The conclusion that can be drawn for the airline data is that seasonality accounts for the bulk of the variation in the original data.

TABLE 4-33 PERCENTAGE CHANGE TEST (RANDOM COMPONENT)

| | Percentage Change from Previous Month[a] | | | | | | | | | | |
Year	Jan.	Feb.	Mar.	Apr.	May	June	July	Aug.	Sept.	Oct.	Nov.	Dec.
1949	0	.4	−.4	3.5	−2.6	.1	−.8	0	.6	1.2	.3	−1.6
1950	−2.1	4.4	−1.1	.6	−5.9	5.3	1.9	−1.4	1.5	−3.7	−2.9	5.0
1951	1.2	−2.2	2.9	−4.0	7.1	−7.0	1.7	−1.0	1.9	−.7	1.5	−1.7
1952	1.5	3.8	−6.2	−1.3	1.3	6.0	−5.2	3.1	−4.0	2.7	1.8	−1.9
1953	−1.9	−.4	3.0	3.4	−2.2	−4.3	−.6	4.0	−.5	1.6	−1.5	−.2
1954	.3	−4.9	6.5	−1.8	1.3	−1.3	1.9	−2.3	0	0	.8	−1.2
1955	2.5	−.4	−2.7	2.0	−1.2	1.3	2.0	−3.2	1.3	−.4	−1.6	2.6
1956	−.9	1.5	−2.5	.1	.5	2.2	−2.1	.8	−.5	−1.1	1.8	−.3

Overall average = 2.10951.

Yearly averages are:

1.1   3.0   2.7   3.2   2.0   1.9   1.8   1.2

[a] *Sample computations* (values taken from Table 4-26):

The first percentage is 0, because there is no preceding month's value for month 1.

The second percentage is $\dfrac{99.6 - 99.2}{99.2} = .4.$

The third percentage is $\dfrac{99.2 - 99.6}{99.6} = .4.$

The overall average of the absolute values of the percentage change is 2.11%.

Trend-cycle component

The final percentage change test is applied to the trend-cycle component. It represents the month-to-month changes in the trend-cycle. For the airline data, these values are shown in Table 4-34. When combined with the values for the percentage change in the random component, these two tests provide one of the most important measures used in Census II—the month for cyclical dominance (MCD). The MCD is the time span for which the ratio of the two averages becomes greater than one.

4/5/5   Month for Cyclical Dominance (MCD)

Tables 4-33 and Table 34 show the percentage change of each month from that of the previous month for the random and trend-cycle components, respectively. The ratio of the average percentage change for all months (without regard to sign) of the random component to that of the trend-cycle component indicates the relative variation of each component. For the airline data the ratio is 1.9 (2.38/1.11), which indicates that the random component dominates the cyclical component 1.9 times.

Using the same computational procedures applied in developing Tables 4.33 and 4.34, percentage changes for 2, 3, 4, and 5 months can be obtained. The ratios of the random and trend-cycle component changes for longer than 1 month's

TABLE 4-34   PERCENTAGE CHANGE TEST (TREND-CYCLE COMPONENT)

					Percentage Change from Previous Month[a]						
Year	Jan.	Feb.	Mar.	Apr.	May	June	July	Aug.	Sept.	Oct.	Nov.	Dec.
1949	0	.2	.2	.2	0	0	0	.2	.4	.6	.7	.7
1950	.7	.7	.9	1.2	1.5	1.6	1.6	1.4	1.2	1.4	1.9	2.5
1951	3.0	3.0	2.3	1.4	.6	.1	.1	.6	1.4	2.0	2.2	2.0
1952	1.3	.7	.4	.5	.8	1.2	1.6	1.7	1.7	1.6	1.7	1.9
1953	2.1	2.1	1.6	.9	.1	−.4	−.6	−.5	−.3	−.3	−.4	−.5
1954	−.1	.6	1.4	2.0	2.1	1.8	1.3	1.0	.9	1.0	1.2	1.4
1955	1.4	1.5	1.6	1.7	1.9	1.8	1.6	1.4	1.2	1.1	1.2	1.3
1956	1.3	1.3	1.3	1.3	1.3	1.2	1.0	.7	.4	.3	.1	.1

Overall average = 1.11759.

Yearly averages are:

.3	1.4	1.6	1.3	.8	1.2	1.5	.8

[a] *Sample computations* (values taken from Table 4-25)

The first percentage is 0 because there is no preceding month's value for month 1.

The second percentage is $\dfrac{125.6 - 125.3}{125.3} = .2$

The third percentage is $\dfrac{125.9 - 125.6}{125.6} = .2.$

The overall average of the absolute values is 1.12.

duration can then be used to determine for how many durations the random component variation exceeds that of the trend-cycle. As the time span increases, the changes in the trend-cycle component tend to become greater, while those of the irregular component become less because of the averaging of random terms. At some point the changes in the random component will about equal the changes in the trend-cycle component. The monthly span for which this occurs is called the month for cyclical dominance (MCD). In the airline data, MCD is 2 (see Table 4-36) because between a time span of 1 month and a time span of 2 months, the fluctuations in the trend-cycle become stronger than the fluctuations in the random component. This relationship can be seen by examining the ratio for a 1-month span (1.9) and a ratio for a 2-month span (.88). It means that over 2 months the trend-cycle dominates the fluctuations of the irregular component.

The MCD provides information that can be used to calculate a series of trend-cycle values with loss of a minimal number of values at the end of the series. Knowing that the MCD is 2 months for the airline data indicates that a 2-month MA of the final seasonally adjusted data should illustrate the movement in the trend-cycle component, since it will eliminate the greatest part of the irregular component. Table 4-35 illustrates this, although in this case a 3-month MA was used in order to center the average. Table 4-35 is similar to Table 4-25 except that Table 4-35 has only 1 value missing and it is very easy to update. In practice,

TABLE 4-35 3-MONTH MOVING AVERAGE (FINAL SEASONALLY ADJUSTED SERIES): ESTIMATE OF TREND-CYCLE COMPONENT

Moving Average of Adjusted Series, MCD Period Centered

Year	Jan.	Feb.	Mar.	Apr.	May	June	July	Aug.	Sept.	Oct.	Nov.	Dec.
1949	0	125	126	127	127	126	126	126	127	129	129	129
1950	130	132	134	133	135	138	142	145	145	145	147	152
1951	158	163	165	170	169	170	167	170	172	177	180	184
1952	189	190	188	185	190	194	199	198	202	206	211	214
1953	215	220	228	233	231	225	223	224	227	226	225	223
1954	219	222	224	233	236	241	243	246	246	249	252	257
1955	261	265	268	270	277	284	289	293	294	297	301	305
1956	312	314	317	319	326	330	334	335	335	337	338	0

Overall average (of their percentage change) = 1.43676.

Overall average of percentage changes without regard to signs is 1.44. This is found as:

$$\sum_{t=2}^{n} \frac{(|FA'_t - FA'_{t-1}|)}{FA'_{t-1}} \bigg/ (n-1) = 1.44.$$

the MCD is usually less than 6, which results in a short moving average with only 1 or at most 2 values missing at the end. Furthermore, to calculate the moving average as new data become available is computationally very easy. That is not true of Table 4-25, which is calculated using Spencer's 15-point formula.

The MCD moving average is the basis for forecasting the trend-cycle. A graphical plot of the moving averages of Table 4-35 is extremely useful in identifying changes in the level of economic activity, the trend-cycle. For the airline series, the graph is shown in Figure 4-3. The last value given in that graph, 340.135, is a rough estimate of the trend-cycle found by averaging the last 2 values of the final seasonally adjusted data of Table 4-24, i.e., periods 95 and 96 were averaged [(340 + 339)/2 = 339.5]. Since that average corresponds to period 95.5, it is half a period behind period 96. Therefore, it can be adjusted by adding to it half the trend change occurring between periods 94 and 95 [(338. − 337.)/2 = .5]. This procedure yields an estimate for the trend-cycle for period 96 of 339.5 + .5 = 340.

Finally, the bottom of Figure 4-3 shows the percentage changes in the trend-cycle for the last two years. These are used to project the trend-cycle for the future periods to be forecast.

4/5/6   Summary Statistics

The final output of Census II is a set of summary statistics related to three aspects of the data:

1. The average percentage change of all components and their ratios.
2. The average duration of positive and negative signs (that is, the average time that it takes for a change in sign to occur) for all components of the series.
3. The average percentage changes of the ratios of the random to the trend-cycle ratios for time spans of 1, 2, 3, 4, and 5 months. These changes reveal the month for cyclical dominance. For the airline data, these summary statistics are shown in Table 4-36 and are self-explanatory from their headings.

In order to forecast, estimates of the trend-cycle must be found. These can be obtained from Figure 4-3 (see also Chapter 12), then multiplied by the corresponding one-year-ahead forecasts of seasonality obtained from Table 4-23. Thus, the forecasts for January, February, and March 1957 (assuming trend-cycles of 342, 345, 347) are

$$F_{J1957} = 342(.919) \ = 314.3,$$

$$F_{F1957} = 345(.87) \quad = 300.15,$$

$$F_{M1957} = 347(1.007) = 349.43.$$

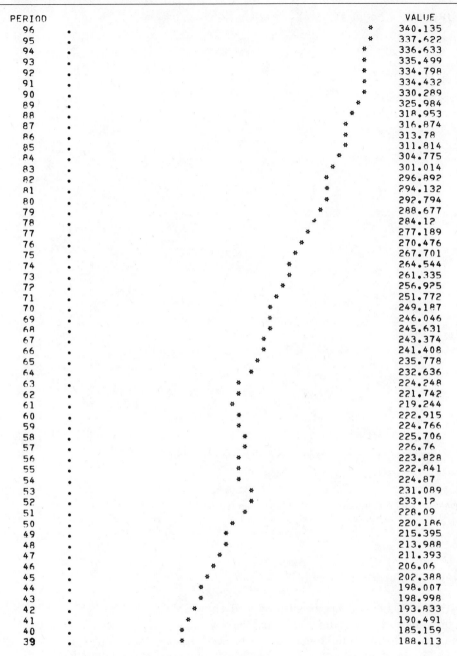

PERIOD		VALUE
96		340.135
95		337.622
94		336.633
93		335.499
92		334.798
91		334.432
90		330.289
89		325.984
88		318.953
87		316.874
86		313.78
85		311.814
84		304.775
83		301.014
82		296.892
81		294.132
80		292.794
79		288.677
78		284.12
77		277.189
76		270.476
75		267.701
74		264.544
73		261.335
72		256.925
71		251.772
70		249.187
69		246.046
68		245.631
67		243.374
66		241.408
65		235.778
64		232.636
63		224.248
62		221.742
61		219.244
60		222.915
59		224.766
58		225.706
57		226.76
56		223.828
55		222.841
54		224.87
53		231.089
52		233.12
51		228.09
50		220.186
49		215.395
48		213.988
47		211.393
46		206.06
45		202.388
44		198.007
43		198.998
42		193.833
41		190.491
40		185.159
39		188.113

FIGURE 4-3 GRAPHIC PLOT OF THE TREND-CYCLE

FIGURE 4-3 *Continued*

```
PERIOD                                                    VALUE
  38      .                    *                        189.516
  37      .                   *                         188.68
  36      .                 *                           183.942
  35      .                *                            179.867
  34      .               *                             176.773
  33      .              *                              171.997
  32      .             *                               169.633
  31      .             *                               167.01
  30      .             *                               170.268
  29      .             *                               169.095
  28      .             *                               170.455
  27      .            *                                164.944
  26      .           *                                 163.292
  25      .          *                                  157.988
  24      .         *                                   151.889
  23      .       *                                     146.664
  22      .       *                                     144.764
  21      .       *                                     145.164
  20      .       *                                     145.071
  19      .       *                                     142.161
  18      .     *                                       137.538
  17      .    *                                        134.909
  16      .  *                                          133.121
  15      .   *                                         134.466
  14      .  *                                          131.583
  13      .  *                                          130.095
  12      .  *                                          128.878
  11      .  *                                          129.427
  10      .  *                                          128.61
   9      .  *                                          126.997
   8      .  *                                          125.741
   7      .  *                                          125.597
   6      .  *                                          125.835
   5      .  *                                          127.268
   4      .  *                                          126.814
   3      .  *                                          126.471
   2      .  *                                          124.75
       I.........I.........I.........I.........I.........I
LOW = 124.75                                     HIGH = 340.135
```

```
% CHANGES IN THE TREND-CYCLE, LAST TWO YEARS
  1.7    1.2    1.2    1.0    2.5    2.5    1.6    1.4    0.4    0.9    1.4    1.2
  2.3    0.6    1.0    0.6    2.2    1.3    1.2    0.1    0.2    0.3    0.3    0.7
```

4/5/7 Summary of Census II

The Census II method has been developed empirically and thoroughly tested with thousands of series. Although it may have some statistical faults, it is intuitive and geared to the practitioner. In this respect, it is the exact opposite of the Box-Jenkins method, which is examined in Chapter 10. Census II is not based on theory, but grew out of empirical developments based on the trial and error of alternative approaches to a great number of series. The Census II method

TABLE 4-36 SUMMARY STATISTICS FROM CENSUS II

```
                AVERAGE % CHANGE

ORIGINAL       TREND-CYCLE     3-M.M.A.    RANDOM  SEAS. ADJ. SER.
8.90942          1.11759        1.43676      2.10951      2.38334

  RANDOM          RANDOM          SEASON
-------------    -------      ------------
TREND-CYCLE     SEASON      TREND-CYCLE
1.88755          .885107       2.13257

  RANDOM       TREND-CYCLE      SEASON
-------       ----------      -------
ORIGINAL       ORIGINAL       ORIGINAL
.236774          .12544           .267508


   AVERAGE DURATION OF POSITIVE AND NEGATIVE SIGNS
ORIGINAL         RANDOM        TREND-CYCLE    3-MONTHS M.A.
2.5              1.31944         23.75           1.82692


        RANDOM/TREND-CYCLE

            SPAN IN MONTHS
     1          2           3           4           5
 1.88755     .877671      .665565      .407453      .303543


MONTHS FOR CYCLICAL DOMINANCE (M.C.D.) = 2
```

is used mainly on macrodata such as official government statistics or aggregate corporate data.

There are many different verions of the Census II method. The one described in this section is the X-9. An X-11 version is currently available, which is very similar to X-9 except for the following five points:

1. The trading days adjustment is not done as phase one of the method, but is calculated later on using regression analysis.
2. The smoothing for strikes, wars, floods, or other unusual events is done more thoroughly than simply excluding extreme values that fall outside the control limits.
3. A Henderson's 5-, 9-, 13- or 23-point weighted moving average is used. The length of the moving average depends upon the average level of the random component. The larger the random component, the more terms included in the Henderson's average. (Henderson's average replaces Spencer's 15-point formula used in the X-9 version.)

4. The user is allowed to choose between an additive and a multiplicative decomposition model.
5. The X-11 method makes many more options available to the user than does X-9.

These differences have made X-11 more elaborate but also more complicated than the X-9 version. The X-9 version was described here because it is much simpler and the substance of the results are very similar.

Decomposition methods are one of the oldest forecasting procedures in use today. They originated around the beginning of this century and were initiated from two different directions. First, it was recognized that to study the serial correlation within or between variable(s), any spurious correlation that might exist because of trend must be eliminated. As early as 1884 Poynting attempted to eliminate trend and some seasonal fluctuations by averaging prices over several years. Hooker (1901) followed Poynting's example, but was more precise in his methods for eliminating trend. His work was followed by Spencer (1904) and Anderson and Nochmals (1914), who generalized the procedure of trend elimination to include higher order polynomials.

A second direction for work in this area originated with economists who worried about the impact of depressions and sought ways to predict them. They felt that the elements of economic activity should be separated so that changes in the business cycle could be isolated from seasonal and other changes. France appointed a committee that in 1911 presented a report analyzing the causes of the 1907 economic crisis. This group introduced the idea of leading and coincidental indicators and attempted to separate the trend from the cycle so that the movement of the latter could be followed.

In the United States this idea was expanded and the concept of constructing barometers of business activity was developed. Furthermore, an attempt to separate the seasonal fluctuation from the rest of the components was made as early as 1915 (Copeland). The process of decomposition, as it is known today, was introduced by Macauley (1930), who in the 1920s introduced the ratio-to-moving averages method that forms the basis of Census II.

4/6 The FORAN System

Another forecasting method based on the principle of decomposition is the FORAN system developed by McLaughlin in the 1960s. The FORAN system has certain advantages over the Census II approach. It can deal with more than one variable simultaneously (it can use any independent variable in addition to time), and it is oriented toward the forecasting needs of business organizations rather than towards the macroseries of government related data.

The FORAN system decomposes a time series into seasonal, cyclical and trend, and irregular elements and provides a summary of the importance or contribution of each of them. One of the strongest points of FORAN is its ability to summarize a number of forecasting results together with descriptions of their accuracy over the last year (12 months). It is then up to the user to determine which forecast, or combination of forecasts, should be used for the final predictions. FORAN extends alternative forecasts for time horizons of 1, 2, and 3 months and provides summary measures of the accuracy of each.

FORAN must be used in conjunction with some other decomposition method because it does not provide the seasonal indices required as inputs to the program. FORAN concentrates on the remaining components of a time series—the trend-cycle and randomness.

According to its developers, FORAN has four main objectives (McLaughlin and Boyle, 1968, pp. 15–16):

1. To evaluate recent trends caused mainly by cyclical factors.
2. To analyze and evaluate the forecasting results of several forecasting methods.
3. To anticipate forthcoming turning points by analyzing the changes of the isolated cyclical component and/or by using leading indicators.
4. To forecast using a number of probabilistic and/or deterministic models as well as subjective predictions. An eclectic approach is employed in which the forecasts of different methods are compared and then combined using a weighting procedure.

REFERENCES AND SELECTED BIBLIOGRAPHY

Anderson, O., and U. Nochmals. 1914. "The Elimination of Spurious Correlation due to Position in Time or Space," *Biometrica*, Vol. 10, pp. 269–76.

Copeland, M. T. 1915. "Statistical Indices of Business Conditions," *Quarterly Journal of Economics*, Vol. 29, pp. 522–62.

Freund, J. E. and F. J. Williams. 1969. *Modern Business Statistics*, Englewood Cliffs, N.J.: Prentice-Hall.

Hadley, G. 1968. *Introduction to Business Statistics*. San Francisco: Holden-Day.

Hooker, R. H. 1901. "The Suspension of the Berlin Produce Exchange and Its Effect upon Corn Prices," *Journal of the Royal Statistical Society*, Vol. 64, pp. 574–603.

Macauley, F. R. 1930. *The Smoothing of Time Series*. National Bureau of Economic Research.

McLaughlin, R. L. 1962. *Time Series Forecasting*. Marketing Research Technique, Series No. 6. American Marketing Association.

McLaughlin, R. L., and J. J. Boyle. 1968. *Short Term Forecasting*. American Marketing Association Booklet.

Poynting, J. H. 1884. "A Comparison of the Fluctuations in the Price of Wheat and in the Cotton and Silk Imports into Great Britain," *Journal of the Royal Statistical Society*, Vol. 47, pp. 345–64.

"Rapport sur les Indices des Crises Economiques et sur les Mesures Résultant de ces Crises." 1911. Ministry of Planning, Paris, France (Government Report).

Shiskin, J. 1957. "Electronic Computers and Business Indicators." *National Bureau of Economic Research*, Occasional Paper 57.

————. 1961. "Tests and Revisions of Bureau of the Census Methods of Seasonal Adjustments." Bureau of the Census, Technical Paper No. 5.

Shiskin, J., A. H. Young, and J. C. Musgrave. "The X-11 Variant of the Census II Method Seasonal Adjustment Program." Bureau of the Census, Technical Paper No. 15.

Spencer, J. 1904. "On the Graduation of the Rates of Sickness and Mortality." *Journal of the Institute of Actuaries*, Vol. 38, p. 334.

Spurr, W. A., and C. P. Bonini. 1967. *Statistical Analysis for Business Decisions*. Homewood, Ill.: Richard D. Irwin.

EXERCISES

1. The following data represent the monthly sales of product A for a plastics manufacturer from 1972 through 1976.

MONTHLY SALES (IN 1000s)

	1972	1973	1974	1975	1976
Jan.	742	741	896	951	1030
Feb.	697	700	793	861	1032
Mar.	776	774	885	938	1126
Apr.	898	932	1055	1109	1285
May	1030	1099	1204	1274	1468
June	1107	1223	1326	1422	1637
July	1165	1290	1303	1486	1611
Aug.	1216	1349	1436	1555	1608
Sept.	1208	1341	1473	1604	1528
Oct.	1131	1296	1453	1600	1420
Nov.	971	1066	1170	1403	1119
Dec.	783	901	1023	1209	1013

a. Plot the time series of sales of product A. Can you identify seasonal fluctuations and/or a trend?

b. Compute the monthly seasonal indices for these data using the ratio-to-trend decomposition method. Do the results support the graphical interpretation of the seasonal pattern?

2. The following are the seasonal indices for exercise 1 calculated by the ratio-to-moving averages method.

	Seasonal Indices		Seasonal Indices
Jan.	79.14	July	117.81
Feb.	70.36	Aug.	122.59
Mar.	77.03	Sept.	123.02
Apr.	91.03	Oct.	118.84
May	104.40	Nov.	98.13
June	114.71	Dec.	82.93

The trend in the data is $T_t = 894.11 + 8.85(t)$, where $t = 1$ is Jan. 1972, and $t = 60$ is Dec. 1976.

Prepare forecasts for the 12 months of 1977 assuming that the cycle will be equal to 100 for the entire year.

3. The following table shows the monthly road casualties (in thousands) in the United Kingdom for the years 1964 through 1971.

	1964	1965	1966	1967	1968	1969	1970	1971
Jan.	26.0	29.0	27.0	27.5	23.9	27.6	26.9	28.4
Feb.	24.5	24.7	26.3	27.2	24.7	23.4	26.6	25.5
Mar.	27.9	31.3	29.8	30.2	27.5	25.0	27.6	26.6
Apr.	29.1	32.4	32.6	28.6	26.7	26.0	27.1	26.2
May	34.7	33.9	35.1	34.1	28.7	31.0	29.8	29.3
June	33.1	35.0	34.4	30.9	30.3	29.3	29.1	28.8
July	36.0	36.4	35.7	34.7	31.3	31.7	32.6	31.2
Aug.	37.5	36.5	33.6	33.7	32.1	32.0	31.6	31.9
Sept.	34.8	34.4	31.9	33.6	31.2	30.0	31.1	28.5
Oct.	35.5	33.9	35.1	31.0	31.4	31.8	33.2	32.2
Nov.	33.4	33.9	33.4	28.9	30.8	33.6	33.6	31.7
Dec.	32.9	36.4	37.6	29.7	30.6	31.6	34.0	31.8

a. Using the data for 1964 through 1970, calculate the seasonal indices of the data using the ratio-to-trend and the ratio-to-moving averages methods. Compare the two. Are they significantly different?

b. What is the behavior of the cyclical factor? Does it vary each year?

c. What is the trend in the data?

d. Prepare forecasts for each month of 1971 using the ratio-to-trend and the ratio-to-moving averages methods. Compare the results. Which method does best?

e. If a Census II program is available, apply it to the first seven years of data. How do the results compare with those of (a) above?

f. Use the Census II results to prepare forecasts for 1971. How do those compare with the results found in (d) above? Which method is the more accurate?

4. a. Using the data of Table 3-12, compute the seasonal indices using the classical decomposition method. How do these indices compare with those given in column 4 of Table 3-12?

b. Find the trend in the data. How does that compare to the trend found in column 5 of Table 3-12?

c. Forecast the next four quarters using classical decomposition. How do these forecasts compare to the forecasts provided by Winters' model?

d. What conclusions, if any, can you make concerning the behavior and accuracy of the results obtained in Table 3-12 and those obtained above from classical decomposition?

5. The following values represent a cubic trend pattern mixed with some randomness. Apply a single 5-period moving average, a single 7-period moving average, a double

3×3 moving average, and a double 5×5 moving average. Which type of moving average seems most appropriate to you in identifying the cubic pattern of the data?

Period	Shipments	Period	Shipments
1	42	9	180
2	69	10	204
3	100	11	228
4	115	12	247
5	132	13	291
6	141	14	337
7	154	15	391
8	171		

PART THREE
REGRESSION METHODS

The techniques of forecasting that use regression analysis are substantially different in their underlying concepts from the techniques of time-series analysis described in Parts Two and Four. The techniques of regression are generally referred to as causal, or explanatory, approaches to forecasting. These techniques attempt to predict the future by discovering and measuring several important independent factors and their effect on the variable to be forecast. The regression approach to forecasting is significantly different from that of time series in that it seeks to discover and measure relationships of interest, then to use them in obtaining forecasts. Because of the higher costs, these methods are generally used in long-range planning and in situations where the value of increased accuracy may warrant the additional expense.

Chapter 5 describes the technique of simple regression involving one independent variable and one dependent variable. The basic concepts involved in terms of estimation procedures and fitting the simple regression model to historical data are presented. Some of the applications of simple regression are also illustrated.

In Chapter 6 the concepts of simple regression are extended to include multiple independent variables in what is called multiple regression analysis. Again, the basic concepts, procedures for application, and statistical measures used in evaluating multiple regression models are described. A number of extensions and limitations of this methodology are also illustrated.

Chapter 7 presents a further extension of regression analysis to the concept of econometric modeling. In econometrics, several multiple regression equations that are interrelated in terms of the independent variables being used and the estimation of individual equations are considered. Some of the methodologies proposed for applying econometric models, as well as specific applications of these techniques, are described in this chapter.

5 SIMPLE REGRESSION

5/1 General Comments on Regression Methods

In Part Two, two major classes of time-series methods were examined—exponential smoothing and decomposition. Various models within each class were presented—models appropriate for different patterns of data and different conditions. The exponential smoothing methods were suggested to be appropriate for immediate or short-term forecasting when large numbers of forecasts are needed, such as at the operating level. On the other hand, the decomposition methods were found to require many more computations. In addition they require the personal attention of the user, who must predict the cycle with only indirect help from information provided by the method. Thus the decomposition approach to forecasting requires more time and is therefore restricted to forecasting fewer items than the simpler smoothing models.

In this and the following two chapters a second approach available to forecasters, that of causal or explanatory methods, will be examined. Simple regression that is restricted to two variables and one equation will be discussed first. Multiple variable relations of one equation will then be examined, and finally multiple relations of many interrelated equations will be considered.

Part Three introduces a new concept in the attempt to forecast: A forecast will be expressed as a function of a certain number of factors that determine its outcome. Such forecasts will not necessarily be time dependent, which allows them to be used for predicting horizons of longer term than appropriate for time series. In addition, developing a causal model facilitates a better understanding of the situation and allows experimentation with different combinations of inputs to study their effect on the forecasts. Causal models by their basic formulation are geared toward intervention, influencing the future through decisions made today. Since the effects of decisions made today are not evident for some time, causal forecasting is more appropriate for time horizons of three months to about two years.

5/2 Different Forms of Functional Relationships

The fact that GNP increases over time can be expressed in a general mathematical form as follows:

$$GNP = f(\text{time}) \tag{5-1}$$

Expression (5-1) implies that the level of GNP is influenced by changes in time and that future values of GNP can be forecast by identifying this time relationship.

A .functional form that relates two variables [GNP and time in (5-1)] does not necessarily have to include time. It can be generalized to include other variables in a causal relationship. In economics for example, the demand for a product (quantity sold) has frequently been found to depend upon the price of the product.

$$\text{Demand of product X} = f(\text{price of product X}). \tag{5-2}$$

Expression (5-2) states that as the price of product X changes, the demand of product X will change too. For most products, an increase in price will decrease the amount sold, while a decrease in price will increase the level of demand.

A functional relationship need not be limited to two variables only. The sales of a company are typically influenced by (depend upon) several factors such as the level of GNP, prices, advertising budget, research and development (R&D) budget, prices of substitute products, etc. Thus, the functional form might be:

$$\text{Sales of XYZ} = f(\text{GNP, prices, advertising, R\&D, prices of substitutes, etc.}) \tag{5-3}$$

The meaning of equation (5-3) is similar to that of equation (5-1) or (5-2), except that sales depend on more than one variable. If the form of relationship among changes in these variables and sales can be discovered, it can subsequently be used for forecasting. The purpose of Part Three is to examine procedures for identifying functional relationships and measuring them so that the pattern connecting the left- and right-hand sides of the equation can be isolated from randomness.

It is customary to call the factor of the left-hand side of equations (5-1), (5-2), or (5-3) the dependent variable and to denote it by Y. Those variables on the right are called independent variables and denoted by X. This convention differs from that used in time-series models where X_t denotes the values of the time series, the dependent variable.

The aim of causal forecasting is to predict the dependent variable by discovering how it relates to one or more independent variables. When there is only one independent variable [as in equations (5-1) and (5-2)], the method of simple regression is appropriate. If additional independent variables are involved [as in equation (5-3)], then multiple regression is available. Both simple and multiple regression involve functional forms of relationships that extend beyond time factors.

Once a functional relationship is assumed to exist between a dependent and an independent variable, two steps must be taken in order to forecast. First, the form of the relationship between the two variables—linear, exponential, quadratic, cubic, etc. (see Figure 5-1)—must be determined. Second, the parameters of the relationship must be estimated. Regression analysis can deal only with linear relationships. This limitation is not as great a disadvantage as it may seem because many nonlinear functions can be transformed into linear functions. A few simple cases can illustrate the point. Consider the case of

$$W = AB^X. \tag{5-4}$$

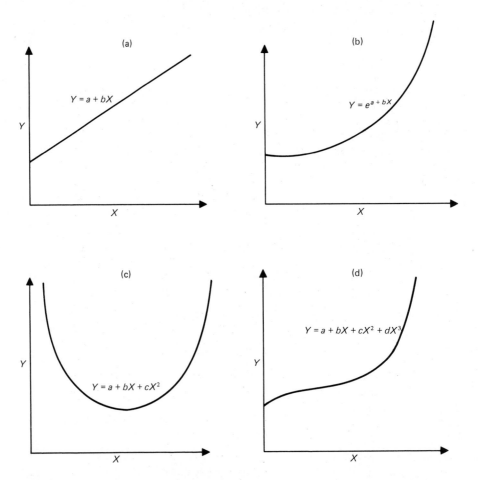

FIGURE 5-1 DIFFERENT FORMS OF FUNCTIONAL RELATIONS: (A) LINEAR, (B) EXPONENTIAL, (C) QUADRATIC, AND (D) CUBIC

Equation (5-4) is an exponential function and thus nonlinear. However, if logarithms are taken of both sides of (5-4), the result is

$$\log W = (\log A) + (\log B)X. \tag{5-5}$$

Now substituting

$$Y = \log W, \qquad a = \log A, \qquad b = \log B,$$

gives $\quad Y = a + bX.$ $\hspace{8cm}$ (5-6)

Equation (5-6) is a linear relationship and its parameters, a and b, can be estimated using simple regression.

A second example of a nonlinear function (relationship) that can be transformed to a linear one is

$$W = e^{a+bX}. \tag{5-7}$$

Taking the natural logarithms of both sides of equation (5-7) gives

$$\log_e W = (a + bX)(\log_e e)$$

$$= a + bX, \quad \text{since } \log_e e = 1.$$

Now letting $\qquad Y = \log_e W$

gives $\qquad Y = a + bX.$ $\hspace{7cm}$ (5-8)

Equation (5-8) is of linear form and thus simple regression could be used to estimate the values of a and b and subsequently to use them to predict future values of Y, the dependent variable.

Before explaining how the values of a and b are estimated, it is useful to examine what they represent. If $X = 0$, then $Y = a + b(0) = a$. Thus, a is the point at which the straight line intersects the Y axis (a is frequently called the intercept). In the linear equation $Y = a + bX$, b is called the slope, and indicates how much Y will change if X changes by 1 unit. Thus, if $a = 10$, $b = 2$, and $X = 100$,

$$Y = 10 + 2(100) = 210.$$

If X increases by one unit, thus becoming 101,

$$Y = 10 + 2(101) = 212.$$

The value of Y changes by 2 units, or the amount of the slope, b.

Finally, a and b are frequently called the regression coefficients. The purpose of regression analysis is to estimate these coefficients and use them to forecast future values of the dependent variable Y. It should be noted that the values of a and b are constant; they do not depend upon time because the relationship $Y = a + bX$ is assumed to be linear and therefore constant.

5/3 Determining the Parameters, *a* and *b*, of a Straight Line

There are several methods that can be used to estimate the values of *a* and *b* in the functional relationship, $Y = a + bX$. Perhaps the most straight-forward technique is simply to plot the historical observations, then draw a line that seems to "fit" those points. The values of *a* and *b* can then be read off the graph. Figure 5-2 is an example of such a graph. Since *a* is the point at which the line intersects the *Y* axis, its value would be around 7, and the value of *b* would simply by the increase in *Y* (the units produced) for a unit increase in *X*. This value can be found by substracting two successive *Y* values and dividing by the change in *X* for those two values.

Although the graphic method might work fairly well in some situations, if there are several hundred observations that are widely scattered it would be extremely difficult to draw a straight line that would give the "best" approximation of the relationship. It would also be preferable to estimate *a* and *b* mathematically so that the same line would always be obtained for a given set of data. This can be done so as to minimize the mean squared errors as was done with the mean and most of the other forecasting methods examined in Chapters 2 and 3. To illustrate this fitting procedure, a simple example with only four observations

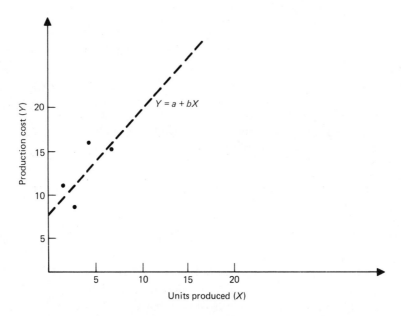

FIGURE 5-2 FORECASTING PRODUCTION COSTS BASED ON THE NUMBER OF UNITS PRODUCED

will be used. The values of these four observations are plotted in Figure 5-2. The dependent variable is assumed to be the total cost of production and the independent variable, the number of units produced. The objective is to determine the relationship between the cost and the number of units produced so that when the number of units to be produced is specified, the cost can be forecasted.

The broken line in Figure 5-2 approximates the straight line $\hat{Y} = a + bX$. The task, of course, is to determine the exact values of a and b using the method of least squares. The rationale of the method of least squares is that the square of the distance between the actual observations and the line should be minimized by the appropriate choice of a and b. In Figure 5-3, the observed (actual) values are labeled as Y_1, Y_2, Y_3, and Y_4; the deviations from the simple regression line are labeled as e_1, e_2, e_3, and e_4; and the points estimated by the regression line are labeled as $\hat{Y}_1$, $\hat{Y}_2$, $\hat{Y}_3$, and $\hat{Y}_4$.

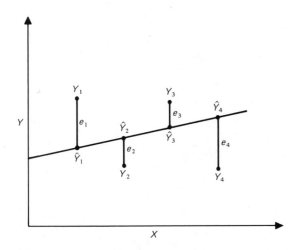

FIGURE 5-3 SIMPLE LINEAR REGRESSION—METHOD OF LEAST SQUARES

In this figure each of the deviations can be computed as $e_i = Y_i - \hat{Y}_i$, and each of the values on the regression line can be computed as $\hat{Y}_i = a + bX_i$. The method of least squares is used to determine the values of a and b in such a way that the mean squared deviations between actual and forecast values $\Sigma e_i^2 = \Sigma(Y_i - \hat{Y}_i)^2$ is as small as possible.

Using the requirement that Σe_i^2 be minimized, one can solve for a and b (see Chapter 5 Appendix, Section 1), obtaining

$$b = \frac{n\Sigma XY - \Sigma X \Sigma Y}{n\Sigma X^2 - (\Sigma X)^2},$$

(5-9)

$$a = \frac{\Sigma Y}{n} - b\frac{\Sigma X}{n},$$

(5-10)

where n = the number of observations (points) used to fit the regression line.

To illustrate the procedure involved in computing a and b, Table 5-1 uses the example shown in Figure 5-2. The relevant computations and the resulting equations for the regression line are obtained using equations (5-9) and (5-10).

TABLE 5-1   SIMPLE REGRESSION COMPUTATIONS

Cost Y	Units X	Y²	X²	XY	$\hat{Y}$	e	$\hat{Y} - \overline{Y}$	e²
8	3	64	9	24	10.93	-2.93	-1.57	8.58
11	2	121	4	22	9.68	1.32	-2.82	1.74
16	5	256	25	80	13.44	2.56	94	6.55
15	7	225	49	105	15.95	-.95	3.45	11.90

$\Sigma Y = 50$ $\Sigma X = 17$ $\Sigma Y^2 = 666$ $\Sigma X^2 = 87$ $\Sigma XY = 231$ $\qquad \Sigma e_i = 0$ $\Sigma(\hat{Y}_i - \overline{Y}) = 0$ $\Sigma e_i^2 = 28.78$

$\overline{Y} = 12.5$ $\qquad \overline{X} = 4.25$ $\qquad\qquad\qquad\qquad\qquad\qquad MSE = \dfrac{28.78}{4}$

$$= 7.195$$

$$b = \frac{n\Sigma XY - \Sigma X \Sigma Y}{n\Sigma X^2 - (\Sigma X)^2} = \frac{4(231) - (50)(17)}{4(87) - (17)^2} = \frac{924 - 850}{348 - 289} = \frac{74}{59} = 1.254,$$

$$a = \frac{\Sigma Y}{n} - b\frac{\Sigma X}{n} = 12.5 - 1.254(4.25) = 12.5 - 5.33 = 7.17,$$

or $a = \overline{Y} - b\overline{X} = 12.5 - 1.254(4.25) = 7.17.$

Thus $\hat{Y} = 7.17 + 1.254X.$

(5-11)

What equation (5-11) states is that given the data in the first and second columns of Table 5-1, values for a and b of 7.17 and 1.254 respectively, give the minimum mean squared error, 7.195. The reader is encouraged to try other values for a and b to compare their mean squared errors. For example, if $a = 10$ and $b = 1.2$, the mean squared error is 11.22, and if $a = 10$ and $b = 1$, the MSE is 7.75.

5/4 The Correlation Coefficient

It often occurs that two variables are related to each other, but it is incorrect to say that the value of one of the variables depends upon or is caused by changes in the value of the other variable. In such a case a relationship can be stated showing the correlation between the two variables. The coefficient of correlation, r, is a relative measure of the association between these two variables. It can vary from 0 (which indicates no correlation) to ± 1 (which indicates perfect correlation). When the correlation coefficient is greater than 0, the two variables are said to be positively correlated, and when it is less than 0 they are said to be negatively correlated. The sign of the correlation coefficient in simple regression is always the same as the sign of the regression coefficient, b.

The correlation coefficient is a number that is calculated using the following formula:

$$r = \frac{n\Sigma XY - \Sigma X\Sigma Y}{\sqrt{[n\Sigma X^2 - (\Sigma X)^2][n\Sigma Y^2 - (\Sigma Y)^2]}}. \tag{5-12}$$

Expression (5-12) has several "nice" properties (see Chapter 5 Appendix, Section 3) that make its application in regression analysis extremely useful. For example, it can be shown that the square of the correlation coefficient, referred to as the coefficient of determination, is the ratio of the variation explained by the regression line over the total variation in the data. That is,

$$r^2 = \frac{\text{sum of explained variation}}{\text{sum of total variation}} = \frac{\Sigma(\hat{Y}_i - \overline{Y})^2}{\Sigma(Y_i - \overline{Y})^2} \tag{5-13}$$

$$= \frac{(n\Sigma XY - \Sigma X\Sigma Y)^2}{[n\Sigma X^2 - (\Sigma X)^2][n\Sigma Y^2 - (\Sigma Y)^2]}.$$

Equation (5-13) indicates the percentage of the total variation that is explained by the regression line. As such, r^2 is a measure of how well the observations fit around the regression line. This fit can be seen from Figure 5-4 where Y_i is some actual data point, $\overline{Y}$ is the mean of all data points, and $\hat{Y}_i$ is the regression equation's estimate for the point Y_i. If for some reason, one did not want to fit a regression line to the data, $\overline{Y}$ (the mean), could still be used as a way of forecasting. The total error of doing so would be $Y_i - \overline{Y}$, since the mean is constant for all possible values. However, with the regression line as a method of forecasting instead of the mean, the error becomes $Y_i - \hat{Y}_i$. Thus, there is a reduction in the total error through use of the regression line.

The difference between the total error ($Y_i - \overline{Y}$) and the error still existing after the regression line is used (unexplained error = $Y_i - \hat{Y}_i$) is $\hat{Y}_i - \overline{Y}$. The regression line does a better job than the mean, in that it explains $\hat{Y}_i - \overline{Y}$ more error, or deviation, than the mean. The total explained and unexplained error can be found in this same manner for all other values. Squaring and summing the

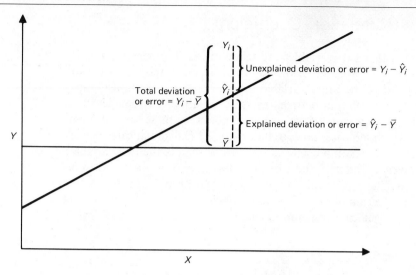

FIGURE 5-4 EXPLANATION OF r^2 IN SIMPLE REGRESSION

explained and total errors provides the information needed to find r^2 in equation (5-13). That ratio of the explained to total variation indicates how much better (in relative terms) the regression line is than the mean.

The sum of the unexplained variations squared, $(Y_i - \hat{Y}_i)^2$, is 0 only when all data points, $\hat{Y}_i$, are on the regression line, Y_i. This implies a perfect fit and gives a value of $r^2 = 1$, as can be seen from equation (5-13). On the other hand, when the explained variation is 0 (implying that the regression line is the same as the mean), r^2 will be equal to 0.

To illustrate the calculation of r and r^2, Table 5-2 shows the computations for the simple example of Table 5-1. The value of r can be found using (5-12) or (5-13) and the terms computed in Table 5-2. Equation (5-12) gives

$$r = \frac{n\Sigma XY - \Sigma X \Sigma Y}{\sqrt{[n\Sigma X^2 - (\Sigma X)^2][n\Sigma Y^2 - (\Sigma Y)^2]}} = \frac{4(231) - (50)(17)}{\sqrt{[4(87) - (17)^2][4(666) - (50)^2]}}$$

$$= \frac{74}{\sqrt{9676}} = .753.$$

Equation (5-13) gives

$$r^2 = \frac{\text{sum of explained variation}}{\text{sum of total variation}} = \frac{\Sigma(\hat{Y}_i - \bar{Y})^2}{\Sigma(Y_i - \bar{Y})^2}$$

$$= \frac{23.20}{40.97} = .566.$$

TABLE 5-2 SAMPLE COMPUTATIONS FOR r AND r^2

Y	X	Y^2	X^2	XY	$\hat{Y}$	Unexplained Deviation $Y - \hat{Y}$	Unexplained Variation $(Y - \hat{Y})^2$
8	3	64	9	24	10.93	−2.93	8.58
11	2	121	4	22	9.68	1.32	1.74
16	5	256	25	80	13.44	2.56	6.55
15	7	225	49	105	15.95	−.95	.90

$\Sigma Y = 50$ $\Sigma X = 17$ $\Sigma Y^2 = 666$ $\Sigma X^2 = 87$ $\Sigma XY = 231$ $\Sigma(Y_i - \hat{Y}) = 0$ $\Sigma(Y_i - \hat{Y})^2 = 17.78$

$\bar{Y} = 12.5$ $\bar{X} = 4.25$

Explained Deviation $\hat{Y} - \bar{Y}$	Explained Variation $(\hat{Y} - \bar{Y})^2$	Total Variation $(Y - \hat{Y})^2 + (\hat{Y} - \bar{Y})^2 = (Y - \bar{Y})^2$
−1.57	2.47	11.05
−2.82	7.95	9.69
.94	.88	7.43
3.45	11.9	12.80

$\Sigma(\hat{Y}_i - \bar{Y}) = 0$ $\Sigma(\hat{Y}_i - \bar{Y})^2 = 23.20$ $\Sigma(Y - \bar{Y})^2 = 40.97$

These results are completely compatible since $(.753)^2 = .566$. The value of r is .753, indicating that the two variables (cost and units produced) are positively correlated. That is, on a scale of -1 to $+1$, this correlation measures .753. On the other hand the value of the coefficient of determination, r^2, is .566, indicating that 56.6% of the total variation of the four data points is explained by the regression line $Y = 7.17 + 1.254X$.

5/5 The Significance of a Regression Equation

In the previous section the concept of the correlation coefficient and its squared value were discussed as measures of how well the observations fit around the regression line. This section goes a step further in exploring the question of significance and whether the results of regression analysis are due to random effects. In the time-series methods described in Part Two, very little was said about their statistical properties, since those methods are empirical in nature. The causal methods, on the other hand, are based on a statistical framework that allows consideration of the following:

1. The overall statistical significance of the regression equation—making sure that the relationship $Y = a + bX$ is not due to chance but is statistically valid.

2. The statistical significance of the regression coefficient b (and a if desired) —determining whether it is significantly different from 0. In the case of simple regression, this indicates whether the regression line is statistically better for forecasting than the mean (since when $b = 0$, the regression relationship becomes $Y = a$, or a constant).

3. Determining how much the estimated values of a and b can vary because of sampling and/or random effects in the data used. If another set of data was selected to estimate the values of a and b, slightly different results might have been obtained, since the data represent a sample from an infinite set of available data.

4. Measuring the dispersion of the data points from the Y values and determining probability limits as to the extent of such variations.

5/5/1 Sampling Distributions

Regression methods are based on the statistical properties of the regression equation and its parameters. From the point of view of classical statistics (as opposed to Bayesian statistics) the estimates are subject to sampling errors whose magnitude can be estimated and used for two important purposes: 1) to test hypotheses of concern and 2) to construct confidence intervals. This section will briefly explain the rationale of sampling distributions that classical statistics uses in doing (1), (2), (3), and (4) above.

The data used in regression analysis is only a small part, i.e., a *sample*, of the possible data, i.e., the *population*. For example, the yearly GNP figures of the last 30 years are only a sample because other older values also exist. Furthermore, even for a new country established only 30 years ago, GNP would be available on a quarterly and monthly basis, as well as annually. Whatever data are selected, they are only a sample of a considerably larger set of data, which in its totality comprises the population. If it were possible to have all data, there would be no need to worry about sampling errors, tests of hypotheses, or confidence intervals. Whatever estimates were obtained would be without error.

In the specific case of simple regression, this would mean that the values found for the two parameters would be the true values for the population. To distinguish these true parameter values from the sampling estimates, a and b, they are usually denoted by the Greek letters α and β. Thus, the regression equation is

$$Y = \alpha + \beta X.$$

The estimated regression equation, on the other hand, is $Y = a + bX$, since a and b are the values estimated from one sample data out of an infinite number of such samples. If a different sample was used from the same population, slightly different values for a and b would be obtained. From statistical theory it is known that all possible values a and b can take are distributed around α and β according to a student-t-distribution, or simply a t-distribution. The mean of this distribution is the true parameter value α or β, and its variance is the variance of the true value around all possible sample values, $E(\alpha - a)^2$ or $E(\beta - b)^2$.

Once the sampling distribution is theoretically known, the testing of hypotheses and the calculation of confidence limits is strictly mechanical. For example, in the case of b, the hypothesis can be made that its value is 0. If that is true, then $Y = \alpha + 0X$. This equation implies two things: first the variable X does not in any way influence Y, and second, the value of Y can be described through a constant, its mean. Thus, when the value of the regression coefficient is not significantly different from 0, variable X is not needed. To determine whether the calculated b is significantly different from 0, the hypothesis that $\beta = 0$ is made and the estimated b is tested to see whether it is statistically different from $\beta = 0$. Knowing the variance of b, this hypothesis can be easily tested to decide if $b = 0$, or $b \neq 0$.

Another sampling distribution used for testing hypotheses is the F-distribution, which indicates whether the overall regression equation is statistically significant. In the case of simple regression the t-test and the F-test are equivalent, since there is only one independent variable. If $b = 0$ then the regression equation is not significant (the t-value computed is equal to the square root of the F-value computed in such an instance). In multiple regression, however, the two tests are aimed at different tasks. It can be that the F-test indicates significance for the regression equation but some of the t-tests are not significantly different from 0.

5/5/2 The F-Test

Consider Figures 5-5, 5-6, and 5-7. From Figure 5-5, it is clear that a linear relationship of the form $Y = a + bX$ exists between time and sales. From Figure 5-6 it is clear that the variable unit cost does not depend on how many units are produced. Therefore, its mean value should be used if variable costs are to be forecast. In Figure 5-7 one must decide whether to use the mean or a regression line to make a forecast. The choice is not obvious from inspection. For this purpose, there is a statistical test based on the F-distribution and known as the F-test, which indicates whether it makes sense from a statistical point of view to use the mean or a regression line to describe the data.

The F-distribution is the ratio of two variances as shown in equation (5-14). If the explained variance is equal to the unexplained, the ratio will be equal to one. This indicates that the regression equation is no better than the mean (see Figure 5-4). As the explained variance increases in magnitude in relation to the unexplained, the F-statistic also increases in value. The F-distribution provides a way for testing the hypotheses that the regression equation will be better than the mean as a method of forecasting. Or viewed in an alternative way, one can find the cutoff point (the F-statistic) where the regression equation is better than the mean as a way of describing the data, *given some probability or confidence interval*. A confidence interval of 95% is usually taken.

$$F = \frac{\dfrac{\text{explained variation}}{k-1}}{\dfrac{\text{unexplained variation}}{n-k}} = \frac{\text{explained variance}}{\text{unexplained variance}} \tag{5-14}$$

$$= \frac{\dfrac{\Sigma(\hat{Y} - \bar{Y})^2}{k-1}}{\dfrac{\Sigma(Y - \bar{Y})^2}{n-k}} \tag{5-15}$$

where n is the sample size (number of observations) and k is the number of variables ($k = 2$ for simple regression).

It should be readily apparent from equation (5-15) that the 95% confidence value for the F-test is dependent on the values of n and k, and the explained

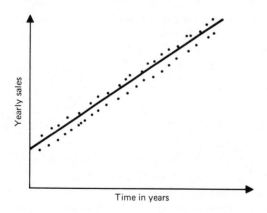

Yearly sales

Time in years

FIGURE 5-5 SIGNIFICANT REGRESSION EQUATION

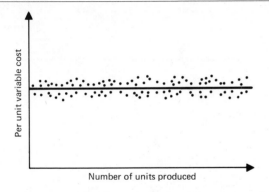

FIGURE 5-6 REGRESSION EQUATION NOT SIGNIFICANT

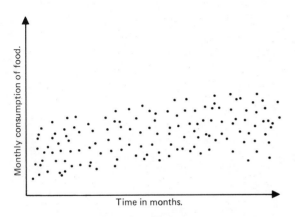

FIGURE 5-7 SIGNIFICANCE OF REGRESSION EQUATION
                UNCERTAIN

an unexplained variances. As n or k gets larger or the unexplained variation gets smaller, the number in the denominator in the F-test gets smaller and thus the F-test increases in value. It also increases when the explained variation gets larger or k gets smaller.

The F-test can be computed for the data presented in Tables 5-1 and 5-2 as shown in Table 5-3. To determine whether the regression line, $Y = 7.17 + 1.254X$, is significant, the F-value computed in Table 5-3, F_c, must be compared with the appropriate value from a table of the F-distribution. (See Appendix I, Table C.) In this case, the F-value (the degrees of freedom are 1 for the numerator and 2 for the denominator) is equal to 18.5 assuming a 95% confidence interval. Since $F_c < F_t$ (2.61 < 18.5), the conclusion is that the regression line could have been obtained by chance, even though $r^2 = .566$. This is due to the small sample

TABLE 5-3 COMPUTATION OF F-STATISTIC

Y	X	$\hat{Y}$	$(Y - \hat{Y})$	$(Y - \hat{Y})^2$	$\hat{Y} - \bar{Y}$	$(\hat{Y} - \bar{Y})^2$
8	3	10.93	−2.93	8.58	−1.57	2.47
11	2	9.68	1.32	1.74	−2.82	7.95
16	5	13.44	2.56	6.55	.94	.88
15	7	15.95	−.95	.90	3.45	11.9
50	17		$\Sigma(Y - Y_c) = 0$	$\Sigma(Y - Y_c)^2 = 17.78$	$\Sigma(Y_c - \bar{Y}) = 0$	$\Sigma(Y_c - \bar{Y})^2 = 23.20$
				Sum of unexplained variation		Sum of explained variation

$$\text{and} \quad F_c = \frac{\dfrac{23.20}{2 - 1}}{\dfrac{17.78}{4 - 2}} = 2.61$$

of only four observations. The values of the F-distribution and the specific one needed for this example, F_t, can be seen in Table C of Appendix I.

A computationally easier way to calculate the value of the F-statistic is

$$F = \frac{\dfrac{r^2}{k - 1}}{\dfrac{1 - r^2}{n - k}}. \tag{5-16}$$

Using (5-16), the F_c for the example is,

$$F_c = \frac{\dfrac{.566}{2 - 1}}{\dfrac{.434}{4 - 2}} = 1.132 = 2.6,$$

the same value obtained from (5-15).

The amount of computation involved in obtaining the values of a, b, r, r^2, F and other statistics that will be discussed later should not be of concern to the reader because all standard computer programs for regression analysis provide these statistics as part of their outputs. The objective here is to present the mechanics of these calculations and their rationale rather than suggest that the computations should be made by hand.

5/5/3 The t-Tests

The values of both a and b are the outcome of a single sample procedure and can therefore differ from the real parameters α and β (see Figures 5-8 and 5-9). It is useful to know the extent of such variation so that confidence intervals can be constructed and tests of hypotheses concerning the true values of α and β can be performed. The t-test is based on values of the student-t-distribution, which represents all possible values that a and b can take as the result of sampling effects. The variances of a and b show the amount of dispersion from their theoretical true value. The square root of the variance divided by the degrees of freedom is called the standard error because it refers to a sampling distribution.

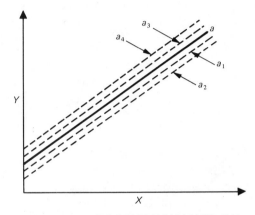

FIGURE 5-8 POSSIBLE VALUES OF a AND THEIR IMPLICATIONS FOR THE REGRESSION LINE

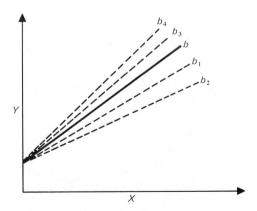

FIGURE 5-9 POSSIBLE VALUES OF b AND THEIR IMPLICATIONS FOR THE REGRESSION LINE

The standard error of a is given by:

$$\sigma_a = \frac{\sigma_u}{\sqrt{n}},$$

(5-17)

where σ_u is the standard deviation of regression often called the standard error of estimate, and is given by

$$\sigma_u = \sqrt{\frac{\Sigma(Y_i - \hat{Y}_i)^2}{n-2}} = \sqrt{\frac{\Sigma e_i^2}{n-2}}.$$

(5-18)

The standard error for b is provided by

$$\sigma_b = \frac{\sigma_u}{\sqrt{\Sigma(X_i - \bar{X})^2}}.$$

(5-19)

If the standard errors of a and b, (5-17) and (5-19) are known, the sampling distributions of a and b can be specified, tests of hypothesis can be conducted, and confidence intervals can be constructed.

Since a and b can vary independently of each other, their combined effect on the regression line at any point, X_i, can be obtained by adding their variances (see Chapter 5 Appendix, Section 2) to obtain

$$\sigma_{a,b} = \sigma_u \sqrt{\frac{1}{n} + \frac{(X_i - \bar{X})^2}{\Sigma(X_i - \bar{X})^2}}.$$

(5-20)

Finally, one may want to determine how far an individual forecast may be from the actual value. This can be found by combining the effects of three possible sources of variation: 1) the variation in a, 2) the variation in b, and 3) the variation of the historical pattern of dispersion around the regression line which is measured by σ_u. These three possible sources of error can be added (see Chapter 5 Appendix, Section 2) to obtain

$$\sigma_{\hat{Y}} = \sigma_u \sqrt{1 + \frac{1}{n} + \frac{(X_i - \bar{X})^2}{\Sigma(X_i - \bar{X})^2}}.$$

(5-21)

As is the case with $\sigma_{a,b}$, the value of $\sigma_{\hat{Y}}$ increases as one moves away from the mean value $\bar{X}$. Thus when $X_i = \bar{X}$, equation (5-20) has its smallest value, becoming equal to equation (5-17),

$$\sigma_{a,b} = \sigma_u \sqrt{\frac{1}{n}}.$$

Similarly, when $X_i = \bar{X}$, equation (5-21) becomes

$$\sigma_{\hat{Y}} = \sigma_u \sqrt{1 + \frac{1}{n}}.$$

(5-22)

The value of equation (5-22) is the smallest the overall dispersion can be and is about equal to σ_u when n is large. On the other hand, the further the forecast is from the mean value, $\bar{X}$, the larger the values of $\sigma_{a,b}$ and $\sigma_{\hat{y}}$, which will create a wider confidence interval around the forecast value (see exercise 1, Figure 5-11).

Through using the standard error of $a(\sigma_a)$ and the standard error of b (σ_b), one can construct probability intervals and test hypotheses of interest. One such hypothesis is: Is the value of a (or b) significantly different from zero? This hypothesis can be tested by using the t-distribution, or t-test.

$$t\text{-test}_a = \frac{a}{\sigma_a}, \qquad t\text{-test}_b = \frac{b}{\sigma_b}.$$

Thus, if the regression equation is

$$Y = 1.5 + 8X,$$

and if $\sigma_a = 1.1$ and $\sigma_b = 1.5$ and $n = 30$ observations,

$$t\text{-test}_a = \frac{1.5}{1.1} = 1.36, \qquad t\text{-test}_b = \frac{8}{1.5} = 5.33.$$

If the computed value of the t-test is larger than the corresponding value from Table B of Appendix I (using say a 95% confidence level), it is concluded that the value of a (or b) is significantly different from zero. If that is not the case, the conclusion is that it is not significantly different from zero.

In the example just mentioned, the t-test from Table B, Appendix I, is 1.701. This is greater than the computed t-test, which indicates that the value of a is not significantly different from zero. The t-test $b = 5.33$ is greater than the one from the table (1.701), indicating that b is significantly different from zero.

A final point deserving attention in concluding this section on significance is the role of the sample size. (The sample size is the number of observations that were used in determining the regression line.) As the sample size increases, the standard error decreases as can be easily seen from equation (5-17) or (5-22); therefore the chances that an individual forecast will be closer to the mean regression line increases. The same is true with the standard error—as the sample size increases, the standard error decreases.

Thus, if one had 100 observations, the confidence interval on a specific forecast would be much narrower than it would be for only 30 observations. Including more observations often means extra cost because data have to be collected and used in the computations. This cost must be balanced against the higher accuracy resulting from more observations. In many cases an optimal sample size can be found that balances these two factors of accuracy and cost. However, in other cases it may simply be impossible to obtain additional observations, in which case the data available must be used.

5/6 Trend Analysis, Time-Series Forecasting

The independent variable in simple regression analysis can be GNP, advertising, price, temperature, time, or any other economic or natural series that can be used in forecasting the dependent variable. When the independent variable is not time, it is a *causal* model, which assumes a cause-effect relationship between the dependent and independent variables. When time is the independent variable in simple regression, as illustrated in Figure 5-10, it is frequently called a *time-series* regression model, which is a special case of the general simple regression equation. In a causal model, future values of the independent variable must be estimated before forecasting. In a time-series model, this is not necessary because the period for which the forecast is to be prepared becomes the value of the independent variable.

A regression time-series model is at a serious disadvantage when fluctuating data such as monthly seasonal values are involved. In such cases, the linear exponential smoothing models of Chapter 3 are much more appropriate. When the forecast is for the long term, however, and annual rather than monthly or quarterly data are available, the fluctuations in the data tend to balance out, and simple regression analysis using time as the independent variable can be used successfully for forecasting. It is worth noting that even though extremely simple, this approach can be very powerful, and is one of the few techniques available for long-range forecasting. Such long-term trend extrapolation includes exponential and S-curves as well as linear trends.

Since the number of annual values available is usually small, a simple graph of the data can give a good approximation of the trend and its future values. It should be understood that no statistical tests or measures of accuracy (for example r^2) can be obtained using such a graphic approach, but the ease of

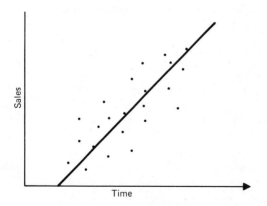

FIGURE 5-10 SIMPLE REGRESSION WITH TIME AS THE
INDEPENDENT VARIABLE

obtaining the results may compensate for that. Finally it should be emphasized that trend analysis is only a *special case* of simple regression analysis that has several advantages as a method of long-term forecasting. (A more detailed treatment of trend extrapolation is given in Chapter 14.)

5/7 The Regression Equation as a Model

Like any other mathematical function, the regression equation, $\hat{Y} = a + bX$, is an abstract model representing some aspect of reality. For example, if Y is sales and X is GNP, reality is being simplified by representing it in terms of the interaction of only two factors. Reality is clearly much more complex than that. Sales are influenced by a myriad of factors—advertising, price, competitors' actions, transportation costs, production costs, R&D expenditures, government policies, etc. An important issue is determining what impact omitting these other factors will have on the results.

In any modeling effort, one can choose to construct a simple model that may not be very accurate or to construct a more complex model that may be more accurate but will be more expensive and complicated. Even the most sophisticated model would still omit some part of reality given the complexity of the real world. To take into consideration the fact that a part of the real process cannot and will not be explained by the regression model, the term u is added to denote the variations in Y that are not explained by the model. The term u is also called *the disturbance term*, *white noise*, *noise*, or the *residual*. Thus u is equivalent to the error used in the simple description

data = pattern + error.

The complete regression equation (denoting the pattern) is not just $\hat{Y} = a + BX$, but $Y = a + bX + u$. The term u is seldom needed for calculations in practice. Its theoretical meaning is that the forecast can vary from the mean or expected value (pattern) of $\hat{Y} = a + bX$ by an amount u, which we estimated in probabilistic terms. The standard deviations and standard errors discussed in the previous sections are the basis for making this estimation of u. The magnitude of u will vary from model to model. In general, the more variables introduced, the smaller the values of u. Multiple regression is usually more accurate than simple regression because it can handle more than one independent variable. However, there is a limit to the number of variables to be employed, since they introduce more complexity and higher cost. A goal in applying regression is to introduce the smallest number of variables (principle of parsimony) and to achieve as small a u as possible.

The term u represents the combined effect of many sources of uncertainty. For example, in quantifying factors, errors of measurement may occur. Also, there are errors in aggregation and sampling biases. One hopes that these can be ignored because they are small and tend to cancel out against each other. However, it is u that represents their combined effect in the theoretical process of going from reality to the regression model.

For the regression equation, $Y = a + bX + u$, to have those characteristics necessary for the statistics described thus far to apply, u must have the following properties:

1. The mean value of u must be equal to zero. This requirement is based on the premise that there are a great number of unimportant factors that influence Y but are not included in the regression equation, which tend to cancel out. Thus, on the average, their sum is equal to zero and cannot be predicted.

2. The error term u must be truly random throughout the range of all observations. That is, successive values of u must be uncorrelated and exhibit no systematic pattern.

3. The disturbance term u must be normally distributed. This requirement is a consequence of the large number of factors influencing Y but not included in the regression equation. It is usually true that extreme variations do not happen as often as lesser ones. Since u is the sum of all such variations, large values should occur infrequently with most values being close to zero. Such a pattern usually results in a normal distribution.

4. The variance of u must be constant. The magnitude of the error term must not increase or decrease within the entire range of observations.

Violations of the above properties of u can cause serious difficulty since the complete regression model, $Y = a + bX + u$, will no longer be correct. As will be seen in Chapter 6, there are ways of making sure that the above rules or assumptions are not violated.

From this point on, the full equation, $Y = a + bX + u$, will be implied, although u will not be included. The same will be true for multiple regression where

$$Y = a + b_1 X_1 + b_2 X_2 + b_3 X_3 + \cdots + b_K X_K$$

will imply inclusion of the error term u.

APPENDIX

MATHEMATICAL SUPPLEMENT

Chapter 5

1. DETERMINING THE VALUES OF *a* AND *b* IN $Y = a + bX$

Assuming n data points denoted by Y_i, the regression equation, $\hat{Y}_i = a + bX_i$, can be estimated so as to minimize the sum of the squared deviations. Defining

$$e_i = Y_i - \hat{Y}_i,$$

then

$$e_i^2 = (Y_i - \hat{Y}_i)^2$$

and

$$\Sigma e_i^2 = \Sigma(Y_i - \hat{Y}_i)^2.$$

By substitution,

$$\Sigma e_i^2 = \Sigma(Y_i - a - bX_i)^2.$$

Applying calculus,

$$\frac{\partial \Sigma e_i^2}{\partial a} = -2\Sigma(Y_i - a - bX_i) = 0, \tag{5-23}$$

$$\frac{\partial \Sigma e_i^2}{\partial b} = -2\Sigma X_i(Y_i - a - bX_i) = 0. \tag{5-24}$$

From (5-23),

$$-\Sigma Y_i + na + b\Sigma X_i = 0. \tag{5-25}$$

From (5-24),

$$-\Sigma X_i Y_i + a\Sigma X_i + b\Sigma X_i^2 = 0. \tag{5-26}$$

Equations (5-25) and (5-26) can be solved simultaneously to obtain the values of a and b. Solving (5-25) for a gives

$$a = \frac{\Sigma Y_i}{n} - b\frac{\Sigma X_i}{n}, \tag{5-27}$$

which substituted into (5-26) yields

$$b = \frac{n\Sigma X_i Y_i - \Sigma X_i \Sigma Y_i}{n\Sigma X_i^2 - (\Sigma X_i)^2}. \tag{5-28}$$

Thus, the values of a and b in (5-27) and (5-28) correspond to the points where the first derivatives of (5-25) and (5-26) are zero; that is, where the sum of the squared errors is at a minimum.

Since the value of b is known through (5-28), it can be substituted into

(5-27) to get a value for *a* as follows:

$$b = \frac{n\Sigma X_i Y_i - \Sigma X_i \Sigma Y_i}{n\Sigma X_i^2 - (\Sigma X_i)^2},$$

$$a = \frac{\Sigma Y_i}{n} - \frac{n\bar{X}\Sigma X_i Y_i - \bar{X}\Sigma X_i \Sigma Y_i}{n\Sigma X_i^2 - (\Sigma X_i)^2}.$$

Equations (5-27) and (5-28) are most often used because they are simpler. The solution point for *a* and *b* is indeed where Σe_i^2 is at a minimum, as can be verified by computing the second derivatives,

$$\frac{\partial \Sigma e_i^2}{\partial a^2} > 0 \quad \text{and} \quad \frac{\partial \Sigma e_i^2}{\partial b^2} > 0.$$

A convenient way of expressing the regression equation is in terms of deviations from the mean values of X and Y. The data are transformed by substituting

$$x_i = X_i - \bar{X} \quad \text{or} \quad X_i = x_i + \bar{X},$$

and $\quad \hat{y}_i = \hat{Y}_i - \hat{Y}' \quad \text{or} \quad \hat{Y}_i = \hat{y}_i + \hat{Y}',$

where $\hat{y}_i'$ is the estimated (predicted) value of $\bar{y}$.

The regression equation, $\hat{Y} = a + bX$, then becomes

$$\hat{y}_i + \hat{Y}' = a + b(x_i + \bar{X}),$$

which simplifies to $\hat{y}_i = a + bx_i + b\bar{X} - \bar{Y}.$

But, since $a = \hat{Y}' - b\bar{X},$

$$y_i = \hat{Y}' - b\bar{X} + bx_i + b\bar{X} - \hat{Y}'$$

and $\hat{y}_i = bx_i.$ (5-29)

Similarly, by substitution

$$\Sigma e_i^2 = \Sigma(y_i - \hat{y})^2$$

$$= \Sigma(y_i - bx_i)^2,$$

$$\frac{d\Sigma_i^2}{db} = -2\Sigma x_i(y_i - bx_i)$$

$$= -2\Sigma x_i y_i + 2b\Sigma x_i^2 = 0,$$

$$b = \frac{\Sigma x_i y_i}{\Sigma x_i^2}.$$ (5-30)

Equation (5-30) is similar to (5-28) except that it is expressed in terms of deviations. Equation (5-27), on the other hand, is not needed because the value of *a* in (5-29) is zero.

2.   VARIANCES IN SIMPLE REGRESSION

Variance in *a*

The variance of a is stated mathematically as $E(a - \alpha)^2$ where α is the true value in the regression equation, $Y_i = \alpha + \beta X_i + u_i$.

Remembering that

$$a = \bar{Y} - b\bar{X},$$

substituting in equation (5-30),

$$a = \bar{Y} - \frac{\Sigma x_i y_i}{\Sigma x_i^2} \bar{X}.$$

Thus $a = \dfrac{\Sigma Y_i}{n} - \bar{X} \dfrac{\Sigma x_i}{\Sigma x_i^2} (Y_i - \bar{Y})$

$$= \Sigma \left(\frac{1}{n} - \bar{X} \frac{x_i}{\Sigma x_i^2} \right) Y_i,$$

since $\bar{X}\bar{Y} \dfrac{\Sigma x_i}{\Sigma x_i^2} = 0,$

and $\Sigma x_i = \Sigma(X_i - \bar{X}) = 0.$

Thus $a = \Sigma \left(\dfrac{1}{n} - \bar{X} \dfrac{x_i}{\Sigma x_i^2} \right)(\alpha + \beta X_i + u_i)$

$$= \alpha \Sigma \left(\frac{1}{n} - \bar{X} \frac{x_i}{\Sigma x_i^2} \right) + \beta \Sigma \left(\frac{1}{n} - \bar{X} \frac{x_i}{\Sigma x_i^2} \right) X_i + \Sigma \left(\frac{1}{n} - \bar{X} \frac{x_i}{\Sigma x_i^2} \right) u_i$$

$$= \alpha - 0 + \Sigma \left(\frac{1}{n} - \bar{X} \frac{x_i}{\Sigma x_i^2} \right) u_i.$$

$$\left[\text{Note that } \frac{\Sigma x_i X_i}{\Sigma x_i^2} = 1, \quad \text{since} \right.$$

$$\left. 1 = \frac{\Sigma x_i^2}{\Sigma x_i^2} = \frac{\Sigma x_i x_i}{\Sigma x_i^2} = \frac{\Sigma x_i(X_i - \bar{X})}{\Sigma x_i^2} = \frac{\Sigma x_i X_i}{\Sigma x_i^2} - \frac{\Sigma x_i \bar{X}}{\Sigma x_i^2} = \frac{\Sigma x_i X_i}{\Sigma x_i^2} - 0. \right]$$

Thus $a = \alpha + \Sigma \left(\dfrac{1}{n} - \bar{X} \dfrac{x_i}{\Sigma x_i^2} \right) u_i,$

or $(a - \alpha) = \Sigma \left(\dfrac{1}{n} - \bar{X} \dfrac{x_i}{x_i^2} \right) u_i,$ (5-31)

and
$$E(a - \alpha) = E\left[\Sigma\left(\frac{1}{n} - \bar{X}\frac{x_i}{\Sigma x_i{}^2}\right)u_i\right]$$

$$= \Sigma\left(\frac{1}{n} - \bar{X}\frac{x_i}{\Sigma x_i{}^2}\right)E(u_i), \qquad (5\text{-}32)$$

since $\Sigma\left(\dfrac{1}{n} - \bar{X}\dfrac{x_i}{\Sigma x_i{}^2}\right)$ is a constant.

Thus $E(a - \alpha) = 0$, since $E(u_i)$ is by definition equal to 0. This shows that a is an unbiased estimator of the true theoretical value of α.

The variance of a is

$$E(a - \alpha)^2 = \left[\Sigma\left(\frac{1}{n} - \bar{X}\frac{x_i}{\Sigma x_i{}^2}\right)E(u_i)\right]^2 \qquad [\text{from (5-32)}]$$

$$= \Sigma\left(\frac{1}{n^2} - \frac{2}{n}\bar{X}\frac{x_i}{\Sigma x_i{}^2} + \bar{X}^2\frac{x_i{}^2}{\Sigma x_i{}^4}\right)E(u_i{}^2).$$

Since by definition $E(u_i u_j) = 0$ for $i \neq j$,

$$E(a - \alpha)^2 = \left(\frac{n}{n^2} - \frac{2}{n}\bar{X}\frac{\Sigma x_i}{\Sigma x_i{}^2} + \bar{X}^2\frac{\Sigma x_i{}^2}{\Sigma x_i{}^4}\right)E(u_i{}^2)$$

$$= \left(\frac{1}{n} - 0 + \frac{\bar{X}^2}{\Sigma x_i{}^2}\right)E(u_i{}^2),$$

but
$$E(u_i{}^2) = \frac{\Sigma e_i{}^2}{n - 2} = \sigma_u{}^2 \quad \text{or the variance of regression.}$$

Then
$$\sigma_a{}^2 = \left(\frac{1}{n} + \frac{\bar{X}^2}{\Sigma x_i{}^2}\right)\sigma_u{}^2,$$

and
$$\sigma_a = \sigma_u\sqrt{\frac{1}{n} + \frac{\bar{X}^2}{\Sigma x_i{}^2}}. \qquad (5\text{-}33)$$

A simplified version of (5-33) is

$$\sigma_a = \frac{\sigma_u}{\sqrt{n}}.$$

This version holds when a is a constant, since from the central limit theorem, the standard error is the population standard deviation (σ_u) divided by the square root of n. However, if a is a variable, then (5-33) is the exact form for computing its standard error.

Variance in b

From equation (5-30),

$$b = \frac{\Sigma x_i}{\Sigma x_i^2}(\beta x_i + u_i),$$

$$b = \beta\frac{\Sigma x_i^2}{\Sigma x_i^2} + \frac{\Sigma x_i}{\Sigma x_i^2} u_i$$

$$= \beta + \frac{\Sigma x_i}{\Sigma x_i^2} u_i, \quad \text{since } \frac{\Sigma x_i^2}{\Sigma x_i^2} = 1.$$

Then

$$b - \beta = \frac{\Sigma x_i}{\Sigma x_i^2} u_i, \tag{5-34}$$

$$E(b - \beta) = E\left(\frac{\Sigma x_i}{\Sigma x_i^2} u_i\right), \tag{5-35}$$

and

$$E(b - \beta) = \frac{\Sigma x_i}{\Sigma x_i^2} E(u_i), \quad \text{since } \frac{\Sigma x_i}{\Sigma x_i^2} \text{ is a constant.}$$

Thus $E(b - \beta) = 0$, since by definition $E(u_i) = 0$.

Therefore, b is an unbiased estimator of the true population parameter, β.

If equation (5-35) is squared, one obtains

$$E(b - \beta)^2 = \left[E\left(\frac{\Sigma x_i}{\Sigma x_i^2} u_i\right)\right]^2$$

$$= E\left[\left(\frac{x_1}{\Sigma x_i^2} u_1\right)^2 + \left(\frac{x_2}{\Sigma x_i^2} u_2\right)^2 + \cdots + \left(\frac{x_n}{\Sigma x_i^2} u_n\right)^2 + \left(\frac{x_1 x_2}{\Sigma x_i^2} u_1 u_2\right)^2\right.$$

$$\left. + \left(\frac{x_1 x_3}{\Sigma x_i^2} u_1 u_3\right)^2 + \cdots + \left(\frac{x_1 x_n}{\Sigma x_i^2} u_1 u_n\right)^2 + \cdots + \left(\frac{x_{n-1} x_n}{\Sigma x_i^2} u_{n-1} u_n\right)^2\right]$$

$$= E\left(\frac{\Sigma x_i^2}{\Sigma x_i^4} u_i^2 + \frac{\sum\limits_{i>j} x_i x_j}{\Sigma x_i^2} u_i u_j\right)$$

$$= \frac{1}{\Sigma x_i^2} E(u_i^2), \quad \text{since } E(u_i u_j) = 0 \quad \text{for} \quad i \neq j,$$

and

$$E(b - \beta)^2 = \frac{\sigma_u^2}{\Sigma x_i^2} \quad \text{since } E(u_i^2) = \frac{\Sigma e_i^2}{n-2} = \sigma_u^2 \tag{5-36}$$

Combined Variance of *a* and *b*

The combined variance of a and b is

$$E(Y - \hat{Y})^2, \quad \text{where} \quad Y = \alpha + \beta X'$$

and X' is a specific value of X for which a forecast is needed. This combined variance is

$$\sigma_{a,b}^2 = E(\alpha + \beta X' - a - bX')^2$$

$$= E[(\alpha - a) + (\beta - b)X']^2$$

$$= E[(\alpha - a)^2 + 2(\alpha - a)(\beta - b)X' + (\beta - b)^2 X'^2]$$

$$= E(\alpha - a)^2 + 2E(\alpha - a)(\beta - b)X' + E(\beta - b)^2 X'^2$$

$$= \sigma_a^2 + 2\,\text{cov}\,(a,b)X' + \sigma_b^2 X'^2, \tag{5-37}$$

but $\text{cov}\,(a,b) = E(\alpha - a)(\beta - b)$

$$= E\left[\left(-\bar{X}\frac{\Sigma x_i}{\Sigma x_i^2}u_i\right)\left(\frac{\Sigma x_i}{\Sigma x_i^2}u_i\right)\right],$$

based on equations (5-32) and (5-34).

Thus $\text{cov}\,(a,b) = E\left(-\bar{X}\dfrac{\Sigma x_i^2}{\Sigma x_i^4}u_i^2\right) = -\dfrac{\bar{X}}{\Sigma x_i^2}E(u_i^2)$

$$= -\frac{\bar{X}}{\Sigma x_i^2}\sigma_u^2. \tag{5-38}$$

Equation (5-37) then becomes

$$\sigma_{a,b}^2 = \left(\frac{1}{n} + \frac{\bar{X}^2}{\Sigma x_i^2}\right)\sigma_u^2 - \frac{2\bar{X}X'}{\Sigma x_i^2}\sigma_u^2 + X'^2\frac{\sigma_u^2}{\Sigma x_i^2}$$

when equations (5-32), (5-38), and (5-36) are substituted into (5-37).
This can be further refined to give

$$\sigma_{a,b}^2 = \sigma_u^2\left(\frac{1}{n} + \frac{\bar{X}^2}{\Sigma x_i^2} - \frac{2\bar{X}X'}{\Sigma x_i^2} + \frac{X'^2}{\Sigma x_i^2}\right)$$

$$= \sigma_u^2\left(\frac{1}{n} + \frac{(X' - \bar{X})^2}{\Sigma x_i^2}\right),$$

where X' is the individual X value corresponding to the desired Y forecast.

Variance of an Individual Forecast ($\sigma_{\hat{y}}^2$)

The variance for an individual forecast is

$$E(Y - \hat{Y})^2, \quad \text{where} \quad Y = \alpha + \beta X' + u.$$

As with the combined variance of a and b, a specific value for X, say X', is needed. In addition, the term u must be included in the equation, $Y = \alpha + \beta X' + u$, since an individual forecast can fluctuate because of the variance of u.

Thus
$$\sigma_{\hat{y}}^2 = E(Y - \hat{Y})^2 = E(\alpha + \beta X' + u - a - bX')^2$$
$$= E[(\alpha - a) + (\beta - b)X' + u]^2,$$
$$E(Y - \hat{Y})^2 = E[(\alpha - a)^2 + (\beta - b)^2 + u^2 + 2X'(\alpha - a)(\beta - b)$$
$$+ 2(\alpha - a)u + 2X'(\beta - b)u]$$
$$= E(\alpha - a)^2 + E(\beta - b)^2 X'^2 + E(u)^2 + 2X'E(\alpha - a)(\beta - b) + 0 + 0$$
$$= \left(\frac{1}{n} + \frac{\overline{X}^2}{\Sigma x_i^2}\right)\sigma_u^2 + \frac{\sigma_u^2 X'^2}{\Sigma x_i^2} + \sigma_u^2 + 2X'\left(-\frac{\overline{X}}{\Sigma x_i^2}\right)\sigma_u^2,$$

using equations (5-33), (5-36), and (5-38) respectively.

Thus,
$$\sigma_{\hat{y}}^2 = \sigma_u^2\left(\frac{1}{n} + \frac{\overline{X}^2}{\Sigma x_i^2} + \frac{X'^2}{\Sigma x_i^2} + 1 - \frac{2X'\overline{X}}{\Sigma x_i^2}\right)$$

and
$$\sigma_{\hat{y}}^2 = \sigma_u^2\left(1 + \frac{1}{n} + \frac{(X' - \overline{X})^2}{\Sigma x_i^2}\right). \tag{5-39}$$

3. EXPLAINED, UNEXPLAINED, AND TOTAL VARIANCE

The actual value can be written as

$$y_i = \hat{y}_i + e_i, \tag{5-40}$$

where y_i is the true value, $\hat{y}_i$ the estimated value, and e_i the error of estimation. Computing the sum of the squared values gives

$$\Sigma y_i^2 = \Sigma(\hat{y}_i - e_i)^2 \tag{5-41}$$
$$= \Sigma\hat{y}_i^2 + \Sigma e_i^2 - 2\Sigma\hat{y}_i e_i.$$

This can be further reduced to

$$\Sigma y_i^2 = \Sigma\hat{y}_i^2 + \Sigma e_i^2, \tag{5-42}$$

since $\quad -2\Sigma\hat{y}_i e_i = -2\Sigma b x_i e_i$ $\qquad$ [using (5-29)]

$\qquad\qquad = -2b\Sigma x_i(y_i - bx_i)$ $\qquad$ [using (5-40)]

$\qquad\qquad = -2b\Sigma x_i bx_i - 2b^2\Sigma x_i^2$ $\qquad$ [using (5-29)]

$\qquad\qquad = 0.$

The three terms of equation (5-42) are the sum of the total variation, the sum of the explained variation, and the sum of the unexplained variation. The explained part of the variation is

$$\Sigma\hat{y}_i^2 = \Sigma[\hat{y}^2 - (\hat{y}')^2]^2 = \Sigma(\hat{y}^2 - \bar{y})^2,$$

where $\hat{y}'$ is the estimated (predicted) value of $\bar{y}$,

and finally, $\quad \Sigma e_i^2 = \Sigma(y_i - \hat{y}_i)^2$ $\qquad$ [using (5-42)]

$$\qquad\qquad = \Sigma(Y_i - \bar{Y} - \hat{Y}_i + \bar{Y})^2 = \Sigma(Y_i - \hat{Y}_i)^2,$$

which is the sum of the unexplained variation.

The ratio of the explained to total variation is

$$\frac{\Sigma\hat{y}_i^2}{\Sigma y_i^2} = \frac{\Sigma(bx_i)^2}{\Sigma y_i^2} = b^2\frac{\Sigma x_i^2}{\Sigma y_i^2}$$

$$= \frac{(\Sigma x_i y_i)^2}{(\Sigma x_i^2)^2}\frac{\Sigma x_i^2}{\Sigma y_i^2} \qquad \text{[using (5-30)]}$$

$$= \frac{(\Sigma x_i y_i)^2}{\Sigma x_i^2\Sigma y_i^2} = r^2. \qquad (5\text{-}43)$$

Equation (5-43) is the formula for r^2 and is equivalent to

$$r = \frac{n\Sigma XY - (\Sigma X)(\Sigma Y)}{\sqrt{[n\Sigma X^2 - (\Sigma X)^2][n\Sigma Y^2 - (\Sigma Y)^2]}} = \frac{\Sigma xy}{\sqrt{(\Sigma x^2)(\Sigma y^2)}}$$

The value of r^2 as expressed by (5-43) is the ratio of explained variation to the total variation and indicates the percentage of the total variation explained by the regression line. The value of the F-statistic, on the other hand, is the ratio of the explained over the unexplained variance. That is,

$$F = \frac{\dfrac{\Sigma\hat{y}^2}{K-1}}{\dfrac{\Sigma e_i^2}{n-K}}. \qquad (5\text{-}44)$$

$\qquad\qquad\qquad\qquad\qquad\qquad\qquad\qquad\qquad$ [using (5-42)]

since $\qquad r^2 = \dfrac{\Sigma\hat{y}_i^2}{\Sigma y_i^2},$

$$\Sigma \hat{y}_i^2 = r^2 \Sigma y_i^2 \qquad\qquad (5\text{-}45)$$

and $\quad \Sigma e_i^2 = \Sigma y_i^2 - \Sigma \hat{y}_i^2 \qquad\qquad (5\text{-}46)$

$$= \Sigma y_i^2 - r^2 \Sigma \hat{y}_i \qquad\qquad [\text{using } (5\text{-}45)]$$

$$= \Sigma y_i^2 (1 - r^2). \qquad\qquad (5\text{-}47)$$

Substituting (5-45) in the numerator of (5-44), and (5-47) in the denominator of (5-44), the F-value becomes

$$F = \frac{\dfrac{r^2 y_i^2}{K-1}}{\dfrac{(1-r^2) y_i^2}{n-K}} = \frac{\dfrac{r^2}{K-1}}{\dfrac{1-r^2}{n-K}}. \qquad\qquad (5\text{-}48)$$

Equation (5-48) shows how the F-statistic is related to r^2 and gives a simpler means to calculate the value of F.

REFERENCES AND SELECTED BIBLIOGRAPHY

Johnston, J. 1966. *Econometric Methods*. Englewood Cliffs, N.J.: Prentice-Hall.

Klein, L. R. 1968. *An Introduction to Econometrics*. Englewood Cliffs, N.J.: Prentice-Hall.

Pindyck, R. S., and D. L. Rubenfeld, 1976. *Econometric Models and Economic Forecasts*, New York: McGraw-Hill.

"Regression as a Forecasting Aid." 1973. Boston: Intercollegiate Case Clearing House, 9-173-147.

Spurr, W. A., and C. P. Bonini. 1967. *Statistical Analysis for Business Decisions*. Homewood, Ill.: Irwin.

EXERCISES

1. Suppose the following data represent the total costs and the number of units produced by Company XYZ.

    a. Determine the regression line, compute the F- and t-tests, and calculate r and r^2.

	Total Cost (in $1000s)	Units Produced (in 1000s)
	25	5
	11	2
	34	8
	23	4
	32	6

Y	X	Y^2	X^2	XY	e
25	5	625	25	125	0
11	2	121	4	22	−2.3
34	8	1156	64	272	−2.7
23	4	529	16	92	1.9
32	6	1024	36	192	3.1

$\Sigma Y = 125$	$\Sigma X = 25$	$\Sigma Y^2 = 3455$	$\Sigma X^2 = 145$	$\Sigma XY = 703$	$\Sigma e = 0$
$\bar{Y} = 25$	$\bar{X} = 5$				

b. Figure 5-11 shows the confidence intervals corresponding to the above data. Interpret the meaning of the different lines.

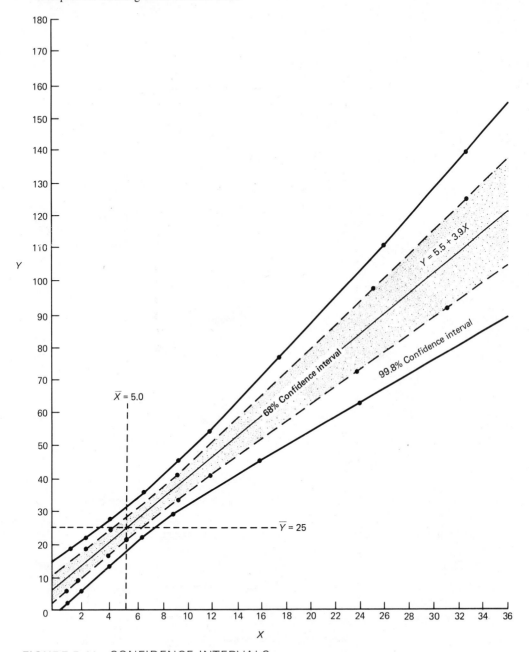

FIGURE 5-11 CONFIDENCE INTERVALS

2. Data on the test scores of various workers and their subsequent production ratings are shown in Table 5-4.

TABLE 5-4 SCORES ON MANUAL DEXTERITY TEST AND PRODUCTION RATINGS FOR 20 WORKERS

Worker	Test Score X	Production Rating Y
A	53	45
B	36	43
C	88	89
D	84	79
E	86	84
F	64	66
G	45	49
H	48	48
I	39	43
J	67	76
K	54	59
L	73	77
M	65	56
N	29	28
O	52	51
P	22	27
Q	76	76
R	32	34
S	51	60
T	37	32

a. Plot these data on a graph with test score as the X-axis and production rating as the Y-axis.

b. Compute the regression coefficient and the value of a for these data.

c. What production rating would you forecast for an individual whose test score was 80?

d. Determine whether the coefficient of regression is significantly different from 0 in this case.

e. Compute the 95% confidence interval for the coefficient of regression.

f. Compute the 95% confidence interval for the forecast you made for the individual whose test score was 80.

g. Determine the coefficient of correlation and the coefficient of determination for this situation. What percentage of the variation in Y is explained by this regression line?

h. Is the overall regression equation significant at the 95% level?

3. Use the data of Table 3-12 and compute a regression equation. Compare the MSE with that of linear exponential smoothing. What do you think are the differences in the forecasting accuracy between linear regression and linear exponential smoothing?

4. Determine the regression equation for the data whose dependent variable has the values for the years given in Table 2-7 and whose independent variable has the GNP values given in Table 2-7. Calculate the F-test, and the t-tests and r^2. Is the regression equation statistically significant? Explain. How good is the fit? Explain.

5. Instead of using the GNP data of Table 2-7 as they are, transform them into a natural logarithmic scale, then estimate the regression equation and compute the F- and t-tests and r^2. Do you prefer this equation to that found in exercise 4? Explain. (A common logarithm transformation involves using the common logarithm of the GNP data rather than the actual values. Thus for 1961 the value is 5.794 (log of 328.327), 5.9058 for 1962, 6.021 for 1963, ..., 6.5985 for 1969, and 6.7095 for 1970).

6 MULTIPLE REGRESSION

6/1 Introduction

Simple regression, as examined in Chapter 5, is a special case of multiple regression. In multiple regression there is one dependent variable (e.g., sales) to be predicted, but there are two or more independent variables. The general form of multiple regression is

$$Y = a + b_1 X_1 + b_2 X_2 + \cdots + b_k X_k \qquad (6\text{-}1)$$

Thus if sales were the variable to be forecast, several factors such as GNP, advertising, prices, competition, R&D budget, and time could be tested for their influence on sales by using regression. If it is found that these variables do influence the level of sales, they can be used to predict future values of sales.

As an example for illustrating the application of multiple regression, Table 6-1 gives sales of California Plate Glass (CPG) Company and some other factors that are thought to influence the company's sales. Based on the technique of simple regression, the company could forecast its future sales using either automobile production, building contracts awarded, or simply the year (time). However, it may be much more complete (and accurate) to assume that both automobile production and building contracts awarded work together in influencing the net sales of the company. Mathematically, such a relationship could be written as

net sales CPG = f (automobile production, building contracts awarded).

This equation simply says that net sales for the company are a *function* of, or depend upon, two independent variables—automobile production and building contracts awarded. Although several different forms of the equation could be written to show the relationships among these variables, a straightforward one that is linear and additive is

$$Y = a + b_1 X_1 + b_2 X_2, \qquad (6\text{-}2)$$

TABLE 6-1 HISTORICAL DATA ON CPG SALES AND RELATED VARIABLES

Year	Net CPG Sales (millions of dollars)	Automobile Production (millions)	Building Contracts Awarded (billions)
1959	280.0	3.909	9.43
1960	281.5	5.119	10.36
1961	337.4	6.666	14.50
1962	404.2	5.338	15.75
1963	402.1	4.321	16.78
1964	452.0	6.117	17.44
1965	431.7	5.559	19.77
1966	582.3	7.920	23.76
1967	596.6	5.816	31.61
1968	620.8	6.113	32.17
1969	513.6	4.258	35.09
1970	606.9	5.591	36.42
1971	629.0	6.675	36.58
1972	602.7	5.543	37.14
1973	656.7	6.933	41.30
1974	778.5	7.638	45.62
1975	877.6	7.752	47.38
1976*	—	6.400	48.51
1977*	—	7.900	51.23
1978*	—	8.400	57.47
1979*	—	8.600	61.03
1980*	—	8.900	66.25

* Data are estimated.

where Y = CPG annual sales,

X_1 = annual automobile production,

and X_2 = annual building contracts awarded.

From equation (6-2) it can readily be seen that if either X_1 or X_2 were eliminated, the equation would be like those handled previously with simple linear regression. Just as the method of least squares was used in Chapter 5 to estimate the values of the coefficients a and b in simple regression, the method of least squares can be used to estimate a, b_1 and b_2. (See Chapter 6 Appendix, Section 1.) In fact, with any number of independent variables the method of least squares can still be used to obtain estimated values of a, b_1, b_2, ..., b_k and several other useful statistics. Simple regression is thus a special case of multiple regression.

6/2 Applying Multiple Regression

To better understand the concepts of multiple regression, the method of least squares will be used to obtain values for a, b_1, and b_2 in equation (6-2) with the data of Table 6-1. It will be assumed that the task is to forecast the company's sales for the next five years (1976 through 1980), and that forecasts will be based in part on the estimated values of automobile production and building contract awards for those years. Using historical observations available in Table 6-1, one would like to determine the values for a, b_1, and b_2 so as to minimize the MSE, then use those estimates of a, b_1, and b_2 to forecast the future values of company sales.

Using this historical information and a multiple regression computer program, the results obtained are

$$a = 19.1, \qquad b_1 = 35.7, \qquad b_2 = 10.9.$$

Thus the equation for forecasting the company's sales can be written as

$$Y = 19.1 + 35.7X_1 + 10.9X_2. \tag{6-3}$$

This equation simply says that based on the historical observations (time period 1959 through 1975) the best model, or equation, is (6-3). It should be noted that the historical values used in developing the equation were in millions of dollars for net sales, in millions of units for automobile production, and in billions of awards for building contracts. It is important to remember that the magnitude of the parameter values depends on the units used in developing them. Thus it is incorrect to interpret equation (6-3) as indicating that auto production is much more important than building contracts in determining company sales simply because 35.7 is much larger than 10.9. If some different units had been used for automobile production, it could well have turned out that the coefficient for X_1 would have been smaller than the coefficient for X_2.

The literal interpretation of the values in equation (6-3) is that when both X_1 and X_2 are 0, company sales (Y) will have a value of 19.1 million (the value of the intercept a), and that when automobile production increases by 1 million units, company sales will increase by 35.7 million dollars (other things being held constant). When building contracts awarded increase by 1 billion, company sales will increase by 10.9 million dollars (again, other things being held constant). Thus the coefficients in the equation simply indicate how changes of one unit in each independent variable will influence the value of the dependent variable, Y.

Once the parameters on the equation have been determined, the equation can be used to forecast the value of annual sales for each of the next five years. This forecast is made by simply substituting the appropriate values for X_1 and X_2 into equation (6-3). These values, for 1976 for example, are 6.4 and 48.51 respectively. Thus the estimates of sales for 1976* would be

$$Y = 19.1 + 35.7(6.4) + 10.9(48.51)$$

$$= 776.3 \ (\text{i.e., } \$776,300,000).$$

Similarly the computations for 1977 through 1980 can be made by simply using the appropriate values for automobile production and building contracts awarded. It should be noted that this approach to forecasting requires estimated values of the independent variables (in this case, X_1 and X_2) for the future years to be forecast. For the two variables used in the above example it seems likely that there would be future estimates because the country involved would probably prepare long-range forecasts of these variables as part of the process of economic planning.

6/3 Multiple Correlation and the Coefficient of Determination

It will be recalled that in the case of simple correlation one could compute a factor called the squared correlation coefficient (or coefficient of determination), which was simply the ratio of the explained variation to the total variation. The same ratio can also be computed in the case of multiple regression, where again it is the explained variation over the total variation but now involves all independent variables. This coefficient of determination, denoted by R^2 (for simple correlation, it was r^2), can take on values from 0 to 1, with the latter representing a situation where all of the variation is explained. The equation used to calculate the coefficient of determination is the same as that used for simple regression:

$$R^2 = \frac{\Sigma(\hat{Y}_i - Y)^2}{\Sigma(Y_i - \bar{\bar{Y}})^2}. \tag{6-4}$$

Returning to the example of the annual sales of the CPG Company, the coefficient of determination computed using formula (6-4) is .976. This means that

---

* It should be noted that this forecast for 1976 is being made without first checking the significance of the parameters on which that forecast will be based. This topic will be taken up in Section 6/4.

97.6% of the variation in annual sales is explained by the combined variation in automobile production and building contracts awarded.

In addition to the coefficients of determination, the simple correlation coefficients between any pair of variables can be calculated as shown in Table 6-2, which is called a simple correlation matrix. Furthermore, a combined correlation coefficient (called multiple correlation) can be computed. In the case of two independent variables, the multiple correlation coefficient (R) will be

$$R = \sqrt{\frac{r_{12}^2 + r_{13}^2 - 2r_{12}r_{13}r_{23}}{1 - r_{23}^2}}, \tag{6-5}$$

where r_{12} is the simple correlation coefficient between sales and auto production (0.56),

r_{13} is the correlation between sales and building contracts (0.99),

and r_{23} is the correlation between auto production and building contracts (0.53).

Thus, $$R = \sqrt{\frac{(0.56)^2 + (0.99)^2 - 2(0.56)(0.99)(0.53)}{1 - (0.53)^2}} = .988,$$

and of course $R^2 = .988^2 = .976$.

The simple correlation matrix is of value in multiple regression because it gives information as to how different pairs of variables are correlated. This information is used in deciding which variables are the most appropriate ones to include in the multiple regression equation. The multiple correlation and coefficient of determination are also useful information, since they indicate how well the entire relationship expressed by the regression equation explains changes in the dependent variable.

6/4 Tests of Significance

The statistical significance of the results of multiple regression analysis must be established before these results can be used in forecasting. The determination of the values of coefficients in the regression equation is based on a sample of historical observations. The purpose of the tests of significance is to determine the confidence that can be placed in the regression results obtained and their applicability to the entire population of possible values.

Although there are many tests of significance, this chapter will deal only with the two described for simple regression:

1. The F-test indicates whether the overall regression equation is significant (i.e., whether a functional relationship is present between the dependent variable and the combined effects of the independent variables). As

TABLE 6-2 SIMPLE CORRELATION MATRIX FOR TABLE 6-1 VARIABLES

	CPG Sales	Automobile Production	Building Contracts
CPG sales	1.00	.56	.99
Auto production	.56	1.00	.53
Building contracts	.99	.53	1.00

explained in Chapter 5, the value of the *F*-test is the ratio of the *explained variance* over the *unexplained variance*. This relationship can be written mathematically in two equivalent forms:

$$F = \frac{\Sigma(\hat{Y}_i - \bar{Y})^2}{\Sigma(Y_i - \hat{Y})^2},$$

or $F = \dfrac{\dfrac{R^2}{k-1}}{\dfrac{1-R^2}{n-k}},$ where R^2 is the coefficient of determination.

For the CPG example the computed *F* value is:

$$F_c = \left(\frac{.976}{3-1}\right)\bigg/\left(\frac{1-.976}{17-3}\right) = \left(\frac{.976}{.024}\right)\left(\frac{14}{2}\right)$$

$$= 284.9.$$

From the table of *F*-values, $F_t = 3.74$ for a 95% confidence interval and for 2 and 14 degrees of freedom. Since $F_c > F_t$, the conclusion is that the overall relationship between the dependent variable and the two independent variables is significant. Thus, $Y = 19.1 + 35.7(X_1) + 10.9(X_2)$ can be considered as a forecasting tool and eventually used if the *t*-tests corresponding to X_1 and X_2 are also significant.

2. The second test determines the significance of the individual coefficients of the regression equation (a, b_1, b_2). Essentially, the question is whether the value of each coefficient is significantly different from 0 or whether it simply occurred by chance. This test consists of determining the variance for each of the coefficients, then using the square root of that, the standard error, to determine whether the value of the coefficient is significantly different from 0. The results of the *t*-test computations for the CPG example are given in Table 6-3.

   The rule for determining whether a coefficient is significantly different from 0 at a specified confidence level (95% for example) is to

TABLE 6-3   TESTS OF SIGNIFICANCE ON THE PARAMETERS IN
EQUATION (6-3)

Coefficient	Value	Standard Error	t-Test (value/standard deviation)
a	19.1	51.9	$.37 = (19.1/51.9)$
b_1	35.7	10.1	$3.55 = (35.7/10.1)$
b_2	10.9	.97	$11.17 = (10.9/.97)$

compare the computed t with the value from Table B, Appendix I, for $n - k$ degrees of freedom. Since the value from that table is $t_t = 1.753$, and the computed t-value t_c, for the intercept a, is 0.37 (which is smaller than the table value) this implies that a is not significantly different from 0. The values of the t-test computed for b_1 and b_2 are 3.55 and 11.17 respectively. In both cases these are larger than the t-test from the table ($t_t = 1.753$). Thus, for equation (6-3) it can be concluded that the coefficient a is not significantly different from 0, but that both b_1 and b_2 are significantly different from 0. The fact that the value of a, the constant term, is not significantly different from 0 indicates that there is no reason to assume that the value 19.1 is any more accurate than simply using the value of 0. Thus one may choose to rewrite the forecasting equation as

$$Y = 35.7X_1 + 10.9X_2.$$

It should be noted that while this procedure works when the constant term is not significant, it is not the recommended procedure when an independent variable is not significant. In this latter case, a new model excluding that independent variable must be fitted because in practice collinearity may exist, making refitting necessary.

In addition to significance tests, one can also construct confidence intervals around the regression equation (see Chapter 6 Appendix, Section 2). These intervals are based on the standard deviation of regression. The different types of confidence levels, their development, and their equations were explained in Chapter 5.

6/5   Transformations

It was indicated in Chapter 5 that a major advantage of regression analysis (either simple or multiple) is that it can describe many forms of nonlinear functions through the transformation of the original data into some linear form. In this section the use of such transformations will be expanded and illustrated by demonstrating the estimation of nonlinear forms, providing guidelines for recognizing when they exist in the data, and transforming them into linear forms.

6/5/1 Semilog Transformation

In business and economic series it is often true that a constant rate of growth prevails. This can happen with the sales of a company, GNP, consumption patterns, etc. For example, if the growth in GNP is 5% a year, it implies a compounded yearly rate of growth of 5%, a pattern that is exponential. Table 6-4 shows the revenues of an antipollution company (Lanard) which follows a typical exponential pattern of growth. (These data are graphed in Figure 6-1.) Regression can be used to estimate a forecasting equation for this nonlinear pattern and to find the exact rate of growth.

As Figure 6-1 shows, the pattern of actual revenues is far from linear. However, an exponential pattern can be described by the following form:

$$\text{revenues} = e^{a+bX}, \tag{6-6}$$

where X is time (1946 = 1, 1947 = 2, ..., 1975 = 30).

Equation (6-6) is equivalent to (6-7) except that the $\log_e$'s, natural or base e logarithms, have been taken off both sides:

$$\log_e (\text{revenues}) = a + bX[\log_e (e)], \tag{6-7}$$

$$\text{or} \quad Y = a + bX, \tag{6-8}$$

$$\log_e (\text{revenues}) = Y, \text{ and } \log_e(e) = 1.$$

Thus, applying a semilogarithm transformation to (6-6) gives the linear form required for a regression equation as described by (6-8).

Transforming the original sales figures to the corresponding natural logarithm ($\log_e$), a simple regression between the transformed revenue figures (column 4 of Table 6-4) and time, X, can be used to estimate the values of a and b. This is a typical simple regression model, and the resulting parameter values can be found to be

$$Y = 4.54 + .083X.$$

The computed F-test is 964 and $R^2 = .972$. Both t-tests are significant as shown in Table 6-5. To estimate the sales for 1975, this regression equation can be used as follows:

$$Y = 4.54 + .083(30) = 7.03.$$

However, since $\quad Y = \log_e (\text{revenues}),$

$$\text{revenues} = \text{antilog}_e (Y),$$

TABLE 6-4 REVENUES OF LANARD COMPANY

(1) Year	(2) Time Period X	(3) Sales (in $1000s)	(4) Natural Logarithm of Sales Y
1946	1	115.182	4.74652
1947	2	67.6176	4.21387
1948	3	104.482	4.64901
1949	4	126.062	4.83678
1950	5	154.174	5.03808
1951	6	174.861	5.16399
1952	7	193.988	5.26779
1953	8	186.968	5.23094
1954	9	223.893	5.41117
1955	10	251.291	5.52661
1956	11	261.78	5.5675
1957	12	232.868	5.45047
1958	13	266.132	5.58399
1959	14	308.049	5.73026
1960	15	283.709	5.64795
1961	16	324.676	5.78283
1962	17	422.233	6.04556
1963	18	387.273	5.95913
1964	19	448.078	6.10497
1965	20	517.24	6.24851
1966	21	558.97	6.3261
1967	22	588.052	6.37682
1968	23	581.686	6.36593
1969	24	685.469	6.5301
1970	25	744.772	6.61308
1971	26	792.753	6.67551
1972	27	826.263	6.71691
1973	28	900.894	6.80339
1974	29	1026.42	6.93383
1975	30	1093.86	6.99746

or revenues = antilog$_e$ (7.03) = 1130.

Similarly, the revenues for 1976 can be estimated as

$$Y = 4.54 + .083(33) = 7.279,$$

and revenues = antilog$_e$ (7.279) = 1480.

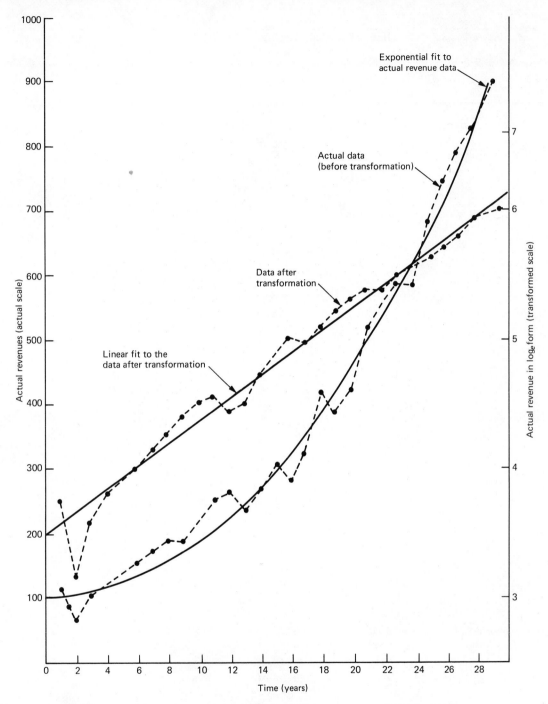

FIGURE 6-1 REVENUES OF LANARD COMPANY—LINEAR AND SEMILOG SCALES

TABLE 6-5   DEPENDENT VARIABLE, $\log_e$ (REVENUES), OF LANARD—
SEMILOG FIT

Variable	Regression Coefficient	Standard Error	t-Test
Constant (a)	4.53804	4.72203E-02	96.1035
Time (b)	8.25889E-02	2.65986E-03	31.0501

$R^2 = 0.972$	$R = 0.986$	F-Test $= 964.1$

$\log_e$ (sales) Actual	Predicted	Residuals	Percentage Error
4.74652	4.62063	.125889	2.65324E−02
4.21387	4.70322	−.489348	−.116128
4.64901	4.78581	−.136793	−2.94242E−02
4.83678	4.86839	−3.16192E−02	−6.53725E−03
5.03808	4.95098	8.70982E−02	.017288
5.16399	5.03357	.130421	2.52558E−02
5.26779	5.11616	.151633	2.87849E−02
5.23094	5.19875	3.21882E−02	6.15342E−03
5.41117	5.28134	.129829	2.39929E−02
5.52661	5.36393	.162682	2.94361E−02
5.5675	5.44652	.120987	.021731
5.45047	5.52911	−7.86356E−02	−1.44273E−02
5.58399	5.6117	−2.77035E−02	−4.96124E−03
5.73026	5.69428	3.59745E−02	6.27799E−03
5.64795	5.77687	−.128924	−2.28267E−02
5.78283	5.85946	−7.66358E−02	−1.32523E−02
6.04556	5.94205	.103505	1.71208E−02
5.95913	6.02464	−6.55107E−02	−1.09933E−02
6.10497	6.10723	−2.26188E−03	−3.70498E−04
6.24851	6.18982	5.86874E−02	9.39224E−03
6.3261	6.27241	5.36885E−02	8.48684E−03
6.37682	6.355	2.18198E−02	3.42174E−03
6.36593	6.43758	−7.16534E−02	−1.12558E−02
6.5301	6.52017	9.92990E−03	1.52063E−03
6.61308	6.60276	1.03154E−02	1.55985E−03
6.67551	6.68535	−9.84049E−03	−1.47412E−03
6.71691	6.76794	−5.10283E−02	−7.59608E−03
6.80339	6.85053	−.047142	−6.92920E−03
6.93383	6.93312	7.10964E−04	1.02536E−04
6.99746	7.01571	−1.82433E−02	−2.60713E−03

TABLE 6-6 SIMPLE LINEAR REGRESSION OF REVENUES AND TIME FOR LANARD

Variable	Coefficients	Standard Error	t-Test
Constant	−60.3383	32.5956	−1.85112
Actual sales	31.5265	1.83607	17.1707

$R^2 = 0.913$	$R = 0.956$	F-Test = 294.8

Actual	Predicted	Residuals	Percentage Error
115.182	−28.8117	143.994	1.25014
67.6176	2.7148	64.9028	.959851
104.482	34.2413	70.2404	.672275
126.062	65.7679	60.2944	.47829
154.174	97.2944	56.8797	.368932
174.861	128.821	46.0405	.263297
193.988	160.347	33.6401	.173414
186.968	191.874	−4.90576	−2.62385E − 02
223.893	223.401	.492798	2.20104E − 03
251.291	254.927	−3.63629	−1.44705E − 02
261.78	286.454	−24.6734	−9.42523E − 02
232.868	317.98	−85.1122	−.365496
266.132	349.507	−83.3746	−.313283
308.049	381.033	−72.9845	−.236925
283.709	412.56	−128.851	−.454166
324.676	444.086	−119.411	−.367785
422.233	475.613	−53.3802	−.126424
387.273	507.139	−119.867	−.309514
448.078	538.666	−90.5878	−.20217
517.24	570.192	−52.9526	−.102375
558.97	601.719	−42.749	−7.64782E − 02
588.052	633.245	−45.1932	−7.68524E − 02
581.686	664.772	−83.0857	−.142836
685.469	696.298	−10.8291	−1.57981E − 02
744.772	727.825	16.9474	2.27551E − 02
792.753	759.352	33.4012	4.21332E − 02
826.263	790.878	35.3848	4.28251E − 02
900.894	822.405	78.4894	8.71239E − 02
1026.42	853.931	172.485	.168046
1093.86	885.458	208.398	.190517

The parameter b in $Y = a + bX$ is the slope of the line and indicates the number of units increase in Y that occurs with a one-unit increase in X. On the other hand, b in $Y = e^{a + bX}$ approximates the percentage growth in Y caused by a one-unit increase in X. Thus .083 indicates that the revenues of Lanard have been growing about 8.3% a year on the average (the actual growth is $8.3 + (8.3)^2/2 + (8.3)^3/6 = .0865$).

A natural question arising from the above examples is how to choose the most appropriate transformation to apply to the original data from the very large number of nonlinear functions available. One approach can be illustrated by assuming that a regression between the actual revenues of Lanard and time is run without any transformation. The result is shown in Table 6-6. What is interesting to note is the pattern in the residuals and the percentage error. About one-fourth of the residuals have a positive sign in the beginning, followed by about half with a negative sign, and finally the last quarter again have a positive sign. This shows a definite nonrandom pattern, which implies that the actual data are above the regression line in the beginning, then below, and finally above again. This pattern is a clear indication that the linear form does not fit the data well. Another indication is the percentage error, which is initially large, becomes smaller, changes sign, then rises, declines, and finally rises again. (Still another indication of the inappropriateness of a linear model to describe the data is given by the Durbin-Watson test, which will be discussed in the Chapter 6 Appendix, Section 3.)

From Figure 6-2, it can be seen that if the actual data is an exponential

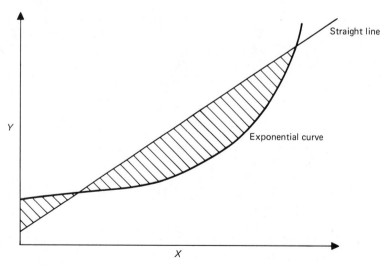

FIGURE 6-2 LINEAR APPROXIMATION OF EXPONENTIAL PATTERN

curve, describing it by using a straight line will give the type of error pattern and percentage errors observed in Table 6-6. In order to identify the best transformation, several possible functional forms can be plotted, previous knowledge can be applied, or the residuals can be examined. Some combination of these procedures is usually best for determining what pattern remains in the residuals once a linear form has been fitted to the data.

6/5/2 Polynomial Transformations

To further illustrate the use of nonlinear functions, the production run cost figures of the Carlisle Corporation (Table 6-7) can be examined to find the functional relationship between the total cost and the number of units produced. Economic theory would suggest that cost functions are either linear

TABLE 6-7 PRODUCTION COSTS FOR CARLISLE

Number of Units Produced (in 1000s) X_1	Total Cost of Production (in $1000s) Y	Number of Units Produced (in 1000s) X_1	Total Cost of Production (in $1000s) Y
7.3865	2094.15	7.89939	2295.63
11.1283	3015.36	11.3904	3201.87
9.16186	2407.32	10.5926	2789.65
6.21721	2045.15	11.9572	3488.61
13.2652	4157.27	3.44103	2000.95
9.87053	2751.86	9.45951	2648.15
8.21257	2312.08	9.88421	2732.38
7.38249	2250.33	15.4036	5841.19
7.93566	2264.81	4.68518	1968.65
1.92551	2054.94	3.9589	2001.01
2.6833	2078.63	7.19952	2125.95
11.4996	3271.48	15.8771	6317.62
8.09594	2199.07	8.96216	2393.23
5.565	1984.25	14.0068	4743.59
7.79677	2209.25	10.2914	2843.17
10.7661	3032.66	6.09008	2026.48
13.9806	4634.34	10.2778	2882.33
3.33987	2101.53	15.3664	5728.24

or cubic. Both linear regression with the actual data and with the cubic transformation can be used to determine which form best fits the actual cost figures. The linear cost function is straightforward—the dependent variable is cost, and the independent variable is number of units produced. The resulting regression is

$$\text{cost} = 420.09 + 277.96X, \qquad (6\text{-}9)$$

where X is the number of units produced.

As shown in Table 6-8, the computed F-test is 105.7, the t-test is 1.6, the t-test$_b$ is 10.28, and $r^2 = .757$.

The next step is to compare the results with the cubic fit to decide which

TABLE 6-8   LINEAR FIT TO THE CARLISLE COST DATA OF TABLE 6-7

Regression number 1 : Dependent variable is total cost.

Variable	Coefficients	Standard Error	t-Test
Constant	420.087	261.512	1.60638
Linear term: X_1	277.964	27.0341	10.282

$R^2 = 0.757$	$R = 0.870$	$F\text{-Test} = 105.7$

Actual	Predicted	Residuals	Percentage Error
2094.15	2473.27	−379.112	−.181034
3015.36	3513.34	−497.977	−.165146
2407.32	2966.75	−559.429	−.232386
2045.15	2148.25	−103.099	−5.04114E − 02
4157.27	4107.32	49.9497	.012015
2751.86	3163.74	−411.872	−.14967
2312.08	2702.88	−390.804	−.169027
2250.33	2472.15	−221.817	−9.85707E − 02
2264.81	2625.91	−361.105	−.159442
2054.94	955.308	1099.63	.535115
2078.63	1165.95	912.683	.439079
3271.48	3616.57	−345.092	−.105485
2199.07	2670.46	−471.396	−.214362
1984.25	1966.96	17.2888	8.71304E − 03
2209.25	2587.31	−378.055	−.171123
3032.66	3412.67	−380.006	−.125304

TABLE 6-8 Continued

Actual	Predicted	Residuals	Percentage Error
4634.34	4306.19	328.151	7.08087E − 02
2101.53	1348.45	753.077	.358347
2295.63	2615.83	−320.205	−.139485
3201.87	3586.19	−384.319	−.120029
2789.65	3364.45	−574.802	−.206048
3488.61	3743.76	−255.146	−7.31367E − 02
2000.95	1376.57	624.378	.312041
2648.15	3049.49	−401.339	−.151555
2732.38	3167.54	−435.161	−.159261
5841.19	4701.73	1139.47	.195074
1968.65	1722.4	246.25	.125086
2001.01	1520.52	480.492	.240125
2125.95	2421.29	−295.341	−.138922
6317.62	4833.34	1484.28	.234943
2393.23	2911.24	−518.016	−.216451
4743.59	4313.47	430.125	.090675
2843.17	3280.72	−437.549	−.153895
2026.48	2112.91	−86.427	−4.26488E − 02
2882.33	3276.93	−394.599	−.136903
5728.24	4691.38	1036.87	.18101

Durbin-Watson Statistic = 2.00646.

of the two is better. This comparison can be made using the F-test or R^2 values for each regression model. The cubic form is

$$\text{cost} = a + b_1X_1 + b_2X_1{}^2 + b_3X_1{}^3. \tag{6-10}$$

Letting $\quad X_2 = X_1{}^2$

and $\quad X_3 = X_1{}^3,$

equation (6-10) becomes

$$\text{cost} = a + b_1X_1 + b_2X_2 + b_3X_3. \tag{6-11}$$

Equation (6-11) is a linear function based on the transformation of $X_1{}^2$ and $X_1{}^3$ of (6-10). These values are given in Table 6-9 and by defining as X_2

TABLE 6-9 CARLISLE COST DATA TRANSFORMED FOR CUBIC FIT

Total Cost	X_1	$X_2 = X_1^2$	$X_3 = X_1^3$
2094.15	7.3865	54.5604	403.01
3015.36	11.1283	123.838	1378.1
2407.32	9.16186	83.9396	769.043
2045.15	6.21721	38.6536	240.318
4157.27	13.2652	175.965	2334.2
2751.86	9.87053	97.4274	961.66
2312.08	8.21257	67.4462	553.907
2250.33	7.38249	54.5011	402.354
2264.81	7.93566	62.9747	499.746
2054.94	1.92551	3.70757	7.13895
2078.63	2.6833	7.20009	19.32
3271.48	11.4996	132.242	1520.73
2199.07	8.09594	65.5442	530.642
1984.25	5.565	30.9693	172.344
2209.25	7.79677	60.7896	473.962
3032.66	10.7661	115.908	1247.88
4634.34	13.9806	195.457	2732.61
2101.53	3.33987	11.1548	37.2555
2295.63	7.89939	62.4004	492.926
3201.87	11.3904	129.74	1477.79
2789.65	10.5926	112.204	1188.53
2488.61	11.9572	142.975	1709.58
2000.95	3.44103	11.8407	40.7442
2648.15	9.45951	89.4824	846.46
2732.38	9.88421	97.6977	965.665
5841.19	15.4036	237.271	3654.82
1968.65	4.68518	21.9509	102.844
2001.01	3.9589	15.6729	62.0475
2125.95	7.19952	51.833	373.173
6317.62	15.8771	252.082	4002.33
2393.23	8.96216	80.3203	719.843
4743.59	14.0068	196.19	2748
2843.17	10.2914	105.912	1089.99
2026.48	6.09008	37.0891	225.875
2882.33	10.2778	105.632	1085.66
5728.24	15.3664	236.125	3628.38

TABLE 6-10 LINEAR FIT TO THE CARLISLE COST DATA OF TABLE 6-9 (LINEAR, QUADRATIC, AND CUBIC TERMS INCLUDED)

Variable	Coefficients	Standard Error	t-Test
Constant	2156.56	98.2032	21.9602
Linear: X_1	−32.7729	41.3519	−.792537
Quadratic: X_2	−7.37235	5.07644	−1.45227
Cubic: X_3	1.61959	.185994	8.70778

$R^2 = 0.998$	$R = 0.999$	F-Test = 42382.4

Actual	Predicted	Residuals	Percentage Error
2094.15	2164.96	−70.8038	$-3.38102E-02$
3015.36	3110.84	−95.479	$-3.16642E-02$
2407.32	2483.	−75.6816	$-3.14381E-02$
2045.15	2057.05	−11.9075	$-5.82231E-03$
4157.27	4205.	−47.7295	−.011481
2751.86	2672.3	79.5615	$2.89119E-02$
2312.08	2287.28	24.8021	$1.07272E-02$
2250.33	2164.46	85.8704	$3.81589E-02$
2264.81	2241.6	23.2079	$1.02472E-02$
2054.94	2077.69	−22.7493	$-1.10705E-02$
2078.63	2046.83	31.7989	.015298
3271.48	3267.71	3.76123	$1.14970E-03$
2199.07	2267.44	−68.3743	$-3.10924E-02$
1984.25	2024.99	−40.7455	$-2.05345E-02$
2209.25	2220.5	−11.2509	$-5.09261E-03$
3032.66	2970.26	62.3972	$2.05751E-02$
4634.34	4683.11	−48.7725	$-1.05241E-02$
2101.53	2025.21	76.3227	$3.63177E-02$
2295.63	2235.98	59.6519	.025985
3201.87	3220.19	−18.314	$-5.71976E-03$
2789.65	2907.14	−117.49	$-4.21165E-02$
3488.61	3479.45	9.16309	$2.62657E-03$
2000.95	2022.48	−21.537	$-1.07634E-02$
2648.15	2557.77	90.3799	$3.41294E-02$
2732.38	2676.35	56.0312	$2.05064E-02$
5841.19	5821.82	19.3721	$3.31646E-03$

TABLE 6-10 Continued

Actual	Predicted	Residuals	Percentage Error
1968.65	2007.75	−39.1026	−1.98627E − 02
2001.01	2011.76	−10.7516	−5.37307E − 03
2125.95	2142.87	−16.9177	−7.95772E − 03
6317.62	6259.92	57.6982	9.13290E − 03
2393.23	2436.55	−43.3218	−1.81018E − 02
4743.59	4701.77	41.8223	8.81658E − 03
2843.17	2803.79	39.3779	.01385
2026.48	2049.36	−22.8828	−1.12919E − 02
2882.33	2799.3	83.0303	2.88066E − 02
5728.24	5788.66	−60.415	−1.05469E − 02

and X_3 they can be linearly related to the total dollar cost. The regression results for this transformed data are shown in Table 6-10. The regression equation there is

$$\text{cost} = 2156.56 - 32.77X_1 - 7.37X_2 + 1.62X_3.$$

However, the t-test of X_1 is $-.793$, which is not significant, suggesting that X_1 has little influence on costs in this model and can therefore be dropped. After dropping X_1, the regression model can be reestimated as shown in Table 6-11, to obtain

$$\text{cost} = 2081.77 - 11.34X_2 + 1.76X_3.$$

This regression has an R^2 of .998, an F-test of 28598.2, and all the t-tests are significant. The R^2 of the cubic fit explains 99.8% of the total variations in cost, while that of the linear fit explains only 91.3%. This indicates that the cubic fit is better for forecasting future costs.

To estimate the cost of 10,000 units using the regression in Table 6-11 gives

$$\text{cost} = 2081.77 - 11.34(10^2) + 1.76(10^3)$$

$$= 2081.77 - 11.34(100) + 1.76(1000)$$

$$= \$2,707,770.$$

The choice of the appropriate transformation was aided in this case by economic theory. Oftentimes, higher order polynomials are also estimated by linear regression analysis. Several other nonlinear forms that are important in economic and management applications are described in the remainder of this section.

TABLE 6-11 LINEAR FIT TO THE CARLISLE COST DATA OF TABLE 6-9 EXCLUDING X_1 (QUADRATIC AND CUBIC TERMS ONLY)

Variable	Coefficients	Standard Error	t-Test
Constant	2081.77	27.0072	77.082
Quadratic: X_2	−11.3394	.839461	−13.5079
Cubic: X_3	1.761	5.21765E-02	33.7508

$R^2 = 0.998$ $\qquad$ $R = 0.999$ $\qquad$ F-Test = 28598.2

Actual	Predicted	Residuals	Percentage Error
2094.15	2172.79	−78.6301	−3.75474E−02
3015.36	3104.35	−88.9888	−2.95118E−02
2407.32	2484.22	−76.9019	−.031945
2045.15	2066.66	−21.5096	−1.05174E−02
4157.27	4196.95	−39.6807	−9.54488E−03
2751.86	2670.48	81.3857	2.95748E−02
2312.08	2292.39	19.6844	8.51374E−03
2250.33	2172.3	78.0334	3.46764E−02
2264.81	2247.72	17.085	7.54367E−03
2054.94	2052.3	2.64033	1.28487E−03
2078.63	2034.14	44.4859	2.14016E−02
3271.48	3260.23	11.2495	3.43867E−03
2199.07	2272.99	−73.9253	−3.36166E−02
1984.25	2034.09	−49.8455	−2.51206E−02
2209.25	2227.1	−17.8441	−.008077
3032.66	2964.95	67.7144	2.23284E−02
4634.34	4677.52	−43.1787	−9.31712E−03
2101.53	2020.88	80.644	.038374
2295.63	2242.22	53.4039	2.32633E−02
3201.87	3212.97	−11.0957	−3.46538E−03
2789.65	2902.44	−112.793	−4.04328E−02
3488.61	3471.08	17.5303	.005025
2000.95	2019.25	−18.3031	−9.14720E−03
2648.15	2557.7	90.4456	3.41543E−02
2732.38	2674.47	57.9128	.021195
5841.19	5827.39	13.8008	2.36266E−03
1968.65	2013.96	−45.3167	−2.30192E−02
2001.01	2013.31	−12.2997	−6.14674E−03

TABLE 6-11   Continued

Actual	Predicted	Residuals	Percentage Error
2125.95	2151.17	−25.2162	−1.18611E−02
6317.62	6271.39	46.2275	7.31724E−03
2393.23	2438.62	−45.3979	−1.89693E−02
4743.59	4696.31	47.2891	9.96904E−03
2843.17	2800.24	42.9246	1.50974E−02
2026.48	2058.96	−32.4832	−1.60293E−02
2882.33	2795.81	86.5229	3.00184E−02
5728.24	5793.82	−65.5732	−1.14474E−02

6/5/3   Logarithmic Transformation

If the function to be estimated is of the form $Z = AB^X$ (see Figure 6-3), taking logs of both sides gives

$$\log Z = \log A + X \log B. \tag{6-12}$$

Letting $Y = \log Z$,

$a = \log A$,

$b = \log B$,

equation (6-12) becomes

$$Y = a + bX. \tag{6-13}$$

As in the Lanard example of Table 6-4, the log of the dependent variable can be regressed against the values of X to obtain the values of a and b. The adjustments then needed to apply the results can be illustrated by assuming that the following regression coefficients have been obtained:

$$a = 0.301, \qquad b = -1.4332.$$

Thus, $Y = 0.301 - 1.4332X$,

since $a = \log A$

and $b = \log B$.

Thus $A = \text{antilog}(a) = \text{antilog}(0.301) = 2.0$,

$B = \text{antilog}(b) = \text{antilog}(-1.4332) = .038$,

and $\qquad Y = 2.0 + .038X.$

So if $\qquad X = 10,$

$\qquad Y = 2 + .038(10) = 2.38.$

And since $\qquad Y = \log Z,$

$\qquad Z = \text{antilog}\,(Y) = \text{antilog}\,(2.38) = 239.9.$

Logarithmic transformations are particularly useful because the slope of the transformed function (6-13) can be used to approximate the growth rate and estimate elasticities (the percentage change in Y caused by a percentage change in X). Both are extremely useful in making policy decisions.

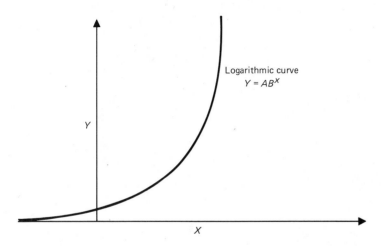

Logarithmic curve
$Y = AB^X$

FIGURE 6-3 GRAPH OF LOGARITHMIC CURVE

6/5/4 Reciprocal Transformation

In order to estimate the total per unit cost, a reciprocal transformation (see Figure 6-4) can be used as shown in equation (6-14):

$$Y = a + \frac{b}{W}, \qquad\qquad (6\text{-}14)$$

where Y is the per unit total cost and W is the number of units products.

Letting $\quad X = \dfrac{1}{W},\quad$ equation (6-14) becomes

$\qquad Y = a + bX.$

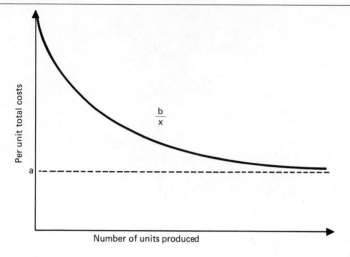

FIGURE 6-4 GRAPH OF A RECIPROCAL RELATIONSHIP

As an illustration of such a transformation, when

$$a = 1.12 \quad \text{and} \quad b = 150,$$

and the objective is to estimate the per unit total cost for 50 units, the following is obtained:

$$Y = 1.12 + 150\left(\frac{1}{50}\right) = 4.12.$$

In this instance, a is the per unit variable cost, while b is the fixed cost for a given level of production.

6/5/5 Double (Reciprocal and Logarithmic) Transformations (S-Curve)

The sales of some products follow an S-curve pattern. This pattern implies a slow start, a steep growth in sales, then a long period of saturation like that illustrated in Table 6-12 and Figure 6-5.

One functional form of an S-curve of this type is

$$Z = e^{a - (b/t)} \tag{6-15}$$

Taking the log of both sides, this becomes

$$\log_e Z = a - \frac{b}{t}$$

or $\quad \log_e Z = a - bX,$

where $\quad X = \dfrac{1}{t}.$

Finally $\quad Y = a - bX,$ $\hfill$ (6-16)

where $\quad Y = \log_e Z.$

Equation (6-16) is of linear form so the values of a and b can be estimated using regression.

As an illustration of the S-curve transformation, Table 6-12 shows the data and the transformed values for Universal's TV sales. Table 6-13 shows the

TABLE 6-12   UNIVERSAL'S SALES OF COLOR TELEVISIONS

Time	Sales	1/Time	$\log_e$ (Sales)
1	.023	1	−3.77226
2	.157	.5	−1.85151
3	.329	.333333	−1.1117
4	.48	.25	−.733969
5	1.205	.2	.186479
6	1.748	.166667	.558472
7	1.996	.142857	.691145
8	2.509	.125	.919884
9	2.366	.111111	.861201
10	2.94	.1	1.07841
11	2.8714	9.09091E−02	1.0548
12	2.9346	8.33333E−02	1.07657
13	3.1346	7.69231E−02	1.1425
14	3.24	7.14286E−02	1.17557
15	3.148	6.66667E−02	1.14677
16	3.522	.0625	1.25903
17	3.54	5.88235E−02	1.26413
18	3.31	5.55556E−02	1.19695
19	3.547	5.26316E−02	1.2661
20	3.374	.05	1.2161
21	3.3745	.047619	1.21625
22	3.401	4.54545E−02	1.22407
23	3.6971	4.34783E−02	1.30755
24	3.493	4.16667E−02	1.25076

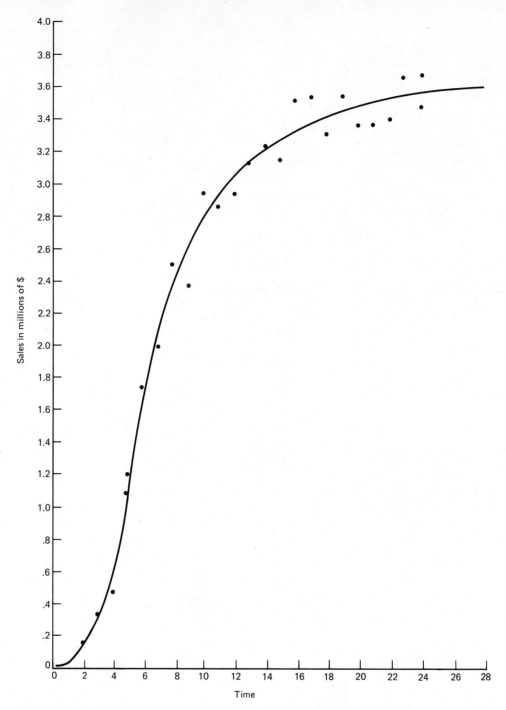

FIGURE 6-5 GRAPH OF UNIVERSAL'S COLOR TV SALES FROM
TABLE 6-12—S-CURVE

regression results for the model (6-16), where Y is (log$_e$ sales) and X is $1/t$. The R^2 for this regression is .976 and both the F- and t-tests are significant. Thus for forecasting purposes,

$$Y = e^{1.478-(5.786/t)} \qquad (6\text{-}17)$$

Equation (6-17) is a nonlinear equation that can be used for predicting the long-term behavior of products or technologies. In period 30, for example, Y(sales) will be

$$Y = e^{1.478-(5.786/30)}$$

$$= 3.613.$$

TABLE 6-13 REGRESSION MODEL FOR TRANSFORMED S-CURVE OF TABLE 6-12

Variable	Mean	Standard Deviation	Correlation Coefficients	
			3	4
3	.157332	.209559	1.000	-.976
4	.567637	1.24234	-.976	1.000

Variable	Coefficient	Standard Error	t-Test
Constant	1.478	7.11033E − 02	20.7867
(3) 1/time	-5.78627	.275028	-21.0389

$R^2 = 0.953$	$R = 0.976$	F-Test $= 442.6$

6/6 The Assumptions of Regression Analysis

Four basic assumptions must be met before the correctness of the results of regression analysis is verified:

1. linearity
2. independence of residuals
3. homoscedasticity
4. normality of residuals

In the previous section it was shown that nonlinear functions can be transformed into linear forms and thus the assumption of linearity is not as restricting as it often seems. However, it should be noted that there is *no* way of applying regression analysis if the function *cannot* be transformed into a linear form. The last assumption (normality of residuals) is also not very restricting because residuals are the outcome of a large number of unimportant factors that influence the dependent variable only slightly (otherwise they should have been included in the regression equation). On average, their influence will be canceled out. This is exactly the pattern described by a normal curve. Thus, it is usually valid to assume that the error term, u, is normally distributed. If the number of observations is greater than 30 and if the other assumptions are met, the residuals will be normally distributed. When the assumption of normality of residuals is in question, no appropriate statistical tests are available; however, the residuals can be plotted to determine whether they are approximately normally distributed and their range (largest minus smallest value) can be computed to determine whether it is close to 6.0, the range expected for a normal distribution.

To determine the validity of the other two assumptions, a more detailed analysis is required. Their violation can have serious consequences because they usually provide clues as to 1) the most appropriate functional form, and 2) the optimal number of variables to be included in the regression equation.

6/6/1 Independence of Residuals

Violation of the assumption of independence of residuals implies that there is some serial correlation (autocorrelation) among successive residuals. That is, e_t is not independent of $e_{t-1} \ldots, e_{t-i+1} \ldots, e_{t+1}, e_{t+2}, \ldots, e_{t+n}$. Lack of independence does not affect the values of the estimated parameters, but can affect their estimated variances. Lack of independence in the residuals implies that R^2, the F-test or the t-tests will be larger or smaller if the autocorrelation is positive and larger if it is negative.

Autocorrelation can result from 1) the incorrect specification (the inclusion of a "nonoptimal" number of variables), which causes a dependence among the independent variables, or 2) the incorrect functional form, or 3) strong trends in the variables. Autocorrelation can be seen visually by plotting the residuals. (If they are not randomly distributed but have some pattern, autocorrelation is implied.) There is also a statistical test (Durbin-Watson, or D-W test) that can be used to test for the existence of autocorrelation. If the computed value of the D-W test is between $D\text{-}W_u$ and $4 - (D\text{-}W_u)$ (see Chapter 6 Appendix, Section 3) it can be concluded that there is no autocorrelation. The exact limits of the D-W tests can be read from a Durbin-Watson table (see Table D, Appendix I) of values as shown in the chapter appendix, Section 3. Approximate limits for $D\text{-}W_u$ and $4 - (D\text{-}W_u)$ are 1.5 to 2.5 respectively.

The autocorrelation of the residuals can be corrected by taking first differences, introducing additional variables, or changing the functional form. For example, the computed D-W statistic of the linear fit shown in Table 6-6 is .219. When the functional form was correctly specified as in Table 6.5, the D-W value is 2.006. Since the former value is outside $D\text{-}W_u$ and $4 - (D\text{-}W_u)$, and the latter is inside, the change in functional form does eliminate autocorrelation in the residuals. If neither a new variable nor a change of the functional form can eliminate autocorrelation among the residuals, then the method of first differences can be used.

The following example illustrates the method of first differences. Suppose there are five observations for three variables as shown below.

Y	X_1	X_2
35	5	10
39	8	12
26	6	11
45	4	12
40	7	14

The first difference of the above set of data is obtained by subtracting the first observation (all variables) from the second, the second from the third, and so on. The result is as follows:

4	3	2
−13	−2	−1
19	−2	1
−5	3	2

It should be observed that the new data set has $n - 1$ observations, since one observation is lost in the process of differencing. Even though in the majority of cases one of the three solutions will correct the existence of autocorrelation, it sometimes may be necessary to go to more complicated procedures (see Johnson 1972, pp. 243–66). It should be reemphasized that a regression equation whose residuals are not independent may have larger or smaller F-test, t-test, R^2, standard deviations, and standard error compared to a nonautocorrelated series.

6/6/2 Constant Variance

If the residuals are not evenly distributed around the regression line for the entire range of observations, the assumption of constancy of variance, which is known as *homoscedasticity*, is violated. Figure 6-6 gives a graphic illustration

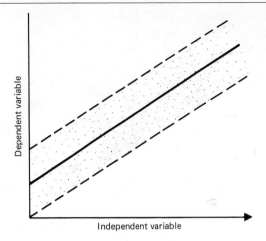

FIGURE 6-6 CONSTANT VARIANCE IN THE RESIDUALS
(HOMOSCEDASTICITY)

of the meaning of constant variance, and Figures 6-7 and 6-8 show two cases of regression equations with nonconstant variances (*heteroscedasticity*).

Heteroscedasticity can be caused by incorrect specification or by the use of the wrong functional form. It can be detected by examining the percentage errors of the regression model. (See, for example, Tables 6-5 and 6-6). If the percentage errors have approximately the same magnitude for the entire range of

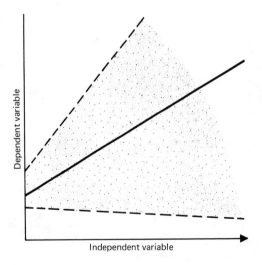

FIGURE 6-7 HETEROSCEDASTIC VARIANCE IN THE RESIDUALS

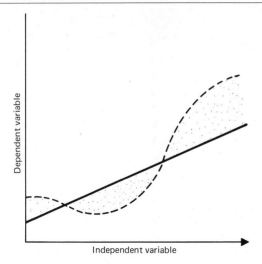

FIGURE 6-8 HETEROSCEDASTIC VARIANCE AND PATTERN IN
THE RESIDUALS

observations, no heteroscedasticity is implied. If that is not the case it is necessary
either to introduce or to eliminate some variables or to introduce some transformation so that the percentage errors will be uniform across all observations.

It is often the case that both autocorrelation and heteroscedasticity exist
concurrently as in Figure 6-8. In such a case the D-W test can provide an
indication of heteroscedasticity. However, one problem can exist without the
other, which necessitates examination of the percentage errors in addition to
using the D-W test.

6/7 Multicollinearity

Multicollinearity is a computational problem that develops when two or
more of the independent variables are highly correlated. The result is a near
singular (close to zero) matrix that has the effect of trying to divide a number
by an extremely small absolute quantity (close to zero). (See the appendix to
this chapter.) The result of the division is an extremely large number that the
computer cannot handle. If multicollinearity exists, the regression results can be
highly erroneous, causing serious errors in forecasting. Fortunately it is easy to
detect and correct multicollinearity.

Multicollinearity is indicated when one or more of the t-tests are small (not
significant) *and* the values of R^2 or the F-test are very large. If this is the case,

the correlation matrix must be examined and all but one of the highly correlated independent variables must be removed. (As a general rule, a simple correlation coefficient of more than about .7 between any two independent variables can cause multicollinearity problems.) Multicollinearity can be also detected if the percentage of variation explained by some variable is negative. It is possible to have highly correlated independent variables and still have a regression equation without multicollinearity problems. As long as all t-tests are significant—even though some independent variables are highly correlated—there is no serious multicollinearity. For example, Table 6-14 shows the simple correlation matrix of the variables in Table 6-9. The correlation between the two independent variables 3 and 4 is .985, but all t-tests in Table 6-11 are significant indicating that there is no problem of multicollinearity. Furthermore, $R = .999$, which is greater than .985, and using the rule of thumb that no serious multicollinearity is present when $R > r_m$ suggests that no multicollinearity exists for the data of Table 6-11.

TABLE 6-14 CORRELATION COEFFICIENTS—LINEAR, QUADRATIC, AND CUBIC TERMS

Terms	Variable	Variables			
		2	3	4	1
Linear	2	1.000	.973	.921	.870
Quadratic	3	.973	1.000	.985	.958
Cubic	4	.921	.985	1.000	.992
Total cost	1	.870	.958	.992	1.000

Multicollinearity is a frequent problem in economic and business data because of the high correlation with time among the different factors such as population, GNP, personal disposable income (PDI), sales, inventories, profits, costs, etc. It is important to recognize the existence of multicollinearity while collecting data; otherwise a large part of the data could not be used because of the high correlation existing among the different variables. Dealing with economic or business data, therefore, presents an interesting problem. One can usually find variables that are highly correlated among themselves and thus of limited value for multiple regression, or others with very little correlation, which are also of limited value for multiple regression. Both provide only limited information, since the former are similar, and the latter do not relate with each other. The independent variables most needed are those with a middle range of correlations between them, but these are the hardest to find.

6/8 Model Specification

Suppose one wants to estimate the sales of Company XYZ. The first step is to develop a model expressing sales as a function of a number of factors. A talk with the marketing manager and the sales vice-president indicates that the most influential factors affecting the sales of the company are as shown in the following model:

> sales = f(PDI, dealers allowances, prices, R&D, capital investments,
>   advertising, sales expenses, total industry advertising,
>   random effects).

The second step is to collect data for each of the eight independent variables and the dependent variable. Table 6-15 presents semiannual data for each of these variables for the period 1957 through 1975.

The third step is to run the data in a multiple regression program to verify the existence of the above relationship and estimate the values of its parameters.

Table 6-16 shows the results for this regression. It can be seen that not all factors are significant. The computed t-tests for variables 2, 4, 7, and 8 are lower than the corresponding value from Table B of Appendix I, $t_t = 1.699$ (for a 95% confidence level and 29 d.f.).

This implies either a lack of relationship between variables 2, 4, 7, and 8 and sales or multicollinearity between independent variables since both R^2 and the F-test are large.

To make sure that multicollinearity does not exist, one must examine the simple correlation matrix in Table 6-17. As this table shows, variables 1 and 7 are highly correlated (.903), and thus one of them must be excluded. It is preferable to omit variable 7 because its correlation with the dependent variable, 9, is smaller (.667) than that between 1 and 9 (.742). The simple correlation matrix also shows that variables 2 and 4 might well be omitted from the regression equation because their correlations with the dependent variable (.009 and .031 respectively) are too small to represent a significant contribution in the results.*

Next, a new regression model can be fitted using 1, 3, 5, 6, 8 as the independent variables. However, even this run results in one variable, 8, not being significant as shown in Table 6-18. The t-test for this variable, -1.48, is smaller than the necessary t-test from Table B, Appendix I, 1.699.

Omitting variable 8 and fitting the revised regression model gives t-tests that are all significant as shown in Table 6-19. The F-test $= 471.2$ is highly significant, since the corresponding F-test from Table C of Appendix I is 2.69

---

* It is possible that the effect of other variables will mask the correlation of an independent variable with the dependent variable. In such cases it may be of benefit to include that variable in the regression model as long as its t-test is significant.

TABLE 6-15 SALES AND RELATED DATA FOR COMPANY XYZ (SEMIANNUAL)

	(1) PDI (in $1,000,000s)	(2) Dealers Allowances (in $1,000,000s)	(3) Price (in $1000s)	(4) R&D Budget (in $1000s)	(5) Capital Investments (in $1000s)	(6) Adver- tising (in $1000s)	(7) Sales Expenses (in $1000s)	(8) Total Industry Advertising Budget (in $1000s)	(9) Sales (in $1000s)
1957	398	138	56.2058	12.1124	49.895	76.8621	228.8	98.2057	5540.39
	369	118	59.0443	9.33042	16.5959	88.8056	177.45	224.953	5439.04
1958	268	129	56.7236	28.7481	89.1829	51.2972	166.4	263.032	4290.
	484	111	57.8627	12.8916	106.738	39.6473	258.05	320.928	5502.34
1959	394	146	59.1178	13.3815	142.552	51.6517	209.3	406.989	4871.77
	332	140	60.1113	11.0859	61.2876	20.5476	180.05	246.996	4708.08
1960	336	136	59.8398	24.9579	−30.3855	40.1534	213.2	328.436	4627.81
	383	104	60.0523	20.8096	−44.5867	31.6456	200.85	298.456	4110.24
1961	285	105	63.1415	8.48533	−28.3735	12.457	176.15	218.11	4122.69
	277	135	62.3026	10.7301	75.7238	68.3076	174.85	410.467	4842.25
1962	456	128	64.922	21.8743	144.03	52.4536	252.85	93.0063	5740.65
	355	131	64.8577	23.5062	112.904	76.6778	208.	307.226	5094.1
1963	364	120	63.5919	13.894	128.347	96.0677	195.	106.792	5383.2
	320	147	65.6145	14.8659	10.097	47.9795	154.05	304.921	4888.17
1964	311	143	67.0228	22.494	−24.7606	27.2319	180.7	59.6123	4033.13
	362	145	66.9049	23.3698	116.748	72.6681	219.7	238.986	4941.96
1965	408	131	66.1843	13.0354	120.406	62.3129	234.65	141.074	5312.8
	433	124	67.8651	8.03304	121.823	24.7122	258.05	290.832	5139.87
1966	359	106	68.8892	27.0486	71.0553	73.9126	196.3	413.636	4397.36
	476	138	71.4177	18.2208	−4.18678	63.2737	278.85	206.454	5149.47
1967	415	148	69.2775	7.74224	−46.9355	28.6762	207.35	79.5662	5150.83
	420	136	69.7334	10.1361	7.62145	91.3635	213.2	428.982	4989.02
1968	536	111	73.1628	27.3709	127.509	74.0169	296.4	273.072	5926.86
	432	152	73.365	15.5281	−49.5742	16.1628	245.05	309.422	4703.88
1969	436	123	73.05	32.4918	100.098	42.9984	275.6	280.139	5365.59
	415	119	74.9102	19.7127	−40.1857	41.1346	211.25	314.548	4630.09
1970	462	112	73.2007	14.8358	68.1537	92.518	282.75	212.058	5711.86
	429	125	74.1615	11.3694	87.963	83.287	217.75	118.065	5095.48
1971	517	142	74.2838	26.751	27.0888	74.8921	306.8	344.553	6124.37
	328	123	77.1409	19.6038	59.3436	87.5103	210.6	140.872	4787.34
1972	418	135	78.591	34.6881	141.969	74.4712	269.75	82.8552	5035.62
	515	120	77.0938	23.202	126.42	21.2711	328.25	398.425	5288.01
1973	412	149	78.2313	35.7396	29.5587	26.4941	258.05	124.027	4647.01
	455	126	77.9296	21.5891	18.0075	94.6311	232.7	117.911	5315.63
1974	554	138	81.0394	19.5692	42.3523	92.5448	323.7	161.25	6180.06
	441	120	79.8485	15.5037	−21.5585	50.048	267.15	405.088	4800.97
1975	417	120	80.6394	34.9238	148.45	83.1803	257.4	110.74	5512.13
	461	132	82.2843	26.5496	−17.5842	91.2214	266.5	170.392	5272.21

TABLE 6-16 REGRESSION RESULTS FOR TABLE 6-15 (DEPENDENT VARIABLE IS 9—SALES)

Variable	Coefficients	Standard Error	t-Tests
Constant	2926.09	612.386	4.77817
1 (PDI)	3.80918	1.5289	2.49146
2 (dealers allowances)	5.06469	3.13835	1.61381
3 (price)	−17.1261	7.99831	−2.14121
4 (R&D)	−10.2588	6.27417	−1.63509
5 (capital investments)	1.51548	.746549	2.02998
6 (advertising)	8.05355	1.77837	4.52861
7 (sales expenses)	3.86459	2.70223	1.43015
8 (total industry advertising)	−.539407	.377653	−1.42831

$R^2 = 0.912$ F-Test = 1144.
Standard deviation of estimate = 243.247   Durbin-Watson statistic = 2.39146

TABLE 6-17 SIMPLE CORRELATION MATRIX—COMPANY XYZ

Variable	\multicolumn{9}{c}{Correlation Coefficients}

Variable	1	2	3	4	5	6	7	8	9
1	1.000	−.069	.555	.160	.131	.199	.903	−.020	.742
2	−.069	1.000	.028	.005	−.149	−.119	−.051	−.145	.009
3	.555	.028	1.000	.438	−.063	.252	.630	−.182	.285
4	.160	.005	.438	1.000	.217	.102	.361	−.128	.031
5	.131	−.149	−.063	.217	1.000	.277	.228	−.063	.410
6	.199	−.119	.252	.102	.277	1.000	.132	−.197	.526
7	.903	−.051	.630	.361	.228	.132	1.000	−.019	.667
8	−.020	−.145	−.182	−.128	−.063	−.197	−.019	1.000	−.175
9	.742	.009	.285	.031	.410	.526	.667	−.175	1.000

(d.f. for the numerator are $k - 1 = 5 - 1 = 4$ and for the denominator are $n - k = 38 - 5 = 33$). The regression equation is, therefore, statistically significant and equal to

$$Y = 3276.55 + 5.696(X_1) - 15.178(X_3) + 1.551(X_5) + 7.574(X_6), \qquad (6\text{-}18)$$

TABLE 6-18 REGRESSION RESULTS FOR COMPANY XYZ

Regression Number 4.		Dependent Variable is 9 (sales).	
Variable	Coefficients	Standard Error	t-Tests
Constant	3517.45	419.618	8.3825
1 (PDI)	5.82732	.736256	7.9148
3 (price)	−17.0858	6.96489	−2.45313
5 (capital investments)	1.49732	.693524	2.15901
6 (advertising)	7.19557	1.76254	4.08251
8 (total industry advertising)	−.575587	.388884	−1.4801

$R^2 = 0.795$	$R = 0.892$	F-test $= 621.2$
Standard error of estimate $= 255.263$	Durbin-Watson statistic $= 2.36581$	

where X_1 is PDI (personal disposable income),

X_3 is price per ton (in dollars),

X_5 is advertising (in thousands of dollars),

and Y is semiannual sales (in thousands of dollars).

The R^2 of .781 indicates that the regression equation (6-18) explains 78.1% of the total variation, or in other words, that variations in X_1, X_3, and X_5 explain 78.1% of the variation in sales.

After a significant regression equation has been identified, it must be verified that none of the assumptions have been violated:

1. Equation (6-18) is indeed linear.
2. The number of observations is more than 30, so one can assume normality in the residuals.
3. The D-W test is 2.31, which is within the acceptance limits of 1.72 to 2.38. Therefore there is no first-order correlation, indicating that the residuals are independent of each other. (See Chapter 6 Appendix, Section 3 for a discussion of the D-W tests.)
4. Looking at the percentage of error column in Table 6-19 it can be seen that it is about constant.

Thus it can be concluded that (6-18) is a significant and meaningful regression equation that can be used for either forecasting or policymaking purposes.

TABLE 6-19 FURTHER REGRESSION RESULTS FOR COMPANY XYZ

Dependent Variable is 9.

Variable	Coefficients	Standard Error	t-Tests
Constant	3276.55	393.685	8.32276
1	5.6957	.74394	7.65613
3	−15.1783	6.96706	−2.17859
5	1.55114	.704959	2.20033
6	7.57419	1.77507	4.26698

$R^2 = 0.781$ $\qquad\qquad$ $R = 0.884$ $\qquad\qquad$ F-test $= 471.2$

Standard deviation of estimate $= 259.829$

Actual	Predicted	Residuals	Percentage of Error
5540.39	5349.89	190.501	$3.43841E - 02$
5439.04	5180.44	258.598	$4.75449E - 02$
4290	4468.9	−178.895	$-4.17005E - 02$
5502.34	5620.87	−118.53	$-2.15417E - 02$
4871.77	5235.68	−363.912	$-7.46982E - 02$
4708.08	4505.83	202.256	$4.29594E - 02$
4627.81	4539.03	88.7833	$1.91847E - 02$
4110.24	4717.04	−606.794	$-.14763$
4122.69	3991.78	130.914	$3.17545E - 02$
4842.25	4543.44	298.814	$6.17097E - 02$
5740.65	5509.08	231.57	$4.03385E - 02$
5094.1	5069.99	24.1051	$4.73197E - 03$
5383.2	5311.28	71.9158	$1.33593E - 02$
4888.17	4482.32	405.854	$8.30277E - 02$
4033.13	4198.47	−165.336	$-4.09943E - 02$
4941.96	5054.38	−112.418	$-2.27476E - 02$
5312.8	5254.56	58.2349	$1.09612E - 02$
5139.87	5088.84	51.0201	$9.92636E - 03$
4397.36	4945.73	−548.365	$-.124703$
5149.47	5376.45	−226.977	$-4.40777E - 02$
5150.83	4733.14	417.69	$8.10918E - 02$
4989.02	5314.13	−325.107	$-6.51645E - 02$
5926.86	5977.36	−50.4986	$-8.52030E - 03$

TABLE 6-19 Continued

Actual	Predicted	Residuals	Percentage of Error
4703.88	4669.05	34.821	$7.40262E-03$
5365.59	5132.04	233.55	$4.35273E-02$
4630.09	4752.48	-122.386	$-2.64328E-02$
5711.86	5603.36	108.498	$1.89951E-02$
5095.48	5361.63	-266.15	$-5.22326E-02$
6124.37	5702.99	421.383	$6.88044E-02$
4787.34	4728.74	58.606	$1.22419E-02$
5035.62	5248.74	-213.121	$-4.23227E-02$
5288.01	5396.88	-108.87	$-2.05881E-02$
4647.01	4682.28	-35.2639	$-7.58850E-03$
5315.63	5429.94	-114.307	$-2.15039E-02$
6180.06	5968.57	211.487	$3.42208E-02$
4800.97	4922.02	-121.043	$-2.52122E-02$
5512.13	5287.97	224.161	$4.06669E-02$
5272.21	5316.98	-44.7695	$-8.49161E-03$

Durbin-Watson statistic $= 2.31183$.

6/9 Lagged Variables

In order to estimate sales for some future period using equation (6-18), values for PDI, price, capital expenditure, and advertising must be known for that period. The whole usefulness of forecasting can be questioned, since the burden is being shifted from prediction of the dependent variable to prediction of the independent variables. This problem can often be solved through use of lagged variables. In the example of Company XYZ, PDI and price could be lagged one period, which enables forecasting one period in advance with the present level of PDI or price. The argument for this procedure is that there is a time delay between changes in PDI or between changes in prices and their influence on sales.

Most of the regression programs allow the user to try different lags (1, 2, or more periods) and tests their appropriateness and significance so that the most appropriate one can be chosen. Equation (6-18) as well as the data matrix of Table 6-15 are in fact for lagged values of PDI and price. That is, the appropriate time indices are

$$Y_t = 327655 + 5.696X_{1,t-1} - 15.178X_{3,t-1} + 1.551X_{5,t} + 7.574X_{6,t},$$

and actual values are available for X_1 and X_3 for period 3.

Through the above equation one can predict sales figures one period ahead with the current values of PDI and price. For variables X_5 and X_6 there is little problem because both the advertising and capital expenditure budgets are known in advance (through budget figures), and their magnitudes can be used as accurate estimates of actual expenditures. Serious problems may result from the introduction of lagged variables, and these problems must be considered before including such variables.

6/10 Dummy Variables

Often there are certain factors that are not naturally quantified. This is true with wars, the seasons, months of the year, or special events such as strikes, etc. However, the influence of such qualitative factors can be extremely important in forecasting and cannot be ignored. Dummy variables are a common way of quantifying qualitative factors. A dummy variable can take only two values— 0 or 1—and is often called a binary variable. It takes the value 1 when the event occurs, and 0 at all other times. For example, to take into consideration the effects of World War II, a dummy variable could be created as follows:

Year	Sales	PDI	Dummy Variable
1938	238	135	0
1939	242	138	0
1940	248	140	1
1941	262	145	1
1942	300	148	1
1943	312	152	1
1944	350	158	1
1945	294	160	0
1946	295	162	0

A dummy variable can be considered as a special case of an independent variable. The only difference is that it can only take two values, 0 and 1. Therefore, if it is used and its influence is statistically important, it can help to explain part of the variation of the dependent variable. Furthermore, since a dummy variable can be considered as another independent variable, it can be treated as such in terms of t-tests, selections, multicollinearity, etc.

To use dummy variables all possible combinations a given event can assume must be enumerated and made mutually exclusive, then a dummy variable must be assigned to all but one of the combinations. For example, suppose that one wants to consider the seasonal impact on monthly sales. With twelve months, eleven dummy variables can be assigned with the twelfth month as the base. Table 6-20 shows the sales of champagne of a French company and illustrates how dummy variables can be assigned to each month. In the month of October, all dummy variables are 0, indicating that October is the base month. The dummy variables can be regressed against the sales, and their statistical significance tested.

The resulting equation is

$$Y = 7048 - 2.195X_1 - 2.612X_2 - 1.978X_3 - 1.849X_4 - 1.685X_5 - 1.617X_6$$

$$- 2.242X_7 - 4.188X_8 - 1.261X_9 + 2.761X_{11} + 4.926X_{12} - .0226X_{13},$$

where Y is sales,

X_1 is a dummy variable for January taking the value of 1 when we forecast for January, and the value of 0 when a forecast for any other month is wanted,

X_2 is a dummy variable for February,

X_3 is a dummy variable for March,

  .
  .
  .

X_{12} is a dummy variable for December,

X_{13} is time.

(Note that X_{10} is omitted, making October the base month).

The R^2 of the above equation is .890, and both the F-test and all the t-tests are significant.

To forecast for the month of October, the value of Y will be

$$Y = 7.048 - .0226X_{13},$$

since there is not a dummy variable for October.

To forecast for March, the equation will be

$$Y = 7.048 - .0226X_{13} - 1.978(1),$$

since the dummy variables of all other months will take the value 0. Thus, if $X_{13} = 85$, the forecast for March will be $Y = 7.048 - .0226(85) - 1.978 = 3.149$. For August, $Y = 7.048 - .0226X_{13} - 4.188(1) = 7.048 - .0226(85) - 4.188 = .939$.

TABLE 6-20 ASSIGNING DUMMY VARIABLES FOR SEASONAL FACTORS

	Champagne Sales	Jan. X_1	Feb. X_2	Mar. X_3	Apr. X_4	May X_5	June X_6	July X_7	Aug. X_8	Sept. X_9	Nov. X_{11}	Dec. X_{12}	Time X_{13}
Nov.	5.89	0	0	0	0	0	0	0	0	0	1	0	1
Dec.	1.43	0	0	0	0	0	0	0	0	0	0	1	2
Jan.	4.30	1	0	0	0	0	0	0	0	0	0	0	3
Feb.	5.31	0	1	0	0	0	0	0	0	0	0	0	4
Mar.	4.62	0	0	1	0	0	0	0	0	0	0	0	5
Apr.	4.79	0	0	0	1	0	0	0	0	0	0	0	6
May	4.58	0	0	0	0	1	0	0	0	0	0	0	7
June	3.56	0	0	0	0	0	1	0	0	0	0	0	8
July	4.35	0	0	0	0	0	0	1	0	0	0	0	9
Aug.	12.67	0	0	0	0	0	0	0	1	0	0	0	10
Sept.	9.85	0	0	0	0	0	0	0	0	1	0	0	11
Oct.	6.98	0	0	0	0	0	0	0	0	0	0	0	12
Nov.	5.95	0	0	0	0	0	0	0	0	0	1	0	13
Dec.	1.65	0	0	0	0	0	0	0	0	0	0	1	14
Jan.	4.53	1	0	0	0	0	0	0	0	0	0	0	15
Feb.	4.87	0	1	0	0	0	0	0	0	0	0	0	16
Mar.	5.01	0	0	1	0	0	0	0	0	0	0	0	17
Apr.	4.68	0	0	0	1	0	0	0	0	0	0	0	18
May	4.29	0	0	0	0	1	0	0	0	0	0	0	19
June	3.15	0	0	0	0	0	1	0	0	0	0	0	20
July	3.93	0	0	0	0	0	0	1	0	0	0	0	21
Aug.	13.08	0	0	0	0	0	0	0	1	0	0	0	22
Sept.	9.84	0	0	0	0	0	0	0	0	1	0	0	23
Oct.	6.42	0	0	0	0	0	0	0	0	0	0	0	24
Nov.	5.22	0	0	0	0	0	0	0	0	0	1	0	25
Dec.	1.74	0	0	0	0	0	0	0	0	0	0	1	26
Jan.	4.22	1	0	0	0	0	0	0	0	0	0	0	27
Feb.	3.89	0	1	0	0	0	0	0	0	0	0	0	28
Mar.	2.93	0	0	1	0	0	0	0	0	0	0	0	29
Apr.	3.74	0	0	0	1	0	0	0	0	0	0	0	30
May	3.37	0	0	0	0	1	0	0	0	0	0	0	31
June	2.90	0	0	0	0	0	1	0	0	0	0	0	32
July	2.64	0	0	0	0	0	0	1	0	0	0	0	33
⋮	⋮	⋮	⋮	⋮	⋮	⋮	⋮	⋮	⋮	⋮	⋮	⋮	⋮
Dec.	2.21	0	0	0	0	0	0	0	0	0	0	1	82
Jan.	2.28	1	0	0	0	0	0	0	0	0	0	0	83
Feb.	3.04	0	1	0	0	0	0	0	0	0	0	0	84

In a similar manner, dummy variables can be used for almost any qualitative event. Their number should be one less than the number of qualitative factors included in the model. (It is possible to use as many dummy variables as the number of qualitative factors, but that would introduce a redundancy and lack of parsimony, since one less dummy variable could have been used to enumerate all possible combinations of events.)

6/11 Summary

Regression analysis is a powerful method of estimation and the most commonly used causal approach to forecasting. It is quite flexible and can include any number of factors in the forecasting model. It also provides substantial information for policymaking and can be used for simulating future environmental conditions. Regression can be used as a time-series model or as a mixed causal and time-series method. However, its main usefulness and applicability is in the area of causal or explanatory forecasting. Regression analysis is backed by statistical theory, is based on economic principles, and can handle qualitative factors. Interest in it has been growing rapidly in the last three decades both in theoretical developments and practical applications. Its increased role has been aided by the introduction of the second and third generation of computers, which can handle the computational requirements of regression easily.

APPENDIX

MATHEMATICAL SUPPLEMENT

Chapter 6

1. OBTAINING THE VALUES OF THE COEFFICIENTS OF REGRESSION

By using the least squares method one can derive the values of a, b_1, and b_2 of a multiple regression equation:

$$\Sigma e_i^2 = (Y - Y_c)^2, \quad \text{but} \quad Y_c = a + b_1 X_1 + b_2 X_2.$$

Thus, $\quad \Sigma e_i^2 = \Sigma(Y - a - b_1 X_1 - b_2 X_2)^2,$

$$\frac{\partial \Sigma_i^2}{\partial a} = -2\Sigma(Y - a - b_1 X_1 - b_2 X_2), \tag{6-19}$$

$$\frac{\partial \Sigma_i^2}{\partial b_1} = -2\Sigma X_1(Y - a - b_1 X_1 - b_2 X_2), \tag{6-20}$$

and $\quad \dfrac{\partial \Sigma_i^2}{\partial b_2} = -2\Sigma X_2(Y - a - b_1 X_1 - b_2 X_2). \tag{6-21}$

Removing the parentheses and equating equations (6-19), (6-20) and (6-21) to zero, gives

$$\left. \begin{array}{l} \Sigma Y = na - b_1\Sigma X_1 - b_2\Sigma X_2, \\[4pt] \Sigma X_1 Y = a\Sigma X_1 - b_1\Sigma X_1{}^2 - b_2\Sigma X_1 X_2, \\[4pt] \Sigma X_2 Y = a\Sigma X_2 - b_1\Sigma X_1 X_2 - b_2\Sigma X_2{}^2. \end{array} \right] \tag{6-22}$$

In (6-22) there are three simultaneous equations with three unknowns (a, b_1, b_2). These can be solved to obtain the values of a, b_1, b_2, ..., b_k. However, doing so involves a tremendous amount of substitutions and is impractical without the use of matrix algebra and the computer. (The reader might attempt to solve for the values of a, b_1, and b_2 to realize the extent of the work involved). Matrix algebra can be used as follows:

$$\mathbf{Y} = \mathbf{Xb} + \mathbf{e},$$

where

$$\mathbf{Y} = \begin{bmatrix} Y_1 \\ Y_2 \\ Y_3 \\ . \\ . \\ . \\ Y_n \end{bmatrix} \qquad \mathbf{X} = \begin{bmatrix} 1 & X_{21} & X_{31} & . & . & . & X_{k1} \\ 1 & X_{22} & X_{32} & . & . & . & X_{k2} \\ 1 & X_{23} & X_{33} & . & . & . & X_{k3} \\ . & . & & . & . & . & . \\ . & . & & . & . & . & . \\ . & . & . & & . & . & . \\ 1 & X_{2n} & X_{3n} & & & & X_{kn} \end{bmatrix}$$

$$\mathbf{b} = \begin{bmatrix} b_1 \\ b_2 \\ b_3 \\ . \\ . \\ . \\ b_k \end{bmatrix} \qquad \text{and} \quad \mathbf{e} = \begin{bmatrix} e_1 \\ e_2 \\ e_3 \\ . \\ . \\ . \\ e_n \end{bmatrix}$$

where $\mathbf{Y}$ is an $n \times 1$ matrix,

$\mathbf{X}$ is an $n \times k$ matrix,

$\mathbf{b}$ is an $k \times 1$ matrix,

and $\mathbf{e}$ is an $k \times 1$ matrix.

(For the remainder of this section, Y, X, b, and e will be used to denote matrices.)

To obtain the values of b, the sum of squared deviations must be minimized:

$$\Sigma e_i^2 = e'e = (Y - Xb)'(Y - Xb),$$

where e', $(Y - Xb)'$, is the transpose of e. Thus

$$e = \begin{bmatrix} e_1 \\ e_2 \\ . \\ . \\ . \\ e_n \end{bmatrix} \qquad e' = [e_1 e_2, \dots, e_n]$$

$$e'e = (Y' - b'X')(Y - Xb)$$

$$= Y'Y - Y'Xb - b'X'Y + b'X'Xb$$

$$= Y'Y - 2b'X'Y + b'X'Xb,$$

since $b'X'Y$ is a scalar and is therefore equal to its transpose, $Y'Xb'$.

$$\frac{\partial e'e}{\partial b} = -2X'Y + 2X'Xb = 0,$$

$$X'Y = X'Xb, \tag{6-23}$$

and $$\boxed{b = (X'X)^{-1}X'Y} \tag{6-24}$$

where $(X'X)^{-1}$ is the inverse of $(X'X)$.

For example, if there are two independent variables, the results are given by

$$Y = \begin{bmatrix} Y_1 \\ Y_2 \\ Y_3 \\ . \\ . \\ . \\ Y_n \end{bmatrix} \qquad X = \begin{bmatrix} 1 & X_{21} & X_{31} \\ 1 & X_{22} & X_{32} \\ 1 & X_{23} & X_{33} \\ . & . & . \\ . & . & . \\ . & . & . \\ 1 & X_{2n} & X_{3n} \end{bmatrix} \qquad X' = \begin{bmatrix} 1 & 1 & 1 & \ldots & 1 \\ X_{21} & X_{22} & X_{23} & \ldots & X_{2n} \\ X_{31} & X_{32} & X_{33} & \ldots & X_{3n} \end{bmatrix}$$

$$X'X = \begin{bmatrix} 1 & 1 & 1 & \ldots & 1 \\ X_{21} & X_{22} & X_{23} & \ldots & X_{2n} \\ X_{31} & X_{32} & X_{33} & \ldots & X_{3n} \end{bmatrix} \begin{bmatrix} 1 & X_{21} & X_{31} \\ 1 & X_{22} & X_{32} \\ 1 & X_{23} & X_{33} \\ . & . & . \\ . & . & . \\ . & . & . \\ 1 & X_{2n} & X_{3n} \end{bmatrix}$$

$$= \begin{bmatrix} n & \Sigma X_2 & \Sigma X_3 \\ \Sigma X_2 & \Sigma X_2{}^2 & \Sigma X_2 X_3 \\ \Sigma X_3 & \Sigma X_2 X_3 & \Sigma X_3{}^2 \end{bmatrix} \tag{6-25}$$

$$X'Y = \begin{bmatrix} 1 & 1 & 1 & \ldots & 1 \\ X_{21} & X_{22} & X_{23} & \ldots & X_{2n} \\ X_{31} & X_{32} & X_{33} & \ldots & X_{3n} \end{bmatrix} \begin{bmatrix} Y_1 \\ Y_2 \\ Y_3 \\ . \\ . \\ . \\ Y_n \end{bmatrix}$$

$$= \begin{bmatrix} \Sigma Y \\ \Sigma X_2 Y \\ \Sigma X_3 Y \end{bmatrix} \tag{6-26}$$

Substituting the values of (6-25) and (6-26) into (6-23) gives

$$
\begin{bmatrix} \Sigma Y \\ \Sigma X_2 Y \\ \Sigma X_3 Y \end{bmatrix} = \begin{bmatrix} n & \Sigma X_2 & \Sigma X_3 \\ \Sigma X_2 & \Sigma X_2{}^2 & \Sigma X_2 \Sigma X_3 \\ \Sigma X_3 & \Sigma X_2 X_3 & \Sigma X_3{}^2 \end{bmatrix} \begin{bmatrix} b_1 \\ b_2 \\ b_3 \end{bmatrix} \tag{6-27}
$$

Equations (6-27) is equivalent to (6-22) except that $a = b_1$, and X_1 and X_2 are now X_2 and X_3.

A solution for b could also be obtained directly using the matrix notation of (6-24).

2.   THE VARIANCE OF THE b's

Substituting $Y = X\beta + u$, where β is the matrix (vector) of the true population values of the regression parameters into equation (6-24) gives

$$b = (X'X)^{-1}X'(X\beta + u)$$

$$= (X'X)^{-1}X'X\beta + (X'X)^{-1}X'u$$

$$= \beta + (X'X)^{-1}X'u.$$

Taking expected values gives

$$E(b) = E(\beta) + (X'X)^{-1}X'E(u),$$

$$E(b - \beta) = (X'X)^{-1}X'E(u) = 0,$$

$$E[(b - \beta)(b - \beta)'] = E[(X'X)^{-1}X'u][(X'X)^{-1}X'u]'$$

$$= E[(X'X)^{-1}X'uu'X(X'X)^{-1}]$$

$$= (X'X)^{-1}X'E(uu')X(X'X)^{-1}$$

$$= \text{var}\,(R)(X'X)^{-1}X'X(X'X)^{-1},$$

$$\text{var}\,(b) = \text{var}\,(R)(X'X)^{-1}.$$

In a similar way, the other variances can also be obtained.

3.   THE DURBIN-WATSON TABLES

The Durbin-Watson (D-W) statistic tests the hypothesis that there is no autocorrelation present in the residuals. Like the F-test and t-tests, the computed value $(D\text{-}W_c)$ of the Durbin-Watson test is compared with the corresponding values from Table D of Appendix I. The two values $(D\text{-}W_L$ and $D\text{-}W_u)$ are read from a D-W table that corresponds to the degrees of freedom of the data. The D-W distribution is symmetrical around 2, its mean value. Thus confidence intervals can be constructed involving the five regions shown in Figure 6-9 and

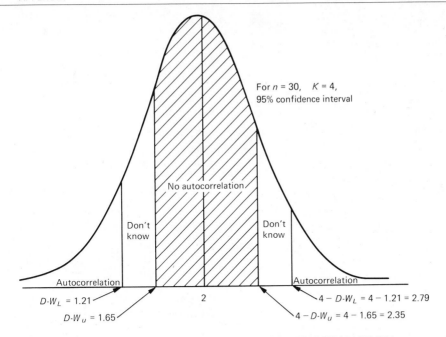

For $n = 30$, $K = 4$,
95% confidence interval

No autocorrelation

Don't know

Don't know

Autocorrelation

Autocorrelation

$D\text{-}W_L = 1.21$

$D\text{-}W_u = 1.65$

2

$4 - D\text{-}W_L = 4 - 1.21 = 2.79$

$4 - D\text{-}W_u = 4 - 1.65 = 2.35$

FIGURE 6-9 GRAPH OF DURBIN-WATSON DISTRIBUTION

using $D\text{-}W_L$ and $D\text{-}W_u$. The five intervals are:

1. less than $D\text{-}W_L$
2. between $D\text{-}W_L$ and $D\text{-}W_u$
3. between $D\text{-}W_u$ and $4 - D\text{-}W_u$
4. between $4 - D\text{-}W_u$ and $4 - D\text{-}W_L$
5. more than $4 - D\text{-}W_L$

If the computed $D\text{-}W_c$ is either in interval (1) or (5), the existence of auto-correlation is indicated. If $D\text{-}W_c$ is in interval 3, no autocorrelation is present. If it is in either 2 or 4, the test is inconclusive as to whether autocorrelation exists.

For example, if there are four variables and 30 observations, then

$$D\text{-}W_L = 1.21, \quad \text{and} \quad D\text{-}W_u = 1.65.$$

If $D\text{-}W_c$ is less than 1.21 or more than

$$4 - D\text{-}W_L = 4 - 1.21 = 2.79,$$

there is autocorrelation. If $D\text{-}W_c$ is between 1.65 and $4 - D\text{-}W_u = 2.35$, there is *no* autocorrelation.

If $D\text{-}W_c$ is between 1.21 and 1.65 or between 2.35 and 2.79, the test is inconclusive.

REFERENCES AND SELECTED BIBLIOGRAPHY

Christ, C. F. 1966. *Econometric Models and Methods*. New York: John Wiley & Sons.

Goldberger, A. S. 1964. *Econometric Theory*. New York: John Wiley & Sons.

Johnston, J. 1972. *Econometric Methods*, Englewood Cliffs, N.J.: Prentice-Hall.

Klein, L. R. 1968. *An Introduction to Econometrics*, Englewood Cliffs, N.J.: Prentice-Hall.

Pindyck, R. S., and D. L. Rubenfeld. 1976. *Econometric Models and Economic Forecasts*, N.Y.: McGraw-Hill.

EXERCISES

1. Table 6-21 presents the results of a regression run. What should be done next? Interpret the final regression equation.

TABLE 6-21   RESULTS OF REGRESSION RUN 1

Variable	B	Standard Error	t-Tests
Constant	357835.	30740.8	11.6404
1	1007.43	524.846	1.91947
2	−56089.2	43008.2	−1.30415
3	21165.1	34096.	.62075
4	−88410.9	35825.1	−2.46785
5	22488.2	35428.	.634759
6	−35399.5	34087.5	−1.03849
7	−21218.7	33351.4	−.636216
8	−122709.	36535.8	−3.35859
9	−3048.89	30339.1	−.100494
10	−57311.	37581.	−1.525
11	−70596.2	38493.5	−1.83398
12	−184778.	36655.7	−5.04089
13	.417727	$6.84181E-02$	6.1055
14	−.216098	$6.53552E-02$	−3.30651

TABLE 6-21 Continued

Variable	B	Standard Error	t-Tests
15	.297009	$3.34643E-02$	8.87541
16	$1.19271E-02$	$3.37776E-02$	.353106
17	$-6.85211E-02$	$3.26835E-02$	-2.0965

$R^2 = 0.943$ $R = 0.971$ F-test $= 31.04$

Standard of regression $= +3.85012E+04$

Degrees of freedom for numer. $= 17$ For denumer. $= 30$

Do you wish the residuals to be printed? No

Durbin-Watson statistic $= 2.27202$

Mean square error $= 9.26623E+08$

Mean percentage error (absolute value) $= 6.76519$

2. Table 6-22 shows the results of another regression run. Interpret these results. What should be done next? What is the final regression equation?

TABLE 6-22 RESULTS OF REGRESSION RUN 2

Variable	B	Standard Error	t-Tests
Constant	344785.	14132.3	24.3969
1	924.084	475.315	1.94415
4	-70236.6	22411.	-3.13402
8	$-101069.$	22304.5	-4.53134
11	$-57996.$	23415.1	-2.47686
12	$-167619.$	22703.2	-7.38306
13	.452488	$4.87001E-02$	9.29132
14	$-.299787$	$4.60195E-02$	-6.51433
15	.321898	$2.96835E-02$	10.8443
17	$-5.47201E-02$	$2.96047E-02$	-1.84835

$R^2 = 0.922$ $R = 0.960$ F-test $= 52.25$

Standard of regression $= +4.00570E+04$

Degrees of freedom for numer. $= 9$ For denumer $= 38$

Durbin-Watson statistic $= 2.272$

3.   Given the data in Table 6-23 (both in actual and $\log_e$ form) for the annual sales of the Multinational Company, obtain a forecast for periods 31 through 35.

TABLE 6-23   ACTUAL AND TRANSFORMED DATA

Period	Sales ($1000s)	$\log_e$ of Sales ($1000s)
1	190.464	5.24946
2	182.916	5.20903
3	246.464	5.50722
4	257.848	5.55237
5	269.559	5.59679
6	345.317	5.84446
7	355.322	5.87302
8	412.509	6.02226
9	431.081	6.0663
10	488.551	6.19144
11	572.552	6.3501
12	643.672	6.46719
13	745.539	6.61411
14	793.442	6.67638
15	922.705	6.82731
16	1028.09	6.93546
17	1125.45	7.02594
18	1266.94	7.14436
19	1490.92	7.30715
20	1637.97	7.40121
21	1814.12	7.50336
22	2082.59	7.64137
23	2315.33	7.74731
24	2585.58	7.85771
25	2932.67	7.98367
26	3330.37	8.11084
27	3690.01	8.21339
28	4179.63	8.33798
29	4740.36	8.46387
30	5331.38	8.58137

4. Given the following two regression equations, explain their validity and their possible use as forecasting equations. What steps should be taken (if any) to correct each of them?

Regression Equation I

Dependent Variable is 9

Variable	Coefficients	Standard Error	t-Tests
Constant	2373.76	626.208	3.79068
1	4.80277	.92865	5.17177
2	8.21194	4.2512	1.93167
3	−16.2377	10.2959	−1.57711
4	−9.27401	7.27363	−1.27502
6	14.8215	1.97564	7.50211

$R^2 = 0.771$ $R = 0.878$ F-test $= 505.1$
Standard deviation of estimate $= 293.806$ D.F. $= 30$
Durbin-Watson statistic $= 1.85057$

Regression Equation II

Dependent Variable is 9

Variable	Coefficients	Standard Error	t-Tests
Constant	2324.77	631.292	3.68256
1	4.84998	.937211	5.17491
2	9.30384	4.20578	2.21216
3	−19.9515	9.97423	−2.00031
6	14.2219	1.93809	7.33811

$R^2 = 0.759$ $R = 0.871$ F-test $= 389.7$
Standard deviation of estimate $= 296.751$ D.F. $= 31$
Durbin-Watson statistic $= 1.24742$

7 ECONOMETRIC MODELS AND FORECASTING

THE PREVIOUS TWO chapters have dealt with the causal approaches to forecasting of simple and multiple regression. Applying simple regression requires little statistical knowledge, limited data, and only moderate computational effort. (Most programmable calculators are adequate for the computations.) Multiple regression, on the other hand, requires a much greater level of sophistication, considerably more data, and a computer to do the computations. While use of simple regression can be made a mechanical task that can be entrusted to a clerical level of operations, multiple regression requires a more highly qualified person. These differences are very important in the practical use of forecasting.

In the same way that simple regression is a special case of multiple regression, the latter is a special case of econometric models. While multiple regression involves a single equation, econometric models can include any number of simultaneous multiple regression equations. The term *econometric models* will be used in this book to denote systems of linear equations involving several interdependent variables. It should be noted that this is not the only usage of the term *econometrics*, since there are those who use it as a general term to cover simple, multiple, and systems of multiple regression equations. The more limited definition used in this chapter appears to be the most common usage at this time.

The objective of this chapter is not to provide the level of detailed information needed to fully utilize these models, but to interpret their use in a practical sense. Such a task is difficult given the mathematical and statistical level assumed in this book. However, this chapter will seek to review the main ideas and concepts underlying econometric models, present the main advantages and difficulties involved, describe the statistical methods used, and finally discuss the role of econometric methods as a forecasting tool.

7/1 The Basis of Econometric Modeling

Regression analysis assumes that each of the independent variables included in the regression equation are determined by outside factors, that is, they are exogenous to the system. In economic or organizational relationships, however, such an assumption is often unrealistic. To illustrate this point, one can assume that sales = f(GNP, price, advertising). In regression, all three independent variables are assumed to be exogenously determined; they are not influenced by the level of sales itself or by each other. This is a fair assumption as far as GNP is concerned which, except for very large corporations, is not influenced directly by the sales of a single firm. However, for price and advertising there is unlikely to be a similar lack of influence. For example, if the per unit cost is proportional to sales volume, different levels of sales will result in different per unit costs. Furthermore, advertising expenditures will certainly influence the per unit price of the product offered, since production and selling costs influence the per unit price. The price in turn influences the magnitude of sales, which can consequently influence the level of advertising. These interrelationships point to the mutual interdependence among the variables of such an equation. Regression analysis is incapable of dealing with such interdependence if it is to be preserved as part of the explanatory model.

The above relationship can be more correctly expressed by a system of simultaneous equations that can deal with the interdependence among the variables.

Although very simplistic, these interdependencies might be represented by the following econometric model:

$$
\left.
\begin{aligned}
&\text{sales} = f(\text{GNP, price, advertising}),\\
&\text{production cost} = f(\text{number of units produced, inventories, labor costs,}\\
&\qquad\qquad\qquad\text{material cost}),\\
&\text{selling expenses} = f(\text{advertising, other selling expenses}),\\
&\text{advertising} = f(\text{sales}),\\
&\text{price} = f(\text{production cost, selling expenses, administrative}\\
&\qquad\qquad\text{overhead, profit}).
\end{aligned}
\right\}
\qquad (7\text{-}1)
$$

In place of one regression equation expressing sales as a function of three independent variables, the set of five simultaneous equations in (7-1) expresses sales and the independent variables as a function of each other and other exogenous factors. The relationship among these variables can be represented graphically as shown in Figure 7-1.

The basic premise of econometric modeling is that everything in the real world depends upon everything else. The world is becoming more aware of this interdependence, but the concept is very difficult to deal with at an operational level. Management systems, MIS, and the systems approach in general are concrete illustrations of the increasing concern of scientists for the interdependence among organizational units. Changing *A* not only affects *A* and its immediate system, but also the environment in general. The practical question is, of course, where to stop considering these interdependencies.

One could develop an almost infinite number of interdependent relationships, but data collection, computational limitations, and estimation problems restrict one in practice to a limited number of relationships. In addition, the marginal understanding, or forecasting accuracy, does not increase in proportion to the effort required to include an additional variable or equation after the first few. In econometric models, a major decision is determining how much detail to include, since more detail inevitably means more complexity.

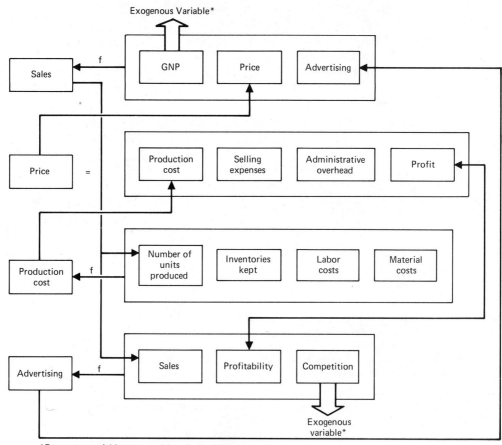

*Exogenous variables are not determined within the system.

FIGURE 7-1 SIMPLE ECONOMETRIC MODEL

In an econometric model one is faced with many tasks similar to those in multiple regression analysis. These tasks include:

1. determining which variables to include in each equation (specification)
2. determining the functional form (i.e., linear, exponential, logarithmic, etc.) of each of the equations
3. estimating in a simultaneous manner, the parameters of the equations
4. testing the statistical significance of the results
5. checking the validity of the assumptions involved.

Steps 2, 4, and 5 do not differ in their basic approach from those of multiple regression, and therefore will not be discussed again in this chapter. Steps 1 and 3 will be examined in Sections 7/4 and 7/3 respectively, to illustrate their important aspects. Before such a discussion, it is useful to review the advantages and disadvantages of econometric methods for forecasting.

7/2 The Advantages and Drawbacks of Econometric Methods

The main advantage of econometric models lies in their ability to deal with interdependencies. If a government, for example, would like to know the results of a 10% tax reduction aimed at stimulating a recessionary economy, it has few alternatives other than econometric models. A tax cut will have direct and immediate effects on increasing personal disposable income and probably decreasing government revenues. It will also tend to influence the price level, unemployment, savings, capital spending, etc. Each of these will in turn influence personal disposable income and therefore taxes of subsequent years. Through a series of chain reactions, the 10% decrease will affect almost all economic factors. These interdependencies must be considered if the effect of the tax cut is to be accurately predicted.

Econometric models are invaluable tools for increasing the understanding of the way an economic system works and for testing and evaluating alternative policies. These goals, however, are somewhat different from forecasting, where the main objective is predicting rather than understanding per se. Complex econometric models do not always perform better in forecasting than simpler time-series approaches. It is important to distinguish between econometric models used for policy purposes and econometric models used for forecasting. They are two different things. In the former usage, there is little doubt as to the usefulness and uniqueness of econometric models. For forecasting usage they must be examined more carefully and in the right perspective (see Chapter 16).

Econometric models for forecasting are generally much simpler and involve fewer equations than those designed for policy study. The main purpose of forecasting versions is to derive values for the independent variables so that they do not have to be estimated. In the simple econometric model of equations (7-1), for example, two of the variables—price and advertising—can be estimated internally. Thus there is no need to specify their values in order to forecast sales. GNP, on the other hand, still needs to be specified because it is determined outside or exogenously.

Whether intended for policy or forecasting purposes, econometric models are considerably more difficult to develop and estimate, as will be seen in Sections 7/4 and 7/3, than other available statistical methods. The difficulties are of two types:

1. technical aspects, involved in specifying the equations and estimating their parameters, and
2. cost considerations, related to the amount of data needed and the computing and human resources required.

In the final analysis, the question is whether the extra burden required for developing and running an econometric model justifies the costs involved. It is the authors' experience that the answer is *yes* if the user is a government, *maybe* if it is a large organization interested in policy considerations, and *no* if it is a medium or small organization or if the econometric model is intended for forecasting purposes only. The above guidelines do not apply to buying the services of one of the several econometric models now available commercially (Chase Econometrics, Data Resources, Inc., General Electric Forecasting Service, Wharton Econometric Forecasting Associates, etc.). Generally, the cost of using such services is only a small fraction of that of developing and operating one's own econometric model.

One of the major weaknesses of econometric models is the absence of a set of rules that can be applied across different situations. This lack makes the development of econometric models highly dependent upon the specific situation and requires the involvement of a skilled and experienced econometrician. Finally, once a model is developed it cannot be left to run on its own with no outside interference. Continuous monitoring of the results and updating for periodic changes are needed. These disadvantages have limited the application of econometrics to forecasting in medium and small organizations.

7/3 Estimation Procedures Used by Econometric Models

In all estimating procedures it is important to obtain unbiased estimators. That means that as the sample size increases, the accuracy of the estimators must increase too. Thus, when the sample size is equal to the population size (as for a complete census), the estimates would be the values of the real population parameters.

The presence of bias in estimators can be checked by using basic procedures of statistics. The estimators of the parameters $a, b_1, b_2, \ldots, b_k$ obtained in multiple regression can be shown to be unbiased. Unfortunately, in systems of simultaneous equations, this is not the case, as can be illustrated using a classic income determination model. Consider:

$$C_t = a + bY_t + u_t, \tag{7-2}$$

$$Y_t = C_t + Z_t, \tag{7-3}$$

where C_t is consumption expenditure at period t,

Y_t is income (GNP) at period t,

Z_t is nonconsumption expenditure (such as government spending) at period t,

u_t is the error or disturbance term at period t.

Equation (7-2) states that consumption is a function of income, while equation (7-3) states that income is determined by consumption and government spending. Thus the independent variable, Y_t, of (7-2) is determined partly by the level of consumption (an endogenous variable) and partly by the outside factor, government spending (an exogenous variable). These two types of variables can be distinguished in a system of simultaneous equations—the endogenous (C_t, Y_t) and the exogenous (Z_t). A problem arises from the fact that the endogenous variables are related to each other. This relationship causes dependence between the dependent variable and the error term, u_t, which appears as a dependence among successive values of u_t. This dependence violates one of the assumptions of ordinary least squares (OLS) used in regression analysis.

The dependence between C_t and u_t in equation (7-2) can be seen by applying the OLS method to (7-2) and (7-3) and separately estimating the values of a and b.

Substituting (7-3) into (7-2),

$$C_t = a + b(C_t + Z_t) + u_t$$

or $$C_t - bC_t = a + bZ_t + u_t,$$

$$C_t(1 - b) = a + bZ_t + u_t,$$

and $$C_t = \frac{a}{1 - b} + \frac{b}{1 - b}Z_t + \frac{u_t}{1 - b}. \tag{7-4}$$

Letting $$a_1 = \frac{a}{1 - b} \quad \text{and} \quad b_1 = \frac{1}{1 - b},$$

$$Y_t = a_1 + b_1 Z_t + \frac{u_t}{1 - b}. \tag{7-5}$$

Equation (7-4) and its equivalent, (7-5), imply that there is a dependence between the dependent variable C_t and the error term, u_t. This dependence results in biased estimation of a_1 and b_1 in (7-5) as well as biased estimators for a and b of the original equations (7-2) and (7-3). The bias exists for both small and large sample sizes and can be predicted if one is willing to assume that the process variance is known. Its existence means that OLS cannot be used reliably to forecast when systems of simultaneous equations are involved.

7/3/1 Alternative Estimation Procedures

In order to avoid bias in estimation, alternative procedures have been introduced that can be applied with varying degrees of effort and success. The relative advantages and weaknesses of these methods have been debated extensively in the literature, but it is clear that their applicability depends on the characteristics of each particular situation. (See Chow 1964 and Nagar 1959.) Several of the major alternative estimation procedures for econometric models are described below.

The full information maximum likelihood (FIML) method of estimation attacks the problem of interdependence among the different endogenous variables directly rather than in sequential steps as is done in many other methods. It constructs a matrix, W, which includes all exogenous and endogenous variables, and using a set of complex procedures based on maximum likelihood methods, solves for the parameters of the equations. The FIML estimation procedure was one of the first attempts to solve the problem of estimating the parameters of econometric models, but is one of the more difficult and expensive approaches of those currently available.

Close to FIML is the *limited information maximum likelihood* (LIML) method, which recognizes only part of the interdependence by estimating the values of each of the equations one at a time but only with respect to the exogenous variables. In each successive estimation, all previous information (estimated values) is substituted into the equation being estimated, accounting in a limited way for the existing dependence.

At the other extreme in terms of computational difficulties and theoretical rigor is the method of *indirect least squares* (ILS). It is similar to the OLS method but is applied to the reduced form of equations (7-2) and (7-3). The reduced form of a system of simultaneous equations can be obtained by successive substitutions of the original equations until all endogenous variables have been expressed as functions of only the exogenous variables. Equation (7-4) is of reduced form, since it expresses C_t, the dependent variable, in terms of the exogenous independent variable only, Z_t:

$$C_t = \frac{a}{1-b} + \frac{b}{1-b} Z_t + \frac{u_t}{1-b}. \tag{7-6}$$

Equation (7-3) can be expressed in a reduced form too by substituting (7-2) into (7-3)

$$Y_t = a + bY_t + Z_t + u_t,$$

$$Y_t(1 - b) = a + Z_t + u_t,$$

and
$$Y_t = \frac{a}{1 - b} + \frac{1}{1 - b} Z_t + \frac{u_t}{1 - b}. \tag{7-7}$$

Equations (7-6) and (7-7) are the reduced forms of (7-2) and (7-3). Through the substitutions

$$a_1 = \frac{a}{1 - b}, \quad b_1 = \frac{b}{1 - b} \quad \text{and} \quad b_2 = \frac{1}{1 - b} \quad \text{in (7-6) and (7-7),}$$

the following are obtained:

$$C_t = a_1 + b_1 Z_t + \frac{u_t}{1 - b}, \tag{7-8}$$

$$Y_t = a_1 + b_2 Z_t + \frac{u_t}{1 - b}. \tag{7-9}$$

Equations (7-8) and (7-9) can be solved by OLS, since the only variable involved is Z, which is exogenous. The resultant estimators of a_1, b_1, and b_2 are unbiased and consistent when n, the sample size, is sufficiently large. However, the values of a and b, which will be found through a_1 and b_2, are biased but not inconsistent, an advantage over the OLS method. Even though the concept of ILS is rather simple, its computational complexities have led most researchers to use two-stages least squares in place of ILS.

The *two-stages least square* (2SLS) method lies somewhere between the FIML and the ILS. It combines some of the advantages and limitations of both, but at the same time it is practical, the estimated values are ·not inconsistent, and the bias is small if the sample size is sufficiently large. In practice it is used more than any other method for simultaneous equation estimation, since it performs well when n is small and does better than FIML when the equations are misspecified (see Summers 1965).

In 2SLS one must first choose one of the endogenous variables as the independent one—Y in the previous example—then try to eliminate the dependence of C on u. This is achieved by applying OLS to the reduced form of equation (7-9) so that the values of a_1 and b_2 can be found. These are then substituted into the original equation (7-2) as follows:

$$C_t = a + bY_t + u_t, \tag{7-10}$$

$$Y_t = a_1 + b_2 Z_t. \tag{7-11}$$

Substituting Y_t of (7-11) into (7-10) gives

$$C_t = a + ba_1 + bb_2 Z_t + u_t,$$

or $$C_t = a_3 + b_3 Z_t + u_t,$$ (7-12)

where $a_3 = a + ba_1$ and $b_3 = bb_2.$

Equation (7-12) includes only exogenous variables and C_t is not dependent on u_t. Thus, it is an unbiased and consistent form of estimation. The problem with 2SLS is that it does not take into consideration the full extent of interdependence among the different equations, since it is applied in a sequential manner, causing some of the dependence to be lost.

Finally, one can apply *three-stages least squares* (3SLS), which is generally more efficient than 2SLS except in some circumstances. This method accounts for the interdependence of equations in a more holistic way than 2SLS. The advantage of greater asymptotic efficiency applies only when the sample size is very large, and the method has little practical value for all but a limited number of cases, even though computationally it is not much more involved than the 2SLS.

7/4 Specification and Identification

An econometric model includes a number of simultaneous equations, each of which includes several variables. Specification of the right kind and number of variables is important. If an important variable is not included in a single equation, nonrandom errors will occur because an important factor influencing the dependent variable will have been omitted. In single equations situations, misspecification can be easily understood. In econometric models the task is much more difficult because absence of an important variable will influence all equations and result in nonrandom (i.e., autocorrelated) residuals but give no indication of the equation(s) generating them. Similarly, the mere fact that there are many equations increases the chances of misspecification.

Identification of the exogenous factors needed in ILS and 2SLS is not always without problems, nor is it a completely objective choice. One must arbitrarily decide on the degree of influence of the different factors (variables) involved and choose those that are least determined within the system. In the income determination example of (7-2) and (7-3), government spending, Z_t, was selected as the exogenous variable not because it is influenced by the level of income or consumption, but rather because the mutual dependence is less than that between income and consumption. If a more detailed model were used, it might be better to make Z_t endogenous and select some other factor such as monetary policy as the exogenous variable.

Although in practice the definition of endogenous and exogenous variables may be nontrivial, once it is done, at least one equation must be specified for each of the endogenous variables. When the number of equations is equal to the number of endogenous variables, the model is referred to as just specified. When there are fewer endogenous variables than equations, the model is under-specified and one of the variables must be arbitrarily set to some value—it must become an exogenous factor—so that estimation will be possible. If the number of endogenous variables is greater than the number of equations, the model is overspecified. This latter form is most often used for estimating the parameters of simultaneous equations.

Another point relating to specification and the choice of exogenous and endogenous variables for econometric models is that of identification. Statistical data do not represent values of a single equation but are the combined result of a number of them. For example, consider a simple demand and supply function represented by a system of two equations:

$$Q_d = a + bp + u, \tag{7-13}$$

$$Q_s = a_1 + b_1 p + u, \tag{7-14}$$

where Q_d is the quantity demanded,

Q_s is the quantity supplied,

p is the corresponding price,

and u is the error term.

The statistical data available do not represent either (7-13) or (7-14). Rather, they are the points of intersection of the two equations, since this is the only point recorded. For example, in a stock market situation, the exact range of the demand and supply is not known, but only the point of their intersection represented by a specific transaction. The same is true for most recorded data. Approaches for identifying the supply and demand functions separately must be developed.

It can be observed that some equations vary more widely than others. This variation will have an effect on the value of u, which will be larger in those equations. For example, one could assume (or show from past data) that the supply of agricultural products varies more widely because of prevailing weather conditions than because of fluctuating demand. If a factor could be identified that correlates with the magnitude of weather variations, it could be included in the supply equation, (7-14), and varied proportionally to the supply. If an exogenous factor, such as the amount of rainfall or the number of sunny days (call it r), is important in determining variations in supply, that factor should be included in (7-14):

$$Q_s = a_1 + b_1 p + b_2 r + u. \tag{7-15}$$

The role of r in equation (7-15) is a dual one. It can identify equation (7-14) from equation (7-13), and at the same time it can be used as an exogenous variable when applying methods such as 2SLS, which use the reduced form requiring exogenous variables. Demand and supply of agricultural products are rather easy to identify and therefore specify correctly. However, this is not true in many cases where identification can become a critical issue. With sales data, for example, it is difficult to distinguish demand and supply because demand figures include sales and unfilled demand when supply is less than demand. Another difficulty arises because there are several levels of inventory between the producer and the final consumers, which distort the data and introduce true lags. All these factors make the identification of demand and supply equations and variables a difficult task.

Whatever the complications that arise in specification and identification, their solution is well documented (see Fisher 1966), and they are not as serious as the problems arising in the estimation process. Those problems, together with the need for appropriate data, are the biggest challenge to development and estimation of econometric models.

7/5 Development and Application of Econometric Models

Econometric models are an interesting application of interdisciplinary research involving statisticians and economists. The mixture of the two has created a new discipline known as econometrics. Econometrics is interested in measuring economic theory through statistical methods. Econometric models involving systems of simultaneous equations are the most advanced and sophisticated part of the profession. The special problems encountered in specification and identification and in estimation as well as the size and complexity of the task, make the econometrician's job a challenging one.

Econometrics is mainly concerned with macroeconomic models. It was not until the late 1960s that the econometric model approach was used for forecasting purposes. The first econometric model had been built in 1939 by Tinbergen, but it was not until 1955 and the advent of computers that a comprehensive model of the U.S. economy was constructed by Klein and Goldberger (1955). This model became the prototype for the development of most other econometric models.

Initially, econometric models used yearly data, which created a serious problem because not enough data were available. In addition, aggregation destroyed intrayear effects, such as seasonal or cyclical variations, and minimized the usefulness of the models as a forecasting tool. These flaws were corrected through development of quarterly econometric models, the best known of which is the Oxford model, developed by Klein et al. in 1961. The Oxford model has been the basis for several of the quarterly models presently used by different forecasting econometric services.

The 1960s witnessed an expansion in the size and complexity of econometric models. This was climaxed by the construction of the Brookings model, which contains more than 200 equations (see Duesenberry et al. 1965). Economic activity was divided into industrial sectors, and separate equations were included for consumption, investment, foreign trade, government transactions, etc. Through the mid-1970s, the Brookings model was by far the biggest and most complete of all econometric models, making it particularly well suited for testing and evaluating the impact of alternative economic policies.

Simultaneously there have been efforts to construct small models that can be used with limited amounts of data at reduced cost (see von Hohenbalken and Tintner 1962). These small models have also been used for forecasting purposes (see Friend and Jones 1964). Smaller models tend to require the estimation of fewer exogenous factors before they can be used, since they tend to be more economical but not necessarily less accurate.

To summarize, econometric models are difficult and costly to build and operate. They are generally aimed towards policymaking and their usefulness in forecasting is somewhat controversial (see Lesser 1966). These characteristics have limited the development of econometric models by individual companies. However, econometric forecasts, and even simulation, can be purchased through several services at economical rates. These professional firms market their use as an alternative or complementary procedure to the other techniques discussed in this book.

7/5/1 An Example of an Econometric Model

One of the difficulties in describing applications of econometric models to business forecasting is that they are generally proprietary and detailed information is not readily available. However, many of these applications are described in the literature in terms of their structure and purpose. One such application is "Scrap: Prices and Issues" by K. T. Wise (1975). This particular article reports on the application of econometric modeling to predicting prices and quantities (supply and demand) for iron and steel scrap. This section will describe the general structural form of this model and some of its applications in practice.

The prices of scrap iron and steel have often behaved in unexpected ways. Since these prices and their resulting impact on supply and demand have a major effect on the profits of companies in the steel, scrap, and related industries, there are a substantial number of organizations concerned with their forecasting. As the actual values shown in Figure 7-2 indicate, domestic scrap usage (and exports) have not always moved consistently with prices, and vice versa. At times scrap prices have risen, even though scrap consumption has decreased. At other times prices have fallen, while usage has increased. These seemingly inconsistent patterns of market behavior can be explained when the full complexity of the scrap market is understood. Many inportant factors interact simultaneously, however, making simple analysis impossible and defying intuition. The econometric approach to predicting scrap volumes and their prices is one way of handling these complexities. Through the concepts of econometrics that have been described previously, such a model can simultaneously account for the interaction of such factors as steel output, pig iron cost, exports of scrap, government policy, technological advances, and inventories.

The particular model described here was developed by Charles River Associates of Cambridge, Massachusetts, for its customers. It basically provides the following for those who use its outputs:

1. A source of scrap prices for one- and two-year, and sometimes longer, profit forecasts.
2. A source of market information to help top management keep tabs on their scrap purchasing operation.
3. A source of short-term price forecasts to enable inventory speculation. The model provides information corroborating that provided by scrap purchasers to treasurers and top management who must approve funds for large-scale inventory buildup.
4. Some special long-term scrap price forecasts that are suitable for use in preparing new facility plans.

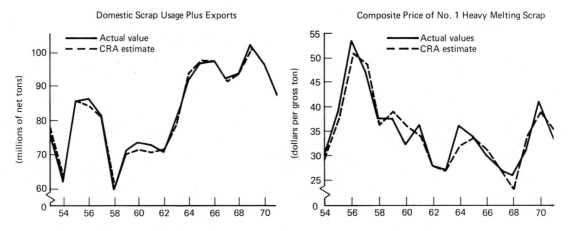

FIGURE 7-2 ECONOMETRIC FORECASTS VERSUS ACTUALS FOR QUANTITY AND PRICE MOVEMENTS OF FERROUS SCRAP

Source: Charles River Associates. Reprinted by permission.

In terms of the performance of this particular econometric model, Figure 7-2 summarizes actual domestic scrap usage plus exports from 1954 to 1971 and also provides actual and forecast values of the composite price of scrap for that same period. Clearly, these results indicate the relative accuracy of such an approach in this particular situation.

One of the key determinants of the success of such a forecasting use of an econometric model is the basic design of the model itself. Before an econometric model can be developed a structural representation of the items that it represents and the various factors that it needs to include must be built. For the scrap situation such a structural representation is shown in Figure 7-3. This figure includes those items that affect scrap demand and supply, and items of general economic influence.

Once the basic structural relationship of different variables has been determined, the data can be collected. These data will be used in the same way that observations were used in estimating multiple regression coefficients in Chapter 6. In many instances these data must come from published sources or be generated for the specific model in question. As indicated previously, one of the reasons for the proprietary nature of many microeconometric models, such as the one for forecasting ferrous scrap quantities and prices, is that the data are expensive to collect and are proprietary.

A major advantage claimed by those who develop econometric models for forecasting purposes is that those same models can be used to perform extensive analysis relevant to other issues of decision making. For example, in the case of the ferrous scrap model, there may be developments on the supply or demand side or changes in government legislation that will affect the quantities and price of ferrous scrap. These can be converted into assumptions suitable for incorporation in the model and tested in terms of the model's sensitivity to those changes. Such a use can add substantially to the value of econometric modeling.

7/5/2 Incorporating an Econometric Model into the Practice of Forecasting

In the previous section a specific illustration of a microeconometric model was described. In that instance the output of the model was forecasts of prices and quantities for ferrous scrap. In many instances, additional steps in forecasting and planning can be closely tied to the use of the econometric model. One such application reported in *Sales and Marketing Management* (1975) is illustrated in Figure 7-4.

In this particular example there are several different forecasting and decision-making models that have been linked together to more completely integrate the forecasting and planning tasks. The econometric model provides

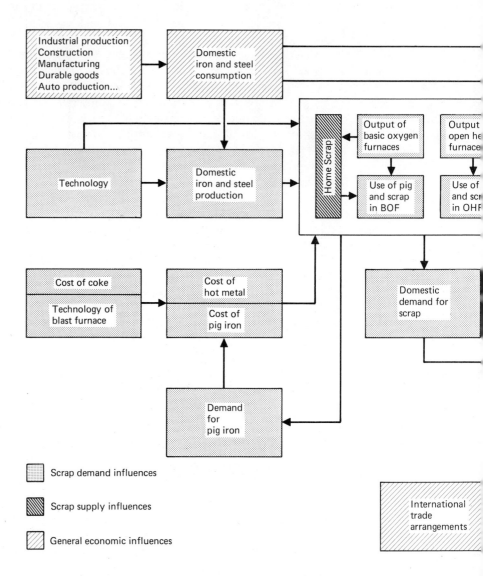

FIGURE 7-3 FACTORS INCLUDED IN ECONOMETRIC MODEL
OF FERROUS SCRAP
Source: Charles River Associates. Reprinted by permission.

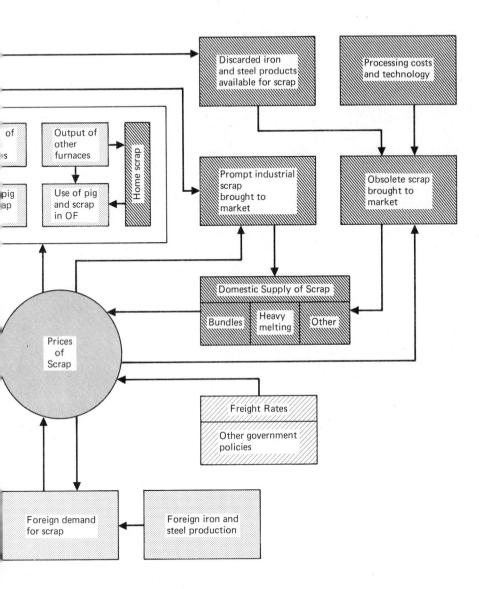

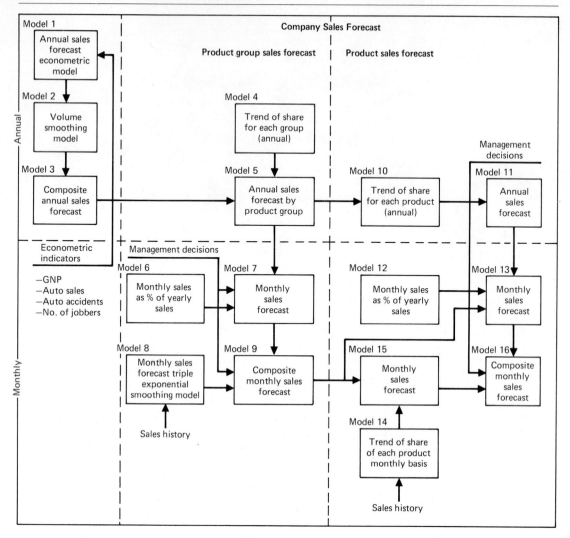

FIGURE 7-4 INTEGRATING ECONOMETRIC FORECASTS WITH OTHER FORECASTS

annual sales forecasts that can be used as the starting point for the planning process. (The organizational aspects of such integration are discussed further in Chapter 15.)

Thus, the econometric model expresses the relationship between company sales and a variety of economic indicators, such as GNP, personal consumption expenditures, and capital spending plans. A second model can be used at a more micro level to provide smooth estimates of monthly sales by product and seasonal factors for those, as well as perhaps incorporating still a third model based on a single multiple regression equation that will show the impact of past promotion on sales.

These three different forms of forecasting can then be used as the major source of input for projecting annual sales by product group. These forecasts can, in turn, serve as the basis for decisions being made at more detailed levels and for setting up performance review and evaluation procedures.

REFERENCES AND SELECTED
BIBLIOGRAPHY

Aaker, David. 1971. *Multivariate Analysis in Marketing*. Belmont, Calif.: Wadsworth.

Chow, G. C. 1964. "A Comparison of Alternative Estimators for Simultaneous Equations." *Econometrica*, Vol. 32, pp. 532–53.

Duesenberry, J. S., G. Fromm, L. R. Klein, and E. Kuh (eds.). 1965. *The Brookings Quarterly Econometric Model of the United States*. Chicago: Rand-McNally.

Fisher, F. M. 1966. *The Identification Problem in Econometrics*, New York: McGraw-Hill.

Friend, J., and R. C. Jones. 1964. "Short-Run Forecasting Models Incorporating Anticipatory Data," in *Models of Income Determination* (National Bureau of Economic Research). Princeton: Princeton University Press.

Johnston, J. 1972. *Econometric Methods*, 2d ed. N.Y.: McGraw-Hill.

Klein, L. R. (ed.), *Essays in Industrial Economics*, Volumes 1–3, Economics Research Unit, Department of Economics, Wharton School of Finance and Commerce, University of Pennsylvania, 1969–1971.

Klein, L. R., and A. S. Goldberger. 1955. *An Econometric Model of the United States, 1929–1952*. Amsterdam: North-Holland Publishing Co.

Klein, L. R., *et al.*, *An Econometric Model of the United Kingdom*. Oxford: Blackwell.

Lesser, C. E. V. 1966. "The Role of Macro-Models in Short-Term Forecasting." *Econometrica*, Vol. 34, pp. 862–72.

————. 1968. "A Survey of Econometrics." *Journal of the Royal Statistical Society*, Series A, Vol. 131, pp. 530–66.

Malinvaud, E. 1966. *Statistical Methods of Econometrics*. Amsterdam: North-Holland Publishing Co.

Murphy, James L. 1973. *Econometrics*. Homewood, Ill.: Irwin.

Nager, A. L. 1959. "The Bias and Moment Matrix of the General K-Class Estimators of the Parameters in Simultaneous Equations." *Econometrica*, Vol. 27, pp. 575–95.

Pindyck, R. S., and D. L. Rubenfeld. 1976. *Econometric Models and Economic Forecasts*. N.Y.: McGraw-Hill.

Sales and Marketing Management. 1975. "Special Report: Forecasting for Higher Profits."

Summers, R. 1965. "A Capital-Intensive Approach to the Small Sample Properties of Various Simultaneous Equation Estimators." *Econometrica*, Vol. 33, pp. 1–41.

Tinbergen, J. 1939. *Business Cycles in the United States of America, 1919–32*. Geneva: League of Nations.

von Hohenbalken, B., and G. Tintner. 1962. "Econometric Models of the O.E.E.C. Member Countries, the United States and Canada, and their Application to Economic Policy." *Weltwirtschaftliches Archiv*, Vol. 89, pp. 29–86.

Wise, K. T. 1975. "Scrap: Prices and Issues." *Iron and Steelmaker*, May, pp. 23–32.

PART FOUR

AUTOREGRESSIVE/MOVING AVERAGE (ARMA) TIME-SERIES METHODS

With the advent of widespread computer applications in organizations, the much more general and statistically based methods of time-series analysis known as autoregressive/moving average (ARMA) processes could be developed and applied in forecasting. Part Four covers the complete range of those ARMA approaches currently in use. The essence of these approaches is similar to smoothing and decomposition methods in that they are based on historical time-series analysis. However, the approach used in identifying the patterns in such historical time series and the methodology for extrapolating those into the future is unique to ARMA processes.

While these autoregressive/moving average approaches are theoretically and statistically very appealing, their complexity has in many instances hindered their widespread adoption as a basis for forecasting in organizations. In order to use these methodologies, substantial analysis of historical time-series data must be performed, appropriate models must be estimated, and those models must be applied to forecasting purposes. While several useful guidelines have been developed to handle each of these tasks, there is still a substantial need for experience and some trial and error in successfully using these approaches.

Chapter 8 presents the basis of all autoregressive/moving average schemes. This chapter includes a discussion of autocorrelation analysis, stationarity (and its achievement), and seasonality. Chapter 9 discusses the authors' own approach to estimating the parameters for autoregressive/moving average models. This approach, known as generalized adaptive filtering, is one that can be used in a fairly intuitive fashion initially and can then be upgraded and made more rigorous as the forecaster gains additional experience with it.

Chapter 10 examines the Box-Jenkins approach to autoregressive/moving average forecasting applications, and Chapter 11 looks at the extension of univariate ARMA processes to multivariate time series. Through these extensions, ARMA approaches can in fact be used as causal models, much as multiple regression can be. While still in their early stages of development, such multivariate time-series approaches are likely to find increased use in the next decade.

8 TIME-SERIES ANALYSIS

8/1 Introduction to Autoregressive Schemes

In Part Two of this book, two major categories of time-series forecasting techniques were examined—smoothing and decomposition. Smoothing methods base their forecasts on the principle of averaging (smoothing) past errors by adding a percentage of the error to a percentage of the previous forecast. Mathematically, single smoothing methods are of the form:

$$F_{t+1} = F_t + \alpha(X_t - F_t). \tag{8-1}$$

Equation (8-1) can be expanded by substituting $F_t = F_{t-1} + \alpha(X_{t-1} - F_{t-1})$.

$$\text{Thus} \quad F_{t+1} = F_{t-1} + \alpha(X_{t-1} - F_{t-1}) + \alpha(X_t - F_t). \tag{8-2}$$

Substituting for F_{t-1} in the first term of (8-2) gives

$$F_{t+1} = F_{t-2} + \alpha(X_{t-2} - F_{t-2}) + \alpha(X_{t-1} - F_{t-1}) + \alpha(X_t - F_t). \tag{8-3}$$

The results of further expanding this substitution should be clear. Given some initial forecast, call it F_{t-2}, new forecasts can be obtained by adding a percentage of the errors between the actual and forecast values (e.g., $X_{t-2} - F_{t-2}$) to this initial forecast. Since some of the errors will be negative and some positive, the final forecast, F_{t+1}, will be close to the actual pattern of data, on average.

Time-series decomposition methods are based on the principle of "breaking down" a time series into each of its components of seasonality, trend, cycle, and randomness and then forecasting by predicting each component separately (except randomness, which cannot be predicted) and recombining those predictions. Both smoothing and decomposition methods express their forecasts as a function of time only.

In Part Three, another approach to forecasting, causal or explanatory methods, was discussed. The three methods examined there are similar in concept, but differ in the level of sophistication they require. In their general form, regression methods attempt to forecast variations in some variable of interest, the dependent variable, based on variations in a number of other factors.

In multiple regression, the causal or explanatory model is of the form:

$$Y = a + b_1 X_1 + b_2 X_2 + \cdots + b_k X_k + u \tag{8-4}$$

In this chapter, the focus will be on some of the same principles used in regression methods and their application to time-series methods. Thus, a combination of the methodologies and their concepts will be examined.

In equation (8-4), $X_1, X_2, \ldots, X_k$ can represent any factors such as GNP, advertising, prices, money supply, etc. Suppose, however, that these variables are defined as $X_1 = Y_{t-1}$, $X_2 = Y_{t-2}$, $X_3 = Y_{t-3}$, $\ldots$, $X_k = Y_{t-k}$. Equation (8-4) then becomes

$$Y_t = a + b_1 Y_{t-1} + b_2 Y_{t-2} + \cdots + b_k Y_{t-k} + u_t. \tag{8-5}$$

Equation (8-5) is still a regression equation, but differs from (8-4) in that the right-hand side variables of (8-4) are different independent factors, while those of (8-5) are previous values of the dependent variable Y_t. These are simply time-lagged values of the dependent variable, and therefore the name autoregression (AR) is used to describe equations or schemes of the form of (8-5). By examining equation (3-7) which is shown below, it can be seen that the method of single exponential smoothing has a form very similar to (8-5).

$$F_{t+1} = \alpha X_t + \alpha(1 - \alpha)X_{t-1} + \alpha(1 - \alpha)^2 X_{t-2} + \alpha(1 - \alpha)^3 X_{t-3} + \alpha(1 - \alpha)^4 X_{t-4} \cdots. \tag{3-7}$$

In forecasting with exponential smoothing the past values are weighted by using the coefficients (parameters) α, $\alpha(1 - \alpha)$, $\alpha(1 - \alpha)^2$, $\alpha(1 - \alpha)^3$, $\ldots$.

One question that arises from considering equation (8-5) is why regression that is applied to a time series (i.e., autoregression) should be treated differently from the regression used in causal models. The answer is twofold:

1. In autoregression the basic assumption of the independence of the residuals can be easily violated, since the independent variables of equation (8-5) usually depend upon each other.
2. Determining the number of past terms of Y_t to include in equation (8-5) is not an easy task.

For these reasons autoregression can be effectively coupled with moving average terms to form a very general and highly accurate class of time series models called autoregressive/moving average (ARMA) schemes or processes.

8/2 Identifying the Characteristics of a Time Series

In Chapter 3 it was shown that smoothing methods should not be used indiscriminately, but rather that the characteristics of the time series should be identified in order to select the right smoothing methods. A similar phase should precede use of the ARMA models that will be discussed in the next three chapters. Identifying characteristics of a series such as stationarity, seasonality, etc., require a systematic approach. One such process is called time-series analysis and utilizes the autocorrelation coefficients for different time lags of the variable to be forecast.

Equation (8-5) consists of a dependent variable, Y_t, and k right-hand side variables, $Y_{t-1}, Y_{t-2}, \ldots, Y_{t-k}$, all of which are past values of the dependent variable. The simple correlations between Y_t and Y_{t-1}, Y_t and Y_{t-2}, Y_t and Y_{t-3}, or any Y_t and Y_{t-k} can be found as described previously for regression. Since these correlations refer to the same (auto) variable, but of different time periods (lags), they are called autocorrelations. Their meaning is exactly the same as that of correlations. The autocorrelation of Y_t and Y_{t-1}, for example, indicates how variable Y_t and Y_{t-1} are related to each other.

If one had a completely random series and computed the correlation of Y_t and Y_{t-1}, it would be close to zero, since each value of the time series would be unrelated to other values. Autocorrelation coefficients close to zero indicate a time series whose successive values are not related to each other. On the other hand, the autocorrelation of successive values, Y_t and Y_{t-1}, of the noiseless time series—1, 2, 3, 4, ..., 20—would be expected to be very high, since there is a high degree of dependence between successive values. Looking at autocorrelations for time lags of more than one period would provide additional information on how values of a given time series are related.

Suppose monthly data for a time series is available and one wants to know whether the series is seasonal. If it is seasonal, data for periods that are 12 months apart would be related to each other. For example, in seasonal data all Januaries may be higher than the average and all Augusts may be lower. If this is the case, the autocorrelation between Y_t and Y_{t-12} will show it with a large value. If the autocorrelation of 12 time lags is close to zero, it will indicate the absence of a relationship between the same months of successive years and therefore a lack of seasonal pattern. In a similar manner the autocorrelations of other time lags can be used to learn the following about the data:

1. Are the data random?
2. Are the data stationary?
3. If nonstationary, at what level do they become stationary?
4. Are the data seasonal?
5. If seasonal, what is the length of seasonality?

The above characteristics can be determined in a routine manner using auto-correlation analysis. The procedure for this analysis will be examined in the next sections.

8/3 Autocorrelation Coefficients

The meaning of autocorrelation coefficients can best be seen using a graphic illustration and considering the mathematics involved. As an example, suppose that variable Y_t denotes the demand for product A and for the past ten time periods has been observed to have the values shown in column 2 of Table 8-1.

TABLE 8-1   TIME SERIES OF DEMAND FOR PRODUCT A

(1) Time (or period) t	(2) Original Variable Y_t	(3) One Time Lag Variable Y_{t-1}	(4) Two Time Lag Variable Y_{t-2}
1	13	8	15
2	8	15	4
3	15	4	4
4	4	4	12
5	4	12	11
6	12	11	7
7	11	7	14
8	7	14	12
9	14	12	—
10	12	—	—

Based on the data in Table 8-1, Y_t might be expressed as

$$Y_t = a + b_1 Y_{t-1} + b_2 Y_{t-2} + u_t. \tag{8-6}$$

Equation (8-6) is an AR time-series model expressing Y_t as a linear combination of its two preceding values. Variables Y_{t-1} and Y_{t-2} are constructed easily by moving the values forward one and two periods respectively. That results in losing one value for Y_{t-1} and two values for Y_{t-2}. The autocorrelations between Y_t and Y_{t-1}, and Y_t and Y_{t-2} can be computed without difficulty. The autocorrelation of Y_t and Y_{t-1} will indicate how successive values of the same variable relate to each other, and the autocorrelation of Y_t and Y_{t-2} will indicate how successive values two periods apart (two time lags) relate to each other.

The simple correlation coefficient between Y_t and Y_{t-1} can be found using (2-19) or its equivalent, (5-12), as restated below in (8-7).

$$r_{Y_t, Y_{t-1}} = \frac{\sum\limits_{t=1}^{n-1} (Y_t - \bar{Y}_t)(Y_{t-1} - \bar{Y}_{t-1})}{\sigma_{Y_t} \sigma_{Y_{t-1}}}, \tag{8-7}$$

where

$$\sigma_{Y_t} = \sqrt{\frac{\Sigma(Y_t - \bar{Y}_t)^2}{n-1}} \tag{8-8}$$

and

$$\sigma_{Y_{t-1}} = \sqrt{\frac{\Sigma(Y_{t-1} - \bar{Y}_{t-1})^2}{n-1}}. \tag{8-9}$$

The result for the data in Table 8-1 is

$$r_{Y_t, Y_{t-1}} = \frac{-27}{12(11.6)} = -.19 \quad \text{(one time lag)}$$

and

$$r_{Y_t, Y_{t-2}} = .22 \quad \text{(two time lags)}.$$

Equation (8-7) can be simplified and made more directly applicable to time-series autocorrelations by making the assumption that the series Y_t is stationary, so that $\bar{Y}_t = \bar{Y}_{t-1}$. In most cases the fact that Y_{t-1} has one less observation will only make a small difference, which can usually be ignored, particularly if the series is stationary (contains no trend). Similarly equation (8-8) and (8-9) will generally have about the same value.

Using these simplifying assumptions, equation (8-7) becomes

$$r_{Y_t, Y_{t-1}} = \frac{\sum\limits_{t=1}^{n-1} (Y_t - \bar{Y}_t)(Y_{t-1} - \bar{Y}_t)}{\sigma_{Y_t}^2} \tag{8-10}$$

$$= \frac{\sum\limits_{t=1}^{n-1} (Y_t - \bar{Y}_t)(Y_{t-1} - \bar{Y}_t)}{\sum\limits_{t=1}^{n} (Y_t - \bar{Y}_t)^2}. \tag{8-11}$$

The assumption of stationarity provides an additional advantage in that the autocorrelation coefficient between Y_{t-1} and Y_{t-2} will be the same as between Y_t and Y_{t-1} because the means will be the same and Y_{t-1} will on average be equal to Y_t or Y_{t-2}. Equation (8-11) is general and can be used for all time lags of one period for a time series. Thus, (8-11) can be written as:

$$r_1 = \frac{\sum\limits_{t=1}^{n-1} (Y_t - \bar{Y_t})(Y_{t-1} - \bar{Y_t})}{\sum\limits_{t=1}^{n} (Y_t - \bar{Y_t})^2},$$

(8-12)

where r_1 denotes the autocorrelation coefficient of one time lag.

Similarly the autocorrelations for $2, 3, 4, \ldots, m$ time lags can be found and denoted by r_k. These can be computed using the general equation,

$$r_k = \frac{\sum\limits_{t=1}^{n-k} (Y_t - \bar{Y})(Y_{t+k} - \bar{Y})}{\sum\limits_{t=1}^{n} (Y_t - \bar{Y_t})^2}.$$

(8-13)

In equation (8-13) the summation of Y_{t+k} has been reordered from that in (8-12). This does not affect the results, since stationarity has been assumed. Equation (8-13) can be interpreted exactly as the correlation coefficient for regression—the square of (8-13) is the ratio of explained to total variation indicating whether the autoregression line between Y_t and Y_{t+k} is better than the mean line of $\bar{Y_t}$, and by how much on a relative scale between zero and one.

Before further interpreting the autocorrelation coefficients and their use in time-series analysis, it is instructive to see how autocorrelation coefficients can be calculated using equation (8-13) and the original data series. For the series in column 2 of Table 8-1,

$$r_1 = \frac{(13-10)(8-10)+(8-10)(15-10)+(15-10)(4-10)+\cdots+(14-10)(12-10)}{(13-10)^2+(8-10)^2+(15-10)^2+(4-10)^2+\cdots+(14-10)^2+(12-10)^2}$$

$$= \frac{3(-2)+(-2)(5)+5(-6)+5(-6)+(-6)(2)+\cdots+(4)(2)}{3^2+(-2)^2+5^2+(-6)^2+\cdots+4^2+2^2}$$

$$= \frac{-27}{144} = -.188.$$

Equation (8-13) is clearly computationally a more efficient way to calculate autocorrelations than equation (8-7). Furthermore, it has properties that facilitate identification of nonstationarity when it exists in the data.

Using equation (8-13) r_2, r_3, etc., can also be computed. For example, the value of r_2 is

$$r_2 = \frac{(13-10)(15-10)+(8-10)(4-10)+(15-10)(4-10)+\cdots+(7-10)(12-10)}{(13-10)^2+(8-10)^2+(15-10)^2+\cdots+(14-10)^2+(12-10)^2}$$

$$= \frac{(-3)(5) + (-2)(-6) + 5(-6) + \cdots + (-3)(2)}{3^2 + (-2)^2 + 5^2 + \cdots + 4^2 + 2^2}$$

$$= \frac{-29}{144} = -.201.$$

The autocorrelation coefficients for r_3 and r_4 are .181 and $-.132$, respectively.

8/4 The Sampling Distribution of Autocorrelations

Table 8-2 gives the values of a time series consisting of 36 observations. This series was constructed using random numbers between 0 and 100. Suppose, however, that this fact were not known. It could be determined by applying the concept of autocorrelations discussed in the previous two sections.

TABLE 8-2 TIME SERIES WITH 36 VALUES

Period	Value	Period	Value	Period	Value
1	23	13	86	25	17
2	59	14	33	26	45
3	36	15	90	27	9
4	99	16	74	28	72
5	36	17	7	29	33
6	74	18	54	30	17
7	30	19	98	31	3
8	54	20	50	32	29
9	17	21	86	33	30
10	36	22	90	34	68
11	89	23	65	35	87
12	77	24	20	36	44

Theoretically, all autocorrelation coefficients for a series of random numbers must be zero. This, however, assumes an infinite sample. The 36 observations in Table 8-2 are only one of many possible samples of 36 random numbers. If another set of 36 random numbers had been selected, they would have somewhat different autocorrelation coefficients. If an infinite number of samples of 36 random numbers were taken and their autocorrelation coefficients for 1, 2, 3, ..., 10 time lags were averaged, the resulting values would all be very close to zero. If ρ_k is used to denote the autocorrelation for the entire population then auto-correlations for different samples of values should form a distribution around ρ_k. The distribution can be determined using statistical theory.

As shown by Anderson (1942), Bartlett (1946), Quenouille (1949), and others, the autocorrelation coefficients of random data have a sampling distribution that can be approximated by a normal curve with mean zero and standard error $1/\sqrt{n}$. This information can be used to develop tests of hypotheses similar to those of the F-test and the t-tests examined in Chapters 5 and 6. These can be used to determine whether some r_k comes from a population whose value is zero at k time lags. Since n is 36 in Table 8-2, the standard error is $1/\sqrt{36} = .167$. This means that 95% of all sample-based autocorrelation coefficients must lie within a range specified by the mean plus or minus 1.96* standard errors. That is, the data series can be concluded to be random if the calculated autocorrelation coefficients are within the limits

$$-1.96(.167) \leq r_k \leq +1.96(.167),$$

$$-.327 \leq r_k \leq .327.$$

Figure 8-1 shows the autocorrelation coefficients for the data in Table 8-2 for time lags of 1, 2, 3, ..., 10. The two dotted lines perpendicular to the horizontal axis are the upper and lower 95% confidence limits for a random series $(-.327, +.327)$. All ten autocorrelation coefficients do lie within these limits, confirming what in this case was already known—the data are random.

The concept of a sampling distribution is of critical importance in time-series analysis. The autocorrelation coefficient corresponding to a time lag of seven periods in Figure 8-1 is .275. This value is different from 0 because of chance in the actual sample of data used. The sampling distribution provides guidelines as to what is chance and what is a significant relationship. The value of .275 is not statistically significant from 0. However, if this value had been obtained for 360 observations instead of 36, the standard error would have been only .053 and the confidence limits would have been $\pm.105$, instead of $\pm.333$. In that case an r_7 of .275 would have indicated the presence of a pattern, since it falls outside the confidence limits. Of course, with 360 random values, it would be very unlikely to observe such a high r value. Owing to chance, the auto-correlation values will be slightly different from those theoretically expected, necessitating the use of such confidence limits. Success in time-series analysis depends in large part on interpreting the results from autocorrelation analysis and being able to distinguish the pattern from randomness in the data.

---

* The value of 1.96 is found by looking at Table A, Appendix I, of areas under the normal curve. Since it is close to 2, it is often approximated by 2.

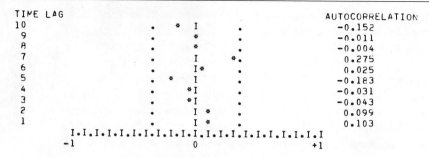

```
TIME LAG                                                   AUTOCORRELATION
10               .    *   I          .                        -0.152
 9               .        *          .                        -0.011
 8               .        *          .                        -0.004
 7               .        I       *. .                         0.275
 6               .        I*         .                         0.025
 5               .    *   I          .                        -0.183
 4               .       *I          .                        -0.031
 3               .       *I          .                        -0.043
 2               .        I *        .                         0.099
 1               .        I *        .                         0.103
      I.I.I.I.I.I.I.I.I.I.I.I.I.I.I.I.I.I.I.I
     -1                   0                   +1
```

FIGURE 8-1 AUTOCORRELATIONS FOR SERIES IN TABLE 8-2

8/5 Autocorrelation Analysis

8/5/1 Determining Randomness of Data (or Residuals)

As seen in the previous section, autocorrelations can be used to determine whether a set of data is random. The autocorrelation coefficients of several time lags are examined to see if any of them are significantly different from zero. It is useful to plot the autocorrelation coefficients as in Figure 8-1 as one step in determining whether any pattern exists. (Those of Figure 8-1 have none.)

Once a forecasting model has been fitted, autocorrelations can be computed for the series residual errors to determine whether they are random. For example, in Table 3-11 it is clear that the forecasting errors using linear exponential smoothing were not random—there is a definite pattern in the errors indicating that the model chosen was not an appropriate one. While the pattern in the errors in Table 3-11 was obvious, in many cases it is not. A standard approach for determining whether the errors are random is to compute the autocorrelations of the errors.

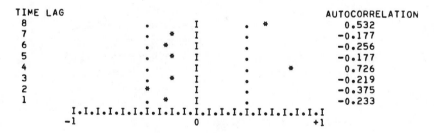

```
TIME LAG                                                   AUTOCORRELATION
 8               .        I          .    *                    0.532
 7               .    *   I          .                        -0.177
 6               .   *    I          .                        -0.256
 5               .    *   I          .                        -0.177
 4               .        I          .        *                0.726
 3               .    *   I          .                        -0.219
 2               .*       I          .                        -0.375
 1               .   *    I          .                        -0.233
      I.I.I.I.I.I.I.I.I.I.I.I.I.I.I.I.I.I.I.I
     -1                   0                   +1
```

FIGURE 8-2 AUTOCORRELATIONS FOR RESIDUAL SERIES
              FROM TABLE 3-11

Figure 8-2 shows the autocorrelations for the residuals of the single exponential smoothing model of Table 3-11. It can be seen that the autocorrelation corresponding to a time lag of four periods is $r_4 = .726$, indicating that there is a pattern in the residuals. This result is expected, since the export data in Table 3-11 are seasonal and single smoothing cannot deal with seasonality. The autocorrelation for a time lag of eight periods is also large and outside the random limits suggesting a recurrence of the quarterly pattern every two years.

Figure 8-3 shows the autocorrelations for the residuals remaining after using Winters' linear and seasonal smoothing methods. This method has eliminated the seasonal pattern completely and has produced residuals for which the autocorrelations are almost random (however not completely).

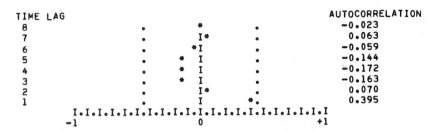

FIGURE 8-3 AUTOCORRELATIONS FOR RESIDUAL SERIES AFTER USING WINTERS' LINEAR AND SEASONAL SMOOTHING METHODS

From Figures 8-2 and 8-3 it can be seen that there are no major problems in determining whether a series of data (or residual errors) are random. It can be done by computing the autocorrelations and plotting them to see whether they are significantly different from zero.

8/5/2 Existence of Stationarity

The characteristic of stationarity* in a data series can be easily identified by examining the autocorrelation coefficients. The autocorrelations of stationary data drop to zero after the second or third time lag, while for a nonstationary series they are significantly different from zero for several time periods. When represented graphically, the autocorrelations of nonstationary data show a trend going diagonally from right to left as the number of time lags increases.

---

* *Stationarity* means that there is no growth or decline in the data. The data must be horizontal along the *x*-, or time, axis. In other words the data fluctuate around a constant mean, independent of time.

Figure 8-4 shows the graph of autocorrelations for a nonstationary series. The autocorrelations of one to five time lags are not significantly different from zero and the existence of a trend (see broken line) can be clearly seen.

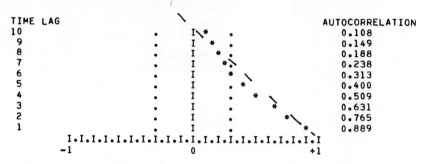

```
TIME LAG                                                    AUTOCORRELATION
10                          .   I\*   .                          0.108
 9                          .   I  *   .                         0.149
 8                          .   I   *  .                         0.188
 7                          .   I    */.                         0.238
 6                          .   I    * \                         0.313
 5                          .   I    . *  \                      0.400
 4                          .   I    .  *  \                      0.509
 3                          .   I    .      *                    0.631
 2                          .   I    .    *\                      0.765
 1                          .   I    .      *\                    0.889
     I.I.I.I.I.I.I.I.I.I.I.I.I.I.I.I.I.I.I.I.I
    -1                      0                      +1
```

FIGURE 8-4 AUTOCORRELATION COEFFICIENTS OF A NONSTATIONARY SERIES

The existence of a trend in the data means that successive values are highly correlated with each other. In such an instance the autocorrelation for one time lag should be large. The autocorrelation of two time lags should be large also, but not as much so for two reasons:

1. In terms of percentage (which is what correlation measures) the increase among successive values of two time lags is smaller than that of one.
2. There will be one less term in the numerator of (8-13) when the autocorrelation of two time lags is computed, while the denominator will have the same number of terms. Similarly, r_3 will be large, since successive values of three periods apart relate to each other when there is a trend, but it will be smaller than r_1 and r_2 for the same reasons.

The autocorrelations for many nonstationary series will be a straight line if no randomness or other variations are present, and will fluctuate around a

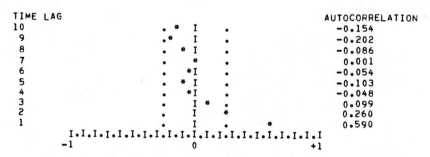

```
TIME LAG                                                    AUTOCORRELATION
10                  .  *  I    .                                -0.154
 9                  .*     I    .                               -0.202
 8                  .   *  I    .                               -0.086
 7                  .      *     .                               0.001
 6                  .     *I     .                              -0.054
 5                  .    *  I    .                              -0.103
 4                  .     *I     .                              -0.048
 3                  .      I *   .                               0.099
 2                  .      I    *                                0.260
 1                  .      I    .        *                       0.590
     I.I.I.I.I.I.I.I.I.I.I.I.I.I.I.I.I.I.I.I.I
    -1                      0                      +1
```

FIGURE 8-5 AUTOCORRELATION COEFFICIENTS OF A STATIONARY SERIES

straight line when other variations do exist. Figure 8-4 indicates a nonstationary series, since the autocorrelations do not drop to zero after the second or third value and show a trend. Figure 8-5, on the other hand, shows the autocorrelations corresponding to a stationary but nonrandom series. After two time lags the autocorrelations are not significantly different from zero. The significant autocorrelations for time lags of one and two periods imply the existence of some pattern other than trend.

8/5/3 Removing Nonstationarity

Trends of any kind tend to introduce spurious autocorrelations that dominate the autocorrelation pattern. It is imperative, therefore, to remove the nonstationarity from the data before proceeding further with time-series analysis. Removing trends can be routinely achieved through the method of *differencing*.*

Consider the simple series 2, 4, 6, 8, ..., 20, consisting of a linear trend and no randomness. Subtracting consecutive values, $4 - 2$, $6 - 4$, $8 - 6$, ..., $20 - 18$, gives as the first differences, the series 2, 2, 2, ..., 2. This series is clearly stationary. Thus to achieve stationarity, a new series is created that consists of the differences between successive periods:

$$X'_t = X_{t+1} - X_t. \tag{8-14}$$

The new series, X'_t, will have $n - 1$ values and will be stationary if the trend in the original data X_t is linear (of first order).

Taking the first difference of the data used in Figure 8-4 gives a series whose autocorrelations are shown in Figure 8-6. In Figure 8-6 the first and second

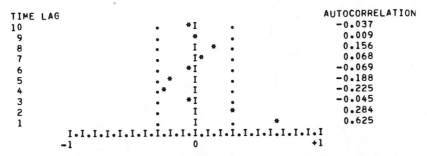

FIGURE 8-6 AUTOCORRELATIONS OF FIRST DIFFERENCES OF NONSTATIONARY DATA (SEE FIGURE 8-4)

---

* In Chapter 4 an alternative method for removing trends was discussed. That method divided the trended data by the moving average to obtain a series without trend. The method of *differencing* is an alternative, more computationally efficient procedure and is better suited for ARMA models.

autocorrelation coefficients are significantly different from zero but the rest are not, which indicates that the series of first differences has transformed the data into stationary form.

If the autocorrelations of the first differenced data do not drop to zero after the second or third lag, it indicates that stationarity has not yet been achieved and therefore first differences of the first differenced data can be taken:

$$X_t'' = X_{t+1}' - X_t'. \tag{8-15}$$

X_t'' is referred to as the series of second differences. This series will have $n - 2$ values.

Substituting (8-14) into (8-15) yields

$$X_t'' = (X_{t+2} - X_{t+1}) - (X_{t+1} - X_t),$$
$$X_t'' = X_{t+2} - 2X_{t+1} + X_t. \tag{8-16}$$

The process of differencing can be applied to the data of Table 8-3, which is known to include a second level, or degree, of nonstationarity. As part of this example the mechanics of differencing can also be reviewed.

Column 3 of Table 8-3 is the first differences, which are found using equation (8-14):

$$X_1' = X_2 - X_1 = 5.3 - 2.44 = 2.88,$$
$$X_2' = X_3 - X_2 = 8.97 - 5.3 = 3.67,$$

    .

    .

    .

$$X_{11}' = X_{12} - X_{11} = 92.13 - 79.63 = 12.5.$$

It is not possible to calculate X_{12}'; therefore the first differenced series has only $n - 1$ observations.

The second differences in Table 8-3, column 4, are found using equation (8-15):

$$X_1'' = X_2' - X_1' = 3.67 - 2.86 = .81,$$
$$X_2'' = X_3' - X_2' = 4.91 - 3.67 = 1.24,$$

    .

    .

    .

$$X_{10}'' = X_{11}' - X_{10}' = 12.5 - 12.27 = .23.$$

TABLE 8-3 SAMPLE TIME SERIES WITH FIRST AND SECOND
DIFFERENCES

(1) Period	(2) Time Series	(3) First Difference	(4) Second Difference
1	2.44	2.86	.81
2	5.3	3.67	1.24
3	8.97	4.91	.79
4	13.88	5.7	1.71
5	19.58	7.41	1.55
6	26.99	8.96	.95
7	35.95	9.91	−.07
8	45.86	9.84	1.82
9	55.7	11.66	.61
10	67.36	12.27	.23
11	79.63	12.5	—
12	92.13	—	—

Again, it is not possible to calculate X''_{11} or X''_{12}, resulting in the loss of two values in the series of second differences.

The values of the second differences could have been found using equation (8-16):

$$X''_1 = X_3 - 2X_2 + X_1 = 8.97 - 2(5.3) + 2.44 = .81,$$

$$X''_2 = X_4 - 2X_3 + X_2 = 13.88 - 2(8.97) + 5.3 = 1.24,$$

$$\cdot$$
$$\cdot$$
$$\cdot$$

$$X''_{10} = X_{12} - 2X_{11} + X_{10} = 92.13 - 2(79.63) + 67.36 = .23.$$

If nothing were known about the time-series data of Table 8-3, a first step in analysis would be to compute the autocorrelations for the original time-series data in column 2. These autocorrelations are shown in Figure 8-7. It is clear that the data are not stationary because of the trend in the autocorrelations. Next the differenced data of column 3 can be used and their autocorrelations calculated. The results are shown in Figure 8-8. These autocorrelations do not behave much differently from those of Figure 8-7. That is, they do not drop to zero rapidly, suggesting nonstationarity in the series of first differenced data. It is necessary, therefore, to take another difference (first difference of the first difference, or a second difference) and find the autocorrelations of the second differenced data shown in column 4 of Table 8-3. The autocorrelations of the second difference are shown in Figure 8-9 and indicate stationarity at this level.

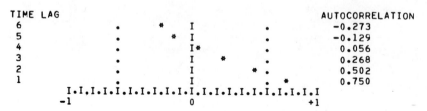

FIGURE 8-7 AUTOCORRELATIONS OF ORIGINAL DATA (SEE TABLE 8-3)

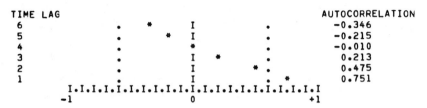

FIGURE 8-8 AUTOCORRELATIONS OF FIRST DIFFERENCED DATA (SEE TABLE 8-3)

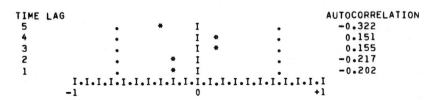

FIGURE 8-9 AUTOCORRELATIONS OF SECOND DIFFERENCED DATA (SEE TABLE 8-3)

Achieving stationarity can be reduced to a rather mechanical task of taking successive differences until the autocorrelations drop to zero within two or three time lags. In practice, it is seldom necessary to go beyond second differences, because real data generally involve nonstationarities of only the first or second level.

8/5/4 Recognizing Seasonality

Seasonality is defined as a pattern that repeats itself over fixed intervals of time. The sales of heating oil, for example, are high in winter and low in summer, indicating a 12-month seasonal pattern. If the pattern is a consistent one, the autocorrelation coefficient of 12-month lags will have a high positive value indicating the existence of seasonality. If it were not significantly different from zero, it would indicate that months one year apart are unrelated (random) with no consistent pattern emerging from one year to the next. Such data would not be seasonal.

For stationary data, seasonality can be found by identifying those auto-correlation coefficients of more than two or three time lags that are significantly different from zero. Any autocorrelation that is significantly different from zero implies the existence of a pattern in the data. To recognize seasonality, one must look for such high autocorrelations.

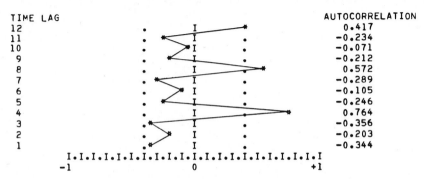

```
TIME LAG                                            AUTOCORRELATION
12                          I          *                0.417
11               *          I          •               -0.234
10               *          I          •               -0.071
 9               *          I             *            -0.212
 8                          I                *          0.572
 7               *          I          •               -0.289
 6                 *        I          •               -0.105
 5                *         I          •               -0.246
 4                          I                  *        0.764
 3             *            I          •               -0.356
 2                *         I          •               -0.203
 1               *          I          •               -0.344
        I.I.I.I.I.I.I.I.I.I.I.I.I.I.I.I.I.I.I.I.I
       -1                   0                   +1
```

FIGURE 8-10   AUTOCORRELATION COEFFICIENTS OF QUARTERLY DATA

The autocorrelation coefficients shown in Figure 8-10 indicate a clear seasonal pattern of four periods duration (four quarters). It can be seen that $r_4 = .764$, which is significantly different from zero. Similarly $r_8 = .572$ is significant and $r_{12} = .417$ is on the border of the limits. The periodic character of seasonality can be seen by the fact that $r_4 > r_8 > r_{12}$ and all three are significantly different from zero. Actually, the autocorrelation $r_4 = .764$ suffices to indicate seasonality with a length of four periods. The additional fact that r_8 and r_{12} are large confirms it.

Seasonality can be easily seen in a graph of autocorrelations or by simply looking at the autocorrelations of different time lags if it is the only pattern present. Seasonality is not always easy to identify when it is combined with other patterns such as trend. The stronger the trend, the less obvious the seasonality will be, since spurious autocorrelations result from the existence of nonstationarity in the data. This problem can be avoided by only determining seasonality when the data are stationary. As a rule, the presence of a trend in the data indicates that the data should be transformed to a stationary series using the method of differencing before determining seasonality.

Figure 8-11 shows a set of autocorrelations for a nonstationary data series. The trend can be easily seen in the autocorrelations. The autocorrelation corresponding to a four-period time lag is $r_4 = .589$. Its value is larger than the previous two, and similarly, r_8 is larger than the two preceding it. This suggests the existence of seasonality, but does not clearly identify it. After detecting the trend, the series must be differenced and the autocorrelations of the differenced series must be calculated. The result is the graph shown previously in Figure 8-10. The differenced series is stationary, since no autocorrelation coefficients except the seasonal ones are significantly different from zero. Figure 8-10 shows a clear seasonal pattern whose length is four periods. As is frequently the case, it was not necessary to plot the data to determine which smoothing model to use and the length of seasonality, since autocorrelation analysis answered both questions.

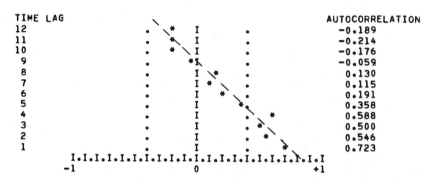

FIGURE 8-11   AUTOCORRELATION COEFFICIENTS OF QUARTERLY DATA WITH STRONG TREND

Not all autocorrelations for data with trend and seasonality will behave as shown in Figures 8-10 and 8-11. When the trend is much stronger in comparison to seasonality, the autocorrelations of the original data may fall on a line. On the other extreme, the seasonality may be clear and dominate the trend. Thus as a first step in autocorrelation analysis, nonstationarity must be removed. Once that is done, other patterns can be examined. Three cases are possible:

1. The autocorrelations may behave as those of Figure 8-1. (None is significantly different from zero.)
2. The autocorrelations may show some pattern, such as in Figure 8.5. (Only the first two or three autocorrelations are significant.)

3. The autocorrelations may be similar to those in Figure 8-10, which show a seasonal pattern.

8/6 The χ^2-Test

Box and Pierce (1970) have developed a test (known as the Box-Pierce Q-statistic) that is capable of determining whether several autocorrelation coefficients are significantly different from zero. This test is based on the χ^2 (chi-squared) distribution of the autocorrelation coefficients. If the computed value of the test is less than that from the table of values of the χ^2 statistic (see Table E of Appendix I), the autocorrelations used to calculate the test are not significantly different from zero. This indicates that the data generating the autocorrelations are random. If the computed χ^2-test (i.e., Q-statistic) is larger than the value from the table, the autocorrelations are significantly different from zero, indicating the existence of some pattern.

The Q-statistic is computed as

$$\chi^2\text{-test} = n \sum_{k=1}^{m} r_k^2, \tag{8-17}$$

where m is the largest time lag included.

The smaller the autocorrelations, the smaller the value of χ^2.

The chi-squared value for the autocorrelations of Figure 8-8 ($n = 12$) is

$$\chi^2 = 12[.751^2 + .452^2 + .213^2 + (-.01)^2 + (-.215)^2 + (-.347)^2]$$

$$= 12(.98) = 11.76.$$

Similarly, the χ^2 corresponding to Figure 8-9 is

$$\chi^2 = 12[(-.202)^2 + (-.217)^2 + .155^2 + .151^2 + (-.322)^2]$$

$$= 12(.238) = 2.86.$$

The fact that the χ^2 corresponding to Figure 8-9 is much smaller indicates that the autocorrelations of Figure 8-9 are much closer to being random that those of 8.8.

The χ^2-test can be applied as a first approximation in determining the extent of randomness in the autocorrelations and consequently in the data. This χ^2-test also holds true when applied to the autocorrelations of residual errors. If the computed value of the χ^2 of the residuals is smaller than the value from the χ^2 table (for the given degrees of freedom), the hypothesis that the auto-correlations are not significantly different from zero is supported, indicating that the residuals are randomly distributed and that the model used is a good one, since only random errors remain.

8/7 Partial Autocorrelations

Partial autocorrelations are used to measure the degree of association between X_t and X_{t-g} when the effect of other time lags on X is held constant. Their singular purpose in time-series analysis is to help identify an appropriate ARMA model for forecasting. (In fact, they have been constructed just for this use.)

Partial autocorrelations are defined as the last autoregressive term of an AR(m) model. Thus, $\hat{\phi}_1, \hat{\phi}_2, \hat{\phi}_3, \ldots, \hat{\phi}_{m-1}, \hat{\phi}_m$ are the m partial autocorrelations of any AR process as can be seen in equations (8-18) through (8-22).

$$X_t = \hat{\phi}_1 X_{t-1} + e_t, \tag{8-18}$$

$$X_t = \phi_1 X_{t-1} + \hat{\phi}_2 X_{t-2} + e_t, \tag{8-19}$$

$$X_t = \phi_1 X_{t-1} + \phi_2 X_{t-2} + \hat{\phi}_3 X_{t-3} + e_t, \tag{8-20}$$

.

.

.

$$X_t = \phi_1 X_{t-1} + \phi_2 X_{t-2} + \cdots + \hat{\phi}_{m-1} X_{t-m+1} + e_t, \tag{8-21}$$

$$X_t = \phi_1 X_{t-1} + \phi_2 X_{t-2} + \cdots + \phi_{m-1} X_{t-m+1} + \hat{\phi}_m X_{t-m} + e_t. \tag{8-22}$$

It would of course be possible to solve this set of equations for $\hat{\phi}_1$, $\hat{\phi}_2$, $\hat{\phi}_3, \ldots, \hat{\phi}_{m-1}, \hat{\phi}_m$ to determine their values. The computations required, however, would be extremely time consuming. Therefore it is more satisfactory to obtain estimates of $\hat{\phi}_1, \hat{\phi}_2, \hat{\phi}_3, \ldots, \hat{\phi}_{m-1}, \hat{\phi}_m$ based on their autocorrelation coefficients. These estimations can be made by the following method.

If both sides of (8-18) are multiplied by X_{t-1}, the result is

$$X_{t-1} X_t = \hat{\phi}_1 X_{t-1} X_{t-1} + X_{t-1} e_t. \tag{8-23}$$

Taking the expected value of (8-23) yields

$$\gamma_1 = \phi_1 \gamma_0, \tag{8-24}$$

since $E(X_{t-1} X_t) = \gamma_1$, $E(X_{t-1} X_{t-1}) = \gamma_0$, and $E(X_{t-1} e_t) = 0$ by definition. (This process is further described in the Chapter 9 Appendix, Section 2.)

If both sides of (8-24) are divided by γ_0, the result is

$$\rho_1 = \hat{\phi}_1, \tag{8-25}$$

since $\rho_k = (\gamma_k / \gamma_0)$. Thus $\hat{\phi}_1 = \rho_1 = r_1$. That is, the partial autocorrelation of one time lag is ρ_1, or its sample estimate, r_1. In general, multiplying both sides of (8-18) through (8-22) by γ_{t-k}, taking expected values and dividing by γ_0 yields a set of simultaneous equations (called the Yule-Walker equations), which can be solved for $\hat{\phi}_1$, $\hat{\phi}_2$, $\hat{\phi}_3$, ..., $\hat{\phi}_{m-1}$, and $\hat{\phi}_m$. These values can then be used as estimates of the partial autocorrelations of up to m time lags. (Efficient recursive estimation procedures do exist for obtaining a solution to these equations.)

After one understands what partial autocorrelations are and how they can be obtained, the next concern is how to use them in identifying an appropriate ARMA model. If the underlying process generating a given series is an AR(1) model, it should be understood that only $\hat{\phi}_1$ will be significantly different from zero, while $\hat{\phi}_2$, $\hat{\phi}_3$, ..., $\hat{\phi}_{m-1}$, $\hat{\phi}_m$ will not be statistically significant. If the true generating process is AR(2), then only $\hat{\phi}_1$ and $\hat{\phi}_2$ will be significant, and the remaining estimated values will not be significant. The same can be said regarding higher-order AR processes.

In other words, because of the way in which $\hat{\phi}_1$, $\hat{\phi}_2$, $\hat{\phi}_3$, ..., $\hat{\phi}_{m-1}$, $\hat{\phi}_m$ are constructed, they will be significantly different from zero only up to the order of the true AR process generating the data. In model identification, it is then assumed that if there are only two significant partial autocorrelations, the generating process is of second order and the order of the forecasting model should be AR(2). If there are p significant partial autocorrelations, then the order should be AR(p).

For identification purposes, therefore, if the process is an autoregressive one (its autocorrelation coefficients decline to zero exponentially), the partial autocorrelations can be examined to determine the order of the process. That order is equal to the number of significant partial autocorrelations.

If the generating process is MA rather than AR, then the partial autocorrelations will not indicate the order of the MA process, since they are constructed to fit an AR process. In fact, they introduce a dependence from one lag to the next that makes them behave in a manner like that of autocorrelations for an AR process. That is, the partial autocorrelations will decline to zero exponentially. For identification purposes, when the partial autocorrelations do not exhibit a drop to random values after p time lags but instead decline to zero exponentially, it can be assumed that the true generating process is an MA one.

In summary, when there are only p partial autocorrelations that are significantly different from zero, the process is assumed to be an AR(p). When the partial autocorrelations tail off to zero exponentially, the process is assumed to be an MA one.

8/8 Summary of Time-Series Analysis

This chapter has shown that time-series analysis can be performed in a fairly mechanical manner using autocorrelations. The process is straightforward and requires only a minimum of human input. It consists of the following steps:

1. Find the autocorrelation coefficients of the original series. If they drop to zero quickly—after the second or third value—it indicates that the data are stationary at their original form. Thus, look for any patterns [see (3) below]. If they do not drop to zero, it indicates nonstationarity [see (2) below].

2. When the autocorrelations suggest nonstationarity, take the first differences of the original data and calculate their autocorrelations. If they indicate stationarity, look for any remaining pattern [see (3) below]. If they are still nonstationary, take the first differences again and examine their autocorrelations. For most practical purposes a maximum of two differences will transform the data into a stationary series.

3. If the data are stationary, examine their autocorrelations. If some with time lags of greater than three are significant, it indicates a seasonal pattern with length corresponding to the time lag of the largest autocorrelation. If the first three autocorrelations are significant, it suggests some other nonseasonal pattern (see Chapter 10). Finally, if none of the autocorrelations are significantly different from zero, it suggests that no pattern exists and that what remains is randomness.

It must be remembered that the graph of autocorrelations is completely different from the graph of the data. The graph of the data is a visual aid to help identify the behavior of the pattern. The autocorrelations are a summary of the pattern existing in the data. The graph of the autocorrelations can reveal a great deal about the data and their characteristics. With the wide availability of computers, calculating the autocorrelations is not the cumbersome job it used to be. This makes the job of time-series analysis relatively easy.

Finally, a word of caution: when the pattern of the data is nonseasonal, stationarity is indicated when all autocorrelations of more than two or three time lags are not significantly different from zero. When the data are seasonal, however, this rule may not always hold. The seasonal pattern may cause some autocorrelations of more than two or three lags to be nonzero. In such cases, it is better to examine how the autocorrelations distribute around zero on the graph, rather than relying on how fast they drop to zero. The same is true for the χ^2-test. A lower value will usually mean a less random series, but not always. Combined trend, seasonality, and randomness can distort its value.

REFERENCES AND SELECTED BIBLIOGRAPHY

Anderson, R. L. 1942. "Distribution of the Serial Correlation Coefficient." *Annals of Mathematical Statistics*, Vol. 13, pp. 1–13.

Bartlett, M. S. 1946. "On the Theoretical Specification of Sampling Properties of Autocorrelated Time Series." *Journal of the Royal Statistical Society*, Series B, Vol. 8, p. 27.

Box, G. E. P., and G. M. Jenkins. 1976. *Time Series Analysis: Forecasting and Control*, Revised Edition. San Francisco: Holden-Day.

Box, G. E. P., and D. A. Pierce. 1970. "Distribution of the Residual Autocorrelations in Autoregressive-Integrated Moving-Average Time Series Models." *Journal of the American Statistical Association*, Vol. 65, pp. 1509–26.

Makridakis, S., and S. Wheelwright. 1978. *Interactive Forecasting*. Second Edition, San Francisco, Calif.: Holden-Day.

Nelson, C. R. 1973. *Applied Time Series Analysis*. San Francisco: Holden-Day.

Quenouille, M. H. 1949. "The Joint Distribution of Serial Correlation Coefficients." *Annals of Mathematical Statistics*, Vol. 20, pp. 561–71.

Wold, H. 1954. *A Study in the Analysis of Stationary Time Series*. Stockholm: Almquist & Wiksell (1st edition 1938).

EXERCISES

1.   Use the data of Table 8-1, column 2, to verify that the autocorrelation coefficients for time lags of 3 and 4 periods are .181 and $-.132$ respectively. What is the meaning of $r_3 = .181$ of $r_4 = .132$?

2.   Using the simple noiseless series of 1, 2, 3, 4, 5, 6, 7, 8, 9, 10, calculate the autocorrelation coefficients for time lags of 1, 2, 3, 4, and 5 periods. Plot these autocorrelations and explain why they lie on a diagonal line going from larger to smaller values as the time lag is extended.

3.   Figure 8-1 shows the first ten autocorrelations for a series of 36 random numbers. Figure 8-12 shows the autocorrelations for 360 random numbers, and Figure 8-13 shows the autocorrelations for 1000 random numbers. Explain the difference in the three figures. Do they all indicate randomness in the data? Why are the dotted lines of different distances from the mean of zero? Why are the autocorrelation coefficients different in each figure when they all refer to random numbers?

4.   Table 8-4 shows a time series composed of 60 values. This series is the basis for the autocorrelation coefficients shown in Figures 8-4 and 8-6. Plot this series to identify its trend. Compute the first differences and plot the resulting series. Explain why the differenced series does not have a trend. Using a computer, find the autocorrelations for time lags of 1, 2, 3, and 4 periods for both the original and the differenced series.

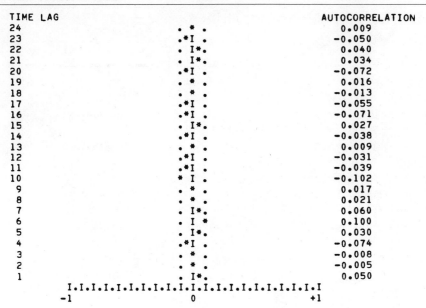

```
TIME LAG                                        AUTOCORRELATION
24                  . * .                           0.009
23                  .*I .                          -0.050
22                  . I*.                           0.040
21                  . I*.                           0.034
20                  .*I .                          -0.072
19                  . * .                           0.016
18                  . * .                          -0.013
17                  .*I .                          -0.055
16                  .*I .                          -0.071
15                  . I*.                           0.027
14                  .*I .                          -0.038
13                  . * .                           0.009
12                  .*I .                          -0.031
11                  .*I .                          -0.039
10                  * I .                          -0.102
 9                  . * .                           0.017
 8                  . * .                           0.021
 7                  . I*.                           0.060
 6                  . I *                            0.100
 5                  . I*.                           0.030
 4                  .*I .                          -0.074
 3                  . * .                          -0.008
 2                  . * .                          -0.005
 1                  . I*.                           0.050
      I.I.I.I.I.I.I.I.I.I.I.I.I.I.I.I.I.I.I.I.I.I.I.I
      -1                  0                  +1
```

FIGURE 8-12   AUTOCORRELATION COEFFICIENTS OF
                   360 RANDOM NUMBERS

```
TIME LAG                                        AUTOCORRELATION
24                  .I*                             0.031
23                  .I*                             0.068
22                  .*.                             0.014
21                  .*.                             0.009
20                  .*.                            -0.019
19                  *I.                            -0.072
18                  *I.                            -0.038
17                  .I*                             0.055
16                  .*.                            -0.008
15                  .*.                             0.016
14                  .I*                             0.032
13                  .I*                             0.036
12                  .*.                            -0.020
11                  *I.                            -0.034
10                  .*.                            -0.006
 9                  .I*                             0.027
 8                  *I.                            -0.044
 7                  .I*                             0.026
 6                  .*.                            -0.023
 5                  *I.                            -0.033
 4                  *I.                            -0.027
 3                  .*.                             0.009
 2                  .*.                            -0.014
 1                  .I*                             0.030
      I.I.I.I.I.I.I.I.I.I.I.I.I.I.I.I.I.I.I.I.I.I.I.I
      -1                  0                  +1
```

FIGURE 8-13   AUTOCORRELATION COEFFICIENTS OF
                   1000 RANDOM NUMBERS

TABLE 8-4 TIME SERIES WITH 60 VALUES

Period	Observation	Period	Observation	Period	Observation
1	9.560	21	60.500	41	85.280
2	12.480	22	63.290	42	84.440
3	13.640	23	66.550	43	86.590
4	18.800	24	68.650	44	88.050
5	25.040	25	72.660	45	90.830
6	30.330	26	71.250	46	93.050
7	34.080	27	65.480	47	94.650
8	40.100	28	62.680	48	96.660
9	42.400	29	56.600	49	96.300
10	41.360	30	49.900	50	96.090
11	39.250	31	49.820	51	99.270
12	38.200	32	51.870	52	104.770
13	41.470	33	57.740	53	105.510
14	46.140	34	58.240	54	105.190
15	52.620	35	58.310	55	109.160
16	59.010	36	59.910	56	110.780
17	60.200	37	62.610	57	115.770
18	58.530	38	69.070	58	122.750
19	56.980	39	77.360	59	126.850
20	57.820	40	80.390	60	132.570

9 GENERALIZED ADAPTIVE FILTERING

9/1 Analyzing and Forecasting a Time Series

In the last chapter it was shown that a time series can be analyzed using autocorrelations. Such analysis can determine whether the series is

1. random
2. stationary
3. nonstationary (and at what level of differencing it becomes stationary)
4. seasonal (and the length of seasonality)

In the first part of this chapter, time-series analysis will be applied to the data of Table 9-1. Forecasts for that time series will then be prepared with several

---

TABLE 9-1 OBSERVATIONS OF A SAMPLE TIME SERIES FOR 20 PERIODS

Period	Time Series Value (X_t)	Period	Time Series Value (X_t)	Period	Time Series Value (X_t)
1	4.200	8	1.700	15	7.960
2	5.800	9	2.020	16	6.780
3	6.900	10	2.710	17	5.070
4	7.620	11	3.630	18	5.040
5	5.570	12	5.180	19	6.020
6	3.340	13	7.110	20	7.610
7	2.000	14	8.260		

alternative methods. Finally, the category of methods known as autoregressive/ moving average will be examined as a way to improve forecasting efficiency.

The first step in any new time-series forecasting situation is to study it either by plotting the data or by using autocorrelation analysis. Even though plotting is simpler, it is often not as efficient or precise. Figure 9-1 shows a plot of the data from Table 9-1, which clearly exhibit some pattern. To further determine the behavior of the series, autocorrelation analysis can be performed.

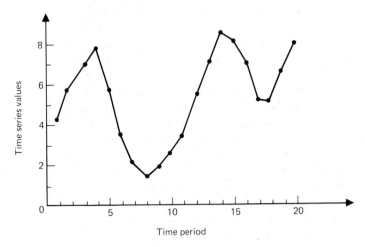

FIGURE 9-1 PLOT OF SAMPLE TIME SERIES SHOWN IN TABLE 9-1

Figure 9-2 shows the autocorrelations for time lags, on the original data, of one to ten periods. The data appear to be stationary, since the autocorrelations drop to 0 quickly ($r_3 = -.01$, $r_4 = -.23$). The autocorrelations for 5, 6, and 7 time lags are a little larger—in absolute value—but not outside the 95% confidence

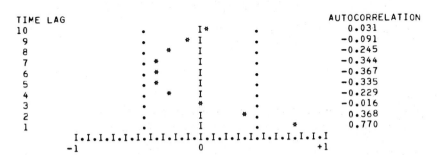

FIGURE 9-2 AUTOCORRELATIONS OF SERIES SHOWN IN TABLE 9-1

limits. Completely accurate judgments about the time series pattern cannot be made on 20 data points. Ideally, 40 to 50 observations are needed to know whether the pattern indicated in Figures 9-1 and 9-2 continues and is of fixed length. However, even with 20 points Figure 9-2 is an excellent description of the data plotted in Figure 9-1.

The pattern in autocorrelations that can be seen in Figure 9-2 and the fact that the autocorrelation for a time lag of one period is significantly different from zero suggests the existence of some pattern. If this pattern can be identified, it can then be used for forecasting purposes. For purposes of illustration several forecasting methods will be applied to the time series data of Table 9-1 and Figure 9-1.

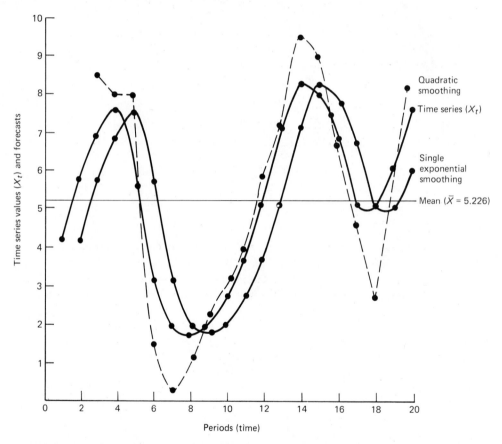

FIGURE 9-3 PLOT OF THE TIME SERIES OF TABLE 9-1 AND FORECASTS OBTAINED FROM THE MEAN AND SINGLE AND QUADRATIC EXPONENTIAL SMOOTHING

9/1/1 Forecasting with the Mean

Suppose the first method to be applied is to use the mean for forecasting, ignoring the fact that the mean should be used as a last resort and only when the data is random. In this case the mean value is

$$\overline{X} = \frac{\sum\limits_{i=1}^{20} X_i}{20} = \frac{104.52}{20} = 5.226.$$

As shown in Figure 9-3, the mean is a straight line and therefore cannot forecast the pattern of the data. If one were not aware of this limitation, the next step would be to find the autocorrelations of the residuals ($X_i - 5.226$) to determine whether they are randomly distributed. These are shown in Figure 9-4 and it is obvious that they are not random. Their pattern is exactly the same as that of Figure 9-2. Thus as was expected, the mean has done nothing to remove the existing pattern.

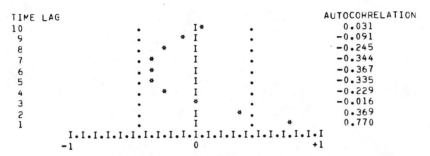

FIGURE 9-4 AUTOCORRELATIONS OF RESIDUALS WITH THE MEAN USED AS A FORECASTING MODEL (DATA OF TABLE 9-1)

As a way to double-check the above conclusions, the χ^2 (Q-statistic) of the ten autocorrelations in Figure 9-4 can be computed. Its value, using equation (8-17), is 24.32. The corresponding value from Table E of Appendix I (9 degrees of freedom and a 95% confidence level) is 16.92. Since $\chi_c^2 > \chi_t^2$, it is again concluded that the residuals are not randomly distributed. Thus, the mean is not an appropriate model for this time series.

9/1/2 Forecasting with Exponential Smoothing

As a second model for forecasting, single exponential smoothing can be tried, since the data are stationary and the evidence of a seasonal pattern is not statistically very strong. (Only one autocorrelation in Figure 9-2 was outside the confidence interval.) Using simple exponential smoothing requires finding the best value of α. For the series of Table 9-1, the best α has a value of one. Thus the best forecast is

$$F_{t+1} = 1X_t + 0(X_t - F_t) = X_t.$$

This model has previously been called *Naive 1* and uses the most recent value as the forecast for next period.

Once this model has been applied, the next question is whether the method produces random residuals. Finding the autocorrelations of the residuals as shown in Figure 9-5 indicates that there is still some pattern remaining. The computed χ^2 value is 24.63, which is larger than 16.92, the corresponding value from the χ^2 table (see Table E, Appendix I), thus suggesting nonrandomness and a nonappropriate model.

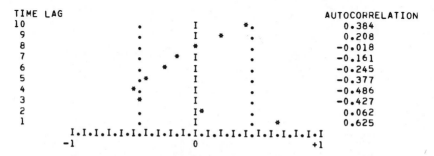

TIME LAG	AUTOCORRELATION
10	0.384
9	0.208
8	-0.018
7	-0.161
6	-0.245
5	-0.377
4	-0.486
3	-0.427
2	0.062
1	0.625

FIGURE 9-5 AUTOCORRELATION OF RESIDUALS WITH SINGLE EXPONENTIAL SMOOTHING USED AS A FORECASTING METHOD (DATA OF TABLE 9-1)

In terms of accuracy, the mean squared error (MSE) from the mean is 4.23, while that from single smoothing is 1.691. Thus the latter method improves the accuracy considerably, but still leaves a pattern in the residuals. Single exponential smoothing lags behind in its forecasts—something characteristic of single smoothing—and is unable to predict turning points, as can be seen in Figure 9-3. This lag causes systematic errors that can be further forecast. The next step is to look for another smoothing method that may be better. Unfortunately, there are very few clues as to what method that may be.

Brown's quadratic smoothing (see Section 3/7) may do better, since it can handle certain kinds of turning points. Applying this method, one finds that the best α is .9, which is unusually high owing to the almost noiseless pattern in the data of Table 9-1. The MSE for Brown's quadratic smoothing is 1.291, and the residuals are random as indicated by Figure 9-6. The χ^2 computed for these autocorrelations is 7.42, suggesting random residuals, since it is well below the corresponding value of 16.92 from Table E, Appendix I.

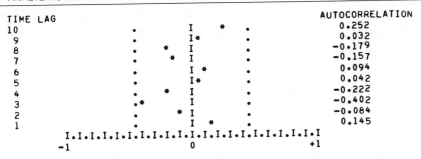

```
TIME LAG                                              AUTOCORRELATION
10                        I       *    .                  0.252
 9                        I*           .                  0.032
 8               *        I            .                 -0.179
 7                   *    I            .                 -0.157
 6                        I  *         .                  0.094
 5                        I*           .                  0.042
 4                   *    I            .                 -0.222
 3              .*        I            .                 -0.402
 2                   *    I            .                 -0.084
 1                        I    *       .                  0.145
      I.I.I.I.I.I.I.I.I.I.I.I.I.I.I.I.I.I.I.I.I
      -1                  0                  +1
```

FIGURE 9-6 AUTOCORRELATIONS OF RESIDUALS OF BROWN'S QUADRATIC EXPONENTIAL SMOOTHING METHOD (DATA OF TABLE 9-1)

Brown's quadratic smoothing does well in following the pattern but over-acts to turning points as can be seen from Figure 9-3. This method does catch up quickly with the actual series and fluctuates around the actual values rather than continuously trailing, as was the case with single exponential smoothing. From a statistical point of view, Brown's quadratic smoothing is an appropriate forecasting method for the data of Table 9-1, even though the improvement in the MSE between the quadratic and the single smoothing is only .4.

The problem with smoothing methods in a situation like this is that they either give good results when applied to the original data or else there is little that can be done to improve them. An advantage of the ARMA models that will be examined later in this chapter is their flexibility in sequential application. An ARMA approach makes several models available to fit different types of pattern, and these models can be applied in several iterations in order to remove any remaining pattern. Most importantly, the ARMA approach systematically provides information at each step of the process that can be used to determine what progress is being made and what steps should be taken next.

9/1/3 Forecasting with Regression

A third model that can be applied in forecasting the data of Table 9-1 is that of regression. This model requires creating independent variables that are past values of the dependent variable. Two possibilities will be examined in this case—using one and two independent variables. The data are shown in Table 9-2. Note that when one or two independent variables are used, one or two observations respectively are lost.

Application of simple regression to Y_t and Y_{t-1} using the data of the second and third columns in Table 9-2 gives

$$Y_t = 1.043 + .831 Y_{t-1}. \tag{9-1}$$

TABLE 9-2 DATA USED IN REGRESSION WITH ONE AND TWO INDEPENDENT VARIABLES (DEPENDENT VARIABLE FROM TABLE 9-1)

| | One Independent Variable | | | Two Independent Variables | |
| | Dependent | Independent | | First Independent | Second Independent |
Period	Dependent	Independent	Dependent	First Independent	Second Independent
1	—	—	—	—	—
2	10.6	11	—	—	—
3	9.36	10.6	9.36	10.6	11
4	7.62	9.36	7.62	9.36	10.6
⋮	⋮	⋮	⋮	⋮	⋮
19	6.02	5.04	6.02	5.04	5.07
20	7.61	6.02	7.61	6.02	5.04

The F-test for this regression model is 31.52, the t-test of b is significant, and the R^2 is .65. These results imply a statistically significant equation with a fairly good fit—65% of the variation in Y_t is explained by the variation in Y_{t-1}.

Applying multiple regression to Y_t, Y_{t-1}, and Y_{t-2} produces

$$Y_t = 1.619 + 1.52 Y_{t-1} - .831 Y_{t-2}. \qquad (9\text{-}2)$$

The F-test for this model is 60.7, all t-tests are significant, and the R^2 is .89, indicating a good fit. These results can be compared with the smoothing method results using MSE. For simple regression [equation (9-1)] the MSE is 1.54 and for multiple regression [equation (9-2)] the MSE is .508. The MSE of simple regression is better than that for the mean and for single exponential smoothing, while that of multiple regression is the smallest of all models fitted. A plot of the forecasts from simple and multiple regression is shown in Figure 9-7. Multiple regression does a reasonable job of following the pattern of the data closely and predicting the turns. However, single regression trails the pattern and the turning points, as did exponential smoothing.

In the next section equations corresponding to (9-1) and (9-2) will be applied, but a different optimization procedure than the linear least square method employed by regression will be used. The new optimization process estimates the regression coefficients a, b_1 or a, b_1, b_2 with a *nonlinear least squares fit*. In addition, autoregression can avoid many of the problems that exist when standard regression is applied to time-series data. These problems include:

1. The parameters of equation (9-2) are unbiased, but Y_{t-1} and Y_{t-2} are are not independent of each other, which results in autocorrelated

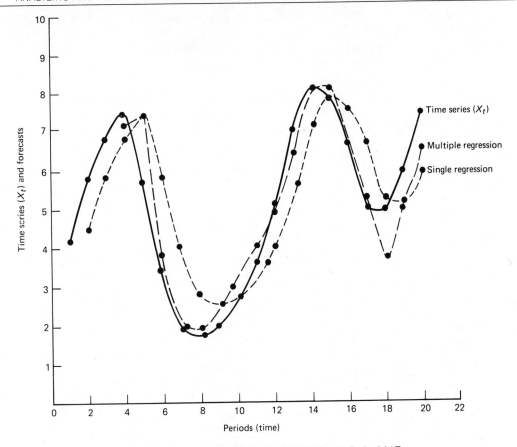

FIGURE 9-7 PLOT OF THE TIME SERIES OF TABLE 9-1 AND
FORECASTS OBTAINED FROM SIMPLE AND
MULTIPLE REGRESSION

residuals. As indicated in Chapter 6, that invalidates the statistical tests
and measures normally used. (The fact that the residuals are not
independent for Figure 9-7, can be seen from the Durbin-Watson test,
which is 1.25.)

2. Since Y_{t-1} and Y_{t-2} are highly correlated with each other, $r = .897$,
   multicollinearity may exist. This possibility can be detected in equation
   (9-2) from the fact that the correlation coefficient between Y_t and Y_{t-2}
   is positive, $r = .857$, while the corresponding regression coefficient, b_2,
   has a negative sign, an indication that multicollinearity may exist.
   Furthermore, $R = .8$, while $r = .897$. The fact that $r > R$ is also an
   indication of multicollinearity. Removing Y_{t-2} from the equation gives
   equation (9-1), which does not have the statistical problems of (9-2) or

multicollinearity, but which does not do as well as (9-2) in regard to MSE.

3. It is not clear whether simple or multiple regression should be used. If multiple regression is used, it is unclear as to how many independent variables should be included.

4. Because of these problems, one cannot be certain whether the regression of the form (9-2) is appropriate, can be improved, or has any statistical value whatsoever.

These serious weaknesses can be overcome by using autoregression and the ARMA methodology. The only disadvantage of this method is increased computational requirements.

9/2 Autoregressive Models

In Section 8/1 of the previous chapter the general class of autoregressive (AR) models were introduced. These are of the form

$$X_t = \phi_1 X_{t-1} + \phi_2 X_{t-2} + \phi_3 X_{t-3} + \cdots + \phi_p X_{t-p} + e_t. \tag{9-3}$$

Equation (9-3) differs from the general regression equation of (6-1) only in that the independent variables are past values of the dependent variable. Equations (9-1) and (9-2) were autoregressive in this respect, but in those instances the regression parameters were estimated through a linear least squares method, while the autoregressive parameters of (9-3) are found using a nonlinear least squares method. Also the variances of (9-1) and (9-2) were calculated in one way and those of (9-3) in another way that takes into account the fact that the independent variables are correlated with each other. These are major differences.

There are also three minor differences between (9-3) and (6-1): The autoregressive equation (9-3) does not contain a constant term; the dependent variable is called X_t instead of Y_t; and the regression coefficients are named ϕ_i instead of b_i. The elimination of the constant term is accomplished either by expressing the X_i in deviation form from their mean ($X_i' = X_i - \overline{X}$), in which case the constant is equal to zero, or by allowing the coefficients to adjust for the constant term. The second and third differences involve only a change of notation. The notation Y_t and b_i could have been used, but the new notation is more consistent with what has been used so far in this book and the literature on such time-series methods.

The general AR(p) model of equation (9-3) can take several forms depending upon the order of p. When $p = 1$, it is a first order AR model, or AR(1). In general, the model is written as AR(p). Before an AR model can be used, its order p must be specified. The appropriate value for p, which specifies the number of terms to be included, can be found by examining the autocorrelation coefficients. The nature of an AR(p) model can be better understood by examining its mathematical form. For example, an AR(1) model can be written as

$$X_t = \phi_1 X_{t-1} + e_t. \tag{9-4}$$

Equation (9-4) becomes

$$X_t = \phi_1{}^2 X_{t-2} + \phi_1 e_{t-1} + e_1 \tag{9-5}$$

when $\quad X_{t-1} = \phi_1 X_{t-2} + e_{t-1}\quad$ is substituted into (9-4).

Similarly, $\quad X_{t-2} = \phi_1 X_{t-3} + e_{t-2}\quad$ can be substituted into (9-5) to obtain

$$X_t = \phi_1{}^2(\phi_1 X_{t-3} + e_{t-2}) + \phi_1 e_{t-1} + e_t,$$

$$X_t = \phi_1{}^3 X_{t-3} + \phi_1{}^2 e_{t-2} + \phi_1 e_{t-1} + e_t. \tag{9-6}$$

Continuing the substitution of X_{t-i} to the first observation gives

$$X_t = \phi_1^{n-1} X_{t-n+1} + \phi_1^{n-2} e_{t-n+2} + \cdots + \phi_1{}^3 e_{t-3} + \phi_1{}^2 e_{t-2} + \phi_1 e_{t-1} + e_t. \tag{9-7}$$

It can be seen from equation (9-7) that an AR(1) process *weights past errors* in an exponentially decreasing manner. In this respect it is similar to single exponential smoothing, which *weights past time-series values* in an exponentially decreasing manner. [See equation (3-7).]

An AR(2) model can be written as

$$X_t = \phi_1 X_{t-1} + \phi_2 X_{t-2} + e_t. \tag{9-8}$$

Equation (9-8) can also be expressed in terms of past errors. The weighting will be similar to (9-7), except that the errors involve cross products of errors of successive periods. For example, a partial substitution gives

$$X_t = (\phi_1{}^2 + \phi_2)\phi_1 X_{t-3} + (\phi_1{}^2 + \phi_2)\phi_2 X_{t-4} + \phi_1{}^2 \phi_2 e_{t-2} + \phi_1 e_{t-1} + e_t. \tag{9-9}$$

The general AR(p) model shown in (9-3) provides an extremely flexible and versatile time-series method. It represents a general class of models that can deal with almost all types of data simply by specifying p.

As an illustration of the autoregressive procedures, suppose that an AR(2) model is to be fitted to the data of Table 9-1. This model is

$$X_t = \phi_1 X_{t-1} + \phi_2 X_{t-2} + e_t. \tag{9-10}$$

Application of (9-10) requires estimates for the values of the autoregressive parameters ϕ_1 and ϕ_2. The criterion to be used in selecting values for ϕ_1 and ϕ_2 is to make the MSE as small as possible. By rearranging terms in (9-10), this error is

$$e_t = X_t - (\phi_1 X_{t-1} + \phi_2 X_{t-2}), \tag{9-11}$$

and the goal is to minimize

$$\frac{\Sigma e_i^2}{n-2}.$$

(9-12)

For the data series of Table 9-1, the AR(2) model, (9-10), is found to be

$$X_t = 1.52X_{t-1} - .84X_{t-2}.$$

(9-13)

The MSE for this model is .509. The computed χ^2 value is 6.9, indicating randomness in the residuals. The autocorrelations for the residuals can be seen in Figure 9-8. The AR(2) model, therefore, provides results that are as good as those of the regression model (9-2). Additionally, the AR(2) model, (9-13), is

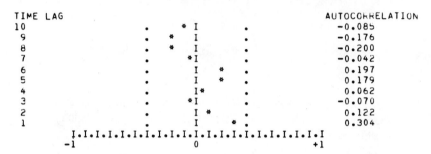

FIGURE 9-8 RESIDUAL AUTOCORRELATIONS OF THE AR(2)
MODEL OF EQUATION (9-13)

statistically problem free. As will be shown in Chapter 10, this approach also supplies enough information so that the best ARMA (p, q) model can be determined. For the data of Table 9-1, the best ARMA (p, q) model is the AR(2) shown in equation (9-13). The only drawback of (9-13) is that it takes much longer to estimate the parameters ϕ_1 and ϕ_2 than it would take to estimate the corresponding parameters b_1 and b_2 of the regression equation (9-2). A plot of the AR(2) forecasts of (9-11) are shown in Section 9/6/2, Figure 9-10.

9/3 The Method of Adaptive Filtering

Adaptive filtering can be applied as an AR method of the form (9-3). The parameters ϕ_1 and ϕ_2 are estimated through a nonlinear least squares approach by using the method of steepest descent (see Chapter 9 Appendix, Section 3). This method, as will be illustrated shortly, starts with an initial set of Φ_i values and proceeds to adjust them using equation (9-15), which is given below. It has been shown by Widrow (1966), that by repeatedly using (9-15) under the necessary conditions, parameter values that result in successively smaller MSE can be easily attained (see Chapter 9 Appendix).

A particularly attractive characteristic of adaptive filtering is its ability to adjust the parameters of the AR equation as new data become available. In other words, the ϕ_i are not fixed as in (9-3) but can vary slightly from one period to the next. The complete expression of the adaptive filtering AR model is therefore

$$X_t = \phi_{1t}X_{t-1} + \phi_{2t}X_{t-2} + \phi_{3t}X_{t-3} + \cdots + \phi_{pt}X_{t-p} + e_t. \tag{9-14}$$

Adaptive filtering is to the general AR model of (9-3) what adaptive-response-rate exponential smoothing is to single exponential smoothing. In one case, α_t varies [see equations (3-9) and (3-10)], while in the other it is constant.

Some of the advantages of adaptive filtering are that it is simple, it can be used with a minimum number of data points, it has few constraints connected with its use, and most important, it is a truly self-adaptive method that can adjust automatically to changing data patterns. The formula for adapting the parameters of (9-14) according to the method of steepest descent is

$$\phi'_{it} = \phi_{it-1} + 2Ke_tX_{t-i}, \tag{9-15}$$

$$i = 1, 2, \ldots, p,$$

$$t = p + 1, p + 2, \ldots, n,$$

where ϕ'_i is the new adapted parameter, ϕ_{it-1} is the old parameter, K is a learning constant that determines the speed of adaptation, and e_t and X_{t-i} are used as in other time-series methods: e_t is the residual error and X_{t-i} is the time-series value at period $t - i$.

Expression (9-15) will approach the optimal parameter values (the ones that minimize MSE), as long as K lies within certain limits. To speed convergence to the optimum values, a K as close to 1 as possible will usually require fewer iterations of (9-15) to achieve a minimum MSE. However, such a K value can result in divergence: instead of a smaller MSE on each iteration, the MSE increases. To avoid this problem, K must be set equal to or smaller than $1/p$. As will be shown in the appendix to this chapter, Section 1, when that is done and the data are standardized, convergence towards a minimum MSE is assured.

The application of adaptive filtering will first be illustrated for its simplest form, which can be used effectively with a minimum of previous knowledge about the method. The one requirement to use adaptive filtering in its simple form is to specify the order of the AR process ($p = 1, 2, \ldots$). Even if the order is specified incorrectly, the method will work, although the results may be suboptimal.

The simple randomless series 1, 2, 1, 2, 1, 2, $\ldots$, 1, 2 (20 values) will be used to illustrate the calculations needed to find optimal values for the parameters. Since the series is randomless, the process of adjusting the parameters through equation (9-15) will continue until the residual errors become zero.

Using two parameters ($p = 2$), with initial values $\phi_1 = \phi_2 = 1/p = .5$ and setting k equal to $1/p$, the training process can be initiated. If equation (9-15) is repeatedly applied as shown in Table 9-3, the values of ϕ_1 and ϕ_2 slowly change each time (9-15) is applied, continuously reducing the error. When the errors become zero, the optimal parameter values have been found ($\phi_1 = 0$, $\phi_2 = 1$), and these can be used to forecast. The only complication that arises is that the values of e_t and X_{t-i} in (9-15) must be standardized for reasons to be explained later. Table 9-3 shows all the parameters and values involved. The standardization constant is 2.2361. The values of e_t, X_{t-1}, and X_{t-2} are divided by this constant to obtain the standardized values. The optimal parameter values, $\phi_1 = 0$ and $\phi_2 = 1$, can then be used to forecast period 21:

$$F_{21} = \phi_1 X_{20} + \phi_2 X_{19}$$

$$= 0(2) + (1)(1) = 1.$$

The forecast for period 22 is

$$F_{22} = \phi_1 X_{21} + \phi_2 X_{20}$$

$$= 0(1) + 1(2) = 2.$$

TABLE 9-3 A DETAILED RUN OF ADAPTIVE FILTERING FOR THE NOISELESS SERIES 1, 2, 1, 2, ..., 1, 2

Period	ϕ_1	ϕ_2	X_t	X_{t-1}^*	X_{t-2}^*	e_t	e_t^*
			First Training Cycle				
3	.300	.400	1.000	.894	.447	−.500	−.224
4	.480	.760	2.000	.447	.894	.900	.402
5	.192	.616	1.000	.894	.447	−.720	−.322
6	.307	.846	2.000	.447	.894	.576	.258
7	.123	.754	1.000	.894	.447	−.461	−.206
8	.197	.902	2.000	.447	.894	.369	.165
9	.079	.843	1.000	.894	.447	−.295	−.132
10	.126	.937	2.000	.447	.894	.236	.106
11	.050	.899	1.000	.894	.447	−.139	−.084
12	.081	.960	2.000	.447	.894	.151	.068
13	.032	.936	1.000	.894	.447	−.121	−.054
14	.052	.974	2.000	.447	.894	.097	.043
15	.021	.959	1.000	.894	.447	−.077	−.035
16	.033	.984	2.000	.447	.894	.062	.028
17	.013	.974	1.000	.894	.447	−.049	−.022

TABLE 9-3 *Continued*

Period	ϕ_1	ϕ_2	X_t	X_{t-1}^*	X_{t-2}^*	e_t	e_t^*
18	.081	.989	2.000	.447	.894	.040	.018
19	.008	.983	1.000	.894	.447	−.032	−.014
20	.014	.993	2.000	.447	.894	.025	.011

			Second Training Cycle				
3	.005	.989	1.000	.894	.447	−.020	−.009
4	.009	.996	2.000	.447	.894	.016	.007
5	.003	.993	1.000	.894	.447	−.013	−.006
6	.006	.997	2.000	.447	.894	.010	.005
7	.002	.996	1.000	.894	.447	−.008	−.004
8	.004	.998	2.000	.447	.894	.007	.003
9	.001	.997	1.000	.894	.447	−.005	−.002
10	.002	.999	2.000	.447	.894	.004	.002
11	.001	.998	1.000	.894	.447	−.003	−.002
12	.001	.999	2.000	.447	.894	.003	.001
13	.001	.999	1.000	.894	.447	−.002	−.001
14	.001	1.000	2.000	.447	.894	.002	.001
15	.000	.999	1.000	.894	.447	−.001	−.001
16	.001	1.000	2.000	.447	.894	.001	.000
17	.000	1.000	1.000	.894	.447	−.001	−.000
18	.000	1.000	2.000	.447	.894	.001	.000
19	.000	1.000	1.000	.894	.447	−.001	−.000
20	.000	1.000	2.000	.447	.894	.000	.000

* Denotes standardized values.

If three parameters are used in place of two, the results do not change much, except that it takes more iterations for the errors to drop to zero. The model is not parsimonious, but for those who can specify a parsimonious model there is no problem. For others, it is an advantage to be able to obtain accurate results even when the best model has not been specified. The optimal parameter values when three parameters are used are $\phi_1 = 0$, $\phi_2 = 1$, and $\phi_3 = 0$. Thus

$$F_{21} = \phi_1 X_{20} + \phi_2 X_{19} + \phi_3 X_{18}$$
$$= 0(1) + 1(1) + 0(2) = 1.$$

Unfortunately, real time series are not randomless. However, the adaptive filtering process remains the same except that the method stops when no further improvement in MSE is achieved. Section 4 of the Chapter 9 Appendix shows a small program that can be used to apply simple adaptive filtering even in a small programmable calculator.

In the remainder of this chapter the method of adaptive filtering in its most generalized form will be discussed and ways of achieving more accurate forecasts will be explored. None of these innovations are required to use the simple adaptive filtering method and program. These innovations are refinements aimed at tuning the method and obtaining better results and are not essential to the method's use.

To further illustrate the use of adaptive filtering, the data of Table 9-1 will again be forecast. The model applied will be the AR(2) one,

$$X_t = \phi_{1t}X_{t-1} + \phi_{2t}X_{t-2} + e_t. \tag{9-16}$$

At the outset, initial estimates for ϕ_1 and ϕ_2 must be specified. (The t subscript will be dropped from now on, since it is always the same as that of X_t.) Starting parameter values can be obtained from the autocorrelation coefficients (see Chapter 9 Appendix, Section 2). For the data in this example, the initial values will be $\phi_1 = 1.20$ and $\phi_2 = -.55$, so equation (9-16) becomes

$$X_3 = 1.20X_2 + (-.55)X_1 + e_t. \tag{9-17}$$

One starts at period 3 because two observations are needed to calculate a forecast. Equation (9-17) gives

$$X_3 = 1.20(5.8) + (-.55)(4.2) + e_3,$$

$$X_3 = 4.65 + e_3,$$

and $e_3 = X_3 - 4.65$

$$= 6.9 - 4.65 = 2.25. \tag{9-18}$$

Once e_t is known, it can be used in equation (9-15) to obtain another set of weights (parameters). Suppose that $K = .008$ (for reasons to be explained later), then (9-15) becomes

$$\phi_1' = \phi_1 + 2Ke_3X_2 = 1.20 + 2(.008)(2.25)(5.8) = 1.409,$$

$$\phi_2' = \phi_2 + 2Ke_3X_1 = -.55 + 2(.008)(2.25)(4.2) = -.399.$$

These new parameters can be used in equation (9-16) to forecast period 4:

$$X_4 = 1.409(6.9) - .399(5.8) + e_4 = 7.408 + e_4,$$

$$e_4 = 7.62 - 7.408 = .212. \tag{9-19}$$

Two new weights corresponding to period 4 can now be obtained using equation (9-15):

$$\phi_1 = 1.409 + 2(.008)(-212)(6.9) = 1.432,$$

$$\phi_2 = -.399 + 2(.008)(.212)(5.8) = -.379.$$

The forecast for period 5 is

$$X_5 = 1.432(7.62) - .379(6.9) + e_5$$

$$= 8.30 + e_5,$$

and $\quad e_5 = 5.57 - 8.30 = -2.728.$ \hfill (9-20)

If one continues to adjust the parameters, the errors for periods 6, 7, 8, and 9 are found to be 2.398, $-.227$, .460, and .549 respectively. On the average, there will be an error reduction, although, depending on the amount of randomness, every iteration may not give a reduction. As equation (9-15) is applied repeatedly, a point will be reached at which no further reduction in the MSE will be possible. At this point the training of the parameters can be terminated and those final values can be used in forecasting. In equation (9-16), the optimal parameters are

$$X_{21} = 1.042X_{20} + .3X_{19} + e_{21}. \qquad (9\text{-}21)$$

The forecast for period 21 is therefore

$$X_{21} = 1.042(7.6) + .3(6.02) + e_{21}$$

$$= 9.725 + e_{21}.$$

The procedure involved in obtaining an optimal set of weights is very simple, although the arithmetic can become cumbersome when many data points are involved and a high degree of an AR process is desired, as is the case with seasonal data. Two points require further consideration:

1. selecting the degree of the AR model
2. choosing a value for the learning constant, K

The procedure for handling (1) is to set $p = 2$ or $p = 3$ when the data are not seasonal and $p = L$ (where L is the length of seasonality) for seasonal data. If the user of adaptive filtering wants to specify the AR process more precisely, a knowledge of the identification process of the Box-Jenkins methodology will be required. This topic will be discussed in the next chapter, since it is relevant for all ARMA models and depends on an examination of the autocorrelations. The value of K is determined by finding the largest values of each p term of the time series used in equation (9-15) and letting K be equal to or smaller than

$$K \leq \frac{1}{\left[\sum_{i=1}^{p} X_i^2 \right]_{\max}}.$$

For the data of Table 9-1, the two maximum values are $X_{14} = 8.26$ and $X_{15} = 7.96$. Thus,

$$K \le \frac{1}{8.26^2 + 7.96^2} = .008.$$

It has been shown by Widrow (1966, p. 34) that

$$K \le \frac{1}{\left[\sum\limits_{i=1}^{p} X_i^2\right]_{max}}$$

guarantees convergence. The only problem that may arise is that future values of X_t may be larger than those already observed. To avoid a problem of too large a K and to achieve a more uniform convergence that is independent of the fluctuations of subparts of data, the X_t values can be standardized after every training of a new set of weights using equation (9-15). That is, a standardized value is found for every $p(X_{t-1}$ to $X_{t-p})$ value. Standardization makes computations slightly more time consuming, but has the advantages of eliminating the need to store past values for purposes of finding the maximum set of X_t values and of making K independent of future values. An additional advantage of this standardization is that K can then be set equal to or less than $1/p$ (see Chapter 9 Appendix, Section 1) as a way of assuring convergence.

One way of standardizing the data is shown in Table 9-4.

TABLE 9-4 STANDARDIZING TIME-SERIES VALUES

(1) Period	(2) X_t	(3) X_t^2	(4) $\sqrt{\Sigma X_t^2} = c$ (5)	(6) $X_t^* = X_t/c$	(7) X_t^2	(8) $\sqrt{\Sigma X_t^2} = c$ (9)	(10) $X_t^* = X_t/c$
1	4.2	17.64	7.16	.5865			
2	5.8	$+$ $33.64 = \sqrt{51.28} = 7.16$		.8099	33.64	9.01	.6437
3	6.9		7.16	.9637	$+$ $47.61 = \sqrt{81.25} = 9.01$		.7658
4	7.62					9.01	.8457
5	5.57						
⋮	⋮						
20	7.61						

The first step is to square the X_t values of as many terms as the number of parameters (degree of AR). Column 3 shows the squares of X_1 and X_2. Next, the square root of their sum is found as shown in columns 4 and 5. This value, 7.16, can be called the standardization constant. Each time-series value is divided by this constant. The result of the division, column 6, is the standardized values, X_t^*, which are used in training the weights. Thus,

$$X_t^* = \frac{X_t}{\sqrt{\sum_{i=1}^{p} X_i^2}}. \tag{9-22}$$

Now the value of K for this standardized series can be specified as $K \le 1/p = .5$, and that value can be used in applying equation (9-15) to the standardized data.

For the standardized data of column 6 in Table 9-4,

$$X_3^* = 1.20(X_2^*) + (-.55)(X_1^*) + e_t^*$$

$$= 1.20(.8099) - .55(.5865) = .649,$$

and $e_3 = .9637 - .649 = .32.$

Using equation (9-22) in (9-15) yields

$$\phi_1' = 1.20 + 2(.5)(.32)(.8099) = 1.58,$$

$$\phi_2' = -.55 + 2(.5)(.32)(.5865) = -.27.$$

For period 4 and the standardized values in column 10 of Table 9-4, this gives

$$X_4^* = 1.580(.7658) - .270(.6437) + e_4^*$$

or $X_4^* = 1.04 + e_4^*$

and $e_4^* = .8457 - 1.04 = -.19.$

Other values for the errors are $e_5^* = .16$, $e_6^* = .16$, $e_7^* = 0$, $e_8^* = .13$, and $e_9^* = .05$. These errors are standardized with their actual values being $e_1 = 2.29$, $e_2 = 1.71$, $e_3 = -1.64$, $e_4 = 1.51$, $e_5 = 0$, $e_6 = .506$, $e_7 = .132$, $e_8 = .08$, $e_9 = .1014$. The errors obtained by using the standardized X_t^* values are decreasing on the average and are smaller than those obtained by not standardizing the data.

In a similar manner additional forecasts can be computed and the parameters can be trained, thus further reducing the MSE. The optimal parameter values of $\phi_1 = 1.042$ and $\phi_2 = .3$ shown in (9-21) were found by standardizing the data and performing four training cycles. That is, once all data up to the twentieth observation were used in training—a full cycle—the process was restarted from the beginning and continued until four complete cycles had been done. The resulting MSE of the fourth and final cycle was .821, achieved with a K of .75. Using a K larger than $1/p$ (1/2 in this case) does not necessarily mean that no optimal set of parameters will be found. Using a K as specified in (9-22) simply guarantees convergence under the worst of circumstances. Since the data of Table 9-1 contain little randomness, a value of K larger than $1/p$ (but smaller than 1) increases the speed of adaptation to the optimal set of weights.

Figure 9-9 shows the autocorrelations of the residuals of the AR(2) model of (9-17). The χ^2 computed is 8.25 indicating that statistically the model can be considered an appropriate one.

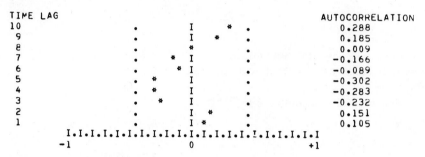

TIME LAG   AUTOCORRELATION
10   •   I   *   •   0.288
9   •   I   *   •   0.185
8   •   *   •   0.009
7   •   * I   •   −0.166
6   •   *   I   •   −0.089
5   •   *   I   •   −0.302
4   •   *   I   •   −0.283
3   •   *   I   •   −0.232
2   •   I *   •   0.151
1   •   I *   •   0.105
        I.I.I.I.I.I.I.I.I.I.I.I.I.I.I.!.I.I.I.I.I
           −1   0   +1

FIGURE 9-9 RESIDUAL AUTOCORRELATIONS OF THE AR(2) MODEL OF EQUATION (9-17)

9/4 Moving Average Models

There may be some data patterns that cannot be isolated with an AR(p) model where p is fairly small. Fortunately, however, there is another type of general model, called moving average (MA), which can fill the gap. In 1938, Wold proved that any discrete time series can be expressed as an AR model and/or an MA model. His work opened the field of ARMA models, but it took the third generation of computers to make ARMA models applicable on an operational level. MA models provide forecasts of X_t based on a linear combination of past errors, in contrast to AR models, which express X_t as a linear function of p actual past values of X_t. The general MA model is

$$X_t = e_t - \theta_1 e_{t-1} - \theta_2 e_{t-2} - \cdots - \theta_q e_{t-q}.$$ (9-23)

Equation (9-23) is called a moving average (MA) model in the literature, but has nothing to do with the moving averages examined in Chapter 3 or those used in Chapter 4 in decomposing a time series. The sum of $\theta_1 + \theta_2 + \theta_3 \ldots + \theta_q$ does not necessarily add to one, nor are the values of θ_i "moving" with new observations as with a moving average computation. The name is thus confusing but will be used here to be consistent with the literature.

An MA(1) model is

$$X_t = e_t - \theta_1 e_{t-1}.$$ (9-24)

Alternatively, $\quad X_t = e_t - \theta_1(X_{t-1} + \theta_1 e_{t-2})$,

since $\quad\quad\quad X_{t-1} = e_{t-1} - \theta_1 e_{t-2} \quad$ or $\quad e_{t-1} = X_{t-1} + \theta_1 e_{t-2}$.

Thus, $\quad\quad\quad\quad X_t = e_t - \theta_1 X_{t-1} - \theta_1^2 e_{t-2}$. $\quad\quad\quad\quad\quad\quad$ (9-25)

Substituting the value of e_{t-2} into equation (9-25) gives

$$X_{t-2} = e_{t-2} - \theta_1 e_{t-3}$$

or $\quad e_{t-2} = X_{t-2} + \theta_1 e_{t-3}$. $\quad\quad\quad\quad\quad\quad\quad\quad\quad\quad$ (9-26)

Substituting equation (9-26) into (9-25) yields

$$X_t = e_t - \theta_1 X_{t-1} - \theta_1^2(X_{t-2} + \theta_1 e_{t-3})$$
$$= e_t - \theta_1 X_{t-1} - \theta_1^2 X_{t-2} + \theta_1^3 e_{t-3}. \quad\quad\quad\quad (9\text{-}27)$$

Continuing this substitution, equation (9-27) becomes

$$X_t = e_t - \theta_1 X_{t-1} - \theta_1^2 X_{t-2} - \theta_1^3 X_{t-3} - \cdots - \theta^{n-1} X_{t-n-1} - \theta_1^n X_{t-n}. \quad (9\text{-}28)$$

Clearly, an MA(1) model is equivalent to single exponential smoothing as given by equation (3-7).

An MA(2) model is written as

$$X_t = e_t - \theta_1 e_{t-1} - \theta_2 e_{t-2}. \quad\quad\quad\quad\quad\quad\quad (9\text{-}29)$$

Equation (9-29) can be expressed in a form similar to (9-28), and that will include cross terms of $X_t X_{t-i}$.

TABLE 9-5 OBSERVATIONS OF A TIME SERIES FOR 20 PERIODS

Period	Time Series	Period	Time Series
1	10.5	11	10
2	10.1	12	8.9
3	8.8	13	8.2
4	9.9	14	10.2
5	11.3	15	8.8
6	12.2	16	8.4
7	11.3	17	9.6
8	9.8	18	10.2
9	9.7	19	10.6
10	9.5	20	11.1

Note: The mean of the data is 9.955.

An MA(3) model is written as

$$X_t = e_t - \theta_1 e_{t-1} - \theta_2 e_{t-2} - \theta_3 e_{t-3}, \tag{9-30}$$

while the general MA(q) model is as shown in equation (9-23).

To illustrate the use of an MA process, an MA(1) model will be applied to the data of Table 9-5. In order to use equation (9-24) the parameter θ_1 of the MA(1) equation must be estimated. This estimation is done by trial and error, as was illustrated for AR models. That is, different θ_1 values are tried until the one that minimizes the MSE is found. The trial and error is guided, since θ_1 must fall within a small range of values ($|\theta_1| < 1$) and a good initial estimate can be obtained (see Chapter 9 Appendix, Section 2) to start the search process. For the data of Table 9-5, the best θ_1 is $-.72$. This yields an MSE of .701 and residuals with a computed χ^2 of 4.14, which can be concluded to be random.

9/5 Applying the Method of Adaptive Filtering in MA Models

As explained in Section 9/3, a basic purpose of adaptive filtering is to calculate optimal parameters for an AR model. In a similar manner, the method can also find optimal parameters for an MA model. The only difference between the two is that AR models include terms involving X_i, while MA models include terms involving e_i. In order to optimize the parameters in the MA model, equation (9-15) can be used in the following form:

$$\theta'_{it} = \theta_{it-1} + 2Ke_t(-e_{t-i}), \tag{9-31}$$

$$i = 1, 2, \ldots, p \qquad t = p + 1, p + 2, \ldots, n.$$

The changes in notation in going from equations (9-15) to (9-31) are as follows:

1. Instead of ϕ'_{it} and ϕ_{it-1} the parameters are θ'_{it} and θ_{it-1}.
2. Instead of X_{t-i}, the error terms, e_{t-i}, are used.
3. The sign of X_{t-i} is changed, since all of the parameters in equation (9-3) have a positive sign while those of (9-23) have a negative sign.

Thus, equation (9-31) can be written as

$$\theta_{it} = \theta_{it-1} - 2Ke_t^* e_{t-i}^*, \tag{9-32}$$

where e_t^* and e_{t-i}^* are the standardized error values obtained in a manner similar to that shown in Table 9-4.

Equation (9-32) can now be used to obtain the optimal parameter value for the MA(1) shown in (9-24). That is,

$$X_t = e_t - \theta_t e_{t-1}. \tag{9-33}$$

Using the data of Table 9-5 and assuming a starting value of $-.84$ (see Chapter 9 Appendix, Section 2), one can calculate as follows:

$$X'_2 = e_2 - \theta_1 e_1,$$

or $\quad e_2 = X'_2 + \theta_1 e_1 = .145 - .84(1) = -.695,$

where $\quad X'_2 = X_2 - \bar{X} = 10.1 - 9.955 = .145$

and $\quad e_1 = 1.$

(A more precise estimate for e_1 can be made, but this will suffice as a starting point.)

In order to use equation (9-32), the errors must be standardized as were the X_t values of equation (9-31). The standardized errors are:

$$e_1 = 1 \qquad e_1{}^2 = 1 \qquad e_1^* = 1/1.218 = .821$$

$$e_2 = -.695 \qquad \underline{e_2{}^2 = .483} \qquad e_2^* = -.695/1.218 = -.571$$

$$\sum_{i=1}^{2} e_i{}^2 = 1.483$$

$$\sqrt{\Sigma e_i{}^2} = 1.218$$

Equation (9-32) can now be used to obtain revised parameter value, θ'_1:

$$\theta'_1 = \theta_1 - 2K e_2^* e_1^*$$

$$= -.84 - 2(.25)(-.571)(.821) = -.606$$

(using $K = .25$).

Consequently, the error for period 3 is

$$e_3 = X'_3 + \theta_1 e_2 = -1.155 + (-.606)(-.695) = .734.$$

Next the errors, e_3 and e_2, must be standardized to be used in (9-32). That is,

$$e_2 = -.695 \qquad e_2{}^2 = .483 \qquad e_2^* = .695/1.011 = -.688$$

$$e_3 = -.734 \qquad \underline{e_3{}^2 = .539} \qquad e_3^* = -.734/1.011 = -.726$$

$$\sum_{i=1}^{2} e_i{}^2 = 1.022$$

$$\sqrt{\Sigma e_i{}^2} = 1.011$$

The updated θ_1 value is

$$\theta'_1 = \theta_1 - 2K e_3^* e_2^* = -.606 - 2(.25)(-.726)(-.688) = -.855,$$

and the error for period 4 is

$$e_4 = X'_4 + \theta_1 e_3 = -.055 + (-.855)(-.734) = .573.$$

This procedure can be continued until the twentieth observation is reached. (Table 9-6 summarizes the relevant values for these iterations for the data of Table 9-5.)

TABLE 9-6   ADAPTIVE FILTERING COMPUTATIONS FOR MA(1) MODEL (DATA OF TABLE 9-5)

| Period | MA Parameter | | Standardization Constant $\sqrt{\Sigma e_i^2}$ | Standardized Errors | | Actual Errors Period t e_t |
	Old θ_t	New θ_t		Period t e_t^*	Period $t-1$ e_{t-1}^*	
2	−.840	−.606	1.218	−.571	.821	−.695
3	−.606	−.855	1.011	−.726	−.688	−.734
4	−.855	−.613	.931	.615	−.788	.573
5	−.613	−.829	1.147	.866	.499	.994
6	−.829	−1.064	1.734	.819	.573	1.421
7	−1.064	−1.006	1.431	−.117	.993	−.167
8	−1.006	−.968	.167	.076	−.997	.013
9	−.968	−.944	.268	−.999	.048	−.267
10	−.944	−1.185	.335	−.604	−.797	−.203
11	−1.185	−.949	.350	.815	−.579	.285
12	−.949	−.846	1.356	−.978	.210	−1.325
13	−.846	−1.041	1.469	−.431	−.902	−.634
14	−1.041	−.806	1.105	.819	−.574	.905
15	−.806	−.610	2.090	−.901	.433	−1.884
16	−.610	−.713	1.927	−.210	−.978	−.405
17	−.713	−.793	.411	−.161	−.987	−.066
18	−.793	−.687	.305	.976	−.217	.297
19	−.687	−.919	.532	.829	.559	.441
20	−.919	−1.138	.861	.859	.512	.740

The final model is

$$X_t = e_t - (-1.138)e_{t-1} + 9.955, \qquad (9\text{-}34)$$

where 9.955 is the mean of the data.

The MSE of equation (9-34) is .637 and the χ^2 of the autocorrelations of the residuals is 2.48. Thus the adaptive filtering optimization has done better than the previous fixed parameter MA(1) model used in Section 9/4. The MSE can be further improved by making a second cycle through the data, i.e., starting at period 2 with $\theta_1 = -1.138$ as the initial estimate and updating using equation (9-32). At the end of the second cycle the MSE is .54, the χ^2 computed is 2.19, and the model is

$$X_t = e_t - (.962)e_{t-1} + 9.955. \tag{9-35}$$

9/6 Mixed Autoregressive Moving Average Models

In addition to AR(p) models and MA(q) models, it is possible to mix AR and MA models in the same equation. This mixture provides the most general class of models, which are called ARMA models. AR and MA processes are special cases of this class. An AR(2) model, for example, can be expressed as an ARMA $(2, 0)$ model and an MA(1) model as an ARMA $(0, 1)$ model. The most general ARMA model is of order p and q. It is found by simply combining equations (9-3) and (9-23), obtaining

$$X_t = \phi_1 X_{t-1} + \phi_2 X_{t-2} + \cdots + \phi_p X_{t-p} + e_t - \theta_1 e_{t-1} - \theta_2 e_{t-2} \cdots - \theta_q e_{t-q}. \tag{9-36}$$

Specifically, an ARMA $(1, 1)$ is

$$X_t = \phi_1 X_{t-1} + e_t - \theta_1 e_{t-1}. \tag{9-37}$$

Equation (9-37) corresponds to

$$X_t = -\theta_1 X_{t-1} + \phi_1^2 X_{t-2} + \phi_1 \theta_1 X_{t-2} + e_t + \phi_1 e_{t-1} - \theta_1^2 e_{t-2} - \phi_1 \theta_1 e_{t-2}. \tag{9-38}$$

Equation (9-38) combines AR and MA influences and is obtained by substituting

$$X_{t-1} = \phi_1 X_{t-2} + e_{t-1} - \theta_1 e_{t-2}$$

and $\quad e_{t-1} = X_{t-1} - \phi_1 X_{t-2} + \theta_1 e_{t-2}$

into (9-37).

An ARMA $(2, 1)$ is

$$X_t = \phi_1 X_{t-1} - \phi_2 X_{t-2} + e_t - \theta_1 e_{t-1},$$

and so forth.

It can be seen from (9-38) that ARMA models use combinations of past values and past errors involving several terms and both AR and MA parameters. Because of this comprehensive nature, their combined performance is better than can be obtained using an AR(1) and an MA(1) separately (although this possibility is available).

9/6/1 A Mixed ARMA Adaptive Filter

Optimization using the steepest descent method can be applied to mixed ARMA models. To revise the parameters, equation (9-15) is used for the AR values and equation (9-32) for the MA values. That is,

$$\phi'_{it} = \phi_{it-1} + 2Ke_t X_{t-i} \tag{9-39}$$

and $\quad \theta'_{it} = \theta_{it-1} - 2Ke_t e_{t-i}.$ $\qquad\qquad$ (9-40)

For example, to fit an ARMA $(1, 1)$ model to the data of Table 9-1 involves use of

$$X_t = \phi_1 X_{t-1} + e_t - \theta_1 e_{t-1}. \tag{9-41}$$

To begin requires initial values for ϕ_1 and θ_1, an initial value for e_1, and a value for K. The use of adaptive filtering in this situation can be distinguished from single AR or MA processes by referring to it as *generalized adaptive filtering*.

Suppose $\phi_1 = .478$, $\theta_1 = 1.09$ (see Chapter 9 Appendix, Section 2, for starting procedures), $e_1 = 1$ and $K = .1$. The equation (9-41) can be written as

$$e_2 = X'_2 - \phi_1 X'_1 + \theta_1 e_1 \tag{9-42}$$

for period 2, where $X'_2 = X_2 - \bar{X} = 5.8 - 5.226 = .574$, and $X'_1 = 4.2 - 5.226 = -1.03$. Then

$$e_2 = .574 - .478(-1.03) + (-1.09)(1) = -.026.$$

In order to use equations (9-39) and (9-40), the e_t and X_t values must be standardized in such a way that ϕ_1 and θ_1 of (9-42) will converge to the optimal values. Also, since e_t is in both (9-39) and (9-40), a common standardization constant is required. To achieve this a standardization constant including both X_t's and e_t's is computed:

$e_1 = \quad 1$	$e_1{}^2 = \quad 1$	$e_1^* = 1/1.433 \qquad = \quad .6978$
$e_2 = \quad -.026$	$e_2{}^2 = \quad .001$	$e_2^* = \quad -.026/1.433 = -.0178$
$X'_1 = -1.026$	$X'^2_1 = +1.053$	$X'_1 = -1.026/1.433 = -.7160$
	$\overline{\Sigma e_i{}^2 + \Sigma X_i'^2 = \quad 2.054}$	
	$\sqrt{2.054} = 1.433$	

where $\quad X_i = X_i - \bar{X}.$

The parameters ϕ_1 and θ_1 can now be updated using equations (9-39) and (9-40).

$$\phi'_1 = \phi_1 + 2(.1)e_2^* X'_1 = .478 + 2(.1)(-.018)(-.7160) = .48,$$

$$\theta'_1 = \theta_1 - 2(.1)e_2^* e_1^* = -1.09 - 2(.1)(-.018)(.698) = -1.09.$$

Next the error for period 3 is computed as

$$e_3 = X'_3 - \phi_1 X'_2 + \theta_1 e_2 = 1.674 - .48(.574) + (-1.09)(-.018) = 1.43.$$

Once e_3 is known, the process can be repeated. The standardization constant can be computed and the values entering equations (9-39) and (9-40) can be standardized:

$$e_2 = -.026 \qquad\qquad e_2{}^2 = .001 \qquad e_2^* = -.026/1.54 = -.017$$

$$e_3 = 1.43 \qquad\qquad e_3{}^2 = 2.03 \qquad e_3^* = 1.43/1.54 = .928$$

$$X'_2 = .574 \qquad\qquad \underline{X'^2_2 = .329} \qquad X'^*_2 = .574/1.54 = .373$$

$$\Sigma e_i{}^2 + \Sigma X_i{}^2 = 2.36$$

$$\sqrt{2.36} = 1.54$$

and $\quad \phi'_1 = \phi_1 + 2(.10)e_3^* X'^*_2 = .48 + 2(.10)(.928)(.373) = .55,$

$\qquad \theta'_1 = \theta_1 - 2(.10)e_3^* = -1.09 + 2(.10)(.928)(-1.08).$

In a similar way the calculations can be continued until the last value, period 20, is reached. That will complete a training cycle at which point

$$X_{21} = .57X_{20} + e_{21} - (-.87)e_{20} + 5.226, \tag{9-43}$$

where 5.226 is the mean of the data.

This first training cycle has an MSE of 3.21. If desired, two more training cycles can be carried out to produce a minimum MSE of 1.13. The parameters upon completion of the third cycle are

$$X_{21} = .68X_{20} + e_{21} - (-.78)e_{20} + 5.226. \tag{9-44}$$

The parameter values of (9-44) are slightly different from those of (9-43), as would be expected in light of the concept of adaptive filtering in which new, adjusted parameters yield an MSE lower than previous ones.

The complete calculations for the first training cycle are shown in Table 9-7.

9/6/2 A Sequential ARMA Adaptive Filter

So far it has been shown that adaptive filtering can be applied with AR, MA, and mixed ARMA models. There are only slight differences in going from one type of model to another as illustrated by the sample calculations. Thus adaptive filtering provides a complete method for iteratively determining the parameter values of any general ARMA model using equations (9-39) and/or (9-40). Although this approach to time-series analysis is very complete theoretically, another factor is very important in practical forecasting situations. This factor is the complexity of a given method, or the ease with which a method can be learned

TABLE 9-7 ADAPTIVE FILTERING COMPUTATIONS TO OBTAIN THE ARMA PARAMETERS OF EQUATION (9-43)

Period	AR Parameters		MA Parameters		Standard-ization Constant	Standardized Values			Actual Error
	ϕ_1	ϕ_1'	θ_1	θ_1'		e_t^*	e_{t-1}^*	$X_{t-1}'^*$	
2	.48	.48	−1.09	−1.09	1.43	−.02	.70	−.72	−.03
3	.48	.55	−1.09	−1.08	1.54	.93	−.02	.37	1.43
4	.55	.54	−1.08	−1.08	2.20	−.03	.65	.76	−.07
5	.54	.48	−1.08	−1.08	2.55	−.35	−.03	.94	−.88
6	.48	.44	−1.08	−1.17	1.45	−.76	−.61	.24	−1.10
7	.44	.51	−1.17	−1.21	2.44	−.45	−.45	−.77	−1.10
8	.51	.54	−1.21	−1.22	3.45	−.15	−.32	−.94	−.53
9	.54	.58	−1.22	−1.23	3.62	−.18	−.15	−.97	−.64
10	.58	.57	−1.23	−1.23	3.27	.04	−.20	−.98	.12
11	.57	.59	−1.23	−1.23	2.54	−.12	.05	−.99	−.31
12	.59	.50	−1.23	−1.21	2.07	.62	−.15	−.77	1.29
13	.50	.50	−1.21	−1.26	1.33	.27	.96	−.03	.35
14	.50	.59	−1.26	−1.28	2.53	.65	.14	.74	1.65
15	.59	.54	−1.28	−1.25	3.65	−.32	.45	.83	−1.18
16	.54	.62	−1.25	−1.22	3.36	.46	−.35	.81	1.55
17	.62	.55	−1.22	−1.15	3.71	−.81	.42	.42	−3.00
18	.55	.54	−1.15	−1.05	4.49	.74	−.67	−.03	3.34
19	.54	.55	−1.05	−.95	4.25	−.62	.79	−.04	−2.61
20	.55	.57	−.95	−.87	5.21	.85	−.50	.15	4.44

and applied by a newcomer to the field. Mixed ARMA models are theoretically complete, but it is difficult to know when to use an AR(p), an MA(q), or a mixed ARMA(p, q) model. There are, of course, rules by which one can identify the appropriate model, and these rules will be examined in detail in the next chapter, but the identification process requires expert knowledge. In addition, the computations involved in estimating initial parameter values for MA models are extensive (see Chapter 9 Appendix, Section 2). Thus the addition of MA terms introduces concerns that can be avoided by the approach described in this section. This approach uses a sequential ARMA procedure that minimizes the identification problem and uses secondary MA processes. There may be some loss of accuracy in this sequential approach, but this loss is compensated for by the reduced complexity of the method.

The approach can be described by starting with the AR(p) model,

$$X_t = \phi_1 X_{t-1} + \phi_2 X_{t-2} + \cdots + \phi_p X_{t-p} + e_t. \tag{9-45}$$

If the AR(p) model of equation (9-45) is fit to a given data series, there will be an error, e_t, for each period ($t = p + 1, p + 2, \ldots, n$). These residual errors may be randomly distributed, in which case the model is adequate. If the errors exhibit some pattern (identified by examining their autocorrelations), one can continue by finding that pattern and using it to forecast. That can be done by applying another adaptive filtering process to the residual terms of equation (9-45), which involves expressing the residuals as a function of previous residual values. Thus, if the e_t are not randomly distributed, they are expressed as

$$e_t = \hat{e}_t - \theta_1 e_{t-1} - \theta_2 e_{t-2} - \cdots - \theta_q e_{t-q}, \tag{9-46}$$

and the parameters of equation (9-46) are estimated with adaptive filtering. Fitting the model in (9-46) results in a new set of residuals, $\hat{e}_t'$, which will either be random (in which case one stops) or will contain a pattern (in which case one continues with another model to identify the pattern in the $\hat{e}_t'$). Theoretically, one can continue with as many sequential models as needed, although in practice it seldom goes beyond three. Thus, the third model would be

$$\hat{e}_t = \hat{e}_t' - \theta_1 \hat{e}_{t-1} - \theta_2 \hat{e}_{t-2} - \cdots - \theta_q \hat{e}_{t-q}. \tag{9-47}$$

To illustrate the concept of sequential application of ARMA models using adaptive filtering, the data series of Table 9-1 will be examined. Originally, several models were fitted to the data of Table 9-1. One of them was an AR(2) model whose parameters were optimized both by trial and error and through the adaptive filter approach. The final parameters, given in equation (9-21) of Section 9/3, were

$$X_t = 1.042 X_{t-1} + .3 X_{t-2} + e_t. \tag{9-48}$$

The errors of (9-48), found by solving (9-48) for e_t, are

$$e_t = X_t - 1.042 X_{t-1} - .3 X_{t-2}. \tag{9-49}$$

Since $1.042 X_{t-1} + .3 X_{t-2}$ is the forecast of the AR(2) model, it is consistent with previous definitions of the error of

$$e_t = X_t - F_t.$$

The errors for this example are shown in Table 9-8.

The autocorrelations for these residuals are shown in Figure 9-9 and are random. However, suppose that some pattern remained (there is a slight pattern in the residuals even though it is not statistically significant) and that one wanted to predict it further using the three-parameter model,

$$e_t = \hat{e}_t - \theta_1 e_{t-1} - \theta_2 e_{t-2} - \theta_3 e_{t-3}, \tag{9-50}$$

where the e_t values are the last column of Table 9-8.

TABLE 9-8 ACTUAL AND FORECAST VALUES AND ERRORS FOR THE
AR(2) MODEL OF EQUATION (9-48)

Period	Actual	Forecast	Error
3	6.90	7.39	−.49
4	7.62	8.00	−.38
5	5.57	8.24	−2.67
6	3.34	2.57	.77
7	2.00	2.13	−.13
8	1.70	1.16	.54
9	2.02	1.64	.38
10	2.71	2.48	.23
11	3.63	3.71	−.08
12	5.18	4.81	.37
13	7.11	7.57	−.46
14	8.26	9.50	−1.24
15	7.96	9.05	−1.09
16	6.78	7.23	−.45
17	5.07	5.60	−.53
18	5.04	3.56	1.48
19	6.02	5.46	.56
20	7.61	7.27	.34

Either equation (9-39) or (9-40) can be used to optimize θ_1, θ_2, and θ_3. It makes no difference which is used since the e_t are independent of the X_t, and the former can be treated as a new series. For illustrative purposes, equation (9-50) will be treated as an AR model, since it is simpler and involves fewer computations in finding initial values than the MA model. Treating the e_t's as X_t's, (9-39) can be used directly to optimize the parameters. Thus equation (9-50) is equivalent to

$$\hat{X}_t = \phi_1 \hat{X}_{t-1} + \phi_2 \hat{X}_{t-2} + \phi_3 \hat{X}_{t-3} + \hat{e}_t. \qquad (9\text{-}51)$$

The initial values of ϕ_1, ϕ_2, and ϕ_3 are (see Chapter 9 Appendix, Section 2) .13, .17, and −.27 respectively. Knowing the initial ϕ_1, ϕ_2, and ϕ_3 values, the error for period 6 can be computed by solving equation (9-51) for $\hat{e}_t$. Period 6 is the starting point because (9-51) has three parameters, while (9-48) has two ($p + q = 2 + 3 = 5$).

Hence, $\hat{e}_6 = \hat{X}_6 - \phi_1 \hat{X}_5 - \phi_2 \hat{X}_4 - \phi_3 \hat{X}_3$

$$= .77 - .13(-2.67) - .17(-.38) - (-.27)(-.49) = 1.04,$$

where the values of $e_6 = \hat{X}_6$, $e_5 = \hat{X}_5$, $e_4 = \hat{X}_4$, and $e_3 = \hat{X}_3$ are taken from the last column of Table 9-8.

The standardized values of $\hat{X}_3$, $\hat{X}_4$, and $\hat{X}_5$ are:

$$\hat{X}_3 = -.49 \qquad \hat{X}_3{}^2 = .24 \qquad \hat{X}_3^* = -.49/2.74 = -.179$$

$$\hat{X}_4 = -.38 \qquad \hat{X}_4{}^2 = .14 \qquad \hat{X}_4^* = -.38/2.74 = -.139$$

$$\hat{X}_5 = -2.67 \qquad \hat{X}_5{}^2 = 7.13 \qquad \hat{X}_5^* = -2.67/2.74 = -.974$$

$$\overline{\qquad \Sigma \hat{X}_i{}^2 = 7.51 \qquad} \quad \hat{e}_6^* = 1.04/2.74 = .38$$

$$\sqrt{7.51} = 2.74$$

The adjusted parameters are then

$$\phi_1' = \phi_1 + 2K\hat{e}_6^*\hat{X}_5^* = .13 + 2(.1)(.38)(-.974) = .05,$$

TABLE 9-9 COMPUTATIONS TO OBTAIN THE SEQUENTIAL ARMA MODEL OF EQUATION (9-52)

Period	$\hat{X}_t = e_t$ Value	Standard-ization Constant	Old Parameters ϕ_1	ϕ_2	ϕ_3	New Parameters $\phi_1{}'$	$\phi_2{}'$	$\phi_3{}'$	Errors
1	—	—	—	—	—	—	—	—	—
2	—	—	—	—	—	—	—	—	—
3	−.49	—	—	—	—	—	—	—	—
4	−.38	—	—	—	—	—	—	—	—
5	2.67	—	—	—	—	—	—	—	—
6	.77	2.74	.13	.17	−.27	.05	.16	−.28	1.04
7	−.13	2.80	.05	.16	−.28	.06	.15	−.28	.14
8	.54	2.78	.06	.15	−.28	.06	.14	−.26	−.32
9	.38	.95	.06	.14	−.26	.13	.12	−.16	.57
10	.23	.68	.13	.12	−.16	.14	.14	−.17	.09
11	−.08	.70	.14	.14	−.17	.13	.13	−.19	−.08
12	.37	.45	.13	.13	−.19	.10	.23	−.03	.42
13	−.46	.44	.10	.23	−.03	−.08	.26	−.14	−.48
14	−1.24	.60	−.08	.26	−.14	.28	−.02	−.08	−1.38
15	−1.09	1.37	.28	−.02	−.08	.37	.01	−.11	−.73
16	−.45	1.72	.37	.01	−.11	.38	.02	−.10	−.07
17	−.53	1.71	.38	.02	−.10	.39	.06	−.06	−.46
18	1.48	1.30	.39	.06	−.06	.29	−.03	−.28	1.64
19	.56	1.63	.29	−.03	−.28	.29	−.03	−.28	−.01
20	.34	1.67	.29	−.03	−.28	.29	−.02	−.28	−.08

$$\phi'_2 = \phi_2 + 2K\hat{e}^*_6\hat{X}^*_4 = .17 + 2(.1)(.38)(-.139) = .16,$$

$$\phi'_3 = \phi_2 + 2K\hat{e}^*_6\hat{X}^*_3 = -.27 + 2(.1)(.38)(-.179) = -.28,$$

and the error for period 7 is

$$\hat{e}_7 = -.13 - .05(.77) - .16(-2.67) - (-.28)(-.38) = .14.$$

Using this new error value and standardizing the series values, the steepest descent formula of (9-39) can be applied to continue the training of the parameters until an optimal set of values is obtained.

Table 9-9 shows the values computed in reaching the optimal weights of equation (9-52) for period 21:

$$\hat{X}_{21} = .294\hat{X}_{20} - .024\hat{X}_{19} - .28\hat{X}_{18} + \hat{e}_{21}. \tag{9-52}$$

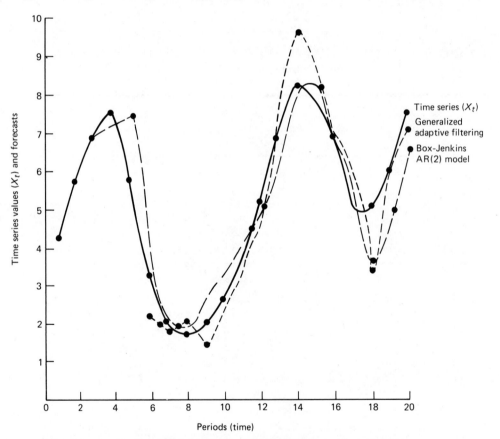

FIGURE 9-10 PLOT OF THE SERIES OF TABLE 9-1 AND THE FORECASTS OBTAINED BY THE AR(2) MODEL (9-11) AND GENERALIZED ADAPTIVE FILTERING (9-52)

The MSE of the model in equation (9-52) is .489, which is a substantial improvement from the MSE of .821 of the AR(2) adaptive filtering model. The χ^2 of the autocorrelations of the residuals in Table 9-8 is 5.28, indicating their randomness. A graph of the sequential model of (9-52) and the AR(2) model of equation (9-11) can be seen in Figure 9-10.

9/7 Seasonal ARMA Models

Seasonal models can be used in a manner similar to that described thus far for nonseasonal series. For mixed models, the exact order of the ARMA process—p and q—and the length of seasonality must be specified (see Chapter 10). The sequential ARMA models are much simpler to apply. One starts by specifying as many parameters as the length of seasonality and then inspecting the autocorrelation of residuals. If they are random, the model is adequate; if they are not random, a model with as many weights as the time lag corresponding to the largest (absolute value) autocorrelation coefficient is specified.

To illustrate the simple procedure of a sequential ARMA model, the nonstationary, seasonal data used in Figure 8-11 will be examined. These data were analyzed in Section 8/5/4 and found to be seasonal with a length of seasonality equal to four and stationary at the first level of difference. Figure 9-11 shows the autocorrelations for these data. The trend can be seen going diagonally from right to left indicating nonstationarity and the need to compute the first differences.

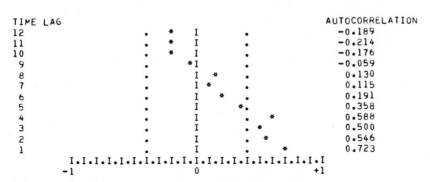

FIGURE 9-11 AUTOCORRELATIONS OF DATA USED IN
FIGURE 8-11

Figure 9-12 shows the autocorrelations of the first differenced data. These data are stationary, since the autocorrelations fluctuate around zero, except for those corresponding to seasonality. The length of seasonality is four, since the largest autocorrelation of .763 corresponds to a time lag of four periods, the second largest corresponds to a time lag of eight periods, etc.

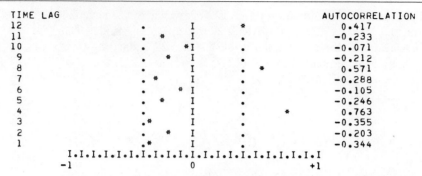

```
TIME LAG                                          AUTOCORRELATION
12              .        I        *                   0.417
11           .     *     I              .            -0.233
10           .        *I              .             -0.071
 9           .     *     I              .            -0.212
 8           .        I        .   *               0.571
 7           .  *     I              .            -0.288
 6           .     *  I              .            -0.105
 5           .     *  I              .            -0.246
 4           .        I        .        *          0.763
 3           .*        I              .            -0.355
 2           .     *  I              .            -0.203
 1           .*        I              .            -0.344
      I.I.I.I.I.I.I.I.I.I.I.I.I.I.I.I.I.I.I.I.I
       -1                 0                +1
```

FIGURE 9-12 AUTOCORRELATIONS OF FIRST DIFFERENCED
DATA SHOWING A STATIONARY PATTERN

Therefore an AR(4) model is chosen to be fitted to the first differenced data, $(X_t - X_{t-1})$. After ten training cycles, the results are

$$(X_t - X_{t-1}) = .039(X_{t-1} - X_{t-2}) - .149(X_{t-2} - X_{t-3}) - .147(X_{t-3} - X_{t-4})$$
$$+ 1.06(X_{t-4} - X_{t-5}).$$

The MSE of this model is 981.1 and the autocorrelations of the residuals are as shown in Figure 9-13.

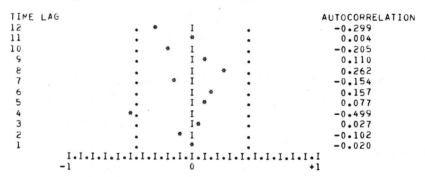

```
TIME LAG                                          AUTOCORRELATION
12              .     *     I              .         -0.299
11              .        *              .            0.004
10              .     *     I              .         -0.205
 9              .        I  *              .          0.110
 8              .        I     *          .          0.262
 7              .     *  I              .           -0.154
 6              .        I  *           .            0.157
 5              .        I  *           .            0.077
 4              *.        I              .           -0.499
 3              .        I*              .            0.027
 2              .     *  I              .           -0.102
 1              .        *              .           -0.020
      I.I.I.I.I.I.I.I.I.I.I.I.I.I.I.I.I.I.I.I.I
       -1                 0                +1
```

FIGURE 9-13 AUTOCORRELATIONS OF RESIDUALS OF THE
AR(4) MODEL

The autocorrelations again indicate the significant value at r_4. Another sequential training is then made by specifying a four-parameter model. The parameter values found after one training cycle are

$$\phi_1 = .108, \qquad \phi_2 = -.159,$$

$$\phi_3 = .136, \qquad \phi_4 = -.623.$$

The MSE for this model is 576.7, the residuals are randomly distributed, and the χ^2 computed value is 5.6. If the residuals were not random at this stage, one could continue with another training.

9/8 Summary Comments on Generalized Adaptive Filtering

Forecasting with adaptive filtering was first reported by the authors in two articles that appeared in 1973. At that time adaptive filtering was used in an AR form only, as shown in Figure 9-14. In another paper (1977), the authors extended the concept to sequential ARMA models and nonstationary time series. Concurrently there have been several applications of the method both among academicians and practitioners. The work of Lewis (1973 and 1975) has been noted among them. In 1975 Long extended the concept of the method to include mixed ARMA models that led to the generalization of the method so it could deal with all types of processes and data. Finally, in a workshop on adaptive filtering, use of the method in a multivariate form (see Chapter 11) was reported. This chapter is an attempt to synthesize what is presently known about adaptive filtering and present it in a way that can be understood and used by non-specialists. The computer program shown in the chapter appendix, Section 4, is included so that the application of the method by potential users will be further facilitated.

Generalized adaptive filtering has three main advantages—its simplicity, economy, and self-adapting procedure. The last advantage makes the method unique among major time-series forecasting methods, such as those of Box-Jenkins, which "freeze" the parameter values of the ARMA model. The method of generalized adaptive filtering combines the positive characteristics of exponential smoothing models—simplicity and economy—with all the flexibility of the ARMA models. In addition, it provides the additional characteristic (unique among ARMA approaches) of automatically adjusted parameters. Even though the method is new, it has been used extensively by both academicians and practitioners. There are no real practical problems in applying the method as long as K is set equal to or less than $1/p$ for AR models, $1/q$ for MA models, and $1/(p + q)$ for mixed ARMA models. The optimization will converge when this is the case, even if the series is nonstationary or the wrong ARMA degree is specified. In some instances the optimization procedure may be suboptimal, but it will converge when this sufficient condition for stability in the optimization process is met.

There are certain directions in which the authors think generalized adaptive filtering would benefit from further evolution. First, the method needs a better theoretical basis as far as the statistical properties of the filter are concerned. Since the parameters are not fixed, it is difficult to use the classical statistical concepts applied when stationarity exists and the ARMA models have fixed parameter values. Second, more work is needed regarding specification of the best value for K. Even though the value of K sufficient for convergence is known, that K value may not be the best in terms of MSE, since quite often other K values give a considerably smaller MSE. Finally, additional usage of the procedure will identify other possible weaknesses and generate improvements that will make the method more effective and efficient.

APPENDIX

MATHEMATICAL SUPPLEMENT

Chapter 9

This appendix will show the following:

1. the sufficient conditions for convergence in the adaptive filtering algorithm
2. the procedure by which initial values for AR, MA, or mixed ARMA models can be obtained
3. the basis of the adaptive filtering algorithm as an optimization technique
4. a computer program for simple adaptive filtering

1. SUFFICIENT CONDITIONS FOR CONVERGENCE OF THE ADAPTIVE FILTERING ALGORITHM (AFA)

Widrow (1966, p. 25) has shown that a sufficient condition for convergence of the adaptive filtering algorithm (AFA) is

$$0 < K < \frac{1}{\lambda_{max}}, \tag{9-53}$$

where λ_{max} is the maximum eigenvalue of the correlation matrix for all X_t and X_{t-k} ($k = 1, 2, \ldots, p$). In order to apply equation (9-53), the maximum eigenvalue must be known, which is difficult if not impossible. Convergence is also assured as long as the MSE reduction is greater than zero and does not exceed 200% (see Widrow, 1966, p. 31). This condition is equivalent to assuring that the learning constant, K, is within the bounds (see Widrow, 1966, pp. 31–34):

$$0 < K < \frac{1}{\sum\limits_{i=t-p}^{t-1} X_i^2}, \tag{9-54}$$

where $t = p + 1, p + 2, \ldots, n$.

Condition (9-54) refers to AR processes only. For MA models, e_i^2 should be substituted for X_i^2, to obtain

$$0 < K < \frac{1}{\sum\limits_{i=t-q}^{t-1} e_i^2}. \tag{9-55}$$

Finally for mixed ARMA models, both X_i^2 and e_i^2 should be included in the denominator, giving

$$0 < K < \frac{1}{\sum\limits_{i=t-p}^{t-1} X_i^2 + \sum\limits_{i=t-q}^{t-1} e_i^2}. \tag{9-56}$$

It is relatively easy to assure that condition (9-54), (9-55), or (9-56) is met. For example, if the data are divided by the largest value, the range of the limits for K will be known for most practical purposes. The only problem may be for new values after period n, which are much larger than past ones. This approach also has the drawback that dividing by the biggest value in the data may be too conservative, since (9-54), (9-55), and (9-56) are sufficient but not necessary conditions. A more efficient way to deal with this problem is to standardize or normalize each set of p, q, or $p + q$ values. Standardizing can be done by dividing by the largest of values in the summation, so that all other values will be smaller than 1. With this standardization, the two extreme cases are:

1. All values, including both e_i and X_i, are equal. In this case the standardized values will all be equal to 1 and the summation equal to p or q in case of (9-54) or (9-55) and $p + q$ in (9-56). This will obviously be the largest value the summations can take. Thus, it will suffice to set K equal to $1/p$, $1/q$, or $1/(p + q)$ respectively.
2. All values are 0 except one. This situation presents no problem since K is less than 1, a condition included in (1).

The procedure that the authors prefer for standardizing the data values has been shown repeatedly in this chapter. It involves dividing each set of p, q, or $p + q$ values by the square root of the sum of the squared X_i, e_i, or X_i and e_i values. The reason for this approach is computational—it is easier than finding the maximum value. The range of values is the same as in (1) and (2) above. Thus in (1), each standardized value is

$$X_i^* = \frac{X_i}{\sqrt{\Sigma X_i^2}} = \frac{C}{\sqrt{pC^2}} = \frac{\cancel{C}}{\cancel{C}\sqrt{p}} = \frac{1}{\sqrt{p}}, \tag{9-57}$$

where $X_i = C$ is a constant. Since there are p standardized values, summing equation (9-57) gives

$$\Sigma X_i^{*2} = \frac{p}{\sqrt{p}} = \frac{\sqrt{p}\sqrt{p}}{\sqrt{p}} = \sqrt{p}.$$

To meet the condition of (9-54), the value of K must be such that

$$0 < K < \frac{1}{\sqrt{p^2}} = \frac{1}{p}.$$

In a similar manner conditions (9-55) and (9-56) are satisfied if

$$0 < K < \frac{1}{q} \quad \text{or} \quad 0 < K < \frac{1}{p+q}.$$

Finally it can be shown that

$$0 < K < \frac{1}{\Sigma X_i^2}$$

is a sufficient condition for convergence. That is done by defining the error reduction as

$$\Delta e_t \equiv \mu e_t,$$

where μ is the error reduction and Δ_e is the incremental change in error. For the AR case,

$$e_t = X_t - \phi_1 X_{t-1} - \phi_2 X_{t-2} - \cdots - \phi_p X_{t-p},$$

$$e_t' = X_t - \phi_1' X_{t-1} - \phi_2' X_{t-2} - \cdots - \phi_p X_{t-p},$$

where e_t and e_t' are found by solving (9-3) and ϕ_i' is the modified parameter, adjusted using (9-15) and e_t' is the new error.

Obviously $\Delta e_t = e_t' - e_t = (X_t - \phi_1' X_{t-1} - \phi_2' X_{t-2} - \cdots - \phi_p' X_{t-p})$

$$- (X_t - \phi_1 X_{t-1} - \phi_2 X_{t-2} - \cdots - \phi_p X_{t-p})$$

$$= (\phi_1' - \phi_1) X_{t-1} + (\phi_2' - \phi_2) X_{t-2} + \cdots + (\phi_p' - \phi_p) X_{t-p}.$$

Solving (9-15) for $\phi_i' - \phi_i$ yields

$$\phi_i' - \phi_i = 2K e_t X_{t-i}.$$

Thus,

$$\Delta e_t = (2K e_t X_{t-1}) X_{t-1} + (2K e_t X_{t-2}) X_{t-2} + \cdots + (2K e_t X_{t-p}) X_{t-p}$$

$$= 2K e_t (X_{t-1}^2 + X_{t-2}^2 + X_{t-3}^2 + \cdots + X_{t-p}^2)$$

$$= 2K e_t \sum_{i=1}^{p} X_{t-i}^2.$$

But

$$\Delta e_t = \mu e_t.$$

Thus, $\quad 2K e_t \sum_{i=1}^{p} X_{t-i}^2 = \mu e_t \quad$ and $\quad K = \dfrac{\mu e_t}{2 e_t \sum_{i=1}^{p} X_{t-i}^2}.$

If the maximum possible average increase could be determined, the maximum value of K so that this increase would never be exceeded would be known. If K is greater than 0 and smaller than 2—the increase is restricted to 0 to 200%—

then

$$0 < K < \frac{1}{\displaystyle\sum_{i=1}^{p} X_{t-i}^2}.$$

The above condition for the learning constant K is not difficult to achieve, since the range of error reduction can be controlled. If it is 0 one stops, and if it becomes greater than 200% (which will never actually happen) one can stop or make K smaller.

2. INITIAL VALUES FOR THE PARAMETERS OF AR, MA, AND MIXED ARMA MODELS

Finding appropriate initial parameter values for ARMA models is not a necessary condition for successful applications, since optimal parameter values will be found starting with almost any initial conditions. (In ARMA models fitted by using approaches other than adaptive filtering the parameters must satisfy some constraints.) In the adaptive filtering AR(2) model of equation (9-16) for example, we could have set $\phi_1 = \phi_2 = .5$ rather than letting $\phi_1 = 1.2$ and $\phi_2 = -.55$ [see (9-17)]. However, doing so would have required more cycles to arrive at optimal parameter values than using good initial estimates. The purpose of this section is to examine procedures for obtaining "good" initial estimates.

Initial Estimates for AR Models

In equation (9-3), the general AR(p) model was represented as

$$X_t = \phi_1 X_{t-1} + \phi_2 X_{t-2} + \phi_3 X_{t-3} + \cdots + e_3. \tag{9-58}$$

If both sides of equation (9-58) are multiplied by X_{t-k}, where $k = 1, 2, 3, \ldots, p$, the result is

$$X_{t-k} X_t = \phi_1 X_{t-k} X_{t-1} + \phi_2 X_{t-k} X_{t-2} + \phi_3 X_{t-k} X_{t-3} + \cdots + \phi_p X_{t-k} X_{t-p} + X_{t-k} e_t. \tag{9-59}$$

Taking the expected value of both sides of equation (9-59) and assuming stationarity gives

$$\gamma_k = \phi_1 \gamma_{k-1} + \phi_2 \gamma_{k-2} + \phi_3 \gamma_{k-3} + \cdots + \phi_p \gamma_{k-p}, \tag{9-60}$$

where γ_k is the covariance between X_t and X_{t-k}. This is so because $E(X_{t-k} X_t)$ is, by definition [see (2-18)], the covariance between the variables X_{t-k} and X_t, where the variables are k time periods apart. Similarly $E(X_{t-k} X_{t-1})$ is γ_{k-1}, since

X_{t-k}, and X_{t-1} are $k-1$ periods apart, and so on. Finally $E(X_{t-k}e_t)$ is zero, since the errors are random and uncorrelated with past X_{t-k} values.

Next, both sides of equation (9-60) can be divided by the variance of X_t,

$$\sigma_X{}^2 = \gamma_0 = \frac{\Sigma(X_i - \bar{X})^2}{n-1}.$$

The result is

$$\rho_\kappa = \phi_1\rho_{\kappa-1} + \phi_2\rho_{\kappa-2} + \phi_3\rho_{\kappa-3} + \cdots + \phi_p\rho_{\kappa-p}, \tag{9-61}$$

since by definition [see (8-13)]

$$\rho_\kappa = \frac{\gamma_\kappa}{\gamma_0}.$$

If $\kappa = 1, 2, 3, \ldots, p$ in (9-61), the following system of equations, known as the Yule-Walker equations, is obtained:

$$\left.\begin{array}{l} \rho_1 = \phi_1 + \phi_2\rho_1 + \phi_3\rho_2 + \cdots + \phi_p\rho_{p-1} \\ \rho_2 = \phi_1\rho_1 + \phi_2 + \phi_3\rho_1 + \cdots + \phi_p\rho_{p-2} \\ \rho_3 = \phi_1\rho_2 + \phi_2\rho_1 + \phi_3 + \cdots + \phi_p\rho_{p-3} \\ \quad \cdot \\ \quad \cdot \\ \quad \cdot \\ \rho_p = \phi_1\rho_{p-1} + \phi_2\rho_{p-2} + \phi_3\rho_{p-3} + \cdots + \phi_p \end{array}\right] \tag{9-62}$$

Since the theoretical values for $\rho_1, \rho_2, \ldots, \rho_p$ are unknown, they are replaced by their estimates $r_1, r_2, \ldots, r_p$. Equation (9-62) can then be solved for $\phi_1, \phi_2, \phi_3, \ldots, \phi_p$ to obtain initial estimates for AR models. In Section 9/3, for example, equation (9-17) used as initial parameter values $\phi_1 = 1.20$ and $\phi_2 = -.55$. These were found starting from Figure 9-2, where the estimates $\rho_1 = r_1 = .77$ and $\rho_2 = r_2 = .368$ could be used as follows:

$$\rho_1 = \phi_1 + \phi_2\rho_1,$$

$$\rho_2 = \phi_1\rho_1 + \phi_2. \tag{9-63}$$

Solving equation (9-63) for ϕ_1 and ϕ_2 gives

$$\phi_1 = \frac{r_1(1 - r_2)}{1 - r_1{}^2}, \tag{9-64}$$

$$\phi_2 = \frac{r_2 - r_1{}^2}{1 - r_1{}^2}. \tag{9-65}$$

Substituting the values of r_1 and r_2 in equations (9-64) and (9-65) yields

$$\phi_1 = \frac{.77(1 - .368)}{1 - .77^2} = 1.1954 \doteq 1.20,$$

$$\phi_2 = \frac{.368 - .77^2}{1 - .77^2} = -.5524 \doteq -.55.$$

Following a similar procedure, one can obtain initial values for any $AR(p)$ model. (Note that if $p = 1$, then equation (9-62) simply becomes $p_1 = \phi_1$, or $\phi_1 = r_1$).

Initial Estimates for MA Models

The $MA(q)$ model is written as

$$X_t = e_t - \theta_1 e_{t-1} - \theta_2 e_{t-2} - \theta_3 e_{t-3} - \cdots - \theta_q e_{t-q}. \tag{9-66}$$

Multiplying both sides of equation (9-66) by X_{t-k} yields

$$X_{t-k} X_t = (e_t - \theta_1 e_{t-1} - \theta_2 e_{t-2} - \theta_3 e_{t-3} - \cdots - \theta_q e_{t-q})$$
$$\times (e_{t-k} - \theta_1 e_{t-k-1} - \theta_2 e_{t-k-2} - \theta_3 e_{t-k-3} - \cdots - \theta_q e_{t-k-q}). \tag{9-67}$$

Taking expected values on both sides of equation (9-67) gives

$$\gamma_k = E[(e_t - \theta_1 e_{t-1} - \theta_2 e_{t-2} - \theta_3 e_{t-3} - \cdots - \theta_q e_{t-q})$$
$$\times (e_{t-k} - \theta_1 e_{t-k-1} - \theta_2 e_{t-k-2} - \theta_3 e_{t-k-3} - \cdots - \theta_q e_{t-k-q})]. \tag{9-68}$$

$$\gamma_k = E(e_t e_{t-k} - \theta_1 e_t e_{t-k-1} - \theta_2 e_t e_{t-k-2} - \cdots - \theta_q e_t e_{t-k-q}$$
$$- \theta_1 e_{t-1} e_{t-k} + \theta_1^2 e_{t-1} e_{t-k-1} + \cdots + \theta_1 \theta_q e_{t-1} e_{t-k-q}$$
$$- \theta_2 e_{t-2} e_{t-k} + \theta_2 \theta_1 e_{t-2} e_{t-k-1} + \cdots + \theta_2 \theta_q e_{t-2} e_{t-k-q}$$
$$\qquad \vdots \qquad\qquad \vdots \qquad\qquad\qquad \vdots$$
$$- \theta_q e_{t-q} e_{t-k} + \theta_q e_{t-q} e_{t-k-1} + \cdots + \theta_q^2 e_{t-q} e_{t-k-q}). \tag{9-69}$$

The expected value of equation (9-69) will depend upon the value of k. **If $k = 0$**, equation (9-69) becomes

$$\gamma_0 = E(e_t e_{t-0}) + \theta_1^2 E(e_{t-1} e_{t-0-1}) + \theta_2^2 E(e_{t-2} e_{t-0-2}) + \cdots + \theta_q^2 E(e_{t-q} e_{t-0-q}). \tag{9-70}$$

All other terms of equation (9-69) drop out because by definition

$$E(e_t e_{t+i}) = 0 \quad \text{for} \quad i > q$$

and $\quad E(e_t e_{t+i}) = \sigma_e^2 \quad \text{for} \quad i < q.$

Thus, (9-70) becomes

$$\gamma_0 = \sigma e^2 + \theta_1{}^2 \sigma e^2 + \theta_2{}^2 \sigma e^2 + \theta_3{}^2 \sigma e^2 + \cdots + \theta_q{}^2 \sigma e^2. \tag{9-71}$$

Factoring out σe^2, equation (9-71) can be rewritten as

$$\gamma_0 = (1 + \theta_1{}^2 + \theta_2{}^2 + \theta_3{}^2 + \cdots + \theta_q{}^2)\sigma e^2. \tag{9-72}$$

Equation (9-72) is the variance of the MA(q) process.

If $k = 1$, equation (9-69) becomes

$$\gamma_1 = -\theta_1 E(e_{t-1}e_{t-1}) + \theta_1\theta_2 E(e_{t-2}e_{t-2-1}) + \cdots \theta_{q-1}\theta_q E(e_{t-q-1}e_{t-q-1}),$$

$$\gamma_1 = -\theta_1\sigma e^2 + \theta_1\theta_2\sigma e^2 + \cdots + \theta_{q-1}\theta_q\sigma e^2.$$

All other terms are 0 because $E(e_t e_{t+i}) = 0$ for $i > q$.

In general **for $k = k$**, equation (9-69) becomes

$$\gamma_k = -\theta_k e^2 + \theta_1\theta_{k+1}\sigma e^2 + \theta_2\theta_{k+2}\sigma e^2 + \cdots + \theta_{q-k}\theta_q\sigma e^2,$$

or $$\gamma_k = (-\theta_k + \theta_1\theta_{k+1} + \theta_2\theta_{k+2} + \cdots \theta_{q-k}\theta_q)\sigma e^2. \tag{9-73}$$

Dividing (9-72) into (9-73) gives

$$\rho_k = \frac{\gamma_k}{\gamma_0} = \frac{(-\theta_k + \theta_1\theta_{k+1} + \theta_2\theta_{k+2} + \cdots \theta_{q-k}\theta_q)\sigma e^2}{(1 + \theta_1{}^2 + \theta_2{}^2 + \theta_3{}^2 + \cdots + \theta^2 q)\sigma e^2}. \tag{9-74}$$

If $q = 1$, equation (9-74) becomes

$$\rho_k = \frac{-\theta_k}{1 + \theta_1{}^2},$$

since all other terms include indexes greater than 1, which do not exist in an MA(1) model. Thus

$$\rho_1 = \frac{-\theta_1}{1 + \theta_1{}^2}. \tag{9-75}$$

Equation (9-75) can be solved for θ_1 to obtain

$$\rho_1 + \rho_1\theta_1{}^2 + \theta_1 = 0.$$

Replacing ρ_1 by its estimate, r_1, gives

$$r_1\theta_1{}^2 + \theta_1 + r_1 = 0. \tag{9-76}$$

Solving equation (9-76) gives two values for θ_1. The one whose absolute value is smaller than 1 is chosen as the initial value of θ_1.

In Section 9/5 an MA(1) model was used. As represented by equation (9-33), the initial value was set equal to $-.84$. Since r_1 for the data was .49, this initial value for θ_1 was found using (9-76):

$$.493\theta_1{}^2 + \theta_1 + .493 = 0.$$

But, $$\theta_1 = \frac{-b \pm \sqrt{b^2 - 4ac}}{2a},$$

where $$a = .493, \qquad b = 1, \qquad \text{and} \qquad c = .493.$$

Therefore $$\theta_1 = \frac{-1 - \sqrt{1^2 - 4(.493)(.493)}}{2(.493)} \approx -1.183,$$

or $$\theta_1 = \frac{-1 + \sqrt{1^2 - 4(.493)(.493)}}{2(.493)} = -.845.$$

The value of $\theta_1 = .845$ is selected, since the absolute value of -1.183 is greater than 1.

For an MA(2) process, equation (9-74) becomes

$$\rho_1 = \frac{-\theta_1 + \theta_1\theta_2}{1 + \theta_1{}^2 + \theta_2{}^2} = \frac{-\theta_1(1 - \theta_2)}{1 + \theta_1{}^2 + \theta_2{}^2}, \qquad (9\text{-}77)$$

$$\rho_2 = \frac{-\theta_2}{1 + \theta_1{}^2 + \theta_2{}^2}. \qquad (9\text{-}78)$$

All other terms of (9-74) are 0 because they involve θ_k parameters for $k > 2$, which do not exist in an MA(2) model.

In an MA(3) process, the relevant equations are

$$\left. \begin{array}{l} \rho_1 = \dfrac{-\theta_1 + \theta_1\theta_2 + \theta_2\theta_3}{1 + \theta_1{}^2 + \theta_2{}^2 + \theta_3{}^2} \\[4mm] \rho_2 = \dfrac{-\theta_2 + \theta_1\theta_2}{1 + \theta_1{}^2 + \theta_2{}^2 + \theta_3{}^2} \\[4mm] \rho_3 = \dfrac{-\theta_3}{1 + \theta_1{}^2 + \theta_2{}^2 + \theta_3{}^2} \end{array} \right] \qquad (9\text{-}79)$$

Equations (9-77) and (9-78) constitute a system of nonlinear simultaneous equations whose solution is not trivial. The same is true with (9-79), where solving for θ_1, θ_2, and θ_3 is difficult and must be done by using an iterative procedure. The estimates obtained from these equations are not as accurate as those of AR models for a variety of reasons. However, they can still be used as good initial estimates for MA models.

Initial Estimates for Mixed ARMA Models

To obtain initial estimates for mixed ARMA models, equations (9-61) and (9-68) must be combined and the expected value taken:

$$\gamma_k = \phi_1 E(X_t X_{t-k}) + \cdots + \phi_p E(X_{t-p} X_{t-k}) + E(e_t X_{t-k})$$
$$- \theta_1 E(e_{t-1} X_{t-k}) - \cdots - \theta_q E(e_{t-q} X_{t-k}). \tag{9-80}$$

If $k > q$, the terms $E(e_t X_{t-k}) = 0$, which leaves

$$\gamma_k = \phi_1 \gamma_{k-1} + \phi_2 \gamma_{k-2} + \cdots + \phi_p \gamma_{k-p}.$$

This is simply equation (9-61).

When $k < q$, the past errors and the X_{t-k} will be correlated and the autocovariances will be affected by the moving average part of the process, requiring that it be included.

The variance and autocovariances of an ARMA(1, 1) process are therefore,

$$X_t = \phi_1 X_{t-1} + e_t - \theta_1 e_{t-1}. \tag{9-81}$$

Multiplying both sides of (9-81) by X_{t-k} gives

$$X_{t-k} X_t = \phi_1 X_{t-k} X_{t-1} + X_{t-k} e_t - \theta_1 X_{t-k} e_{t-1}. \tag{9-82}$$

Taking the expected values of (9-82) results in

$$E(X_t - kX_t) = \phi_1 E(X_{t-k} X_{t-1}) + E(X_{t-k} e_t) - \theta_1 E(X_{t-k} e_{t-1}).$$

If $k = 0$, this is

$$\gamma_0 = \phi_1 \gamma_1 + E[(\phi_1 X_{t-1} + e_t - \theta_1 e_{t-1}) e_t] - \theta_1 E[(\phi_1 X_{t-1} + e_t - \theta_1 e_{t-1}) e_{t-1}],$$

since $X_t = \phi_1 X_{t-1} + e_t - \theta_1 e_{t-1}$,

$$\gamma_0 = \phi_1 \gamma_1 + \sigma e^2 - \theta_1 (\phi_1 - \theta_1) \sigma e^2. \tag{9-83}$$

Similarly, if $k = 1$,

$$\gamma_1 = \phi_1 \gamma_0 - \theta_1 \sigma e^2. \tag{9-84}$$

Solving equations (9-83) and (9-84) for γ_0 and γ_1 yields

$$\gamma_0 = \frac{1 + \theta_1{}^2 - 2\phi_1 \theta_1}{1 - \phi_1{}^2}, \tag{9-85}$$

$$\gamma_1 = \frac{(1 - \phi_1 \theta_1)(\phi_1 - \theta_1)}{1 - \phi_1{}^2}. \tag{9-86}$$

Dividing (9-86) by (9-85) gives

$$\rho_1 = \frac{(1 - \phi_1 \theta_1)(\phi_1 - \theta_1)}{1 + \theta_1{}^2 - 2\phi_1 \theta_1}. \tag{9-87}$$

Finally, if $k = 2$, the autocorrelation function, (9-61), becomes

$$\rho_2 = \phi_1 \rho_1, \tag{9-88}$$

or $\phi_1 = \dfrac{\rho_2}{\rho_1}$.

From equations (9-87) and (9-88) initial estimates can be obtained. However, solving (9-87) is not trivial and requires a time-consuming iterative procedure.

The initial estimates of $\phi_1 = .478$ and $\theta_1 = -1.09$ used in equation (9-42) of Section 9/6/1 were obtained by substituting for ρ_1 and ρ_2, their sample estimates $r_1 = .77$, $r_2 = .368$ found in Figure 9-2. Then

$$\phi_1 = \frac{r_2}{r_1} = \frac{.368}{.77} = .478.$$

Estimating θ_1 must be done iteratively by starting with a θ_1 value, seeing if it satisfies equation (9-87), and if not, trying another value. The value finally obtained is $\theta_1 = -1.09$, which satisfies (9-87) as an equality. That is,

$$.77 = \frac{(1 - .478)(-1.09)(.478) - (-1.09)}{1 + (-1.09)^2 - 2(.478)(-1.09)}.$$

3.   THE BASIS OF THE ADAPTIVE FILTERING ALGORITHM

The method of steepest descent consists of starting at some point on the MSE surface, then moving toward the bottom of the surface following an iterative procedure,

$$W_i' = W_i - K \overline{\nabla e^2} \tag{9-89}$$

where W_i can either be an AR or an MA parameter and $\overline{\nabla e^2}$ is the gradient vector of $\overline{e^2}$ (see Wilde, 1964).

AR Processes

Widrow (1966, pp. 7–13) has developed an approximation for $\overline{\nabla e^2}$ by using e^2 in an average mode [this amounts to saying that (9-89) will be true on the average of several errors] and using the derivative of e^2 with respect to ϕ_i as an approximation of the gradient vector. Solving equation (9-3) for e_t gives

$$e_t = X_t - \phi_1 X_{t-1} - \phi_2 X_{t-2} - \cdots - \phi_p X_{t-p}, \tag{9-90}$$

and squaring equation (9-90) gives

$$e_t^2 = (X_t - \phi_1 X_{t-1} - \phi_2 X_{t-2} - \cdots - \phi_p X_{t-p})^2. \tag{9-91}$$

Then $\dfrac{\partial e_t^2}{\partial \phi_i} = 2e_t \dfrac{\partial e_t}{\partial \phi_i},$ \qquad (9-92)

and $\dfrac{\partial e_t^2}{\partial \phi_i} = 2e_t(-X_{t-i}),$

since $\quad \dfrac{\partial e}{\partial \phi_i} = -X_{t-i}\quad$ using (9-90).

Thus, $\quad \dfrac{\partial e_t^2}{\partial \phi_i} = -2e_t X_{t-i}.$ $\hfill (9\text{-}93)$

Substituting $\quad \overline{\nabla}\mathbf{e}^2 = \dfrac{\partial e_t^2}{\partial \phi} = -2e_t X_{t-i}\quad$ in (9-89) gives

$$\phi_i' = \phi_i + 2k e_t X_{t-i}. \hfill (9\text{-}94)$$

Equation (9-94) is the adaptive filtering steepest descent algorithm used for AR processes throughout this chapter.

MA Processes

An MA process is represented as

$$X_t = e_t - \theta_1 e_{t-1} - \theta_2 e_{t-2} - \cdots - \theta_q e_{t-q}. \hfill (9\text{-}95)$$

Thus $\quad e_t = X_t + \theta_1 e_{t-1} + \theta_2 e_{t-2} + \cdots + \theta_q e_{t-q}, \hfill (9\text{-}96)$

and $\quad \dfrac{\partial e_t^2}{\partial \theta_i} = 2e_t \dfrac{\partial e_t}{\partial \theta_i} \hfill (9\text{-}97)$

$$= 2e_t e_{t-i}, \quad \text{since} \quad \dfrac{\partial e_t}{\partial \theta_i} = e_{t-i}. \hfill [\text{using (9-96)}]$$

Thus $\quad \overline{\nabla}\mathbf{e}^2 = 2e_t e_{t-i}.$

This can be substituted into (9-89) to obtain

$$\theta_i' = \theta_i - 2k e_t e_{t-i}. \hfill (9\text{-}98)$$

Formula (9-98) corresponds to (9-92) but is for MA processes.

Mixed ARMA Models

Finally, for mixed ARMA models

$$X_t = \phi_1 X_{t-1} + \phi_2 X_{t-2} + \cdots + \phi_p X_{t-p} + e_t - \theta_1 e_{t-1} - \theta_2 e_{t-2} - \cdots - \theta_q e_{t-q},$$

and $\quad e_t = X_t - \phi_1 X_{t-1} - \phi_2 X_{t-2} - \cdots - \phi_p X_{t-p} + \theta_1 e_{t-1} + \theta_2 e_{t-2} + \cdots - \theta_q e_{t-q}.$

$\hfill (9\text{-}99)$

As shown in (9-93), $\dfrac{\partial e_t^2}{\partial \phi_i} = -2e_t X_{t-i}$.

If independence between the θ_i and the ϕ_i is assumed, then

$$\frac{\partial e_t^2}{\partial \theta_i} = 2e_t e_{t-i}, \quad \text{as shown in (9-97).}$$

Thus for mixed ARMA models,

$$\phi_i' = \phi_i + 2k e_t X_{t-i}, \qquad \theta_i' = \theta_i - 2k e_t e_{t-i}. \tag{9-100}$$

This amounts to applying (9-94) and (9-98) concurrently.

4. A COMPUTER PROGRAM FOR SIMPLE ADAPTIVE FILTERING

The BASIC language program shown in Figure 9-14 can be used to estimate the p parameter values of simple adaptive filtering. The program can be used for almost any type of data. If nonstationarity is strong, a small value of k should be used (rather than leaving line 80 as $k = 1/p$). Otherwise the program can be used routinely. Better results will be obtained if the data are transformed to a stationary series. However, the method will work (converge) with a non-stationary series as well. The program standardizes the values by finding the sum of the squared values (line 270), then taking the square root of that sum (line 290).

Figure 9-15 shows the statements (marked with an asterisk) needed to modify the program so that the largest of the set of p values is found. This modification requires fewer training cycles than simply using the program in its present form. However, it also requires 15% more computational time. Thus, in the final analysis the program shown in Figure 9-14 is about 5% faster than the same program with the modifications of Figure 9-15. A final standardization approach, finding the largest value of all the data and using it as the standardization constant, is much less efficient, requiring about 50% more computer time than the program shown in Figure 9-14. The changes needed to modify the program in this way are shown in Figure 9-16.

The program shown in Figure 9-14 with its standardization constant (lines 270 and 290) is preferable to the two alternative approaches for standardizing the data because generally it is computationally more efficient. The other two methods of standardizing the data shown in Figures 9-15 and 9-16 can be used however, and there may be circumstances in which they yield computationally more efficient results. The sample run in Table 9-10 illustrates the results obtained by executing the program listed in Figure 9-14.

```
10   REM INPUT THE PARAMETER AND DATA IN THE STATEMENTS FOLLOWING REM
20   DIM X[174], W[12], E[150]
30   REM N=NUMBER OF DATA POINTS IN THE TIME SERIES (MAXIMUM 150)
40   N=20
50   REM P=DREDER OF AUTOREGRESSIVE PROCESS, I.E. AR(P), (MAXIMUM 12)
60   P=2
70   REM K=LEARNING CONSTANT SET IT IN ANY OTHER VALUE THAN 1/P IF SO DESIRED
80   K=1/P
90   FOR I=1 TO N
100    READ X[I]
110    NEXT 1
120    FOR I=1 TO P
130    W[I]=1/P
140    NEXT I
150    REM L1=NUMBER OF TRAINING ITERATIONS (CYCLES)
160    L1=100
170    PRINT "TRAINING          MSE                 PARAMETERS"
180    PRINT "ITERATION               OF ADAPTIVE FILTERING MODEL"
190    S1=1, E+37
200    FOR L=1 TO L1
210    S=0
220    H1=0
230    FOR I=P+1 TO N
240    F=0
250    FOR J=1 TO P
260    F=F+W[J]*X[1-J]
270    H1=H1+X[I-J]*X[1-J]
280    NEXT J
290    H1=SOR (H1)
300    REM E(I)=ERROR, X(I)=ACTUAL VALUE, F=FORECAST, I=P+1 TO N
310    E[I]=X[I]-F
320    FOR J=1 TO P
330    REM UPDATING THE PARAMETERS OF AR(P) WITH (9-15), H1=STANDARDIZATION
340    REM CONSTANT STANDARDIZING E(I) AND X(I-J) BEFORE USED NEXT LINE
350    W[J]=W[J]+2*K*E[I]/H1*X[I-J]/H1
360    NEXT J
370    S=S+E[I] 42
380    NEXT I
390    PRINT USING " #, 3D, 6X, 8D, 4D, 4X"; L, 8/(N-P+1)
400    FOR J=1 TO P
410    PRINT USING 420; W[J]
420    IMAGE #, 6 (3D.3D, 2X)
430    NEXT J
440    REM IF THE MSE DOES NOT DECREASE BY AT LEAST 1/1000 STOP THE TRAINING
450    IF S+.0001 >S1 THEN 490
460    S1=S
470    PRINT
480    NEXT L
490    M=6
500    REM M=NUMBER OF FORECASTS DESIRED MAXIMUM 24
510    PRINT LIN(2); "PERIOD          FORECAST"
520    FOR I=N+1 TO N+M
530    F=0
540    FOR J=1 TO P
550    F=F+W[J]*X[I-J]
560    NEXT J
570    X[I]=F
580    PRINT I, F
590    NEXT I
600    REM INPUT N DATA VALUES IN THE DATA STATEMENT BELOW
610    DATA 2, 4, 6, 8, 10, 12, 14, 16, 18, 20, 22, 24, 26, 28, 30, 32, 34, 36, 38, 40
620    END
```

FIGURE 9-14 PROGRAM LISTING FOR SIMPLE ADAPTIVE FILTERING

```
*220    H1=-1
 230    FOR 1=P+1 TO N
 240    F=0
 250    FOR J=1 TO P
 260    F=F+W[J]*X[I-J]
*270    IF H1 >= ABS(X[I-J]) THEN 290
*280    H1=ABS(X[I-J])
 290    NEXT J
 300    REM E(I)=ERROR, X(I)=ACTUAL VALUE, F=FORECAST, 1=P+1 TO N
```

* Modifications to the program shown in Figure 9.14.

FIGURE 9-15   MODIFICATIONS NEEDED TO USE THE LARGEST VALUE OF EACH SET OF p DATA VALUES AS THE NORMALIZED CONSTANT

TABLE 9-10   TEST RUN OF THE PROGRAM SHOWN IN FIGURE 9-14 (DATA SHOWN IN LINE 610)

Run Affin Training Iteration	MSE	Parameters of Adaptive Filtering Model	
1	.8691	.631	.445
2	.7060	.704	.368
3	.6324	.774	.294
4	.5665	.840	.225
5	.5074	.902	.159
6	.4545	.961	.097
7	.4071	1.016	.039
8	.3647	1.069	−.017
9	.3266	1.119	−.070
10	.2926	1.166	−.120
11	.2621	1.211	−.167
12	.2348	1.253	−.211
13	.2103	1.293	−.254
14	.1884	1.331	−.294
15	.1687	1.367	−.331
16	.1511	1.401	−.367
17	.1354	1.433	−.401
18	.1213	1.463	−.433
19	.1086	1.498	−.464

TABLE 9-10 *Continued*

Run Affin Training Iteration	MSE	Parameters of Adaptive Filtering Model	
20	.0973	1.519	−.492
⋮	⋮	⋮	⋮
70	.0004	1.969	−.968
71	.0004	1.971	−.969
72	.0003	1.973	−.971
73	.0003	1.974	−.972
74	.0003	1.975	−.974
75	.0002	1.977	−.975
76	.0002	1.978	−.977
77	.0002	1.979	−.978
78	.0002	1.980	−.979
79	.0001	1.981	−.980
80	.0001	1.982	−.981
81	.0001	1.983	−.982
82	.0001	1.984	−.983
83	.0001	1.985	−.984
84	.0001	1.986	−.985
85	.0001	1.987	−.986
86	.0001	1.987	−.987
87	.0001	1.988	−.987
88	.0001	1.989	−.988
89	.0000	1.989	−.989
90	.0000	1.980	−.989

Period	Forecast
21	42.0012
22	44.0046
23	46.0115
24	48.0228
25	50.0397
26	52.0692

```
  80   K=1/P
 *90   H1=-1
 100   FOR I=1 TO N
 110   READ X[I]
*120   IF H1 >= ABS(X[I]) THEN 140
*130   H1=ABS(X[I])
 140   NEXT I
 150   FOR I=1 TO P
 160   W[I]=1/P
 170   NEXT I
 180   REM L1=NUMBER OF TRAINING ITERATIONS (CYCLES)
 190   L1=200
 200   PRINT "TRAINING        MSE              PARAMETERS"
 210   PRINT "ITERATION              OF ADAPTIVE FILTERING MODEL"
 220   S1=1.E+37
 230   FOR L=1 TO L1
 240   S=0
 250   FOR I=P+1 TO N
 260   F=0
 270   FOR J=1 TO P
 280   F=F+W[J]*X[I-J]
 290   NEXT J
 300   REM E(I)=ERROR, X(I)=ACTUAL VALUE, F=FORECAST, I=P+1 TO N
```

* Modification to the program shown in Figure 9.14.

FIGURE 9-16 MODIFICATIONS NEEDED TO USE THE LARGEST
VALUE OF ALL THE DATA AS THE NORMALIZED
CONSTANT

REFERENCES AND SELECTED BIBLIOGRAPHY

Lewis, C. D. 1973. "Advances in the Development of the Adaptive Filtering Forecasting Technique." University of Aston, Working Paper No. 15.

————. 1975. *Demand Analysis and Inventory Control*. Westmead, England: Saxon House.

Long, A. J. "An Extended Version of the Adaptive Filtering Forecasting Model." Unpublished working paper.

Makridakis, S., and S. Wheelwright. 1977. "Adaptive Filtering: An Integrated Autoregressive-Moving Average Filter for Time Series Forecasting." To be published in *Operational Research Quarterly*.

Wheelwright, S., and S. Makridakis. 1973. "An Examination of the Use of Adaptive Filtering in Forecasting." *Operational Research Quarterly*, Vol. 24, No. 1, pp. 55–64.

————. 1973. "Forecasting with Adaptive Filtering." *Revue Francaise d'Automatique, Informatique et Recherche Operationnelle*, March, Vol. 1, pp. 32–52.

Widrow, B. 1966. "Adaptive Filters I: Fundamentals." Stanford University Technical Report No. 67 64-6. Systems Theory Laboratory.

Wilde, D. J., and C. Beighter. 1964. *Foundations of Optimization*. Englewood Cliffs, N.J.: Prentice-Hall, pp. 271–339.

Wold, H. 1954. *A Study in the Analysis of Stationary Time Series*. Stockholm: Almquist & Wiksell (1st edition, 1938).

EXERCISES

1. Given the values $X_1 = 2$, $X_2 = 1$, $X_3 = .5$, $X_4 = 1.5$, $X_5 = 2.2$, $X_6 = 2$:

    a. Use an AR(1) model and calculate ϕ_1 by trial and error in such a way as to minimize the MSE.

    b. Use the adaptive filtering algorithm:

    $$\phi'_1 = \phi_1 + 2ke_t X_{t-1}$$

    in order to find the optimal ϕ_1 value.

2. Fit an AR(1) model to the data of Table 9-1. Do the autocorrelations of the residuals indicate randomness? Why or why not?

3. Fit an MA(1) model to the data of Table 9-1. What is your evaluation of the fit?

4. Fit an AR(1) model to the time series $1, 2, 3, 4, \ldots, 9, 10$ without differencing the series. Is the resulting AR(1) model correct? Why or why not?

5. The data of Table 9-11 are the shipments (in thousands of Swiss francs) for the years 1972–1975 of a stereo manufacturing firm. Estimate the sales for the year 1976.

TABLE 9-11 SHIPMENTS OF STEREO EQUIPMENT (IN THOUSANDS OF SWISS FRANCS)

Period	Observation	Period	Observation	Period	Observation
1	306.484	17	378.727	33	888.805
2	302.106	18	880.048	34	919.453
3	411.565	19	597.645	35	792.481
4	367.781	20	584.510	36	897.562
5	429.078	21	1177.776	37	623.915
6	571.375	22	726.806	38	1138.371
7	310.863	23	711.482	39	1517.098
8	389.673	24	728.995	40	1063.939
9	542.915	25	718.049	41	1234.695
10	440.024	26	788.103	42	1214.992
11	356.836	27	1044.236	43	1234.695
12	490.375	28	720.239	44	1147.128
13	571.375	29	562.618	45	1357.288
14	586.699	30	1077.074	46	1418.585
15	799.049	31	573.564	47	1582.422
16	604.212	32	742.130	48	1979.014

6.   Apply the method of adaptive filtering to the data of Table 3-6.

10 THE BOX-JENKINS METHOD

AUTOREGRESSIVE/MOVING AVERAGE (ARMA) models have been studied extensively by George Box and Gwilym Jenkins (1970), and their names frequently have been used synonymously with general ARMA processes applied to time-series analysis, forecasting, and control. Autoregressive (AR) models were first introduced by Yule (1926) and later generalized by Walker (1931), while moving average (MA) models were first used by Slutzky (1937). It was the work of Wold (1938), however, that provided the theoretical foundations of combined ARMA processes, and thus should be considered as the most valuable in the field. Building on Wold's work, ARMA models have developed in two directions—efficient identification and estimation procedures (for AR, MA, and mixed ARMA processes) and extension of the results to include seasonal time series.

Box and Jenkins (1970) have effectively put together in a comprehensive manner the relevant information required to understand and use univariate time series ARMA models like those described in the last chapter. The basis of their approach is summarized in Figure 10-1 and consists of three phases—identification, estimation and testing, and application.

In the remainder of this chapter, each of the three phases of Figure 10-1 will be examined and practical examples illustrating their application (the Box-Jenkins methodology) to univariate time-series analysis will be given.

10/1 Identification

The purpose of the identification phase is to select a specific ARMA model from the general class of ARMA (p, q) processes shown in equation (9-36) as

$$X_t = \phi_1 X_{t-1} + \phi_2 X_{t-2} + \cdots + \phi_p X_{t-p} + e_t - \theta_1 e_{t-1} - \theta_2 e_{t-1} - \cdots - \theta_q e_{t-q}. \tag{10-1}$$

The choice of the appropriate p and q values requires examining the autocorrelation and partial autocorrelation coefficients calculated for the data. The concept and use of autocorrelation coefficients have been explored in previous chapters. How-

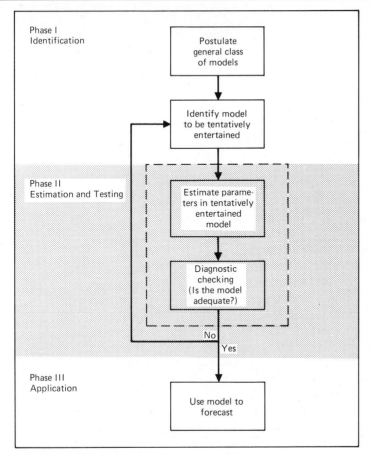

FIGURE 10-1 SCHEMATIC REPRESENTATION OF THE BOX-JENKINS APPROACH

ever, partial autocorrelations, briefly mentioned in Chapter 8, have not been discussed in detail; therefore they will be described before returning to the question of how specific ARMA model can be selected among the general ARMA (p, q) class of equation (10-1).

10/1/1   Partial Autocorrelation Coefficients

Suppose $q = 0$ in equation (10-1) and $p = 0, 1, 2, 3, \ldots, p$, consecutively. Equation (10-1) then becomes

$$X_t = e_t, \tag{10-2}$$

$$X_t = \phi_1 X_{t-1} + e_t, \tag{10-3}$$

$$X_t = \phi_1 X_{t-1} + \phi_2 X_{t-2} + e_t, \tag{10-4}$$

$$X_t = \phi_1 X_{t-1} + \phi_2 X_{t-2} + \phi_3 X_{t-3} + e_t, \tag{10-5}$$

.

.

.

$$X_t = \phi_1 X_{t-1} + \phi_2 X_{t-2} + \phi_3 X_{t-3} + \cdots + \phi_p X_{t-p} + e_{tn}. \tag{10-6}$$

If the real order of equation (10-3) is $p = 0$, ϕ_1 will have a value that will not be significantly different from zero. Thus, if one were to calculate ϕ_1, it would be found that the process is an AR(0). However, if the real order is $p = 1$, the value of ϕ_1 calculated in (10-3) will be significantly different from zero. If equation (10-4) is used, when the real order is $p = 1$, ϕ_2 will not be statistically significant. Using similar reasoning, if the real order is $p = 2$, then ϕ_1 will be significantly different from zero, ϕ_2 will also be significant, but ϕ_3 will not be, since the real AR process is of only second order. In general the pth parameter of an AR(p) process will only be significantly different from zero when the AR process is at least of order p or higher.

In general the real order of an AR process is unknown, but one could compute ϕ_1 using (10-3), ϕ_2 using (10-4), ϕ_3 using (10-5), etc. If ϕ_1 is not significantly different from zero, the process is AR(0). If ϕ_1 is significant but ϕ_2 is not, the process is AR(1). Similarly if ϕ_p is significant but ϕ_{p+1} is not, the process is AR(p).

Calculating the values of $\phi_1, \phi_2, \phi_3, \ldots, \phi_p$ from (10-3), (10-4), (10-5), $\ldots$, (10-6) can be very time consuming. However, it is possible to obtain estimates using equation (9-61) for $k = 1, 2, 3, \ldots, p$. When $k = 1$, (9-61) becomes

$$\rho_1 = \phi_1 \rho_0 \quad \text{and} \quad \phi_1 = \rho_1, \tag{10-7}$$

since $\rho_0 = 1$ (ρ_1 is the autocorrelation coefficient of one time lag).

When $k = 2$, (9-61) becomes [see also (9-62)]

$$\rho_1 = \phi_1 + \phi_2 \rho_1 \quad \text{and} \quad \rho_2 = \phi_1 \rho_1 + \phi_2. \tag{10-8}$$

Solving (10-8) for ϕ_2 yields

$$\phi_2 = \frac{\rho_2 - \rho_1^2}{1 - \rho_1^2}. \tag{10-9}$$

Equation (10-9) is the same as (9-65) when $r_1 = \rho_1$ is substituted (i.e., sample estimates are used for ρ_1 and ρ_2).

If $k = 3$, equation (9-61) becomes

$$\left.\begin{aligned}
\rho_1 &= \phi_1 + \phi_2\rho_1 + \phi_3\rho_2, \\
\rho_2 &= \phi_1\rho_1 + \phi_2 + \phi_3\rho_1, \\
\rho_3 &= \phi_1\rho_2 + \phi_2\rho_1 + \phi_3.
\end{aligned}\right\} \qquad (10\text{-}10)$$

Substituting $r_1 = \rho_1$, $r_2 = \rho_2$, and $r_3 = \rho_3$ and solving equation (10-10) provides a value for ϕ_3 that can be used as an estimate in determining the order of the AR process. Similarly, letting $k = p$, one could compute ϕ_p using the p partial autocorrelations of a set of time-series data.

Identifying the order of an AR process can be done by examining their partial autocorrelations. The order will simply be equal to the number of partial autocorrelations significantly different from zero. The partial autocorrelations up through p time lags will be significant, while the remaining will be close to zero. This cutoff, p, will be the order of the AR process.

Moving average processes do not behave as (10-3), (10-4), (10-5), or (10-6). Attempting to estimate $\phi_1, \phi_2, \phi_3, \ldots, \phi_p$ in such cases is fitting the wrong model to the data. In moving average processes the different X_t values are dependent on each other; therefore an infinite number of ϕ_i terms would be required to fit an AR model to MA data. For MA data the values of the partial autocorrelation parameters will initially be large and their magnitude will decrease as the time lag increases. Thus, the partial autocorrelations of an MA process do not have a cutoff after p time lags as in the AR process, but they continue and slowly trail off to zero. That is, there is an exponential decrease in the partial autocorrelations going from large to smaller values as the time lag of the autocorrelations lengthens.

Some typical patterns for partial autocorrelations can be seen in Figure 10-2.

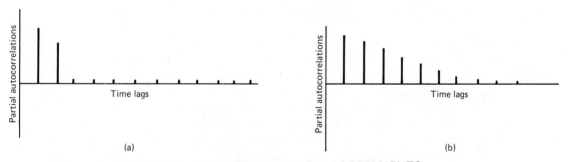

(a)   (b)

FIGURE 10-2 PARTIAL AUTOCORRELATION COEFFICIENTS: (A) TWO PARTIAL AUTOCORRELATIONS ARE SIGNIFICANTLY DIFFERENT FROM ZERO, THE REMAINING ARE NOT. THE CUT OFF AFTER TWO TIME LAGS SUGGESTS AN AR(2) MODEL. (B) PARTIAL AUTOCORRELATIONS DROP TO ZERO EXPONENTIALLY, SUGGESTING AN MA MODEL

10/1/2 Autocorrelation Coefficients

Fortunately, the autocorrelation and partial autocorrelation functions of AR and MA models behave very differently. The autocorrelation coefficients of an AR process behave as those of Figure 10-2(b)—they trail off; those of an MA process exhibit the pattern of Figure 10-2(a)—they drop to zero after q time lags. (Note that this is just the reverse of the behavior of the partial autocorrelation coefficients for AR and MA processes.)

Autocorrelation coefficients show the degree of association among values of the same variable but for different time lags. In AR processes such an association exists, and its magnitude determines the order of the process. In an AR(1) process, for example,

$$X_t = \phi_1 X_{t-1} + e_t, \tag{10-11}$$

$$\text{or} \quad X_t = \rho_1 X_{t-1}. \tag{10-12}$$

If $\rho_1 = \phi_1$ is substituted into (10-11) the result is (10-12). (Note that e_t is omitted because the expected or average value is being considered.)

Equation (10-12) states that X_t and X_{t-1} (one time lag) are related through ρ_1, or its estimate r_1. Since it is also the case that

$$X_{t-1} = \rho_1 X_{t-2}, \tag{10-13}$$

substituting (10-13) into (10-12) gives

$$X_t = \rho_1(\rho_1 X_{t-2})$$

$$= \rho_1^2 X_{t-2}. \tag{10-14}$$

Thus, X_t and X_{t-2} are related through ρ_1^2, or r_1^2. Similarly

$$X_t = \rho_1^s X_{t-s}. \tag{10-15}$$

Clearly, the autocorrelations of an AR(1) process will trail off gradually in an exponential manner as the time lag between X_t and X_{t-s} increases.

For an AR(p) process ($p > 1$) the behavior of the autocorrelation coefficients is similar, even though the autocorrelations trail off a little more slowly. That can be seen by substituting equations (9-64) and (9-65) to obtain an AR(2) process.

For an MA process, the association among successive X_t values is limited to the order of the MA model. In an MA(1), for example,

$$X_t = e_t - \theta_1 e_{t-1}. \tag{10-16}$$

Equation (10-16) states that X_t is related to X_{t-1} only through e_{t-1} and not through any of the remaining terms. Thus, the autocorrelation coefficients of time lags longer than one do not exist (are not significantly different from zero). Hence, there must be a cutoff in the autocorrelation coefficients after one time lag.

If the process is MA(2), X_t is related only to e_{t-1} and e_{t-2} (and therefore X_{t-1} and X_{t-2}). Thus, the first two autocorrelations should be significantly different from zero and the remaining ones should drop to zero. In general, if the process is MA(q), the first q autocorrelations will be significantly different from zero, while the others will not. Figure 10-3 illustrates the typical behavior of autocorrelation coefficients.

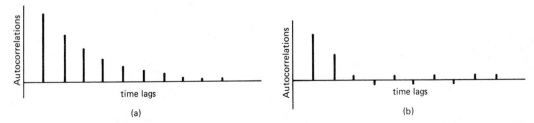

FIGURE 10-3 AUTOCORRELATION COEFFICIENTS: (A) AUTOCORRELATIONS DROP OFF TO ZERO EXPONENTIALLY, SUGGESTING AN AR MODEL. (B) ONLY THE FIRST TWO AUTOCORRELATIONS ARE SIGNIFICANTLY DIFFERENT FROM ZERO, SUGGESTING AN MA(2) MODEL.

10/1/3 Using Both the Autocorrelation and Partial Autocorrelation Coefficients

The information in Figures 10-2 and 10-3 is complementary. For example, Figure 10-2(b) indicates the process is MA and Figure 10-3(b) identifies its order as 2. Similarly, 10-3(a) implies an AR process, while 10-2(a) identifies its order as 2. Thus, for pure AR or MA processes one can first look for the trailing off, which will be in either the autocorrelations or partial autocorrelations. If it is in the former, it indicates an AR process [Figure 10-3(a)] and if in the latter it indicates an MA process [Figure 10-2(b)]. One then looks for the time lag where the values drop to zero, which identifies the degree of the process.

Figures 10-2 and 10-3 present only one possible case of the behavior of autocorrelation and partial autocorrelation coefficients. There are many variations although they have similar patterns. If ϕ_1 is negative, for example, ρ_1 in equation (10-13) will be negative, while ρ_1^2 in equation (10-14) will be positive. Thus, the autocorrelations will alternate in sign and trail off to zero, and the one significant partial autocorrelation will be negative. If the process is an AR(2) and ϕ_1 is positive and ϕ_2 negative, the autos and partials will behave in a slightly different pattern. However, only two partials will be significantly different from zero, while the autos will trail off to zero in some alternating fashion.

Figure 10-4 shows the expected behavior of the autocorrelation and partial autocorrelation coefficients of AR(1), AR(2), MA(1), and MA(2) models. Higher order models will behave in similar ways but will have more than two significant coefficients in either the autocorrelation or partial autocorrelation functions.

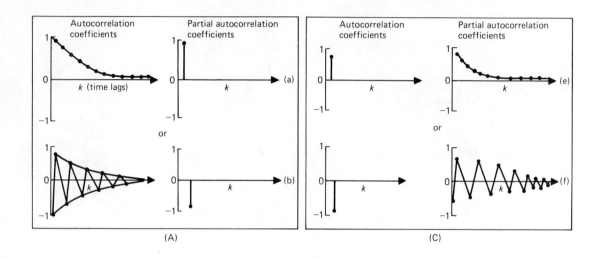

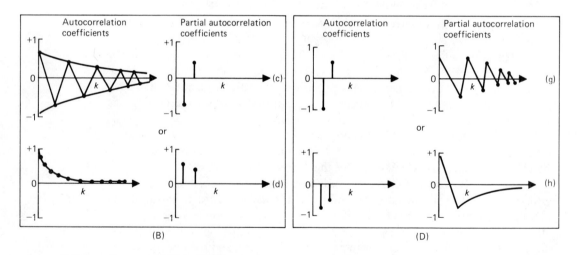

FIGURE 10-4   AUTOCORRELATION AND PARTIAL AUTOCORRELATION FUNCTIONS: (A) AR(1) MODELS, (B) AR(2) MODELS, (C) MA(1) MODELS, AND (D) MA(2) MODELS

10/1/4   Mixed ARMA Processes

ARMA processes combine the characteristics of AR and MA schemes, both in terms of the formulation of an ARMA model and in the behavior of the autocorrelation and partial autocorrelation coefficients. One must literally add together the AR and MA autocorrelations and partial autocorrelations coefficients to obtain the corresponding ones for ARMA models. Thus, for an ARMA(1, 1) model, Figures 10-4(a) and 10-4(e) can be combined to obtain the pattern shown in Figure 10-5.

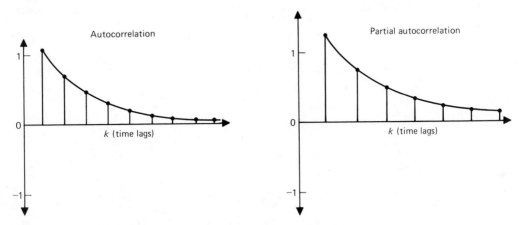

FIGURE 10-5   AUTOCORRELATION AND PARTIAL AUTOCORRELATION COEFFICIENTS OF AN ARMA (1, 1) PROCESS

Figure 10-5 takes the shape of the autocorrelation of 10-4(e) and partial autocorrelation of 10-4(a). The single autocorrelation and partial autocorrelation that are significantly different from zero are included as part of Figure 10-5. Thus, the only time that both the autos and partials will trail off to zero will be when the real process is a mixed ARMA one.

Figure 10-6 indicates the other possible patterns obtained for an ARMA(1, 1) process. These are simply the different possible combinations of AR(1) and MA(1) patterns from Figure 10-4.

10/1/5   Identifying a Tentative ARMA(p, q) Model

A major phase in the Box-Jenkins methodology is identifying an appropriate ARMA(p, q) model by examining the autocorrelation and partial auto-

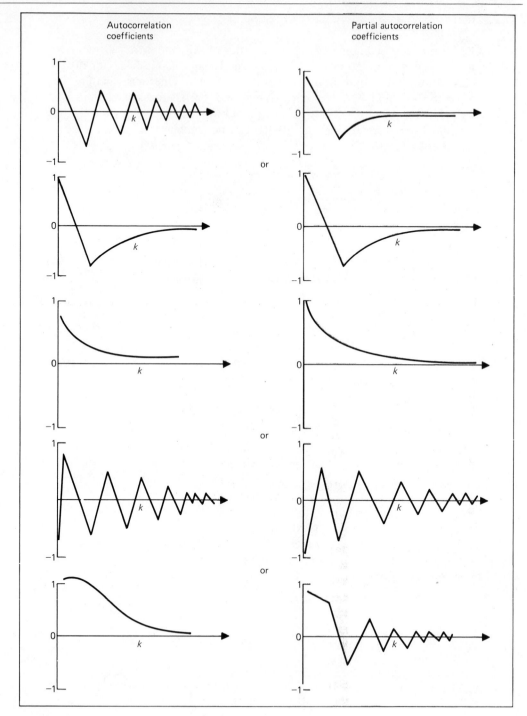

FIGURE 10-6 AUTOCORRELATION AND PARTIAL
AUTOCORRELATION FUNCTIONS OF A MIXED
ARMA (1, 1) MODEL

correlation coefficients of the time series. Although this procedure is straight-forward, it cannot be reduced to a mechanical level. It requires human judgment, and unfortunately it does not always result in a correct identification of a single model for two reasons:

1. The autos and partials may not clearly indicate a specific model.
2. They may indicate more than one model.

In practice, the autos and partials do not always behave according to a clear pattern because of randomness in the data. The behavior of autos and partials indicated in the previous section is theoretical and assumes no noise. When there is noise, the autos or partials may be higher or lower than their theoretical value. Since the amount of variation caused by randomness is not known at the outset, the pattern in the autos and partials is used to infer a "tentative" $ARMA(p, q)$ model.

It is known that the autos and partials are normally distributed with mean zero and standard error $1/\sqrt{n}$. Based on this knowledge, confidence intervals can be constructed and used to determine the chances that a given auto or partial will be significantly different from zero. A 95% confidence interval will require an auto or partial to be more than about $2/\sqrt{n}$ in order to be significant. This can be used as a rough rule to determine the true behavior of the auto and partial correlations. In the remainder of this chapter, several examples illustrating identification of the model will be examined. Before doing so however, it is useful to outline the three-step procedure involved.

1. *Obtaining a stationary series.* If the time series is not stationary, spurious autocorrelations will result that will hinder the model identification procedure. Therefore, if the series is not stationary, it must be transformed to a stationary series by taking the appropriate level of differences. (See Section 8/5/3.)
2. *Examining the autocorrelations and partial autocorrelations* (preferably in graphic form). One must identify the correlations that drop off exponentially (i.e., trail off) to zero. If this trailing off happens among the autocorrelation coefficients, an AR process is implied; if it happens among the partial autocorrelations, an MA process is implied; and if both drop off exponentially, a mixed ARMA process is indicated.
3. *Examining the remaining correlations* (those that do not drop off to zero) *to determine the order of the AR or MA process.* This determination is made by counting the number of autocorrelations or partial auto-correlations significantly different from zero. For a mixed ARMA process, the AR order is determined from the partials and the MA order is determined from the autos.

By executing these three steps, one can identify an $ARMA(p, q)$ model for the stationary series. This process can be illustrated by using the data series

TABLE 10-1   TIME SERIES WITH 24 OBSERVATIONS

Period	Observation	Period	Observation	Period	Observation
1	22.665	9	107.930	17	184.705
2	32.861	10	116.722	18	194.733
3	43.623	11	124.937	19	204.726
4	54.606	12	133.885	20	215.358
5	65.140	13	144.446	21	225.484
6	76.421	14	154.768	22	234.735
7	87.345	15	165.617	23	246.186
8	98.158	16	175.654	24	258.504

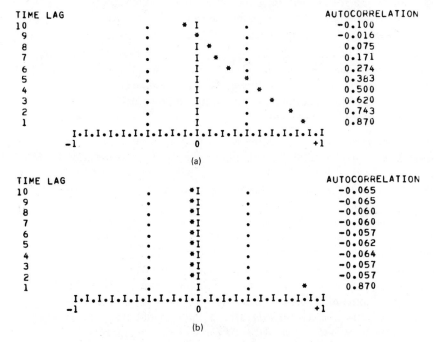

FIGURE 10-7   ORIGINAL DATA OF TABLE 10-1: (A) AUTOCORRELATIONS SUGGESTING A NONSTATIONARY SERIES AND (B) PARTIAL AUTOCORRELATIONS. THE PARTIALS HAVE LITTLE MEANING BECAUSE THEY ARE DOMINATED BY NONSTATIONARITY

in Table 10-1. As the first step in determining the ARMA model that best describes the series, one examines a graph of the autos and partials (see Figure 10-7). The fact that the autocorrelations do not drop to zero quickly (i.e., after the second or third lag), suggests nonstationarity in the original data.

The next step is to take the first differences and then recalculate the autos and partials, as shown in Figure 10-8. The autos now suggest stationarity (they drop to zero very fast), and one can look for the trailing off of the autos and partials. This trailing off occurs for the partials which, as can be seen from Figure 10-8(b), drop exponentially to zero alternating in sign, much like the pattern in Figure 10.4(f). This pattern implies an MA process.

Consequently, the next step is to look at the autocorrelation coefficients where it is clear that only one autocorrelation is significantly different from zero (i.e., outside the dotted lines, $\pm 2/\sqrt{n}$). The conclusion is that the order of the MA process is 1 and that the process is MA(1) or equivalently, ARMA(0, 1).

As a second example of the identification process, Figure 10-9 shows the autos and partials of the data of Table 9-1. There is only one significant auto-

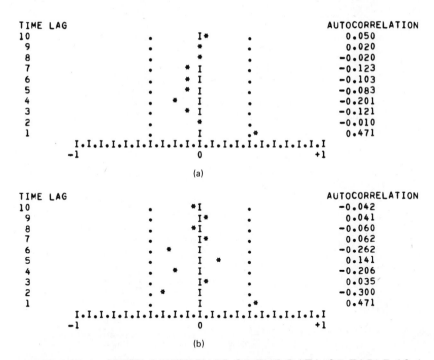

FIGURE 10-8   FIRST DIFFERENCE OF THE DATA OF TABLE 10-1: (A) AUTOCORRELATIONS AND (B) PARTIAL AUTOCORRELATIONS. THE RESULTS SUGGEST AN MA(1) OR ARMA(0, 1) MODEL.

correlation coefficient, which suggests stationarity of the original data. As the figure shows, the autos trail off to zero, suggesting an AR process. (The dropping off is not perfect because of randomness, but it is there.) The next step is to look at the partials. Two of them are significantly different from zero. Thus, the process is AR(2) or equivalently, ARMA(2, 0). This is in fact the model that was used in Chapter 9 and explains why that model worked so well.

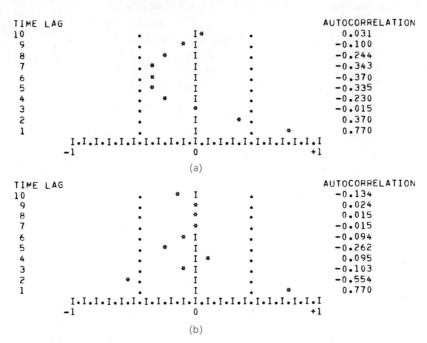

```
TIME LAG                                              AUTOCORRELATION
10               .           I*         .                 0.031
 9               .        *  I          .                -0.100
 8               .     *     I          .                -0.244
 7               .   *       I          .                -0.343
 6               .   *       I          .                -0.370
 5               .   *       I          .                -0.335
 4               .     *     I          .                -0.230
 3               .           *          .                -0.015
 2               .           I    *    .                  0.370
 1               .           I          .      *          0.770
      I.I.I.I.I.I.I.I.I.I.I.I.I.I.I.I.I.I.I.I.I
     -1                      0                 +1
                            (a)
```

```
TIME LAG                                              AUTOCORRELATION
10               .        *  I          .                -0.134
 9               .           *          .                 0.024
 8               .           *          .                 0.015
 7               .           *          .                -0.015
 6               .        *  I          .                -0.094
 5               .     *     I          .                -0.262
 4               .           I  *       .                 0.095
 3               .        *  I          .                -0.103
 2               *  .        I          .                -0.554
 1               .           I          .      *          0.770
      I.I.I.I.I.I.I.I.I.I.I.I.I.I.I.I.I.I.I.I.I
     -1                      0                 +1
                            (b)
```

FIGURE 10-9   DATA OF TABLE 9-1: (A) AUTOCORRELATIONS AND (B) PARTIAL AUTOCORRELATIONS. AN ARMA(2) OR ARMA(2, 0) PROCESS IS INDICATED.

10/2 Estimating the Parameters of an ARMA Model

Once the decision to fit an ARMA(0, 1) model to the first differences of the data of Table 10-1 has been made, one must estimate the value of the parameter of the MA(1) model. That involves finding the value of θ_1 in equation (10-17) that minimizes the MSE:

$$\nabla X_t = e_t - \theta_1 e_{t-1},$$

(10-17)

where $\nabla X_t = X_{t+1} - X_t$ (i.e., the first difference of the original data of Table 10-1, expressed in terms of deviations around the mean).

It is known that $-1 < \theta_1 < 1$ and therefore one can try different values of θ_1 in this range, compute the MSE and choose the value, θ_1^*, which gives the minimum MSE. Figure 10-10 shows the MSE for different values of θ_1. The optimal θ_1^* is $-.88$, which gives an MSE of about .507 (see Figure 10-10).

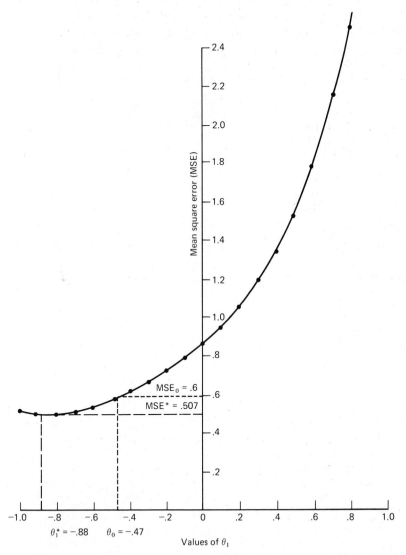

FIGURE 10-10 THE MSE FOR DIFFERENT θ_1 VALUES FOR THE DIFFERENCED DATA OF TABLE 10-1

In order to avoid the time consuming and computationally cumbersome job of finding the best θ_1 by trial and error, one can start with an initial estimate based on a function involving the autocorrelations (see Chapter 9 Appendix, Section 2). For this specific example the initial estimate is $\theta_0 = -.47$, which corresponds to an MSE of .6. From this starting point, it is much easier to move to the optimal value of $-.88$ than it would be to search the entire range between -1 and $+1$.

Instead of employing a simple trial and error procedure to find the best θ_1, it is usually more efficient to apply a method based on the Gauss-Newton constrained optimization approach (such as the Marquardt algorithm). A major difficulty in applying ARMA models is that because of the iterative trial and error procedure involved, considerable computations are required when the order of the model increases beyond one.

For the series in Table 10-1, the final model is therefore,

$$\nabla X_t = e_t - .88e_{t-1}. \tag{10-18}$$

The next step is to check whether the model of (10-18) is an appropriate one.

10/3 Diagnostic Checking of the Estimated Model

Once equation (10-18) has been estimated, its appropriateness in describing the data is determined by examining the residuals of (10-18),

$$e_t = \nabla X_t - .88e_{t-1}.$$

The autocorrelations for these residuals, shown in Figure 10-11, do not denote any pattern (i.e., all autocorrelations are within the dotted lines). Further-

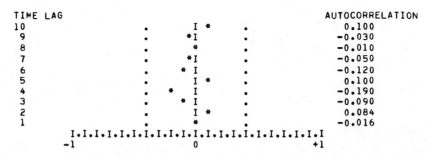

```
TIME LAG                                            AUTOCORRELATION
10                    .        I *      .               0.100
 9                    .       *I       .              -0.030
 8                    .        *       .              -0.010
 7                    .       *I       .              -0.050
 6                    .      * I       .              -0.120
 5                    .        I *      .               0.100
 4                    .    *   I       .              -0.190
 3                    .      * I       .              -0.090
 2                    .        I *      .               0.084
 1                    .        *       .              -0.016
          I.I.I.I.I.I.I.I.I.I.I.I.I.I.I.I.I.I.I.I
          -1                   0              +1
```

FIGURE 10-11   AUTOCORRELATIONS OF RESIDUALS AFTER AN MA(1) MODEL IS FITTED TO THE FIRST DIFFERENCED DATA OF TABLE 10-1

more, the χ^2 of the autocorrelations is 2.06, while the corresponding value from the Table E, Appendix I, for 22 degrees of freedom and a 95% confidence level is 12.3. Since $\chi_c^2 < \chi_t^2$ one can conclude that the MA(1) model shown in equation (10-18) is an appropriate one for forecasting future values of the time series of Table 10-1.

To illustrate the case for which an inadequate model is identified in phase I, suppose that the autos and partials are interpreted incorrectly and it is decided to fit an ARMA(1, 1) model to the original data of Table 10-1. The optimal ARMA(1, 1) model is

$$X_t = .95X_{t-1} + e_t - .94e_{t-1}. \qquad (10\text{-}19)$$

The autocorrelations of the residuals for this model, shown in Figure 10-12, indicate a clear pattern, suggesting that equation (10-19) is not an appropriate model. It would therefore be necessary to go back to phase I and attempt to identify a better model.

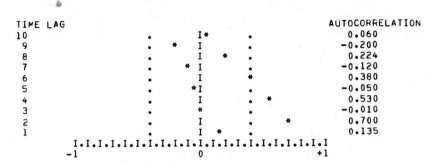

TIME LAG		AUTOCORRELATION
10		0.060
9		−0.200
8		0.224
7		−0.120
6		0.380
5		−0.050
4		0.530
3		−0.010
2		0.700
1		0.135

FIGURE 10-12 AUTOCORRELATIONS OF RESIDUALS AFTER AN ARMA(1, 1) MODEL IS FITTED TO THE ORIGINAL DATA OF TABLE 10-1

Suppose a different type of mistake were made in the identification process after taking the first difference. Instead of choosing an MA(1), an MA(2) was selected. This is not as bad a mistake as fitting an ARMA(1, 1) to the original data. The estimated value of the second MA parameter turns out to be very close to zero, which makes the MA(2) model almost equivalent to the MA(1) of equation (10-18). The only problem here is one of parsimony—using more parameters than necessary. This means fewer degrees of freedom and more computations, which are needless if the second MA parameter adds nothing to the fit.

Similarly, one might have decided to use an ARMA(1, 1) model for the first differenced data. This model is not better than the MA(1) model either, since the value of the AR parameter is very close to zero. It is advisable to use the model with fewest parameters when more than one model gives residuals that are randomly distributed and whose MSE's are approximately equal.

Estimation and checking completes the second phase of the Box-Jenkins approach. The final phase is to use the estimated and checked model to forecast future values of the time series.

10/4 Using an ARMA Model to Forecast

To illustrate the forecasting utilization of an ARMA model, the MA(1) model developed for the data of Table 10-1 will be used. The model was found in equation (10-18) to be

$$\nabla X_t = e_t - .88e_{t-1}.$$

Since there are 24 data points, it is useful to consider the task of preparing forecasts for periods 25, 26, 27, and 28, assuming period 24 results are available. The forecast for period 25 is found by using

$$\nabla X_{25} = e_{25} - .88e_{24}. \tag{10-20}$$

Since $\nabla X_{25} = X_{25} - X_{24},$ \hfill (10-21)

equation (10-21) can be substituted into (10-20) to yield

$$X_{25} - X_{24} = e_{25} - .88e_{24},$$

or $X_{25} = X_{24} + e_{25} - .88e_{24}.$ \hfill (10-22)

However, it will be recalled that the X_t have been expressed in a deviation form around their mean, $\bar{X}$. That is, $X_t = X_t^0 - \bar{X}$. Thus,

$$X_{25} = X_{25}^0 - \bar{X}. \tag{10-23}$$

Substituting (10-23) into (10-22) gives

$$X_{25}^0 = \bar{X} + X_{24} + e_{25} - .88e_{24} \tag{10-24}$$

$$= 10.254 + 258.504 - .88(-.776)$$

$$= 269.44 + e_{25}.$$

Where the value of $\bar{X}$ is found by averaging the data of Table 10-1, X_{24} is the most recent actual value from this table, and e_{24} is known from applying the model to all past values.

For period 26,

$$X_{26}^0 = \bar{X} + X_{25} + e_{26} - .88e_{25}. \tag{10-25}$$

However, neither the real values for X_{25} nor e_{25} are known at period 24.

This suggests that the forecasting value of an MA(1) model is limited for time horizons of more than one period ahead. It is possible to assume that $e_{25} = 0$ and use the estimated value of X_{25} from equation (10-24) as the actual value for (10-25). This is called bootstrapping and eventually allows one to obtain forecasts for as many periods into the future as desired. For example, in this case

$$X_{26}^0 = 10.254 + 269.44 + e_{26} = 279.674 + e_{26},$$

$$X_{27}^0 = 10.254 + 279.674 + e_{27} = 289.948 + e_{27},$$

and $\quad X_{28}^0 = 10.254 + 289.948 + e_{28} = 300.202 + e_{28}.$

In a similar way, one can forecast using other models and various degrees of differencing. However, one must be careful to:

1. add the mean if the data have been expressed in the form of deviations from the mean
2. take into account the level of differencing applied to the data

This latter consideration becomes a little difficult when more than first differencing is used when AR processes are applied. Standard computer programs do both (1) and (2) automatically and give the user the number of forecasts requested. However, to illustrate what is involved in forecasting, an example of an AR(2) model developed for second differenced data will be examined. The model has been found to be

$$\nabla^2 X_t = .5(\nabla^2 X_{t-1}) - .3(\nabla^2 X_{t-2}) + e_t, \tag{10-26}$$

where $\nabla^2 X_t$ is used to denote the second difference of X_t, which simplifies to

$$
\begin{aligned}
\nabla^2 X_t &= \nabla X_t - \nabla X_{t-1} \\
&= (X_t - X_{t-1}) - (X_{t-1} - X_{t-2}) \\
&= X_t - X_{t-1} - X_{t-1} + X_{t-2} \\
&= X_t - 2X_{t-1} + X_{t-2}.
\end{aligned} \tag{10-27}
$$

Similarly

$$\nabla^2 X_{t-1} = X_{t-1} - 2X_{t-2} + X_{t-3}, \tag{10-28}$$

and $\quad \nabla^2 X_{t-2} = X_{t-2} - 2X_{t-3} + X_{t-4}.$ \hfill (10-29)

Substituting (10-27) for the left-hand side of (10-26) and substituting (10-28) and (10-29) for the right-hand side of (10-26) gives

$$X_t - 2X_{t-1} + X_{t-2} = .5(X_{t-1} - 2X_{t-2} + X_{t-3}) - .3(X_{t-2} - 2X_{t-3} + X_{t-4}) + e_t.$$

Collecting terms, one gets

$$X_t = 2.5X_{t-1} - 2.3X_{t-2} + 1.1X_{t-3} - .3X_{t-4} + e_t.$$

In this example, the mean is .727 and the last four data values are

$$X_{24} = 140, \qquad X_{23} = 114, \qquad X_{22} = 133, \qquad X_{21} = 158.$$

Using the above and adding the mean one gets as a forecast for period 25,

$$X_{25}^0 = .727 + 2.5(140) - 2.3(114) + 1.1(133) - .3(158) + e_{25}$$

$$= 187.427.$$

A bootstrap forecast can be obtained for period 26 by assuming $X_{25} = 187.427$ and computing

$$X_{26} = .727 + 2.5(187.427) - 2.3(140) + 1.1(114) - .3(133) + e_{26}$$

$$= 232.795.$$

Similarly we can assume that the forecasts for periods 25 and 26 are the actual values and obtain a forecast for X_{27}, the value 271.433, etc.

To summarize, the Box-Jenkins methodology consists of three phases. In phase I an appropriate ARMA(p, q) model is identified. In phase II the parameters of the model are estimated and the model is tested to see whether the residuals of that model are random. That is done by calculating the autocorrelations for the residuals and determining whether they are randomly distributed around their mean of zero. In the last phase, the appropriate model is used to forecast future values of the time series. It will be recalled that Figure 10-1 shows a schematic of this procedure.

10/5 Seasonal ARMA Models

Seasonal time series add another dimension of difficulty to forecasting with an ARMA model because in addition to the period-to-period pattern there is a longer, repetitive pattern in the series occurring every Lth period (where L is the length of seasonality). To predict the seasonal pattern, seasonal parameters must be included. As in the nonseasonal models, these can be either of an autoregressive or moving average form. (Mixed processes can also be considered, but they are not usually necessary in practice.)

To express and understand seasonal ARMA models, the concept of the backshift operator, B, must be introduced. This operator has no mathematical meaning, but is used to facilitate the writing of different types of models that would otherwise be extremely difficult to express. The backshift operator is defined as $B^m Y_t$. For example,

$$BX_t = X_{t-1} \qquad \text{or} \qquad Be_t = e_{t-1}$$

$$B^2 X_t = X_{t-2} \qquad\qquad B^2 e_t = e_{t-2}$$

$$B^3 X_t = X_{t-3} \qquad\qquad B^3 e_t = e_{t-3}$$

$$\begin{matrix} . & . & & . & . \\ . & . & & . & . \\ . & . & & . & . \end{matrix}$$

$$B^m X_t = X_{t-m} \qquad\qquad B^m e_t = e_{t-m}$$

An ARMA model can be expressed in terms of the backshift operator. An AR(1) model, for example, can be written as

$$X_t = \phi_1 X_{t-1} + e_t$$

or $\quad X_t - \phi_1 X_{t-1} = e_t.$ (10-30)

However, since

$$X_{t-1} = BX_t,$$

equation (10-30) can be rewritten as

$$X_t - \phi_1 BX_t = e_t$$

and $\quad (1 - \phi_1 B)X_t = e_t.$

Similarly, for an AR(2) model,

$$X_t - \phi_1 X_{t-1} - \phi_2 X_{t-2} = e_t.$$

Since $\quad X_{t-1} = BX_t$

and $\quad X_{t-2} = B^2 X_t,$

this can be rewritten as

$$X_t - \phi_1 BX_1 - \phi_2 B^2 X_t = e_t,$$

and $\quad (1 - \phi_1 B - \phi_2 B^2)X_t = e_t.$ (10-31)

Now suppose one has an AR(2) model and that the first differences have been used. That is,

$$(X_t - X_{t-1}) = \phi_1(X_{t-1} - X_{t-2}) + \phi_2(X_{t-2} - X_{t-3}) + e_t.$$

Since $\quad X_{t-1} = BX_t, \qquad X_{t-1} = BX_{t-2}, \qquad$ and $\qquad X_{t-2} = BX_{t-3},$

this can be rewritten as

$$BX_t = \phi_1 BX_{t-1} + \phi_2 BX_{t-2} + e_t.$$ (10-32)

Also, since

$$X_t = BX_{t-1} \qquad \text{and} \qquad X_t = B^2 X_{t-2},$$

Equation (10-32) becomes

$$X_t - BX_t = \phi_1 BBX_t + \phi_2 BB^2 X_t = e_t,$$

$$\text{or} \quad (1 - B)X_t - \phi_1 B^2 X_1 - \phi_2 B^2 X_t = e_t. \tag{10-33}$$

If $(1 - B)X_t$ is used as a common factor, (10-33) becomes

$$X_t(1 - B)(1 - \phi_1 B - \phi_2 B^2) = e_t,$$

which in a resequenced form is

$$(1 - B)(1 - \phi_1 B - \phi_2 B^2)X_t = e_t. \tag{10-34}$$

Equation (10-34) is the equivalent of an AR(2) process (i.e., $1 - \phi_1 B - \phi_2 B^2$) on the first differenced data (i.e., $1 - B$). This type of expression is possible because ARMA models are multiplicative.

Similarly, MA or mixed ARMA processes can be expressed in terms of the backshift operator, B. An MA(1) process is

$$X_t = e_t - \theta_1 e_{t-1}.$$

Since $e_{t-1} = Be_1,$

this can be rewritten as

$$X_t = e_t - \theta_1 Be_t$$

$$\text{or} \quad X_t = (1 - \theta_1 B)e_t. \tag{10-35}$$

Similarly, an MA(2) process is written as

$$X_t = (1 - \theta_1 B - \theta_2 B^2)e_t. \tag{10-36}$$

An MA(2) for first differenced data is

$$(1 - B)X_t = (1 - \theta_1 B - \theta_2 B^2)e_t. \tag{10-37}$$

An ARMA(1, 1) is

$$(1 - \phi_1 B)X_t = (1 - \theta_1 B)e_t. \tag{10-38}$$

An ARMA(1, 1) with first order differencing is

$$(1 - B)(1 - \phi_1 B)X_1 = (1 - \theta_1 B)e_t. \tag{10-39}$$

An ARMA(1, 2) with second order differencing is

$$(1 - 2B + B^2)(1 - \phi_1 B)X_t = (1 - \theta_1 B - \theta_2 B^2)e_t. \tag{10-40}$$

The use of the backshift operator may seem awkward at first glance, but after some exposure to the idea, it becomes easy to deal with. The operator without a parameter denotes differencing whose level is equal to the highest exponent of B. If, however, it is next to a parameter it denotes an ARMA process.

The order and type of process can be identified from the exponent of B and the type of parameter. (If it is Φ_i, an AR is represented; if it is Θ_i, an MA process is represented.)

Suppose one has a set of seasonal data. Assuming a multiplicative model, the ARMA process that one might attempt to fit will consist of two parts:

1. the regular nonseasonal part that has been examined previously in this chapter
2. some seasonal parameters

In terms of identification, one can ignore the seasonality of the data initially and choose an ARMA model as before. In terms of identifying the seasonal pattern (and choosing a seasonal process) one ignores the nonseasonal part and determines whether the seasonality is determined by an AR or MA process. As a more specific illustration, assume that the nonseasonal part is an ARMA(1, 1) with no differencing [see (10-38)]. If the data show a monthly seasonal pattern, the complete model becomes

$$(1 - \phi_1 B)(1 - \phi_{12} B^{12})X_t = (1 - \theta_1 B)e_t \tag{10-41}$$

or $\quad (1 - \phi_1 B)X_t = (1 - \theta_1 B)(1 - \theta_{12}B^{12})e_t,$ (10-42)

where $\quad (1 - \phi_{12}B^{12})X_t = X_t - \phi_{12}B^{12}X_t.$

That is,

$$X_t = \phi_{12}X_{t-12}. \tag{10-43}$$

Similarly

$$(1 - \theta_{12}B^{12})e_t = e_t - \theta_{12}B^{12}e_t$$

$$= e_t - \theta_{12}e_{t-12}. \tag{10-44}$$

Thus, (10-41) or (10-42) include seasonal parameters that use the X_t or e_t of 12 months ago to take into account seasonality.

An MA(2) seasonal process with one level of differencing [see (10-37)] can take one of the following two forms:

$$(1 - B)(1 - \phi_{12}B^{12})X_t = (1 - \theta_1 B - \theta_2 B^2)e_t$$

$\Downarrow$	$\Downarrow$	$\Downarrow$
One level of differencing	Seasonal parameter in AR	MA(2) nonseasonal

$$(1 - B)X_t = (1 - \theta_1 B - \theta_2 B^2)(1 - \theta_{12}B^{12})e_t$$

$\Downarrow$	$\Downarrow$	$\Downarrow$
One level of differencing	MA(2) nonseasonal	Seasonal parameter in MA

TABLE 10-2 INDUSTRY SALES FOR PRINTING AND WRITING PAPER

Period	Observation	Period	Observation	Period	Observation
1	562.674	41	701.108	81	742.000
2	599.000	42	790.079	82	847.152
3	668.516	43	594.621	83	731.675
4	597.798	44	230.716	84	898.527
5	579.889	45	617.189	85	778.139
6	668.233	46	691.389	86	856.075
7	499.232	47	701.067	87	938.833
8	215.187	48	705.777	88	813.023
9	555.813	49	747.636	89	783.417
10	586.935	50	773.392	90	828.110
11	546.136	51	813.788	91	657.311
12	571.111	52	766.713	92	310.032
13	634.712	53	728.875	93	780.000
14	639.283	54	749.197	94	860.000
15	712.182	55	680.954	95	780.000
16	621.557	56	241.424	96	807.993
17	621.000	57	680.234	97	895.217
18	675.989	58	708.326	98	856.075
19	501.322	59	694.238	99	893.268
20	220.286	60	772.071	100	875.000
21	560.727	61	795.337	101	835.088
22	602.530	62	788.421	102	934.595
23	626.379	63	889.968	103	832.500
24	605.508	64	797.393	104	300.000
25	646.783	65	751.000	105	791.443
26	658.442	66	821.255	106	900.000
27	712.906	67	691.605	107	781.729
28	687.714	68	290.655	108	880.000
29	723.916	69	727.147	109	875.024
30	707.183	70	868.355	110	992.968
31	629.000	71	812.390	111	976.804
32	237.530	72	799.556	112	968.697
33	613.296	73	843.038	113	871.675
34	730.444	74	847.000	114	1006.852
35	734.925	75	941.952	115	832.037
36	651.812	76	804.309	116	345.587
37	676.155	77	840.307	117	849.528
38	748.183	78	871.528	118	913.871
39	810.681	79	656.330	119	868.746
40	729.363	80	370.508	120	993.733

10/6 An Application of Seasonal ARMA Processes

   Table 10-2 shows the industry sales (in thousands of francs) for printing and writing paper between the years 1963 and 1972. These data can be used to prepare a forecast for 1973. In the first phase the pattern of the data must be identified.

   Figure 10-13 shows the autocorrelation coefficients of the original data of Table 10-2. It can be seen that the data are not stationary in their original form, since almost all the coefficients are positive. Furthermore, several autocorrelations (r_1, r_3, r_9, r_{11}, r_{12}, r_{13}, r_{23}, r_{24}, r_{25}) are significantly different from zero. Once it is determined that there is nonstationarity, there is no reason to compute the partial autocorrelations, since the latter are used only to identify the right model. Thus the next step is to obtain a stationary series.

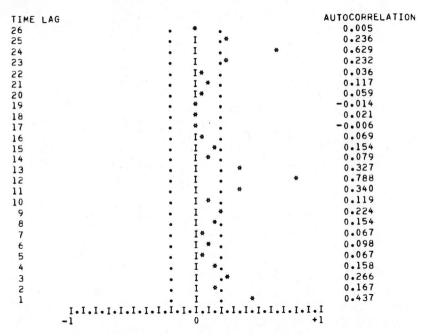

TIME LAG	AUTOCORRELATION
26	0.005
25	0.236
24	0.629
23	0.232
22	0.036
21	0.117
20	0.059
19	−0.014
18	0.021
17	−0.006
16	0.069
15	0.154
14	0.079
13	0.327
12	0.788
11	0.340
10	0.119
9	0.224
8	0.154
7	0.067
6	0.098
5	0.067
4	0.158
3	0.266
2	0.167
1	0.437

FIGURE 10-13 AUTOCORRELATIONS OF ORIGINAL DATA OF TABLE 10-2

   Figure 10-14 shows the autocorrelations for the series of first differences. Things have improved; the slight trend pattern of Figure 10-13 has been eliminated and the autos are distributed evenly around zero, indicating that the first differences have removed the period-to-period nonstationarity. However, there are some very significant coefficients, notably r_{12} and r_{24}. That means stationarity on a period-to-period basis has been achieved, but not on the longer seasonal length of 12 periods. In other words, the seasonal autocorrelation coefficients (r_{12}, r_{24}, r_{36}, etc.) do not behave as the nonseasonal ones (r_1, r_2, r_3, etc.). It is difficult to determine whether the seasonal autos drop to zero fast enough, since to do so requires several seasonal coefficients, which are difficult to calculate and require a lot of data points. However, in Figure 10-14 it is clear that both r_{12} and r_{24} are too large, and that r_{24} is not close to zero at all. Thus, one would conclude that there is nonstationarity between successive seasonal periods (separated by a time lag of 12 months). This longer-term trend must be removed by taking long-term differences—differences whose length is 12 periods apart.

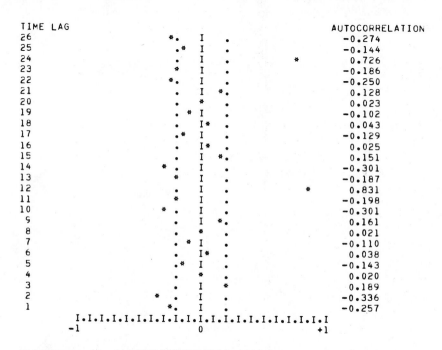

TIME LAG	AUTOCORRELATION
26	-0.274
25	-0.144
24	0.726
23	-0.186
22	-0.250
21	0.128
20	0.023
19	-0.102
18	0.043
17	-0.129
16	0.025
15	0.151
14	-0.301
13	-0.187
12	0.831
11	-0.198
10	-0.301
9	0.161
8	0.021
7	-0.110
6	0.038
5	-0.143
4	0.020
3	0.189
2	-0.336
1	-0.257

FIGURE 10-14 AUTOCORRELATIONS OF FIRST DIFFERENCE OF DATA OF TABLE 10-2

A long-term difference, frequently referred to as a "long" difference, is written as

$$X_t - X_{t-12} = X_t - B^{12}X_t = (1 - B^{12})X_t.$$

For the data of Table 10-2, the 12-period difference is shown in the last column of Table 10-3.

TABLE 10-3 A LONG DIFFERENCE (OF 12 PERIODS) FOR THE DATA OF TABLE 10-2

Period	Actual Values	X_t	X_{t-12}	$(1 - B^{12})X_t$
1	562.674	634.712	562.674	72.038
2	599.000	639.283	599.000	40.283
3	668.516	712.182	668.516	43.667
4	597.798	621.557	597.798	23.759
5	579.889	621.000	579.889	41.111
6	668.233	675.989	668.233	7.756
7	499.232	501.322	499.232	2.090
8	215.187	220.286	215.187	5.099
9	555.813	560.727	555.813	4.914
10	586.935	602.530	586.935	15.596
11	546.136	626.379	546.136	80.243
12	571.111	605.508	571.111	34.397
13	634.712	646.783	634.712	12.071
14	639.283	658.442	639.283	19.158
15	712.182	712.906	712.182	.723
16	621.557	687.714	621.557	66.157
17	621.000	723.916	621.000	102.917
18	675.989	707.183	675.989	31.194
19	501.322	629.000	501.322	127.678
20	220.286	237.530	220.286	17.245
21	560.727	613.296	560.727	52.568
22	602.530	730.444	602.530	127.914
23	626.379	734.925	626.379	108.546
24	605.508	651.812	605.508	46.304
⋮	⋮	⋮	⋮	⋮
105	791.443	849.528	791.443	58.084
106	900.000	913.871	900.000	13.871
107	781.729	868.746	781.729	87.017
108	880.000	993.733	880.000	113.733
109	875.024	—	—	—
110	992.968	—	—	—
111	976.804	—	—	—
112	968.697	—	—	—
113	871.675	—	—	—
114	1006.852	—	—	—
115	832.037	—	—	—
116	345.587	—	—	—
117	849.528	—	—	—
118	913.871	—	—	—
119	868.746	—	—	—
120	993.733	—	—	—

From Table 10-3 it can be seen that 12 values are lost, since one must start at X_{13} to take the initial long difference, $X_{13} - X_1$. The long differenced series, therefore, has 108 data points. To determine whether they are stationary, the autocorrelation coefficients are computed as shown in Figure 10-15.

```
TIME LAG                                                    AUTOCORRELATION
26                        .     *    .                           0.009
25                      . *   I      .                          -0.108
24                      . *   I      .                          -0.104
23                      . *   I      .                          -0.110
22                      .  *I         .                         -0.061
21                      .* I         .                          -0.148
20                      .* I         .                          -0.164
19                      .* I         .                          -0.143
18                      .* I         .                          -0.154
17                      .     *       .                         -0.001
16                      .* I          .                         -0.134
15                      .* I          .                         -0.155
14                      . * I         .                         -0.115
13                      .     *       .                         -0.004
12             *        .     I       .                         -0.383
11                      .     *       .                          0.023
10                      .    I*       .                          0.030
9                       .    I  *   .                            0.077
8                       .    I*     .                            0.053
7                       .    I   *.                              0.137
6                       .    I *  .                              0.120
5                       .    I*    .                             0.028
4                       .    I   *. .                            0.128
3                       .    I    *                              0.195
2                       .    I  *.                               0.170
1                       .    I *  .                              0.077
            I.I.I.I.I.I.I.I.I.I.I.I.I.I.I.I.I.I.I.I
            -1                 0                 +1
```

FIGURE 10-15 AUTOCORRELATIONS FOR LONG DIFFERENCE OF DATA OF TABLE 10-2

The autocorrelations of Figure 10-15 are very close to zero except for the one significant autocorrelation corresponding to a time lag of 12 periods, $r_{12} = -.383$. One might, therefore, conclude stationarity at the level of one long difference. However, this is not the case. Careful examination of Figure 10-15 indicates a trend pattern because the first 11 autos are above zero and all others are below. Even though this pattern seems minimal, its presence should arouse suspicion. The problem is that autocorrelation coefficients are influenced by high degrees of dependence. In the same way that a trend hinders identification of other patterns and must be removed before remaining patterns can be recognized, strong seasonality can hinder identification of other patterns. The data must be stationary before anything can be determined about the pattern of the data. Thus, even though the autos of Figure 10-15 appear at first glance not to be different from zero, the slight trend pattern should make one think that there may be something wrong. The easiest way to disperse the doubts in this situation is to combine the long difference shown in Figure 10-15 with the short shown in Figure 10-14. That requires taking both a short and long difference at the same time. However, before doing so, it is instructive to assume that one did not detect anything wrong with Figure 10-15 and to see what happens when one proceeds to identify an appropriate model. That requires computing the partial autocorrelations and choosing an appropriate ARMA model. Figure 10-16 shows the partial autocorrelations for this example. These partials behave in a manner similar to that for the autos.

Identifying an ARMA model from Figures 10-15 and 10-16 is not easy. The nonseasonal coefficients exhibit no pattern whatsoever, suggesting that the nonseasonal model is $(1 - B^{12})X_t = e_t$.

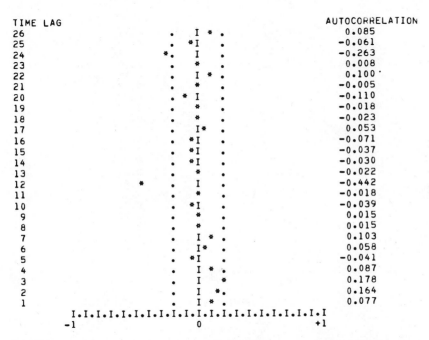

TIME LAG		AUTOCORRELATION
26	I *	0.085
25	*I	-0.061
24	*. I	-0.263
23	*	0.008
22	I *	0.100
21	*	-0.005
20	* I	-0.110
19	*	-0.018
18	*	-0.023
17	I*	0.053
16	*I	-0.071
15	*I	-0.037
14	*I	-0.030
13	*	-0.022
12	* I	-0.442
11	*	-0.018
10	*I	-0.039
9	*	0.015
8	*	0.015
7	I *	0.103
6	I*	0.058
5	*I	-0.041
4	I *	0.087
3	I *	0.178
2	I *.	0.164
1	I *	0.077

```
I.I.I.I.I.I.I.I.I.I.I.I.I.I.I.I.I.I.I.I.I
-1                  0                  +1
```

FIGURE 10-16 PARTIAL AUTOCORRELATIONS FOR LONG DIFFERENCE OF DATA OF TABLE 10-2

The seasonal coefficients (partials) do show some pattern with r_{12} and r_{24} being significant. It appears that r_{24} is dropping exponentially to zero, and that if r_{36} were computed it would have been even closer to zero. Thus, indications are that r_{12}, r_{24}, and r_{36}, etc., trail off to zero. Since this trailing off is in the partials, it suggests an MA model. The order of the model is 1, since the only significant autocorrelation is r_{12}. Having determined that the seasonal part of the process is generated by an MA(1) process, one gets $(1 - \theta_{12}B^{12})e_t$. Combining the identified nonseasonal and seasonal models gives

$$(1 - B^{12})X_t = (1 - \theta_{12}B^{12})e_t. \tag{10-45}$$

The next task is to estimate θ_{12} and to calculate the autocorrelations of the resulting residuals. As shown in Figure 10-17, the autocorrelations of the residuals are found to exhibit a trend, since they are almost all positive. Even if no trend had been suspected in Figure 10-15, the results of Figure 10-17 would have clearly identified the problem.

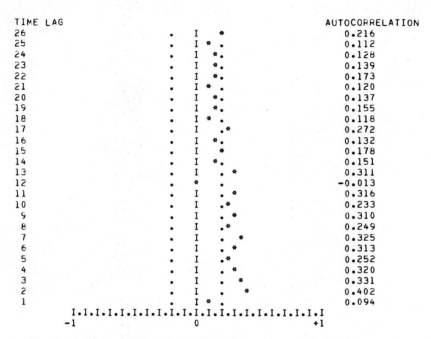

FIGURE 10-17   RESIDUAL AUTOCORRELATIONS OF MODEL (10-45) FOR ONE LONG DIFFERENCE OF DATA OF TABLE 10-2

Taking a short difference in addition to the long in order to eliminate the remaining trend presents no extra problems; it simply involves differencing more terms. This simultaneous difference is equivalent to

$$(1 - B)(1 - B^{12})X_t. \tag{10-46}$$

⇓   ⇓

one short-term   one long-term
difference (i.e.,   difference (i.e.,
every 1 period)   every 12 periods)

Figure 10-18 shows the autocorrelation coefficients obtained for the series given by (10-46). These are more dispersed around zero than those of Figure 10-15 and show no trend pattern. Except for r_1, r_{11}, r_{12} and r_{13}, their dispersion around zero appears to be random. That indicates stationarity at the level of one short and one long difference. Thus the next step can be taken—calculating the partials to determine the appropriate model. Figure 10-19 shows the partial autocorrelations for this series.

Looking at Figures 10-18 and 10-19, the appropriate ARMA model for the data can be easily identified. First, one ignores the seasonal coefficients and concentrates on the nonseasonal pattern. Figure 10-19 shows an exponential decay of the nonseasonal coefficients (partials). This pattern in the partial autocorrelations means an MA process. Next, one looks at the autos of Figure 10-18 where only one nonseasonal autocorrelation is significantly different from zero ($r_1 = -.552$), indicating that the order of the MA process is 1. This model can be written as

$$(1 - B)(1 - B^{12})X_t = (1 - \theta_1 B)e_t, \tag{10-47}$$

where the left-hand side of (10-47) is the same as (10-46).

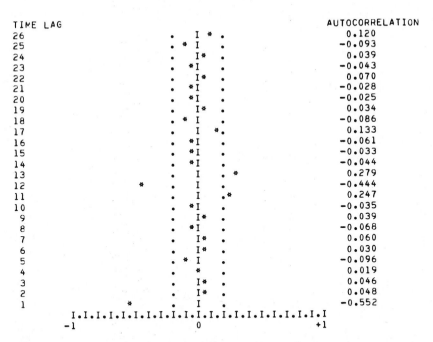

FIGURE 10-18 AUTOCORRELATIONS FOR ONE SHORT AND ONE LONG DIFFERENCE OF DATA OF TABLE 10-2

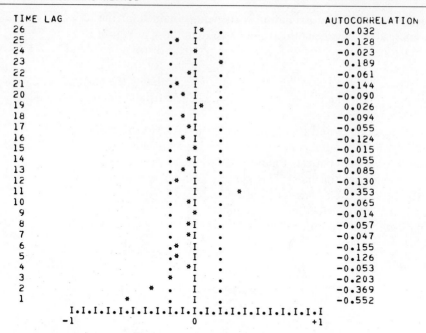

```
TIME LAG                                                    AUTOCORRELATION
26                          .   I*  .                            0.032
25                         .*  I    .                           -0.128
24                         .   *    .                           -0.023
23                         .   I    *                            0.189
22                         .  *I    .                           -0.061
21                         .*  I    .                           -0.144
20                         .  * I   .                           -0.090
19                         .   I*   .                            0.026
18                         . * I    .                           -0.094
17                         .  *I    .                           -0.055
16                         . * I    .                           -0.124
15                         .   *    .                           -0.015
14                         .  *I    .                           -0.055
13                         . * I    .                           -0.085
12                         .*  I    .                           -0.130
11                         .   I    .   *                        0.353
10                         .  *I    .                           -0.065
 9                         .   *    .                           -0.014
 8                         .  *I    .                           -0.057
 7                         .  *I    .                           -0.047
 6                         .* I     .                           -0.155
 5                         .* I     .                           -0.126
 4                         .  *I    .                           -0.053
 3                         .  *I    .                           -0.203
 2                         *  .  I  .                           -0.369
 1              *               .  I  .                         -0.552
     I.I.I.I.I.I.I.I.I.I.I.I.I.I.I.I.I.I.I.I.I.I.I
    -1                          0                    +1
```

FIGURE 10-19 PARTIAL AUTOCORRELATIONS FOR ONE SHORT
AND ONE LONG DIFFERENCE OF DATA OF
TABLE 10-2

The subsequent step is to identify the seasonal pattern by examining the coefficients—r_{12}, r_{24}, r_{36}, etc.—in both the autos and partials. It appears that the partials trail off to zero, since $r_{12} = .354$ and $r_{24} = .189$. It would have been desirable to know r_{36}, r_{48}, and even r_{60}, but this is often not possible. Since only r_{12} is significant in the autocorrelations, the initial judgment is that the seasonal parameter should be the MA,

$$(1 - \theta_{12}B^{12})e_t.$$ (10-48)

Combining the nonseasonal (10-47) with (10-48) results in

$$(1 - B)(1 - B^{12})X_t = (1 - \theta_1 B)(1 - \theta_{12}B^{12})e_t.$$ (10-49)

$\Downarrow$ $\Downarrow$ $\Downarrow$ $\Downarrow$

one short difference   one long difference   MA(1)   MA seasonal

The steps of the identification phase are now completed:

1. The series has been made stationary by taking the appropriate number(s) of short- and/or long-term differences.

2. A nonseasonal ARMA model has been identified.

3. A seasonal AR or MA model has been identified.

In the second phase one estimates θ_1 and θ_{12} and checks the autocorrelations of the residuals for randomness. The parameter values are found by a standard nonlinear estimation program (see for example Marquardt 1963):

$$\theta_1 = .8255, \qquad \theta_{12} = .6123.$$

Equation (10-49) then becomes

$$(1 - B)(1 - B^{12})X_t = (1 - .8255)(1 - .6123B^{12})e_t. \qquad (10\text{-}50)$$

The autocorrelations of the residuals of (10-50) are shown in Figure 10-20. These appear to be random, and therefore it can be concluded that (10-50) is a correct model that can be used for forecasting purposes. (The computed χ^2 is

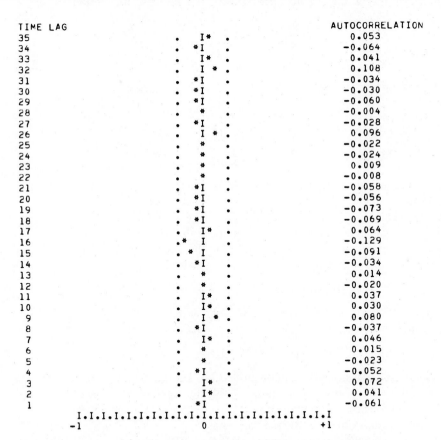

TIME LAG		AUTOCORRELATION
35	I*	0.053
34	*I	-0.064
33	I*	0.041
32	I *	0.108
31	*I	-0.034
30	*I	-0.030
29	*I	-0.060
28	*	-0.004
27	*I	-0.028
26	I *	0.096
25	*	-0.022
24	*	-0.024
23	*	0.009
22	*	-0.008
21	*I	-0.058
20	*I	-0.056
19	*I	-0.073
18	*I	-0.069
17	I*	0.064
16	* I	-0.129
15	* I	-0.091
14	*I	-0.034
13	*	0.014
12	*	-0.020
11	I*	0.037
10	I*	0.030
9	I *	0.080
8	*I	-0.037
7	I*	0.046
6	*	0.015
5	*	-0.023
4	*I	-0.052
3	I*	0.072
2	I*	0.041
1	*I	-0.061

I.I.I.I.I.I.I.I.I.I.I.I.I.I.I.I.I.I.I.I.I

-1   0   +1

FIGURE 10-20 AUTOCORRELATIONS OF RESIDUALS OF MODEL (10-50)

11.9, and the corresponding value from Table E, Appendix I, for 32 degrees of freedom and a 95% confidence level is 18.5.)

Finally, equation (10-50) can be used for forecasting. The relationship, however, is complex, involving many terms of X_t and e_t. Normally, the forecasts will be given directly by the computer program being used. However, equation (10-50) will be expanded to show the use of past values of X_t and past errors e_t in forecasting.

Equation (10-50) is equivalent to

$$(1 - B^{12} - B + B^{13})X_t = [1 - .6123B^{12} - .8255B + .8255(.6123)B^{13}]e_t. \qquad (10\text{-}51)$$

Collecting terms and expressing (10-51) in terms of X_t gives

$$X_t = X_{t-1} + X_{t-12} - X_{t-13} + e_t - .8255e_{t-1} - .6123e_{t-12} + .5054e_{t-13}.$$

Since the most recent data is for period 120, the forecast for period 121 is

$$X_{121} = X_{120} + X_{109} - X_{108} + e_{121} - .8255e_{120} - .6123e_{109} + .5054e_{108}.$$

This becomes $X_{121} = 946.11$,

since $X_{120} = 993.733, \qquad X_{109} = 875.024, \qquad X_{108} = 880.000,$

$$e_{120} = 69.9, \qquad e_{109} = -14.4, \qquad e_{108} = 12.3.$$

Similarly, $X_{122} = 996.705, \qquad X_{123} = 1029.98,$

$$X_{124} = 981.83, \qquad X_{125} = 929.5, \text{ etc.}$$

A question of concern with seasonal ARMA models is whether to place the seasonal parameter in the MA or AR part. The difficulty in making this decision is that one usually has neither enough data to make a reliable identification nor enough time to calculate numerous autos and partials. When the question is unclear, it is advisable to try both possibilities. For the example above, the model that has the seasonal parameter in the AR portion is

$$(1 - B)(1 - B^{12})(1 - \phi_{12}B^{12})X_t = (1 - \theta_1 B)e_t. \qquad (10\text{-}52)$$

The parameters of (10-52) are found to be $\phi_{12} = .8717$ and $\theta_1 = -.1272$, and equation (10-52) can be rewritten as

$$(1 - B)(1 - B^{12})(1 - .8717)X_t = [1 - (-.1272)B]e_t. \qquad (10\text{-}53)$$

Unfortunately (10-53) is not an adequate model. The computed $\chi^2 = 36.59$, and the corresponding value from the χ^2 table (Table E, Appendix I) for 32 degrees of freedom is 18.5. These values indicate that the residuals are not random, and this conclusion is substantiated by the fact that $r_{12} = -.405$, which is significantly different from zero. Furthermore, the MSE = 2594, while the MSE from (10-50) is 1935. All indications are thus that (10-50) with the seasonal in the MA portion is more appropriate than (10-53), which has the seasonal in the AR portion.

10/7 Achieving Stationarity in Variance

A final concern when using the Box-Jenkins methodology to fit ARMA models is the need to achieve stationarity in the variance of the time series. Economic and business series usually vary in relation to percentages. That is, the magnitude of the fluctuations is proportional to the magnitude of the actual values. This pattern can be seen clearly from the data of Table 10-4, which shows the shipments of a company that manufactures pollution equipment.

TABLE 10-4 SHIPMENTS OF POLLUTION EQUIPMENT BETWEEN 1964 AND 1975 (IN THOUSANDS OF FRENCH FRANCS)

Period	Observation	Period	Observation	Period	Observation
1	122.640	44	459.024	87	2411.628
2	120.888	45	543.120	88	1510.224
3	164.688	46	567.648	89	1876.392
4	147.168	47	613.200	90	1792.296
5	171.696	48	791.904	91	1307.868
6	228.636	49	305.724	92	1705.572
7	124.392	50	713.064	93	1945.596
8	155.928	51	1156.320	94	2219.784
9	217.248	52	829.572	95	2528.136
10	176.076	53	865.488	96	3534.660
11	142.788	54	1318.380	97	1546.140
12	196.224	55	971.484	98	2246.064
13	228.636	56	817.308	99	2930.220
14	234.768	57	1079.232	100	2462.436
15	319.740	58	1013.532	101	2551.788
16	241.776	59	986.376	102	3140.460
17	151.548	60	1264.068	103	2437.032
18	352.152	61	997.764	104	2109.408
19	239.148	62	1415.616	105	3853.523
20	233.892	63	1709.952	106	2840.868
21	471.288	64	1443.648	107	3164.112
22	290.832	65	1619.724	108	3946.380
23	284.700	66	2120.796	109	3044.976
24	291.708	67	923.304	110	3957.768
25	287.328	68	860.232	111	4552.571
26	315.360	69	1639.872	112	3651.167
27	417.852	70	1106.388	113	3861.408
28	288.204	71	1161.576	114	5048.388

TABLE 10-4 *Continued*

Period	Observation	Period	Observation	Period	Observation
29	225.132	72	1034.556	115	2990.664
30	430.992	73	960.972	116	2677.056
31	229.512	74	1214.136	117	5566.103
32	296.964	75	1492.704	118	3661.680
33	355.656	76	991.632	119	2435.280
34	367.920	77	1025.796	120	3550.428
35	317.112	78	1399.848	121	2215.404
36	359.160	79	818.184	122	3312.156
37	249.660	80	865.488	123	4289.771
38	455.520	81	1547.892	124	3218.424
39	607.068	82	1003.020	125	3193.020
40	425.736	83	960.972	126	3542.544
41	494.064	84	1568.040	127	2169.852
42	486.180	85	1065.216	128	1536.504
43	494.064	86	1107.264	129	3454.944
				130	2351.184

The heavy line in Figure 10-21 is the plot of the actual data of Table 10-4. It can be seen clearly that the fluctuations increase as one moves from left to right on the graph. Until December 1969, the value of shipments was low and so were the fluctuations. From December 1969 until May 1971, shipments increased and so did their variations from one month to the next. The same pattern continues until 1975 when both shipments and fluctuations are largest. This variation in the magnitude of the fluctuations with time is referred to as nonstationarity in the variance of the data. It must be corrected (i.e., a stationary variance achieved) before fitting an ARMA model to the series.

The main approach for achieving stationarity in variance is through a logarithmic or power transformation of the data. The dotted line in Figure 10-21 is a logarithmic transformation of the actual data. It is plotted on the scale shown on the right side of the graph. [For example, $X_{10} = 176.076$, which corresponds to $\log_e (176.076) = 5.171$.] It is clear that the magnitude of the fluctuations in the logarithmic transformed data does not vary with time. Even the fluctuations in the very beginning of the series are not much different from those at the end. Thus one can say that the logarithmic transformation has achieved a series that is stationary in its variance. Once this stationarity in variance is achieved the Box-Jenkins methodology of Figure 10-1 can be applied. If this is mistakenly

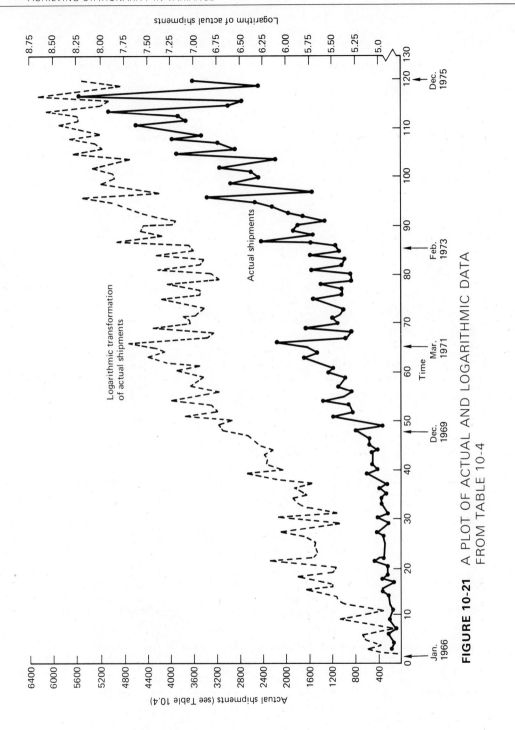

FIGURE 10-21 A PLOT OF ACTUAL AND LOGARITHMIC DATA FROM TABLE 10-4

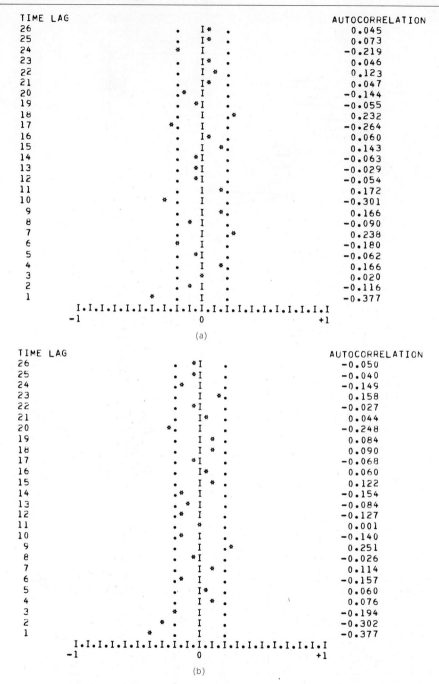

FIGURE 10-22   DATA OF TABLE 10-4 WITH ONE SHORT AND
ONE LONG DIFFERENCE: (A)
AUTOCORRELATIONS AND (B) PARTIAL
AUTOCORRELATIONS

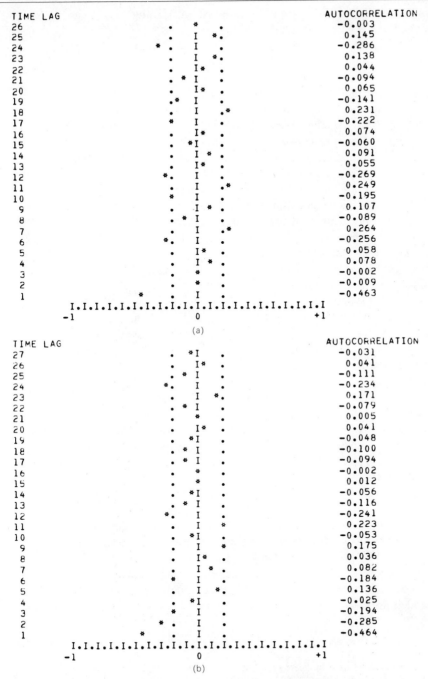

FIGURE 10-23 LOGARITHMIC TRANSFORMATION WITH ONE
SHORT AND ONE LONG DIFFERENCE FOR DATA
OF TABLE 10-4: (A) AUTOCORRELATIONS AND
(B) PARTIAL AUTOCORRELATIONS

done without first achieving stationarity in the variance, misleading results can be obtained.*

Achieving stationarity in variance is not a simple task in many instances. A straightforward logarithmic transformation may "over-transform" the data, necessitating a power transformation (such as square root). Unfortunately, there are no good practical methods for making such power transformations, even though on a theoretical level there are several approaches available (see Bartlett 1947 and Box and Cox 1964). All these methods are based on trying alternative transformations, which is often time consuming and impractical.

Figure 10-22 shows the autos and partials obtained after taking one short and one long difference for the data of Table 10-4. At this level, the data are stationary in their mean as indicated by their autocorrelation coefficients. (These drop to zero after the first coefficient and then are distributed around zero.) However, there are some problems that are not well explained in these values. For example, there are significant autocorrelations at time lags of 7, 10, 17, and 18. There may be some explanation for why r_{18} is significant, but r_7, r_{10}, and r_{17} would not be expected to be significant when monthly data are involved. The problem is simply the lack of stationarity in variance.

Figure 10-23 uses the logarithms of the data of Table 10-4 as the base series. There are many similarities between Figures 10-22 and 10-23, but also some notable differences. First, r_{12} and r_{24} in Figure 10-23 are significantly larger than they were in Figure 10-22. Second, the coefficients r_{10} and r_{17} are not significantly different from zero in Figure 10-23. Third, r_7 is still significant, but so is r_6. This now makes sense, since the model is multiplicative and r_1 and r_6 interact (both negative), making r_7 significantly positive. Clearly, Figure 10-23 makes more sense given the actual data, which is known to be seasonal, and it is better to base the model identification on the transformation series. It should be noted that even without knowing anything about nonstationarity in the mean, Figure 10-22 should arouse some suspicions that something might be wrong.

As a final illustration of the Box-Jenkins methodology, a model for the log data of Table 10-4 can be identified based on the autos and partials of Figure 10-23. Because the partials trail off, an MA process can be assumed, and since there is only one significant auto (except for the seasonal ones), an MA(1) model is implied. It is difficult to determine whether the seasonal coefficient should be in the AR or MA portions, since r_{12} and r_{24} for both the autos and partials do not drop to zero. (That may even suggest nonstationarity in the mean.) Thus, it is necessary to try both MA and AR seasonal parameters. The two alternative models are

$$(1 - B)(1 - B^{12})X_t = (1 - \theta_1 B)(1 - \theta_{12}B^{12})e_t \qquad (10\text{-}54)$$

---

* Chatfield and Prothero reported in a case study that the results they obtained from using the Box-Jenkins methodology were very unsatisfactory. Box and Jenkins in a discussion session following the presentation of the paper felt that the reason for the poor results was simply that the wrong transformation was used (see Chatfield and Prothero 1973).

and $\quad (1 - B)(1 - B^{12})(1 - \phi'_{12}B^{12})X_t = (1 - \theta'_1 B)e_t,$ (10-55)

where X_t is the logarithm of the data of Table 10-4

and $\quad \theta_1 = .64$ and $\theta_{12} = .72$ in (10-54),

while $\quad \phi'_{12} = .691$ and $\theta'_1 = -.116$ in (10-55).

Of the two models, (10-54) provides the better fit. No autocorrelations of residuals are significantly different from zero and no obvious pattern exists among the autocorrelations. Thus, the final model is

$$(1 - B)(1 - B^{12})X_t = (1 - .64B)(1 - .72B^{12})e_t.$$

REFERENCES AND SELECTED BIBLIOGRAPHY

Bartlett, M. S. 1947. "The Use of Transformations." *Biometrica*, Vol. 3, pp. 39–52.

Box, G. E. P., and D. R. Cox. 1964. "An Analysis of Transformations." *Journal of the Royal Statistical Society*, Vol. 26, Series B, pp. 211–53.

Box, G. E. P., and G. M. Jenkins. 1970. *Time Series Analysis, Forecasting and Control.* San Francisco: Holden-Day (rev. ed. 1976).

Chatfield, C. 1975. *The Analysis of Time Series: Theory and Practice.* London: Chapman and Hall.

Chatfield, C., and D. L. Prothero. 1973. "Box-Jenkins Seasonal Forecasting: Problems in a Case Study." *Journal of the Royal Statistical Society*, Vol. 136, Series A, Part 3, pp. 295–336.

Durbin, J. 1959. "Efficient Estimation of Parameters in Moving-Average Models." *Biometrica*, Vol. 46, pp. 306–16.

Hannan, E. J. 1963. "The Estimation of Seasonal Variation in Economic Time Series." *Journal of the American Statistical Association*, Vol. 58, pp. 31–44.

Jenkins, G. M., and D. G. Watts. 1968. *Spectral Analysis and its Applications.* San Francisco: Holden-Day.

Mabert, V. A. 1975. *An Introduction to Short Term Forecasting Using the Box-Jenkins Methodology.* Publication No. 2. Atlanta, Ga.: American Institute of Industrial Engineers (Production Planning and Control Division).

Marquardt, D. W. 1963. "An Algorithm for Least Squares Estimation of Nonlinear Parameters." *Journal of the Society for Industrial and Applied Mathematics*, Vol. 11, pp. 431–41.

Nelson, C. R. 1973. *Applied Time Series Analysis for Managerial Forecasting.* San Francisco: Holden-Day.

Slutzky, E. 1937. "The Summation of Random Causes as the Source of Cyclic Processes." *Econometrica*, Vol. 5, pp. 105–46.

Sorenson, H. W. 1973. "Least-Squares Estimation: from Gauss to Kalman." *IEEE Spectrum*, Vol. 7, July, pp. 63–68.

Thompson, H. E., and G. C. Tias. 1969. "Analysis of Telephone Data: a Case Study of Forecasting Seasonal Time Series." *Proceedings of the Conference on Time Series Models for Marketing Forecasts*, University of Wisconsin, May.

Walker, A. M. 1931. "On the Periodicity in Series of Related Terms." In *Proceedings of the Royal Society of London*, A 131, pp. 518–32.

Wold, H. 1954. *A Study in the Analysis of Stationary Time Series.* Stockholm: Almquist & Wiksell (1st ed. 1938).

Yule, G. U. 1926. "Why Do We Sometimes Get Nonsense-Correlations Between Time Series? A Study in Sampling and the Nature of Time Series." *Journal of the Royal Statistical Society.* Vol. 89, pp. 1–64.

EXERCISES

1. Table 10-5 gives the quarterly sales of MRAC Company for 1967 through 1975.

TABLE 10-5 QUARTERLY SALES OF MRAC COMPANY FOR THE YEARS 1967 THROUGH 1975

Period	Observation	Period	Observation	Period	Observation
1	2575.800	13	2953.430	25	3329.890
2	2606.680	14	2986.450	26	3361.130
3	2639.000	15	3017.050	27	3392.070
4	2671.000	16	3048.120	28	3423.520
5	2702.380	17	3079.180	29	3455.050
6	2733.890	18	3109.000	30	3487.140
7	2765.740	19	3143.240	31	3516.750
8	2796.710	20	3171.630	32	3550.370
9	2829.000	21	3205.110	33	3580.560
10	2859.800	22	3235.900	34	3611.470
11	2892.200	23	3266.950	35	3644.170
12	2921.900	24	3297.650	36	3674.310

Using Figures 10-24 and 10-25, answer the following questions:

a. At what level do you consider the series to be stationary?

b. What do you consider to be the most appropriate model for the series?

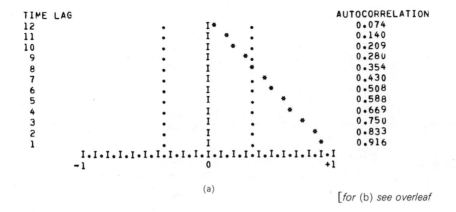

```
TIME LAG                                    AUTOCORRELATION
12                  .      I*    .             0.074
11                  .      I  *  .             0.140
10                  .      I   * .             0.209
 9                  .      I   *.              0.280
 8                  .      I     *             0.354
 7                  .      I   . *             0.430
 6                  .      I   .  *            0.508
 5                  .      I   .   *           0.588
 4                  .      I   .    *          0.669
 3                  .      I   .     *         0.750
 2                  .      I   .      *        0.833
 1                  .      I   .       *       0.916
    I.I.I.I.I.I.I.I.I.I.I.I.I.I.I.I.I.I.I.I.I
   -1                      0              +1
```

(a)

[for (b) see overleaf

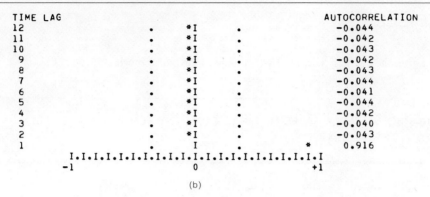

```
TIME LAG                                              AUTOCORRELATION
12              •      *I       •                          -0.044
11              •      *I       •                          -0.042
10              •      *I       •                          -0.043
 9              •      *I       •                          -0.042
 8              •      *I       •                          -0.043
 7              •      *I       •                          -0.044
 6              •      *I       •                          -0.041
 5              •      *I       •                          -0.044
 4              •      *I       •                          -0.042
 3              •      *I       •                          -0.040
 2              •      *I       •                          -0.043
 1              •       I       •              *            0.916
        I.I.I.I.I.I.I.I.I.I.I.I.I.I.I.I.I.I.I.I.I.I.I
        -1               0                    +1
```

(b)

FIGURE 10-24   ORIGINAL DATA OF TABLE 10-5: (A)
AUTOCORRELATIONS AND (B) PARTIAL
AUTOCORRELATIONS

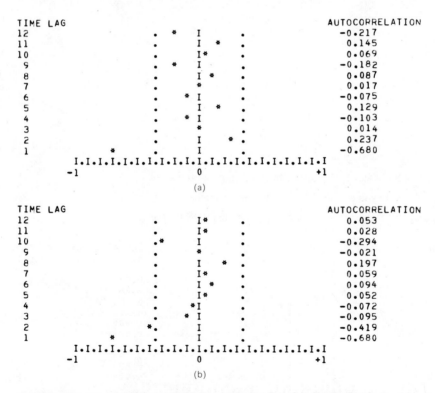

```
TIME LAG                                              AUTOCORRELATION
12            •    *     I       •                         -0.217
11            •          I   *   •                          0.145
10            •          I*      •                          0.069
 9            •    *     I       •                         -0.182
 8            •          I  *    •                          0.087
 7            •          *       •                          0.017
 6            •       *  I       •                         -0.075
 5            •          I   *   •                          0.129
 4            •       *  I       •                         -0.103
 3            •          *       •                          0.014
 2            •          I     * •                          0.237
 1          *    •          I    •                         -0.680
        I.I.I.I.I.I.I.I.I.I.I.I.I.I.I.I.I.I.I.I.I.I.I
        -1               0                    +1
```

(a)

```
TIME LAG                                              AUTOCORRELATION
12            •          I*      •                          0.053
11            •          I*      •                          0.028
10            •*         I       •                         -0.294
 9            •          *       •                         -0.021
 8            •          I    *  •                          0.197
 7            •          I*      •                          0.059
 6            •          I  *    •                          0.094
 5            •          I*      •                          0.052
 4            •         *I       •                         -0.072
 3            •       *  I       •                         -0.095
 2            •     *•    I       •                        -0.419
 1          *    •          I    •                         -0.680
        I.I.I.I.I.I.I.I.I.I.I.I.I.I.I.I.I.I.I.I.I.I.I
        -1               0                    +1
```

(b)

FIGURE 10-25   FIRST DIFFERENCED DATA OF TABLE 10-5: (A)
AUTOCORRELATIONS AND (B) PARTIAL
AUTOCORRELATIONS

c. Find initial estimates for the model you identified in (b). (See Chapter 9 Appendix, Section 2 for formulas.)

d. Figure 10-26 shows the autocorrelations of the residuals from an AR model fitted to the first differenced data. Do you consider the model appropriate? If yes, why? If not, what is needed to correct any deficiencies?

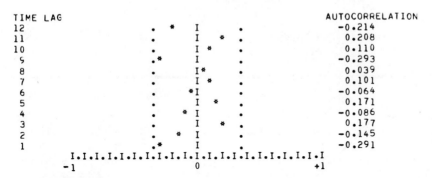

FIGURE 10-26 AUTOCORRELATIONS OF RESIDUALS OF AN AR MODEL

e. Figure 10-27 shows the autocorrelations of the residuals from an MA model. What would you propose to correct this model?

FIGURE 10-27 AUTOCORRELATIONS OF RESIDUALS OF AN MA MODEL

2. Table 10-6 gives U.S. car registrations for the years 1964 through 1970. Figure 10-28 gives the autocorrelations and partial autocorrelations for one long- and one short-term difference of the data in Table 10-6.

a. Using Figure 10-28, identify an appropriate model.

b. Write this model in terms of the backshift operator.

c. Assume some values for the model's parameters and prepare a forecast for the next two months.

d. If you have a computerized version of the Box-Jenkins program available, run it to determine whether you have identified an appropriate model and to obtain forecasts for the next 12 months.

TABLE 10-6   REGISTRATION OF PASSENGER CARS IN THE UNITED STATES (IN THOUSANDS)

	1964	1965	1966	1967	1968	1969	1970
Jan.	613.84	667.01	606.57	616.13	657.93	657.62	619.14
Feb.	550.32	631.11	721.59	538.89	604.62	607.53	578.42
Mar.	636.88	798.66	878.80	670.78	724.98	681.21	741.13
Apr.	812.32	895.92	822.57	786.08	859.44	876.02	768.35
May	780.72	841.42	777.19	821.49	824.29	880.14	784.39
June	754.32	841.54	752.52	805.56	800.60	841.87	900.86
July	724.20	833.55	832.73	753.31	871.99	815.30	837.71
Aug.	648.68	766.72	743.62	725.73	744.38	718.84	683.15
Sept.	565.43	589.53	573.76	550.15	705.32	733.36	612.14
Oct.	658.45	745.82	766.65	710.07	880.25	955.55	719.03
Nov.	563.52	793.85	732.11	641.31	757.02	757.54	537.15
Dec.	756.71	908.71	800.32	737.37	972.98	912.49	606.67

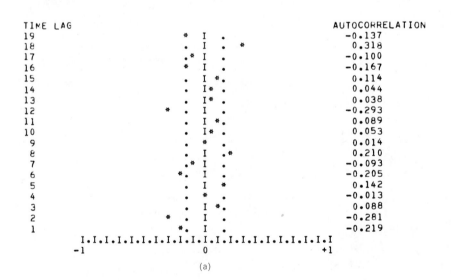

(a)

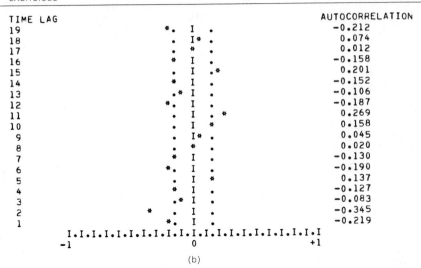

```
TIME LAG                                            AUTOCORRELATION
19            *.  I  .                                 -0.212
18             .  I* .                                  0.074
17             .  *  .                                  0.012
16            *  I  .                                  -0.158
15             .  I  .*                                 0.201
14            *  I  .                                  -0.152
13            .* I  .                                  -0.106
12           *.  I  .                                  -0.187
11             .  I  .*                                 0.269
10             .  I  *                                  0.158
 9             .  I* .                                  0.045
 8             .  *  .                                  0.020
 7            *  I  .                                  -0.130
 6           *.  I  .                                  -0.190
 5             .  I  *                                  0.137
 4            *  I  .                                  -0.127
 3            .* I  .                                  -0.083
 2         *   .  I  .                                 -0.345
 1          *.  I  .                                   -0.219
      I.I.I.I.I.I.I.I.I.I.I.I.I.I.I.I.I.I.I
      -1              0              +1
```

(b)

FIGURE 10-28 ONE LONG AND ONE SHORT DIFFERENCE FOR DATA OF TABLE 10-6: (A) AUTOCORRELATIONS AND (B) PARTIAL AUTOCORRELATIONS

3. Forecast for periods 122 to 132 using equation (10-51) obtained in Section 10/6. The residual errors of the last 12 periods are $e_{108} = 12.3$, $e_{109} = -14.4$, $e_{110} = 90.0$, $e_{111} = .2$, $e_{112} = 65.6$, $e_{113} = -18.8$, $e_{114} = 53.5$, $e_{115} = 9.6$, $e_{116} = -59.1$, $e_{117} = 4.7$, $e_{118} = -28.3$, $e_{119} = 19$, and $e_{120} = 69.9$. The actual values of X_t can be seen in Table 10-2.

4. Table 10-7 shows a list of normal random numbers generated with a mean of zero and a variance of one.

TABLE 10-7 A LIST OF 50 NORMAL RANDOM NUMBERS ($\mu = 0$, $\sigma^2 = 1$)

.01	1.38	.53	1.58	1.32
1.04	.33	-.20	1.90	.72
-.27	-1.43	-1.15	-.07	1.69
.28	-.01	.94	-2.10	.09
.91	1.76	.84	-1.13	.92
1.67	-1.03	-1.71	1.18	-.59
-.76	-.27	-.97	.59	1.55
-1.07	-1.07	1.27	-.60	.79
1.27	1.25	-.99	-.99	.15
-.94	1.37	-.00	-.57	-1.98

a. Using the normal random numbers of Table 10-7, generate an AR(1) model with $\phi_1 = .6$.

b. Generate an MA(1) model with $\theta_1 = -.6$.

c. Compare the graphs of (a) and (b). What can you say about the differences of the two models?

d. Generate an ARMA(1, 1) model with $\phi_1 = .6$ and $\theta_1 = -.6$.

e. Generate an AR(2) model with $\phi_1 = -.8$ and $\phi_2 = .3$ and an MA(2) model with $\theta_1 = -.8$ and $\theta_2 = .3$. Graph the two models and compare them.

11 MULTIVARIATE TIME-SERIES ANALYSIS

11/1 Introduction

The models examined so far in Part Four have been univariate analysis and forecasting of a *single* time series. In this chapter a procedure analogous to that used for univariate time-series analysis but extended to more than one variable will be described. Because multivariate time-series analysis and forecasting is a relatively new field, only limited results are available from practical applications. Even though this chapter will focus on bivariate models, its theoretical extension to several (multivariate) series should be apparent.

Multivariate ARMA (MARMA) models combine the characteristics of both the univariate processes examined in Chapters 9 and 10 and those of multiple regression examined in Chapter 6. Thus, they combine the time-series approach to forecasting with the causal approach. That makes them a powerful tool when the appropriate conditions exist for their use. The main objective in using MARMA models is not explanatory in nature, even though successful attempts to use them in this way have been reported (see Zellner and Palm 1974). Rather, their aim is to identify some leading indicator(s) of the series to be forecast that can be used to improve the predictions over those attainable with a univariate model.

The general form of a MARMA model is:

$$Y_t - \delta_1 Y_{t-1} - \delta_2 Y_{t-2} - \cdots - \delta_r Y_{t-r} = \omega_0 X_{t-b} - \omega_1 X_{t-b-1} - \cdots - \omega_s X_{t-b-s}$$
$$+ \zeta_0 Z_{t-c} - \zeta_1 Z_{t-c-1} - \cdots - \zeta_v Z_{t-c-v}$$
$$+ \xi_0 W_{t-d} - \xi_1 W_{t-d-1} - \cdots - \xi_u W_{t-d-u} + e_t.$$

$$(11\text{-}1)$$

As shown in (11-1) the dependent variable, Y_t is expressed as a function of previous values of Y [left-hand side of (11-1)] and previous values of one or more independent variables (e.g., X, Z, W). The form of MARMA models that will be examined in detail in this chapter is that involving only two variables (time series), given by:

$$Y_t - \delta_1 Y_{t-1} - \delta_2 Y_{t-2} - \cdots - \delta_r Y_{t-r} = \omega_0 X_{t-b} - \omega_1 X_{t-b-1} - \cdots - \omega_s X_{t-b-s} + e_t.$$

(11-2)

Equation (11-2) includes $r + s + 1$ terms. The parameters of these terms must be estimated with a nonlinear estimation procedure similar to that employed in Chapters 9 and 10. The estimated equation can then be used to forecast future values of Y_t.

In expression (11-2), Y_t is the dependent variable whose future values are to be predicted. It is also called the output variable or output series. X_t is the independent variable and frequently is called the input series or the leading indicator because it leads the dependent variable by b time lags. The parameter b is called the delay lag, or the lead of X_t to Y_t. If $b > 0$, X_t is a leading indicator, and Y_t can be forecast using X_t. If $b = 0$, X_t is of little value for forecasting, since it is not known beforehand. If $b < 0$, Y_t is a leading indicator of X_t, and thus X_t will be of no value in forecasting Y_t.

The procedure for forecasting with a MARMA model is very similar to that described in Chapter 10, Figure 10-1. From the general class of models shown in equation (11-1), or (11-2), a specific model that best describes the observed data at hand must be identified. In such a model the parameters r, s, and b must be specified. These parameters are then estimated and a diagnostic test is made of the residual errors to determine whether the model postulated is an adequate one. The major difficulty in using a MARMA model is in identification, since the process used is not as precise as that used for univariate ARMA models. The estimation and testing phases are very similar for both univariate and multivariate ARMA models, although the latter require considerably more computations than the former.

11/2 Bivariate Time-Series Analysis

The autocorrelation coefficients of a time series can be used to identify the pattern in the series and to select the appropriate ARMA model. These autocorrelation coefficients describe the degree of association between values of the variable for different time lags. In bivariate time-series analysis, the concept of autocorrelation is extended to aid in identifying the degree of association between values of the dependent variable and values of the independent variable for different time lags. This is called *cross autocorrelation*. Conceptually, it is similar to combining the simple correlation coefficient (which indicates the degree of association between Y and X) with the autocorrelation (which indicates the degree of association between values for various time lags). The cross autocorrelations can be used to determine whether Y and X are stationary. More importantly, they can be used to identify an appropriate MARMA model. That process will be discussed in the next section. The remainder of this section will describe the concept of cross autocorrelation, or cross autos, and illustrate them through a few selected examples.

The cross autocovariance between X_t and Y_t defines the degree of association between values of X at time t and values of Y at time $t + k$ ($k = 0, 1, 2, 3, \ldots$). Similarly, the cross autocovariance between Y_t and X_t defines the degree of association between values of Y at time t and values of X at time $t + k$ ($k = 1, 2, 3, \ldots$). If X_t is a leading indicator of Y_t, for $k > 0$ some cross autocovariances, $C_{XY}(k)$, must be significantly different from zero. This occurs because X_t is correlated with Y_{t+k} ($k = 0, 1, 2, 3, \ldots$). It can best be seen from expression (11-3), which shows the cross autocovariance between X_t and Y_t:

$$C_{XY}(k) = \frac{\sum_{t=1}^{n-k} (X_t - \bar{X})(Y_{t+k} - \bar{Y})}{n - 1} \qquad k = 0, 1, 2, 3, \ldots. \tag{11-3}$$

The cross autocovariance between Y and X will not be significantly different from zero if X_t is a leading indicator of Y_t, since current values of Y cannot be correlated with future values of X_t. Convention in the multivariate literature is to express the cross autocovariance between Y and X with a negative k and the subscript XY. Thus, $C_{YX}(k) = C_{XY}(-k)$ or $C_{XY}(k), k = -1, -2, -3, \ldots$. Using this convention the expression for the cross autocovariance between Y and X becomes

$$C_{XY}(k) = \frac{\sum_{t=1}^{n+k} (Y_t - \bar{Y})(X_{t-k} - \bar{X})}{n - 1}, \qquad k = -1, -2, -3, \ldots. \tag{11-4}$$

The cross autocovariance is an absolute measure that can be standardized by dividing by the product of the standard deviation of X and the standard deviation of Y. That yields the cross autocorrelation of k time lags, $r_{XY}(k)$ ($k = 0, \pm 1, \pm 2, \pm 3, \pm 4, \ldots$). Thus,

$$r_{XY}(k) = \frac{C_{XY}(k)}{S_X S_Y}, \qquad k = 0, \pm 1, \pm 2, \pm 3, \ldots, \tag{11-5}$$

where $\qquad S_X = \sqrt{\dfrac{\sum_{i=1}^{n} (X_i - \bar{X})^2}{n - 1}}, \qquad S_Y = \sqrt{\dfrac{\sum_{i=1}^{n} (Y_i - \bar{Y})^2}{n - 1}}.$

Equation (11-5) can be used in two important ways: (1) to determine whether the series, X and Y, are stationary, and (2) to identify an appropriate

MARMA model. These uses will be illustrated after a numerical example has been examined to illustrate calculations involved in computing the cross autos. The values for this example are given in Table 11-1.

TABLE 11-1 VALUES USED IN CALCULATING THE CROSS AUTOS

(1) Period	(2) X_t	(3) $X_t - \bar{X}$	(4) Y_t	(5) $Y_t - \bar{Y}$	(6) $Y_{t+1} - \bar{Y}$	(7) $Y_{t+2} - \bar{Y}$
1	12.77	4.37	22.00	−7.82	19.78	−6.78
2	11.56	3.16	49.60	19.78	−6.78	8.49
3	9.67	1.27	23.04	−6.78	8.49	4.87
4	8.83	.43	38.31	8.49	4.87	.81
5	8.02	−.38	34.69	4.87	.81	−3.34
6	12.25	3.85	29.01	.81	−3.34	−5.77
7	4.76	−3.64	26.48	−3.34	−5.77	6.94
8	9.27	.87	24.05	−5.77	6.94	−15.54
9	3.23	−.517	36.76	6.94	−15.54	—
10	3.66	−4.74	14.28	−15.54	—	—
	$\bar{X} = 8.40$		$\bar{Y} = 29.82$			

Computation of the cross autocovariance of zero time lags requires cross multiplication of columns 3 and 5 of Table 11-1. That is,

$$C_{XY}(0) = \frac{\sum_{t=1}^{10} (X_t - \bar{X})(Y_t - \bar{Y})}{10}.$$

Substituting the values from columns 3 and 5 gives

$$C_{XY}(0) = \frac{(4.37)(-7.82) + 3.16(19.78) + 1.27(-6.78) + \cdots + (-4.74)(-15.54)}{10},$$

$$C_{XY}(0) = \frac{63.4125}{10} = 6.341.$$

Since $S_X = 3.304$ and $S_Y = 9.638$,

$$r_{XY}(0) = \frac{6.341}{(3.304)(9.638)} = .199.$$

Similarly, the cross auto of one time lag (the cross auto between X_t and Y_{t+1}) is

$$C_{XY}(1) = \frac{\sum_{t=1}^{9} (X_t - \bar{X})(Y_{t+1} - \bar{Y})}{10}.$$

Substituting the values of $(X_t - \bar{X})$ and $(Y_{t+1} - \bar{Y})$ from columns 3 and 6 in Table 11-1 yields

$$C_{XY}(1) = \frac{(4.37)(19.78) + (3.16)(-6.78) + (1.27)(8.49) + \cdots + (-.517)(-15.54)}{10},$$

$$C_{XY}(1) = \frac{172.737}{10} = 17.274,$$

and $\quad r_{XY}(1) = \frac{17.274}{(3.304)(9.638)} = .542.$

Similarly $C_{XY}(2)$ and $r_{XY}(2)$ are obtained using columns 3 and 7 of Table 11-1.

$$C_{XY}(2) = \frac{\sum_{t=1}^{8} (X_t - \bar{X})(Y_{t+2} - \bar{Y})}{10} = \frac{(4.38)(-6.78) + (3.16)(8.49) + \cdots + (.87)(-15.54)}{10}$$

$$= \frac{-56.661}{10} = -5.666,$$

and $\quad r_{XY}(2) = \frac{-5.666}{(3.304)(9.638)} = -.178.$

The cross autocovariance and cross autocorrelation between Y and X of one time lag are

$$C_{YX}(1) = C_{XY}(-1) = \frac{\sum_{t=1}^{n-1} (Y_t - \bar{Y})(X_{t+1} - \bar{X})}{10}$$

$$= \frac{(-7.82)(3.16) + (19.78)(1.27) + (-6.78)(.43) + \cdots + (6.94)(-4.74)}{10},$$

$$C_{XY}(-1) = \frac{9.97881}{10} = .9979,$$

and $\quad r_{XY}(-1) = \frac{.9979}{(3.304)(9.638)} = .031.$

The values of $C_{XY}(-2)$ and $r_{XY}(-2)$ are

$$C_{XY}(-2) = \frac{\sum_{t=2}^{n-1}(Y_t - \bar{Y})(X_{t+2} - \bar{X})}{10} = \frac{(-7.82)(1.27)+(19.78)(.43)+\cdots+(-5.77)(-4.74)}{10}$$

$$= \frac{60.079}{10} = 6.0079.$$

and $\quad r_{XY}(-2) = \dfrac{6.0079}{(3.304)(9.638)} = .189.$

Figure 11-1 shows the cross autos of time lags $0, \pm 1, \pm 2, \pm 3, \pm 4, \pm 5$ for the data of columns 2 and 4 of Table 11-1.

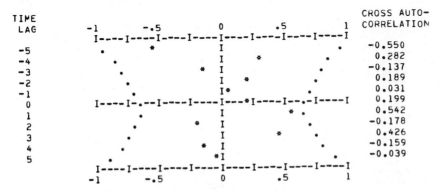

FIGURE 11-1 CROSS AUTOCORRELATIONS OF DATA OF TABLE 11-1

Bartlett (1955) has developed approximate formulas for variances and covariances between cross autos that can be used to test hypotheses of interest when the assumption of normality is satisfied. As will be seen in the next section, for practical purposes, the patterns of cross autos of a series that has been reduced to white noise (i.e., to a random series) and for a series that is not white noise, are of interest because these two series allow identification of an appropriate pattern and estimation of initial parameter values. The regular autocorrelations of the random series cannot, by definition, be significantly different from zero, while those of the nonrandom series may well be. Thus, concerning the joint variation between the two series (one random, the other not necessarily random), it will be the same as the variance of the nonrandom series, adjusted for degrees of freedom:

$$\text{Var}\left[r_{XY}(k)\right] = \frac{1}{n-k}, \tag{11-6}$$

and the standard deviation

$$\text{SD}\left[r_{XY}(k)\right] = \frac{1}{\sqrt{n-k}} \tag{11-7}$$

The dotted lines in Figure 11-1 are the values of (11-7) multiplied by 1.96 (i.e., 95% confidence intervals) for $k = 0, \pm 1, \pm 2, \pm 3, \pm 4,$ and ± 5.

The behavior of cross autos concerning nonstationarity is completely analogous to that of univariate autocorrelations. When X_t or Y_t are nonstationary the cross autos will not decrease to zero quickly (within three or four time lags), suggesting that either X_t or Y_t requires differencing. Determination of which variable needs differencing is made by calculating the regular autocorrelation coefficients of X_t and Y_t.

11/3 Identification of an Appropriate MARMA Model and Initial Estimation of Its Parameters

Cross autos play an important role in helping to identify an appropriate model from the general class shown in equation (11-2). (A model is defined by the values of r, s, and b and the type of the noise model for e_t, which is not necessarily white noise.) Cross autos also can provide initial estimates for the values of $\delta_1, \delta_2, \ldots, \delta_r$ and $\omega_0, \omega_1, \ldots, \omega_s$. (That is similar to the function of regular autos, which provide initial estimates for each coefficient in univariate ARMA models.)

11/3/1 Prewhitening X_t and Y_t

Equation (11-2) can be rewritten as

$$Y_t = \delta_1 Y_{t-1} + \delta_2 Y_{t-2} + \cdots + \delta_r Y_{t-r} + \omega_0 X_{t-b} - \omega_1 X_{t-b-1} - \cdots - \omega_s X_{t-b-s} + e_t. \tag{11-8}$$

Thus, Y_t is represented by a weighted sum of its own prior values and prior values of X_t. However, Y_t and X_t are each univariate time series that have been generated by some univariate ARMA process. In other words,

$$Y_t = \phi_1 Y_{t-1} + \phi_2 Y_{t-2} + \cdots + \phi_p Y_{t-p} + e_t - \theta_1 e_{t-1} - \cdots - \theta_q e_{t-q}, \tag{11-9}$$

$$\text{and} \quad X_t = \phi_1' X_{t-1} + \phi_2' X_{t-2} + \cdots + \phi_p' X_{t-p} + e_t - \theta_1' e_{t-1} - \cdots - \theta_q' e_{t-q} \tag{11-10}$$

The order and parameter values of (11-9) and (11-10) are not necessarily the same, although if X_t is to be a good leading indicator of Y_t, equation (11-9) should be similar to equation (11-10). Since (11-9) and/or (11-10) may have seasonal terms and/or be nonstationary, (11-8) is considerably more complicated than its univariate counterparts. Two different variables are involved, each one of which may have some nonstationary ARMA (p, q) generating process with observations available only on Y_t and X_t.

The following example will clarify further the types and forms of variation taking place in equation (11-8). Suppose $r = 1$, $s = 1$, $b = 3$ in (11-8) while the generating process of X_t and Y_t can be described by a nonseasonal, stationary AR(2) model. Expression (11-8), then, becomes

$$Y_t = \delta_1 Y_{t-1} + \omega_0 X_{t-3} - \omega_1 X_{t-4} + e_t. \tag{11-11}$$

(Notice that when $s = 1$ there are two terms involving X_t in (11-11); there are r terms of Y_{t-i} and $s + 1$ terms of X_{t-b}.)

The univariate generating processes are

$$X_t = \phi_1 X_{t-1} + \phi_2 X_{t-2} + e_t^* \tag{11-12}$$

and $$Y_t = \phi_1 Y_{t-1} + \phi_2 Y_{t-2} + e_t'. \tag{11-13}$$

Substituting (11-12) and (11-13) into (11-11) yields

$$Y_t = \delta_1(\phi_1 Y_{t-2} + \phi_2 Y_{t-3} + e_{t-1}') + \omega_0(\phi_1 X_{t-4} + \phi_2 X_{t-5} + e_{t-3}^*)$$
$$- \omega_1(\phi_1 X_{t-5} + \phi_2 X_{t-6} + e_{t-4}^*) + e_t. \tag{11-14}$$

The Y_t observed is that generated by (11-14), while the corresponding X_t is that generated by (11-12) when the model is of the form described by (11-11).

Fortunately, X_t includes only one type of pattern or variation in its ARMA generating process. That is not the case with Y_t, which includes three types of patterns or variations—variations caused by its own generating process, equation (11-9); variations caused by the generating process for X_t, (11-10); and variations caused jointly by previous values of Y_t and of X_{t-b}, (11-8). The totality of these variations for the specific example of (11-12) and (11-13) is given by (11-14). Unless these three patterns or variations can be separated, there is little that can be done to identify the generating process of (11-11). In some sense the joint relationship of Y_t and X_t is buried within the Y_t and X_t variation and cannot be discovered unless all other types of variations, except that between Y_t and X_t variation, have been eliminated. To eliminate the variations within Y_t and within X_t, the two series must be prewhitened by manipulating them until the variation within each of them has been eliminated as far as possible.

Since X_t includes only that pattern or variation caused by the ARMA generating process, that pattern or variation can be identified by fitting an appropriate ARMA model to X_t. That process is described in Chapters 9 and 10 (see Figure 10-1). Once an adequate ARMA model—one that produces randomly distributed residuals—has been fitted to X_t, subsequent steps can work with the residuals of X_t rather than the original X_t series. Since the criterion for judging the adequacy of the ARMA model used on X_t is randomly distributed residuals, working with the resulting residuals assures a series consisting of a pure white noise. This series will be denoted by X_{et}.

If X_t is to be an effective leading indicator of Y_t, the generating process for Y_t should be similar to that for X_t. Therefore the same model developed for X_t could be applied to Y_t to obtain the residuals, Y_{te}. The series Y_{te} consists of more than white noise, since Y_t includes types of variation in addition to that caused by the univariate generating process of Y_t. Fitting an appropriate ARMA model to X_t, then applying that same ARMA model to Y_t to obtain X_{et} and Y_{et} is referred to as prewhitening. Figure 11-2 presents a flowchart of the basic steps in developing a MARMA model, including the prewhitening phase.

For the model postulated in (11-14), the prewhitening process is performed as follows:

1. Estimate ϕ_1 and ϕ_2 in (11-12) as shown in Chapters 9 and 10.
2. Solve (11-12) for e_t^*. Suppose it is found that $\phi_1 = .8$ and $\phi_2 = -.5$, then

$$e_t^* = X_t - .8X_{t-1} + .5X_{t-2}. \tag{11-15}$$

Additionally $X_{et} = e_t^*$ and is the prewhitened series for X_t.
3. Solve (11-13) for e_t', obtaining

$$e_t' = Y_t - .8Y_{t-1} + .5Y_{t-2}. \tag{11-16}$$

Then $Y_{et} = e_t'$ and is the prewhitened Y_t series.
4. Y_{et} is not necessarily white noise, as can be seen by substituting (11-15) and (11-16) into (11-11), which yields:

$$Y_{et} = \delta_1 e_{t-1}' + \omega_0 e_{t-3} - \omega_1 e_{t-4}, \tag{11-17}$$

$$Y_{et} = \delta_1 Y_{et-1} + \omega_0 X_{et-3} - \omega_1 X_{et-4}. \tag{11-18}$$

5. X_{et-3} and X_{et-4} are white noise and therefore uncorrelated with each other.

Expression (11-18) has other properties that will be seen in the next section. These form the basis for identifying r, s, and b.

Having the values of X_{et} and Y_{et} completes the prewhitening phase (see Figure 11-2). With the within X_t and within Y_t variations eliminated, the between X_t and Y_t variation described by (11-8) can be identified and analyzed.

11/3/2   Relation between the Cross Autocorrelation Coefficients and the Parameters of a MARMA Model

The relationship between the cross auto and the parameters of a MARMA model can be best understood by looking at (11-8) and assuming that $r = 1$,

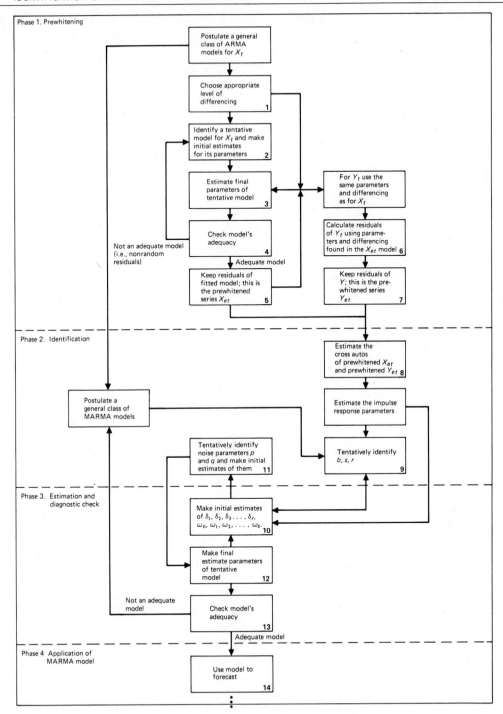

FIGURE 11-2 THE BASIC STEPS IN DEVELOPING A MARMA MODEL

$s = 0$, and $b = 0$. Expression (11-8) then becomes

$$Y_t = \delta_1 Y_{t-1} + \omega_0 X_t. \tag{11-19}$$

If it is further presumed that $\omega_0 = 1$, equation (11-19) becomes

$$Y_t = \delta_1 Y_{t-1} + X_t. \tag{11-20}$$

However, if X_t is prewhitened, it is white noise, and (11-20) is equivalent to

$$Y_t = \delta_1 Y_{t-1} + e_t. \tag{11-21}$$

Equation (11-21) is simply an AR(1) process. Thus, the autocorrelation coefficients of (11-21) will behave as those of an AR(1) model. (They will decline exponentially to zero if $\delta_1 > 0$ and decline exponentially to zero but alternate in sign, if $\delta_1 < 0$.) For equation (11-20) finding the cross autos of Y_t and X_t is equivalent to finding the regular autos of (11-21), given the way this example was constructed. Thus, the cross autos of (11-19) will behave the same as an AR(1) process when $r = 1$, $s = 0$, $b = 0$, and $\omega_0 = 1$. The goal is to explain the behavior of the cross autos when r, s, and b take different values and $\omega_0 \neq 1$.

If $\omega_0 = 2$, for example, equation (11-21) will still be an AR(1) process except that e_t becomes $2e_t$. That will not change the basic behavior of the regular autos, since $2e_t$ is still randomness. It is always true that the value of ω_0 will not affect the behavior of the cross autos, but may make identification of that basic behavior more difficult.

If $r = 2$, equation (11-21) will have two parameters, δ_1 and δ_2, and will behave as an AR(2) process—decline exponentially, decline exponentially alternating between plus and minus, decline as a sine wave, or decline as an alternating sine wave. If $r = 3$, equation (11-21) will behave as an AR(3) model, etc. Since the cross autos and regular autos are equivalent if $s = 0$ and $b = 0$ and if Y_{et} and X_{et} are the series, the cross autos will behave as an AR(r) model.

When $b = 1$, equation (11-19) becomes

$$Y_t = \delta_1 Y_{t-1} + \omega_0 X_{t-1}$$

or $\quad Y_{et} = \delta_1 Y_{et-1} + \omega_0 e_{t-1}. \tag{11-22}$

But e_{t-1} is white noise so theoretically (or when n is large) its correlation with Y_{et} will not be significantly different from zero. Thus, the autocorrelation for a time lag of zero in equation (11-22) will be zero and, similarly, the cross auto between Y_{et} and X_{et} will also be zero. When $b = 1$ however, the autos or cross autos of 1 time lag may be significantly different from zero. If $b = 3$ the time lags of 0, 1, and 2 will not be significant, etc. The AR(1) pattern of (11-22) will, therefore, commence at 1 time lag. That is, the regular autos in (11-22) or the cross autos between Y_{et} and X_{et} will not be significantly different from zero for the first $b - 1$ time lags. Thus, significant autos or cross autos will not exist for $b - 1$ time lags.

In order to see the influence of s on the cross autos, equation (11-11) will be used with $r = 1$, $s = 1$, and $b = 3$. Prewhitening (11-11) yields (11-18). Equation (11-18) is similar to (11-19) except that it includes an extra term $[s = 1$, versus $s = 0$ of (11-19)$]$. The role of this extra term, $\omega_1 X_{et-4}$, is to delay the start of the regular AR(1) pattern by one period; the AR(1) pattern will not start until period $b + 1$ (or $b + s$ in general). This can be understood better if (11-19) is compared to (11-18). Equation (11-19) behaves as an AR(1) process, for reasons explained. Equation (11-18), on the other hand, has an extra term, $\omega_1 X_{et-4}$, which will upset the AR(1) pattern and will delay its start.

In summary, the values of r, s, and b influence the behavior of the cross autos as follows:

1. For k time lags ($k < b$), the cross autos will not be significantly different from zero. Thus, b is identified as the time lag corresponding to the first significant cross auto.
2. For s time lags, the cross autos will not show a clear pattern, even though they may well be significant. The value of s is inferred from the difference between b and the point at which the pattern of the cross autos starts. Thus, if $b = 3$ and the pattern of cross autos commences at 5, $s = 2$.
3. The value of r is identified by examining the pattern of cross autos after time lag $b + s$ and inferring the order of AR(r) process that has generated this pattern.

11/3/3 The Impulse Response Parameters

Using the backshift operator, B, described in Chapter 10, expression (11-2) can be written as

$$Y_t - \delta_1 B Y_t - \delta_2 B^2 Y_t - \cdots - \delta_r B^r Y_t = \omega_0 X_{t-b} - \omega_1 B X_{t-b} - \cdots - \omega_s B^s X_{t-b} + e_t. \quad (11\text{-}23)$$

$$\text{or} \quad (1 - \delta_1 B - \delta_2 B^2 - \cdots - \delta_r B^r) Y_t = (\omega_0 B^b - \omega_1 B^{b+1} - \cdots - \omega_s B^{b+s}) X_t + e_t \quad (11\text{-}24)$$

$$\text{and} \quad Y_t = \frac{(\omega_0 B^b - \omega_1 B^{b+1} - \cdots - \omega_s B^{b+s})}{(1 - \delta_1 B - \delta_2 B^2 - \cdots - \delta_r B^r)} X_t$$

by ignoring e_t for a moment. If expressed in terms of the prewhitened Y_{et} and X_{et},

$$Y_{et} = \frac{(\omega_0 B^b - \omega_1 B^{b+1} - \cdots - \omega_s B^{b+s})}{(1 - \delta_1 B - \delta_2 B^2 - \cdots - \delta_r B^r)} X_{et}. \quad (11\text{-}25)$$

Thus, the MARMA model becomes a ratio of two polynomials. This representation has no mathematical significance and is used to facilitate writing and analyzing MARMA models. However, it can be observed that Y_t is a function of previous values of X_t. This form is written as

$$Y_t = v_0 X_t + v_1 X_{t-1} + v_2 X_{t-2} + \cdots + \varepsilon'_t, \tag{11-26}$$

where ε'_t is white noise.

When Y_t and X_t are prewhitened, (11-26) becomes

$$Y_{et} = v_0 X_{et} + v_1 X_{et-1} + v_2 X_{et-2} + \cdots + \varepsilon_t. \tag{11-27}$$

Multiplying both sides of (11-27) by X_{et-k} yields

$$X_{et-k} Y_{et} = v_0 X_{et-k} X_{et} + v_1 X_{et-k} X_{et-1} + v_2 X_{et-k} X_{et-2} + \cdots + X_{et-k} \varepsilon_t. \tag{11-28}$$

Taking expected values of (11-28) yields

$$\gamma_{X_e Y_e}(k) = v_k \sigma_{Xe}^2 \quad \text{for} \quad k = 0, 1, 2, \ldots.$$

Since X_{et-k} is white noise, on the average it is uncorrelated with values at periods other than $t - k$. If $k = 0$, for example, the expected value of (11-28) becomes

$$E(X_{et} Y_{et}) = v_0 E(X_{et} X_{et}), \qquad \gamma_{XeYe}(0) = v_0 \sigma_{Xe}^2,$$

since $E(X_{et} X_{et}) = \sigma_{Xe}^2$ and $E(X_{et} X_{et-i}) = 0$ for $i \neq 0$.

Similarly when $k = 1$ the expectation of (11-28) is

$$E(X_{et-1} Y_t) = v_1 E(X_{et-1} X_{et-1}),$$

since $E(X_{et-1} X_{et-1-i}) = 0$ for $i \neq 0$.

Thus, $\gamma_{XeYe}(1) = v_1 \sigma_{Xe}^2.$

Dividing both sides of (11-28) by $S_{Xe} S_{Ye}$ yields

$$\frac{\gamma_{XeYe}(k)}{S_{Xe} S_{Ye}} = \frac{v_k S_{Xe}^2}{S_{Xe} S_{Ye}}. \tag{11-29}$$

The left-hand side of (11-29) was defined in (11-5) as the cross auto-correlation. Thus, (11-29) is the equivalent of

$$\rho_{XeYe}(k) = \frac{v_k S_{Xe}}{S_{Ye}} \tag{11-30}$$

and $v_k = \rho_{XeYe}(k) \dfrac{S_{Ye}}{S_{Xe}}.$ \hfill (11-31)

Expression (11-31) relates the parameters of (11-27) to the cross autos. The parameters of (11-27) are called impulse response parameters because they will cause a change in Y_{et} after some change in X_{et} has occurred (as long as $b > 0$). The theoretical autocorrelations needed in (11-31) are, of course, not known. However, their sample estimates can be found. These estimates are not efficient for small sample sizes but are the only clues available in identifying an appropriate MARMA model. Thus, an important relation that can be estimated is

$$v_k = r_{XeYe}(k)\frac{S_{Ye}}{S_{Xe}},$$

(11-32)

where r_{XeYe} are sample estimates of the theoretical cross autos e_{XeYe}.

Expression (11-32) indicates that the impulse response parameters of (11-27) are proportional to the cross autocorrelations of corresponding time lags multiplied by a constant. The constant is the ratio of the two standard deviations. Its value is usually larger than zero, because the variance of the independent, pre-whitened series, X_{et} includes only randomness caused by the X_t generating process, while the variance of Y_{et} also includes between X_t and Y_t randomness. Thus, v_k starts at zero time lags and positive cross autos will usually be scaled upwards in order to define values for the impulse response parameters, v_k.

Using the data of Table 11-1 and their cross autos (Figure 11-1), one can calculate the impulse response parameters as shown in Table 11-2.

TABLE 11-2 CALCULATING THE IMPULSE RESPONSE PARAMETERS FOR DATA OF TABLE 11-1

K	$r_{XY}(K)$	S_Y/S_X	Impulse Response Parameters $= r_{XY}(K) * S_Y/S_X$
0	.199	9.638/3.304 = 2.917	.58
1	.542	2.917	1.58
2	−.178	2.917	−.519
3	.426	2.917	1.243
4	−.159	2.917	−.464
5	−.039	2.917	−.114

If one rewrites equation (11-26) as

$$Y_{et} = (v_0 + v_1 B + v_2 B^2 + \cdots)X_{et},$$

(11-33)

the mathematical relationship between v_k and δ_r and ω_r can be seen by equating (11-26) and (11-25) to obtain

$$(v_0 + v_1 B + v_2 B^2 + \cdots)X_{et} = \frac{(\omega_0 B^b - \omega_1 B^{b+1} - \cdots - \omega_s B^{b+s})}{(1 - \delta_1 B - \delta_2 B^2 - \cdots - \delta_r B^r)}X_{et}$$

or

$$(v_0 + v_1 B + v_2 B^2 + \cdots) = \frac{(\omega_0 B^b - \omega_1 B^{b+1} - \cdots - \omega_s B^{b+s})}{(1 - \delta_1 B - \delta_2 B^2 - \cdots - \delta_r B^r)}.$$

(11-34)

Expression (11-34) shows the relationship between the impulse response parameters and the parameters of the MARMA model. This equation can be used for two purposes: (1) It can be solved for $v_0, v_1, v_2 \ldots$ to verify mathematically the behavior of the cross autos as described in Section 11/3/2, and (2) by calculating (11-33) it can provide initial estimates for $\omega_0, \omega_1, \ldots, \omega_s$ and $\delta_1, \delta_2, \ldots, \delta_r$, once the impulse response parameters, $v_0, v_1, v_2, \ldots$, are known.

Using the products on the left-hand side of (11-34) and equating powers of B to their counterparts on the right-hand side yields estimates of $v_0, v_1, v_2, \ldots$. These estimates are

$$\left.\begin{aligned} v_j &= 0 \quad \text{for } j < b, \\ v_j &= \omega_0 \quad \text{for } j = b. \end{aligned}\right\}$$

Depending on the order of r and s, the values of v_j will exhibit some pattern starting at $j = b + s$. Thus, when $r = 2$, $s = 1$, $b = 3$, and

			Remarks
$j = 0$	$v_0 = 0$	$j < b$	All v_j are equal to 0.
$j = 1$	$v_1 = 0$	$j < 3$	
$j = 2$	$v_2 = 0$		
$j = 3$	$v_3 = \omega_0$	$j = b = 3$	There is no pattern in v_j for $s = 1$ terms.
$j = 4$	$v_4 = -\omega_1 + \delta_1 v_3$		Pattern in v_j starts
$j = 5$	$v_5 = \delta_1 v_4 + \delta_2 v_3$	$j \geq b + s + 3 + 1$	and continues.
$j = 6$	$v_6 = \delta_1 v_5 + \delta_2 v_4$		
$j = 7$	$v_7 = \delta_1 v_6 + \delta_2 v_5$		
$\cdot$	$\cdot$		$\cdot$
$\cdot$	$\cdot$		$\cdot$
$\cdot$	$\cdot$		$\cdot$

Similarly, when $r = 2$, $s = 3$, $b = 4$, and

			Remarks
$j = 1$		$j < b$	All v_j are 0.
$j = 2$	$v_1 = v_2 = v_3 = 0$	$j < 4$	
$j = 3$			
$j = 4$	$v_4 = \omega_0$	$j = b = 4$	There is no pattern in v_j
$j = 5$	$v_5 = \omega_1 + \delta_1 v_4$	$b < j < b + s = 4 + 7$	for $s = 3$ terms.
$j = 6$	$v_6 = -\omega_2 + \delta_1 v_5 + \delta_2 v_4$		

$j = 7$ $v_7 = -\omega_3 + \delta_1 v_6 + \delta_2 v_5$ $j \geq b + s = 3 + 4 = 7$ Pattern in v_j starts
$j = 8$ $v_8 = -\delta_1 v_7 + \delta_2 v_6$ and continues.
$j = 9$ $v_9 = -\delta_1 v_8 + \delta_2 v_7$
$j = 10$ $v_{10} = -\delta_1 v_9 + \delta_2 v_8$

Box and Jenkins (1970, p. 350) report the values of v_j for all combinations of r and s up to the order of two. The interested reader unfamiliar with solving equation (11-34) can refer to Box and Jenkins (1976) for the values the v_j take for various values of r, s, and b. From these values and using the estimates of the impulse response parameters calculated based on the cross autos of the prewhitened series, one can find initial estimates of $\delta_1, \delta_2, \delta_3, \ldots, \delta_r$ and $\omega_0, \omega_1, \omega_2, \ldots, \omega_s$ by solving (11-34).

11/3/4   Identifying an Appropriate MARMA Model— Some Examples

For purposes of illustration, 100 values of X_t were generated from normal random numbers with a mean of zero and a variance of one. For this series,

$$X_t = e_t, \tag{11-35}$$

where $e_t = N(0, 1)$. (These are normally distributed random values whose mean is zero and variance is one.)

The values of Y_t were calculated as

$$Y_t = -.8 Y_{t-1} + 1.5 X_{t-1}. \tag{11-36}$$

Since X_t is random noise, (11-36) includes two prewhitened series with $r = 1$, $b = 1$, and $s = 0$. Figure 11-3 shows the cross autos between Y_t and X_t and the impulse response parameters.

If the generating process of (11-35) and (11-36) were unknown, several facts could still be implied from Figure 11-3. First, Y_t and X_t are stationary, since the cross autos damp to zero rapidly. Second, X is a leading indicator of Y, since for positive time lags there are several significant cross autos. Third, a MARMA model can be identified as follows:

1. Since the first significant cross auto is at $k = 1$, $b = 1$.
2. From both the cross autos and the impulse response parameters, v_j, r seems to be equal to one. That is so because the cross autos, or the

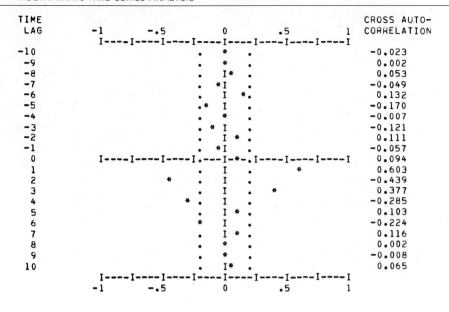

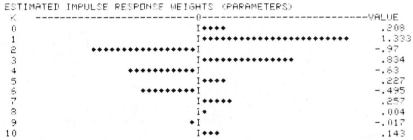

ESTIMATED IMPULSE RESPONSE WEIGHTS (PARAMETERS)

FIGURE 11-3 CROSS AUTOS AND IMPULSE RESPONSE PARAMETERS OF 100 VALUES GENERATED BY EQUATIONS (11-35) AND (11-36)

impulse response parameters, die out exponentially to zero, alternating in sign. [That occurs because δ_1 ($-.8$) is negative.]

3. Also $s = 0$, or $s = 1$, although it is difficult to determine which. It could be that v_1 is the starting point of the pattern or that v_2 is. From Figure 11-3 it is not clear. The solution is to try an $s = 0$. If that does not produce a satisfactory model, then $s = 1$ can be tried.

4. If $s = 0$, initial estimates for ω_0 and δ_1 can be found by solving equation (11-34) for ω_0 and δ_1, which gives

$$\omega_0 = v_1 = 1.333$$

and $\delta_1 = \dfrac{v_2}{v_1} = \dfrac{-.97}{1.333} = -.728.$

[Notice that $\omega_0 = 1.333$ and $\delta_1 = -.728$ are pretty close to the values of 1.5 and $-.8$ used to generate (11-36).]

If $s = 1$, solving (11-34) for ω_0, ω_1 and δ_1 yields

$$\omega_0 = \omega_1 = 1.333,$$

$$\delta_1 = \frac{v_3}{v_2} = \frac{.834}{-.97} = -.86,$$

and $\omega_1 = -v_2 + \delta_1 v_1 = .97 - .86(1.333) = -.176.$

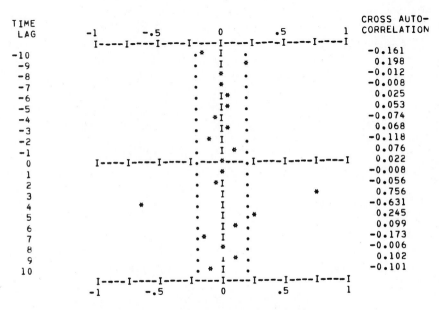

```
TIME                                                              CROSS AUTO-
LAG       -1        -.5        0        .5        1      CORRELATION
          I----I----I----I----I----I----I----I----I
 -10                          .* I   .                      -0.161
  -9                          .  I  .*                       0.198
  -8                          .  *  .                       -0.012
  -7                          .  *  .                       -0.008
  -6                          .  I* .                        0.025
  -5                          .  I* .                        0.053
  -4                          . *I  .                       -0.074
  -3                          .  I* .                        0.068
  -2                          . * I  .                      -0.118
  -1                          .  I * .                       0.076
   0      I----I----I----I.---*---.I----I----I----I          0.022
   1                          .  *  .                       -0.008
   2                          . *I  .                       -0.056
   3                          .  I  .              *         0.756
   4              *           .  I  .                       -0.631
   5                          .  I  .*                       0.245
   6                          .  I * .                       0.099
   7                          .* I  .                       -0.173
   8                          .  *  .                       -0.006
   9                          .  I * .                       0.102
  10                          . * I  .                      -0.101
          I----I----I----I----I----I----I----I----I
          -1        -.5        0        .5        1
```

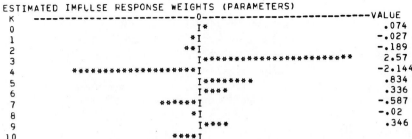

```
ESTIMATED IMPULSE RESPONSE WEIGHTS (PARAMETERS)
 K   ----------------------------0----------------------------VALUE
 0                               I*                            .074
 1                              *I                            -.027
 2                             **I                            -.189
 3                               I*********************** **   2.57
 4        *******************I                               -2.144
 5                               I********                     .834
 6                               I****                         .336
 7                          ******I                           -.587
 8                              *I                            -.02
 9                               I****                         .346
10                           ****I
```

FIGURE 11-4 CROSS AUTOS AND IMPULSE RESPONSE
PARAMETERS OF 100 VALUES GENERATED BY
EQUATIONS (11-35) AND (11-37)

Figure 11-4 is very similar to 11-3 except that Y_t has been generated by

$$Y_t = -.8Y_{t-1} - .4Y_{t-2} + 2.5X_{t-3}. \qquad (11\text{-}37)$$

The X_t values have been generated from normal deviates as described in (11-35). Obviously, $b = 3$, $r = 2$, and $s = 0$ in (11-37).

Upon examining Figure 11-4, one can easily determine that $b = 3$. The value of r could be 1 or 2, but most likely it is 2 since v_5 and v_6, and v_6 and v_7 occur in pairs. The most likely value for s is 0, since the pattern in the cross autos or the impulse response parameters starts almost immediately (from period 3).

The cross autos or impulse response parameters of the two examples illustrated in Figures 11-3 and 11-4 provide enough information to identify an appropriate pattern. In this case it can be seen to be the right one, since the generating process of Y_t is known. Even in such a simple case with only a small amount of randomness involved, the values of s and r are not obvious. In most practical situations, data identification of the right pattern is much more difficult. The values of $r_{XY}(K)$ or v_K are not efficient estimators of ρ_K or the real impulse response parameters. As a result, mistakes are often possible. Fortunately, the residuals of any selected model can be checked for randomness, and when it is not present, another model can be fitted. This process may require extra effort and additional computer time, which can be avoided through good initial estimation of the parameters of the MARMA model. However, this process only occurs once, and using and rerunning the model will require very little extra work.

Figure 11-5 shows the impulse response parameters for various combinations of r (0, 1, 2, 3, 4, 5), s (0, 1, 2, 3), and b (0, 1, 2) when the parameter values are $\delta_1 = .7$, $\delta_2 = -.6$, $\delta_3 = .6$, $\delta_4 = -.4$, $\delta_5 = -.2$ and $\omega_0 = 1.8$, $\omega_1 = .7$, $\omega_2 = -.5$, and $\omega_3 = -.6$. Figure 11-5 should be studied carefully before attempts are made to identify an appropriate MARMA model. It shows the typical behavior of impulse response parameters when randomness is not present. When randomness is present the behavior of the impulse response parameters is more complicated and difficult to identify.

Table 11-3 shows the weekly production figures of a company that is interested in forecasting the value of its billings. Since scheduled production will influence future billings, the approach of MARMA models was used to determine if better forecasting results could be achieved. (Even though there is limited variation in the billings, those concerned wanted forecasts to be as accurate as possible.) Table 11-4 shows the figures of weekly billings for the same 120-week time span.

To determine whether the weekly figures of scheduled production, X_t, are random noise their autocorrelation coefficients are calculated. As shown in Figure 11-6(a), these autos suggest that X_t is not random but shows some definite pattern. [Figure 11-6(b) shows the partial autos.] No differencing seems necessary,

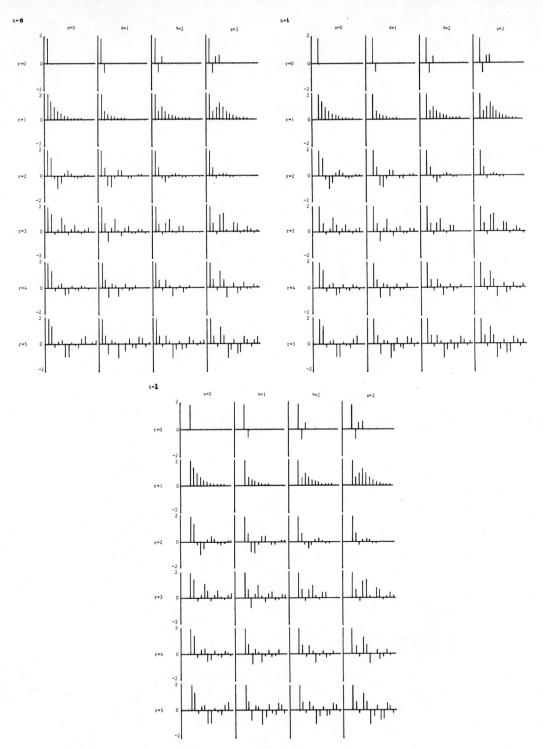

FIGURE 11-5 THE IMPULSE PARAMETERS, v_k, WHEN $\delta_1 = .7$, $\delta_2 = .6$, $\delta_3 = -.4$, $\delta_5 = -.2$, AND $\omega_1 = .7$, $\omega_2 = -.5$, AND $\omega_3 = -.6$

TABLE 11-3 WEEKLY PRODUCTION SCHEDULE FIGURES, X_t (IN THOUSANDS OF UNITS)

Period	Observation	Period	Observation	Period	Observation
1	50.900	41	51.849	81	47.942
2	49.112	42	49.635	82	48.715
3	48.791	43	50.549	83	48.746
4	50.114	44	48.722	84	49.058
5	52.127	45	49.824	85	51.504
6	50.706	46	51.045	86	48.549
7	51.100	47	50.943	87	49.037
8	50.164	48	50.249	88	49.361
9	49.998	49	50.538	89	50.291
10	51.269	50	50.569	90	47.061
11	48.894	51	50.671	91	47.768
12	52.673	52	51.360	92	47.585
13	53.406	53	49.646	93	48.311
14	51.192	54	49.415	94	48.049
15	50.114	55	48.940	95	45.933
16	49.968	56	50.746	96	49.883
17	53.321	57	48.912	97	46.565
18	51.683	58	49.358	98	44.731
19	49.843	59	47.812	99	47.420
20	51.464	60	49.362	100	49.694
21	51.671	61	50.630	101	49.590
22	50.456	62	52.009	102	52.368
23	50.395	63	48.907	103	49.560
24	52.591	64	49.114	104	50.955
25	51.916	65	52.602	105	52.251
26	49.967	66	53.808	106	48.975
27	51.100	67	49.900	107	49.408
28	50.214	68	48.454	108	51.122
29	47.217	69	49.372	109	50.942
30	48.172	70	46.517	110	50.302
31	50.618	71	47.724	111	49.741
32	51.055	72	49.661	112	51.061
33	52.299	73	48.638	113	47.548
34	51.282	74	52.285	114	51.425
35	50.533	75	51.087	115	50.690
36	50.628	76	48.851	116	50.206
37	51.531	77	47.761	117	50.505
38	48.488	78	45.251	118	49.662
39	46.747	79	49.121	119	49.906
40	49.301	80	48.933	120	49.626

TABLE 11-4 WEEKLY BILLING FIGURES, Y_t (IN MILLIONS OF DOLLARS)

Period	Observation	Period	Observation	Period	Observation
1	103.000	41	94.262	81	88.770
2	103.916	42	85.900	82	90.126
3	100.115	43	86.393	83	92.812
4	101.577	44	97.544	84	92.246
5	100.812	45	101.861	85	95.298
6	96.455	46	106.499	86	100.044
7	98.459	47	104.903	87	102.806
8	101.856	48	104.643	88	112.437
9	98.898	49	103.684	89	106.934
10	99.189	50	103.667	90	106.283
11	99.455	51	103.087	91	102.776
12	98.775	52	96.766	92	100.181
13	103.087	53	95.956	93	92.541
14	100.569	54	95.719	94	86.056
15	105.557	55	96.644	95	85.623
16	109.592	56	93.025	96	89.016
17	105.883	57	92.576	97	96.537
18	102.970	58	95.205	98	95.561
19	94.108	59	100.016	99	106.057
20	97.793	60	101.049	100	103.590
21	99.117	61	104.115	101	94.572
22	101.337	62	101.299	102	93.528
23	101.926	63	98.391	103	98.715
24	103.925	64	99.020	104	103.129
25	103.674	65	103.847	105	112.684
26	100.041	66	99.947	106	109.569
27	101.488	67	97.395	107	110.798
28	97.475	68	104.410	108	110.503
29	88.786	69	111.124	109	102.000
30	88.079	70	104.956	110	96.259
31	90.521	71	95.525	111	95.155
32	92.665	72	92.163	112	94.168
33	92.890	73	83.464	113	95.973
34	98.968	74	82.083	114	96.456
35	103.838	75	89.417	115	98.481
36	110.873	76	100.043	116	94.707
37	110.924	77	111.950	117	100.683
38	108.998	78	115.786	118	103.935
39	105.282	79	109.128	119	105.390
40	105.015	80	102.147	120	108.281

since the autos drop to zero quickly. Furthermore, the exponential dampening occurs for the autocorrelation coefficients. That suggests an AR model of order 1, since there is only one significant partial autocorrelation.

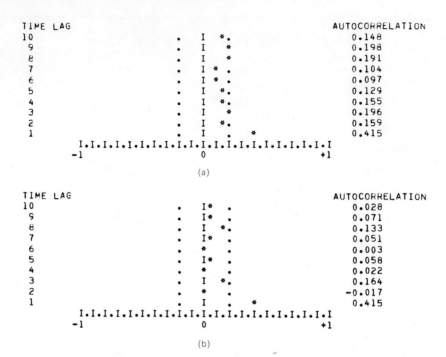

```
TIME LAG                                                      AUTOCORRELATION
10                         .  I  *.                               0.148
 9                         .  I  *                                0.198
 8                         .  I  *                                0.191
 7                         .  I *  .                              0.104
 6                         .  I *  .                              0.097
 5                         .  I  *.                               0.129
 4                         .  I  *.                               0.155
 3                         .  I   *                               0.196
 2                         .  I  *.                               0.159
 1                         .  I    .      *                       0.415
           I.I.I.I.I.I.I.I.I.I.I.I.I.I.I.I.I.I.I.I
          -1                0                +1
```

(a)

```
TIME LAG                                                      AUTOCORRELATION
10                         .  I*  .                               0.028
 9                         .  I*  .                               0.071
 8                         .  I  *.                               0.133
 7                         .  I*  .                               0.051
 6                         .  *   .                               0.003
 5                         .  I*  .                               0.058
 4                         .  *   .                               0.022
 3                         .  I  *.                               0.164
 2                         .  *   .                              -0.017
 1                         .  I    .      *                       0.415
           I.I.I.I.I.I.I.I.I.I.I.I.I.I.I.I.I.I.I.I
          -1                0                +1
```

(b)

FIGURE 11-6 DATA OF TABLE 11-3: (A) AUTOCORRELATIONS OF X_t AND (B) PARTIAL AUTOCORRELATIONS OF X_t

The tentative model for X_t is therefore

$$X_t = \phi_1 X_{t-1} + e_t. \qquad (11\text{-}38)$$

The best value for ϕ_1 is .41 and the residuals in (11-38) are therefore

$$e_t = X_t - .41X_{t-1}, \qquad (11\text{-}39)$$

where X_t is expressed in terms of deviation from the mean.

As shown in Figure 11-7, the autocorrelations of these residuals indicate that e_t is white noise. Therefore, e_t can be used as the prewhitened series, X_{et}.

The prewhitened series, X_{et}, is shown in Table 11-5. Note that Table 11-5 has only 119 values, since 1 value is lost when equation (11-39) is calculated. To illustrate the computation of (11-39) and subsequently Table 11-5, the values

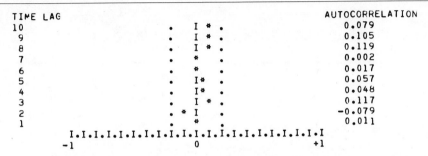

FIGURE 11-7 AUTOCORRELATIONS OF RESIDUALS OF
EQUATION (11-38)

of e_2 and e_3 will be examined in detail. First, e_2 is restated as

$$e_2 = X_2 - .41X_1$$

$$= (X_2 - \bar{X}) - .41(X_1 - \bar{X}),$$

since the model of (11-38) is in terms of deviations from the mean X value. This gives

$$e_2 = (49.112 - 49.882) - .41(50.9 - 49.882) = -1.187$$

and $e_3 = (48.791 - 49.882) - .41(49.112 - 49.882) = -.775.$

In a similar way the remaining values of e_t are found. Their values are printed in Table 11-5. Notice that all the e_t have been moved up one period to account for the one observation lost because equation (11-39) must start at period two.

The same model estimated for X_t is applied on the Y_t values of Table 11-4. Thus,

$$e'_t = Y_t - .41Y_{t-1}. \tag{11-40}$$

Restated in terms of deviation from the mean, this is

$$e'_t = (Y_t - \bar{Y}) - .41(Y_{t-1} - \bar{Y}).$$

Thus, $e'_2 = (103.916 - 99.701) - .41(103 - 99.701) = 2.862$

and $e'_3 = (100.115 - 99.701) - .41(103.916 - 99.701) = -1.315,$

etc.

The prewhitened series, $Y_{et} = e'_t$, and its values are shown in Table 11-6.

The cross autocorrelations and the impulse response parameters then are found between the series X_{et} and the series in Table 11-6. They are shown in Figure 11-8, which becomes the major tool in the identification of an appropriate MARMA model.

TABLE 11-5   PREWHITENED SERIES $X_{et} = e_t$ OF EQUATION (11-39)

Period	Observation	Period	Observation	Period	Observation
1	−1.187	41	−1.053	81	−.372
2	−.775	42	.768	82	−.658
3	.679	43	−1.434	83	−.358
4	2.150	44	.418	84	1.960
5	−.096	45	1.186	85	−1.998
6	.880	46	.585	86	−.299
7	−.218	47	−.068	87	−.174
8	.000	48	.506	88	.622
9	1.339	49	.418	89	−2.988
10	−1.557	50	.507	90	−.958
11	3.197	51	1.154	91	−1.430
12	2.380	52	−.842	92	−.629
13	−.135	53	−.370	93	−1.189
14	−.305	54	−.750	94	−3.198
15	−.008	55	1.250	95	1.620
16	3.404	56	−1.324	96	−3.318
17	.391	57	−.127	97	−3.791
18	−.777	58	−1.855	98	−.350
19	1.598	59	.329	99	.821
20	1.140	60	.962	100	−.214
21	−.159	61	1.820	101	2.606
22	.277	62	−1.847	102	−1.341
23	2.499	63	−.368	103	1.205
24	.924	64	3.035	104	1.929
25	−.749	65	2.810	105	−1.879
26	1.183	66	−1.591	106	−.102
27	−.167	67	−1.436	107	1.434
28	−2.801	68	.075	108	.552
29	−.617	69	−3.156	109	−.014
30	1.437	70	−.779	110	−.313
31	.871	71	.664	111	1.236
32	1.936	72	−1.153	112	−2.818
33	.409	73	2.914	113	2.500
34	.077	74	.219	114	.175
35	.479	75	−1.525	115	−.007
36	1.343	76	−1.698	116	.490
37	−2.070	77	−3.761	117	−.476
38	−2.563	78	1.137	118	.114
39	.705	79	−.637	119	−.266
40	2.205	80	−1.551		

TABLE 11-6   PREWHITENED SERIES $Y_{et} = e_t'$ OF EQUATION (11-40)

Period	Observation	Period	Observation	Period	Observation
1	2.862	41	−11.572	81	−5.093
2	−1.315	42	−7.649	82	−2.964
3	1.706	43	3.299	83	−4.631
4	.342	44	3.044	84	−1.346
5	−3.702	45	5.912	85	2.148
6	.088	46	2.415	86	2.964
7	2.664	47	2.809	87	11.462
8	−1.686	48	1.956	88	2.011
9	−.183	49	2.332	89	3.616
10	−.036	50	1.760	90	.376
11	−.825	51	−4.324	91	−.781
12	3.765	52	−2.542	92	−7.358
13	−.520	53	−2.447	93	−10.709
14	5.500	54	−1.424	94	−8.484
15	7.490	55	−5.423	95	−4.913
16	2.126	56	−4.388	96	1.216
17	.734	57	−1.575	97	−2.843
18	−6.933	58	2.158	98	8.054
19	.384	59	1.218	99	1.283
20	.198	60	3.862	100	−6.724
21	1.876	61	−.212	101	−4.071
22	1.554	62	−1.966	102	1.545
23	3.311	63	−.144	103	3.832
24	2.241	64	4.425	104	11.577
25	−1.290	65	−1.454	105	4.545
26	1.647	66	−2.407	106	7.051
27	−2.959	67	5.654	107	6.252
28	−10.003	68	9.492	108	−2.130
29	−7.147	69	.572	109	−4.385
30	−4.415	70	−6.331	110	−3.135
31	−3.273	71	−5.826	111	−3.669
32	−3.926	72	−13.147	112	−1.459
33	2.059	73	−10.961	113	−1.717
34	4.437	74	−3.061	114	.111
35	9.476	75	4.558	115	−4.494
36	6.643	76	12.109	116	3.029
37	4.695	77	11.063	117	3.831
38	1.769	78	2.831	118	3.953
39	3.026	79	−1.419	119	6.247
40	−7.618	80	−11.934		

From Figure 11-8 the value of b is easily identified as 3. The order of r is probably 2 or higher, since there is a trailing off of the cross autos and impulse

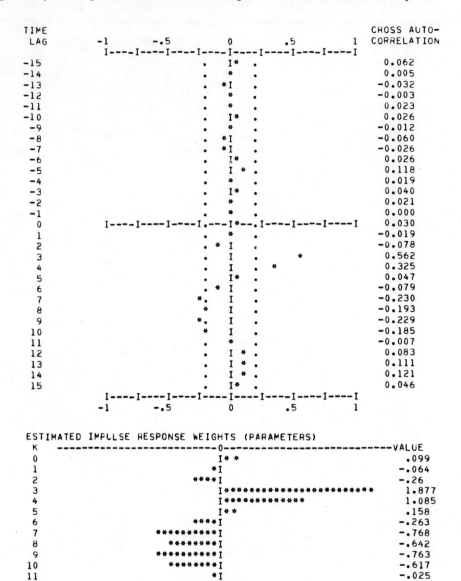

```
TIME                                                    CROSS AUTO-
LAG     -1       -.5        0        .5        1     CORRELATION
        I----I----I----I----I----I----I----I----I
-15                        .  I*  .                      0.062
-14                        .  *   .                      0.005
-13                        . *I   .                     -0.032
-12                        .  *   .                     -0.003
-11                        .  *   .                      0.023
-10                        .  I*  .                      0.026
 -9                        .  *   .                     -0.012
 -8                        . *I   .                     -0.060
 -7                        . *I   .                     -0.026
 -6                        .  I*  .                      0.026
 -5                        .  I *  .                     0.118
 -4                        .  *   .                      0.019
 -3                        .  I*  .                      0.040
 -2                        .  *   .                      0.021
 -1                        .  *   .                      0.000
  0     I----I----I----I.----I*--.I----I----I----I       0.030
  1                        .  *   .                     -0.019
  2                        . * I  c                     -0.078
  3                        .  I   .      *               0.562
  4                        .  I   . *                    0.325
  5                        .  I*  .                      0.047
  6                        . * I  .                     -0.079
  7                       *.  I   .                     -0.230
  8                        *  I   .                     -0.193
  9                       *.  I   .                     -0.229
 10                        *  I   .                     -0.185
 11                        .  *   .                     -0.007
 12                        .  I * .                      0.083
 13                        .  I * .                      0.111
 14                        .  I * .                      0.121
 15                        .  I*  .                      0.046
        I----I----I----I----I----I----I----I----I
        -1       -.5        0        .5        1
```

```
ESTIMATED IMPULSE RESPONSE WEIGHTS (PARAMETERS)
K       --------------------------0-------------------------VALUE
0                                I* *                        .099
1                                *I                         -.064
2                             ****I                         -.26
3                                I************************    1.877
4                                I*************              1.085
5                                I**                         .158
6                             ****I                         -.263
7                       **********I                         -.768
8                         ********I                         -.642
9                       **********I                         -.763
10                       ********I                          -.617
11                               *I                         -.025
12                               I****                       .276
13                               I*****                      .37
14                               I*****                      .404
15                               I**                         .154
```

FIGURE 11-8   CROSS AUTOS AND IMPULSE RESPONSE
PARAMETERS

response parameters in a sine wave form that is characteristic of $r = 2$, $r = 3$, and $r = 4$. The value of s is more difficult to identify. It is most likely that it is 1 or 2, although there is some chance that it is 0. Unfortunately, it is not clear whether the sine pattern starts at time lag 4, 5, or 3.* Assuming $b = 3$, $r = 2$, and $s = 2$, initial estimates for δ_1, δ_2, ω_0, ω_1, and ω_2 can be found from the impulse response parameters by solving equation (11-34). This gives the following:

Parameters are zero for $b < 3$.	$v_1 = v_2 = 0$	$v_j = 0 \qquad j < b$	
Pattern has not been settled.	$v_3 = \omega_0$ $v_4 = \delta_1 v_3 - \omega_1$	No pattern for $s = 2$ terms	(11-41) (11-42)
Pattern in parameters starts at v_5; before v_5 the pattern is not yet settled.	$v_5 = \delta_1 v_4 + \delta_2 v_3 - \omega_2$ $v_6 = \delta_1 v_5 + \delta_2 v_4$ $v_7 = \delta_1 v_6 + \delta_2 v_5$	Pattern starts at $b + s$	(11-43) (11-44) (11-45)

From equation (11-41), it is found that $\omega_0 = v_3 = 1.877$. Expressions (11-44) and (11-45) can be solved for δ_1 and δ_2, yielding

$$\delta_1 = \frac{v_5 v_6 - v_4 v_7}{v_5{}^2 - v_4 v_6} = \frac{.158(-.263) - 1.085(-.768)}{.158^2 - 1.085(-.263)} = 2.55,$$

$$\delta_2 = \frac{v_7 - \delta_1 v_6}{v_5} = \frac{(-.768) - 2.55(-.263)}{.158} = -.616.$$

Substituting the values of δ_1 and δ_2 in (11-42) and (11-43) yields estimates for ω_1 and ω_2 respectively. These are

$$\omega_1 = -v_4 + \delta_1 v_3 = -(1.085) + 2.55(1.877) = 3.701$$

and $\quad \omega_2 = -v_5 + \delta_1 v_4 + \delta_2 v_3 = -.158 + 2.55(1.085) + (-.616)(1.877)$

$$= 1.453.$$

Thus, initial estimates of the MARMA model's parameters are found from the estimate impulse response parameters.

---

* It should be noted that the concept of pattern is not being used in the impulse response parameters the same way that Box and Jenkins (1970, p. 378) use it. According to Box and Jenkins's definition, the pattern starts at $b + s - r + 1 = 3 + 2 - 2 + 1 = 4$, i.e., at v_4. That may be so, but v_4 does not contain both δ_1, and δ_2, so the pattern is in a transient state. It is therefore more logical to put the beginning of the pattern at v_5 ($b + s = 3 + 2 = 5$) and say that v_3 and v_4 (two values of s) are not settled. This can be seen from expressions (11-41) through (11-45).

11/3/5 Identifying an Appropriate Noise Model

So far in this chapter we have demonstrated and illustrated the following:

1. The relationship between a dependent and an independent variable can be found by prewhitening both variables and finding the cross autocorrelation between them.
2. From the cross autos, the impulse response parameters can be found simply by scaling the cross autos.
3. From both the cross autos and the impulse response parameters an appropriate model of the form (11-46) can be tentatively identified.
4. Initial estimates for the parameters of the tentatively identified model can be made.

If $\hat{\delta}_1, \hat{\delta}_2, \ldots, \hat{\delta}_r, \hat{\omega}_0, \hat{\omega}_1, \ldots, \hat{\omega}_s$ are the initial (or final) estimates of the parameters, the forecast value, $\hat{Y}_t$, will be

$$\hat{Y}_t = \hat{\delta}_1 \hat{Y}_{t-1} + \hat{\delta}_2 \hat{Y}_{t-2} + \cdots + \hat{\delta}_r \hat{Y}_{t-r} + \hat{\omega}_0 X_{t-b} - \hat{\omega}_1 X_{t-b-1} - \cdots - \hat{\omega}_s X_{t-b-s}. \qquad (11\text{-}46)$$

The actual value of the dependent variable is Y_t, thus the difference between the two is the residual error, e_t, and

$$e_t = Y_t - \hat{Y}_t, \qquad (11\text{-}47)$$

$$e_t = Y_t - \hat{\delta}_1 \hat{Y}_{t-1} - \hat{\delta}_2 \hat{Y}_{t-2} - \cdots - \hat{\delta}_r \hat{Y}_{t-r} - \hat{\omega}_0 X_{t-b} + \hat{\omega}_1 X_{t-b-1} + \cdots + \hat{\omega}_s X_{t-b-s},$$

$$(11\text{-}48)$$

where both Y_t and X_t are expressed as deviations from their means, i.e., $Y_t = Y_t - \bar{Y}$ and $X_t = X_t - \bar{X}$.

The value of e_t in equations (11-47) or (11-48) may be white noise (completely random) or it may exhibit some pattern that can be identified and used for forecasting purposes. In the general case, e_t will behave according to some ARMA (p, q) model that can be identified by looking at the autocorrelations of the series of residuals, e_t, given by (11-47). There is often a problem, however, in computing e_t. It can be done by using the initial estimates of the parameters computed from the impulse response function or by finding more refined estimates and using them in (11-48) to identify the noise model.

In the last example taken up in the previous section, the initial estimates for the MARMA model were

$$\delta_1 = 2.55, \qquad \delta_2 = -.616,$$

$$\omega_0 = 1.877, \qquad \omega_1 = 3.701, \qquad \omega_2 = 1.453.$$

If these estimates are substituted into equation (11-48), they yield a series of residual errors, e_t. Unfortunately, these initial estimates are not always efficient, and they may give a noise pattern in e_t that results in the errors getting larger and larger in such a way that they become meaningless. It is possible that the noise model can be identified beforehand (see Box and Jenkins 1970, pp. 384–85). However, such procedures are difficult to implement in practice and are computationally cumbersome. An alternative used by the authors is to find ordinary regression estimates for the model shown in (11-48), once r, s, and b have been identified. Such estimates are calculated using the variables, X and Y appropriately differenced (or using Xe_t and Ye_t). (See Tables 11-3 and 11-4.) These estimates are much more efficient than the initial estimates found from the impulse response

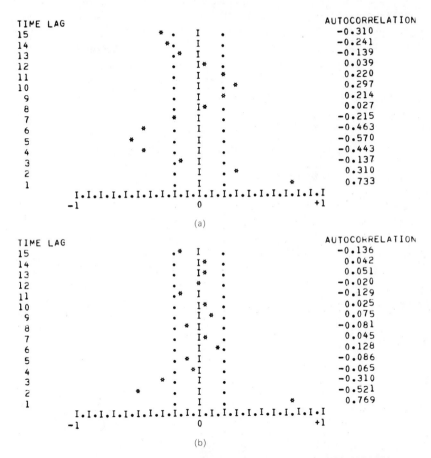

FIGURE 11-9   NOISE MODEL OF EQUATION (11-48) WHEN ORDINARY REGRESSION ESTIMATES ARE USED FOR MODEL PARAMETERS: (A) AUTOCORRELATIONS AND (B) PARTIAL AUTOCORRELATIONS (SEE TABLE 11-8 FOR VALUES).

parameters and do not necessarily require more computing time (see Table 11-10 of Section 11/4/2 for values). In addition, such estimates are very close to the final estimates, which speeds the nonlinear estimation of the final parameters. Thus, the authors have found that there are considerable computational gains from using ordinary regression estimates as initial estimates rather than those coming from the impulse response parameters. The parameters found can be seen in Table 11-10. The autocorrelations of the residuals of the regular regression model fitted to the prewhitened series (when $r = s = 2$ and $b = 3$) are shown in Figure 11-9. From these autos and partials a noise model can be estimated following the procedure discussed in Chapter 10. (This involves a regular, univariate, identification process.) First, the fact that the exponential decline is in the autocorrelations (it appears as a sine wave) suggests an AR model. Secondly, there are three significant partials. That suggests an order of 3. Thus, the noise model is AR(3). Initial estimates for ϕ_1, ϕ_2, and ϕ_3 can be found by solving the Yule-Walker equations explained in Chapter 9 to obtain $\phi_1 = 1.324$, and $\phi_2 = -.595$. Using the regression parameters as initial estimates, the complete MARMA model is now available and takes the following form:

$$\hat{Y}_t = 1.374\hat{Y}_{t-1} - .668\hat{Y}_{t-2} + 2.118X_{t-3} - 1.686X_{t-4} + .038X_{t-5} + e_t, \tag{11-49}$$

where both $\hat{Y}_t$ and X_t are in deviation form; and

$$e_t = 1.008e_{t-1} - .159e_{t-2} - .31e_{t-3} + e'_t, \tag{11-50}$$

where e'_t is now white noise.

In the next section, the final estimates of the parameters of a specific MARMA model, such as that given by (11-49) and (11-50), will be estimated by two methods: the method of steepest descent used in adaptive filtering (see Chapter 9) and a standard (Marquardt's) nonlinear estimation algorithm. As with all MARMA models, the final step is to verify that the resulting residuals are white noise.

11/4   Estimation of the Parameters of a Specific MARMA Model and Diagnostic Checking

In the previous section, the complete identification of an appropriate MARMA model was discussed and its rationale was described by explaining and illustrating the behavior of cross autos for various values of r, s, and b. This process was shown verbally and then mathematically by solving (11-34) and finding the v_j values. Furthermore, procedures for obtaining initial estimates for $\delta_1, \delta_2, \ldots, \delta_r$ and $\omega_0, \omega_1, \ldots, \omega_s$ from the impulse response parameters, or better ones by regression, were discussed. Finally, examples were used to illustrate these procedures for identification and parameter estimation. In this section the estimation of refined parameter values will be described so that a final MARMA model relating Y and X can be found and used to forecast future Y values.

11/4/1   Standard Nonlinear Estimation

Estimation of final parameter values is the most routine portion of MARMA model development, but is also the most demanding computationally. The estimation begins with (11-49), or any other set of initial parameter values. The values, $e_t = Y_t - \hat{Y}_t$, are then calculated. The third step is to find values for e_t' by solving (11-50). The parameter values that minimize the MSE resulting from e_t' are then chosen to be the final estimates. The algorithm most often used for this last step is the Marquardt (1963) method of constrained optimization, which is a combination of the Gauss-Newton and the steepest descent iterative approaches. The essence of the method is a guided trial and error approach that facilitates the achievement of a minimum MSE. The method is similar to the steepest descent algorithm already discussed in detail in Chapter 9, except that it changes the parameter values only after the MSE from all the data has been calculated. The steepest descent method as it is used in adaptive filtering, on the other hand, updates the parameters after each data point, which gives convergence to a minimum MSE with considerably fewer computations.

Using nonlinear optimization, final parameter values are found. If the residuals, e_t', of the final model are white noise and if the cross autocorrelations between residuals and prewhitened independent variable show no pattern, it implies that the model originally identified is adequate. This procedure will be applied to the example used in the previous section after some potential pitfalls in the procedure are described.

The difficulty with nonlinear estimation is that there may be more than one minimum. It is possible, therefore, to arrive at a situation in which the minimum MSE that has been achieved is only a local one. (Existing methods cannot guarantee that a global minimum has been found.) To avoid this problem it is important either to test combinations of parameters and find those giving a minimum MSE or to start with good initial estimates of the parameter values, then improve them. That will minimize the possibility of reaching a local minimum, since the MSE for the initial parameter values will not be much different from the MSE of the global minimum (an additional reason to use ordinary regression estimates as initial estimates).

Finally, it should be noted that in the fitting phase the parameter values estimated by the different methods give similar results; the estimates obtained by regular regression and those coming from the Yule-Walker equations give MSE values not very different from those resulting from the computationally cumbersome procedure of nonlinear estimation.

Some of the calculations necessary to compute the parameter values required in estimating the MSE (and in deciding in which direction the parameter values should be changed) are shown in Table 11-7. Taking period 30 as an example, the calculations in Table 11-7 can be illustrated as follows:

1. Obtain the value of $\hat{Y}_t$ using equation (11-49):

$$\hat{Y}_{30} = 1.374\hat{Y}_{29} - .668\hat{Y}_{28} + 2.118X_{27} - 1.686X_{26} + .038X_{25}$$

$$= (1.374)(1.68) - .668(5.53) + 2.118(1.22) - 1.686(.08) + 0.38X_{25}$$

$$= (1.374)(1.68) - 668(5.53) + 2.118(1.22) - 1.686(.08) + 0.38(2.03)$$

$$\hat{Y}_{30} = 1.13 \quad \text{(see column 6)}.$$

2. Obtain the errors, $Y_t - \hat{Y}_t$, or

$$e_{30} = Y_{30} - \hat{Y}_{30} = 11.62 - 1.13 = -12.75 \quad \text{(see column 7)}.$$

3. Forecast the error using equation (11-50),

$$\hat{e}_{30} = 1.008e_{29} - .159e_{28} - .31e_{27}$$

$$= 1.008(-12.59) - .159(-7.76) - .31(-2.36)$$

$$\hat{e}_{30} = -10.73 \quad \text{(see column 8)}.$$

4. Add the forecast noise term to the forecast, $\hat{Y}_t$, obtained in (1),

$$F_{30} = \hat{Y}_{30} + \hat{e}_{30} = 1.13 - 10.73 = -9.60.$$

5. Add the mean Y value to the total forecast,

$$F_{30} = \overline{Y} - 9.60 = 90.10 \quad \text{(see column 9)}.$$

6. Find the total error, e'_t,

$$e'_{30} = Y_{30} + \overline{Y} - F_{30} = 88.08 - 90.10 = -2.02$$

(see column 10).

Finally, it is necessary to find the MSE by taking the sum of the final errors squared as shown in column 10 and dividing this sum by the number of terms used, i.e., 115. This MSE value provides a statistical measure of how well the parameter values of (11-49) and (11-50) fit the time-series data. If the MSE can be improved, new parameter values will be specified and the same calculations shown in Table 11-7 will be repeated until a minimum MSE has been achieved. Figure 11-10 shows the autocorrelations of the residuals of the final model fitted and of the residuals and the prewhitened independent variable, X_{et}. Both suggest that the model used is an adequate one.

TABLE 11-7 CALCULATION OF RELEVANT VALUES IN MARMA MODELS

(1)	(2)	(3)	(4)	(5)	(6)	(7)	(8)	(9)	(10)
								Total Forecast of MARMA Model	Total Error of MARMA Model:
	Depend-ent Variable	In Deviation Form	Indepen-dent Variable	In Deviation Form	Forecast Using (11-46)	Error in (11-48) $Y_t - \hat{Y}_t$	Forecast of Error in (11-48)	$\hat{Y}_t + \hat{e}_t + \overline{Y}$	e_t' in
Period	Y_t	$Y_t = Y_t - \overline{Y}$	X_t	$X_t = X_t - \overline{X}$	$\hat{Y}_t$	$[(3) - (6)]$	(11-48)	(11-48)	(11-50)
1	103	3.30	50.9	1.02	—	—	—	—	—
2	103.92	4.22	49.11	−.77	—	—	—	—	—
3	100.12	.42	48.79	−1.09	—	—	—	—	—
4	101.58	1.88	50.11	.23	—	—	—	—	—
5	100.81	1.11	52.13	2.25	—	—	—	—	—
6	96.45	−3.25	50.71	.82	−.97	−2.27	.00	98.73	−2.27
7	98.46	−1.24	51.10	1.22	.96	−2.21	−2.29	98.37	.09
8	101.86	2.15	50.16	.28	6.30	−4.14	−1.86	104.14	−2.28
9	98.90	−.80	50.00	.12	5.98	−6.78	−3.12	102.56	−3.66
10	99.19	−.51	51.27	1.39	5.28	−5.80	−5.49	99.49	−.30
11	99.45	−.25	48.89	−.99	1.84	−2.09	−3.48	98.06	1.39
12	98.78	−.93	52.67	2.79	−1.18	.26	.92	99.44	−.66
13	103.09	3.39	53.41	3.52	−.10	3.49	2.39	101.99	1.10
14	100.57	.87	51.19	1.31	−3.78	4.65	4.12	100.05	.52
15	105.56	5.86	50.11	.23	2.51	3.35	4.05	106.26	−.70
16	109.59	9.89	49.97	.09	8.69	1.20	1.55	109.95	−.35
17	105.88	6.18	53.32	3.44	7.21	−1.02	−.76	106.14	−.26
18	102.97	3.27	51.68	1.80	2.51	.76	−2.26	99.95	3.02
19	94.11	−5.59	49.84	−.04	−1.52	−4.07	.56	98.73	−4.63
20	97.79	−1.91	51.46	1.58	3.38	−5.29	−3.91	99.17	−1.38
21	99.12	−.58	51.67	1.79	3.68	−4.26	−4.92	98.46	.65
22	101.34	1.64	50.46	.57	−.19	1.83	−2.19	97.32	4.02
23	101.93	2.22	50.39	.51	.77	1.46	4.16	104.62	−2.70
24	103.92	4.22	52.59	2.71	2.30	1.92	2.50	104.50	−.58
25	103.67	3.97	51.92	2.03	.91	3.06	1.14	101.75	1.92
26	100.04	.34	49.97	.08	−.10	.44	2.33	101.93	−1.89
27	101.49	1.79	51.10	1.22	4.15	−2.36	−.64	103.21	−1.72
28	97.47	−2.23	50.21	.33	5.53	−7.76	−3.40	101.83	−4.36
29	88.79	−10.92	47.22	−2.66	1.68	−12.59	−7.58	93.80	−5.01
30	88.08	−11.62	48.17	−1.71	1.13	−12.75	−10.73	90.10	−2.02
⋮	⋮	⋮	⋮	⋮	⋮	⋮	⋮	⋮	⋮
100	103.59	3.89	49.69	−.19	−2.71	6.60	5.82	102.81	.78
101	94.57	−5.13	49.59	−.29	−9.22	4.09	5.07	95.55	−.98
102	93.53	−6.17	52.37	2.49	−7.52	1.34	1.19	93.38	.15
103	98.71	−.99	49.56	−.32	−.61	−.37	−1.34	97.75	.97
104	103.13	3.43	50.96	1.07	3.79	−.36	−1.86	101.63	1.50
105	112.68	12.98	52.25	2.37	11.36	1.62	−.72	110.34	2.34
106	109.57	9.87	48.97	−.91	8.20	1.67	1.81	109.71	−.14
107	110.80	11.10	49.41	−.47	6.58	4.51	1.54	107.82	2.98
108	110.50	10.80	51.12	1.24	6.77	4.04	3.78	110.25	.25
109	102.00	2.30	50.94	1.06	−.98	3.28	2.83	101.56	.44
110	96.26	−3.44	50.30	.42	−5.24	1.80	1.26	95.72	.54
111	95.16	−4.55	49.74	−.14	−3.16	−1.38	.04	96.58	−1.43
112	94.17	−5.53	51.06	1.18	−.71	−4.83	−2.69	96.30	−2.13
113	95.97	−3.73	47.55	−2.33	.29	−4.02	−5.20	94.79	1.18
114	96.46	−3.25	51.43	1.54	−.09	−3.15	−2.86	96.75	−.30
115	98.48	−1.22	50.69	.81	2.43	−3.65	−1.04	101.09	−2.60
116	94.71	−4.99	50.21	.32	−3.54	−1.45	−1.93	94.23	.47
117	100.68	.98	50.50	.62	.76	.22	.09	100.56	.13
118	103.93	4.23	49.66	−.22	2.43	1.80	1.58	103.72	.22
119	105.39	5.69	49.91	.02	2.22	3.47	2.23	104.15	1.24
120	108.28	8.58	49.63	−.26	2.22	6.35	3.15	105.07	3.21

11/4/2 Estimation and Forecasting with Adaptive Filtering

As discussed in Chapter 9, adaptive filtering utilizes the method of steepest descent as an optimization procedure to achieve a minimum MSE. The method consists of repeatedly applying equation (9-15). [See (11-51), where the parameters refer to the MARMA equation (11-2) or to the AR noise model of (11-54). When the noise parameters are of an MA type, then equations (9-32) and (9-51) apply.]

The values of $\delta_1, \delta_2, \ldots, \delta_r, \omega_0, \omega_1, \omega_2, \ldots, \omega_s$, and $\phi_1, \phi_2, \ldots, \phi_p$ are updated using (11-51), and if there are MA parameters, $\theta_1, \theta_2, \ldots, \theta_g$ are updated using (11-52). [The model being used as an example in this chapter does not involve MA noise parameters and therefore (11-52) is not needed.]

$$\omega'_{it} = \omega_{it-1} + 2ke_t Z_{t-i}, \tag{11-51}$$

$$\theta'_{it} = \theta_{it-1} - 2ke_t e_{t-i}, \tag{11-52}$$

for $i = 1, \ldots, D$ and $t = D + 1, \ldots, n$,

where ω_{it} can be δ_i, ω_i or ϕ_i, and

Z_{t-i} is the series value corresponding to this parameter variable.

All values in (11-51) and (11-52) are applied for each set of D terms.

Thus, the corresponding general **MARMA** model for adaptive filtering is:

$$Y_t = \delta_{1t} Y_{t-1} + \delta_{2t} Y_{t-2} + \cdots + \delta_{rt} Y_{t-r} + \omega_{0t} X_{t-b} - \omega_{1-b-st} X_{t-b-s} + e_t, \tag{11-53}$$

where $e_t = \phi_{1t} e_{t-1} + \phi_{2t} e_{t-2} + \cdots + \phi_{pt} e_{t-p} + e'_t. \tag{11-54}$

Using the example of the specific model that has been carried through in the previous sections, one can see that these equations are similar to (11-49) and (11-50). Thus, for the initial period, $\hat{Y}_6$, the equation is

$$\hat{Y}_6 = +1.374\hat{Y}_{-1} + .668\hat{Y}_{-2} + 2.118X_{t-3} - 1.686X_{t-4} + .038X_{t-5} + e_t \tag{11-55}$$

and $e_t = 1.008e_{t-1} - .159e_{t-2} - .31e_{t-3} + e'_t. \tag{11-56}$

Expression (11-51) can be used to update the parameters of (11-55), to calculate e_t, and to update the parameters in (11-56). One word of caution: the sign of $2ke_t Z_{t-i}$ will vary (be positive or negative) depending upon the sign of the parameter in (11-53) or (11-54).

The example used previously can now be used to illustrate these steps. Starting with the initial values calculated by regression and the Yule-Walker equations, the calculations required for parameter estimation and the corresponding errors are shown in Table 11-8. These values were developed by using a $K = .01$ and four training cycles to obtain a minimum MSE. Table 11-9 gives the parameter values resulting from these calculations. The final parameter values are shown in Table 11-10. The noise residuals from these parameter values are

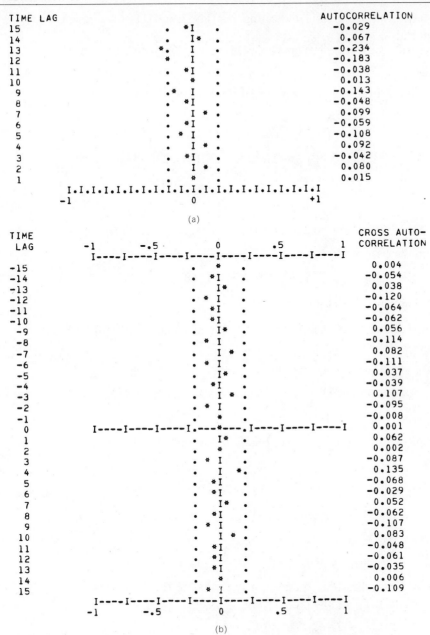

FIGURE 11-10   (A) RESIDUAL AUTOCORRELATIONS AND (B)
CROSS AUTOCORRELATIONS BETWEEN
RESIDUALS AND PREWHITENED INDEPENDENT
VARIABLES X_{et}

random as can be seen in Figure 11-11, indicating that (11-55) and (11-56) represent an adequate model.

The calculations used to develop Tables 11-8 and 11-9, with period 30 as an example, are as follows:

1. Calculate $\hat{Y}_t$ by using the appropriate form of equation (11-53) with updated parameters:

$$\hat{Y}_{30} = \delta_{1,29}\hat{Y}_{29} + \delta_{2,29}\hat{Y}_{28} + \omega_{0,29}X_{27} - \omega_{1,29}X_{26} - \omega_{2,29}X_{25}$$

$$= (1.355)(1.81) + (-.681)(5.77) + (2.105)(1.22) - (1.664)(.08)$$

$$- (-.009)(2.03),$$

$$\hat{Y}_{30} = .973 \quad \text{(see column 4, Table 11-8)}.$$

[See Table 11-9 at Period 29 for parameters $\delta_{1,29}, \delta_{2,29}, \ldots, \omega_{2,29}$.]

2. Obtain the error at Period 30, $e_t = Y_t - \hat{Y}_t$:

$$e_{30} = Y_{30} - \hat{Y}_{30} = -11.62 - .973 = -12.60$$

(see column 5, Table 11-8).

3. Forecast the error by using the equivalent of equation (11-54) with updated parameter values:

$$\hat{e}_{30} = 1.023(e_{29}) - .177(e_{28}) - .325(e_{27})$$

$$= 1.020(-12.73) - .179(-7.99) - .325(-2.49) = -10.74$$

$$= -10.74 \quad \text{(see column 6)}.$$

4. Add the two forecasts, $\hat{Y}_t + \hat{e}_t$, to obtain an overall MARMA forecast:

$$F_{30} = \hat{Y}_{30} + \hat{e}_{30}$$

$$= .973 - 10.74 = -9.77 \quad \text{(see column 7)}.$$

5. Find the total MARMA error, $e'_t = Y_t - F_t$:

$$e'_{30} = Y_{30} - F_{30}$$

$$= -11.62 - 9.77 = -1.85 \quad \text{(see column 8)}.$$

6. Once the error has been found, use it to update the parameters, δ_1, δ_2, ω_0, ω_1, ω_2, ϕ_1, ϕ_2 and ϕ_3:

$$\delta_{1,30} = \delta_{1,29} + 2Ke'^*_{30}\hat{Y}^*_{30-1}$$

$$= 1.355 + 2(.01)[(-1.85)/12.73](1.81/12.73)$$

$$= 1.354,$$

TABLE 11-8 RELEVANT VALUES FOR ESTIMATING MARMA
FORECASTS AND UPDATING THE PARAMETER VALUES
OF EQUATIONS (11-53) AND (11-54)

(1)	(2)	(3)	(4)	(5)	(6)	(7)	(8)
			Forecast Using (11-9)	Error in (11-53) $e_t = Y_t - \hat{Y}_t$	Forecast of Error in (11-53)	Total MARMA Forecast: $\hat{Y}_t + \hat{e}_t$	Total MARMA Error: e_t' in (11-54)
Period	$Y_t = Y_t - \bar{Y}$	$X_t = X_t - \bar{X}$	$\hat{Y}_t$	[(2) − (4)]	in (11-54)]	[(4) + (6)]	[(6) − (7)]

				First Iteration Cycle			
6	−3.25	.82	−.97	−2.27	.00	−.97	−2.27
7	−1.24	1.22	.97	−2.21	−2.29	−1.32	.08
8	2.15	.28	6.45	−4.29	−1.87	4.58	−2.43
9	−.80	.12	6.20	−7.00	−3.27	2.93	−3.73
10	−.51	1.39	5.38	−5.90	−5.77	−.39	−.12
11	−.25	−.99	1.77	−2.01	−3.59	−1.83	1.58
12	−.93	2.79	−1.35	.43	1.06	−.29	−.64
13	3.39	3.52	−.22	3.61	2.56	2.34	1.05
14	.87	1.31	−3.83	4.70	4.21	.38	.49
15	5.86	.23	2.58	3.28	4.06	6.64	−.79
16	9.89	.09	8.90	.99	1.43	10.34	−.45
17	6.18	3.44	7.35	−1.17	−1.01	6.34	−.16
18	3.27	1.80	2.46	.81	−2.37	.09	3.17
19	−5.59	−.04	−1.60	−3.99	.70	−.91	−4.69
20	−1.91	1.58	3.39	−5.30	−3.79	−.40	−1.51
21	−.58	1.79	3.80	−4.38	−4.99	−1.19	.60
22	1.64	.57	−.13	1.77	−2.34	−2.47	4.11
23	2.22	.51	.79	1.44	4.26	5.05	−2.82
24	4.22	2.71	2.35	1.87	2.50	4.85	−.63
25	3.97	2.03	.99	2.99	1.08	2.06	1.91
26	.34	.08	.01	.33	2.29	2.30	−1.96
27	1.79	1.22	4.28	−2.49	−.75	3.53	−1.75
28	−2.23	.33	5.77	−7.99	−3.47	2.30	−4.53
29	−10.92	−2.66	1.81	−12.73	−7.70	−5.89	−5.03
30	−11.62	−1.71	.97	−12.60	−10.74	−9.77	−1.85
⋮	⋮	⋮	⋮	⋮	⋮	⋮	⋮

TABLE 11-8 *Continued*

(1)	(2)	(3)	(4)	(5)	(6)	(7)	(8)
						Total	Total
			Forecast	Error in	Forecast	MARMA	MARMA
			Using	(11-53)	of Error	Forecast:	Error: e_t'
			(11-9)	$e_t = Y_t - \hat{Y}_t$	in (11-53)	$\hat{Y}_t + \hat{e}_t$	in (11-54)
Period	$Y_t = Y_t - \bar{Y}$	$X_t = X_t - \bar{X}$	$\hat{Y}_t$	[(2) − (4)]	[(11-54)]	[(4) + (6)]	[(6) − (7)]

Last (fourth) Iteration Cycle

100	3.89	−.19	−1.76	5.65	5.76	4.00	−.11
101	−5.13	−.29	−7.80	2.67	4.00	−3.80	−1.33
102	−6.17	2.49	−6.28	.10	−.39	−6.66	.49
103	−.99	−.32	.57	−1.56	−2.35	−1.78	.79
104	3.43	1.07	5.16	−1.73	−2.61	2.55	.88
105	12.98	2.37	12.79	.20	−1.60	11.19	1.79
106	9.87	−.91	10.11	−.25	1.06	11.17	−1.31
107	11.10	−.47	8.25	2.85	.31	8.56	2.54
108	10.80	1.24	8.12	2.69	2.99	11.10	−.30
109	2.30	1.06	.02	2.28	2.42	2.44	−.14
110	−3.44	.42	−5.34	1.90	.94	−4.40	.96
111	−4.55	−.14	−4.30	−.25	.67	−3.62	−.92
112	−5.53	1.18	−2.35	−3.19	−1.40	−3.75	−1.78
113	−3.73	−2.33	−1.47	−2.25	−4.00	−5.47	1.74
114	−3.25	1.54	−1.60	−1.64	−1.71	−3.31	.06
115	−1.22	.81	1.38	−2.60	−.21	1.17	−2.39
116	−4.99	.32	−3.74	−1.26	−1.71	−5.45	.46
117	.98	.62	.61	.37	−.32	.29	.69
118	4.23	−.22	2.78	1.45	1.49	4.27	−.04
119	5.69	.02	2.83	2.85	1.89	4.72	.97
120	8.58	−.26	2.93	5.65	2.64	5.57	3.01

$$\delta_{2,30} = \delta_{2,29} + 2Ke_{30}'^* Y_{30-2}^*$$

$$= -.681 + 2(.01)[(-1.85)/12.73](5.77/12.73)$$

$$= -.682,$$

$$\omega_{0,30} = \omega_{0,29} + 2Ke_{30}'^* X_{30-3}^*$$

$$= 2.105 + 2(.01)[(-1.85)/12.73](1.22/12.73)$$

$$= 2.104,$$

$$\omega_{1,30} = \omega_{1,29} + 2Ke'^{*}_{30}X^{*}_{30-4}$$

$$= 1.664 + 2(.01)[(-1.85)/12.73](.08/12.73)$$

$$= 1.664,$$

$$\omega_{2,30} = \omega_{2,29} + 2Ke'^{*}_{30}X^{*}_{30-5}$$

$$= -.009 + 2(.01)[(-1.85)/12.73](2.03/12.73)$$

$$= -.009,$$

TABLE 11-9 ESTIMATED PARAMETER VALUES

Period	Parameters of $\hat{Y}_t$					Noise Parameters of $\hat{e}_t$		
	δ_1	δ_2	ω_0	ω_1	ω_2	ϕ_1	ϕ_2	ϕ_3
	First Iteration Cycle							
6	1.374	−.668	2.160	1.657	.001	1.008	−.159	−.310
7	1.374	−.668	2.160	1.657	.001	1.008	−.159	−.310
8	1.365	−.659	2.139	1.659	−.009	1.008	−.159	−.310
9	1.353	−.661	2.137	1.663	−.009	1.016	−.155	−.306
10	1.353	−.661	2.137	1.663	−.009	1.016	−.155	−.306
11	1.356	−.657	2.137	1.662	−.009	1.012	−.159	−.309
12	1.356	−.658	2.137	1.662	−.009	1.013	−.158	−.307
13	1.355	−.657	2.138	1.662	−.009	1.013	−.159	−.310
14	1.355	−.658	2.137	1.661	−.009	1.016	−.159	−.312
15	1.357	−.658	2.135	1.661	−.008	1.012	−.161	−.312
16	1.356	−.657	2.134	1.662	−.008	1.011	−.163	−.314
17	1.356	−.657	2.134	1.662	−.008	1.011	−.163	−.314
18	1.362	−.650	2.134	1.661	−.011	1.010	−.163	−.311
19	1.358	−.662	2.134	1.661	−.009	1.009	−.160	−.313
20	1.361	−.667	2.127	1.661	−.008	1.016	−.162	−.311
21	1.362	−.668	2.128	1.660	−.008	1.014	−.164	−.310
22	1.373	−.658	2.128	1.655	−.019	1.001	−.179	−.322
23	1.374	−.665	2.125	1.655	−.015	.998	−.170	−.311
24	1.373	−.665	2.124	1.656	−.015	.997	−.172	−.308
25	1.389	−.660	2.128	1.643	−.026	1.010	−.162	−.296
26	1.385	−.670	2.125	1.646	−.018	.996	−.170	−.303
27	1.385	−.674	2.115	1.648	−.016	.995	−.182	−.310
28	1.364	−.674	2.105	1.661	−.013	1.008	−.183	−.325
29	1.355	−.681	2.105	1.664	−.009	1.020	−.179	−.325
30	1.354	−.682	2.104	1.664	−.009	1.023	−.177	−.325
⋮	⋮	⋮	⋮	⋮	⋮	⋮	⋮	⋮

TABLE 11-9 *Continued*

Period	Parameters of $\hat{Y}_t$					Noise Parameters of $\hat{e}_t$		
	δ_1	δ_2	ω_0	ω_1	ω_2	ϕ_1	ϕ_2	ϕ_3
	Last (fourth) Iteration Cycle							
100	1.448	−.699	2.096	1.687	.087	1.064	−.172	−.352
101	1.449	−.699	2.100	1.685	.087	1.061	−.177	−.354
102	1.448	−.700	2.099	1.686	.088	1.061	−.176	−.353
103	1.447	−.702	2.099	1.686	.089	1.061	−.175	−.351
104	1.447	−.704	2.099	1.686	.090	1.060	−.175	−.350
105	1.454	−.704	2.102	1.687	.090	1.058	−.177	−.350
106	1.452	−.705	2.103	1.687	.090	1.058	−.177	−.349
107	1.455	−.701	2.103	1.687	.089	1.058	−.177	−.350
108	1.454	−.701	2.103	1.687	.089	1.058	−.177	−.350
109	1.454	−.701	2.103	1.687	.089	1.058	−.177	−.350
110	1.454	−.699	2.103	1.688	.089	1.058	−.176	−.349
111	1.457	−.699	2.102	1.687	.088	1.057	−.178	−.351
112	1.463	−.692	2.100	1.689	.088	1.057	−.180	−.354
113	1.458	−.701	2.101	1.687	.085	1.051	−.180	−.350
114	1.458	−.701	2.101	1.687	.085	1.051	−.181	−.350
115	1.466	−.694	2.096	1.686	.087	1.059	−.170	−.335
116	1.468	−.696	2.093	1.685	.087	1.055	−.172	−.338
117	1.464	−.695	2.094	1.687	.086	1.054	−.175	−.340
118	1.464	−.695	2.094	1.687	.086	1.054	−.175	−.340
119	1.471	−.693	2.095	1.685	.082	1.058	−.174	−.343
120	1.490	−.674	2.099	1.683	.077	1.077	−.164	−.340

$$\phi_{1,30} = \phi_{1,29} + 2Ke'^*_{30}e^*_{30-1}$$

$$= 1.020 + 2(.01)[(-1.85)/12.73](-12.73/12.73)$$

$$= 1.023,$$

$$\phi_{2,30} = \phi_{2,29} + 2Ke'^*_{30}e^*_{30-2}$$

$$= 1.79 + 2(.01)[(-1.85)/12.73](-7.99/12.73)$$

$$= -.177,$$

TABLE 11-10   FINAL PARAMETER ESTIMATES

Parameter of Model	Initial Estimate from Impulse Response Parameters	Initial Estimate from Ordinary Regression Estimates	Marquardt's Nonlinear Estimation Method	Adaptive Filtering's Steepest Descent Method
Transfer function parameters:				
δ_1	2.55	1.374	1.545	1.49
δ_2	−.616	−.668	−.790	−.674
ω_0	1.877	2.118	2.105	2.099
ω_1	3.701	1.686	1.976	1.683
ω_2	1.453	−.038	−.059	.077
		From the Yule-Walker Equations		
Noise parameters (AR):				
ϕ_1	—	1.008	.963	1.077
ϕ_2	—	−.159	−.163	−.164
ϕ_3	—	−.31	−.326	−.340

$$\phi_{3,30} = \phi_{3,29} + 2Ke_{30}^{\prime*}e_{30-3}^{*}$$

$$= -3.25 + 2(.01)[(-1.85)/12.73](-2.49/12.73)$$

$$= -.325,$$

where $e_{30}^{\prime*} = e_{30}^{\prime}/12.73$. (That is, $e_{30}^{\prime}$ is standardized by dividing it by the largest value in the data used to update the parameter values, $\delta_s^{\prime}$, $\omega_s^{\prime}$, or $\phi_0^{\prime}$. Similarly, $\hat{Y}_{30-i}$, X_{30-i}, and e_{30-i} are standardized and those standardized values denoted with a superscript.)

The updated parameters then can be used in period 31 to find the forecast and the errors associated with it. This updating is continued until the end of the data. Table 11-9 shows the parameter values and their updating for the first training cycle. It takes four such cycles to achieve a minimum MSE.

Figure 11-11 shows the autocorrelation of residuals of the final (fourth) training cycle. As can be seen from Figure 11-11, the final cycle produces residuals that are randomly distributed, implying that the model resulting from the updating process is adequate.

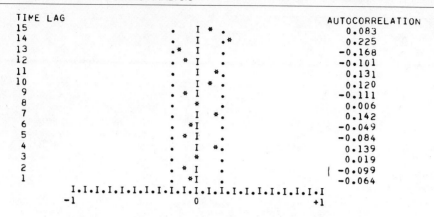

FIGURE 11-11 AUTOCORRELATIONS OF RESIDUALS OF ADAPTIVE FILTERING MARMA MODEL

The final parameter values (see Table 11-10) can be used to forecast future periods. For example, the forecast for period 121 for adaptive filtering is

$$F_{121} = \hat{Y}_{121} + \hat{e}_{121} = .928 + 5.125 = 6.05,$$

since, $\quad \hat{Y}_{121} = 1.49\hat{Y}_{120} - .674\hat{Y}_{119} + 2.099X_{118} - 1.683X_{117} - .077X_{116}$

$$= 1.49(293) - .674(2.83) + 2.099(-.22) - 1.683(.62) - .077(.32)$$

$$= .928$$

and $\quad \hat{e}_{121} = 1.077e_{120} - .164e_{119} - .34e_{118}$

$$= 1.077(5.65) - .164(2.85) - .34(1.45) = 5.125.$$

Since all values are expressed in the form of deviation from the mean, the actual forecast is

$$F_{121} = F_{121} + \overline{Y} = 6.05 + 99.7 = 105.75$$

(see Table 11-8 for values of $\hat{Y}_{121-i}, \hat{X}_{121-i}, e_{121-i}$).

11/4/3 Forecasting

Forecasting with **MARMA** models often involves applying the final parameter values to periods for which data are not available. Depending upon the time delay, b, forecasting in such instances is based on past values of X_t. It is at this point that the true benefits of a **MARMA** model can be realized. If X_t is a good leading indicator of Y_t, then Y_t can be accurately forecast when cyclical changes occur and even X_t values can be forecast using the univariate model generating X_t.

11/5 Identification of *r, s,* and *b* by Contracting the Cross Autocorrelations of the Estimates

As has been indicated, the greatest problem in applying MARMA models lies in the identification of an appropriate model. Randomness in the data mixes with the pattern and makes identification through the cross autos and the impulse response parameters difficult. Priestley (1971) reports an approach for identifying *r, s,* and *b* that is based on differencing or averaging the prewhitened dependent variable. The idea is that differencing or averaging will reduce randomness and clarify the pattern. Even though Priestley's approach requires some trial and error steps, it can be used effectively in cases where serious doubt exists as to the order of *r, s,* and *b.*

The starting point in Priestley's approach is the cross autos between the prewhitened series, Y_{et} and X_{et}. From graphs of these series, it must be determined whether they decline slowly and smoothly to zero or whether they decline to zero while oscillating around zero. In the former case, a difference operator (i.e., second, third difference, etc.) should be applied. In the latter case, a moving average ($N = 2$, $N = 3$, etc.) should be taken. Usually the behavior of the autos will be sufficiently clear to indicate whether differencing or a moving average is required. If it is not clear, both may need to be tried and the one that results in cross autos that are closer to zero will be used. This approach is similar to using different levels of differencing in order to make a series stationary. The user must determine the "best" level of differencing by seeing how fast the autocorrelations drop to zero and how they behave afterwards. In a similar way, the user must decide whether differencing or a moving average makes the cross autos drop to zero faster.

Once the choice between differencing and a moving average has been made, one continues by increasing the order of differencing (from second to third, etc.) or increasing the length of the moving average ($N = 3$, $N = 4$, etc.) until no further improvement can be made in terms of further contracting the cross autos. Then *r, s,* and *b* are identified as follows:

1. The order (value) of *r* is equal to the level of differencing or the length of the moving average, *N,* at which no further contraction of the cross autos is possible.
2. The order of *s* is equal to the number of cross autos of (1) that are significantly different from zero.
3. The order of *b* is equal to the period at which the cross autos of (1) reach their "peak."

As an illustration, Figures 11-12 and 11-13 can be examined and compared to Figure 11-8. Figure 11-8 shows the cross autos between (11-40), Table 11-6, and (11-39), Table 11-5. From this graph of the cross autos, it was previously inferred that $r = 2$, $s = 1$ or $s = 2$, and $b = 3$. An examination of Figures 11-12 and 11-13 reveals the same models but the identification is now easier and the order of s can be inferred to be 2, with some confidence.

The cross autos of Figure 11-8 decline to zero while oscillating. This pattern indicates the need to use a moving average operator on the prewhitened series, Y_{et}. Taking a moving average with $N = 2$, the cross autos of the averaged series, Y_{et}, with the series, X_{et}, can then be found. These cross autos are shown in Figure 11-12.

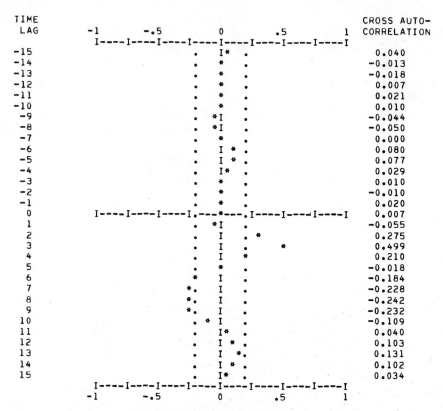

TIME LAG		CROSS AUTO-CORRELATION
-15		0.040
-14		-0.013
-13		-0.018
-12		0.007
-11		0.021
-10		0.010
-9		-0.044
-8		-0.050
-7		0.000
-6		0.080
-5		0.077
-4		0.029
-3		0.010
-2		-0.010
-1		0.020
0		0.007
1		-0.055
2		0.275
3		0.499
4		0.210
5		-0.018
6		-0.184
7		-0.228
8		-0.242
9		-0.232
10		-0.109
11		0.040
12		0.103
13		0.131
14		0.102
15		0.034

FIGURE 11-12 CROSS AUTOS WHEN A MOVING AVERAGE ($N = 2$) IS APPLIED TO THE PREWHITENED SERIES, Y_{et}, OF TABLE 11-6. THE SERIES X_{et} REMAINS THE SAME AS IN TABLE 11-5.

The cross autos of Figure 11-12 are closer to zero (i.e., they have been "contracted") than those of Figure 11-8. Thus $N = 2$ is better from the point of view of contracting the cross autos than was $N = 1$, as shown in Figure 11-8.

The cross autos of Figure 11-12 are also smoother, containing fewer jumps than those of Figure 11-8.

To determine whether a moving average with $N = 2$ is sufficient, Figure 11-13 can be examined. This figure is analogous to Figure 11-12 except that the length of moving average is $N = 3$.

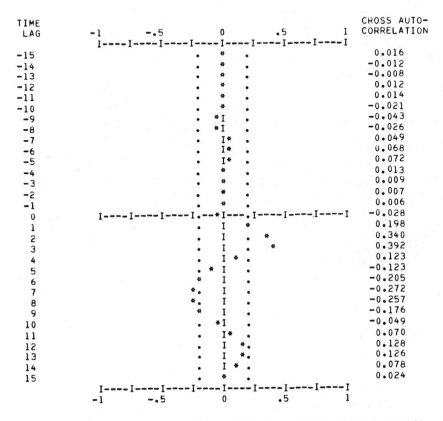

```
TIME                                                     CROSS AUTO-
LAG    -1        -.5        0        .5        1         CORRELATION
       I----I----I----I----I----I----I----I----I
-15                          .    *    .                    0.016
-14                          .    *    .                   -0.012
-13                          .    *    .                   -0.008
-12                          .    *    .                    0.012
-11                          .    *    .                    0.014
-10                          .    *    .                   -0.021
 -9                          .  *I     .                   -0.043
 -8                          .  *I     .                   -0.026
 -7                          .   I*    .                    0.049
 -6                          .   I*    .                    0.068
 -5                          .   I*    .                    0.072
 -4                          .    *    .                    0.013
 -3                          .    *    .                    0.009
 -2                          .    *    .                    0.007
 -1                          .    *    .                    0.006
  0    I----I----I----I.--*I---.I----I----I----I          -0.028
  1                          .   I   *                      0.198
  2                          .   I    .  *                  0.340
  3                          .   I    .   *                 0.392
  4                          .   I *  .                     0.123
  5                          . * I    .                    -0.123
  6                          *    I    .                   -0.205
  7                         *.    I    .                   -0.272
  8                         *. .  I    .                   -0.257
  9                          *    I    .                   -0.176
 10                          .  *I     .                   -0.049
 11                          .   I*    .                    0.070
 12                          .   I *.  .                    0.128
 13                          .   I *.  .                    0.126
 14                          .   I *  .                     0.078
 15                          .    *    .                    0.024
       I----I----I----I----I----I----I----I----I
      -1        -.5        0        .5        1
```

FIGURE 11-13   CROSS AUTOS WHEN $N = 3$ (SEE FIGURE 11-12)

Figure 11-13 is not very different from Figure 11-12. There is no additional contraction in the cross autos, indicating that taking a moving average of $N = 3$ does not give any significant improvement over $N = 2$. In other words, Figure 11-12 should be used to identify the appropriate model. Since the maximum cross autocorrelation occurs with $N = 2$, then $r = 2$. There are two cross autos significantly different from zero in Figure 11-12, indicating that the value of s is 2. The peak cross auto is at a time lag of three, and therefore the value of b is 3.

11/6 Other Multivariate Models

Up to this point, this chapter has discussed multivariate autoregressive/moving average (MARMA) models using the bivariate case as an illustration. The rather difficult process of identifying, estimating, and checking a MARMA model (see Figure 11-2) was explained and illustrated through several examples. The main difficulty in applying MARMA processes lies in the identification phase where b (delay lag), r (number of past terms of the dependent variables), and s (number of past terms of the independent variable minus one) must be specified together with the noise parameters. Once this is done, the remainder of the procedure for a MARMA model is similar to that for a univariable ARMA model (see Chapters 9 and 10).

Even though the methodology described theoretically in this chapter can be extended to any number of independent variables, so far the models used have been bivariate. There are several questions to be answered before a fully multivariate approach can be applied to practical situations. The state of the art is still embryonic and much has to be learned before two or three independent variables can be used with ease. A final question which will have to be answered is that of the additional usefulness (in terms of greater accuracy) of MARMA models over univariate ARMA models. Additional research work and experience with MARMA models is clearly needed before they can be comfortably used for day-to-day application. (Forecasters using ARMA models should not fall into the same trap as econometricians who, during the 1960s, thought that the more complex their forecasting models, the more accurate they would be.) A cost-benefit analysis is needed to determine whether the additional accuracy of MARMA models will compensate for the additional complexity. In the remainder of this section other MARMA methods will be examined whose full potential, the authors believe, will be realized in the future, making them useful forecasting tools.

11/6/1 Intervention Analysis

Intervention analysis is an extension of MARMA concepts. It has been made widely known through an article entitled "Intervention Analysis with Applications to Economic and Environmental Problems," in which Box and Tiao (1975) suggest an approach for recognizing the interventions (effects) of some independent variable on a dependent variable of interest. Their approach is aimed at answering questions such as How will sales be affected if the price is increased by 20%? or How will sales be affected if a promotional campaign is started on July 1? These types of questions can be considered by using multiple regression. However, multiple regression assumes a steady state where transitional effects have been eliminated. In practice, one is as interested in the transition period as in periods where the new equilibrium has been reached. The effects of the Arab oil embargo, for example, were not felt overnight. It was almost a year before their full impact was felt by many world economies.

Intervention analysis is aimed at identifying the type of response a dependent variable will exhibit, given some step change in an independent variable(s). Box and Tiao (1975) have shown the impulse response on the dependent variable for different types of changes. The objective is to identify an appropriate model using a process similar to that described in Section 11/3 and to estimate its parameters. If the diagnostic check on the residuals of the intervention model shows no pattern, it indicates that the identified model is adequate and that the effects of the intervention (the step or other drastic change) are as postulated; otherwise, a new intervention response model must be specified. Finally, Glass et al. (1975) have written a book on the subject providing a detailed treatment of this approach and providing examples of its application.

11/6/2 Kalman Filters

The forecasting models examined in this book can be classified into two categories: (1) fixed models having fixed parameters and fixed variances; and (2) fixed models with varying parameters and variances. The first category includes all forecasting methods discussed so far with the exception of adaptive-response-rate exponential smoothing and adaptive filtering. (Although these two methods postulate a fixed model, they adapt the parameter values to deal with changing conditions in the data.)

Fixed models with fixed parameters require stationarity of both the mean and the variance throughout the entire range of observations. That is why so much effort is spent to make the data stationary in their mean (through differencing) and in their variance (through appropriate power—logarithmic, square root, etc.—transformations). Otherwise, the results are not meaningful from a statistical point of view. Classical statistical estimation theory has not been able to directly remove the assumption of stationarity, which causes problems of significant practical consequence. For example, when the data pattern changes as with a step or trend, or when there are transient shifts, classical statistical theory will treat those as random effects or temporary shifts. If the changes are permanent, a new forecasting model will have to be specified to deal with the new equilibrium conditions. However, the model will only be good for those new equilibrium conditions when fixed patterns exist.

Classical statistical methods must be used in conjunction with other control processes (see Section 3/10/6; Page 1957, 1961; and Barnard 1959) if permanent or significant changes in the data are to be identified. Methods based on classical statistics cannot sense a shift by themselves and once a shift has taken place, the model will do badly because it will still be tuned to the specification of the old set of data.

Adaptive-response-rate exponential smoothing and adaptive filtering, on the other hand, can deal much better with step changes and transient situations because they update their parameters in a way that takes account of changes in pattern. Furthermore, they can deal with changes in trend much better than fixed model/fixed parameter methods. However, even these two methods cannot do as well as the Kalman filters, which can deal with variable models, variable parameters, and variable variances simultaneously.

Classical statistical estimation attempts to minimize the MSE of the fitted model. This criterion is appropriate for the past, but may be inappropriate for the future. If the criterion is to minimize the MSE of the model fitted to historical data, classical estimation can provide a minimum MSE by assuming a fixed model with fixed parameters and fixed variances. However, when the MSE of the future is to be minimized, adaptive-response-rate exponential smoothing, adaptive filtering, or the Kalman filters can do as well for future periods as classical estimation procedure, even when the data pattern does not change. In addition, these methods may do much better when there are changes in the pattern of the data, since such changes will be identified and used in forecasting.

For example, when β in (3-11) is set equal to zero, the adaptive-response-rate exponential smoothing becomes analogous to single exponential smoothing and the initial α will be constant. Similarly, adaptive filtering becomes analogous to the Box-Jenkins method when $k = 0$, or k takes an arbitrarily small positive value, since the change in the parameter values from one period to the next will be zero or extremely small [see (9-15) and (9-32)]. However, when b and k are between 0 and 1 respectively, the parameters will change from one period to the next in a way consistent with changes in the data. Finally, experience and judgment about the future can be incorporated through b and k. For example, when patterns are thought to be changing, the values of b or k can be changed to make the system more responsive to these changes. On the other hand, when the pattern is thought to be continuing as in the past, the values of b or k can be reduced. That gives additional flexibility in forecasting in adapting the model to the situation.

Kalman filters are the most general approach to statistical estimation and prediction. It has been shown by Harrison and Stevens (1975a) that all forecasting methods are special cases of Kalman filters. These filters can deal with changes in the model, the parameters, and the variances. The difficulty with Kalman filters is that many technical questions have not yet been answered satisfactorily. The approach itself has grown out of engineering. Consequently, many statisticians and operations researchers know little about it or find it difficult to understand because it is most often described in *state space notation*. With the exception of the work of Harrison and Stevens (1971, 1975a, and 1975b) little research has been reported on the applicability of Kalman or other filters to forecasting (see Schneeweiss 1971, Chang and Fyffe 1971, and Mehra 1973). Furthermore, many practical difficulties still exist as to initial estimates for parameters, variances, and covariances and for the transition matrix. In order to point out these problems and to show the substantial potential of the Kalman filters, a nontechnical introduction to the topic will be presented here. The interested reader is encouraged to examine the references suggested in the end of the chapter for an in-depth study of Kalman filters.

Kalman filtering consists of combining two independent estimates to form a weighted estimate or prediction. One estimate can be a prior prediction or an estimate based on prior knowledge, and the other a prediction based on new information (new data). The purpose of the Kalman filter is to combine these two pieces of information to obtain an improved estimate. It is similar to the Bayesian approach, which combines prior and sampling information to form a posterior distribution (see Raiffa 1968). The name *Bayesian forecasting* is used by Harrison and Stevens as synonymous with *Kalman filters*.

In order to illustrate the Kalman filter, the simple univariate case will be examined first, then its extension to multivariate data for fixed models will be described. Finally, its application for a model of varying characteristics will be illustrated.

Univariate data

If F_t is the forecast for period t, and X_t is the latest available information, the forecast for period $t + 1$ can be expressed as a weighted sum of F_t and X_t,

$$F_{t+1} = \omega X_t + (1 - \omega)F_t. \tag{11-57}$$

Equation (11-57) is the same as equation (3-5) of single exponential smoothing. If the variance of X_t and F_t, say σ_x^2 and σ_F^2, is known, the overall variance of (11-57) can be calculated as the weighted square sum of σ_x and σ_F. That is

$$\sigma^2 = (1 - \omega)^2 \sigma_F^2 + \omega^2 \sigma_x^2. \tag{11-58}$$

Expression (11-58) can be differentiated with respect to ω to obtain the value of the parameter ω for which (11-58) is a minimum. This gives

$$\frac{d\sigma^2}{d\omega} = -2(1 - \omega)\sigma_F^2 + 2\omega\sigma_x = 0. \tag{11-59}$$

Solving for ω^* gives:

$$\omega^* = \frac{\sigma_F^2}{\sigma_F^2 + \sigma_x^2}. \tag{11-60}$$

If equation (11-60) is substituted into (11-57), the result is

$$F_{t+1} = \frac{\sigma_F^2}{\sigma_F^2 + \sigma_x^2} X_t + \left(1 - \frac{\sigma_F^2}{\sigma_F^2 + \sigma_x^2}\right) F_t$$

$$= \frac{\sigma_F^2}{\sigma_F^2 + \sigma_x^2} X_t + \frac{\sigma_x^2}{\sigma_F^2 + \sigma_x^2} F_t \qquad (11\text{-}61)$$

$$= \frac{\sigma_F^2 X_t + \sigma_x^2 F_t}{\sigma_F^2 + \sigma_x^2}. \qquad (11\text{-}62)$$

If the variance of X_t, σ_x^2, is the same as the variance of F_t, σ_F^2, and if X_t and F_t are to be weighted equally [see (11-60)] using weights of 1/2, then as long as the uncertainty does not change, equation (11-61) will result in a constant α value of

$$\omega = \frac{\sigma_F^2}{\sigma_F^2 + \sigma_x^2} = 1/2.$$

However, if the uncertainty about the future increases, the variance of σ_x^2 will become larger. That will increase the denominator of the right-hand side terms of (11-61) and the numerator of the second term of (11-61). Thus, relatively more weight will be given to F_t than to X_t. The opposite is true if the uncertainty about the future decreases ; relatively more weight will be given to X_t and relatively less to F_t.

The ratio of the variances plays a role completely analogous to that of α_t in adaptive-response-rate exponential smoothing [see (3-10)] or ϕ_{it} in adaptive filtering [see (9-15)]. Thus, in the case of a Kalman filter, ω_t (the equivalent of X_t) is given by

$$\omega_t = \frac{\sigma_F^2}{\sigma_F^2 + \sigma_x^2}. \qquad (11\text{-}63)$$

There is an operational difficulty in reconciling (11-63) and (3-10), however. Expression (3-10) can be calculated from past data, while expression (11-63) requires knowledge of the variance, σ_x^2, which is not readily available. Furthermore, the terms of (3-10) can be routinely supplied, while some provisions must be made to estimate σ_x^2 as an input to (11-63).

Furthermore, an estimate of the overall variance of F_{t+1}, σ_{F+1}^2, can be updated by substituting (11-60) into (11-58) to obtain

$$\sigma_{F+1}^2 = \left(1 - \frac{\sigma_F^2}{\sigma_F^2 + \sigma_x^2}\right)^2 \sigma_F^2 + \left(\frac{\sigma_F^2}{\sigma_F^2 + \sigma_x^2}\right)^2 \sigma_x^2$$

$$= \frac{\sigma_x^4 \sigma_F^2}{(\sigma_F^2 + \sigma_x^2)^2} + \frac{\sigma_F^4 \sigma_x^2}{(\sigma_F^2 + \sigma_x^2)^2}, \qquad (11\text{-}64)$$

$$\sigma_{F+1}^2 = \frac{\sigma_x^2 \sigma_F^2}{\sigma_F^2 + \sigma_x^2}. \qquad (11\text{-}65)$$

Expression (11-65) indicates that the variance at period $t + 1$ can be updated by combining the variance of up to period t, $\sigma_F{}^2$, with the variance of period t, $\sigma_x{}^2$. Expression (11-65) can be put into a more convenient form by expressing it as a function of ω^* using (11-60).

Rearranging (11-60) by subtracting unity from both sides and multiplying by minus, gives

$$(1 - \omega^*) = \frac{\sigma_F{}^2 + \sigma_x{}^2}{\sigma^2} - \frac{\sigma_F{}^2}{\sigma_F{}^2 + \sigma_x{}^2} = \frac{\sigma_x{}^2}{\sigma_F{}^2 + \sigma_x{}^2}. \tag{11-66}$$

Substituting (11-66) into its equivalent form of (11-65) gives

$$\sigma_{F+1}^2 = \sigma_F{}^2 \frac{\sigma_x{}^2}{\sigma_F{}^2 + \sigma_x{}^2} = \sigma_F{}^2(1 - \omega^*). \tag{11-67}$$

In terms of the Kalman filters discussed so far, the following can be said:

1. An updated estimate combining new and old information can be made.
2. The weights combining new and old information are a function of the variances.
3. Both the estimates and their variances can be computed recursively (Kalman filtering is an infinite memory filter).
4. There will be some difficulties in obtaining estimates of the variance of X_t.

Multivariate data

The multivariate Kalman filter is analogous to the univariate form and can be obtained by replacing scalers by matrices. This gives

$$\mathbf{F}_{t+1} = \mathbf{W}\mathbf{X}_t + (\mathbf{I} - \mathbf{W})\mathbf{F}_t \tag{11-68}$$

Equation (11-68) is similar to (11-57) except that $\mathbf{F}_{t+1}$, $\mathbf{X}_t$ and $\mathbf{F}$ are vectors, $\mathbf{W}$ is the vector of weights and I is the identity matrix. Going from equation (11-68) to the expressions required for updating the weight vector $\mathbf{W}$ and the variance-covariance matrix (in the multivariate case the covariances between the $\mathbf{X}_t$ estimates must be estimated in addition to the variances) is not much different from the univariate case except that it involves matrix algebra.

The Kalman filter examined so far provides for varying parameters and variances, but still assumes a fixed model. This last constraint can be removed by introducing the transition matrix, $\phi_{t,t+1}$, which indicates how the parameters of the model change from period t to period $t + 1$. The forecasting error of period t is

$$\mathbf{F}_t = \mathbf{X}_t - \mathbf{e}_t.$$

The data for period t, $\mathbf{X}_t$, can be expressed as the actual pattern, $\mathbf{X}'_t$, plus the error, $\mathbf{u}_t$. Thus

$$\mathbf{X}_t = \mathbf{H}_t\mathbf{X}'_t + \mathbf{u}_t, \tag{11-69}$$

where $\mathbf{H}_t$ is the observation matrix at period t.

The best forecast of the pattern for period $t + 1$, assuming some change in the model, is given by

$$\mathbf{X}'_{t+1} = \boldsymbol{\phi}_{t,t+1}\mathbf{X}'_t + \mathbf{Z}_t, \tag{11-70}$$

where $\boldsymbol{\phi}_{t,t+1}$ is the transition matrix showing how the model changes from period t to $t + 1$ and $\mathbf{Z}_t$ is white noise affecting the real process generating the $\mathbf{X}_t$.

Equations (11-69) and (11-70) describe the Kalman filtering system in its most general form. They can be solved recursively using equations (11-71), (11-72), and (11-73).

Given some initial estimates, an estimate $\hat{\mathbf{X}}'_t$ of $\mathbf{X}'_t$ can be made as

$$\hat{\mathbf{X}}'_t = \boldsymbol{\phi}_{t-1,t}\hat{\mathbf{X}}'_{t-1} + \mathbf{K}_1(\mathbf{X}_t - \mathbf{H}_t\boldsymbol{\phi}_{t-1,t}\hat{\mathbf{X}}'_{t-1}, \tag{11-71}$$

where the gain, $\mathbf{K}_t$, is

$$\mathbf{K}_t = \mathbf{P}_{t-1,t}\mathbf{H}_t^T(\mathbf{H}_t\mathbf{P}_{t/t-1}\mathbf{H}_t^T + \mathbf{R}_t)^{-1} \tag{11-72}$$

(the superscript T denotes the transpose of H, and -1 denotes the inverse of the expression in the parentheses),

$$\text{where} \quad \mathbf{P}_{t-1,t} = \boldsymbol{\phi}_{t-1,t}\mathbf{P}_{t-1}\boldsymbol{\phi}^T_{t-1,t} + \mathbf{Q}_{t-1}, \tag{11-73}$$

where $\mathbf{Q}_{t-1}$ is the covariance of $\mathbf{Z}_t$ in (11-70).

In addition to estimating the variance-covariance matrix, the transition matrix, $\boldsymbol{\phi}_{t-1,t}$, must also be estimated. That may be difficult, but Harrison and Stevens (1971, 1975a, and 1975b) claim that the system is quite robust to the transition matrix values, and that they can therefore be set to fixed values, since they have a minimal effect on the results. However, if that is true then the forecasting system will not be responsive to changes or it will overreact to them, depending upon the way the transition matrix is set up.

11/7 Conclusions

In this chapter a wide range of multivariate ARMA models has been presented. Unfortunately, their utilization for forecasting is still in a period of testing and research with the exception of bivariate ARMA models, which can be used with fewer difficulties than the other models. The properties, advantages, and weaknesses of these models are not well known and much more must be done before multivariate time-series methods can be applied routinely to business and economic forecasting situations. Except for some applications of bivariate MARMA models (Zellner and Palm 1974, Barth et al. 1975, Subba-Rao et al. 1975) not much work has been reported in the literature. The following practical problems are associated with MARMA models: (1) they are very difficult to use; (2) they are costly to apply for day-to-day forecasting purposes; (3) the required lead/lag relationships between the variables often are not constant; and (4) their advantages, in terms of better accuracy, over univariate ARMA models have not been proven beyond reasonable doubt.

Multiple time-series analysis has been studied since the early 1950s (see Whittle 1953 and Quenouille 1957). As was the case with univariate models, however, MARMA methods did not become widely known until Box and Jenkins's work appeared in 1970. Only more recently has extensive interest in MARMA models appeared. Box and Jenkins have contributed substantially by providing a unified terminology, although they refer to MARMA models as transfer functions, a term used mainly in control engineering. MARMA models will undoubtedly evolve with time to provide a more complete methodology for dealing with estimation and prediction problems. The Kalman filters, examined only briefly here, could provide the unifying force to bring together many diverse forecasting methodologies.

REFERENCES AND SELECTED BIBLIOGRAPHY

Anderson, B. D. O. 1971. "A Qualitative Introduction to Wiener and Kalman-Bucy Filters." In *Proceedings of The Institute of Radio and Electricity Engineering, Australia.* March 1971, pp. 93–103.

Barnard, G. A. 1959. "Control Charts and Stochastic Processes." *Journal of the Royal Statistical Society*, Series B, Vol. 21, pp. 239–71.

Barth, J., M. Phaup, and D. A. Pierce. 1975. "Regional Impact of Open-Market Operations on Member Bank Reserves." *Journal of Economics and Business*, Fall, pp. 36–40.

Bartlett, P. S. 1955. *Stochastic Processes.* Cambridge, England: Cambridge University Press.

Box, G. E. P., and G. M. Jenkins. 1976. *Time Series Analysis Forecasting and Control*, rev. ed. San Francisco: Holden-Day (earlier edition 1970).

Box, G. E. P., and G. C. Tiao. 1975. "Intervention Analysis with Applications to Economic and Environmental Problems." *Journal of the American Statistical Association*, Vol. 70, No. 349, pp. 70–79.

Chang, S. H., and D. E. Fyffe. 1971. "Estimation of Forecast Errors for Seasonal-Style-Goods Sales." *Management Science*, Vol. 18, No. 2, pp. B89–B96.

Gelb, A. 1974. *Applied Optimal Estimation.* Cambridge, Mass.: MIT Press.

Glass, G. V., V. L. Wilson, and J. M. Gottman. 1975. *Design and Analysis of Time-Series Experiments.* Colorado. Colorado University Press.

Harrison, P. J., and C. F. Stevens. 1971. "A Bayesian Approach to Short-Term Forecasting." *Operational Research Quarterly*, Vol. 22, No. 4. pp. 341–62.

———. 1975a. "Bayesian Forecasting," University of Warwick, Working Paper No. 13.

———. 1975b. "Bayesian Forecasting in Action: Case Studies," University of Warwick, Working Paper No. 14.

Kalman, R. E. 1960. "A New Approach to Linear Filtering and Prediction Problems." *Journal of Basic Engineering*, D82, March, pp. 35–44.

Kalman, R. E., and R. S. Bucy. 1961. "New Results in Linear Filtering and Prediction Theory." *Journal of Basic Engineering*, D83, March, pp. 95–107.

Marquardt, D. W. 1963. "An Algorithm for Least-Squares Estimation of Nonlinear Parameters." *Journal of the Society for Industrial and Applied Mathematics*, Vol. 2, pp. 431–41.

Mehra, R. K. 1973. "A Mechanical Forecasting System for Financial Variables Using Kalman Filtering and Maximum Likelihood Estimation." Progress Report No. 1. New York: Baker Weeks. February.

Pack, D. J. 1974. "Computer Programs for the Analysis of Univariate Time Series Models and Single Input Transfer Function Models Using the Methods of Box and Jenkins." Ohio State University, December.

———. 1975. "Revealing the True Nature of Time Series Interrelationships." Working Paper. Ohio State University.

Page, E. S. 1957. "On Problems in Which a Change in Parameters Occurs at an Unknown Point." *Biometrica*, Vol. 4, 1957, pp. 249–260.

———. 1961. "Cumulative Sum Charts." *Technometrics*, Vol. 3, pp. 1–10.

Priestley, M. B. 1971. "Fitting Relationships between Time Series." In *International Statistical Institute Proceedings*. Washington, D.C.

Quenouille, M. H. 1957. *The Analysis of Multiple Time Series*. New York: Hafner Publishing Co.

Raiffa, H. 1968. *Decision Analysis*. Reading, Mass.: Addison-Wesley.

Schneeweiss, C. A. 1971. "Smoothing Production by Inventory—An Application of the Wiener Filtering Theory." *Management Science*, Vol. 17, No. 7, pp. 472–99.

Subba-Rao, U. V., R. Schroth, and A. Fask. 1975. "Application of Box-Jenkins Transfer Function Methodology to Marketing Problems." Presented at the 1975 Joint Institute of Management Sciences/Operations Research Society of America Conference.

Trigg, D. W., and D. H. Leach. 1967. "Exponential Smoothing with an Adaptive Response Rate." *Operational Research Quarterly*, Vol. 18, pp. 53–59.

Whittle, P. 1953. "The Analysis of Multiple Stationary Time Series." *Journal of the Royal Statistical Society*, B, Vol. 15, pp. 125–39.

Zellner, A., and F. Palm. 1974. "Time Series Analysis and Simultaneous Equation Econometric Models." *Journal of Econometrics*, Vol. 2, pp. 17–54.

PART FIVE
QUALITATIVE AND TECHNOLOGICAL METHODS

Although this portion of the book continues to discuss methodologies for forecasting, the techniques it describes are substantially different from those described in previous chapters. The main distinction is that, rather than basing forecasts exclusively on historical data and the information they contain, these methodologies seek to make effective use of judgmental processes and management experience and knowledge in arriving at forecasts.

Chapter 12 examines the problems associated with predicting business cycles and, more generally, turning points. One of the most useful techniques developed in this area and described in Chapter 12 is the use of leading indicators. Other methods that are more subjective in nature and that seek to combine managerial judgment with the results of quantitative forecasts are also described.

Many of the more subjective methods of forecasting are described in Chapter 13. These are frequently used when an organization first approaches the forecasting function. They tend not to require substantial computations and mathematical background and thus can be used very directly. However, experience has shown that these techniques can produce much more accurate and suitable results when used with systematic procedures and guidelines than when used on a strictly informal basis.

In Chapter 14 the forecasting methodologies commonly referred to as technological, or qualitative, methods are described. These approaches seek to use the creative potential of experts in order to more thoroughly identify long-run outcomes and to aid in the long-range planning process. Additionally, some of these methodologies are normative in nature and seek to identify desired future outcomes and alternative plans for achieving them, as well as simply providing forecasts of what is likely to be. Several different approaches, the best known of which is the Delphi method, are described in Chapter 14. A relatively new approach, that of catastrophe theory, is also described. The authors feel this method will gain much greater acceptance in the next few years because of its ability to predict behavior where multimodality exists in terms of the outcome, rather than simply predicting the most likely outcome and some distribution around that.

12 PREDICTING THE CYCLE

12/1 Introduction

Economic activity generally exhibits a longer-term cyclical pattern called the *business cycle* (periods of expansion followed by periods of contraction). The duration and intensity of such a cyclical pattern varies from one cycle to another and is extremely difficult to predict. Schumpeter 1939, a noted economist, has claimed that there are cycles of one to ten years' duration within longer cycles of about thirty years' duration. Prediction of cyclical changes is extremely critical to many organizations but is generally the component of a time series that is hard to predict accurately (see Chapter 4). This poor accuracy is due mainly to the length and intensity of cycles, which vary radically from one cycle to the next (see, for example, Table 12-4).

To illustrate the importance and influence of the cycle on forecasting accuracy, the data for monthly sales of writing paper in France of Table 10-2 and the Box-Jenkins model shown in equation (10-50) will be used to prepare a forecast for the twelve months of 1973. Forecasts using the method of generalized adaptive filtering (GAF) will also be prepared to illustrate that the cyclical component problem is not dependent on a single method, but is rather influenced by the pattern of the cycle itself.

The year 1973 was fairly normal for the French economy. There was a minor slowdown in the rate of growth in September and October, but in November the economy resumed its normal growth. Table 12-1 shows the forecasts obtained using Box-Jenkins and generalized adaptive filtering for up to twelve months ahead. These forecasts were found using 120 data points (up through December 1972). Since the actual values for 1973 are known, a comparison can be made of the accuracy of the two forecasting methods. Table 12-1 shows this comparison using the *mean absolute percentage error* (MAPE). The MAPE for either forecasting method is between 5% and 6%.

434

TABLE 12-1 FORECASTING ACCURACY OF BOX-JENKINS AND GENERALIZED ADAPTIVE FILTERING FOR THE TWELVE MONTHS OF 1973 (DATA OF TABLE 10-2)

Month	Period	Actual Sales	Box-Jenkins		Generalized Adaptive Filtering	
			Forecast	% Error	Forecast	% Error
Jan.	121	946.23	946.11	.01	908.63	3.97
Feb.	122	1013.38	996.70	1.65	1000.99	1.22
Mar.	123	1051.97	1029.98	2.09	973.05	7.5
Apr.	124	1019.86	981.83	3.73	973.51	4.54
May	125	1007.72	929.50	7.76	861.09	14.55
June	126	1020.73	1022.41	−.16	1016.12	.45
July	127	867.26	868.72	−.17	843.84	2.69
Aug.	128	326.12	423.36	−29.82	357.24	−9.55
Sept.	129	911.28	894.53	1.84	859.4	5.69
Oct.	130	960.00	978.55	−1.93	896.7	6.59
Nov.	131	870.00	907.49	−4.31	860.47	1.09
Dec.	132	915.00	999.30	−9.21	994.71	−8.72
				MAPE = 5.22%		MAPE = 5.55%

It is interesting now to see the effect of a change in the cycle on the forecasting accuracy in this situation. If one assumes that only the data up through 1973 are known (132 values), forecasts for the twelve months of 1974 can then be obtained using the Box-Jenkins approach and the generalized adaptive filtering approach. The results are shown in Table 12-2.

Table 12-2 indicates that both models did well up through October of 1974, and then the errors increased substantially. (Through October the MAPE for the Box-Jenkins forecasts is 5.42% and for GAF is 6.26%, both within the same range as the 1973 errors.) The forecasting performance deteriorates from an accuracy point of view, if the last four months of 1974 and the first two months of 1975 are forecast as shown in Table 12-3. The MAPE is 41.36% and 34.56% for Box-Jenkins and GAF respectively. In contrast to the 1973 performance and the first eight months of 1974, these are very inaccurate forecasts.

From previous chapters, it will be recalled that formal forecasting methods attempt to separate randomness and pattern and then extrapolate the latter. Thus, at the end of 1972 (see Table 12-1), the method simply extrapolates the pattern of trend-cycle of the previous years. As long as the trend-cycle continues to behave

TABLE 12-2 FORECASTING ACCURACY OF BOX-JENKINS AND GENERALIZED ADAPTIVE FILTERING FOR THE TWELVE MONTHS OF 1974

Month	Period	Actual Sales	Box-Jenkins		Generalized Adaptive Filtering	
			Forecast	% Error	Forecast	% Error
Jan.	133	975.	961.98	1.33	926.31	4.99
Feb.	134	1039.59	1020.42	1.84	1011.78	2.67
Mar.	135	1174.84	1054.59	10.24	1041.71	11.33
Apr.	136	973.27	1014.22	−4.21	1028.4	−5.67
May	137	1063.44	977.20	8.11	1009.75	5.04
June	138	1110.79	1038.62	6.50	1028.77	7.38
July	139	834.24	884.83	−6.06	872.93	−4.64
Aug.	140	381.42	398.02	−4.35	334.73	12.24
Sept.	141	965.79	917.51	5.00	912.90	5.47
Oct.	142	926.18	986.91	−6.56	955.58	−3.18
Nov.	143	724.34	907.86	−25.34	857.72	−18.42
Dec.	144	703.69	981.79	−39.52	909.42	−29.24
				MAPE = 9.92%		MAPE = 9.19%

as in the past, forecasting will be quite accurate. However, at the end of 1973 there is no way for the typical time-series forecasting method to know that there will be a downturn in October, November, and December of 1974. Since such a downturn has not occurred in the past in a consistent manner, a time-series quantitative method cannot predict it. That accounts for the large errors at the end of 1974 and the beginning of 1975 (see Table 12-3) that were found using 140 data points and forecasting up to 6 periods ahead.

Forecasting requires two types of predictions. The first is for the continuation of existing conditions, as shown in Table 12-1. The other involves the prediction of turning points, as necessitated by the data shown in Tables 12-2 and 12-3. In the first case, one or more of the quantitative time-series methods described in previous chapters will do well. In such cases, one simply predicts a continuation of the cyclical pattern. However, when the first signs of cyclical changes appear, additional work is required to predict those changes of the cycle. Some of the different approaches that are available to predict such turning points will be discussed in this chapter. Several things should be clear, however: forecasting will be more difficult, errors are likely to be larger, and much more time

TABLE 12-3 FORECASTING ACCURACY OF BOX-JENKINS AND GENERALIZED ADAPTIVE FILTERING FOR SEPTEMBER 1974 THROUGH FEBRUARY 1975

Month	Period	Actual Sales	Box-Jenkins		Generalized Adaptive Filtering	
			Forecast	% Error	Forecast	% Error
1974						
Sept.	141	965.79	934.09	3.3	961.73	.44
Oct.	142	926.18	999.13	−7.9	968.49	−4.59
Nov.	143	724.34	919.27	−26.97	862.47	−19.13
Dec.	144	703.69	993.27	−41.08	907.29	−28.87
1975						
Jan.	145	560.00	1011.12	−80.56	965.54	−72.42
Feb.	146	570.00	1073.53	−88.39	1036.95	−81.56
				MAPE = 41.36%		MAPE = 34.56%

and effort will be required for effecting forecasting than is the case when no cyclical changes are in sight.

The remainder of this chapter will describe briefly business cycles and their causes and will discuss some of the methods available for predicting fluctuations in the economic cycle. As subjective as those methods are, they can be extremely useful because the stakes are high when an inaccurate prediction is made of the level of economic activity.

12/2 Business Cycles

Business cycles have received attention since the early stages of the western economic system and probably have been studied more extensively than any other economic phenomenon. The reason for such interest has been the human misery and suffering that business cycles cause when their downswings reach depression magnitudes. Classical economists have accepted the existence of cycles, feeling that they are temporary deviations from equilibrium that can correct themselves without outside interference. The classical economist's viewpoint has been expressed in Say's law, which asserts that supply creates its own demand. In other words, supply and demand are equal and deviations are only temporary.

The classical viewpoint has troubled many, mainly because depressions have appeared often during the last two centuries. The work of Keynes has probably had the most profound effect on government thinking about the causes and cures of inflation and depression cycles. Keynes advocated direct government interference through fiscal and monetary policies in order to maintain the economic equilibrium. Keynes's view has been widely adopted today and many governments actively intervene in the economic arena. It has generally been thought that Keynesian policies have been successful in averting depressions. Until the 1970s it was even believed that, modified as they were, they could avert all serious recessions. Some economists even believed that recessions were a thing of the past (see Beman 1976). The 1974–75 recession, the most serious since the 1930s, has reopened the question and made both government officials and private citizens realize that business cycles and their effects are here to stay. Attempts to predict the cycle have received renewed attention recently and will undoubtedly be improved substantially in the next few years.

Table 12-4 shows the economic cycles in the United States between 1850 and 1976. An examination of the table reveals the following:

1. The length of an expansion in economic activity can vary from 10 to 105 months. Even in the postwar period, which is thought to have been relatively free of major economic upheavals, the duration of expansion varies from 25 to 105 months.
2. The length of a contraction in economic activity has varied from 7 to 65 months. In the postwar period, however, the range of variation is much shorter, 9 to 13 months. This is an encouraging sign suggesting that governments may have been more successful in combating recessions.
3. The duration of a full cycle also varies considerably, ranging from 28 to 117 months.

Table 12-4 particularly reveals the futility of trying to predict the cycle mechanically, simply by analyzing the behavior of past cycles. After a lengthy study of cycles, Mitchell (1951) concluded that there may be some features common to all cycles, but at the same time each cycle is unique. It is with this background that one attempts to predict changes in the cycle. There are no quantitative approaches that will guarantee success, since cycles are unique and the length and intensity of each one varies. Rather, subjective methods must be coupled with judgment and the continuous monitoring of macroeconomic statistics in order to predict cyclical fluctuations. Unlike quantitative methods, the success of such predictions depends largely on the personal skills of the forecaster who must learn and develop the ability to deal with cyclical factors. Fortunately, several methods are available that provide a great deal of information about the state of economic activity and its future direction. These methods will be presented in the remainder

TABLE 12-4 U.S. BUSINESS CYCLES 1850 THROUGH 1976

Business Cycle			Duration (months) of:		
Trough	Peak	Trough	Expansion	Contraction	Full Cycle
Dec. 1854	June 1857	Dec. 1858	30	18	48
Dec. 1858	Oct. 1860	June 1861	22	8	30
June 1861	Apr. 1865	Dec. 1867	46	32	78
Dec. 1867	June 1869	Dec. 1870	18	18	36
Dec. 1870	Oct. 1873	Mar. 1879	34	65	99
Mar. 1879	Mar. 1882	May 1885	36	38	74
May 1885	Mar. 1887	Apr. 1888	22	13	35
Apr. 1888	July 1890	May 1891	27	10	37
May 1891	Jan. 1893	June 1894	20	17	37
June 1894	Dec. 1895	June 1897	18	18	36
June 1897	June 1899	Dec. 1900	24	18	42
Dec. 1900	Sept. 1902	Aug. 1904	21	23	44
Aug. 1904	May 1907	June 1908	33	13	46
June 1908	Jan. 1910	Jan. 1912	19	24	43
Jan. 1912	Jan. 1913	Dec. 1914	12	23	35
Dec. 1914	Aug. 1918	Mar. 1919	44	7	51
Mar. 1919	Jan. 1920	July 1921	10	18	28
July 1921	May 1923	July 1924	22	14	36
July 1924	Oct. 1926	Nov. 1927	27	13	40
Nov. 1927	Aug. 1929	Mar. 1933	21	43	64
Mar. 1933	May 1937	June 1938	50	13	63
June 1938	Feb. 1945	Oct. 1945	80	8	88
Postwar Cycles					
Oct. 1945	Nov. 1948	Oct. 1949	37	11	48
Oct. 1949	July 1953	Aug. 1954	45	13	58
Aug. 1954	July 1957	Apr. 1958	35	9	44
Apr. 1958	May 1960	Feb. 1961	25	9	34
Feb. 1961	Nov. 1969	Nov. 1970	105	12	117
Nov. 1970	Aug. 1974*	June 1975	45	10	56

* There is some disagreement as to whether the start of the recession was November 1973 or August 1974. The latter has been assumed here.

of this chapter, and in the next chapter an approach will be described for combining the results of these methods with the subjective feelings of the decision maker to obtain a unique forecast of the cycle.

12/3 Causes of Business Cycles

There are numerous theories as to what causes cycles in economic activity. These theories cite causes ranging from random events, such as a good or bad harvest, to necessary readjustments in the economic system. Economists who have studied this topic include Dauten and Valentine (1974, Parts 1 and 2), Evans (1969, Part II), Schumpeter (1939), Mitchell (1913 and 1951), and Mass (1976). In spite of the fact that cycles have been studied extensively there is little agreement as to their real causes and the means of preventing them. For the purposes of this book, it is useful to discuss two possible causes of the business cycle—capital spending and inventory levels—since their influence on forecasting is extremely important.

12/3/1 Capital Spending

Whatever the explanation, business cycles do take place, and government officials as well as private sector managers are aware of their effects on consumer spending. When a slowdown (recession) in the economy is predicted, businesses generally cut back their capital outlays, feeling that consumer spending will be reduced in the near term. If a sufficient number of businessmen take such action, even if a slowdown in consumer spending could have been avoided, a slowdown in economic activity occurs because of a considerable reduction in capital spending that would have otherwise taken place. Thus, a recession can become a self-fulfilling prophecy for psychological reasons. Many people believe that the 1974–75 recession was partially caused by the prediction of a depression. World leaders anticipated a depression because of the oil embargo following the 1973 Arab-Israeli war and the fourfold increase in oil prices. This is not to say that the recession was purely the result of its own anticipation, but rather that its intensity might have been much less had it not been advertised so widely.

In a similar manner, booms of economic activity can be intensified by expectations of booms among enough people. The forecaster of business cycles must, therefore, bear in mind that predictions can intensify recessions or booms and this possibility must be taken into account in the preparation of forecasts.

Government policies are generally aimed at stabilizing the economy. When there are indications of boom or bust conditions, governments through fiscal and/or monetary policies attempt to avert these extremes. As more is learned about the intricate balances of the economic system and as more accurate and timely statistics are obtained about it, governments can act promptly to minimize such swings in activity. Government policies can be applied to slow the rate of growth and achieve a more moderate and balanced economic expansion or to strengthen a sluggish economy. Such actions must be considered by the forecaster, since even the best predictions can be nullified once government actions have been taken to modify the course of events. This situation creates a dilemma for the forecaster of cyclical changes: are the psychological considerations affecting recessions or booms more or less important than government actions aimed at balancing the economy? The answer depends upon the specific circumstances and that is one reason why the prediction of cyclical change is so difficult.

12/3/2 Level of Inventories

In major world economies there is continuous adjustment of inventory levels among wholesalers and retailers in such a way that there is a rather constant ratio of demand to inventory (see Mack 1956 and Barksdale and Hilliard 1975). However, since neither wholesalers nor retailers can forecast cyclical changes with complete accuracy, their inventory levels require frequent adjustment to maintain a constant ratio with actual demand as well as predicted demand. These adjustments have profound effects on the cycle as well as implications for sales forecasting when the cycle changes.

The impact of inventory and sales adjustments becomes even more profound when several levels of inventories are kept between manufacturers and final consumers. The recession finds the inventories too large at all levels and by the time they are readjusted to reflect actual demand levels, the volume of orders is reduced considerably, intensifying the recession. This pattern can be easily seen in the fact that GNP may fall by 3% to 5%, while utilization of production capacity for individual firms may be reduced by as much as 50%.

It has been estimated (Barksdale and Hilliard 1975, pp. 380–82) that it takes an average of five months for firms to realize changes in the cyclical component and react to them by adjusting their inventory levels. That is a long time, and it must be kept in mind while preparing forecasts aimed at predicting the cycle that such adjustments in inventories are a major element in determining the timing of turning points in the cycle. The timing of these adjustments in inventories is difficult to predict, even when one is using anticipatory surveys.

12/4 Anticipatory Surveys

Anticipatory surveys are aimed at collecting information concerning the intentions of consumers or businesses. There are three major types of anticipatory surveys:

1. consumer attitudes and buying plans

2. investment anticipations
3. inventory and sales anticipations

The outcome of these surveys can be used as input to the prediction of the cycle, even though the forecasting accuracy of such surveys is not necessarily better than naive approaches. The forecaster must bear in mind the characteristics and accuracy record of these surveys, each of which is described below.

12/4/1   Consumer Attitudes and Buying Plans

The survey on consumer attitudes and buying plans (CABP) is conducted by the Survey Research Center at the University of Michigan. The survey gathers information on consumer opinions about general economic conditions and consumer buying plans. Although the forecasting record of CABP has been poor in several instances (see Mueller 1963 for example), their record is better than simply using last year's attitudes or sales data as a prediction for next year. When considered as one of many inputs, the survey can reveal a great deal about anticipated consumer actions, which in the final analysis will largely determine the level of economic activity.

12/4/2   Investment Anticipations

There are two widely used investment anticipation surveys. One is prepared by the McGraw-Hill Company and is published the first week of November in *Business Week*. The other is conducted by the Office of Business Economics and the Securities and Exchange Commission (OBE-SEC) of the U.S. government. Of the two, the OBE-SEC has historically been the more accurate. Its only disadvantage is that it does not appear until March of the year to which it applies. Thus, it is of little value in preparing budgets that must be completed before the end of the previous year. The McGraw-Hill survey is much more timely for such use although not as accurate. However, it can become a useful tool since its predictive power often has been satisfactory in the past (Okun 1962, p. 221).

12/4/3   Inventory and Sales Anticipations

Besides the investment anticipation survey, the OBE-SEC also conducts inventory and sales anticipation surveys. There is general agreement that the results of the sales anticipation survey provide little help, since those surveyed are not necessarily good forecasters. [It has been shown that sales anticipations are no better than naive models (Okun 1962, p. 219).] Anticipatory data on inventories have been more accurate and more useful than naive models. They can be used together with the investment and consumers' plans to obtain information about possibly cyclical changes.

12/5 Leading Indicators

Leading indicators are series whose changes in pattern precede those of the specific series being forecast. (Some limited use of leading indicators was seen in Chapter 11 in the discussion of multivariate time series.) There is no such thing as a *perfect* leading indicator. If there were, forecasting would be a trivial task that could be done by using only a leading indicator. There are some series that on average lead others, but they do not always do so, nor is the lead time constant. The problems of identifying a leading indicator and determining what deviation from the average lead time is likely make the use of leading series often unreliable. Evans (1969, p. 460) writes about leading indicators as follows: "The series serves as a valuable historical record and sheds light on the causes of past depressions. But as a practical method of forecasting, the leading indicators cannot be used very effectively or accurately."

As a subsequent step in the development of leading indicator approaches, multiple series have been used as leaders instead of a single series. Also, a composite leading indicator constructed by combining individual series has been suggested. This composite approach has several merits, even though it should still be used with caution. By examining several leading indicators, the risks of missing a cycle or predicting one when none will occur are reduced, since some of the leading series will almost always reach a turning point before the actual series does.

McLaughlin (1975) has proposed a variation of leading indices by advocating the construction of a pyramid of leader and coinciders and then noting the points at which each achieves its low value. This configuration allows one to better see the chances of an upturn. Figure 12-1 (McLaughlin 1975, p. 158) shows some indicator pyramids. The smallest values of each series indicate cycles. It can be seen that this approach has performed very well, since the smaller values indicate a bottoming out of the 1974–75 recession from as early as the end of 1974. (The actual bottom was July 1975 according to U.S. government economists.)

12/6 Paired Indices

Paired indices is another method suggested by McLaughlin and Boyle (1968) for predicting cyclical changes. It combines the concept of leading indicators with that of the percentage change in a series. The basis of the method of paired

Exhibit 10

Indicator Pyramids: 50 Leaders

(a)

Indicator Pyramids: 28 Coinciders

(b)

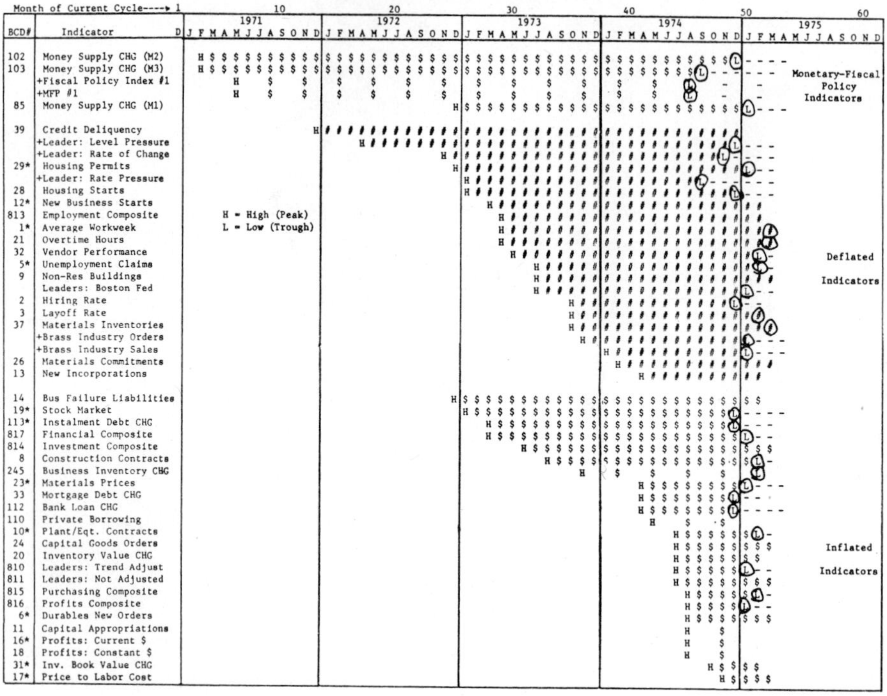

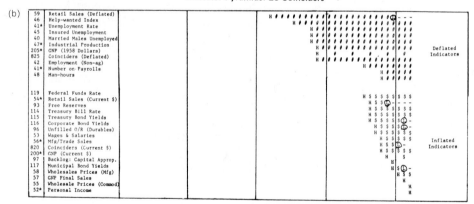

FIGURE 12-1 INDICATOR PYRAMIDS: (A) 50 LEADERS AND (B) 28 COINCIDERS
Source: McLaughlin (1975)

indices can be seen in Figure 12-2, which consists of three graphs, each containing a time series and a leading indicator. Figure 12-2(a) shows the plot of the time series and its leading indicator for the last twelve periods. This is a plot of the

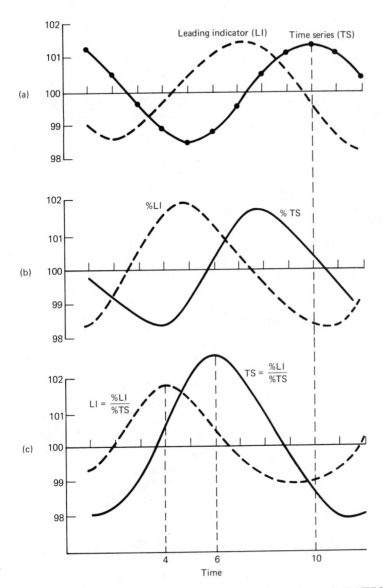

FIGURE 12-2 PAIRED INDICES: (A) INDICES, (B) RATES OF CHANGE, AND (C) PRESSURES
Source: McLaughlin (1975)

trend-cycle values (or just the cycle values), which are standardized so that they fluctuate around 100. (The standardization is accomplished by dividing all data by the mean, then multiplying the resulting values by 100.) Figure 12-2(a) is intended as a graphic presentation of the cyclical behavior of the time series and its leader from which leads can be inferred and their length determined. In the case of Figure 12-2(a), the indicator series leads the time series by three periods. Figure 12-2(b) is merely the period-to-period percentage change of the values in Figure 12-2(a). This second graph highlights changes in the rate of change. In Figure 12-2(a) it can be seen that the time series (or its leader) first decreases rapidly in value, then the rate of decrease slows, becomes zero, slowly increases, increases more rapidly, slows down, becomes zero, etc. This pattern of changes is shown clearly in Figure 12-2(b), where it also seen to lead 12-2(a) by about two periods. That is, assuming no randomness—which unfortunately is never the case with real life data—Figure 12-2(b) leads 12-2(a) by two periods. The trend-cycle changes in 12-2(a) therefore can be forecast using Figure 12-2(b). Finally, Figure 12-2(c) shows the ratio of the leading indicator to the time series (heavy line) and the ratio of the percentage change of the leading indicator to the time series. This pattern is called a pressure by McLaughlin and leads both Figure 12-2(a) and 12-2(b)—(a) by four periods and (b) by almost two. Although one would not expect such perfect behavior of paired indices in practice as those shown in Figure 12-2, even imperfect relationships provide enough information to be helpful in predicting turning points. Often when the leader is not very good, the percentage changes and the pressures may well lead the actual series. In practice it has been found that one- to three-month leads usually can be inferred

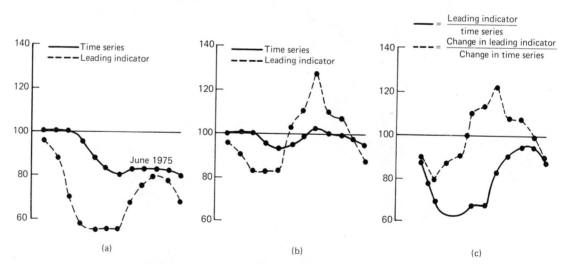

FIGURE 12-3 JUNE 1975: (A) TREND-CYCLE, (B) PERCENTAGE CHANGE IN TREND-CYCLE, AND (C) PRESSURES

so that turning points in the time series can be predicted reasonably well within the time horizon of one to three months.

Figures 12-3, 12-4, 12-5, and 12-6 show an application of the method of paired indices to a specific situation. This application involves the months of June, July, August, and September 1975 when a European firm was in the midst of its

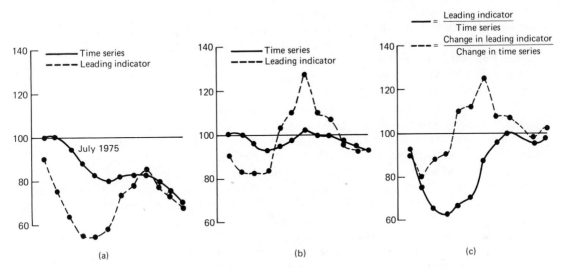

FIGURE 12-4   JULY 1975: (A) TREND-CYCLE, (B) PERCENTAGE CHANGE IN TREND-CYCLE, AND (C) PRESSURES

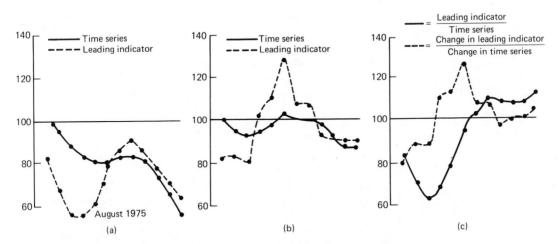

FIGURE 12-5   AUGUST 1975: (A) TREND-CYCLE, (B) PERCENTAGE CHANGE IN TREND-CYCLE, AND (C) PRESSURES

worst recession in several decades. That firm was operating at 60% of capacity and there was a fear among the executives that the worst was yet to come. (In Europe, the 1974–75 recession bottomed several months later than in the United States.) The time series plotted in Figures 12-3 through 12-6 is the set of trend-cycle values (see Chapter 4 for an explanation) of Table 10-4, while the leading indicator is sales orders received by the company.

In June the situation was bleak as can be seen in Figure 12-3, where all three measures are pointing down. In July, both the time series and its leader still point downward as shown in Figure 12-4(a). The percentage changes of the time series and its leader, however, indicate a slowing down in their descent as shown in Figure 12-4(b). Most important, the pressures show a slight turning point [Figure 12-4(c)]. August and September confirm this pattern, indicating a continuing increase in the percentage changes and pressures, even though the trend-cycle of the shipments and orders is still decreasing (see Figures 12-5 and 12-6).

It was not until October and November 1975 that the actual trend-cycle values turned up and verified the evidence of the turn started in July. Unfortunately, one can never be sure that a turn will in fact develop simply because it is signaled by the percentage change indices or the pressures. There are false alarms and sometimes changes take place without warning. As a whole, however, the method of paired indices can be used quite successfully in conjunction with other evidence to signal impending changes in the trend-cycle.

Figure 12-5 will be used as an example of how the numbers used to plot these graphs are obtained. Figure 12-5 refers to August 1975 (period 128 in the

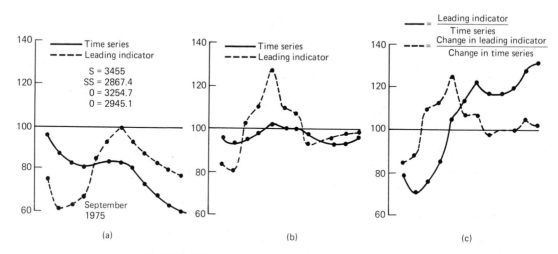

FIGURE 12-6 SEPTEMBER 1975: (A) TREND-CYCLE, (B) PERCENTAGE CHANGE IN TREND-CYCLE, AND (C) PRESSURES

data given in Table 10-4). One would therefore use the first 128 points of Table 10-4 in performing the following calculations:

1. Deseasonalize the time series by finding the seasonal indices (see Chapter 4) of the data, then dividing them into the actual values of Table 10-4. The seasonal indices are shown in Table 12-5, column 3. Thus, the seasonally adjusted value for August 1975 (period 128) is 1975.97 (1536.5/.7776). The value for July (period 127) is 2711.94 (2169.9/.8001), etc. Table 12-5, column 4, shows these seasonally adjusted values of the time series.

2. Calculate the trend-cycle values by applying some form of moving average to the seasonally adjusted data of column 4. A 3×3 moving average (see Section 4/4) has been applied in this case. Other types of moving averages could have been applied, but a 3×3 MA was

TABLE 12-5 RELEVANT VALUES FOR CONSTRUCTING PAIRED INDICES OF FIGURE 12-5

(1) Period	(2) Time Series (see Table 10-4)	(3) Seasonal Index	(4) (2)/(3) Seasonally Adjusted Time Series	(5) Trend- Cycle of Time Series	(6) Percentage Change in Trend- Cycle	(7) (6)+100 Plotted in Figure 12-5(b)	(8) (5)/3902.1 Plotted in Figure 12-5(a)
114 Jan.	5048.1	1.259	4009.8	—	—	—	—
115 Jan.	2990.7	.800	3738.4	—	—	—	—
116 Aug.	2677.1	.778	3441.0	3887.0	—	—	—
117 Sept.	5566.1	1.198	4647.9	3902.1	.38	100.4	100
118 Oct.	3661.7	.944	3877.4	3707.5	−4.99	95.	95.0
119 Nov.	2435.3	.871	2797.6	3387.6	−8.63	91.4	86.8
120 Dec.	3550.4	1.044	3402.2	3187.4	−5.91	94.1	81.7
121 Jan.	2215.4	.767	2888.7	3099.8	−2.75	97.3	79.4
122 Feb.	3312.2	1.025	3230.6	3168.1	2.20	102.2	81.2
123 Mar.	4289.8	1.353	3169.4	3188.7	.65	100.7	81.7
124 Apr.	3218.4	.974	3303.3	3195.7	.22	100.2	81.9
125 May	3193.0	.987	3234.4	3090.9	−3.28	96.7	79.2
126 June	3542.5	1.259	2813.5	2845.8	−7.93	92.1	72.9
127 July	2169.9	.800	2711.9	2521.6	−11.39	88.6	64.6
128 Aug.	1536.5	.778	1976.0	2181.9	−13.47	86.5	55.9

used here because it irons out irregular movements in the data while losing only two data points at the beginning and end of the series. The 3×3 moving values of the trend-cycle are shown in column 5 of Table 12-5. The last two values of column 5 are obtained by taking a three-point weighted moving average $[.3(2813.5) + .4(2711.9) + .3(1976) = 2521.6]$ and a two-point weighted moving average, respectively, adjusted for trend (see Section 4/4).

3. Standardize the trend-cycle values—by dividing each trend-cycle value by the largest trend-cycle value (3902.1) and multiplying the result by 100 to obtain the values in column 8. These values are those plotted as the heavy line in Figure 12-5(a).

4. Find the percentage change in the trend-cycle, by using

$$\%TC_t = \frac{TC_t - TC_{t-1}}{TC_{t-1}} \times 100.$$

Thus for period 117, the percentage change in trend-cycle is

$$\%TC_{117} = \frac{3902.1 - 3887}{3887}(100) = .38.$$

Adding 100 to these values gives column 7 in Table 12-5, which is plotted as the heavy line in Figure 12-5(b).

5. Repeat steps (1), (2), (3), and (4) as above, substituting the leading indicator as the basic data instead of the time series. This process gives the values shown as the broken lines in Figure 12-5(a) and (b).

6. Find the pressure index by dividing the values shown in column 8 of Table 12-5 by the corresponding values for the leading indicator. For period 128, for example, the pressure index is

$$P^*_{128} = \frac{\text{Standardized value of leading indicator}}{\text{Standardized value of time series}}$$

$$= \frac{62.6}{55.9} \times 100 = 112.01,$$

and the pressure of the percentage is

$$P_{128} = \frac{\text{Around 100 percentage change in leading indicator}}{\text{Around 100 percentage change in time series}}$$

$$= \frac{90.15}{86.5} = 104.22.$$

Note that 86.5 is the last value (period 128) in column 7 of Table 12-5, and 90.15 is the corresponding value for the leading indicator.

12/7 Tracking the Evolution of Cycles

Tracking the evolution of cycles and comparing them to previous cyclical patterns is the final method for predicting turning points to be presented. An illustration of this method can be seen in Figure 12-7 which shows the cycles in the Federal Reserve Board Production Index between 1948 and 1976. It shows five complete major cycles (1948–49, 1953–54, 1957–58, 1960–61, and 1969–70) and the latest cycle (1974–75), which was still running its course in December of 1975.

The method for tracking the evolution of cycles is straightforward. It consists of finding the trend-cycle of the series of interest, then determining the periods in which the trend-cycle has peaked historically. The intent is to plot each complete cycle from one peak to the next (or similarly, from one trough to the next). This plotting is done in a way that overlaps each cycle by starting at its peak and then plotting all other values as "periods after the peak" (see Figure 12-7). Finally, to provide a more meaningful comparison, the data are standardized by dividing the time-series values within each cycle by the value of the series at the peak. That gives the peak period the value of 100 and the remaining periods in each cycle values smaller than 100. Following this procedure for all cycles gives an idea of how past cycles have behaved and allows the current cycle (heavy line) to be placed among the previous ones. In Figure 12-7 for example, it can be seen that the 1974–75 recession started slowly but then the level of economic activity declined more rapidly than any of the other postwar cycles. This important information can help the forecaster to determine the intensity and the possible length of the current cycle.

The calculations required to prepare Figure 12-7 are shown in Table 12-6 where both the 1969–70 and 1974–75 cycles are illustrated. The data used are the Federal Reserves Board's Index of Industrial Production. (The base is different for each of the two cycles, but this does not matter since the data are standardized.) Column 3 in Table 12-6 gives the actual values of the series, and column 4 is a three-month moving average of column 3. A three-month moving average is used because the randomness in the series is small. However, for many less aggregated series it may be necessary to use a longer-term average. Finally, in column 5 the trend-cycle values are standardized by dividing all figures of column 4 by 172.8, which is the value at the peak of the cycle. Column 5 is the data plotted in Figure 12-7. (There may be some slight differences between column (5) and the corresponding plot in Figure 12-7 because Figure 12-7 uses the actual data rather than the trend-cycles.) Column (2) shows the periods (months) after the peak and is the x-axis used in the plotting. Columns (7), (8), (9), and (10) are analogous to columns (2), (3), (4), and (5) except that they refer to the 1974–75 cycle. Columns (6) to (10) include the whole cycle, while Figure 12-7 shows only four months after the peak (through December 1974).

In addition to the methods examined so far in this chapter the person in

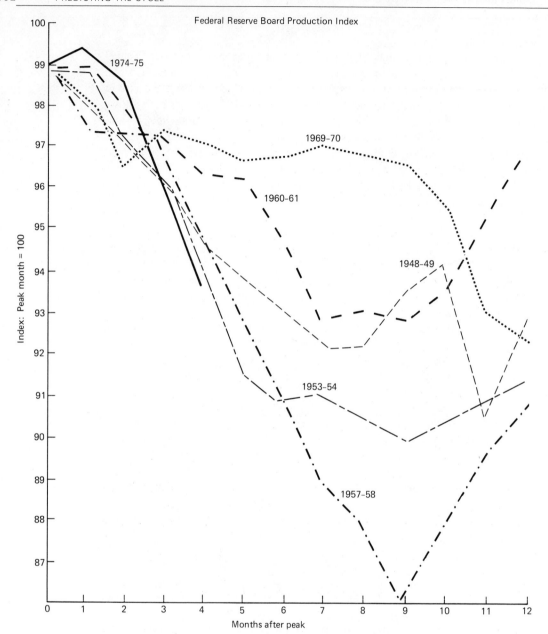

Federal Reserve Board Production Index

FIGURE 12-7   TRACKING THE EVOLUTION OF CYCLES

Source: Quarterly Business Conditions Analysis, *by I. L. Kellner,*
Vice-President, Manufacturing Hanover Trust Company, March 1975.
Reprinted by permission.

TABLE 12-6 COMPUTING THE VALUES REQUIRED TO TRACK THE EVOLUTION OF CYCLES (1969–70 AND 1974–75 CYCLES)

Time		Months after Peak	Time Series	Trend-Cycle	Standardized Trend-Cycle
			1969–70 Recession		
(1)		(2)	(3)	(4)	(5)
1969	Sept.	—	173.9	—	—
Start of	Oct.	0	173.1	172.8	100
Recession	Nov.	1	171.4	171.87	99.46
	Dec.	2	171.1	170.97	98.94
1970	Jan.	3	170.4	170.67	98.77
	Feb.	4	170.5	170.67	98.77
	Mar.	5	171.1	170.6	98.73
	Apr.	6	170.2	170.1	98.44
	May	7	169.	169.33	97.99
	June	8	168.8	169	97.80
	July	9	169.2	169.27	97.96
	Aug.	10	169.8	168.27	97.39
	Sept.	11	165.8	166	96.06
	Oct.	12	162.4	162.97	94.31
			1974–75 Recession		
(6)		(7)	(8)	(9)	(10)
1974	July	—	125.2	—	—
Start of	Aug.	0	125.2	125.27	100
Recession	Sept.	1	125.4	125.07	99.84
	Oct.	2	124.6	123.9	98.91
	Nov.	3	121.7	122.4	97.71
	Dec.	4	120.9	119.57	95.45
1975	Jan.	5	116.1	116.23	92.78
	Feb.	6	111.7	112.33	89.67
	Mar.	7	109.2	109.53	87.44
	Apr.	8	107.7	108.27	86.43
	May	9	107.9	107.05	85.46

charge of predicting the cycle must be continuously informed of economic trends, government initiatives, proposed legislation, and other actions. Hence that person must follow economic publications and be aware of consensus forecasts made by economists, government officials, and private forecasting services. In addition, industry trends also must be followed and analyzed using a top-down approach that starts from the total economic activity and goes down to industry activity and then to total corporate projections.

Predicting the cycle is a complex activity that requires substantial effort and as much information as possible. One should also bear in mind the tendency among forecasters to underestimate the magnitude of cyclical changes—underestimation of actual values in periods of booms and overestimation in periods of recession (see Theil, 1975). Table 12-7 shows some indication of this bias using a comparison taken from Modigliani and Sauerlender (1955).

TABLE 12-7 AVERAGE PREDICTED AND ACTUAL PERCENTAGE CHANGES IN SALES OF MANUFACTURING FIRMS RESPONDING TO OBE-SEC SURVEYS

Asset of Firm	Number of Observations	Average Predicted Change	Average Actual Change
1948			
Above $50 million	26	7.8	14.2
$10–$50 million	58	4.4	11.9
Below $10 million	39	.5	5.8
1949			
Above $50 million	57	1.8	−2.1
$10–$50 million	208	−4.5	−8.6
Below $10 million	211	−1.9	−7.0

Source: F. Modigliani and O. H. Sauerlender, "Economic Expectations and Plans of Firms in Relation to Short-Term Forecasting," in Short-Term Economic Forecasting, vol. 17 of Studies in Income and Wealth (Princeton, N.J.: Princeton University Press, 1955), pp. 288–89. Reprinted by permission.

REFERENCES AND SELECTED BIBLIOGRAPHY

Barksdale, H. C., and J. E. Hilliard. 1975. "A Cross-Spectral Analysis of Retail Inventories and Sales." *Journal of Business*, Vol. 48, No. 3, pp. 365–82.

Beman, L. 1976. "The Chastening of the Washington Economists." *Fortune*, January, pp. 158–66.

Dauten, C. A., and L. M. Valentine. 1974. *Business Cycles and Forecasting*. Cincinnati: South-Western Publishing Co.

Evans, M. K. 1969. *Macroeconomic Activity*. New York: Harper & Row.

Keynes, J. M. 1936. *The General Theory of Employment, Interest, and Money*. New York: Harcourt, Brace and World.

Mack, R. P. 1956. *Consumption and Business Fluctuations*. New York: National Bureau of Economic Research.

McLaughlin, R. L. 1975. "A New Five-Phase Economic Forecasting System." *Business Economics*, September, pp. 49–60.

McLaughlin, R. L., and J. J. Boyle. 1968. *Short-Term Forecasting*. Chicago: American Marketing Association.

Mass, N. J. 1976. *Economic Cycles: An Analysis of Underlying Causes*. New York: John Wiley & Sons.

Mitchell, W. C. 1913. *Business Cycles*. Berkeley, Calif.: University of California Press.

———1951. *What Happens During Business Cycles: A Progress Report*. Studies in Business Cycles. New York: National Bureau of Economic Research.

Modigliani, F., and O. H. Sauerlender. 1955. "Economic Expectations and Plans of Firms in Relation to Short-Term Forecasting." In *Short-Term Economic Forecasting*. Vol. 17 of Studies in Income and Wealth. Princeton, N.J.: Princeton University Press, pp. 288–89.

Mueller, E. 1963. "Ten Years of Consumer Attitude Surveys: Their Forecasting Record." *Journal of the American Statistical Association*, Vol. 58, No. 4.

Okun, A. 1962. "The Predictive Value of Surveys of Business Intentions." *American Economic Review Papers and Proceedings*, Vol. 52, No. 2.

Schumpeter, J. A. 1934. *Theory of Economic Development*. Cambridge, Mass.: Harvard University Press.

———1939. *Business Cycles*, Vol. 1. New York: McGraw-Hill.

Theil, H. 1975. *Economic Forecasts and Policies*. Amsterdam/New York: North-Holland/American Elsevier (1st ed. 1958).

13 SUBJECTIVE ASSESSMENT METHODS

THIS CHAPTER TAKES a somewhat different focus than that of the previous twelve chapters. In one sense, it can be thought of as a transition between forecasting situations for which adequate historical data are available to apply quantitative forecasting techniques and situations for which no relevant historical data are readily available and for which in fact the long-term prospects are for fundamental changes in the historical patterns. The methods commonly applied in these latter cases are referred to as qualitative or technological methods of forecasting. These will be discussed in Chapter 14.

For a number of situations, the aim and focus of forecasting is very similar to what it has been in the previous chapters on quantitative methodologies for forecasting, but the necessary historical data are not available. These situations may range from circumstances involving a new product to simple lack of data collection. In addition, management may have information that is very relevant to forecasting, but it may not be available in the format commonly required for quantitative forecasting techniques. In such instances, forecasts reflecting management's subjective assessments of the situation can often be of substantial benefit.

Some of the methods most commonly used for obtaining such subjective assessments for purposes of forecasting include surveys, market research, individual judgmental assessments, and group composites. Two of the most commonly used methods of the latter type are the *jury of executive opinion* approach and the *sales force composite* method. In each of these methods, those best informed about the likely outcome for the item of interest are asked to make some subjective assessments as to the value of that outcome. It should be stressed that these methods of subjective assessment differ from technological methods along a continuum rather than in terms of absolutes. Clearly the Delphi approach to technological forecasting involves subjective assessments from experts. However, methods like the Delphi approach tend to be aimed at much longer time horizons than the methods that will be discussed in this chapter. Such technological methods also tend to use experts external to the organization in doing the forecasting.

In dealing with subjective assessments, it quickly becomes apparent that a wide range of values can be given for a single event or outcome. In many instances, such as with new product development, this range represents increased uncertainty because there are no historical patterns readily available for extrapolation. However, the range in such forecasts also generally reflects the fact that the quantitative methods incorporate as an integral part of their mathematics some scheme for weighting the historical values. When subjective assessments are used, each individual may use a different scheme for weighting historical experience, and thus the weighting scheme can often be the source of the substantial variation in the forecasts. It is important to distinguish those variations in forecasts that are based on differences in weighting past experience and those that are inherent in the situation itself and the uncertainty it contains.

Because of the generally wide range of outcomes in forecasts based on subjective estimates, decision makers frequently desire to incorporate explicitly that range of uncertainty into their decision making rather than use a single-point estimate as a forecast. That, of course, can also be done with several of the quantitative techniques discussed in previous chapters. For example, a methodology such as regression analysis that provides confidence intervals surrounding a forecast can be thought of as providing a point estimate (the expected outcome) as well as some distribution around that outcome. Although many users of quantitative methods account for such variability in the forecasts either in an implicit manner or through sensitivity analysis to determine the effect of changes in the forecast value on their decision, it is also possible to be more explicit about this variability.

The full range of possible outcomes for the item being forecast can be systematically handled through the technique of decision analysis. This technique involves specifying a range of outcomes for any uncertain quantity—often referred to as a random variable in statistical literature—then determining the expected outcome based on all of the relevant uncertain events. Decision analysis really seeks to combine forecasts that involve a range of possible outcomes into a systematic framework for making decisions. Thus this approach takes explicit account of the variability in those forecasts as an integral part of decision making.

In this chapter, the intent is to describe the most commonly used methods of forecasting that involve subjective assessment, to present the framework of decision analysis, and to illustrate its use as an integral part of forecasting and decision making. This framework will be described first so that it can be used to more effectively understand the type of information to be gathered during subjective assessments and the value of that information. The subsequent sections of the chapter will describe the individual methodologies available for obtaining forecasts based on subjective assessments and the application of those in combination with decision analysis. A rather complete set of literature has grown up around the technique of decision analysis and its use as a decision making tool (as an alternative form of forecasting), and the interested reader is referred to the sources listed in the references at the end of the chapter.

13/1 The Basic Framework of Decision Analysis

The notion of decision analysis is based on the fact that in many management situations decisions must be made sequentially over time. During this process events will occur that will affect which decisions are best at each point in time. Thus the technique of decision analysis is aimed at providing an explicit framework for relating the outcomes of uncertain events to the alternatives that management has available at various times.

Although different criteria can be accommodated with the use of decision analysis, the most common one is that of expected monetary value, such as maximizing expected profits or minimizing expected costs. These objective criteria can be replaced with what are commonly called *preferences* in order to explicitly take account of management's attitude toward risks. This extension of decision analysis will be discussed at the end of the chapter.

In order to deal with uncertainty in a very explicit manner, as decision analysis does, a language must be developed that will allow uncertainty to be expressed in a rigorous and consistent form. Over the last few years the *language of probability* has evolved and has gained general acceptance in handling such uncertainty. The advantage of stating uncertainty explicitly in the language of probability is that the procedures used to deal with it in the decision making process can be clearly stated and applied in a consistent manner. Considerable work has been done on the use of probability to represent uncertainty, but it should be remembered that in this chapter the aim of using probability is simply to improve decision making and more adequately represent reality. Thus it should be used when it helps accomplish that purpose, but should not be used when it merely complicates the situation without improving decision making.

Most managers are familiar with the use of probability in games of chance. For example, if a fair coin is tossed, it is as likely to come up heads as tails. Thus the probability of achieving an outcome of heads is one-half, and that of achieving an outcome of tails is one-half. Similarly, when a fair die is rolled, the probability of realizing each of the six possible outcomes is one-sixth. It can be seen from the previous two examples that in many instances probability can be interpreted in terms of frequency. If a fair coin is tossed one thousand times, approximately one-half or five hundred of those tosses would result in an outcome of heads, and the other five hundred would be tails. Similarly, rolling a die one thousand times would result in a value of one for approximately one-sixth of the one thousand rolls, a value of two for one-sixth of them, and so on. In these examples it is possible to run an experiment (tossing a coin or rolling a die) that would develop a frequency pattern corresponding to these probabilities.

It is this type of probability interpretation that is being used when the confidence interval is determined for a regression line. For example, if a 95% confidence interval is assumed, it means that if more experiments were made, 95% of them would fall within that confidence interval and only about 5% of them would lie outside that interval. It is important, of course, to realize that such probabilities represent only the long-run average. It could be that if in the case of regression analysis two more experiments were added, both of them might happen to be outside the 95% confidence interval. Thus it is important to distinguish between the probability of the actual occurrence of an event or a value and the outcome of that event on a particular experiment or trial.

When probability can be interpreted as the long-run average frequency of an event, historical data can often be used to explicitly obtain the probability distribution. However in many management situations, the interpretation of frequency might apply, but management may not have the historical data available to obtain these frequencies. In such situations, the concept of probability can still be applied. However, such an application is called *subjective probability*, indicating that the probabilities are based on subjective judgments of the decision maker and not on an objective (frequency) analysis of past information.

When a manager says, "There's only one chance in ten that if we submit a bid of $100,000, we will obtain the contract," he is giving a subjective probability estimate. In such a situation, since every contract is different and the competitors' reactions are uncertain, this probability statement must be based on some kind of subjective judgment as to what will happen. If such judgments can be made accurately, they can contribute substantial information to decision making and can actually serve the same purpose that forecasts based on quantitative methods might have provided. (For example, it should be apparent from the chapter on regression analysis that if one had several observations of the bid prices submitted by competitors on a certain type of contract, those observations could be used as the basis for preparing a regression model to estimate the bid prices that might be received on a future contract of that type.) In a bidding situation, if some individual in the company with substantial experience in bidding could tell the manager for each of four different bid prices what the probability would be of winning the contract, that would certainly help the manager in deciding on the appropriate price to submit.

One of the points that needs to be stressed about the difference between subjective and objective probability is that there is no way to check on a single subjective estimate to determine whether or not it is correct. Although it is possible to check for systematic bias over several estimates (this process will be described later), the outcome for a particular event in and of itself does not indicate whether or not the estimator is biased or unbiased.

There are two important properties of probability that the manager must keep in mind in using probability estimates as a part of decision analysis. The first is that if all possible events (that is, all possible outcomes) are considered in a given situation, *the sum of the probabilities assigned to each of those individual events must be equal to one.* For example, in tossing a coin there are two possible outcomes— heads and tails. The probability of heads plus the probability of tails must always equal one. Similarly, there are six possible outcomes in the role of a die. The sum of the probability of each of those six outcomes must equal one. Finally, in the example of bidding on a contract, if there are two possible outcomes, winning the contract and losing the contract, the probability of winning plus the probability of losing must equal one.

The second important property of probabilities to keep in mind is that *the probability assigned to a specific outcome can never be less than zero nor greater than one.* If an outcome is assigned a probability of zero, it implies that the outcome is impossible. Assigning a probability of one implies that the outcome is certain to occur no matter what.

The methodology of decision analysis can be used by the manager as a means of making his decision in a way that explicitly considers the uncertainties involved. A specific example will illustrate the methodology; a company in the cement business must submit a bid on a proposed contract. Suppose that this company is bidding on a single contract that calls for delivery of 100,000 barrels of cement over a period of two months. The management of the company has already decided that it is only necessary to consider three possible bid prices: $2.90 per barrel, $2.50 per barrel, and $2.10 per barrel.

As a starting point in handling this bidding problem, the situation can *first* be diagrammed. The possible actions available can be determined and related graphically by drawing a *decision tree.* For the cement company, the alternative actions are the three possible bid prices of $2.90, $2.50, and $2.10. Depending on the bid that the company submits, there will be a certain probability of winning or losing the contract. The relation between winning or losing the contract and the bid price is shown in the decision tree in Figure 13-1.

In this decision tree diagram a square indicates a decision point and a

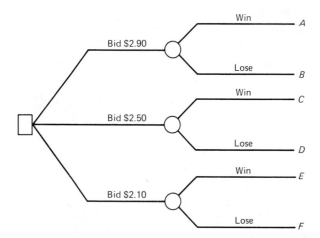

FIGURE 13-1   DECISION TREE FOR CEMENT CONTRACT
BIDDING

circle indicates an uncertain event. The distinction between decisions and uncertain events is important and necessary in this type of analysis. Note that in the decision tree of Figure 13-1, the possible outcomes of each event have been enumerated and the possible decisions have been explicitly identified.

In the *second* step of applying decision analysis, the criterion to be used in decision making is specified. In the example of the cement bidding problem, the company may want to take the action that is likely to lead to the highest profit after tax on this contract. An alternative criterion would be to obtain the largest contribution toward fixed expenses. That is, the company may want to take the action that would maximize its expected contribution from the contract.

It is this latter criterion that will be used in pursuing this example. One of the characteristics of decision analysis is that a single objective criterion must be specified. In most situations, several objectives need to be considered. Although advanced techniques like preference in utility theory have been developed to allow decision analysis to handle situations involving risk and multiple objectives, they are generally complex and difficult to apply. Thus in this section, the discussion will be limited to consideration of a single criterion for decision making.

The *third* step in the application of decision analysis is to determine the value of each of the possible paths in the decision tree. These paths are lettered A through F in Figure 13-1. Three of these paths (B, D, and F) represent losing the contract, and the other three represent winning the contract, although with different bid prices. To evaluate each path, one can start with path A and ask, "What will be the contribution the company will receive if they bid $2.90 per barrel and win the contract?" Since a contract is for a fixed number of barrels (100,000), the company must determine the contribution on each of these barrels when the price is $2.90 and multiply that contribution by the 100,000 barrels.

Suppose the company finds that the direct costs associated with this contract are $1.50 per barrel. The contribution per barrel with a price of $2.90 would be $1.40. Thus the value of path A is $1.40 × 100,000 barrels or $140,000. Next, path B can be examined (a bid of $2.90 and loss of the contract). Since the company will receive no revenue if they lose, a value of $0 can be assigned to this path. (In some instances, there may be costs associated with bidding, even if the contract is lost. However, in this example it will be assumed that there are no such costs.) Similarly, the contributions for paths C, D, E, and F can be computed as $100,000, $0, $60,000, and $0 respectively.

In the *fourth* step probabilities are assigned to those uncertain events included in the decision diagram. These events are represented by a circle in Figure 13-1. Although the company may have some historical information that relates to similar contracts, it is most likely that this particular bidding situation will be somewhat different from previous situations either in terms of competition or the details of the contract. Thus the probabilities would need to be based on management's assessments about the situation and not merely on historical observation. Suppose that the manager has considered the likelihood of winning and losing the bid with each of the three prices, and has come up with the following estimates :* There is one chance in ten of winning, and nine chances in ten of losing if the bid is $2.90. If the bid is $2.50, it appears equally likely that the company will win or lose, and if the bid is $2.10, the chances are nine out of ten of winning, and one out of ten of losing the contract. (It should be emphasized that these are subjective probability estimates and thus there is no way to verify their correctness.)

The *fifth* step in decision analysis is to complete the mathematical evaluation of the various alternative decisions by working backward from the values *A* through *F* (usually called the end point values) to obtain values for the intermediate branches and events, and finally to determine the decision with the highest expected contribution. This process is referred to as *folding back* the decision tree. This folding back process can be illustrated by using the bid option of $2.90. If the company bids $2.90, there is a 10% chance of winning and a 90% chance of losing. Essentially, this means that if the situation were to arise several different times, 10% of the time a bid of $2.90 would result in winning the contract (with a contribution of $140,000), and 90% of the time it would result in losing the contract (with a value of $0). Thus the average of several such occasions would give an expected value of .10 × $140,000 + .9 × $0 = $14,000 in contribution. This value is called the expected value for that decision. It is computed by multiplying the probability of each outcome by the value of that outcome, then summing those products.

One way to consider the computation of the expected value is that the value of winning is weighted by the chances of winning—one-tenth in this case— and the value of losing is weighted by the chances of losing—nine-tenths in this case. This same computational procedure can now be applied to *bid $2.50* and *bid $2.10*, obtaining the expected values of $50,000 and $54,000 respectively. To see just where the analysis stands at this point, the decision tree can be redrawn as shown in Figure 13-2 to incorporate the computations made thus far.

It is useful to review the meaning of the decision diagram in Figure 13-2. It states that if the company makes a bid of $2.90 per barrel, the expected payoff from that decision is a contribution of $14,000. Similarly, a bid of $2.50 has an expected payoff of $50,000 contribution and a bid of $2.10 has an expected payoff of $54,000 contribution. Thus the analysis would indicate that the company would be best off—that is, it would maximize its contribution—if it submitted a bid of $2.10. Note that while this bid will maximize the expected value, since the actual payoff depends on winning or losing the bid—an uncertain event—the company is still not certain whether it will win or lose the bid no matter what action is taken. The analysis has not eliminated the uncertainty, but rather it has sought to explicitly incorporate it into the decision making process.

---

* The next section of this chapter will examine in some detail the alternative ways in which such assessments of the probabilities might be obtained.

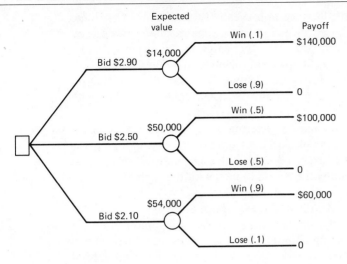

FIGURE 13-2 DECISION TREE WITH COMPUTATIONS FOR CEMENT CONTRACT BIDDING

It may be that in such a situation other considerations will influence the *sixth* step in decision analysis—determining the most appropriate action to be taken. For example, the manager might be concerned about starting a price war if he submits a price of $2.10 per barrel. Since the expected payoff of a bid price of $2.50 is not much lower than the expected payoff for a bid price of $2.10, he might choose to submit the $2.50 price. Alternatively, it may be that the company is operating close to capacity and thus wants the business only if the profit margin is extremely high. That might argue for submitting a bid of $2.90 and simply taking the chances of winning or losing. (This analysis also suggests the expected opportunity loss associated with submitting such a high bid price.) The manager who uses subjective probability as an integral part of decision analysis must still consider other outside factors before making a final decision.

The six steps of decision analysis can now be summarized:

1. Draw the decision tree. The relevant decisions and events must be identified and placed in their proper sequence.
2. Determine the decision criterion. The basis on which the decision will be made must be specified. (For example, maximize cash flow or net profit or minimize costs.)
3. Determine the value of each possible path. This step involves evaluating each of the possible paths contained in the decision tree in terms of the selected decision criterion. The step is completed when an end point value has been obtained for all of the end points in the decision tree.

4. Assign probabilities to the uncertain events. In many instances, these probabilities will be based on subjective estimates made by decision makers involved in the situation. In other cases, they may come from a quantitative forecasting technique that includes confidence intervals as a part of its forecast results, or from subjective assessment procedures that will be described later on. In any event, the rules for dealing with probabilities must be observed in making these assignments.

5. Fold back the end point values to determine the expected value of each decision. This step consists of working from the ends of the tree backward by computing the expected values at each event point, then at each action point selecting the action branch with the highest expected value.

6. Take the best action(s) identified. The example that has been used in this section, while a relatively simple one, is also fairly common in that it describes a typical bidding situation. In many instances, the decision tree will be much more elaborate than in this example, and several sequential decisions will be required. In such instances, this final step involves specifying the sequence of decisions that will be made given various sequences of event outcomes. However, even in these more complicated situations, the basic procedure to be used in determining the optimal course of action is exactly the same as described here.

It should be clear from the above example that obtaining accurate assessments of uncertain events (the items to be forecast) is essential if decision analysis is to provide useful results and guidance for management. The next section of this chapter will focus on several of the different approaches that can be used to obtain subjective assessments for such purposes.

13/2 Methods for Obtaining Subjective Assessments

A wide range of methods for obtaining subjective assessments have been suggested in the literature. A number of the better known of these will be discussed in this section. It should be stressed that these methods are usually just a general set of guidelines and their application depends on the situation. The user of such methods must evaluate the knowledge and information level of those making the assessments and verify their competence so that the degree of confidence that can be placed in such assessments can be determined.

For each of five different procedures—formal surveys, market research, sales force composites, jury of executive opinion, and individual probability assessments—a framework for obtaining subjective assessments will be described.

Specific examples will illustrate the application of these frameworks and the types of variations that might be considered. Finally the question of validating the results will be addressed.

13/2/1 Formal Surveys

The most obvious way to find out what people are going to do and what their intentions are is to ask them. A number of surveys* based on this premise are conducted in the United States and elsewhere. The most important for forecasters include those dealing with business plant and equipment expenditures and those dealing with consumer durables. Each of these will be considered in turn.

Business fixed investment consists of nonresidential structures and producer variables. Statistical series for past expenditures are usually available, but the short-term fluctuations in actual expenditures can be substantial and the pattern can change because of cyclical factors. Many planners and forecasters find it useful to consider surveys aimed at determining the intentions of business in this area, such as the U.S. Department of Commerce–Securities and Exchange Commission Survey published quarterly in the survey of current business. This survey is one of the most widely used in the area of business plant and equipment expenditures. Although the sample is not particularly large, it does provide useful information in many situations.

The Commerce–SEC survey is published in the third month of each quarter. At each publication date, a revised estimate of expenditures for the current quarter and the survey results for the next quarter are published. In December, the estimate for the second quarter of the next calendar year is also included, while the March issue contains estimates for the calendar year even though three months have passed. With these yearly estimates, the revised first quarter estimate and the second quarter estimate, the forecaster can project the expenditures for the last half of the calendar year.

A second survey in the area of business plant and equipment expenditures is that published by McGraw-Hill in *Business Week*. This survey is published twice a year and concentrates on large firms in order to pick up the big capital expenditure programs. Surveying large firms creates some biases when business activity changes direction because in many instances the smaller firms are more likely to be sensitive to short-run changes in business conditions and thus to revise their investment plans.

McGraw-Hill conducts a preliminary survey early in the fourth quarter and releases its results in November. This date is generally late enough that most large firms have pretty well fixed their expenditures for the following year,

---

* See also Chapters 12 and 16 on more information about surveys and their accuracies.

and yet early enough to provide the forecaster with information that is generally useful in planning for the subsequent year. McGraw-Hill then resurveys during the spring of the year and publishes that result in April. Usually this second survey is much more accurate than the first, since most business budgets are operational by then. Both the fall and spring surveys prepared by McGraw-Hill contain forecasts for multiple years in advance. As one might expect, the accuracy of these longer-term surveys has generally been much less than those of the one-year-ahead surveys.

Both the Commerce–SEC survey and the McGraw-Hill survey now include requests for information that serves as an internal check on the firmness and validity of the responses. Essentially, these requests try to cover three questions: (1) Do expenditure plans allow for changes in the price of capital goods? (2) What is the firm's own forecast of sales of GNP? (3) What are its present and preferred rates of capacity utilization?

A third survey of business plant and equipment expenditures is that conducted by the Conference Board. This survey is of capital appropriations and is reported quarterly. It is based on a sample of 1000 manufacturing firms that account for a substantial portion of the total capital expenditures in the United States. The survey picks up plans that are reasonably firm and that appropriations have been made for, since it reports capital appropriations that boards of directors have made commitments to. This survey has been particularly helpful to many forecasters in picking up turning points in the plant and equipment series.

To complement the several available forecasts on business plant and equipment expenditures, a number of surveys of consumer purchasing of durables are also available. As one might expect, individual consumers are somewhat less sophisticated in forecasting and predicting their own expenditures, and thus the results of such surveys tend to be much less accurate than those surveys based on business intentions. However, they can still be very useful in many situations. Perhaps the best known of the consumer surveys are those conducted by the Survey Research Center (SRC) of the University of Michigan. SRC publishes an index that contains information about consumer sentiment (what the consumer thinks about the economy) and consumer buying plans. Several studies have concluded that indices based on attitudes rather than buying plans are most relevant in predicting consumer purchases. Furthermore, these attitudes seem most useful in predicting purchases of automobiles rather than durables.

There are several other sources of consumer surveys currently available. These include Consumer's Union, which publishes its surveys in *Consumer Reports*; the U.S. Bureau of Census, which publishes its survey, "Consumer Buying Intentions," in its current population reports; and Commercial Credit Company, which publishes a quarterly pamphlet, *Consumer Buying Prospects*. Unfortunately, most of these consumer surveys have a problem in adequately recording the consumer's feelings and intentions and determining the firmness of these attitudes. Studies evaluating the effectiveness of such surveys have found that generally they are not very adequate in predicting turning points, but they do give some indication of changes in trend in the near term.

Finally, forecasters can simply conduct their own survey of their customers by mail, telephone, or personal interview. The method used depends on the number of companies to be surveyed and the amount of detail being sought. To increase the accuracy of customer forecasts, many of those conducting such surveys seek to obtain information from more than one source in each customer company that is surveyed. For example, the production manager as well as the purchasing agent may be questioned.

The general goal of such corporate surveys is to determine how much of a given product the consumer firm plans to use. Sometimes the inquiry is limited to the customer's expected use of the company's brand of the product, but other times it may relate to the customer's use of several related items as well.

An example of the use of customer surveys is that of National Lead as reported by the Conference Board (1964). In order to obtain a five-year forecast of its sales of titanium (a pigment used in volume in the paint, paper, rubber, and hard-surface flooring industries) the company uses a customer survey to determine the answer to three questions.

1. Will the products in which titanium is an ingredient increase in sales?
2. Is the average rate of the use of titanium expanding or contracting in each of the using industries?
3. What share of the resulting market can National Lead reasonably expect to get over the five-year period covered by the forecast?

In conducting this survey, National Lead goes directly to executives in the customer companies that use its product titanium. Executives of about 100 companies are interviewed in person, and as many as 300 to 500 more are surveyed by mail. National Lead considers such large samples necessary to ensure the validity of the survey findings. Interviews are conducted by marketing research personnel trained to do this type of work.

In the case of personal interviews, three individuals are contacted in each customer company—the technical research director (or chief engineer), the sales manager (or director of marketing research), and the director of purchases. An attempt is made to elicit different types of information from each of these executives, and both specific and general questions are asked about the above three topics.

Some of the advantages that companies have found in customer surveys is that they provide a better understanding of the customers' motivations and considerations in buying, they enable the company to obtain information in the form and detail desired, and they provide a basis for making a forecast in situations for which historical data either may not be available or may not be relevant. However, there are some disadvantages in this approach. It is clearly difficult to employ in markets where the number of customers is large or the final customers are hard to identify. It also clearly depends on the judgment and cooperation of the customers, and it takes considerable time and money to complete. However, in many instances it may be the best way to proceed with forecasting and planning.

13/2/2 Market Research

There is an extensive literature about market research, and the full range of that literature cannot be surveyed here. However, some comments about market research may be useful to the forecaster faced with a situation for which subjective assessments based on market research are the most suitable form of information for forecasting and planning. Generally, market research encompasses those activities undertaken to learn more about the market for a particular service or product. Because of the costs associated with market testing and market research, it is generally done in only one of a few geographical areas, depending on how much variability there is in customer preference throughout the potential market segment. The primary objectives of market testing in early product stages are to determine (1) whether the new product characteristics will be as well received by the consumer as the assumptions indicate, and if not, (2) what must be done to make the product successful.

Market research should indicate not only why the consumer is or is not buying, but who the consumer is, how he or she is using the product, and what characteristics the consumer thinks are most important in the purchasing decision. (In many instances, the consumer does not use a product primarily for its intended purpose.) Through information on these dimensions, the forecaster can prepare estimates of market potential and market share for various products and services.

As an example of the role of market research, one can consider the situation described by Chambers et al. (1974) involving the picture phone. Forecasts were prepared in the late 1960s that projected sales of the picture phone as entering the rapid growth stage by 1973. It was assumed in these projections that the product features and price would be sufficiently appealing to the customer and that the method of transmission would be both feasible and sufficiently economical to ensure this rapid growth. The picture phone was subsequently introduced for market testing in Pittsburgh and New York City. The market tests showed that the demand was extremely low because of high costs and other related problems, and that significant improvements in transmission methods were needed to achieve lower cost and to make large volumes feasible. It was concluded from the tests that while a large market for picture phones was still likely, it would probably not emerge until at least the late 1970s and then—as the test indicated—the initial market would be for communications within and between corporations.

Another very important use of market research is in determining and identifying those factors that affect or can be used to predict a major variable to be forecast. In one sense, this use of market research might be compared to the initial stages of multiple regression where several independent variables that may be related to the dependent variable are identified and their correlations determined. A major use of market research is simply to identify those independent variables that might be correlated with the dependent variable to be forecast. This identification can be done effectively even when there is no intention of using regression analysis as the forecasting methodology.

An example of this approach is the manufacturer who discovered a relationship between the sales of the industry's major product line and industrial power consumption. With the aid of power companies, the manufacturer was able to obtain power consumption figures for all of the principal markets that the company served. Applying the ratio that had been derived from the test market areas, the manufacturer estimated the total demand in each market segment. This estimate was then compared to actual past performance in order to determine market penetration in each of the markets served. Also, the manufacturer was able to obtain forecasts of probable demand for industrial power in each region and use them as the basis for predicting demand of the company's own products.

Considerable skill is required in designing market research studies that will discover such relationships and determine their validity. Sometimes a single factor may upset an otherwise strong correlation. The trick is to recognize and correct for such factors. For example, a chemical manufacturer found that there was an apparent relation between industrial employment and the sales of one of its products. Based on market research, however, some disturbing variations were identified. Through the appropriate design of this market research, it was discovered that one industry using exceptionally large quantities of the chemical was concentrated in a few localities. It was that high consumption in the one industry and its concentration in a few localities that was causing the distortion of the normal relationship between industrial employment and demand for the company's products. By adjusting regional figures to correct for this distortion, sales and industrial employment were very closely correlated. This correlation allowed industrial employment figures and projections to be used as the basis for forecasting the company's product sales.

In designing market research studies for purposes of forecasting it is important to be very explicit as to what information is needed and what the value of that information will be once it is obtained. Frequently decision analysis can be used to shed light on this latter question. The information that might possibly be obtained from the market research study is assessed and its value in increasing the expected value for the alternative decisions is determined. Clearly the market research is only worthwhile when its value exceeds its cost. The interested reader may want to pursue some of the references cited at the end of this chapter that deal with the value of information as obtained from such market research (see Brown et al. 1974, Raiffa 1968, and Schlaifer 1968).

13/2/3 Sales Force Composite Methods

The sales force composite approach to forecasting consists of obtaining the views of the individual sales people and sales management as to the future sales outlook. This method is frequently used and has been the focus of studies by the Conference Board and others. In describing the technique, the Conference Board (1964) has divided its use into three general categories—the grass roots approach, the sales management technique, and the wholesaler's approach.

In the grass roots approach, the process begins with the collection of each salesperson's estimate of probable future sales in his or her territory. These estimates may be made privately by the salesperson on forms provided for that purpose, or they may be made by the salesperson in consultation with a branch or regional manager. Oftentimes these assessments are associated with the annual budgeting and planning cycle of the company. Once the salespeople have made their individual assessments, the results for the district or region are accumulated and forwarded to the central office where a composite forecast is put together. It is commonly the practice to have the salespeople estimate demand by classes of products and often by customer so that the final composite can provide forecasts on several different dimensions—geographical area, product line, customer size, etc. The checks generally used in application of this approach are based mainly on the judgment and assessment of district salespeople and top management as to the reasonableness of the individual salespeople's estimates. It is also common practice for a corporate staff group to make an independent estimate of demand and use that as a basis for cross-checking the composite results.

The advantages most often cited for the sales force composite approach are that it uses the specialized knowledge of those closest to the marketplace, it places responsibility for the forecasts in the hands of those who can most affect the actual results, and it lends itself to the easy breakdown of the forecasts by territory, product, customer, or salesperson. The disadvantages are in many cases very similar to those found in consumer surveys. Oftentimes salespeople are poor estimators and are either overly optimistic or overly pessimistic. At other times salespeople are unaware of broad economic patterns that may affect demand in their territory for various product lines. (Some companies have sought to overcome this weakness by giving salespeople information on general economic projections before they make their estimates.) Finally, elaborate schemes are sometimes necessary to keep estimates reliable and free from bias.

As an alternative to the grass roots approach of the sales force composite method, the Conference Board suggests the sales management technique. In this approach, the specialized knowledge of the sales executive staff is used rather than assessments by individual salespeople. The rationale is that the sales executives generally possess almost as much information as the individual members of the sales force and the executives can be trained to make better assessments over time. Sometimes this approach involves only such high level executives that it begins to resemble the jury of executive opinion. One of the advantages claimed for using only sales executives rather than individual salespeople is that it reduces the time required to obtain such forecasts. However, it also means that the individual salespeople will not be committed to the forecast nearly as much as they would have been had they prepared their portion of it.

The wholesaler approach to the sales force composite method is generally used by manufacturing concerns that distribute their products through independent channels of distribution rather than directly contacting the users of their products. In such instances, this approach looks very much like the survey method described for National Lead. Essentially it involves asking each distributor of the product for information as to the size and quantity of the company's product lines that they expect to sell in the next quarter or the next year. To promote interest and improve validity of results, some companies who use this approach give their distributors comparisons of previous sales forecasts and actual performance. Alternatively, they may provide similar data designed to encourage the cooperating distributors to evaluate their sales prospects objectively. Some companies have gone one step further: they help their distributors do their own forecasting and planning, and as a spinoff from that, the manufacturing company receives better forecasting information.

13/2/4 Jury of Executive Opinion

The jury of executive opinion approach has also been clearly defined over the past decade by the Conference Board (1964). Recent surveys of actual forecasting practice in business indicates that it is one of the simplest and most widely used forecasting approaches available. In its most basic form, it simply amounts to the corporate executives sitting around a table and deciding as a group what their best estimate is for the item to be forecast. One of the main drawbacks of this approach is that because it puts the estimators in personal contact with one another, the weights assigned to each executive's assessment will depend in large part on the role and personality of that executive in the organization. Thus the executives with the best information will not necessarily have the greatest weight given to their assessments.

When using this approach, a company generally brings together executives from sales, production, finance, purchasing, and administration so as to achieve broad coverage in experience and opinion. A number of companies give the executives involved in this assessment process background data on the economy and various factors within the company that may be useful in assessing forecasts. This factual assistance can help to separate those areas for which judgment is most important from those for which historical information is very relevant. Making this separation often helps the group to move toward a more precise evaluation of the factors that affect the forecast.

In one variation of the jury of executive opinion approach, the jury is periodically requested to submit its estimates in writing. (This variation begins to look very much like the Delphi approach described in Chapter 14.) These written estimates may then be reviewed by the president or an executive vice-president who makes a final assessment on the basis of the opinions expressed, or they may be averaged to arrive at a representative forecast. This approach has the advantage that the president or executive vice-president may have learned from experience which executives are generally biased in which direction and can appropriately weight each individual's estimates.

The advantages most often cited for the jury of executive opinion approach to forecasting are that it provides forecasts quickly and easily, it does not require the preparation of elaborate statistics, it brings together a variety of specialized viewpoints (it pools experience and judgment), and many times it may be the only feasible means of forecasting, especially in the absence of adequate data. As might be expected, the disadvantages are also related to the important role of judgment in this approach. For example, it is often thought to be inferior to more factually based (quantitative) forecasting methods that do not rely so heavily on opinion. In addition, this method requires costly executive time, disperses responsibility for accurate forecasting, and may present difficulties in making breakdowns by products, time intervals, or markets for operating purposes.

13/2/5 Individual Subjective Probability Assessments

The use of subjective probability estimates is another method commonly used for incorporating individual judgment into forecasting. However, this approach splits the forecasting problem somewhat differently than most other methodologies do. Generally, the assessment procedures seek to locate the most likely forecast for some uncertain quantity of random variable. In the case of subjective probability estimates, however, various levels for the outcome of that variable are specified, and the judgmental assessment becomes determining the probability associated with each of those levels of outcome. For example, the company faced with forecasting its sales for a certain product line would specify three or four different levels of sales covering the full range of possible outcomes, and would then subjectively assess the probability associated with each of those levels of outcome.

Considerable work has been done by those who have developed the technique of decision analysis in regard to alternative procedures for assessing probability distributions as an integral part of forecasting and decision making. Rather than cover all of these, this section will summarize some of the main conclusions that have been reached and suggest an approach for calibrating such individual assessments and using that calibration as the basis for developing a probability distribution.

One of the original developers of decision analysis, Robert Schlaifer (1968), has summarized some of the important aspects involved in direct judgmental assessment of subjective probabilities along the following lines:

1. Uncertainty concerning events that individually may have a substantial effect on the item being estimated should be separated wherever possible. The decision maker should not attempt to directly assess a probability distribution for the variable in question that combines several different elements of uncertainty. Rather it is better to apply the individual's judgment and experience to the problem in smaller increments by estimating distributions for each of several different uncertain events, and then combining them through use of decision analysis.

2. An advantage of separating those individual events that may have a substantial effect on the outcome of the uncertain quantity or the variable in question is that the decision maker is likely to feel that for each individual event, the assessed probability should be unimodal and smooth.

3. If the decision maker feels that the probability distribution should be unimodal and smooth for a particular event, the distribution can be assessed by making a few separate assessments at various points on the cumulative function, plotting those points, and then fitting a smooth curve to them.

4. If only a very small probability is to be assigned to any individual value or outcome of an event, the decision maker can assess points on the cumulative function by selecting various fractiles (such as the .25, .5, and .75 fractiles) and specifying the outcome that corresponds to each of those fractiles.

Additionally, the decision maker may be able to improve the accuracy of the subjective probability assessment by relating it to historical frequency and through understanding the rules of probability assessment and the implications of various shapes in those probability distributions more fully. Generally, the experiments have found that even individuals who know a lot about the variable to be forecast may have trouble making subjective probability assessments unless they are given guidance as to how these assessments can be made. Thus an important step in this approach is to guide those making the assessments. They may need to practice by assessing the probability of various levels of the New York Stock Exchange Index or the GNP rather than starting immediately with the key item in a forecast.

A critical aspect in using subjective probability assessments as a part of forecasting is calibrating the individuals making those assessments. If the decision maker or forecaster is to use such subjective estimates developed by people either internal or external to the firm, it must be determined whether those individuals are generally optimistic or pessimistic in their assessment of probabilities and various outcomes. This, of course, cannot be done by simply looking at the after-the-fact results for one or two assessments. Rather several repeated assessments must be obtained, and an evaluation procedure for calibrating bias in them adopted.

To illustrate just how such a calibration procedure might be carried out in practice, it is useful to consider a specific example. In this case, a forest products firm faced with the task of estimating the amount of timber that can be cut from specific parcels of land will be considered. Suppose that one such company follows the procedure of sending an estimator out to examine each such parcel and prepare an estimate of the yield per acre in thousands of board feet. Of course once the parcel is actually harvested, the company will know the yield exactly. The estimator's record on the last ten parcels is shown in Table 13-1. The third column of the table show the ratio of actual to forecast for each parcel (A/F). This ratio can be used to determine both the extent of bias in the estimator's forecast and the dispersion in those forecasts.

In the example shown in Table 13-1, the average A/F value can be computed as .98. This value suggests that the estimator is only slightly biased on the side of overestimating the yield of a given parcel of land. If this pattern were observed consistently, the planner might want to revise the estimator's forecast downward by 2% in each individual instance in order to compensate for this bias.

The dispersion in the subjective assessments shown in Table 13-1 can be determined in two different ways. First, one could compute the standard deviation, which gives a value of .06 and suggests that the estimator is quite precise. (It will be recalled from earlier chapters that for a normal distribution the values will be

TABLE 13-1   SUBJECTIVE ESTIMATE OF FOREST YIELD PER ACRE
(THOUSANDS OF BOARD FEET)

Forecast (estimate)	Actual	Actual/Forecast
170	175	1.03
190	178	.93
165	175	1.06
203	200	.98
169	170	1.01
183	190	1.04
190	180	.95
200	205	1.02
206	200	.97
185	160	.86

within plus or minus three standard deviations of the mean 99% of the time. That indicates the estimator will be within plus or minus 18% of the actual value over 99% of the time.)

Using an alternative means of viewing the dispersion in the estimates, one could draw a cumulative probability graph of the A/F values. The A/F values could be ranked, then plotted in the manner shown in Figure 13-3. This approach has the advantage of being able to determine a distribution for any new estimate. For example, suppose the estimator gave a forecast value of 180 for a new parcel of timber (180,000 board feet per acre). The horizontal axis in Figure 13-3 shows as a second row the range of possible outcomes for the actual value based on the estimator's past record. As can be seen, there is only a 20% chance in this situation that the actual value will lie outside the range 162 through 193. Other probability ranges could also be estimated in the same fashion. Thus the calibration of the forecaster is a practical method for assessing expected bias and dispersion in a subjective estimating situation where individual assessments must be made repeatedly.

Owing to the wide range of approaches that have been suggested for obtaining subjective assessments as the basis for forecasting, it is not surprising that a number of studies have been conducted to estimate the relative accuracy and benefits of these alternative approaches. Several of these are compared in Chapter 16. The general conclusion, however, is that the adequacy of various methods depends more on their being tailored to the situation in question than on any inherent features of the method itself. Thus it is imperative that the forecaster adopting such methods not only know the methods, but understand the situation in which they are to be applied.

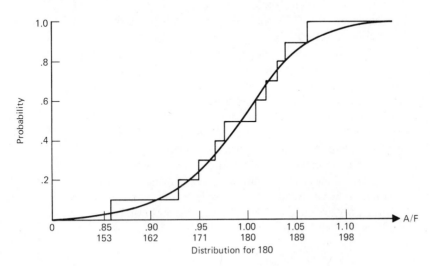

FIGURE 13-3 CALIBRATING A FORECASTER WITH A/F

13/3 Combining Subjective Assessments and Decision Analysis in Practice

As pointed out earlier, decision analysis provides a framework that can be used to effectively integrate subjective assessments and probability distributions into the process of decision making. As an illustration of that, this section will consider a specific example dealing with corporate management of currency exchange risks.* While this particular example deals with currency fluctuations that occurred when countries operated on fixed exchange rates with only periodic adjustments, its application to a wide range of situations should be readily apparent.

The situation faced by Ed Holland, Treasurer of the National Machine Company, in June 1968 is typical of that frequently faced by multinational companies. The National Machine Company was a large established manufacturer of heavy capital equipment. Although its product line was partially diversified across a number of different types of equipment, the company tended to specialize in heavy equipment of an electrical nature such as electric motors, generators, turbines, and electrically powered industrial equipment. Sales were primarily directed to domestic industrial cororations and utilities, although in recent years the firm had begun to expand its international sales, particularly to the developed countries of Western Europe, Japan, and Australia.

As a proportion of sales to foreign customers increased, several new and different problems arose. Most of the firm's senior managers were executives who had progressed upward through the company largely on the basis of their experience in established markets, and they were just learning of the special problems involved in marketing capital equipment abroad. At several times in the past, outside consultants had suggested that National reorganize its management and establish a separate international division. As of 1968, however, the company was still organized along traditional lines with vice-presidents of engineering, sales and production, a controller, and a treasurer, all of whom reported to the president. The international marketing problems were handled in the same manner as domestic sales problems, and the treasurer was responsible for any special problems of international finance.

This latter responsibility raised particular problems for Holland, the corporate treasurer, who was responsible for National's decisions in the foreign exchange markets. Most of the company's sales in a foreign country resulted in a net balance receivable in the local currency of that country. Typical terms of sales of a large electrical generator in Great Britain, for example, might be a significant deposit at the time the contract was signed and the balance due in pounds sterling 60 days after final installation of the generator. Holland's problem arose from

---

*This example is taken from S. C. Wheelwright, "Applying Decision Theory to Improve Corporate Management of Currency Exchange Risks," *California Management Review* (Summer 1975), pp. 41–49. Used by permission.

the delay between the time the contract was signed and the final payment. If the British pound sterling were devalued in this intervening period, the contractual revenue in pounds would represent a significantly smaller number of dollars. It was possible, therefore, to actually lose money on an ostensibly profitable sale because of devaluation.

Holland was concerned about a large sale of electric generators that National had recently completed to a French firm. The balance on the terms of the sale was 25 million francs (about $5 million at the then current exchange rate), which was receivable in a little less than 30 days. The civil unrest and related events in France at that time had increased speculative pressures on the franc and the foreign exchange markets reflected this crisis. In particular, the "spot" rate for the franc was 0.2011 U.S. dollars, just marginally above the lower peg of $0.2010, the rate at which the French government was committed to buy francs rather than let the price fall further. In addition, francs could be bought or sold forward 30 days at $0.2000, significantly below the lower peg.

Holland believed that people were behaving very irrationally and that a devaluation was highly unlikely under existing circumstances. On the other hand, if a devaluation did occur, National was going to lose a significant sum of money. For example, a devaluation of 20% would result in a loss of about $1 million, throwing this particular sale of generators into the red and, moreover, reducing National's annual income before taxes by almost 5% overnight. Because of this dire prospect, Holland was tempted to hedge his risk by selling the 25 million francs in the 30-day forward market, and obtaining a sure $5 million. He was troubled, however, by the apparent costs of this step. Assuming that he did not sell the francs forward and the rather unlikely devaluation did not occur, he could surely exchange the francs in 30 days for at least the lower peg value of $0.2010. Selling them forward was therefore going to cost National a pretty penny—about $25,000 he figured, which would have to be deducted from the profits of the sale. He wondered whether this was an exorbitant price for protection from what was, after all, a very unlikely event.

Since the problem facing Holland was one that recurred frequently, he thought it might be useful to examine some of the decision rules that he might choose to follow in this type of situation. From discussions with corporate treasurers and assistant treasurers with similar responsibilities in other domestic corporations, Holland had identified five major alternatives that might be used as a guide in making decisions in this area. Although combinations of these could also be developed, he wanted initially to examine only the clearly distinctive approaches.

Never hedge

Proponents of the never-hedge decision rule had argued that a company the size of National should never hedge against exchange devaluations because the market for currency futures was perfect, and thus represented the "expectations" of those involved in the market, who obviously knew more about the chances of a devaluation than a corporate treasurer with diverse responsibilities could ever know. In addition, this approach assumed that the company was willing to play the long-run averages.

Always hedge

The always-hedge approach also assumed that the currency futures market was perfect and represented the expectations of the experts, but that in the short run a firm like National would be adverse to taking on the risks of currency devaluations because they could have a significant effect both on corporate earnings and on top management's evaluation of the performance of the treasurer or person in change of such situations. One form of the argument supporting this decision rule, which Holland had heard often, was that the company was in business to take those risks associated with its industry, but not to take on the risks associated with currency devaluation.

Hedge, contingent on amount involved

According to this rule, one never hedged for amounts less than . . . dollars and always hedged for amounts greater than . . . dollars. The arguments for this approach had been a combination of those for the first two, although the emphasis was somewhat different. Although this rule generally assumed that the currency futures market was perfect or nearly so, this assumption was not nearly so important as understanding that most companies will tolerate small losses but few will tolerate large ones, even if justified on some long-run average basis. Implicitly, many of the people who had discussed this approach felt that playing the averages was clearly in the company's best interests, but that for significant amounts it was not practical for a manager to do so.

Hedge, contingent on probability of devaluation

This approach recommended hedging only when the probability of devaluation was greater than some value, *p*. Reflected in this decision rule was the fact that many managers are only willing to bet on things about which they are quite certain. Thus one colleague of Holland's had suggested that even if the average or expected value of not hedging was much less than the average cost of hedging, he would still hedge if the probability of a devaluation was felt to be greater than some value, for instance 5%. This action was justified on the basis that the manager would be viewed unfavorably any time there was a devaluation and he had not hedged.

Hedge, contingent on expected cost

According to this rule, one decided whether to hedge on the basis of the action with the lowest expected cost. The expected value approach generally involved estimating the probability of a devaluation and the likely amount of that devaluation, then through the application of decision analysis determining the expected values associated with hedging and not hedging. Arguments for this approach were that it helped to clarify decision making in any given situation because of the structure that it brought to the problem, that it could clearly identify which action was in the firm's best long-run interests, and that it could indicate the cost associated with taking an action other than the one with the minimum expected cost.

To better understand Holland's problem and the implications of the various alternatives, it is useful first to look at the application of decision analysis to the problem he faced. The six-step procedure outlined previously can be applied to this problem.

As a preliminary step, some additional information must be obtained from Holland about his view of the alternative actions he can take, the nature of the uncertainties associated with his problem, and his assessment of the likelihood of various outcomes for each uncertain event. (In essence, this amounts to handling the forecasting problem as to the amount of the devaluation and the likelihood of various devaluations.)

Suppose that one has met with Holland and that the information he has provided is summarized by the following statement:

> As a starting point, I see my two alternative decisions as either hedging the entire 25 million francs through the use of the currency futures market or not hedging at all and just playing the long-run averages. The major uncertainty, of course, is the exchange rate for the franc in 30 days. It could be close to what it is now, or if a devaluation occurs, it could be worth substantially less.
>
> Regarding the possibility of a devaluation of a certain amount, I find it useful to think about that uncertainty as being divided into three parts. First, I think it depends on whether De Gaulle remains in power. If De Gaulle remains at the helm in France, then I don't think there is any possibility of a devaluation. If there is a change in the government, however, there is a significant chance the new leader will immediately devalue the franc. From talking with others and from my readings, I think there is only one chance in twenty that there will be a new government in the next 30 days. Given that there is a new government, I consider it about equally likely that they will or will not devalue.
>
> As to the third part of the uncertainty, the amount of the devaluation if it does occur, I think that the range of possible devaluations is 5% to 20% and that it could fall just about anywhere in this range. I guess I would consider the numbers 0.16, 0.17, 0.18, and 0.19 dollars to the franc as representative of the possible outcomes, and I feel that they are equally likely to occur.

Finally, if there is no devaluation, I think the best estimate for the "spot" rate for the franc in 30 days is $0.2010, the lower peg. I can't imagine anything in that short a time that would cause it to move much above that level. I should also keep in mind that if I hedge through use of the currency futures market, the franc is currently selling 30 days forward at $0.2000.

From this additional information, the decision tree for Holland's problem can be developed as shown in Figure 13-4. As indicated there, the basic analysis shows that the expected value of taking the action, *hedge*, is $5,000,000, while the expected value of taking the alternative action, *no hedge*, is $5,008,750. Since following the *hedge* option involves no uncertainty, the $5,000,000 associated with that branch is exactly what Holland would have in 30 days. For the other main action branch, there is considerable uncertainty, and the value of $5,008,750 represents a kind of average value. That is, if Holland faced this identical situation many times and always chose not to hedge, on the average the company would end up with this amount. However, for any single occasion like this, the outcome would be somewhere between a low of $4,000,000 (associated with a 20% devaluation) and a high of $5,025,000 (associated with no devaluation). It should be clear that for a person such as Holland, the greater uncertainty associated with

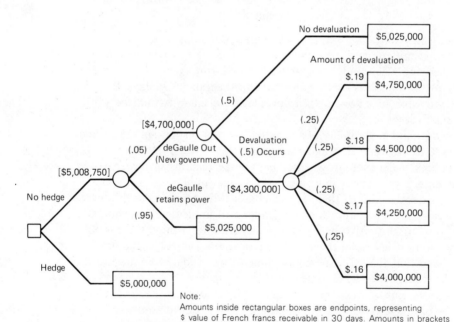

Note:
Amounts inside rectangular boxes are endpoints, representing $ value of French francs receivable in 30 days. Amounts in brackets are expected values. Values in parentheses are probability estimates.

FIGURE 13-4 APPLICATION OF DECISION ANALYSIS TO THE CURRENCY EXCHANGE PROBLEM

no hedge could well be more important than the differences in expected values. As will be shown, this preference can also be included in the basic decision analysis. Before dealing with such extensions, it is interesting to consider some of the other decision rules described previously and commonly applied by corporate financial managers to handle currency exchange risks.

One way of viewing the results of Figure 13-4 is that the technique of decision analysis has been applied to evaluate two commonly used policies in corporate finance—hedge and don't hedge. On an expected value basis, the conclusion is that in this case, National Machine would be better off not to hedge. However, a very relevant question is how this approach deals with the assumptions and arguments generally used in practice to support one policy over the other. It will be recalled that both hedge and no-hedge supporters tend to assume that the forward currency market is perfect and simply reflects the market expectations concerning the future exchange rate. Decision analysis, on the other hand, makes no such general assumption, but rather examines each situation individually and through incorporating the likelihood of a devaluation and its size in the analysis includes a consideration of just how the forward rates compare with the expected cost of not hedging. This makes the technique attractive, because as those who have examined the forward market know, it not only represents the likelihood of devaluations, but also the differences in interest rates in various countries.

The other assumption identified earlier concerning these two approaches involved the company's and the treasurer's attitudes toward risk. The use of decision analysis and expected monetary values clearly assumes that the company is willing to play the long-run averages. However, even when this is not the case, decision analysis can be very useful. One way of adjusting for the attitude towards risk is to use expected monetary value as a type of base case and then have the manager decide if the risks involved with the course of action having the most attractive expected value are such that a course of action involving a somewhat lower expected value, but with lower risk, would be more attractive. This type of adjustment requires that the decision maker consider trade-offs between expected monetary value and risk on a very *ad hoc* basis for each situation. Thus Mr. Holland might consider the risk involved with *not* hedging the 25 million francs and decide that he would rather forego the $8,750 in expected value in order to eliminate that risk.

A much more systematic approach to handling this trade-off between risk and expected value is that of preference theory. This approach amounts to developing a *preference curve* that shows explicitly the trade-offs that one is willing to make between the risk surrounding an uncertain situation and an amount to be received with certainty. This approach can be completely integrated with decision analysis. Once the first three steps of decision analysis have been applied, the endpoint values associated with each possible sequence of events and decisions can be converted into preferences using the preference curve. The folding back can then be done using expected preference rather than expected monetary value. Finally, each expected preference can be converted into a certainty equivalent (the amount that the decision maker would accept for certain in place of the uncertain situation that he faces). Thus, the decision analysis approach can cover both the hedge rule and the no-hedge rule, lending structure to the analysis and giving much more consistent results.

In comparison with the other two decision rules commonly used by corporate financial officers, decision analysis also performs better both on straight financial terms and in dealing with the arguments that support these alternative approaches. The first of these other approaches is that of hedging only when the amount involved is above a certain level. This rule ignores the likelihood of a devaluation and aims simply at eliminating any significant losses associated with a single devaluation. Clearly this rule focuses on the short-term situation rather than the long run. When this approach is followed strictly, it would tell the decision maker to hedge no matter what the cost of doing so, if the amount involved reached a certain level. On the other end, it could well lead him to not hedging on several smaller amounts, when in fact hedging was cheaper than playing the long-run averages. Decision analysis does give a much clearer picture of the trade-offs being made, and even if a firm decides that for amounts over a certain level they should always hedge, at least with decision analysis they can identify the best actions for smaller amounts and determine the cost of their policy for larger amounts.

The final policy that is often encountered in practice is that of hedging whenever the probability of a devaluation gets above a certain level. Clearly this rule takes no account of the costs involved and thus would be difficult or impossible to defend as being in the company's best interests. However, it may make the financial officer feel better to know that he is never letting the chances of getting hurt by a devaluation rise above a certain level. Since decision analysis takes account of both the likelihood of various outcomes as well as the economic results associated with the outcomes, it will give much more consistent recommendations and ones much more in line with the economic aims of the company.

The purpose of this discussion has been to demonstrate that decision analysis is at least theoretically a more appropriate approach for handling the risks of currency devaluations than other approaches commonly used in practice. The rather simple example used here overlooks a number of important considerations with which forecasters and planners must normally deal. These include the range of situations in which decision analysis is applicable, a consideration of the other alternatives available to reduce risk (besides hedging using the futures market), the objectives of the financial manager that may be in conflict with the objectives of the company, and application of the concepts of decision analysis in handling very complex situations of this kind.

In regard to the range of situations in which decision analysis can be used, one of the basic assumptions involved is that the treasurer is faced with a decision at a given time and must make his decision based on the information currently available. While these conditions may hold for a company like National Machine that is dealing with a few large contracts, the situation is quite different for a company that has transactions going on daily in a number of different currencies. There the problem becomes a very dynamic one, and the thorough evaluation of all possible actions and uncertain events may be totally impractical. In such situations, the concepts of decision analysis may still be very useful when incorporated with some of the extensions to be described. However, even in these more complex situations, for the company that has never developed a systematic approach to handling these kinds of risks, decision analysis offers an excellent starting point. Then as experience is gained and the situation is better understood, other techniques can be developed and adopted. Decision analysis is most appropriate for situations of limited complexity, such as the example of National Machine, and as a starting point for any company with very limited experience in making decisions in this area.

The extension of decision analysis to handle other actions in addition to hedging through the futures market is very straightforward. It simply involves including as alternative actions any of the possibilities that management wants to consider, computing the expected value associated with each, then selecting the course of action that is most attractive. Thus, the use of short-term local borrowing, contracts written only in the currency of the parent company, and affiliate loans are all possible ways of coping with the risks of currency devaluation that can be handled using decision analysis.

Related to this consideration of alternative actions is the timing of this type of analysis. It is not hard to see that in a situation like that facing National Machine, the possibility of a devaluation should be considered when pricing the contract and not just 30 days before the final payment is received. In this way, management can determine just what the expected cost of a devaluation in the country in question would be and compensate for that in its pricing policies.

Often one of the most difficult aspects of handling currency exchange risks is the conflict between actions in the company's best interests and actions in the treasurer's best interest. Although it may in fact be advantageous for the company to play the long-run averages, this course of action may be much too risky from the personal perspective of the treasurer. It is one thing for the company to subscribe in theory to the adoption of expected value as a decision criterion and another for the treasurer to have to explain to the president and board of directors that the company sustained a significant devaluation loss because he was operating on the basis of long-run averages. Clearly the behavioral nature of this problem makes it impossible for decision analysis to deal with it completely. However, through the use of this technique, the treasurer can present the situation to top management before the fact so that they can realize the trade-offs that must be made and supply the treasurer with some guidelines for his decisions. Other steps that might be taken to cope with this problem involve setting up a reward system that motivates the treasurer to act in a manner consistent with the best interests of the company and building up a history of performance to be used in evaluating the treasurer on decision making in this area.

The final area to consider in relation to decision analysis is what to do when it is no longer a practical technique for handling a given situation. The most frequent cause of the inadequacy of decision analysis is the absence of subjective probability estimates. Two of the available alternatives are the use of an optimization model that can consider many complexities or the use of a simulation model that can help the treasurer in evaluating those alternatives he feels are worthy of consideration. This latter approach can be developed as a natural extension of decision analysis. In fact, when preceded by a period in which decision analysis is used, it is much more likely that the simulation model will meet with success as a management tool.

The technique of decision analysis offers an excellent framework for dealing with a wide range of complex management forecasting and decision making by clarifying management's perception of the problems surrounding a given situation, identifying the costs of alternative actions, and providing an indication of the opportunity cost of making a decision on a basis other than expected value. From the authors' investigations, companies with a wide range of backgrounds can profitably consider the adoption of the straightforward technique of decision analysis before considering much more complex procedures for forecasting and decision making.

REFERENCES AND SELECTED BIBLIOGRAPHY

Brown, R. V., A. S. Kahr, and C. Peterson. 1974. *Decision Analysis for the Manager.* New York: Holt, Rinehart & Winston.

Chambers, J. C., S. K. Mullick, and D. D. Smith. 1974. *An Executive's Guide to Forecasting.* New York: John Wiley & Sons.

Chisholm, R. K., and G. R. Whitaker. 1971. *Forecasting Methods.* Homewood, Illinois: Irwin.

The Conference Board. 1964. *Sales Forecasting.* Studies in Business Policy, No. 106. New York.

————. 1977. *Sales Forecasting.* New York.

Dalrymple, D. J. 1975. "Sales Forecasting: Methods and Accuracy." Papers from the Marketing Department, Indiana University, Bloomington, Indiana. September.

Hammond, J. S. 1967. "Better Decisions with Preference Theory." *Harvard Business Review,* November–December, pp. 123–41.

Raiffa, H. 1968. *Decision Analysis.* Reading, Mass.: Addison-Wesley.

Schlaifer, R. O. 1968. *Analysis of Decisions Under Uncertainty.* New York: McGraw-Hill.

Ster, T. F. 1966. "Consumer Buying Intentions and Purchase Probability." *Journal of the American Statistical Association,* September.

Theil, H., and R. F. Kosobud. 1968. "How Informative are Consumer Buying Intentions Surveys?" *Review of Economics and Statistics,* Vol. 19, February.

Wheelwright, S. C. 1975. "Applying Decision Theory to Improve Corporate Management of Currency Exchange Risks." *California Management Review,* Summer, pp. 41–49.

Wheelwright, S. C., and S. Makridakis. 1977. *Forecasting Methods for Management.* 2d ed. New York: John Wiley & Sons.

Wotruba, T. R., and M. L. Thurlow. 1976. "Sales Force Participation in Quota Setting and Sales Forecasting." *Journal of Marketing,* Vol. 40, April, pp. 11–16.

EXERCISES

1. American General Films

In August of 1971, Mr. Henry Mott, President of American General Films, was considering which of two financial arrangements he should adopt in connection with the rights to a new film, *New Zealand Safari.* During the previous twelve months, American General had test marketed this film and now had to decide on the financing arrangements it should make with the New Zealand government, the owner of the film.

American General Films was a privately owned firm that specialized in the mass marketing of family-oriented films. Its normal method of operation was to obtain the rights to a film, such as *New Zealand Safari,* from a private producer and then to market it throughout the United States and Canada by offering limited engagements at several theaters in each major population center. The showings of a given film in a major market were scheduled for a two-week period so that TV time could be purchased and used to advertise those theaters at which the movie would play. Thus the aim of the firm's marketing strategy was to saturate a major population center as far as that film was concerned during that two-week limited engagement. This program would then be repeated each year for three or four years or until American General felt that the marginal cost of marketing the film exceeded the marginal revenue. The film was then generally placed in the firm's inactive film library. During the past five years this method of operation had been very successful and had resulted in the firm's achieving an average annual return on investment of 18%.

The situation facing American General in connection with *New Zealand Safari* was a typical one. They had obtained the rights to run a market test on the film early in 1970. That test had now been completed and from its results Mr. Mott felt that he could estimate what the gross receipts would be on the film during its first full year of showings. He thought it was equally likely that these receipts would be greater or less than $3,000,000. He also felt that there was a 25% chance that the receipts would be less than $2,500,000 and a similar likelihood, that they would exceed $3,600,000. In no case did he feel that the first year's gross receipts on the film would exceed $5,500,000 or fall below $1,200,000. Mr. Mott felt certain that American General would want to market the film extensively during the coming year because it was by far the most promising of those they had tested, and their initial agreement with the New Zealand government required that they promote it on a nationwide basis during the coming year. (New Zealand was obviously interested in promoting itself as well as receiving the payment for the rights to the film.)

By September 1, 1971, American General had to sign an agreement with the New Zealand government on the terms of payment for exclusive rights to the film. Two options were available—a fixed payment plan or a variable payment plan. The fixed payment option would require that the company make a single cash payment on October 1, 1971, of $750,000. If this plan were adopted, no additional payments would have to be made.

The alternative plan involved a down payment of $200,000 to be paid on October 1, 1971, and a series of annual cash payments for each of the following five years. The amounts of these subsequent annual payments would depend on the gross receipts of the film during its first full year of promotion (September 1, 1971, through August 31, 1972). If the gross receipts for the first year of promotion were $4,000,000 or less, the variable payment plan would require the $200,000 down payment plus cash payments of 6% of the actual first year gross receipts in 1972, 1973, and 1974 and payments in 1975 and 1976 equaling 3% of first-year gross receipts. If gross receipts exceeded $4,000,000, then under the variable payment plan, American General would have to make the above payments plus an additional payment on October 1, 1972, amounting to 10% of the amount by which first-year gross receipts exceeded $4,500,000.

Although the thought of accepting this second set of terms and then only promoting the film in a limited fashion during the coming year had occurred to Mr. Mott, he had ruled it out both because of the previous agreement with the New Zealand government and because of the company's need to include it as a major part of the coming year's product line.

To help him in deciding which of these two financing arrangements he should accept, Mr. Mott asked an assistant to determine the probability that the lump sum arrangement would be more costly to American General than the alternative arrangement which was based on the first year's gross receipts. Mr. Mott had decided that if the probability exceeded .4, he would make the time payments; otherwise, he would pay the single lump sum.

2. Shasta Timber

For the past two years, Bob Cohen and J. B. Sullivan have been serving as timber estimator apprentices under Al Beers, one of the two master estimators presently retained by

Shasta Timber, a moderately large wood products firm in northern California. The timber estimator is a crucial link in maintaining a steady flow of logs from the forests to the mill, for logging decisions are based on his estimates, and the flow thus established. If the flow is too low, the milling operations are disrupted and, if too high, excessive waste will result. Consequently, a good estimator is a highly valued asset to any company. Shasta will soon begin developing several new areas and a third master estimator will be required to cover these tracts. Mr. Cohen and Mr. Sullivan are prime candidates for this assignment.

A timber estimator surveys the tracts by foot and by helicopter estimating the forest density, the average height of the trees, and the average diameter. From these data and a certain feel that is developed over many years of close association with logging operations, an estimate of the number of cubic feet of usable timber is made. This estimate is given to the manager of the Forest Operations Division who stores it in his locked safe. The division manager is the only person in the company who has access to the estimate as well as to the actual yield from each of the surveyed tracts. The yield is roughly measured when the cut logs are transported from the tract to the mill.

The estimator works in an environment of little feedback, since Shasta does not inquire as to how he made his prediction nor do they tell him the actual yield. In addition, two master estimators are never assigned to survey the same tracts. Thus the estimator does not have a standard against which he can compare his performance. In fact, the only indication that he has been performing well is that he has retained his job. When an estimator goes bad, he is transferred to another area.

The training program operates in precisely the same way except that the master estimator assists in the apprentice's estimates. For the past six months the two apprentices have been operating without Mr. Beer's assistance and their performances are as follows:

Cohen		Sullivan	
Estimate	Actual	Estimate	Actual
1500	1410	1425	1570
1625	1940	1625	2000
1225	1660	1400	1330
1375	1140	1100	1250
1850	1200	1500	1780
1450	1550		

Note: Figures given in cubic feet per acre.

Based on these records, the division manager must decide which apprentice is to be retained.

3. Lyon Plate Glass Company

In late 1972, Jean-Pierre Laurent, a recent graduate of a well-known European business school, inherited a sizable block of stock in the Lyon Plate Glass Company (LPG). LPG was a closely held French corporation in the glass production business. The firm sold most of its products to other industrial companies, particularly auto manufacturers and construction

TABLE 13-2   RELEVANT DATA FOR LYON PLATE GLASS COMPANY

Year	Net Sales LPG (millions of francs)	Automobile Production (in millions)	Building Contracts (in millions)
1956	280.0	3.909	9.43
1957	281.5	5.119	10.36
1958	337.4	6.666	14.50
1959	404.2	5.338	15.75
1960	402.1	4.321	16.78
1961	452.0	6.117	17.44
1962	431.7	5.559	19.77
1963	582.3	7.920	23.76
1964	596.6	5.816	31.61
1965	620.8	6.113	32.17
1966	513.6	4.258	35.09
1967	606.9	5.591	36.42
1968	629.0	6.675	36.58
1969	602.7	5.543	37.14
1970	656.7	6.933	41.30
1971	778.5	7.638	45.62
1972	877.6	7.752	47.38
1973*	—	6.400	48.51
1974*	—	7.900	51.23

* Estimates (forecasts) prepared by the French government.
Note: See Chapter 6 on Multiple Regression for additional information on regression analysis.

operations, although it did have a growing retail business amounting to about one-eighth of its total operation in 1971.

Because the firm's stock was closely held by two families, neither of whose name happened to be Laurent, they were anxious to buy Jean-Pierre's stock rather than take a chance on his wanting a say in the management of the company. Early in 1973, negotiations were completed and Jean-Pierre was faced with choosing between two alternative buy-out plans. (He had definitely decided to sell the stock that his stepmother had left him.)

The first plan was a lump sum agreement that would pay him 8,200,000 francs for this stock. The alternative plan was based on 1973 sales of LPG. (He negotiated this plan because an advisor from a well-known U.S. business school had predicted that 1973 would be another boom year for the French glass industry.) The amount Jean-Pierre would receive under this alternative would be a lump sum of 7,750,000 francs if the sales of LPG were 775 million francs *or less* during 1973. If 1973 sales exceeded this level, he would receive an amount equal to 1% of 1973 sales. Since under both alternatives Jean-Pierre would receive his money in cash

TABLE 13-3 RESULTS OF REGRESSION ANALYSIS FOR LYON PLATE GLASS COMPANY

Run 1 $(Y = A + B_1 X_1)$

Y=LPG Sales X_1=Automobile Production
A= −33.98
B_1=95.11
SEE=125.1
Adjusted R^2=.473

Using these results to forecast Y for 1973 gives the following fractiles:

.01	.10	.25	.50	.75	.90	.99
282.3	415.0	490.4	575.0	659.5	735.2	867.4

Run 2 $(Y = A + B_2 X_2)$

Y=LPG Sales X_2=Building Contracts
A=180.93
B_2=12.69
SEE=54.1
Adjusted R^2=.899

Using these results to forecast Y for 1973 gives the following fractiles:

.01	.10	.25	.50	.75	.90	.99
670.5	727.4	760.0	796.5	833.1	865.6	922.4

Run 3 $(Y = A + B_1 X_1 + B_2 X_2)$

Y=LPG Sales X_1=Automobile Production X_2=Building Contracts
A=19.13
B_1=35.67
B_2=10.86
SEE=42.5
Adjusted R^2=.947

Using these results to forecast Y for 1973 gives the following fractiles:

.01	.10	.25	.50	.75	.90	.99
672.3	716.8	742.7	771.4	800.1	825.9	880.5

on January 30, 1974, he did not feel it was necessary to discount the amounts involved in order to make his decision.

To help him in making his decision, Jean-Pierre had tried to apply much of what he had learned in business school about decision making under uncertainty. Graphically, he viewed his decision as follows:

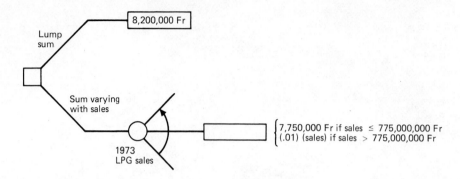

Jean-Pierre saw as his next task determining the possible sales levels for 1973. Because LPG sold mainly to the auto and construction industries, and since the French government prepared forecasts for these two industries, regression analysis looked like a useful forecasting tool. After gathering the data in Table 13-2, Jean-Pierre ran several regressions, the results of which are shown in Table 13-3. He must now decide how to complete the analysis of his problem.

14 QUALITATIVE AND TECHNOLOGICAL METHODS OF FORECASTING

14/1 Introduction

The terms *qualitative* and *technological* are generally used to denote forecasting techniques focused primarily on predicting the environment and technology over the longer term. They contrast with quantitative methods that are employed mainly for economic, marketing, financial, and other business forms of forecasting. Technological methods are not simply an extrapolation of past data patterns, as are many of their quantitative counterparts, nor do they assume constancy of the past pattern into the future. Even though history plays an important role in these methods of forecasting, technological techniques require imagination combined with individual talent, knowledge, and foresight in order to effectively predict long-run changes. The intuition, judgment, imagination, and expertise required for application of these methods are in fact more important than the methods themselves. However, a knowledge of the procedures involved in various qualitative or technological approaches can help in formalizing both thought processes and prediction of the future.

Technological methods of forecasting do not always provide a step-by-step procedure, nor do they give their forecast in terms of a single numerical answer. Use of these methods varies with each situation and requires an understanding of the factors involved and the need to adapt the method to the particular situation. In contrast to quantitative methods, it is the expert who becomes the processor of facts, knowledge, and information, rather than some set of mathematical rules or mathematical model. In his book *Profiles of the Future*, Clark describes the environment within which the technological forecaster must operate as follows:

> He does not try to describe the future, but to define the boundaries within which possible futures must lie. If we regard the ages which stretch ahead of us as an unmapped and unexplored country, what he's attempting to do is to survey its frontiers and to gain some idea of its extent. The detailed geography of the interior must remain unknown until he reaches it. [Clark 1973, p. xi]

As might be expected, the costs of technological or qualitative methods of forecasting are frequently greater than those of quantitative methods, largely because they often require a considerable commitment of time on the part of experts. It is particularly difficult in the case of technological forecasting to trade off the expected costs with the level of accuracy because accuracy is extremely hard to determine. Essentially the problem of accuracy becomes similar to that described for subjective assessments; inaccuracy of a single technological forecast does not indicate the level of accuracy provided by that methodology or that expert. While biases can be identified in technological forecasters, it is an extremely difficult process and requires considerable experience with both the forecaster and the methodology.

In spite of the difficulties and the subjective nature of technological forecasting and its evaluation, it has grown rapidly in its acceptance and application in organizations. In 1969 Jantsch estimated that about 500 to 600 medium and large American companies had established a technological forecasting function as a part of their operations. In 1969 Ayres estimated that about half of the largest 500 companies in the United States were using such forecasting methodologies. Cetron and Ralph reported in 1971 that about 50% of the people responding to their survey on the use of various forecasting methods indicated they used technological approaches.

Some authors have chosen to include long-range planning activities as an integral part of technological forecasting. When such planning activities are included, the number of organizations using these methods is indeed substantial. In 1971 Gerstenfeld reported that 71% of the respondents in his forecasting survey were using such methodologies. Subsequent studies have indicated 70% to 90% of respondents using such techniques, depending on the population being surveyed.

The exact percentage of organizations making use of technological methodologies is not of great importance. However, the fact that these methods have gained widespread acceptance in spite of their drawbacks indicates the importance of the problems with which they deal and the need that organizations feel for improving their forecasting in such situations. It is likely that organizations in the future will feel even more need to use technological forecasting in order to cope with the rapid acceleration of technological innovation and changes in the environment.

Before describing several of the different methods included in the category of qualitative or technological forecasting, it is useful to further define these terms and the items they cover. Since these definitions vary substantially from one writer to another, it is useful to consider definitions from several different authors in order to more completely describe the area covered by these methods and some of their important characteristics.

Prehoda (1967, p. 12) provides a simple intuitive definition of technological forecasting as "the description or prediction of a foreseeable invention, specific scientific refinement or likely scientific discoveries, that promise to serve some useful function. These are functions that meet the requirements of industry and military services, government agencies, and the general needs of society." Cetron (1969, p. 4) defines these methodologies as "a basis for prediction with a level of confidence of a technological achievement in a given time frame with a specific level of support." Jantsch (1969, p. 15) uses as his definition, "the probabilistic assessment on a relatively high confidence level of future technology transfer." Although other writers provide different definitions, most seem to agree that these methodologies distinguish formal prediction with high confidence levels from mere guesses or fiction. Technological forecasting falls into the former category as being systematic and providing greater confidence in the results.

A question that is often raised in a discussion of technological or qualitative methods of forecasting is whether or not they really represent methods at all, or whether they are simply attempts at describing what experts might do anyway. Among the objections raised to these methods is the fact that using the same method with different experts does not produce the same forecasts. Sometimes the divergence in opinion among the experts is so extensive that it is hard to imagine that any substantial confidence could be placed in the results. In addition, following the method gives no assurance that the goal of better forecasts will be achieved. While these are clearly important issues to be considered in determining whether a specific method should be adopted, the fact remains that in many instances these technological methods are the only systematic approaches available. As more experience is gained in the field, other methods will undoubtedly be proposed, many of which will represent substantial improvements over existing approaches. However, in the meantime understanding the methods currently available can be very helpful.

In the remainder of this chapter the distinction made by Roberts (1969) between *exploratory* and *normative* methodologies will be pursued. As explained by Jantsch (1969, p. 15), exploratory forecasts "start from today's assured basis of knowledge and are oriented toward the future, while normative technological forecasting first assesses future goals, needs, desires, missions, etc., and works backwards to the present in order to determine those developments which will be necessary to achieve those goals." A number of the most commonly used exploratory methods will be discussed in the next section. These tend to be more fully developed than the normative methods, which will be discussed in the final section of this chapter.

14/2 Exploratory Methods of Forecasting

14/2/1 Subjective Assessment Methods

Subjective assessment or intuitive approaches to forecasting were the focus of the previous chapter. The basic idea of such methodologies is to make efficient use of the ability of the human mind in processing very diverse pieces of information. Approaches for subjective assessment range from a single individual attempting to forecast the future to the use of committees, panels, polls, and other group work. Generally these subjective assessment approaches do not include much detail as to the actual steps the individuals will follow in their thought processes. Rather, the focus is on obtaining predictions in certain formats so that they can then be integrated with other planning and decision-making processes. As pointed out in the previous chapter, one framework frequently used for structuring predictions is that of decision analysis.

An approach that was not described in the previous chapter, but is close to technological forecasting while still involving subjective assessments is that of brainstorming. Extensive work has been done on creativity and the use of brainstorming sessions to discover new ideas or solve complex problems. Brainstorming aims at freeing individuals from traditional constraints and "sets" that inhibit them from discovering new approaches and new conceptualizations regarding the future. Some of the rules that might be followed in a brainstorming session could include the following:

1. Consider any idea, opinion, or alternative, regardless of its feasibility, relevance, or applicability.
2. Do not criticize any other individual involved in the session for expression of ideas or opinions.
3. Encourage and support the formulation and statement of unusual ideas and thoughts.

One of the dangers in brainstorming is that the discussions may grow so diverse that no alternatives, conclusions, or consensus about the initial problem will be reached. In this respect the leader of the brainstorming session must be highly skilled at directing the group toward the desired outcome without constraining their creative thought processes. This balance can be achieved in part by defining the problem at the outset and specifying the boundaries of interest. However, such restrictions, no matter what their practical value in terms of reaching a conclusion, may limit the creative process.

While considerable material has been written on subjective assessment approaches to technological forecasting, not much has been written as to the accuracy and performance of these approaches. A few general discussions that try to tackle the question of performance evaluation of these approaches have recently appeared in the literature.

In 1955 the Nobel prize-winning British physicist, Sir George Thomson, published a book forecasting future technological developments called *The Foreseeable Future*. The work was based largely on his own assessments of the future regarding those variables that he thought might be most important. The book and its forecasts were recently reevaluated by Prehoda (1975). He reports that Thomson's forecasts have generally turned out to be remarkably accurate with a few noteworthy exceptions where the data Thomson was using were generally incorrect.

Another study that recently reviewed the performance of technological forecasts based on subjective assessment processes was reported in a series of articles, "The Future Revised," published in *The Wall Street Journal*. These articles reviewed the set of forecasts that *The Wall Street Journal* had reported ten years earlier (1965) and identified the accurate and the inaccurate forecasts as well as the reasons for inaccuracies. The series concluded that although the forecasts prepared in the mid-1960s were made with extreme care and with the most sophisticated methodologies available, they proved to be quite unsatisfactory.

One of the reasons this study found a higher level of inaccuracy than the Thomson reevaluation is that *The Wall Street Journal* had reported on forecasts of very specific variables for a long-term time horizon. Essentially, they were seeking to identify changes in pattern rather than to identify what the actual environment and technology would look like. Undoubtedly one factor contributing to the inaccuracies is that the variables themselves have changed. Those preparing the forecasts in the mid-1960s severely limited themselves by sticking to those variables that were important in the 1960s and thought to be the key items for futures planning.

14/2/2 Dramatic Simulations of Reality

Several techniques use dramatic simulations of reality to explore possible futures. Scenario writing, gaming or role playing, and science fiction are examples of these methods.

Scenario writing takes a well-defined set of assumptions, then develops an imaginative conception of what the future would be like if these assumptions were true. In this sense, scenarios are not future predictions by themselves. Rather they present a number of possible alternatives, each one based on certain assumptions and conditions. It is then up to the decision maker to assess the validity of the assumptions in deciding which scenario is most likely to become reality.

Much of the work on scenario writing has been done by Kahn of the Hudson Institute. Kahn (1964, 1976) developed a number of alternative scenarios for the world. In one he assumed that an arms control agreement between the United States and Russia would be reached and that China would follow only a defensive policy, not an offensive policy. Based on these and other assumptions, he developed a scenario describing a future political-social environment, following a predictable sequence of developments, constraints, and ideologies. For this set of assumptions, Kahn predicted a future environment that would be highly stable and peaceful. Under a different scenario, Kahn assumed that Russia would lose control over the world Communist movement, that the European Economic Community would become much stronger and more protectionist in its policies, and so on. The third scenario Kahn described in 1964 was based on the construction of new alliances among the countries and the development or acquisition of nuclear arms by smaller countries. This set of assumptions gives rise to a very different scenario of the world's future environment and its relative stability.

A technological approach that is very similar to that of scenario writing in concept is *gaming* or *role playing*. It consists of using either straight mathematics or combining it with individuals serving as actors in order to determine the effects of an action and reaction pair. For example, the role might involve various competitors, consumers, or another third party and might give some general guidelines for behavior, and then require the participants to develop their own responses to various actions by the central organization. The difficulty in such role playing or gaming is the inability of the person or mathematical model representing the individual player to act as that party would act in reality. However, in many cases the method can suggest a number of alternatives, much as brain-storming would, that would not normally be thought of within the planning organization.

Another approach that is similar to scenario writing, but even more speculative, is that of science fiction. Many of the writers of science fiction literature are actually spinning scenarios as to alternative states of technology and the environment. Historically there have been some writers who have done fairly well at predicting the future. For example, Jules Verne, Karel Ĉapek, Aldous Huxley, and David A. Clarke seem to have been particularly successful in foreseeing future environmental states. The major problem in using such science fiction as a source of information for planning is distinguishing those writings that are pure fantasy from those that are likely to represent reality. It is also often the case that the time horizon for these scenarios is so long that they are of very limited value to an individual organization. For example, if an individual company had accepted Verne's predictions regarding atomic energy and moon flights as being accurate more than 100 years ago when Verne wrote those stories, it would have had little impact on the company's own performance and strategy.

14/2/3 The Delphi Approach

The Delphi approach is undoubtedly the most commonly used of technological or qualitative forecasting methods. This approach, originally developed at the Rand Corporation, is essentially a method for obtaining a refined consensus from a group. In this sense, it is very similar to some of the methodologies discussed in the previous chapter. However, it seeks to be much more systematic in its use of individual assessments and can be used whenever a group consensus is needed, whether for a forecast or for some other type of estimate.

The objective of the Delphi approach is to obtain a reliable consensus of opinion from a group of experts that can be used as a future forecast, while at the same time minimizing the undesirable aspects of group interaction. Two of the main developers of this approach, Helmer and Rescher have described the Delphi method as follows:

> The Delphi technique eliminates committee activity altogether thus further reducing the influence of certain psychological factors, such as specious persuasion, the unwillingness to abandon publicly expressed opinions, and the bandwagon effect of majority opinion. This technique replaces direct debate by a carefully designed program of sequential individual interrogations (best conducted by questionnaires), interspersed with information and opinion feedback derived by computer consensus from the earlier parts of the program. Some of the questions directed at respondents may, for instance, inquire into the "reasons" for previous expressed opinions and a collection of such reasons may then be presented to each respondent in the group, together with an invitation to reconsider and possibly revise his or her earlier estimates.*

Application of the Delphi approach requires a group of experts who are willing to answer specific questions relating to problems, such as the forecasting of a new technological process and the time at which that will take place. However, these experts do not meet to debate the question, but rather are kept apart from one another so that their judgment will not be influenced by social pressure or other aspects of small-group behavior. An example of how this approach has been used will demonstrate its procedural characteristics (Helmer and Rescher 1959).

Phase 1. The experts on the panel were asked in a letter to name inventions and scientific breakthroughs that they thought were both urgently needed and could be achieved within the next 20 years. Each expert was then asked to send his or her list back to the coordinator of the panel. From these lists, a general list of 50 items was compiled.

Phase 2. The experts were then sent a list of the 50 items and asked to place each of those items in one of the five-year time periods into which the next 20 years had been divided. The basis for this categorization was that there would be a 50-50 probability that it would take a longer or shorter period of time for each breakthrough to occur. Again, the experts were asked to sent their responses to the panel coordinator. (Throughout this procedure the experts were kept apart and asked not to contact any of the other members of the panel.)

Phase 3. Letters were again sent to the experts telling them on which items there was a general consensus and giving them the responses falling in the middle 50%, as well as in each of the higher and lower quartiles on those items where there was not a general consensus.

The experts were also asked to state their reason for any widely divergent

---

*O. Helmer and N. Rescher, "On the Epistemology of the Inexact Sciences," *Management Science*, vol. 6, no. 1 (1959), p. 47. Reprinted by permission.

estimates they had made. Several of the experts, as a result of this, reassessed their estimates in a narrower range.

Phase 4. To narrow the range of estimates further, the phase 3 procedure was repeated. At the end of this phase, a number of the original items on the list were grouped together as breakthroughs for which a relatively narrow time estimate of their occurrence had been obtained. Thus, the final result of such a procedure was not only information based on expert opinion as to what breakthroughs were likely to occur, but also information as to when those breakthroughs would most likely be achieved.

The individual answers obtained when the Delphi approach is applied ensure the anonymity that is needed to reduce the effect of the "socially dominant individual," and controlled feedback reduces the redundant or irrelevant noise often found in direct confrontations. Furthermore, the conformity to a majority opinion achieved by committee meetings is avoided through presentation of a statistical group (quartile) response in relation to the feedback of previous estimates. It would be possible also to consider questions of cost as well as questions of timing of breakthroughs and the nature of those breakthroughs.

It should be stressed that the Delphi approach does not necessarily produce a single answer as its output, as is the case with many methods based on questionnaires. Instead of a single consensus, the Delphi approach permits a spread of opinion so that the uncertainties surrounding a situation can be better reflected. The objective is to narrow the quartile range as much as possible without pressuring the experts on the panel to the extent that deviant opinion would no longer be allowed. This can be done in part by asking deviants to justify their position. Helmer describes the use of this characteristic of the approach somewhat further:

> The effect of placing the onus of justifying relatively extreme responses on the respondent has the effect of causing those without strong convictions to move their estimates closer to the median while those who feel they have a good argument for a "deviationist" opinion tend to retain their original estimate and defend it. [Helmer 1966a]

The Delphi method, like any individual forecasting approach, has its disadvantages. The most general complaints against it are its often low level of reliability, its oversensitivity of results to ambiguity in the questionnaire, and the difficulty in assessing the degree of expertise incorporated in its forecast. These disadvantages must be weighed against the advantages that can often be achieved through its use. These objections obviously apply to even less systematic techniques with greater force than they do to the Delphi approach.

There are a variety of situations within business and government in which the Delphi technique can be used with only minor modifications. In the corporate setting, the experts in the group generally come from both within and outside the company. An important aspect of such a group is that each expert need not be well qualified in exactly the same portion of the area of interest. Rather, the experts can be qualified in only subparts of the area, with at least one expert in every subpart. In this way, information can be processed about the entire problem area. The initial questionnaire distributed to the group of experts should seek to establish the general products or production processes for which the forecasts are to be made. The subsequent phases would then give the panel members feedback on the results of the first phase and attempt to have the panel reach a consensus on some of the kinds of products and processes likely to be developed and the timing of these developments. The final phases might seek to further detail some of the specifics of these developments and attempt to discover the most likely alternatives to be developed first.

A number of evaluative studies have been made in recent years in order to summarize experiences with the Delphi technique and some of its advantages and disadvantages. One of the most thorough of these is that prepared by Sackman (1975). He not only attempts to evaluate the Delphi approach, he also seeks to describe some of its variations and some of the alternative procedures that have been found to best overcome shortcomings in the method as it was originally developed. Another interesting summary of experience with Delphi is that prepared by Ament (1970). In this study, a comparison was made of expert panels studying similar problems using the Delphi technique in 1964 and 1969. The conclusions of this study indicate a relative consistency in the forecasts prepared, a shift in median dates of many biological forecasts to earlier time periods, and a shift to later dates for several of the space forecasts. The study also indicated that the spread of the forecast values increased as a function of median time into the future. Thus, the conclusion was that by following the procedures, the same kind of characteristics were observed whether they were followed in the mid-sixties or in the late sixties. A third work, by Linstone and Turoff (1975), also has added to the evaluative literature on the Delphi approach, as well as expanding discussion of its practical applications.

14/2/4   Cross-Impact Matrices

A technological method of forecasting closely related to both the Delphi method and the use of the scenario is that of cross-impact matrices. Although a rather recent development, a number of papers have appeared reporting applications of this methodology. A cross-impact matrix describes two types of data for a set of possible future developments. The first type estimates the probability that each development will occur within some specified time period in the future. The second estimates the probability that the occurrence of any one of the potential developments would have an effect on the likelihood of occurrence of each of the others. In general, the data for such a matrix can be obtained using either subjective assessment procedures or a method such as the Delphi approach.

The aim of cross-impact analysis is to refine the probabilities relating to the occurrence of individual future developments and their interaction with other developments to the point that these probabilities can be used either as the basis for planning or as the basis for developing scenarios that subsequently can be used in planning. An example taken from Rochberg et al. (1970) will help to illustrate this methodology and its application in forecasting. In this example there are four developments that might occur in the next year. These developments are shown at the top of Figure 14-1. In the bottom of that figure, the cross-impact matrix is shown. The upward arrows in certain of the boxes in the matrix indicate where the occurrence of a certain development will increase the probability of one of the other developments. For example, if D-2, *Feasibility of Limited Weather Control*, were to occur then D-1, *One-Month Reliable Weather Forecast*, would become more probable as noted by the upward arrow.

The interaction between the various potential developments shown in

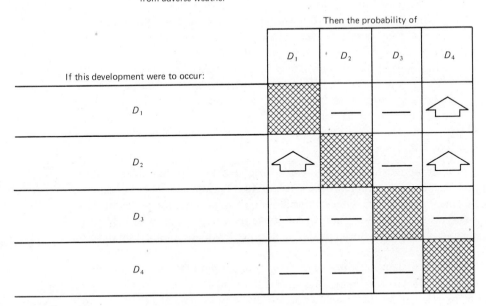

FIGURE 14-1 EXAMPLE OF A CROSS-IMPACT MATRIX

Figure 14-1 are, of course, very complex. The arrows simply indicate the nature of the relationship. Some form of expert opinion and subjective assessment would be needed to quantify that relationship. In addition, the technique of simulation is often used to further refine these probability estimates and their overall impact on the probability that each individual development will occur in the specified time period.

Through appropriate analysis of the problem and use of the guidelines suggested by those who have developed this approach to forecasting, numerical estimates of the probabilities can be filled in for each box in a cross-impact matrix. In addition, formulas can be developed for calculating changes in probabilities that will occur as different developments become a reality. Once this has been done, the matrix can be analyzed using a computer and the technique of simulation. Rochberg (1970) describes the following set of steps for this analysis:

1. Assessing the potential interactions (the cross impacts) among individual events in a set of forecasts in terms of:
    a. direction or mode of the interaction
    b. strength of the interaction
    c. time delay of the effect of one event on another
2. Selecting an event at random and "deciding" its occurrence or non-occurrence on the basis of its assigned probability. (This is simply an application of simulation.)
3. Adjusting the probability of the remaining events according to the interactions assessed in step 1.
4. Selecting another event from among those remaining and deciding its occurrence or nonoccurrence (using its new probability) as before. (Again, this is an application of simulation.)
5. Continuing this process until all events in the set have been decided.
6. "Playing" the matrix in this way many times so that the probabilities can be computed on the basis of the percentage of times an event occurs during these repeated plays.
7. Changing the initial probability of one or more events and repeating steps 2 through 6.

Through application of this procedure, a set of probabilities can be developed that adequately represents the interaction between a number of different developments, each of which is uncertain. This analysis allows such probabilities to take into account the cross-impacts of other events. Clearly, that is of help to the forecaster and planner who must consider a number of different uncertain developments.

One of the first applications of the cross-impact method was that developed by Gordon and Hayward (1968). This application involved 28 events that were judged to be relevant to the decision concerning deployment of the Minuteman Missile System. These 28 events were arrayed in a matrix like that of Figure 14-1 and estimates were obtained for the direction, strength, and time phasing of the effects of the events on each other. The matrix was then run 1000 times on a computer according to the steps outlined above. The results were averaged in order to obtain new estimates of the probability of occurrence of each of the events in the matrix. Those probability shifts identified through this procedure provided the forecasters with some measure of the combined cross-impact effects implicit in the original matrix.

The results of this application to the Minuteman analysis problem indicated that the mutual interaction of the events increased the likelihood of the decision to deploy the system. In addition, a ranking of the events in terms of their final cross-impacted probabilities provided the ingredients for a scenario that subsequently proved to be quite descriptive of the technological and political environment of the 1950s. Thus, despite the simplifications needed to apply the methodology, the findings were consistent with what actually occurred.

While the basic concept of cross-impact matrices is straightforward, the detailed paths involved in its application are generally quite complex. In fact, Amara (1972) points out that one of the major shortcomings of the methodology is that frequently the impact of various developments on each other is sequence-dependent. That is, the probabilities for the impact of one development on another depend on sequences of activity rather than on individual activities. That, of course, greatly increases the magnitude of the problem and the difficulties associated with the application of this methodology. However, in spite of these shortcomings, it is a technique that has found a number of useful applications in both government and business.

14/2/5 Curve Fitting

Curve fitting is a methodology commonly discussed as a quantitative forecasting technique, but it is also an approach that can be effectively used as a technological method. However, there are considerable differences in the approaches taken in both instances. It will be recalled from previous chapters that in the quantitative methods, some form of curve fitting is often done to approximate the basic trend component of a time series. This fitting is usually based on historical data and covers only a few years in most instances. In the case of technological approaches to curve fitting, the time horizon is generally much longer, only a limited number of data points are available, some rather tenuous assumptions must be made, and an interpretation of results is required. However, in some instances, this approach can indeed be most helpful to the forecaster and planner.

The application of curve fitting in predicting the efficiency of man-made illumination (Cetron 1969) can serve as an example of this approach. In this particular application there are only seven data points available, each representing a substantial development in technology that has occurred historically. This small number of data points makes it very tenuous to do any quantitative type of prediction. Furthermore, a simple trend cannot be extrapolated directly because the curve would increase indefinitely. Such an increase is impossible because the efficiency of man-made illumination cannot exceed the theoretical efficiency of light. Thus the trend will have to bend as shown in Figure 14-2.

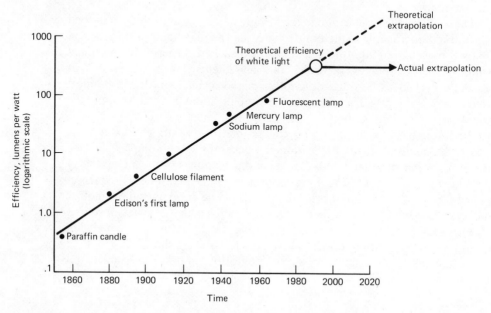

FIGURE 14-2 EFFICIENCY OF MAN-MADE WHITE LIGHT

There are many different shapes of curves that can be used in fitting historical data for technological forecasting. One of the most frequently used forms is that of the S-curve. As indicated in the example shown in Figure 14-3, this curve implies a slow start, a steep growth, and then a plateau that is characteristic of many technological capabilities. This shape of curve is often used in depicting the product life cycle. Chambers et al. (1971) report that the sales of both black and white and color TV have followed such S-patterns. Ayres (1969) and Jantsch (1967) also report a number of applications of different technologies that have followed such S-shaped curves. By connecting the tangents of individual growth curves, an envelope of S-curves can be formed that can be used to predict such things as the maximum speed of transportation. The example in Figure 14-3 shows the behavior of transportation speed from the pony express to the chemical rocket. This curve can be further extrapolated to predict future speeds of nuclear rockets or even presently unknown forms of energy.

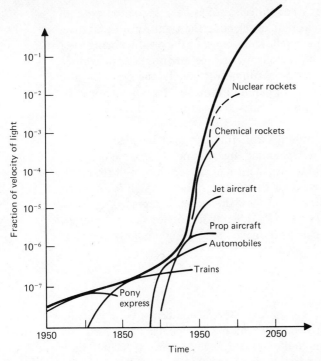

FIGURE 14-3 S-CURVE OF TRANSPORTATION SPEED

Mathematically, there are many different equations that can be used to represent an S-shaped curve. The most common of these are the following:

$$Y = e^{a - (b/t)} \qquad (14\text{-}1)$$

$$Y = \frac{L}{1 + ae^{-bt}} \qquad (14\text{-}2)$$

$$Y = Le^{-ae^{-bt}} \qquad (14\text{-}3)$$

$$Y = (1 - ae^{-bt})^3 \qquad (14\text{-}4)$$

In each instance the parameter A is the intercept of the S-curve, the parameter B is the slope, L is the upper limit (the asymptote), and t is time. Estimating the parameters for equation 14-1 is a rather straightforward matter, as has been shown in previous chapters. In equations 14-2 and 14-3, if $L = 1$, the equation is simplified considerably and can be estimated using the method of least squares after the appropriate transformation has been applied. In equation 14-4, the parameters cannot be estimated using least squares because the functional form cannot be reduced to a linear trend.

A major problem that arises when a decision has been made to apply an S-curve in technological forecasting is that of selecting the right form of S-curve. The solution to this problem depends on the technology or the product being forecast and its characteristics. Through previous experience one might approximate the S-curve form in order to use it for forecasting. Fortunately, the exact form of S-curve necessary for sufficient accuracy for planning is not always critical as can be seen from Figure 14-4. (The choice of one S-curve over another will result in little difference in the arrow.)

There are several other functional forms that can also be used in curve fitting for technological purposes—exponential, logarithmic, double exponential, and others. The problem of determining which form of curve will best fit the available data and give an accurate forecast for the future is always the most difficult part of such applications. One illustration of these difficulties is reported by Ayres (1969) who describes the use of S-curves by two different forecasters. In each instant a different scale was used and this change alone led to strikingly different results.

14/2/6 Analogies

Analogies are attempts to compare historical patterns with existing situations in order to forecast future progress and developments. These forecasts are generally technological in nature and involve changes in various technologies or the environment. There are several types of analogies, including growth analogies, historical analogies, and social physics. Each of these will be discussed in turn.

Growth analogies

Many researchers have shown that the population growth tends to follow a pattern similar to the growth of biological organisms. The same conclusion was reached by Gompertz and Von Bertalanffy. The S-type curve described in the previous section can be used in predicting population growth pattern and its point of stability by using such analogies. The concept of analogy between biological and other kinds of growth has recently been applied to such phenomena as the growth pattern of particular technologies, transportation speeds, the life cycle of individual products, and the growth of government spending.

Cetron (1971) cites Lenz's application of the biological growth analogy (the growth of living organisms in a limited space) in predicting the maximum speed of military aircraft and concludes that Mach 6 performance can be expected in 1979, while Mach 12 speeds can be expected by 1995. These estimates are about 10 years later than those obtained through simple extrapolation of exponential trends, but these latter forms of extrapolation do not bend in the same way that biological growth patterns do.

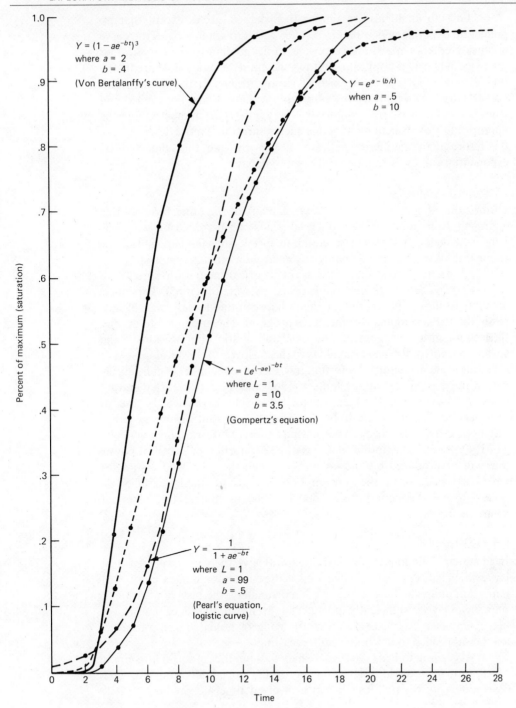

FIGURE 14-4 COMMONLY USED S-CURVES

Growth analogies are similar to S-shaped curves except that no prediction of parameters is required, since with growth analogies the curve is considered known and the purpose is to fit the data to the curve rather than vice versa. This application allows the curve to be used in predicting time estimates for the occurrence of various events in the future. With growth curves, as with S-curves, saturation will eventually be reached and identification of when that will occur is very important in determining the appropriate growth analogy. Whether such saturation is more descriptive of the future than an increasing rate of growth, like that depicted by exponential curves, is a matter still open to debate.

Historical analogies

Historical analogies are more intuitive than any of the other forms of this approach. In many different ways predictions can be based on what has happened in the past. In these common forms, such as superstition or rational thinking, historical analogies are as old as civilization itself.

One attempt to formalize the use of historical analogies for predictive purposes has been made in a book edited by Mazlish (1965). This book attempts to show a number of analogies between the development of railroads and the development of the space program. The attempt is to predict the technological development and social and political implications of the space program by drawing an analogy to these aspects of the development of railroads in the last century. Unfortunately, there are a number of deficiencies in this study, as pointed out by Jantsch (1967) and Ayres (1969), that detract from Mazlish's attempt to apply this approach. However, the use of historical analogies can still be extremely important in many other instances. General Electric has been using a form of historical analogy in its TEMPO project, attempting to forecast the proportion of electrical power that will be produced by nuclear fuels through the year 2060. Estimates have been made using the consumption of fossil fuel and hydroelectric power during the period from 1800 to 1960 as a base for historical comparison.

Social Physics

In a manner analogous to physical or natural laws, there may well be social laws, which if discovered could be used as the basis for making a number of important and valuable predictions. Unfortunately, the task of identifying such social laws is sufficiently difficult that even their existence has not yet been completely verified. However, the concept holds some promise as another approach to technological forecasting.

According to Bell (1964), there may be a number of social laws upon which human behavior, development of the social environment, and development of the political system at a given time are predicated. Bell uses the law of motion of capitalism set forth by Marx as an example of an attempt to identify such a social law. The falling rate of profit on which Marx based the large armies of unemployed, the impoverishment of labor, the centralization of capital, etc., can in fact be thought of as an analogy to a falling object that accelerates in speed and rate of fall because of gravity. The conclusion that Marx reached is that capitalism will fall in the same manner and nothing can stop or slow the rate of increased speed until it crashes. This conclusion is based on the assumption that there are natural laws that govern falling objects whether they be societies or whether they be physical items. Although Marx's specific predictions lack accuracy because he did not recognize the existence of feedback mechanisms that could slow down or reverse such laws of motion as they apply to societies, his predictions are based on an interesting methodology that may be applicable elsewhere.

Bell refers to still another application of the effort to create a social physics in discussing the work of Rappaport as follows:

> He [Rappaport] sets up mathematical models for mass action and descriptive models for conflict situations. One section of the book deals with arms races and the equations that are developed seek to describe the development of actual arms races in the same way that the equations of thermodynamics are meant to describe the behavior of gases. One intention of the new social physics is to set up general probabilistic laws that govern behavior in game-like situations. [Bell 1964, p. 850]

To what extent analogies can be used for technological forecasting is a question that has not yet been thoroughly answered. At the present time they are not used to any great extent, nor have they been used in the past by any large number of forecasters. However, they may be useful in particular situations for which data are not available or other methods simply are not suitable. One advantage of analogies is that they can be used intuitively and without much effort in many situations. Thus, they might be preferred in cases that require a tremendous amount of work before other methodologies can be applied successfully.

14/2/7 Morphological Research

The morphological approach to technological forecasting was developed by the well-known Swiss astronomer, Zwicky, in his efforts to discover new inventions in the field of jet engines. Zwicky claims over 30 industrial applications in addition to a large number of purely theoretical uses of this technique in discovering new technological possibilities. The General Electric TEMPO Center has used a morphological approach in some of its research and the same is true for several projects conducted at the Stanford Research Institute in areas of political and social development.

Morphological research "concerns itself with the development and the practical application of basic methods that will allow us to discover and analyze the structural or morphological interrelationships among objects, phenomena, and concepts and to explore the results obtained for the construction of a sound world" (Zwicky 1962, p. 275). This definition of the morphological method goes beyond simple forecasting applications and represents an approach to systematic thinking and problem solving. Although there may be some arguments about the universality of such an approach, it is clear that the framework can be very useful to those faced with technological forecasting problems. An application of this methodology will help to describe its usefulness.

Zwicky (1962) describes five basic steps comprising the morphological method:

Step 1. The problem must be explicitly formulated and defined.

Step 2. All parameters that may enter into the solution must be identified and characterized.

Step 3. A multidimensional matrix (the Morphological Box) containing all parameters identified in Step 2 must be constructed. This matrix will contain all possible solutions (combinations).

Step 4. All solutions of the Morphological Box should be examined for their feasibility, and analyzed and evaluated with respect to the purposes which are to be achieved.

Step 5. The best solutions identified in Step 4 should be analyzed (possibly through an additional Morphological Study) as to the feasibility of carrying them out with available resources.

As an application of this approach, Zwicky mentions his attempts in the late thirties to identify possible propulsive power plants (jet engines) that could be activated by chemical energy. He distinguishes six parameters that define all possible jet engines of this form:

P_1: The medium through which the jet engine moves. There are four components related to the first parameter.

   P_{11}: denoting that the jet engine moves through a vacuum,

   P_{12}: denoting that the jet engine moves in the atmosphere,

   P_{13}: denoting that the jet engine moves in large bodies of water,

   P_{14}: denoting that the jet engine moves in the solid surface strata of the Earth.

P_2: The type of motion of the propellant relative to the jet engine, with the following four components:

   P_{21}: denoting a propellant at rest,

   P_{22}: denoting a translatory motion,

P_{23}: denoting an oscillatory motion,

P_{24}: denoting a rotary motion.

P_3: The physical state of the propellant, with the following three components:

P_{31}: denoting a gaseous physical state,

P_{32}: denoting a liquid physical state,

P_{33}: denoting a solid physical state.

P_4: The type of thrust augmentation, with the following three parameters:

P_{41}: denoting no thrust augmentation,

P_{42}: denoting internal thrust augmentation,

P_{43}: denoting external thrust augmentation.

P_5: The type of ignition, with the following two parameters:

P_{51}: denoting a self-igniting engine,

P_{52}: denoting an externally ignited engine.

P_6: The sequence of operations, with the following two parameters:

P_{61}: continuous operation,

P_{62}: intermittent operation. [Zwicky 1962, p. 32]

From the above Morphological Box of 6 parameters, 576 combinations $(4 \times 4 \times 3 \times 3 \times 2 \times 2 = 576)$ of jet engines can be identified. These can then be studied for their feasibility and analyzed and evaluated with respect to their ability to achieve a specific set of objectives. The large number of alternatives involved makes it impractical to examine all of them (step 4). Zwicky had either to pick at random some of them for study, or to discover some principle that would relate a number of possible alternatives so he could study them as a group.

Based on this use of morphological analysis, Zwicky was able to suggest several radical new inventions that were at least conceptually sound and many of which were later successfully developed in various stages of jet engine technology. He goes on to describe 16 different patents that were granted to him as a result of his study of the jet engine example and claims that those patents and the inventions they represent were obtained largely as a result of applying this morphological approach.

One of the advantages accompanying the use of morphological research stems from its assessment of the chances that a future technology will be realized. This assessment can be made based on a study of the Morphological Box and is calculated as a function of what Zwicky calls the morphological distance (the number of parameters by which the existing technology differs from a specific one inside the Morphological Box). The greater the distance the smaller will be the chances of that particular technology's being realized. In a similar fashion, technological opportunities can be evaluated as a function of the number of combinations existing within the neighborhood of a certain technology. The greater the number the higher the chances that technology will materialize, either by accident or because it will be needed before some future technological development can be realized.

It should be stressed that morphological research is a kind of checklist that in a systematic manner enumerates all possible combinations of technologies. Its advantage is that it allows the user to identify hidden or rare opportunities for technological possibilities that can be profitably developed. Both the search for new technologies and their chances of successful development can be calculated from the checklist or Morphological Box. Even though simple in nature, the morphological approach can serve as a useful tool to the forecaster in many situations.

Taylor et al. (1967) have combined the morphological approach with scenario writing. A similar combination has also been used by the Hudson Institute where a variety of different types of nuclear threats and possible future worlds have been classified in a Morphological Box. Although few applications of this approach to business situations have been reported, an exercise is included at the end of this chapter that suggests how it might be used in that setting.

14/2/8   Catastrophe Theory

A major new approach to forecasting began developing in the mid-seventies. This approach, called *catastrophe theory*, may eventually become a more quantitative method of forecasting, but its early stages have many attributes that would classify it as a technological or qualitative approach. The aim of catastrophe theory is to fill a significant gap in existing forecasting methodologies.

Most forecasting methodologies look at average values as the basis for prediction. Generally they assume that randomness consists of a large number of unimportant factors that can take on either positive or negative values. The result of these numerous random elements is a unimodal distribution. Such random elements are generally ignored because their expected value is assumed to equal zero.

One of the main rationales for catastrophe theory is that such assumptions about randomness are inappropriate in a number of situations. Catastrophe theory assumes that bimodality (or, in general, multimodality) very often exists in the real world. In such instances the outcome that is observed has as much chance of moving toward one modal point as toward another, so that on average it is very unlikely that it will fall in between those two modes. In fact, the average outcome is extremely unlikely to occur in many instances because it is not one of the modes.

One of the most complete descriptions of the use of catastrophe theory in forecasting is that reported by Zeeman (1976). Using a number of graphics, and concepts from topology, he gives several different examples of phenomena that exhibit bimodality or multimodality. Much of Zeeman's work is based on the original work of Thom (1972), which reports on the initial development and exposition of this approach.

Zeeman describes five properties that characterize phenomena that can be effectively described using this set of concepts:

1. The behavior (the outcome) is always bimodal in some part of its range and sudden jumps are observed between one mode of behavior and the other.
2. The jump from the top sheet of the behavior surface to the bottom sheet does not take place at the same position as the jump from the bottom sheet to the top one, an effect called *hysteresis*.
3. Between the top and bottom sheets there is an inaccessible zone on the behavior axis.
4. The middle sheet representing least likely behavior is usually not important.
5. This model implies a possibility of divergent behavior. [Zeeman 1976, p. 76].

In Zeeman's description of the theory he uses a number of examples based on behavior. These vary from situations involving self-pity and anger to those involving aggression and fear. He also includes some physical examples, such as decompression of an elastic beam that may buckle either downward or upward, depending on which mode is reached. Finally, he considers the transition of a liquid to a gaseous state, a process that is affected by the pressure, temperature, and density during the transition.

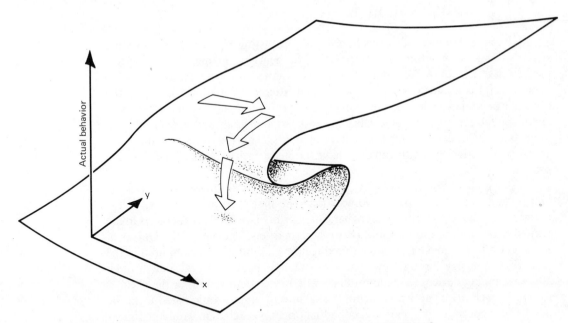

FIGURE 14-5 GRAPHIC REPRESENTATION OF PREDICTING BIMODAL BEHAVIOR WITH CATASTROPHE THEORY

Source: Zeeman (1976)

Graphically, the notion of catastrophe theory and bimodal outcome can be represented as shown in Figure 14-5. The x- and y-axes indicate the two important criteria that can be used to distinguish the two modes of likely behavior. The vertical axis represents the actual behavior that is observed. According to application of the theory, what happens is that as the various levels of x and y (for example, fear and rage) are altered the behavior may change radically if it forces a precipitous drop from one level of the surface to another level. (A low level of fear may cause withdrawal; a high level may cause aggressive behavior.) It is also possible to interpret the implications of Zeeman's five characteristics for applying this approach.

While still a relatively new technique, the fact that this approach fills a substantial gap in existing forecasting methodologies and has been illustrated to effectively explain a number of different outcomes in a wide range of situations suggests that it may find increasing application in the future. Undoubtedly other techniques will also be developed for use in forecasting as the base of experience in the application of existing methodologies is expanded.

14/3 Normative Approaches to Technological Forecasting

Exploratory methods of technological forecasting begin with the existing situation and in an intuitive, extrapolative, or heuristic manner move toward prediction of the future. In so doing, there is assumed to be an almost fatalistic view of what is about to happen. No explicit attempt is made to consider the objective or goal of society or the individual organization and the impact of these factors on the eventual outcome. Clearly, however, such goals and desires serve an important role in determining future developments. Ignoring or not treating such goals and objectives explicitly can often have serious negative effects on the planning process.

A couple of examples can help to illustrate the need for assessing goals or objectives as an integral part of forecasting. The first example is the use of the Universal Product Code (the series of bars often printed on product packages in the United States today) and its adoption by supermarkets. The aim of the Universal Product Code is to make it possible to reduce the amount of labor required in the retail food industry through fewer mistakes at the checkout stand and through having scanning devices read the product code rather than requiring the checker to type in each price and item. Part of the savings originally anticipated from the use of such codes was that marking individual prices on each item would no longer be necessary, since prices could be stored in a central computer and accessed when the product was passed over the scanner and the product code identified.

Unfortunately for those who were heavily committed to this technology, very little research was done on consumer reaction to removal of individual prices on each item, and in the early seventies the industry was surprised to find that consumers were unwilling to have prices simply marked on the shelves but, in fact, would insist they be marked on individual items. This problem could have been foreseen and perhaps at least partially compensated for if the forecasting had looked not only at the development of the technical capabilities required for use of such a system, but also at the goals and objectives in adopting the system and the desires and needs of consumers.

Another example is the development of the supersonic transport (SST) in the United States. During the sixties it was continuously assumed that the problems of adoption of SST technology and aircraft were technical in nature and that once it became feasible and economical the use of such aircraft would become widespread. Again, the reaction of consumers and those elements of the U.S. population who would be affected by the noise and pollution associated with the SST aircraft were not considered in forecasting the adoption of this technology. As is now well known, the SST projects of U.S. manufacturers were, in fact, dropped by the mid-seventies and even the European SST was running into considerable legal difficulty simply in its request for landing rights in the United States, even though technologically the French-English Concorde has been an indisputable success.

In order to overcome some of the problems that can often hinder the actual adoption of technologies and in order to adequately forecast when such adoption will take place, many forecasters have considered the use of normative methods of technological forecasting. Two varieties of such methods will be described in this chapter: relevance trees and systems analysis, and examples will be given of both.

14/3/1 Relevance Trees

The method of relevance trees is not a new development. Its origin dates back to the development of decision theory and the construction of decision trees aimed at aiding the decision maker in selecting the best strategy from among a number of alternatives. Relevance trees use the same concepts and methodologies as decision theory in order to assess the desirability of future goals and to select those areas of development that are necessary in order to achieve the desired goals. Specific technologies can then be singled out for further development and greater commitment of resources can be made to ensure the success of those projects.

One of the earliest and perhaps the best-known application of relevance trees is the PATTERN (planning assistance through technical evaluation of relevance numbers) project that has been used by Honeywell Corporation for military, space, and medical purposes. The aim of the PATTERN approach, as with other types of relevance trees, is to aid planners in identifying the long-range developments that are most important to the accomplishment of specific objectives. The PATTERN computer program sequences the relevance of the objectives and prints out a list of technological breakthroughs that are needed to achieve those objectives. In one sense, the results obtained from a PATTERN application often become self-fulfilling prophecies, since they identify the primary objectives and the means available for their accomplishment.

One of the first applications of PATTERN was in evaluating national objectives for military and space exploration. On the highest level three broad goals were stated: national survival, creation of a credible posture, and favorable world opinion. As a starting point in helping the planners identify the developments necessary to achieve these national objectives, a scenario was prepared identifying all levels of support needed for their successful accomplishment. This scenario was simply a brief description about the future and what the situation might possibly be surrounding related military and scientific developments. The scenario itself was developed by a group of experts involved in long-range planning for the government. The scenario served as a starting point and thus did not need to be accurate in every detail, but rather simply suggested the types of problems that had to be considered in achieving the three goals.

Based on the scenario, a panel of experts was used to develop the relevance tree shown in Figure 14-6. This relevance tree shows the relationship between the primary objectives and the subobjectives and breaks those subobjectives down to a level at which specific technological requirements can be identified. In the example of Figure 14-6, eight such levels have been defined. The elements of the final level represent the breakthroughs required in order to achieve the long-run objectives given in the first level.

Once the relevance tree has been constructed and the criteria for the achievement (and measurement) of the primary objectives have been identified, a panel of experts can be used to determine the relevance and importance of each element of the tree. This process involves relating each element at each level to all others at that same level and evaluating each element's ability to fulfill the existing criteria. Once this assessment has been completed, the results can be tallied and a mean computed by either averaging all answers or using some form of weighting.

Following this phase, the results can be entered into a computer that has previously been programmed to calculate a number of important factors, such as the partial relevance of each element, the local relevance of each branch at each level, and the cumulative total relevance of each branch using a top-down or bottom-up accumulation procedure.

Through this type of PATTERN analysis of objectives, Honeywell has been able to identify a number of high-ranking missions related to space and ocean exploration, military counterinsurgency, arms control, etc. These missions could then be used as the basis for shifting resources among various programs in order to better meet existing goals. In the area of aircraft technology and field guidance, results from the use of this approach indicate that lower costs and better performance have been obtained than would otherwise have been the case.

Relevance trees can be used for evaluating a wide range of projects. How-

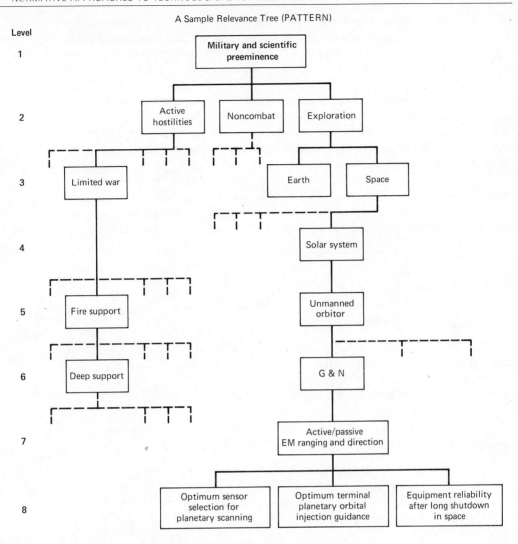

FIGURE 14-6 A SAMPLE RELEVANCE TREE (PATTERN)

ever, it should be realized that the cost of applying this methodology can be significant. Like morphological research, relevance trees involve a large number of alternatives, all of which must be assessed and evaluated. This process requires considerable human and computer resources. To illustrate some of the advantages and disadvantages of this approach, a specific application developed by Alderson and Sproull (1971) in the area of automobile transportation can be considered.

Suppose an auto manufacturer is concerned with predicting future technological innovations related to automobile transportation. Further, assume that the
company is willing to use the PATTERN approach for application of relevance
trees. To facilitate this application, the total task can be divided into a number of
sequential steps.

Step 1. A relevance tree structure must be developed that identifies the
company's objectives, each of the functions involved, requirements to achieve
these objectives and so on. The tree must be extended to a low enough level that
the individual technologies and developments needed to achieve each of the higher
level objectives can be identified.

Step 2. A number of criteria must be established so that priorities in
ordering each of the variables can be determined in a meaningful manner.
Criteria must be established for each level. For illustrative purposes, however,
attention will be focused on level 1, where one might establish the following
four criteria:

    A. reduced cost
    B. increased safety
    C. increased efficiency
    D. increased comfort

Step 3. A panel of experts could be asked to weight the importance of
each criterion in relation to the others. The question might be phrased as follows:
"What is the relative importance (weight) of each of the following criteria in
achieving the higher level objective of providing automobile transportation?"

A second set of questions could then be used to determine the importance
of each element at each level in relation to all other elements at that same level.
At level 1 the following elements might be considered:

    a. accommodate passengers
    b. provide an environment
    c. provide performance monitoring capabilities
    d. provide control capabilities

The comparison might take the form of weighting with regard to each of the four
criteria. Thus, a typical question might be: "In order to reduce the cost of automobile transportation, what is the relative importance (weight) of each of the
following elements?"

When the experts have answered all the questions for all elements at each
level, their answers can be coded and the data entered into a previously programmed
computer that will calculate several useful numbers. Before doing this, however,
it is useful to consider the computations involved in calculating a single relevance
number. The tree itself can be summarized as shown in Figure 14-7.

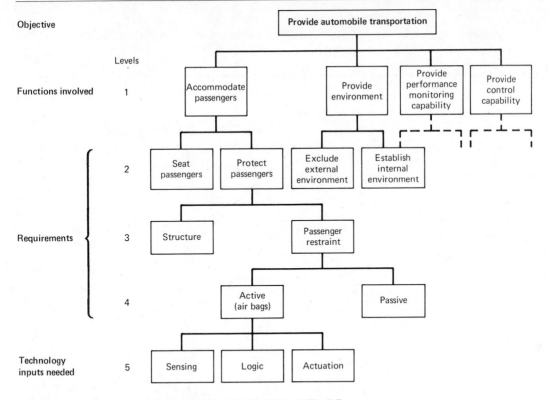

FIGURE 14-7 RELEVANCE TREE STRUCTURE

Step 4. Assuming that the average panel weights for the items assessed in step 3 are as shown in Table 14-1, the individual relevance numbers can be computed.

The partial relevance number (*PRN*) is

PRN = (criterion weight) (element weight).

Thus, $(.20)(.05) = .01$ is a partial relevance number;
$(.20)(.30) = .06$ is another partial relevance number.

A local relevance number for level 1 is

$R_L = \Sigma PRN.$

There are as many local relevance numbers as there are elements at the level. The local relevance numbers for the first level are shown in Table 14-2.

TABLE 14-1   WEIGHTS FOR CRITERIA AND ELEMENTS OF RELEVANCE TREES

	Criteria				
	Reduced Cost	Increased Safety	Increased Efficiency	Increased Comfort	
Criterion weight	.20	.50	.20	.10	= 1.0
	Element Weights (based on specific criterion)				
Elements of level 1					
Accommodate passenger	.05	.25	.40	.35	
Provide environment	.30	.05	.15	.50	
Provide performance monitoring capabilities	.60	.10	.40	.05	
Provide control capabilities	.05	.60	.05	.10	
	1.00	1.00	1.00	1.00	

Summing the partial relevance numbers corresponding to each element, four local relevance numbers that indicate the importance of each element are obtained. From these it can be seen that *provide control protection* is the most important of the four functions, and *provide environment* is the least important function or characteristic of the car—as perceived or judged by the panel members. (The summation of all local relevance numbers is always 1, making such comparisons straightforward.)

Cumulative direct relevance numbers can be calculated as

$$R_D = R_{L,i}(R_{L,i+1}),$$

where $R_{L,i}$ is the local relevance number at level 1 and $R_{L,i+1}$ is the local relevance number of the related (continued) element(s) of the next level. For example, if the local relevance numbers for level 2 are as follows (calculated exactly as for level 1):

seat passengers	.12
protect passengers	.23

TABLE 14-2 LOCAL RELEVANCE NUMBERS FOR LEVEL 1

Criterion	Criterion Weight	Accommodate Passengers		Provide Environment		Provide Performance Monitoring Capabilities		Provide Control Capabilities	
		W*	PRN†	W	PRN	W	PRN	W	PRN
Reduced costs	.20	.05	.01	.25	.06	.40	.12	.35	.01
Increased safety	.50	.25	.125	.05	.025	.10	.05	.60	.30
Increased efficiency	.20	.40	.08	.15	.03	.40	.08	.05	.01
Increased comfort	.10	.35	.035	.50	.05	.05	.005	.10	.01
Local relevance number for level 1			.250		.165		.255		.330

* Weights.
† Partial relevance number.

exclude external environment   .08
establish internal environment   .15,

then the cumulative direct relevance number will be as shown in Table 14-3.

In the second level, the most important of the four elements is *protect passengers* (local relevance number .23), followed by *establish internal environment*. Looking at the cumulative direct relevance numbers, which show the importance of an element up to the level of calculation, *protect passengers* is still the most important element and the second is *seat passengers*.

In a similar manner, the cumulation of relevance numbers can be achieved for each of the levels until the lowest level is reached. The cumulative direct relevance number of the lowest level will become the total direct relevance number indicating the importance of each of the final technological requirements if the higher-level objectives are to be realized.

In the Alderson and Sproull illustration, the element at the last level that has the highest total direct relevance number is that of sensing (see Figure 14-7), with a total direct relevance number of .052. It is followed in importance by a

TABLE 14-3 CUMULATIVE DIRECT RELEVANCE NUMBERS FOR LEVELS 1 AND 2

Corresponding Element of Level 1	Local Relevance Number (level 1)	Element of Level 2	Local Relevance Number (level 2)	Cumulative Direct Relevance Number
Accommodate passengers	.25	Seat passengers	.12	$(.25)(.12) = .03$
Accommodate passengers	.25	Protect passengers	.23	$(.25)(.23) = .05$
Provide environment	.165	Exclude external environment	.08	$(.165)(.15) = .013$
Provide environment	.165	Establish internal environment	.15	$(.165)(.15) = .024$

response element (not shown in Figure 14-7) with .0375 relevance and an information transmission element (not shown in Figure 14-7) with .0358 relevance. The first number implies that there will be a high demand for technological breakthroughs, so that an air bag protecting passengers can be developed. The most critical element will be the sensing device to operate that air bag. In the same manner, the other relevant numbers can be interpreted and used as a basis for selecting future areas of technological pursuit. Through R&D investments and other commitments of resources, these areas can then be developed in order to realize the higher level objectives and missions.

Generally, the computer printout of a PATTERN application provides substantially more information than the few relevance numbers described in this example. This information includes the variance of each element, the weights voted by each of the panel members (and the distribution of those weights), selected ratios permitting the display of the relationship between relevance rankings, measures of dispersion, etc. All of these are aimed at facilitating the identification of future technological needs and concentrating efforts on those areas that are most important.

It is interesting to compare the weighting of criteria developed by U.S. car manufacturers with those developed by some European auto manufacturers for the example shown in Figure 14-7. Reducing cost and increasing efficiency tend to be more important than safety and comfort in the priorities assigned by these European auto companies. As a result, there may be substantial differences in the ranking of technological requirements for the U.S. and European companies. In recent years government legislation and other social changes have made it necessary for all auto manufacturers to move closer together in their product design and specifications than had previously been the case. Thus, U.S. auto manufacturers have moved toward smaller and more efficient cars, while European manufacturers have tended to incorporate additional safety equipment in their autos. However, differences in objectives still play an important role in selecting those technologies to which resources are going to be committed. Relevance trees are one approach for handling such differences and systematically integrating forecasting and planning in regard to them.

14/3/2 Systems Analysis

Systems analysis or the systems approach, as it is commonly called, is aimed at considering a given entity or organization in terms of the interrelationship among its components rather than in terms of the properties of each of the individual elements. In such applications it is the mutual interaction of each unit with other units within the same environment that is of interest. Through attempting to understand the complex pattern of interaction among the elements composing the system, better predictions of future behavior of the system become possible. The difficulty, of course, is to adequately understand the interaction pattern among the elements of the system and its environment, so that they can be used as the basis for prediction.

Generally, one must choose between highly complex models of the system that more accurately explain the interaction pattern but are difficult to construct and even more difficult to manipulate, and simpler models that give only a rough approximation of some of these interactions. An important skill of the system analyst is constructing models that are both feasible and manageable in size and yet adequately represent reality. While several books have been written on the development and application of the systems approach, the aim here is simply to summarize the results of these applications and to relate them to the forecasting task.

The chief aim of system analysis is twofold—to allow the interaction pattern among the different system components to emerge and to avoid obscuring total system considerations in favor of specific demands merely because the system is too large to be easily managed. In order to fulfill this twofold aim the systems analyst must do the following:

1. *Describe the present system.* The interaction pattern of the existing system must be described in such a way that it can be used as the base for model development.
2. *Determine what the system ought to be.* The goals, objectives, and aspirations of those in charge of this system must be identified and analyzed so that they can be used as constraints and guidelines in determining the direction of future developments of the system.

3. *Define alternatives.* Starting from the existing situation, a number of alternative futures must be constructed that can fulfill the system requirements developed in step 2.

4. *Determine feasibility.* The final step in systems analysis is to consider the feasibility of each of the alternatives as to its profitability, its ability to meet system requirements, and its technological feasibility. The profitability is stated in terms of the difference in costs or savings between the existing system and the existing alternatives. The ability to achieve the proposed alternatives is then judged in relation to resource requirements. At this point some alternatives may be rejected. If an alternative is accepted, a complete list of all required resources and capabilities must be developed so that forecasts can be based on con- sideration of them. In this sense, systems analysis can become a thorough study aimed at designing a new system that meets both present and future demands. Since all of the desired characteristics and requirements of a new system are known, the resources can be estimated and used as the basis for predicting and planning what will happen and when. Oftentimes a PERT or critical path analysis can be used for scheduling and estimating these resource requirements.

Methods of system analysis are not widely used for forecasting because of the high costs involved. However, they do incorporate elements of both exploratory and normative forecasting and include occasional feedback features. Thus, they serve as an integrative approach to using several of the different con- cepts that form the basis of a number of technological approaches to forecasting.

There have been some attempts to use systems analysis for forecasting purposes. These have included the pioneering efforts of the Rand Corporation in its project to predict and design future urban environments in the Northeast Corridor transportation system. The U.S. Government has been another user of this approach in its model cities program, as has been the Systems Development Corporation in its design of educational systems.

14/4 Summary

There are numerous other methods of technological or qualitative approaches to forecasting that are less well known and often more complex than those described in this chapter. For example, horizontal or vertical decision matrices can be used to assess priorities among a number of proposed alternatives and to establish project rankings. Another technological method involves establishing (estimating) the net present value of all future returns associated with a number of proposed alternatives. Such alternatives can then be ranked in terms of their net present value. As with decision matrices, this approach is an indirect way of forecasting.

A final technique often used as a combination of technological and quantitative approaches to forecasting is that of industrial or world dynamics. This approach has been developed by Forrester and applied by several others. One such application is that reported by Gross and Ware (1975) concerning energy prospects over the next 25 years. In this study as in others, the aim is to stimulate future environmental conditions. (The process is similar to writing scenarios.) The basic notion is one of feedback control; the changing situation provides feedback so that society and industries can realign themselves in order to respond to the new conditions.

The oil embargo of 1973 is a good example of how such feedback works and some of its limitations. The initial response by many countries was to instigate changes in resource allocations immediately in order to reduce dependence on Middle Eastern oil and to increase energy independence. Clearly, this response illustrates the use of feedback to change the course of future developments. However, by the mid-1970s it was clear in several countries that with the removal of the oil embargo, the removal of the feedback loop had also occurred. Thus, several nations returned to their previous levels of oil imports and in some instances have continued to increase their dependence on Middle Eastern oil. The technique of industrial and world dynamics seeks to simulate such conditions and to use quantitative models in order to develop scenarios of future developments. As more experience is gained in the use of both quantitative and technological methods of forecasting, there will undoubtedly be several new approaches developed and existing techniques described in this chapter and earlier chapters will be further refined.

REFERENCES AND SELECTED BIBLIOGRAPHY

Alderson, R. C., and W. C. Sproull. 1971. "Requirement Analysis, Need Forecasting and Technology Planning, Using the Honeywell PATTERN Technique." In *Industrial Applications of Technological Forecasting*, ed. M. Cetron. New York: John Wiley & Sons.

Amara, R. C. 1972. "Methodology: A Note on Cross-Impact Analysis." *Futures*, September, pp. 267–71.

Ament, R. H. 1970. "Comparison of Delphi Forecasting Studies in 1964 and 1969." *Futures*, March, pp. 35–44.

Ayres, R. U. 1969. *Technological Forecasting and Long-Range Planning*. New York: McGraw-Hill.

Bell, D. 1964. *Daedlus, Journal of the American Academy of Arts and Sciences*, Summer, pp. 845–80.

Bright, J. R., and M. E. F. Schoeman, eds. 1970. *Technological Forecasting*. Canoga Park, Calif.: Information Corporation.

Cetron, M. 1969. *Technological Forecasting*. New York: Gordon & Breach.

————. 1971. *Industrial Applications of Technological Forecasting*. New York: John Wiley & Sons.

Cetron, M., and C. A. Ralph. 1971. *Industrial Application of Technological Forecasting*. New York: John Wiley & Sons.

Chambers, J. C., S. K. Mullick, and D. D. Smith. 1971. "How to Choose the Right Forecasting Technique." *Harvard Business Review*, Vol. 65, July–August.

Clarke, A. C. *Profiles of the Future: An Enquiry into the Limits of the Possible*, rev. ed. New York: Harper & Row.

Gerstenfeld, A. 1971. "Technological Forecasting." *Journal of Business*, Vol. 44, No. 1, January, pp. 10–18.

Gordon, T. J., and H. Hayward. 1968. "Initial Experiment with the Cross-Impact Matrix Method of Forecasting." *Futures*, Vol. 1, No. 2, December.

Gross, A. C., and W. W. Ware. 1975. "Profiles of the Future: Energy Prospects in 1990." *Business Horizons*, June, pp. 5–18.

Hahn, W. A., and K. F. Gordon, eds. 1973. *Assessing the Future and Policy Planning*. New York: Gordon & Breach.

Helmer, O. 1966a. "The Delphi Method for Systematizing Judgments about the Future." Los Angeles: University of California, Institute of Government and Public Affairs, April.

Helmer, O. 1966b. *The Use of The Delphi Technique—Problems of Educational Innovations*. Santa Monica, Calif.: The RAND Corp., December.

Helmer, O., and N. Rescher. 1959. "On the Epistemology of the Inexact Sciences." *Management Science*, Vol. 6, No. 1.

Hueckel, G. 1975. "A Historical Approach to Future Economic Growth." *Science*, Vol. 197, March, pp. 925–31.

Jantsch, E. 1969. *Technological Forecasting in Perspective*. Paris: O.E.C.D.

Jolson, M. A., and G. L. Rossow. 1971. "The Delphi Process in Marketing Decision Making." *Journal of Marketing Research*, Vol. 8, November, pp. 443–48.

Kahn, H. 1964. "Alternative World Futures." Paper HI-342-B IV, Croton-on-Hudson: Hudson Institute. April.

Linstone, H. A., and M. Turoff. 1975. *The Delphi Method: Techniques and Applications*. Reading, Mass.: Addison-Wesley.

Malabre, A. L. 1976. "The Future Revised." *The Wall Street Journal*, Monday, March 15.

Prehoda, R. W. 1967. *Designing the Future*. Philadelphia: Chilton Book Co.

———. 1975. "The Future in Retrospect." *The Futurist*, October, pp. 263–65.

Roberts, E. 1969. "Exploratory and Normative Technological Forecasting: A Critical Appraisal." MIT Working Paper, No. 378-69.

Rochberg, R., T. J. Gordon, and O. Helmer. 1970. "The Use of Cross-Impact Matrices for Forecasting and Planning." Middletown, Conn.: The Institute for the Future, IFF Report R-10. April.

Sackman, H. 1975. *Delphi Critique*. Lexington, Mass.: Lexington Books, D. C. Heath and Company.

Scott, R. F., and D. B. Simmons. 1974. "Programmer Productivity and the Delphi Technique." *Datamation*, May, pp. 71–73.

Sigford, J. V., and R. H. Parvin. 1965. "Project PATTERN: A Methodology for Determining Relevance in Complex Decision-Making." *IEEF Transactions on Engineering Management*, Vol. 12, No. 1. March.

Steiner, G. A. 1969. *Top Management Planning*. London: Macmillan.

Taylor, T. B. et al. 1967. "Preliminary Survey of Non-National Nuclear Threats." *Stanford Research Institute Technical Note*, SSG-TN-5205-83. September.

Tersine, R. J., and W. E. Riggs. 1976. "The Delphi Technique: A Long-Range Planning Tool." *Business Horizons*, April, pp. 51–56.

Thom, Rene. 1972. *Stabilitie Structurelle et Morphogenese*. Reading, Mass.: Benjamin.

Thomson, G. 1955. *The Foreseeable Future*. Cambridge, England: Cambridge University Press.

Withington, F. G. 1975. "Beyond 1984: A Technology Forecast." *Datamation*, January.

Zeeman, E. C. 1976. "Catastrophe Theory." *Scientific American*, April, pp. 65–83.

Zwicky, F. 1962. "Morphology of Propulsive Power." *Monographs on Morphological Research*, No. 1. Pasadena, Calif.: Society for Morphological Research.

Zwicky, F., and G. Wilson. 1967. *New Methods of Thought and Procedure*. New York: Springer Verlag.

EXERCISE

Suppose that a food company is concerned with its future expansion and technological possibilities in the areas of food production and processing. One approach to planning and forecasting in such a company might be that of morphological research. As a first step the following six classes of parameters might be identified.

P_1: Market
P_2: Market territory
P_3: Type of food
P_4: Materials used
P_5: Location of sources of materials
P_6: Manner of obtaining and/or processing materials

Develop a Morphological Box that describes four or five parameters under each of these headings. How many combinations of parameters from each of these six classes does this give? How might one decide which combinations to pursue in order to make this analysis feasible?

PART SIX
INTEGRATING FORECASTING AND PLANNING IN THE ORGANIZATION

It is the authors' belief that although understanding forecasting methodologies and their use is interesting for academic purposes, the real test comes in their applicability in practice and their impact on decision making and planning. The purpose of Part Six is to describe some of the most important issues surrounding effective utilization of forecasting in the organization and some of the relevant empirical results reported in the literature.

In Chapter 15 the nature of the planning function is described, and the requirements of planning are related to the characteristics of forecasting. This chapter seeks to integrate many of the advantages and disadvantages of individual forecasting methods that were described in earlier chapters, with the requirements of specific planning situations.

A number of studies reporting on the application and performance of various forecasting methodologies are described in Chapter 16. The purpose in this chapter is to provide a framework for comparing alternative forecasting methods and to suggest guidelines for selecting those methods most appropriate in a given situation.

In Chapter 17 the data procurement, preparation, and handling functions that are needed to support effective forecasting are discussed. The chapter describes a number of systems for minimizing the roadblocks presented by data handling tasks. In addition, guidelines for providing the necessary organizational resources to support the data requirements of forecasting are discussed.

In Chapter 18 some of the behavioral and organizational problems of effectively using forecasting resources are examined. A number of structures are presented for tackling these common problems, and empirical results showing the need for placing major attention on these topics are presented. The hope is that by the end of this portion, not only will the forecasting methodologies and their applications have been described and understood, but the initial steps required for effectively using them in the organization will also have been presented.

15 FORECASTING AND PLANNING

THIS CHAPTER BEGINS the final segment of the book, which deals with the integration of forecasting into planning and decision making in the organization. Specifically, in this chapter the aim is to provide background on the role of planning in organizations today and to illustrate the role of forecasting as it can be effectively integrated into the management and administrative tasks of planning and decision making.

The chapter is organized into four main sections. The first examines the concept of planning and defines the opportunities and problems of forecasting in connection with planning. Current trends relating to planning and its use by organizations are also examined. These topics are covered first at a conceptual level. In the second section they are dealt with on a much more practical basis by looking at the adaptation required to fit forecasting and planning to specific organizations. Two examples of the role of forecasting in the firm are described: one for the B. F. Goodrich Company and one for the Armstrong Cork Company.

The third segment of this chapter deals in some detail with specific areas in an organization where forecasting can serve as an input to planning and decision making. The time horizon of planning is used as the dimension for categorizing such needs. Several examples of applications are also mentioned in this section.

The final section of the chapter examines the contribution that forecasting can make to the analysis and understanding of administrative and management problems. Essentially this section looks beyond the obtaining of a forecast for a given variable and points out some of the learning that is possible when formalized forecasting procedures are applied.

15/1 The Role of Forecasting in Planning

Thus far in this text it has been assumed that the purpose of forecasting has been relatively simple to define. However, it should be clear to the reader who anticipates becoming a practical user of forecasting that this is not always the case. Although one can focus direct attention on what is to be forecast and the best way to approach that, it is perhaps more instructive to deal first with the topic of planning and its role in the organization. A basic understanding of planning can then aid the forecaster in determining what types of forecasts would be most useful and how one might proceed to define them.

Although there is not a generally accepted definition of planning (Steiner 1969, p. 5), most writers tend to agree that the concept deals with some form of decision making involving the future. The Random House dictionary, for example, defines planning as a method of thinking out acts and purposes beforehand. Drucker (1959, p. 238) describes planning "as the conscious recognition of the futurity of present decisions," while Ackoff (1970, p. 2) talks about planning as a task that is performed in advance of taking actions. Ackoff continues his description by saying that planning is actually anticipatory decision making, even though not all forms of decision making are planning.

A more comprehensive definition of planning describes it as a well-thought-out set of decisions and actions that when followed ensure that the organization in the future will be affected by its environment in a manner consistent with its goals and objectives. This definition views planning as a coordination effort in addition to being a future-oriented decision-making process.

Planning can also be described by indicating what it is *not* (Ewing 1968, pp. 14–17). Although often confused with these functions, planning clearly is not (1) a public relations vehicle, (2) budgeting, (3) forecasting, (4) a mode of reporting, (5) the keeping of a planning department, (6) avoiding risk taking, or (7) improving operating efficiency.

No matter what definition is accepted for planning, it is clear that it concerns itself with future events. The same can also be said for forecasting, which is aimed at providing predictions about the state of events in such a way that the planning process can be performed more accurately. Forecasting is of greatest use when its results can be used to take advantage of future opportunities while avoiding future threats. Mere recognition of a forthcoming event is not in and of itself particularly valuable unless plans and actions are adapted to cope with that event.

Planning can be performed under conditions of certainty, uncertainty, or ignorance about the future. It is in those situations involving uncertainty that forecasting provides the maximum help to planners. When certainty exists, forecasting does not require much effort, since predictions about the future are trivial. When there is ignorance, the most that forecasting can do is provide some clues about future possibilities. However, even such clues cannot be provided unless some information is available on which the forecast can be based. In many organizations the major purpose of forecasting is to reduce uncertainty and minimize ignorance.

Because both forecasting and planning concern themselves with the future, it is important to integrate these two functions within the organization. A knowledge of forecasting techniques is of little value unless they can be effectively applied in the organization's planning process. That requires an examination of the planning activities within an organization so that the types of forecasts required and the techniques available for providing them can be tailored to the organization's needs.

The manner in which organizations and managers plan has received considerable attention in the management literature, and books have been written about both the theory and practice of planning. Mockler (1970) and Naylor and Schauland (1976) give a good overview of some of the concepts used in planning. Unfortunately, most of the planning literature has concerned itself with the various aspects of the planning process—establishing goals, objectives, strategies, etc.— and has largely assumed that forecasting, while important, is readily available. It is the purpose of this chapter and the following three to examine the planning needs for forecasting in more detail and to suggest approaches that can be used to integrate forecasting into planning and provide the required predictive inputs.

Recent years have seen a tremendous increase in the emphasis placed on planning. There are several reasons for this increase. First, when needs and opportunities arise, they should be met without delay. For example, a manufacturer whose product experiences high seasonal demand in the summer months does not want to wait until summer to start producing products for that season. Rather some lead time is needed so that appropriate products can be manufactured in advance and be immediately ready for purchase by consumers. A second impetus for planning is that frequently the future environment can be influenced if certain actions are taken beforehand. For example, the manufacturer can advertise or open new retail outlets in order to increase sales. However, such action is most effective when plans are based on accurate predictions about the future.

Planning not only allows actions to be taken that will meet lead time requirements and that will influence the future environment, it also has by-products that can create a more efficient and effective mode of operation. One such by-product is increased motivation of individuals in the organization. Many companies have found that morale has improved when individuals are involved in planning the future course of the organization, and that organization goals are more likely to be achieved when people understand them and are committed to them. Planning also aids in the coordination of several diverse activities and enables the organization to meet its objectives with a minimum amount of resources.

A number of recently published surveys indicate that planning is used by the majority of business, government, military, and nonprofit organizations in the United States and Western Europe. In almost all cases planning procedures are being used more extensively today than they were a decade ago. While some skeptics have suggested that planning may not be very effective, practice seems to indicate that it is the best alternative available. Usually the decisions about the areas in which planning will take place, the degree of detail in various functional plans, and the level at which plans are coordinated and integrated are much more crucial in today's organizations than simply the decision to plan or not to plan. It is these factors that determine how much the planning activity will cost and whether or not it will be effective.

Some of the reasons commonly given for the adoption of formal planning procedures include the following (Steiner 1969, pp. 15–17):

1. Organizations do not want to be helpless in the face of external marketing forces.
2. The increasing rate of technological innovation requires better planning for survival.
3. The management task is becoming increasingly complex.
4. The environment within which an organization must operate is becoming increasingly complex.
5. Management is seeking to become more systematic in its evaluation of risks and in its decision-making procedures.

15/2 Relating Forecasting and Planning in the Organization

In discussing the role of forecasting in planning, it is important to distinguish between two forecasting situations. In one the forecaster will also prepare the plans and make the decisions; in the other the forecasters are generally part of a staff function and the decision makers and/or planners are in line positions located elsewhere in the organization. The latter is probably the most frequently encountered situation in forecasting because as organizations grow and develop, the need for increased specialization arises. Many of the techniques that have been described in this book require substantial resources and skills to apply. As a result, they tend to be most useful when the planning activity to which they are related has a major impact on and value to the organization. In such cases, the forecasters and/or planners are usually not the same individuals as the decision makers and line managers.

To illustrate the alternative ways in which forecasting as a staff function can be integrated with line management's decision making and planning, forecasting/planning organizations in two firms will be examined: the B. F. Goodrich Company and the Armstrong Cork Company. Although several other variations in organization have been followed in practice, these examples can indicate some of the problems involved in integrating forecasting and planning and some of the alternative procedures for effectively handling these problems.

15/2/1 Putting Forecasting to Work at the B. F. Goodrich Company*

At the B. F. Goodrich Company, organization forecasting is an integral part of the business research department. The group has had an outstanding reputation over the past several years as indicated both by the positions that some of its members have attained in the organization (including chairman and chief executive officer, group vice-president, vice-president, and senior division vice-president), and the fact that requests from outside the company for the industry forecasts prepared by this department greatly exceed requests for information about the company itself.

As a key to understanding the use of forecasts in planning and management at B. F. Goodrich, it is helpful to consider the company's organization, which is shown in Figure 15-1. The vice-president of planning reports to the group vice-president of corporate services. This vice-president of planning is responsible for both the planning and development division as well as the corporate communication division. In addition, he or she serves as a secretary of the management committee. The operations of the company are handled by six operating divisions under two executive vice-presidents.

At B. F. Goodrich, planning is the major use of forecasting. The company has formalized part of its planning procedures into a planning cycle that produces a completed corporate plan in the fourth quarter of each year. This plan states the goals, missions, and objectives of the company and of all the divisions in broad terms—outlining businesses that fall into the categories of harvest, expand, or hold. These categories are based upon the forecasts of the markets that have been made by the company's economists and the forecast of the company's own strengths and weaknesses made by the operating divisions and the corporate support groups.

In the first quarter of each year, the operating divisions receive guidance in the form of market forecasts and a reminder of their portion of the previous corporate plan. In addition, the controller's office provides forecasts of profit and loss statements and sources and uses of funds statements. These latter are used by the treasurer to forecast whether or not the company has the financial capability to carry out the plan.

The vice-president of planning, the treasurer, and the controller then work with various combinations of each division's plan to find one that appears to be workable. When such a plan is developed, it is presented to the management committee and guidelines are released to the division for development of additional strategic plans. The divisions then prepare the next year's detailed operating

---

*This description is adapted from an article prepared by T. W. Blazey, Vice-President and Controller, B. F. Goodrich Company. That article appeared in *Business Economics* (January 1976) pp. 41–44.

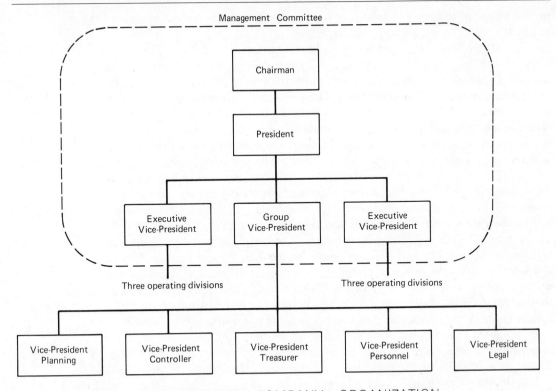

FIGURE 15-1 B. F. GOODRICH COMPANY—ORGANIZATION

budget for submission in the fourth quarter. That completes a full cycle in the planning process, which includes both a revision of the corporate plan and development of division operating budgets.

Forecasting has an important role in this cycle. The two factors whose forecasts are most critical are those of market size and market share, since they determine such things as capacity requirements, size of sales staff, and methods of distribution. Considerable justification is required of individual divisions when they project changes in growth rates or other assumptions that are not completely consistent with the forecasts prepared by the planning division.

Attempts are continually made to upgrade the forecasting in the planning cycle and its value to the individual divisions. One refinement recently made is switching from using constant dollars to current dollars for the last four years of the five-year plan. Previously, they had used a rather simplistic assumption that price increases would offset cost increases. Since that had been found to rarely be the case, a switch to current dollars seemed to be a substantial improvement. This switch, however, required that forecasts also be prepared for cost increases for a number of the raw material items and other inputs to the manufactured products.

The forecasts of the company's economists are used not only in the planning process but also in many of the firm's other operations. For example, the treasury division has a weekly meeting at which the company's economists review and forecast money market conditions. These forecasts are combined with forecasts of receipts and expenditures so that maturity dates of financial paper to be sold can be more effectively planned. Similarly, since the firm has considerable funds exposed to movements in foreign exchange rates, forecasting is also involved in determining how best to hedge and handle those foreign obligations.

Other areas in which forecasts are particularly useful are feedstock prices, transportation costs, and basic raw materials. Depending on the economists' forecasts of both supply and prices of basic commodities, raw material inventories are increased or decreased in order to best meet the firm's needs at minimum cost.

A final area in which the B. F. Goodrich Company has found an important role for forecasting is that of affecting policy for the industry and the economy as a whole. For example, the chief economist and the controller at B. F. Goodrich worked closely with the Cost of Living Council during the early 1970s. It was the company's feeling that existing indices for tires and inner tubes and productivity for the industry were misleading and incomplete. Through the company's efforts in working with the Bureau of Labor Statistics, an improved new tire and inner tube wholesale price index has been established and is being published as of 1976. These are just a few of the uses that B. F. Goodrich has made of forecasting in both its short- and long-range planning.

15/2/2 Forecasting and Planning at the Armstrong Cork Company*

The Armstrong Cork Company is one of the leading producers of interior furnishings for residences as well as commercial and institutional buildings in the United States. With annual sales approaching a billion dollars, Armstrong and its subsidiaries employ some 23,000 people and operate more than 50 plants worldwide.

Armstrong is involved in four principal markets—home improvement and refurbishing, new residential building, commercial and institutional building, and specialty industrial products. The company has chosen to organize its manufacturing activities into six divisions or profit centers. These profit centers are supported by more than a dozen centralized staff departments including a corporate planning department and a corporate economist's office.

---

*This description is adapted from an article prepared by George F. Johnston, Vice-President and Chief Planning Officer, Armstrong Cork Company. That article appeared in *Business Economics* (January 1976), pp. 35–40.

Even though the corporate planning and chief economist groups are separated at Armstrong, the two work closely together to coordinate their various functions. Both are concerned with the future, but from differing points of view. The chief economist department is involved in predicting what is likely to happen with a focus on trends and implications for the company's various businesses. The corporate planning group, on the other hand, is involved in helping managers identify opportunities and problems so that they can achieve a measure of control over what will happen and direct their businesses accordingly.

To better understand the integration of planning and forecasting at Armstrong, it is useful to consider the basic concepts and objectives that it holds for its planning operations. The ultimate goal in planning is the development of both operational plans (two-year time horizon) and strategic plans (five-year time horizon) for each operation and subsidiary and for the company as a whole. These plans are aimed at coordinating marketing, production, personnel, and financial requirements in achieving a predetermined set of goals.

The starting point for initiating the planning process is the concept of business unit planning. This concept provides the framework that is used by general managers to involve a wide range of middle managers in the planning process. The concept of business unit planning focuses on the smallest practical unit for which planning can be performed. That is a single business or collection of related businesses that has its own unique mission, product lines, markets, distribution, competitors, etc., and whose planning and managing generally can be focused on one individual.

The corporate planning department provides a format for the company's general managers to use in the preparation of their business unit plans. The execution of that format involves four distinct phases.

Phase I. In this phase the business unit data base is prepared. The intent is to bring together as much factual data as is available on that specific business unit. Data both external and internal to the firm are included and are generally collected through marketing, marketing research, the controller, and the economic research departments. The economic research department actually provides information that represents a historical analysis of the business unit as well as an analysis of the industry and markets that it serves.

Phase II. This phase involves the assessment of the business unit. Essentially, it is aimed at determining what can realistically be done by the business unit during that planning period. Key elements for success are identified and the competitive constraints and relevant aspects of the environment are recognized. The business unit manager and his staff do much of this work.

Phase III. In this phase objectives, strategies, and action plans are established. As such it is the most crucial step in business unit planning. Essentially, the unit manager is specifying his goals and his plans for achieving them.

During this phase the economic research department makes valuable contributions by providing forecasts of basic assumptions for operational planning purposes, and later in the cycle by providing forecasts of long-range assumptions for strategic planning purposes. These basic assumptions cover general economic forecasts as well as specific market forecasts. In addition, the economic research department provides forecasts of the potential of each individual market segment. For example, general forecasts are developed for a market such as the resilient flooring industry, then for Armstrong's resilient flooring operation, and then for the sheet flooring business unit within that operation. Finally the focus is narrowed further as specific forecasts are developed for individual market segments such as the builder market, the installed residential replacement market, the do-it-yourself market, and the commercial market.

To give business unit managers a perspective for the five-year plan, the economic research department publishes long-range assumptions that are more general in nature than the shorter-range assumptions used in the two-year operating plan. These include forecasts for some of the basic markets and industries served by Armstrong on inflation factors, prices, raw material supplies, and capital expenditures as well as forecasts of economic, social, political, and international factors.

Because of the emphasis that Armstrong puts on this third phase in its planning cycle, it encourages management to allow substantial time to study the assumptions and to prepare specific statements on objectives, strategies, and action plans for both the two-year operational and five-year strategic recommendations. The concept of business unit planning is based on managers developing the most likely plan after reviewing various alternatives. However, it also emphasizes the need to consider contingency planning given today's business climate and the uncertainty in the environment. Here the economic research department again makes a contribution by forecasting alternative paths that the economy might take and the probability of occurrence of each of those alternatives.

Phase IV. This final phase in business unit planning deals with the financial and resource implications of the selected strategic plan. In essence, it is aimed at getting the managers to describe the resources that their plans will require and to assess the availability of these resources and their costs. Much of the input for this phase comes from the business unit manager working with staff departments such as purchasing, production planning, engineering, and finance. At the completion of this phase, all business unit plans are accumulated and adjusted to accommodate the priorities at the division level within the operation or subsidiary and finally within the entire corporation.

Planning at Armstrong has become essentially a year-round activity with operational plans covering sales, profits, and expenses for a two-year time horizon being developed during the September through December months. Those plans then serve as the base for the five-year strategic plans that are developed and consolidated from March through June.

One of the key elements of Armstrong's planning process is the development of contingency plans and the integration of them at the corporate level.

An example of how the economist's office plays a role in helping the chief executive officer deal with contingencies is provided by the situation in January of 1975. With a tight corporate operational plan for 1975, the chief executive was faced with several questions concerning uncertainties about the economy and about the specific segments in which Armstrong was involved. As an aid to the chief executive officer in these considerations, the economist's office described three possible economic paths in terms of the recession, inflation rates, unemployment rates, real GNP, and the impact on Armstrong's markets. Once contingency plans were developed for each of these three scenarios, trigger points were identified and the economy was monitored continually against these alternative paths. When it became apparent early in 1975 that the path the economy was taking was not consistent with the corporate operational plan, a predetermined contingency plan was put into effect. This change helped to minimize disruptions at the corporate level as well as in the individual operating units.

By way of summary, it can be noted that at Armstrong Cork Company the economic research department provides forecasts and other information for developing business unit data bases, then publishes basic assumptions and long-range assumptions for use in the preparation of operational, strategic, and contingency plans. Essentially, it focuses on preparing forecasts of uncontrollable, external influences on the business. Next the corporate planning group concerns itself with helping to systematize, guide, and assist the business unit managers in their planning process. The aim is to help them identify opportunities and threats and prepare plans that are realistic, challenging, and achievable. Once specific operational and strategic plans have been developed and agreed upon for individual business units, divisions, and subsidiaries, the president's office reviews the results and synthesizes them into a total plan for using the resources of the corporation.

In practice this integration of forecasting and planning is much more difficult than it may sound in this description. The Armstrong Cork Company has been making substantial progress in both of these areas. The people at Armstrong feel that forecasting is one of the most valuable tools they have and that as they learn to use it better it will improve both their strategic and operational planning and decision making.

15/3 Forecasting as Input to Planning and Decision Making

The previous sections have shown that forecasting and planning are two highly interrelated areas. Unfortunately, in most firms there is still considerable opportunity to further integrate them and to make them mutually supportive of one another. One of the main problems in accomplishing this goal of integration is simply that of having forecasters understand the opportunities for forecasting in planning and having planners and managers understand the opportunity for forecasting in their own activities. In this section, several specific areas of planning will be examined and at least a partial list will be developed for those areas where forecasting has been found to be most beneficial. It is hoped that this information will enable forecasters and planners to better understand the opportunities for integration. However, it must be remembered that each organization is distinct in terms of its environment, its organization structure, and its existing strategies and plans, and thus considerable adaptation is required for each new situation.

As both the B. F. Goodrich and the Armstrong Cork Company's use of planning and forecasting illustrate, planning can be divided into two types—strategic and operational. The former is concerned more with what the organization desires to be and the latter deals more with how to do better what is already being done. Thus the first is more concerned with overall direction and is aimed at a longer time horizon, while the second deals with maintaining the organization on a day-to-day basis and providing adequate resources to meet the short-term goals of the firm.

One way in which planning can be examined is from the viewpoint of each of the functional areas of management. Under such a scheme, one could examine marketing, production, and financial planning and then consider their forecasting needs. An alternative way of examining planning is in terms of the time horizon covered by those plans. This is the structure that will be used in this section, since it minimizes the duplication that might occur from using a functional categorization or the strategic/operational categorization.

In earlier chapters of this book, four distinct time horizons have been used in talking about forecasting:

immediate term—less than one month
short term—one to three months
medium term—three months to two years
long term—two years or more

This categorization is a convenient one for considering the characteristics and areas of general applicability of quantitative methods of forecasting. Thus there are certain benefits to be gained from using this same scheme when looking at the opportunities for forecasting in planning. However, it should be recognized that the situation has a major impact on which decisions fall into which of these four time horizons. For example, for one company a two-year time horizon may be very long range, while for another it may be short or medium in its range (Steiner 1963, pp. 44–45). Also, for individual managers the meaning of the terms may depend very much on their positions in the organization. Thus for a foreman, immediate planning or forecasting may be related to the next hour, and long-range planning or forecasting may involve a six-month time horizon, while for top management, planning for a few months ahead may be immediate term and long term may cover a span of several years or even decades.

For purposes of discussion, it is useful to define each of these four categories very explicitly, since they will be used in the remainder of this section as the opportunities for forecasting in these categories are examined.

Long-term planning

The time horizon covered by long-term planning is generally *two years or more*. Most of the decisions made in this time horizon tend to be strategic in their focus and are aimed at determining the overall direction the organization will follow. Some of these decisions relate to:

1. determination of goals, objectives, and strategies
2. the level and direction of capital expenditures
3. the acquisition of new sources of funds
4. organization design and structure

To achieve the purposes of long-range planning, a coordinated effort on several fronts is required. Forecasts must be made of demand for products and services, general economic conditions, and technological and competitive conditions. Furthermore, costs of production and distribution

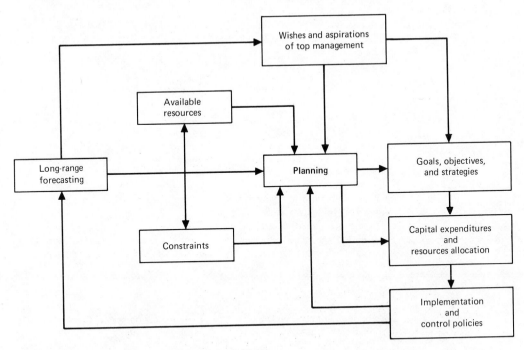

FIGURE 15-2 LONG-RANGE PLANNING

must be estimated and the financial position of the firm must be assessed. (Figure 15.2 indicates the interrelationship of some of the essential tasks involved in long-range planning.)

While the intuition and judgment of top management cannot be replaced by any single formal method of forecasting, such methods can play an invaluable role in supplementing the long-range planning process. Quantitative methods of forecasting can be used to estimate trends in such variables as sales, costs, profits, and growth rates. Through the extrapolation

TABLE 15-1 FORECASTING NEEDS FOR LONG-RANGE PLANNING (TWO YEARS OR MORE)

Organization Unit	Information Needs	Quantitative Forecasting Inputs	Technological Forecasting Inputs
Business			
Marketing	Total sales, major product categories, new product introduction, saturation points of existing products, customers' preferences and tastes	Trends in sales revenues	Saturation points in sales, new product introduction, customers' preferences
Production	Costs, expansion of plant and equipment, ordering of heavy machinery and equipment, demand for production facilities, new technologies	Trends in costs	Evaluation of technologies
Inventory	Total sales, expansion of warehouses, centralized vs. decentralized warehouses	Total sales, total demand for material	Buying habits, future technology of storing
Finance	Total sales, investment selections, capital expenditure, allocations of resources, capital programs, cash flows	Trends in revenues, trends in profits, profitability rate of future investments	—
Purchasing	Contracts for buying raw materials	—	Buying conditions
R&D	Total sales; technological, social, political, and economic conditions of future; new product development; customers' preferences and tastes	—	Technological possibilities, new product development
Top management	Total sales; costs and other expenses; social, political, and economic trends; goals, objectives, and strategies; new products; competition's pricing policies	Trends in market share of competition	Evaluation of competition
Economic			
Economic unit	State and type of economy, level of economic activity, sales of industry	Trends in economy, trends in industry	Type of politico-economic system, saturation points in economic growth

TABLE 15-1 *Continued*

Organization Unit	Information Needs	Quantitative Forecasting Inputs	Technological Forecasting Inputs
Environmental Technological unit	Areas of technological innovations, R&D selections, available technological opportunities	—	Technological breakthroughs, new inventions
Business environment forecasting unit	Social trends, tastes, areas of concern	—	Type of society
	Trends in the rate of taxation, depreciation, and concept of free market	—	Type of political system
	Capital investment, new technologies and R&D selections of competitors	—	Strategies of competitors
	General environmental constraints (pollution level, availability of raw material, etc.)	—	Trends in people's perception of their environment
Methods Available		Regression analysis, econometric models, S-curve transformations, input-output analysis	Scenarios, Delphi approach, morphological research, relevance trees, historical analogies, theoretical limit tests, modified S-curves

of historical data, basic patterns can be identified and used to establish a framework within which long-range planning and contingency plans can be evaluated. It is important in making such extrapolations to provide a mechanism for top management to impose its own judgments about saturation points and turning points on these trends. That requires close contact between forecasters, planners, and top management.

Some of the forecasting needs that appear in long-range planning are shown in Table 15-1. This table shows both the variables that must be considered in planning and the inputs to these variables that quantitative and technological or qualitative forecasting techniques can offer.

Quantitative forecasting methods applied to long-range planning are more accurate when used to predict aggregate levels of variables such as sales and revenues. However, even such aggregate forecasts may prove wrong as the business cycle changes and as other environmental factors are altered. That is one of the reasons technological forecasting methods tend to be used most often in long-range planning. They allow management to formalize its own judgments about the future and the judgment of other experts in such a way that they can be explicitly examined and used as part of the planning process. One of the specific advantages of technological forecasting methods is that unlike their quantitative counterparts, they provide a number of future alternatives or scenarios as inputs to planning.

Medium-term planning

Medium-term planning usually covers a time span of *three months to two years*. It is used mainly to determine the allocation of resources among competing activities and to revise long-range plans in view of more recent developments. Medium-term planning often takes the form of budgeting in which each division, department, or unit is allocated certain resources during the coming year. These allocations are based in part on forecasts of demand, costs, financial position, and competition. With a time horizon of one to two years and critical decisions on resource allocation, medium-term planning must correctly predict the general level of economic activity, since that affects such factors as revenues, profits, costs, and expenditures.

The identification of saturation points and trends are critical factors in long-range planning and require major inputs from forecasting, but in medium-term planning it is economic conditions that must be forecast correctly, since many other factors will depend upon how well the economy does. Forecasting relevant economic variables involves both extrapolating current trends and identifying forthcoming turning points in the economy.

The forecasting required to satisfy medium-term planning needs relies less on technological methods and more heavily on quantitative methods than that for long-range planning. The importance and infrequency of such forecasts (once or twice a year) make it worthwhile to spend more effort and employ more elaborate techniques to obtain accurate predictions than is the case for shorter time horizons. Often it may be wise to use more than one method in order to check and compare the accuracy of results. Some of the methods most frequently used for medium-term planning needs are decomposition, ARMA, and regression techniques. They can be supplemented with anticipatory surveys, publications on the economic outlook, government budgeting plans, and the outcome of econometric models. These methods and information sources combined with management judgment can reveal a great deal about trends and forthcoming turning points in the economy.

Table 15-2 summarizes some of the medium-term planning needs, forecasting inputs requirements, and techniques available for meeting those requirements. As with Table 15-1, this table is only indicative of the general needs and inputs in this area.

TABLE 15-2 FORECASTING NEEDS FOR MEDIUM-TERM PLANNING (THREE MONTHS TO TWO YEARS)

Organization Unit	Information Needs	Quantitative Forecasting Inputs	Technological Forecasting Inputs
Business			
Marketing	Total sales, product categories, prices, general economic conditions	Cyclicality in sales, trend in sales and revenues	Government actions
Production	Costs, budget allocations, buying or ordering equipment and machinery, employment level	Level of utilizing plants and equipment, estimating the costs	Types of technology to apply
Inventory	Possible strikes of suppliers or transportation facilities	Expiration date of union contracts, past behavior of unions	—
Finance	Budget allocations, cash flows	Revenue and costs, level of economic activity, cost of borrowing	Government monetary policies
Purchasing	Demand for products, demand for raw and other materials	Sales level, production level, buying conditions	—
R&D	New product introduction, R&D selections	—	State of technology, financing
Top management	Demand for sales, costs and other expenses, cash position, general economic conditions, controls, objectives	Sales level, costs, cash balances, economic conditions	Competitors' actions, government policies and legislation
Economic			
Economic unit	General economic conditions, turning points in economy, level of economic activity	Government spending, capital outlays, consumer spending	Interest rates, monetary policies
Environmental			
Technological unit	Available technologies	—	Announcement of new inventions or technologies
Business environment forecasting unit	Social attitudes	—	Social norms
	Fiscal and monetary policies	—	Attitude of legislative bodies and the government administration
	New product developments by competitors	—	Type and timing of new products
	Crops	—	Size and quality of crops
Methods Available		Regression analysis, econometric models, decomposition methods, Box-Jenkins, adaptive filtering, anticipatory surveys, leading indicators	Delphi approach

Short-term planning

Short-term planning is used mainly for scheduling purposes and covers a time span of *one to three months*. Its aim is to provide the financial, labor, machine, and material resources required to meet market demands and opportunities. The forecasting inputs needed for this planning include predicting the level of demand and its mix and translating these predictions into production levels and requirements for materials, machines, labor, etc. Because of the short time span between planning and implementation, short-term planning's impact is much more operational than that of either long-term or medium-term planning. It is used most effectively as a co-ordinating and control device for taking corrective action when short-term deviations from longer-term forecasts and plans occur. It is also used to adjust production schedules, determine inventory levels, and maintain an acceptable working capital position for the organization.

The trend element is not particularly important in short-term planning, and cyclical fluctuations in the economy are less important than they are during medium-term planning. It is unlikely that there will be substantial growth or declines in sales, revenues, costs, etc., during the time span of short-term planning. Similarly, turning points in economic activity can occur during a three-month period, but their magnitude will be limited and of lesser importance as the time horizon of planning decreases from a quarterly to a monthly time span. However, the element of seasonal fluctuations can be quite significant in this shorter time horizon. Often the main purpose of short-term planning is to identify seasonal fluctuations and to forecast them. Although that involves the prediction of turning points, it is much easier than predicting turning points caused by cyclical factors or the saturation of trends, because the time length of seasonality is usually constant. These fixed intervals of seasonal turning points can be found by analyzing past data.

The forecasting techniques used for short-term planning are mostly quantitative and usually have the special characteristic of being able to predict seasonal fluctuations. Since forecasts must be provided for a greater number of items, implying a higher usage cost, that affects which methods will be used. Table 15-3 summarizes some of the information needs, forecasting inputs, and applicable methods for short-range planning.

A final category of unexpected or unusual events that must be foreseen for effective short-term planning includes strikes by the suppliers, transportation facilities, or internal personnel; breakdowns of an unusual nature; wars or threats of war; etc. Quantitative forecasting techniques, however, are of little value in predicting such events, and more judgmental approaches are necessary for incorporating them into the planning process.

TABLE 15-3 FORECASTING NEEDS FOR SHORT-TERM PLANNING
(ONE TO THREE MONTHS)

Organization Unit	Information Needs	Quantitative Forecasting Inputs	Technological Forecasting Inputs
Business			
Marketing	Total sales, product categories, major products, prices, effect of advertising and sales promotion	Seasonality in sales, actual sales levels, estimation of advertising recalls	
Production	Total demand, demand of product categories and product groups, scheduling, employment level, costs	Sales by each product, needs for materials, needs for personnel	
Inventory	Demand for material, demand for semifinished products, demand for products, possible strikes	Sales by each product, extent of forecasting error	Results of contract negotiations
Finance	Total demand, inventory levels, cash flows, short-term borrowing, prices	Revenues, expenses, borrowing conditions, inventories	
Purchasing	Demand for products, demand for materials, lead time for purchasing	Production by each product, lead times, quantity discounts	
R&D			
Top management	Total sales, sales breakdowns, pricing		
Economic			
Economic unit	Level of economic activity, turning points	Level of GNP	
Environmental			
Technological unit			
Business environment forecasting unit	Availability of money, interest rates		Government policies
	Competitors' prices, advertising selections, sales promotions, new product introduction	Analyzing and predicting competitors' prices and sales	Timing of advertising campaigns and sales promotions
	Weather conditions	Weather forecasts	
Methods Available		Regression analysis, decomposition methods, Box-Jenkins, adaptive filtering, some smoothing techniques	

Immediate-term planning

Immediate-term planning is concerned with the day-to-day operational aspects of running the organization and generally covers a time span of *less than one month*. It is usually conducted by middle and lower management. The purpose of immediate-term planning is to finely adjust operations through incremental improvements, rather than to change the course of future events. Forecasting is simpler in this time span because immediate-term planning involves fewer fluctuations than does planning for longer time horizons, and predictions usually are for situations for which there is adequate knowledge. For example, the sales of the next day or week can be pretty well determined by the number of orders received ahead of time for shipment in that period. The cash inflows can be estimated by the magnitude of billing, and outflows of cash can be forecast using the level of current buying authorizations. Since the variables to be forecast are more deterministic in nature than those for longer time horizons, that portion of the job of planning is easier. At the same time, however, planning must be done for a large number of items and situations.

A goal of planning for the immediate term is to make sure that demand in the near future can and will be met through existing inventory levels and planned production. That requires shipping to different geographical locations, having cash available where needed to meet expenses, and having adequate material supplies and labor to keep the production process going and the organization running without major obstacles. Even in a small plant producing 1000 items with a production cycle of one week, planning for 1000 items will be required 52 times a year. Predicting the level of demand for 1000 items for each of several geographical areas will require that the forecasting techniques used, if any, be inexpensive and simple to apply. An alternative to using quantitative forecasting methods is to have the planner make judgmental predictions. However, such informal forecasting is not necessarily the cheapest or most efficient mode for predicting the future, even for situations with little uncertainty.

For each planning time horizon there are some critical elements that must be predicted correctly. For long-term planning, these include the identification of trends and saturation points; for medium-term planning predicting the general level of economic activity and turning points in that activity are vital. Predicting seasonal fluctuations is critical for short-term planning, and finally, random fluctuations are a major concern for the immediate term. Day-to-day demand usually is not significantly influenced by trend elements, cyclical factors, or seasonal fluctuations, although there may be other factors that can be identified that account for immediate-term fluctuations. These other factors are often hard to deal with in immediate-term planning and therefore inventories are frequently used to absorb a good part of these fluctuations. However, whether predictable or treated as random, the planner will have to be concerned with these fluctuations and take actions that anticipate their magnitude.

The forecasting methods used most frequently in immediate-term planning include the mean, smoothing techniques, and some of the decomposition and control methods. Since all of these except the smoothing methods require a substantial number of data points and are expensive to use, the smoothing techniques are generally the most appropriate methods when forecasts for a large number of items are required for a short time span. When the number of items is smaller or when increased accuracy has high value, decomposition or control methods may be appropriate.

An alternative approach sometimes used in immediate-term situations is to apply decomposition or control methods to a longer time horizon, and then to subdivide that forecast value among each of the shorter time periods needed for immediate-term planning. Such an approach often can be quite accurate because within a period such as a month, neither the trend nor the cyclical pattern is dominant and the fluctuations caused by seasonality can be allocated to each week by using something like the working-days ratio of each week to the total for the month. If there are large day-to-day or week-to-week fluctuations, it may not be suitable simply to subdivide the monthly forecast, and a more sophisticated approach to dealing with such a situation may need to be devised.

Immediate-term forecasting almost always requires the use of a time-series method because macrodata is seldom available on a basis shorter than a month, and making use of a causal model is expensive. An exception might be when an internal variable (orders received or backlog) is used as a leading indicator to forecast another variable (such as the level of inventory of certain materials), or when the independent variable can be generated or estimated through a sampling procedure (such as shown in Chapter 6 where in one example the weight of the mail received was used in a causal model to estimate the number of orders received).

The use of quantitative methods can be helpful to the immediate-term planner because they can provide timely information and serve as a control device against which actual performances can be compared. Table 15-4 summarizes some of the information needs, forecasting inputs, and appropriate forecasting methods for immediate-term planning.

Tables 15-1 through 15-4 are meant to provide guidelines for the planner rather than to be an exhaustive list of all forecasting input requirements. A complete list can only be compiled after a careful examination of all planning activities of a specific organization and a cost-benefit analysis to determine the feasibility of using judgmental methods, quantitative techniques, or technological approaches. As a starting point for such an

TABLE 15-4 FORECASTING NEEDS FOR IMMEDIATE-TERM PLANNING (LESS THAN ONE MONTH)

Organization Unit	Information Needs	Quantitative Forecasting Inputs	Technological Forecasting Inputs
Business			
Marketing	Sales of each product type, sales by geographical area, sales by customer, competition, prices, inventory levels	Sales by product and geographical region, prices	
Production	Demand of each product, plant loading	Production for each product, inventory level, availability of materials and personnel	
Inventory	Demand of each product, production, demand for materials, demand for semifinished products, weather conditions	Production schedules, sales, extent of forecasting error	
Finance	Sales revenue, production costs, inventory costs, loading indicators, cash inflows, cash outflows	Revenue and expenses, need for short-term borrowing	
Purchasing	Production, cash availability, purchasing of supplies and materials	Cash position, availability of materials in suppliers' warehouses	
Economic			
Economic unit			
Environmental			
Business environment forecasting unit	Sales promotions of competitors		Monitoring competitors' activities
	Weather conditions		
Methods Available		Inventory control, smoothing methods, some decomposition methods, some control methods	

analysis, Table 15-5 provides one summary of the planning needs of an organization categorized by time horizon and service area. Chapter 16 will examine some of the important factors that determine the final choice between (1) informal and formal methods and (2) the selection of the most appropriate formal method.

TABLE 15-5 INFORMATION NEEDS FOR PLANNING

Organization Unit	Time Horizon			
	Immediate Term (less than 1 mo)	Short Term (1–3 mo)	Medium Term (3 mo–2 yr)	Long Term (2 yr or more)
	Quantitative Forecasting			
Business Marketing	Sales of each product type, sales by geographical area, sales by customer, competition, prices, inventory levels	Total sales, product categories, major products, product groups, prices	Total sales, product categories, prices, general economic conditions	Total sales, major product categories, new product introduction, saturation points of existing products, customers' preferences and tastes
Production	Demand of each product, plant loading	Total demands, demand of product categories and product groups, scheduling employment level, costs	Costs, budget allocations, buying or ordering equipment and machinery, employment level	Costs, facility investments, expansion of plant and equipment, ordering of heavy machinery and equipment, demand of production facilities, new technologies
Inventory	Demand of each product, production, demand for material, demand for semifinished products, weather conditions	Demand for materials, demand for semifinished products, demand for products, possible strikes	Possible strikes in suppliers or transportation facilities	Total sales, expansion of warehouses
Finance	Sales revenue, production costs, inventory costs, leading indicators, cash inflows, cash outflows	Total demand, inventory levels, cash flows, short-term borrowing, prices	Budget allocations, cash flows	Total sales, investment selections, capital expenditure, allocations of resources, capital programs, cash flows
Purchasing	Production, cash availability, purchasing of supplies and materials	Demand for products, demand for materials, lead time for purchasing	Demand for products, demand for raw and other materials	Contracts for buying raw materials, customers' preferences and tastes
R&D			New product introduction, R&D selections	Total sales; technological, social, political, and economic conditions of future; new product development

TABLE 15-5 *Continued*

Organization Unit	Time Horizon			
	Immediate Term (less than 1 mo)	Short Term (1–3 mo)	Medium Term (3 mo–2 yr)	Long Term (2 yr or more)
Quantitative Forecasting				
Top management		Total sales, sales breakdowns, pricing	Demand for sales, costs and other expenses, cash position, general economic conditions, control objectives	Total sales; costs and other expenses, social and economic trends; goals, objectives and strategies; new products; pricing policies
Economic Economic unit		Level of economic activity	General economic conditions, turning points in economy, level of economic activity	State and type of economy, level of economic activity, sales of industry
Technological Forecasting				
Environment Technological unit			Available technologies	Areas of technological innovation, R&D selections, available technological opportunities
Business environment forecasting unit			Social attitudes	Social trends, tastes, areas of social concern
		Availability of money, interest rates	Fiscal and monetary policies	Trends in the rate of taxation, depreciation, and concept of free market
	Prices, sales promotions	Prices, advertising selections, sales promotions, new product introduction	New product development	Capital investment, new technologies, R&D selections of competitors
	Weather conditions	Weather conditions	Crops	General environmental constraints (pollution level, availability of raw materials, etc.)

15/4 Contribution of Forecasting to Analysis and Understanding

In each of the chapters that deals with specific methods of forecasting, the aim has been to provide a forecast or range of forecasts for a specific variable or item. Although that is most often the direct application of forecasting, there are frequently other substantial benefits in the analysis and understanding that accompany the application of forecasting methodologies. The extent and potential usefulness of such information depend upon the type of forecasting model applied (causal or time series) and the statistical parameters provided by that technique. In this respect, regression methods have a much higher potential contribution in regard to analysis and understanding than many of the other methodologies. The remainder of this chapter will look at several of the specific areas for which substantial side benefits can arise from the application of a formal forecasting methodology.

15/4/1 The Variance as a Measure of Risk

As shown previously, statistical forecasting methods can use the statistical properties of the data to construct confidence intervals and test different hypotheses about the forecasts. This process involves use of the central limit theorem, which allows the distribution of the forecast values to be approximated with a normal curve. The mean of the normal distribution is the most likely value, and the variance is a measure of the dispersion of all possible values around the mean. The variance is an extremely useful statistic because it summarizes the uncertainties and errors in the estimation of the model's parameters. Further, with these two measures—the mean and the variance—the range of all future values and their probability of occurrence can be predicted.

In addition to its use in constructing a confidence interval for a forecast, the variance of a forecast is a measure of risk and can be utilized as such. It provides an indication of the degree of uncertainty associated with predicting that variable. The planner can use it as a measure of the risk involved and prepare contingency plans for optimistic and pessimistic outcomes. In the short run, this measure of risk can be utilized for inventory and cash management purposes, since its magnitude will be reflected in the extent of over- or under-prediction. Decision models for handling the levels of inventory and cash in an optimal way can be built based on a knowledge of the magnitude of the variance.

A tremendous amount of work has been done on financial portfolio analysis (Markowitz 1959) involving the covariance as a basis for minimizing the risk in a set of investments, or optimizing the return for a given level of risk. In a similar manner, forecasting models can be built to minimize the effects of forecasting errors when a number of items or areas of management are involved.

In other words, it may be possible to decrease the total risk of inaccurate forecasts by examining in a global fashion the variance and covariance of the predictions made on different items. This technique can decrease substantially the effects of over- or under-estimation for the total organization by grouping the forecasts in such a way that their covariance will be as small as possible.

15/4/2 Marginal Analysis

In many forecasting situations, the parameter(s) of the forecasting model contain useful information. In the case of a time-series model of the form

$$Y = a + bX$$

where X is time,

the change in Y caused by a unit change in X is $b(dY/dX)$. Since successive values of X correspond to successive periods, the value of b indicates the change in Y for each time period. For example, if the model is

$$Y = 10 + 250X,$$

where X represents months, and Y represents the sales of product A, then the first derivative is

$$\frac{dY}{dX} = 250.$$

This means that, on the average, there is an increase of 250 units in the sales of product A every month.

Oftentimes the relationship of a variable to time is nonlinear. In such instances, simple transformations can provide information on the growth rate as well as improving forecasting performance. If the values of Y are transformed to their natural logarithms, the result is

$$\log_e Y = a + bX. \tag{15-1}$$

The values of a and b in this equation can be easily estimated using regression analysis or some form of time-series analysis. The parameter b, the slope of the line, can then be shown to be a good estimate of the growth rate.

As an example of how this estimate of the growth rate might be obtained, suppose the following functional form is applied to a set of data:

$$Y = ab^x. \tag{15-2}$$

Taking logs (either natural or common) of both sides of equation (15-2) gives

$$\log Y = \log a + X(\log b). \tag{15-3}$$

This means that if the data of both the dependent and independent variables are transformed into logarithms, estimates for log a and log b could be obtained and used as the parameters of equation (15-3). It can then be shown that a will be the value of Y at period $X = 0$, while $(b - 1)$ will be the growth rate.

As a specific example, suppose one has a quantity of Y_0 units that are increasing at a constant rate of r per period. This can be expressed as

$$Y = Y_0(1 + r)^x, \qquad\qquad (15\text{-}4)$$

where x is the time period $(1, 2, \ldots)$.

If $Y_0 = 100$ and $r = .10$, then equation (15-4) gives

Period	Value of Y	Increase in Y over Previous Period	Growth Rate r
$x = 0$	$Y_0 = 100$	—	—
$x = 1$	$Y_1 = 110$	$(110 - 100) = 10/100 =$	.10
$x = 2$	$Y_2 = 121$	$(121 - 110) = 11/110 =$	.10
$x = 3$	$Y_3 = 133.1$	$(133.1 - 121) = 12.1/121 =$	.10
$x = 4$	$Y_4 = 146.4$	$(146.4 - 133.1) = 13.3/133.1 =$	.10
etc.			

If equation (15-2) is substituted into (15-4), the result is

$$ab^x = Y_0(1 + r)^x. \qquad\qquad (15\text{-}5)$$

Taking the logs of both sides of (15-5) gives

$$\log a + X(\log b) = \log Y_0 + X[\log (1 + r)], \qquad\qquad (15\text{-}6)$$

$$\log a = \log Y_0,$$

and

$$a = Y_0.$$

Thus the initial value of Y (at time $X = 0$) will be equal to the intercept, a.

Similarly

$$\log b = \log (1 + r),$$

$$b = 1 + r,$$

and

$$r = b - 1.$$

This means that the growth rate for a set of data can be found directly by applying equation (15-3) and substracting 1 from b.

If the data cannot be expressed by equation (15-2), but can be better approximated by

$$Y = e^{a+bx}, \tag{15-7}$$

the growth rate can still be found.

This is done by first taking the logs of both sides to obtain

$$\log Y = a + bX(\log e),$$

$$\log Y = a + bX, \tag{15-8}$$

since $\log e = 1$.

From equation (15-8), the values of a and b can be estimated after the data of the dependent variable have been transformed to log.

The log of equation (15-4) is

$$\log Y = \log Y_0 + X[\log(1 + r)] \tag{15-9}$$

Substituting (15-8) into (15-9) gives

$$a + bX = \log Y_0 + X[\log(1 + r)].$$

Thus, $a = \log Y,$

and $b = \log(1 + r). \tag{15-10}$

The antilog of equation (15-10) is

$$e^b = 1 + r,$$

which gives $r = e^b - 1. \tag{15-11}$

This simply says that the constant growth rate r will be equivalent to the exponent of b, minus 1. For growth rates of less than 20%, the estimated value of b in equation (15-7) will be very close to the actual growth rate. Table 15-6 shows the estimated and real growth rates for different values of b. There are no great differences between the two, indicating that the coefficient b is a good estimate of the true growth rate.

A close approximation of (15-11) is

$$r = b + \frac{b^2}{2} + \frac{b^3}{6} + \cdots.$$

When $b = .20$, this gives

$$r = .20 + \frac{(.20)^2}{2} + \frac{(.20)^3}{6} \cdots \cong .221.$$

It can thus be concluded that the coefficient of the transformed dependent variable data ($\log_e$) provides an approximate measure of the growth rate, while an exact measure of the growth can be found using equation 15-2.

TABLE 15-6 ESTIMATION OF GROWTH RATES USING A REGRESSION COEFFICIENT

Value of Regression Coefficient (b) of $\log_e$ Data	Real Growth Rate
0	0
.025	.0253
.05	.0513
.075	.0779
.10	.1052
.125	.133
.15	.162
.175	.191
.20	.221
.225	.252
.25	.284
.275	.317
.30	.350

When a causal instead of a time-series model exists, the parameters of the equation can supply marginal information. Their value can indicate the change in the dependent variable Y caused by a unit change in the independent variable corresponding to that parameter.* Thus, for the causal model

$$Y = a + bX_1 + cX_2,$$

where X_1 is GNP and X_2 is advertising, b will indicate the change in Y accompanying a unit increase in GNP, and c will indicate the change in Y accompanying a unit change in advertising. In terms of policymaking, it may be very useful to know whether the change in Y corresponding to a dollar increase in advertising will cover the cost of that advertising.

15/4/3 Elasticities

Elasticity is an important factor in many situations. It can be estimated easily after a logarithmic transformation (either natural or common) of both

---

* This interpretation is only exact when variables X_1 and X_2 are independent of each other; otherwise this interpretation of the parameters may not be valid.

dependent and independent variables has taken place. For example, for the function

$$Y = ax^b,$$ (15-12)

taking logs of both sides gives

$$\log Y = \log a + b(\log X).$$ (15-13)

In equation (15-13), the values of $\log a$ and b can be calculated and the derivative found as

$$\frac{d \log Y}{d \log X} = b.$$

This indicates the change in $\log Y$ caused by a one-unit change in $\log X$. Since a logarithmic change corresponds to a percentage change in the original data, b can be interpreted as the percentage change in Y caused by a percentage change in X. As such it is a measure that is independent of the absolute value of the units involved.

In equation (15-12) three categories of values for b can be distinguished: $b < 1$, $b = 1$, and $b > 1$. The functional forms corresponding to each of these can be seen in Figure 15-3.

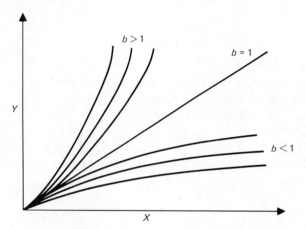

FIGURE 15-3 ALTERNATIVE VALUES FOR THE COEFFICIENT, b

For $b < 1$, a 1% increase in X will cause less than a 1% increase in Y. When $b > 1$, a 1% increase in X will cause more than a 1% increase in Y. Finally, when $b = 1$ equation (15-12) becomes the equivalent of $Y = a + bX$, indicating a constant linear increase in Y for each increase in X. This behavior of Y can be seen in Figure 15-3.

The usefulness of elasticities for policymaking can be further illustrated by an example. Suppose

$$\log Y = \log a + b \log X,$$

where Y is the sales of product A, and X is its price.

If $b = -1.5$, it indicates that every percentage increase in the price of product A will result in a 1.5% decrease in sales. In this case the demand is elastic. On the other hand, if $b = -.5$, an increase in price of 1% will decrease demand by only .5%. This is commonly called inelastic demand. This type of information can provide important data upon which to base pricing decisions. Similar measures can be calculated for other factors as long as the data can be fitted into a form like that of equation (15-12).

15/4/4 Costing

Once a cost function has been estimated, questions relating to fixed, variable, marginal, or per unit costs often can be answered. For example, suppose the estimated total cost function is cubic and of the form

$$\text{Cost} = a + bX + cX^2 + dX^3. \tag{15-14}$$

$$\text{Then} \qquad \text{fixed cost} = a, \tag{15-15}$$

$$\text{variable cost} = bX + cX^2 + dX^3, \tag{15-16}$$

$$\text{per unit variable cost} = (a/X) + b + cX + dX^2, \tag{15-17}$$

$$\text{and} \qquad \text{marginal cost} = b + 2(c)X + 3(d)X^2. \tag{15-18}$$

Decisions on production levels, expansion policies, pricing, and efficiency can be facilitated using the information obtained through cost functions like those above. For example, the optimal production will be at the lowest point of equation (15-17). If sales increase beyond the production level corresponding to the lowest cost, then new plant or equipment might be considered to raise the optimal level. Because of long lead times, a decision to expand must be made well in advance through combined information obtained from growth rates, elasticities, etc. Much of this information needed by top management for long-run policy formulation can be obtained as direct and indirect output from formalized forecasting applications.

15/4/5 Seasonal and Cyclical Considerations

Forecasting methods can discover the seasonal and cyclical behavior of the data. Through such analyses, it is often possible to predict future variations in sales and attribute them to trend, seasonal, or cyclical factors.

Decomposition methods are the most direct and explicit in isolating the seasonal and cyclical part of a set of data. Their output for monthly data consists of 12 seasonal indices whose base is 100. Index values higher or lower than this base indicate expected variations attributable to the season. Similarly cyclical indices are provided that help to explain and predict the effects of cycle.

Regression methods are less explicit in isolating seasonal and cyclical elements. By defining dummy variables to each of the seasons but one, the season without a corresponding dummy variable becomes the base and the parameters of the other variables will indicate seasonal adjustments to that base. Thus a positive coefficient will denote a higher level of sales caused by seasonal effects, and a negative coefficient will denote a lower level. The effects of cyclicality can be estimated by relating the dependent variable to an independent factor, such as GNP, that can be used to explain cyclical changes.

ARMA methods are less explicit in the way they estimate the seasonal effects. These methods do not separate the trend, cyclical, or seasonal effects from each other. Thus, a total forecast is given, which includes all effects without breaking the pattern down into its various components.

Seasonal variations can cause considerable fluctuations in sales that have important policy consequences. For example, the manager making a decision to cut production when a lower level of sales is forecast will want to consider whether a few months later more favorable seasonal factors will cause the sales to pick up again. If so, it may be that inventories should be accumulated to keep a more constant production rate. Similar questions will arise with respect to predicted cyclical fluctuations. Policy questions of this type can be dealt with through knowledge of the seasonal and cyclical factors. Thus not only is the forecast important, but so too are the reasons for that forecast.

15/4/6 Simulation and Sensitivity Analysis

Causal forecasting models are not as easy to use as time-series models. The difficulty is that the values of each of the independent variables used in the model must be estimated before one can forecast. This can be a serious problem because it shifts the burden of forecasting to that of estimating the values of the independent variables. However, this very problem can present many advantages, too. First, marginal analyses can be applied and elasticities for any of the independent variables can be found. In addition, the effects of multiple changes and their influence on the dependent variable can be calculated. For example, suppose that the following model of sales has been determined:

$$\text{Sales} = 250 + .03\,(\text{GNP}) + 3.8\,(\text{Advertising}) - 4.5\,(\text{Price}) + 2.5(\text{R\&D}). \tag{15-19}$$

This model could be used to predict the sales volume under varying decisions regarding advertising, prices, and R&D expenditures. Thus, more than one input can be varied to determine their effects on sales. This use of the model goes beyond forecasting in trying to shape the future, since the values of advertising, prices, and R&D are controllable. They can be set at a level that best fits the organization's plans and goals.

A forecast model like equation (15-19) is one of the most efficient ways to obtain information about the influence of changes in controllable factors (the independent variables) on the dependent variable. Actually it is a form of laboratory simulation that shows how varying the levels of advertising, price, and R&D will influence the sales. From this simulation, a desirable level of sales, advertising, price, and R&D can be selected, and the feasibility of actions needed to achieve that level examined. In this way, equation (15-19) can be used to formulate alternatives for management choice.

More information can be obtained from forecasting techniques than simply a prediction about a single variable. The extent of such information depends upon the particular method used and the extra work put forth to extract it. As a rule, causal models provide more information than time-series models, and statistical models more than nonstatistical. In the end, such advantages must be weighed against the costs in deciding how much information for policymaking purposes should be sought from forecasting applications.

REFERENCES AND SELECTED BIBLIOGRAPHY

Ackoff, R. L. 1970. *A Concept of Corporate Planning*. New York: John Wiley & Sons.

Ayres, R. U. 1969. *Technological Forecasting and Long-Range Planning*. New York: McGraw-Hill.

Baumol, W. J. 1965. *Economic Theory and Operations Analysis*. Englewood Cliffs, N.J.: Prentice-Hall.

Blazey, T. W. 1976. "Putting Forecasts to Work in the Firm." *Business Economics*, January, pp. 41–44.

Centron, M. 1971. *Industrial Applications of Technological Forecasting*. New York: John Wiley & Sons.

Cohen, K. J., and R. M. Cyert. 1965. *The Theory of the Firm: Resource Allocation in a Market Economy*. Englewood Cliffs, N.J.: Prentice-Hall.

Cotton, D. B. 1970. *Company Wide Planning*. London: Macmillan.

Drucker, P. F. 1959. "Long Range Planning." *Management Science*, Vol. 5, April, pp. 238–39.

Ewing, D. C. 1968. *The Practice of Planning*. New York: Harper & Row.

Ewing, D. W. 1969. *The Human-Side of Planning—Tool or Tyrant?* London: Macmillan.

Haas, R. M. 1964. *Long-Range Planning for Small Business*. Small Business Management Research Reports, July.

Holt, C., F. Modigliani, J. F. Muth, and H. A. Simon. 1960. *Planning Production, Inventories and Work Force*. Englewood Cliffs, N.J.: Prentice-Hall.

Hussey, D. E. 1971. *Introducing Corporate Planning*. Oxford: Pergamon Press.

Johnston, G. F. 1976. "Putting Forecasts to Work in the Corporate Planning Function." *Business Economics*, January, pp. 35–40.

McAlpine, T. S. 1969. *Profit Planning and Control*. London: Business Books LMT.

McKenna, J. P. 1965. *Aggregate Economic Analysis*. New York: Holt, Rinehart & Winston.

Markowitz, H. M. 1959. *Portfolio Selection: Efficient Diversification of Investments*. New York: John Wiley & Sons.

Meadows, D. H. 1972. *Limits of Growth*. London: Earth Island Limited.

Miller, E. C. 1971. *Advanced Techniques for Strategic Planning*. Research Study 104. New York: American Management Association.

Mockler, R. J. 1970. "Theory and Practice of Planning," *Harvard Business Review*, March–April, pp. 148–59.

Naylor, T. H., and H. Schauland. 1976. "A Survey of Users of Corporate Planning Models," *Management Science*, Vol. 22, No. 9, pp. 927–37.

Reichard, R. S. 1966. *Practical Techniques of Sales Forecasting*. New York: McGraw-Hill.

Steiner, G. A. 1963. *Managerial Long-Range Planning.* New York: McGraw-Hill.

————. 1969. *Top Management Planning.* London: Macmillan.

von Allmen, E. 1969. *Putting Corporate Planning into Practice.* London: I. & C. T.

Warren, E. 1966. *Long-Range Planning: The Executive Viewpoint.* Englewood Cliffs, N.J.: Prentice-Hall.

16 COMPARISON AND SELECTION OF FORECASTING METHODS

IN THE FIRST fourteen chapters of this book, a number of quantitative and qualitative or technological methods of forecasting were presented. These methods vary widely in terms of the accuracy they can achieve in forecasting, the constraints and requirements they impose on the organization using them, and their complexity and intuitive appeal to the ultimate user. Given the wide choice of alternative forecasting methods available, it is particularly useful for both the forecaster and the user of forecasts to have criteria that can be used in selecting and comparing alternative methodologies. The purpose of this chapter is to discuss such alternative criteria and to draw upon existing literature to illustrate some of the comparative benefits of one method over another in certain situations.

Effective selection of a forecasting methodology for a given situation has two prerequisites. First, a range of alternatives must be understood and recognized. Developing such an understanding has been the purpose of the first fourteen chapters of this book. The methods covered in those chapters represent a fairly complete set of those currently available. The second prerequisite is some systematic procedure for comparing the strengths and weaknesses of alternative methods in different situations. The purpose of this chapter is to provide such a framework.

There are several ways in which criteria for comparing and selecting a forecasting method can be organized. The organization used here is essentially that of establishing a set of priorities for the criteria so that those most important in practice can be considered first. That allows the quick elimination of many methods found to be inappropriate for the most important criterion. Under such a system, accuracy clearly is given top priority. Most analyses and empirical research indicate that selection and evaluation can be and are performed on the basis of accuracy. In this chapter, the question of the measurement of accuracy will be addressed first. Empirical results using various measures of accuracy will then be summarized to illustrate their application and to suggest the relative accuracy of different forecasting methodologies in a range of situations.

Unfortunately, forecasters often terminate the evaluation process after this first criterion of accuracy has been examined. The author's own experience and contacts with practitioners indicate that a number of other criteria are also very important as a part of this evaluation process. These criteria include the pattern of the data to be forecast, the time horizon to be covered in forecasting, the cost of applying alternative methodologies, and the ease of application in organization situations. While each of these criteria will be discussed in detail in this chapter, it is helpful to provide an overview of them so that they can be kept in mind as each individual criterion is discussed. This overview is important because of the interrelationship among criteria and the need to select the forecasting method that best meets all of the dimensions of the given situation.

The *pattern of the data* is important in selecting a forecasting method because, as shown in previous chapters, different methods can cope with only certain kinds of data patterns. There are, of course, methods that can cope with a very wide range of patterns, but these are usually more expensive to use and more difficult to apply; thus a trade-off is involved in using them. Generally, the pattern element can be divided into two main subparts, which can then be subdivided further. The two main subparts are patterns that repeat with time (periodic patterns such as trend and seasonal components) and patterns that represent turning points that do not repeat over fixed time intervals. These latter turning points, caused by business cycles or by other changes in the environment, are an important consideration in selecting a forecasting method, as are periodic patterns.

The *time horizon* criterion for evaluating forecasting methods is closely related to the pattern criterion. As shown in Chapter 15, different planning horizons involve different pattern characteristics and make different demands in terms of the number of items to be forecast and the value of accuracy. Closely related to the time horizon to be forecast is the time that can be taken to actually prepare the forecast. In immediate- and short-term situations, a much quicker turnaround for obtaining the forecast is needed than in situations involving medium- and long-term planning.

The element of *cost* is often one of the key criteria that is traded off against such things as accuracy, ease of application, and the pattern. The costs of forecasting depend very much on the method itself and its inherent complexity as well as on its data requirements and the number of items to be forecast. In discussing this criterion later in the chapter, elements of costs associated with data requirements, computer and human resources, training of the forecasting methodology, and use of the methodology on an ongoing basis will be considered.

Ease of application might be thought of as a criterion that brings together several remaining considerations not covered by the previous four criteria. Included under this heading are such things as the complexity of the method, the timeliness of the forecasts that it provides, the level of knowledge required for application, and the conceptual basis and the ease with which it can be conveyed to the final user of the forecast. As practitioners know, one of the common stumbling blocks in adoption of appropriate forecasting techniques is making the ultimate user comfortable with the technique and its rationale so that the user can effectively judge the results of the forecasting method and their usefulness.

It should be clear from the brief description of these criteria that the assignment of priorities to them in comparing and selecting a forecasting method for a given situation will depend in part on the situation to be forecast and in part on the organization's experience with forecasting. Thus while accuracy is almost universally recognized as being the number one criterion, the relative importance of the others will depend on the situation and the organization.

16/1 The Accuracy of Forecasting Methods

In the majority of practical forecasting situations, accuracy is treated as the overriding criterion for selecting a forecasting method. Accuracy is not only important in itself, but other factors are also frequently reflected in accuracy. (For example, insufficient data or use of a technique that does not fit the pattern of the data will be reflected in less accurate forecasts.) In spite of the fact that accuracy is given prime importance as a factor in the selection process, little systematic work has been done to develop a framework for measuring and evaluating accuracy-related issues. Such a framework would be particularly useful if it could serve as a mechanism for bracketing the accuracy that is possible in a given situation and as an aid in answering the following kinds of questions:

1. What additional accuracy can be achieved in a given situation through use of a formal forecasting technique? (How inaccurate will the forecasts be if they are based on a very simple or naive approach rather than on a more mathematically sophisticated technique?)
2. For a given situation, how much improvement can be obtained in the accuracy of the forecasts? (How close can one come to achieving perfect forecasts?)
3. If the opportunity for achieving greater accuracy in a given situation is understood, how can that knowledge help in selecting the most appropriate forecasting technique?

In this section, a conceptual framework for applying the criterion of accuracy will be developed. Although this framework is applicable mainly in the area of quantitative forecasting methods, its extension to qualitative or technological methods should also become apparent.

16/1/1 Measuring Forecasting Accuracy

One of the difficulties in dealing with the criterion of accuracy in forecasting situations is the absence of a single universally accepted measure of accuracy.

Several alternative measures have been suggested. One that is commonly used by statisticians and in the more statistical methods of forecasting is that of mean squared error (MSE). The MSE is defined as

$$MSE = \frac{\sum\limits_{i=1}^{n} (X_i - F_i)^2}{n},$$ (16-1)

where X_i is the actual value,

F_i is the forecast,

and n is the number of data values.

As pointed out previously, the objective of statistical optimization in forecasting is to choose a model in such a way as to minimize the MSE. Unfortunately, even this measure of accuracy has two significant drawbacks. First, it refers to fitting a model to historical data. Such fitting does not necessarily imply good forecasting. An MSE of zero can always be obtained in the fitting phase by using a polynomial of sufficiently high order or an appropriate Fourier transformation. Overfitting a model to a data series, which is equivalent to including randomness as part of the generating process, is as bad as failing to identify the nonrandom pattern in the data. Comparison of the MSE developed during the fitting phase of forecasting may give little indication of the accuracy of the model in forecasting. As a result, a completely meaningful comparison can be made only after the fact.

A second drawback of the MSE as a measure of forecasting accuracy is related to the fact that different methods use different procedures in the fitting phase. These differences make comparison on a single criterion measure often incomplete. For example, smoothing methods are highly dependent upon initial forecasting estimates, decomposition methods include the trend-cycle in the fitting phase as though it were known; regression methods minimize the MSE by giving equal weight to all observations; generalized adaptive filtering minimizes an evolutionary MSE value, since the weights change with time; and Box-Jenkins minimizes the MSE of a nonlinear optimization procedure. Thus, comparison of such methods that utilize MSE in their fitting procedure in very different ways is of limited value.

In the forecasting phase, the use of MSE as a measure of accuracy can also create problems. It does not facilitate comparison across different time series and for different time intervals, since the MSE is an absolute measure. Furthermore, its interpretation is not intuitive even for the specialist because it involves the squaring of a range of values. Finally, the MSE is not particularly appropriate for making comparisons among formal forecasting methods and naive methods.

For all of the above reasons, alternative measures of accuracy have been proposed, measures that seek to:

1. express accuracy in relative terms

2. allow comparison among formal methods and naive methods of forecasting

Several of these alternative measures of accuracy will be discussed in this
section. One of the most straightforward of them is the percentage error. It is a
relative measure of accuracy that is defined as

$$PE_t = \left[\frac{X_t - F_t}{X_t} \right](100).$$

(16-2)

This equation can be used to compute the percentage error for any time
period. It is then useful to consider combining the percentage error from several
different time periods in order to estimate the accuracy over time. If the percentage
errors are simply added together, positive values will offset negative values and
the average percentage error will be quite small, even though individual errors
may be substantial. An alternative approach commonly used for combining the
individual percentage errors is to take the absolute value of each of them to
obtain the mean absolute percentage error (MAPE). The equation for computing
the MAPE is given by

$$MAPE = \frac{\sum_{i=1}^{n} |PE_i|}{n}.$$

(16-3)

From the point of view of the ultimate user of forecasting, knowing that
the MAPE of a method is 5% means a great deal more than simply knowing
that the MSE is 183. However, even the MAPE itself does not give a good basis
of comparison as to the gains in accuracy made by applying a specific forecasting
method. One basis for making such a comparison is to define some very simple
naive methods against which the performance of more sophisticated methods can
be compared.

The authors have found it useful to define two different naive methods of
forecasting for use as a basis in evaluating other methods in a given situation. The
first is referred to as Naive Forecast 1 or NF1. This method uses as a forecast
the most recent information available concerning the actual value. Thus, if a forecast is being prepared for a time horizon of one period, the most recent actual
value would be used as the forecast for the next period. When this is done, the
MAPE of this method can be expressed as follows:

$$NF1 = \frac{\sum_{i=2}^{n} \left| \frac{(X_i - X_{i-1})}{X_{i-1}} \right|}{n - 1}(100).$$

(16-4)

Only $n - 1$ terms are included in computing the MAPE of this naive
forecast, since forecasting begins with period 2 rather than period 1. The difference
between the MAPE obtained from a more formal method of forecasting and that

obtained using NF1 provides a measure of the improvement attainable through use of that formal forecasting method. This type of comparison is much more useful than simply computing the MAPE of the formal method or the MSE, since it provides a basis for evaluating the relative accuracy of those results.

A second naive method of forecasting has also been found to be extremely useful as a basis for evaluating more formal forecasting methods. This method is referred to as Naive Forecast 2 or NF2 and goes beyond NF1 in that it considers the possibility of seasonality in the series. Since seasonality often accounts for a substantial percentage of the fluctuation in a series, this method can frequently do much better than NF1 and yet is still a very simple straightforward approach. The procedure is to remove seasonality from the original data in order to obtain seasonally adjusted data. Once the seasonality has been removed, NF2 is comparable to NF1 in that it uses the most recent seasonally adjusted value as a forecast for the next seasonally adjusted value. When NF2 is applied, the MAPE can be computed as follows:

$$NF2 = \frac{\sum\limits_{i=2}^{n} \left| \dfrac{(X_i' - X_{i-1}')}{X_{i-1}'} \right|}{n-1} (100), \tag{16-5}$$

where X_i' is the seasonally adjusted value of X_i.

In practice, NF2 allows one to decide whether or not the improvement obtained from going beyond a simple seasonal adjustment of the data is worth the time and cost involved.

Finally, there is one other measure that is useful as a basis for comparing the accuracy of a formal forecasting method with some standard. This measure can be referred to as the optimal forecast, OF. It denotes the minimum possible error that can be achieved by a formal forecasting method. In concept the OF is found by isolating the randomness in a set of data and calculating the MAPE of that randomness. In practice, since the complete pattern is not generally known, the OF must be estimated. When the OF is obtained, it can be used as an indication of the minimum error that can be expected through use of the best possible forecasting method. In this sense, it sets a lower bound on the level of accuracy that can be achieved in a given situation. The MAPE of the optimal forecast can be defined mathematically as follows:

$$MAPE_{OF} = \frac{\sum\limits_{i=2}^{n} \left| \dfrac{(R_i - R_{i-1})}{R_i} \right|}{(n-1)} (100), \tag{16-6}$$

where R_i is the random component of the actual value, X_i.

As an illustration of the use of the MAPE values obtained from NF1, NF2, and OF forecasts, the three series shown in Table 16-1 can be considered. As would be expected, the relative differences in these three comparative measures depend largely on the series being considered. For example, for series A in Table 16-1 the MAPE of NF1 is 26.5%. Because of seasonality in the series, this MAPE drops to 19.8% using NF2. The optimal forecast (one that considers all of the pattern except randomness) gives a MAPE of 8.3%. These differences indicates that substantial improvement over NF1 is possible with NF2, and that further improvements might also be made with more sophisticated methods. However, the best that can be achieved, on the average, is a MAPE of 8.3%.

The results for series B in Table 16-1 indicate that series has a much stronger seasonal component than series A. Thus simply applying NF2 rather than NF1 reduces the MAPE from 32.6% to 10.2%. Since the average randomness in the series gives a MAPE of 9.3%, there is little reason to go beyond NF2 in looking for a more sophisticated (and more accurate) forecasting methodology.

In the case of series C, it can be seen that there is little seasonality present in the series and little pattern of any kind. Thus the change in MAPE obtained in going from NF1 to NF2 is only from 30.4% to 29.3%. Additionally, the randomness in the series gives a MAPE of 28.7% indicating that there is not much room for improvement from using any formal forecasting methodology.

TABLE 16-1 APPLICATION OF ACCURACY CRITERIA IN EVALUATING POTENTIAL IMPROVEMENT FROM FORMAL FORECASTING TECHNIQUES

| Series | Percentage of MAPE for: | | |
	Naive 1	Naive 2	Optimal Forecast
A	26.5	19.8	8.3
B	32.6	10.2	9.3
C	30.4	29.3	28.7

Although the above procedure for computing the mean absolute percentage error for NF1, NF2, and OF forecasts as well as for selected formalized forecasting methodologies is very useful, it still has the disadvantage that it gives equal weight to both small and large errors. In many situations, it is particularly important to avoid large errors in forecasting, since they tend to be much more costly than small errors. The MSE measure avoids this disadvantage by employing a quadratic loss function (it squares the errors). However, its weakness is its absolute characteristic as opposed to a relative measure of accuracy like the MAPE. A measure that considers both the disproportionate cost of large errors and provides a relative basis for comparison with naive methods would be very helpful.

One approach that provides this combination of characteristics is the U-statistic developed by Theil (1966). This statistic allows a relative comparison of formal forecasting methods with naive approaches and also squares the errors involved so that large errors are given much more weight than small errors. The positive characteristic that is given up in moving to Theil's U-statistic as a measure of accuracy is that of intuitive interpretation. This difficulty will become more apparent as the computation of this statistic and its application is examined. Mathematically, Theil's U-statistic is defined as

$$U = \sqrt{\frac{\sum_{i=1}^{n=1} (FPE_{i+1} - APE_{i+1})^2/(n-1)}{\sum_{i=1}^{n=1} (APE_{i+1})^2/(n-1)}}, \qquad (16\text{-}7)$$

where $\quad FPE_{i+1} = \dfrac{F_{i+1} - X_i}{X_i}, \quad$ (This is the predicted relative change.)

and $\quad APE_{i+1} = \dfrac{X_{i+1} - X_i}{X_i}. \quad$ (This is the actual relative change.)

Equation (16-7) is actually very straightforward, as can be seen by simplifying it to the form shown in (16-8). When the values of FPE_{i+1} and APE_{i+1} are substituted into equation (16-7), the result is

$$U = \sqrt{\frac{\sum_{i=1}^{n-1} \left(\dfrac{F_{i+1} - X_i - X_{i+1} + X_i}{X_i}\right)^2 \Big/ (n-1)}{\sum_{i=1}^{n-1} \left(\dfrac{X_{i+1} - X_i}{X_i}\right)^2 \Big/ (n-1)}}$$

$$= \sqrt{\frac{\sum_{i=1}^{n-1} \left(\dfrac{F_{i+1} - X_{i+1}}{X_i}\right)^2 \Big/ (n-1)}{\sum_{i=1}^{n-1} \left(\dfrac{X_{i+1} - X_i}{X_i}\right)^2 \Big/ (n-1)}}. \qquad (16\text{-}8)$$

Comparing the numerator of equation (16-8) with equation (16-3) shows that it is very similar to what was defined previously as the MAPE of a given forecasting method. Also, the denominator is very similar to equations (16-4) and (16-5). Thus the U-statistic is an accuracy measure that incorporates the MAPE of both NF1 and NF2. The only thing that is not included in the U-statistic that was discussed above is the MAPE of the OF.

Theil's U-statistic can be better understood by examining its interpretation.

The value of the U-statistic given by equation (16-7) will be 0 only if $FPE_{i+1} = APE_{i+1}$. That in turn occurs only when the forecasts are exact (give 0 error). Alternatively, the U-statistic will have a value of 1 only when FPE_{i+1} is equal to 0. That would only be the case if the errors in the forecasting method were the same as those that would be obtained by forecasting no change at all in the actual values. That is comparable to assuming an NF1 approach. If FPE_{i+1} is in the opposite direction of APE_{i+1}, the U-statistic will be greater than unity since the numerator will be larger than the denominator. The ranges of the U-statistic can thus be summarized as follows:

$U = 1$: the naive method is as good as the forecasting technique being evaluated.

$U < 1$: the forecasting technique being used is better than the naive method. The smaller the U-statistic, the better the forecasting technique is relative to the naive method.

$U > 1$: there is no point in using a formal forecasting method, since using a naive method will produce better results.

An alternative accuracy measure to the U-statistic and yet one that is very similar in concept to it is that suggested by McLaughlin (1975). McLaughlin refers to his measure of accuracy as a batting average. This measure is not normally squared although it can be. The score of the batting average ranges between 200 and 400 with a value of 300 having a similar interpretation to Theil's U-statistic at a value of unity. McLaughlin's batting average can actually be found from the U-statistic by subtracting it from 4 and multiplying the result by 100. This correspondence in values is shown in Table 16-2.

16/1/2 Forecasting Accuracy of Qualitative or Technological Methods

Much of what has been discussed in the previous section relates specifically to quantitative methods of forecasting. Unfortunately, it is extremely difficult to assess the accuracy of qualitative or technological forecasting methods and to make comparisons among different methods of this type. These methods are difficult to assess because they are very nonstandardized in the type of forecasts they provide. In addition, they rely heavily on the abilities of the forecaster and simply provide a general framework for channeling available resources into a forecast. Knowing that a qualitative forecasting method gives results whose MAPE is 15% is not particularly useful, since the same method used in the same situation by a different individual might yield a MAPE of 5% or 25%.

Unfortunately, the accuracy of various qualitative or technological methods of forecasting in practice is not documented in a way that facilitates easy comparison. However, it is useful to consider the few studies reported in the literature

TABLE 16-2 RELATIVE MEASURES OF FORECASTING ACCURACY

Theil's *U*-Statistic	McLaughlin's Batting Averages	
0	$(4-0) \times 100$	400
.5	$(4-.5) \times 100$	350
1.0	$(4-1) \times 100$	300
1.5	$(4-1.5) \times 100$	250
2.0	$(4-2) \times 100$	200

that deal with such methods, since they are indicative of some of the accuracies that might be anticipated. Oftentimes the studies that are available seek to bridge the gap between quantitative and qualitative forecasting approaches in comparing the accuracy of very diverse methods.

One area in which qualitative forecasts have been analyzed in some detail is that of earnings per share. A number of researchers have compiled histories of the forecasts of earnings per share made by analysts (qualitative predictions) and compared them with the results obtained from more quantitative methods. Some of the typical studies in this area include Green and Segall (1967), Cragg and Malkiel (1968), Elton and Gruber (1972), and Niederhoffer and Regan (1972). In all four of these studies, the researchers conclude that analysts do not do as well in forecasting earnings per share as do more quantitative techniques. This conclusion in each case is based on several different measures of the accuracy of the resulting forecasts, which adds to its validity. These studies also tend to conclude that quantitative forecasting methods can do considerably better than simple naive methods.

The conclusions concerning qualitative forecasts of earnings per share are not unanimous in all cases. Johnson and Schmitt (1974) claim that naive methods outperform the trend and exponential smoothing methods that might commonly be available. Furthermore, they report that analysts can do better than quantitative methods provided the analysts have accurate economic and industry information. A summary of the results reported by Johnson and Schmitt is shown in Table 16-3.

A similar comparison of qualitative forecasting results with quantitative methods has been reported by Mabert (1975). In this instance, the researcher took a company situation in which sales forecasts had been based historically on opinions of the sales force and corporate executives. The accuracy of those forecasts was compared with three different quantitative forecasting methods both in terms of mean absolute deviation and MAPE. The results of this study are summarized in Table 16-4. As can be seen from that table, all three of the quantita-

TABLE 16-3   EFFECTIVENESS OF EARNINGS PER SHARE FORECASTING

Forecast Model	Accuracy (MAPE)			Bias (MPE)		
	1 yr	2 yr	3 yr	1 yr	2 yr	3 yr
Naive	29.3%	38.4%	43.7%	2.7%	5.0%	8.0%
Average (3 yr)*	34.2	41.3	45.3	5.5	8.9	12.7
Linear trend (6 yr)*	29.3	39.8	47.5	−.7	−2.4	−1.1
Linear trend (variable)	36.9	42.4	46.7	6.3	8.8	11.0
Exponential trend (variable)	38.2	43.2	47.3	5.1	3.5	3.1
Single smoothing (Trigg and Leach)	31.1	38.8	43.3	2.4	4.6	7.4
Single smoothing (simulation)	31.7	40.3	45.6	4.6	9.6	11.6
Double smoothing (Chow)	30.9	39.6	45.6	.9	4.1	4.5
Double smoothing (simulation)	32.6	40.8	46.8	1.8	5.8	6.1
Triple smoothing (simulation)	34.2	42.0	47.9	1.9	4.4	5.2

*Three years was found to provide the best base in the average model. Six years was the optimal base in the linear trend model.

Source: T. E. Johnson and T. G. Schmitt, "Effectiveness of Earnings per Share Forecasts," *Financial Management (Summer 1974), p. 69,* © 1974 by the Regents of the University of Wisconsin. Reprinted by permission.

tive methods gave more accurate results over the five-year time period covered by the study than did the company (nonquantitative) forecasts. In addition, Mabert found that in terms of timeliness and the cost of preparing forecasts, the quantitative techniques were again more attractive than the subjective estimates.

A major area of qualitative forecasts that has received considerable attention in the literature is that of anticipatory surveys. In Chapter 12, some of the more common of these techniques were examined and the basic problems of accuracy discussed. In one recent study, Rippe and Wilkinson (1974) examined the forecasting accuracy of the McGraw-Hill anticipatory survey data dealing with investment, sales, and capacity. Those researchers concluded that the McGraw-Hill data were generally less accurate than the Bureau of Economic Analysis–

TABLE 16-4 COMPARISON OF SALES FORECAST ERRORS (MEAN ABSOLUTE DEVIATION)

Year	Company Forecast	Exponential Smoothing	Harmonic Model	Box-Jenkins
1968	5749	5974	5408	4755
1969	3858	4470	4013	4403
1970	4013	2958	2998	3284
1971	6033	5657	5311	4785
1972	9782	8958	8384	8748
Average	5887	5603	5222	5195
MAPE	15.9%	15.1%	14.1%	14.0%

Source: V. A. Mabert, "Statistical Versus Sales Force-Executive Opinion Short Range Forecasts: A Time Series Analysis Case Study," Krannert Graduate School, Purdue University (1975, working paper), pp. 11–12. Reprinted by permission.

Securities and Exchange Commission survey (now known as the BEA survey) of anticipated investments on a one-year time horizon. However, the McGraw-Hill data were found to be more accurate than naive approaches and than some sophisticated econometric models. In addition, the researchers report that more recent anticipatory surveys tend to be more accurate, on average, than older surveys. Tables 16-5, 16-6, and 16-7 summarize the MAPE values obtained for the McGraw-Hill surveys and compare those with the equivalent results for the BEA survey and the U-statistic developed by Theil.

From Tables 16-5 and 16-6 it can be seen that the accuracy in the anticipatory surveys is generally no better than a 10% MAPE. Furthermore, it is clear that the accuracy deteriorates as the forecasting time horizon is lengthened. That is typical of all forecasting methods whether qualitative, technological, or quantitative. Finally, Table 16-7 indicates that the McGraw-Hill survey results are considerably better than naive forecasts, since the great majority of U-statistic values are less than 1.

A final study that can be mentioned in considering the forecasting accuracy of quantitative and of qualitative or technological methods is that reported by Kiernan (1970). That particular study examined the performance of airline industry forecasts of domestic revenue passenger-miles from 1959 through 1968. The results are summarized graphically in Figure 16-1. It is evident from the graph of actual and forecast values that the industry continually underestimated the growth in revenue passenger miles throughout this entire period. However, since the early

TABLE 16-5 MEAN ABSOLUTE PERCENTAGE ERROR OF McGRAW-HILL ANTICIPATORY SURVEY DATA (1948–71* AND 1962–72)

Industry	Anticipated Investment				Anticipated Sales		Anticipated Capacity	
	1 yr	2 yr	3 yr	4 yr	1 yr	4 yr	1 yr	4 yr
				1948–71				
Durables								
Iron and steel	12.60	17.00	22.19	31.05	7.39	22.96	1.78	4.73
Nonferrous metals	12.14	11.50	24.79	29.74	5.41	10.87	1.70	6.21
Electrical machinery	16.47	17.95	19.11	25.49	4.36	7.24	1.68	7.10
Nonelectrical machinery	10.47	17.04	23.47	32.67	5.01	23.24	2.07	4.99
Motor vehicles and parts	10.58	25.30	29.58	29.62	6.69	14.32	1.95	5.26
Other transp. equip.	20.56	30.25	45.17	50.68	3.56	18.65	2.43	9.92
Fabricated mtls. and instru.	8.42	13.99	19.56	20.18	4.29	13.90	1.22	3.75
Stone, clay, and glass	12.24	19.46	15.84	15.08	5.15	14.10	2.66	5.82
Nondurables								
Chemicals	9.54	13.79	15.01	15.40	2.61	8.23	2.93	5.21
Paper and pulp	7.94	18.92	27.93	28.63	3.98	7.68	2.56	6.83
Rubber	10.04	17.08	22.84	22.67	4.56	9.14	2.25	3.67
Petroleum	6.97	10.51	15.86	20.30	2.88	9.77	1.40	4.72
Food and beverages	7.67	12.44	19.31	27.00	2.24	6.61	1.04	3.41
Textiles	11.33	19.55	23.07	25.30	3.57	10.03	1.76	3.99
All manufacturing	6.45	11.59	19.52	24.26	2.65	8.49	1.04	3.71
All business	3.01	9.36	16.43	21.65	†	†	†	†
				1962–72				
Durables								
Iron and steel	8.49	14.70	21.16	29.52	5.20	16.75	1.99	3.74
Nonferrous metals	6.06	10.84	21.07	26.52	5.90	9.60	1.30	4.50
Electrical machinery	6.04	12.43	16.19	24.53	4.21	7.29	1.50	7.72
Nonelectrical machinery	10.55	15.36	20.30	30.46	4.70	17.67	1.26	3.72
Motor vehicles and parts	8.40	21.70	20.47	19.69	6.26	12.01	1.29	4.18
Other transp. equip.	9.09	23.04	38.17	42.62	4.05	17.14	1.24	10.62
Fabricated mtls. and instru.	6.40	11.67	17.51	24.04	4.29	8.92	1.12	3.34
Stone, clay, and glass	14.87	20.52	16.46	15.54	4.27	9.76	3.74	7.09
Nondurables								
Chemicals	3.82	11.09	14.27	17.89	1.91	7.64	4.81	6.35
Paper and pulp	7.32	14.15	27.35	31.56	2.67	3.59	3.36	7.32
Rubber	10.31	16.68	22.12	27.80	3.67	8.41	2.13	3.05
Petroleum	4.55	7.62	10.59	17.63	3.51	13.91	1.46	4.85
Food and beverages	6.55	8.09	15.58	24.56	2.13	5.44	.84	3.56
Textiles	7.91	21.11	28.77	29.90	2.96	9.47	1.51	4.05
All manufacturing	4.17	9.57	17.29	23.53	2.21	6.03	.53	2.24
All business	2.22	9.42	18.29	25.77	†	†	†	†

* Series begin at various years between 1948 and 1955.
† Data not available.

Source: R. D. Rippe and M. Wilkinson, "Forecasting Accuracy of the McGraw-Hill Anticipatory Data," Journal of the American Statistical Association, vol. 69, no. 348 (1974), p. 851. Reprinted by permission.

TABLE 16-6 MEAN ABSOLUTE PERCENTAGE ERROR FOR McGRAW-HILL AND BEA ONE-YEAR INVESTMENT ANTICIPATIONS

Industry	McGraw-Hill	BEA
Durables		
Iron and steel	11.19	10.61
Nonferrous metals	12.14	11.01
Electrical machinery	10.05	6.53
Nonelectrical machinery	9.96	8.44
Motor vehicles and parts	11.65	12.11
Other transp. equip.	14.87	10.79
Fabricated mtls. and instru.	8.42	*
Stone, clay, and glass	12.24	9.06
Nondurables		
Chemicals	9.20	7.17
Paper and pulp	7.94	7.49
Rubber	10.04	7.81
Petroleum	6.17	5.92
Food and beverages	5.41	6.73
Textiles	9.52	13.04
All manufacturing	6.45	3.66

* Data not available.

Source: R. D. Rippe and M. Wilkinson, "Forecasting Accuracy of the McGraw-Hill Anticipatory Data," Journal of the American Statistical Association, vol. 69, no. 348 (1974), p. 852. Reprinted by permission.

1970s, just the opposite has been true, with industry forecasts exceeding actual values. In this particular instance, the major problem can be traced to what is called the product life cycle. This concept hypothesizes an S-shaped curve as demand for an item slowly develops, then grows rapidly, and finally reaches maturity. It appears from Figure 16-1 that the forecasts being made throughout the 1960s by the airline industry assumed that the mature stage would shortly be reached. Then in the early 1970s, when the industry finally decided that maturity was not imminent, in fact it appears that it was, and thus forecasts were above actual values.

TABLE 16-7   THEIL'S *U*-STATISTIC FOR McGRAW-HILL
ANTICIPATIONS (1948–71*)

Industry	Anticipated Investment				Anticipated Sales		Anticipated Capacity	
	1 yr	2 yr	3 yr	4 yr	1 yr	4 yr	1 yr	4 yr
Durables								
Iron and steel	.570	.573	.902	1.110	.842	1.478	.675	.531
Nonferrous metals	.456	.258	.843	.815	.532	.438	.418	.436
Electrical machinery	1.256	.855	.856	.955	.527	.296	.321	.345
Nonelectrical machinery	.615	.894	.987	1.016	.557	.915	.387	.347
Motor vehicles and parts	.476	.806	.860	.845	.611	.582	.580	.510
Other transp. equip.	.764	1.129	1.345	1.382	.545	.881	.528	.496
Fabricated mtls. and instru.	.934	.813	.843	.766	.622	.592	.316	.247
Stone, clay, and glass	.698	.866	.882	.897	.626	.708	.750	.491
Nondurables								
Chemicals	.557	.634	.769	.775	.427	.356	.630	.291
Paper and pulp	.490	.830	1.066	1.031	.723	.585	.725	.494
Rubber	.671	.779	.857	.771	.690	.375	.510	.250
Petroleum	.616	.758	.894	.910	.480	.499	.460	.487
Food and beverages	1.046	1.018	1.151	1.235	.461	.434	.311	.217
Textiles	.740	.920	.995	1.015	.616	.719	.465	.297
All manufacturing	.550	.722	.984	1.021	.439	.438	.258	.275
All business	.356	.681	.911	.972	†	†	†	†

* Series begin at various years between 1948 and 1955.
† Data not available.

*Source: R. D. Rippe and M. Wilkinson, "Forecasting Accuracy of the McGraw-Hill
Anticipatory Data," Journal of the American Statistical Association, vol. 69, no. 348
(1974), p. 853. Reprinted by permission.*

16/1/3   Forecasting Accuracy of Quantitative Methods

Almost all of the quantitative methods discussed in Chapters 3 through 11 can be classified into one of two categories: time series or causal (regression). (Only the multivariate ARMA methods of Chapter 11 do not fall naturally into one of these two categories.) This categorization is a useful one to make in discussing the accuracy of quantitative forecasting methods, since the basis of comparison depends very much on which category is being considered.

During the decade of the 1960s and in the early 1970s, regression methods of forecasting became very popular, partially because of their impressive record of accuracy. Many of these methods were of the econometric type dealing with several variables and several equations. Naylor et al. (1972) suggested it might be

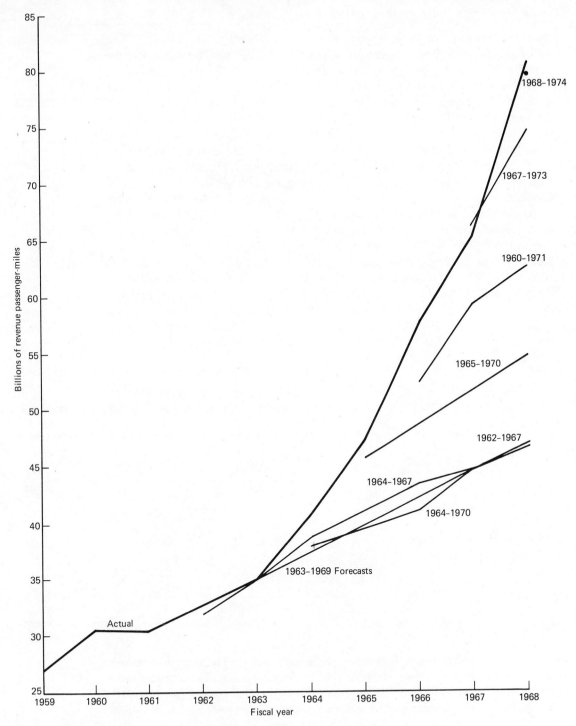

FIGURE 16-1 FAA SIX-YEAR FORECASTS AND ACTUAL SINCE
1961 (BILLIONS OF DOMESTIC REVENUE
PASSENGER-MILES)

*Source: J. D. Kiernan, "A Survey and Assessment of Air Travel
Forecasting," Urban Mass Transportation Project, Arlington, Va.
(April 1970), p. 13. Reprinted by permission.*

appropriate to label the 1960s "the age of the large-scale econometric model." The initial success with these econometric models generated considerable optimism about their forecasting performance over the longer term. Unfortunately, however, the 1960s turned out to be a rather special period for the economy. That period included 105 months of uninterrupted growth and prosperity, which was longer than any other similar period since 1850. The fact that those econometric models performed well during the 1960s is not a good indication of their level of accuracy when economic conditions are changing as they were in the early and mid-1970s.

Since the early 1950s (see Christ 1951), studies have indicated that when structural changes are taking place in the economy, econometric models are not superior to time-series approaches. Even a study conducted in the 1960s (Steckler 1968) found that econometric models were not entirely successful in improving accuracy in forecasting. In another study, Cooper (1972) concluded that econometric models are not in general superior to purely mechanical (time-series) methods of forecasting. Naylor et al. (1972) made a more extensive and detailed comparison of alternative methods and examined the Box-Jenkins approach in contrast to the Wharton econometric model for the years 1963 through 1967. A summary of the results of this study are shown in Table 16-8. The results indicate that the accuracy of ARMA models of the Box-Jenkins methodology is considerably better than the accuracy of the Wharton econometric model.

TABLE 16-8   COMPARISON OF THE WHARTON ECONOMETRIC
MODEL WITH THE BOX-JENKINS APPROACH (1963–67)

	Wharton (average absolute error)	Box-Jenkins (average absolute error)
I_p (investment in billions)	1.09	.59
P (*GNP* price deflator in percentages)	.22	.11
Un (unemployment in percentages)	.186	.109
GNP (in billions)	2.51	2.01

Source: T. H. Naylor, T. G. Seaks, and D. W. Wichern, "Box-Jenkins Methods: An Alternative to Econometric Forecasting," International Statistical Review, vol. 62, no. 5 (December 1972), p. 831. Reprinted by permission.

A more recent study by Nelson (1972) compared econometric (regression) and time-series (ARMA) methods for an even longer time horizon. This comparison was made using the FRB-MIT-PENN econometric model. Nelson (1972, p. 915) concluded that "the simple ARMA models are relatively more robust with respect to post sample predictions than the complex FRB-MIT-PENN models.... Thus if the mean squared error were an appropriate measure of loss, an unweighted assessment clearly indicates that a decision maker would have been best off relying simply on ARMA predictions in the post sample periods" (i.e., in the forecasting phase). The authors are not aware of any studies that reach conclusions opposite to those reached by Nelson, Naylor, Cooper, and others. It thus seems plausible to accept the hypothesis that, in fact, time-series methods can do as well on an accuracy basis as regression methods and that perhaps other criteria must be considered in discriminating between the two. (These types of comparisons will be elaborated in later sections of this chapter.)

Within the sets time-series approaches and regression approaches, studies have also been performed to compare the relative accuracy of individual techniques. In the case of regression and econometric models, both Cooper (1972) and Fromm and Klein (1973) conclude that no single econometric model is overwhelmingly superior to all others. These researchers recognize that differences may exist in the forecasting performance for single items or over a limited time horizon, but on the average, these differences in accuracy do not consistently favor one model over another.

Table 16-9 provides one comparison of these econometric models for the period 1970 through 1974. This comparison comes from McLaughlin (1975) and is based in part on an earlier study reported by McNees (1974). The results in this table are expressed in terms of the batting average measure of accuracy described previously. Table 16-9 indicates a marked similarity in the forecasting accuracy achieved by different models. All of these particular models perform considerably better than a Naive Forecast 1 model but not much better than what McLaughlin refers to as a *fair model*. This latter model is based on a few simple equations included in a straightforward econometric model. However, even in terms of this comparison it must be realized that from the third quarter of 1970 through the second quarter of 1974, the U.S. economy was fairly stable in terms of cyclical influences. The forecasting performance of econometric models tends to be much worse during periods of recession than is indicated by Table 16-9.

A comparison of the relative accuracy of various time-series methods is more difficult than that done above for econometric and regression models. The difficulties arise because there are many more methods to compare and also because different studies have arrived at different and often conflicting conclusions.

In a study reported by Kirby (1966), three different time-series methods were compared—moving averages, exponential smoothing, and regression. Kirby found that in terms of month-to-month forecasting accuracy, the exponential smoothing methods did best; both moving averages and exponential smoothing gave similar results when the forecasting horizon was increased to six months. The regression model included in that study was the best method for longer-term forecasts of one year or more.

In a study reported by Levine (1967), the same three forecasting methods

TABLE 16-9   FORECASTERS' BATTING AVERAGES (THIRD QUARTER 1970–SECOND QUARTER 1974)

	(1) NF1	(2) NF2: Fair	(3) BEA	(4) Chase	(5) DRI	(6) GE	(7) Wharton	(8) ASA- NBER	(9) Models (4) to (7)
				Commercial Services					
Nominal GNP	300	381L	385	388	385	389H	384	384	387
Real GNP	300	352L	362	367	367	370	372H	365	369
Inflation	300	347L	358	361	357	365H	359	357	361
Residential construction	300	313L	336	327	340	335	355H	—	339
Business fixed investment	300	360L	371	381H	363	361	375	—	370
Inventory investment	300	300	305	309	312	289L	316	317H	307
Consumption total	300	382	381L	381L	384	387H	386	—	385
Durables	300	344	341L	347	351	354H	343	347	349
Nondurables/services	300	381	383	379L	380	386H	383	—	382
Unemployment rate	300	332	346H	341	342	340	296L	335	330
Averages (means):									
All variables	300	349L	357	358H	358H	358H	357	—	358H
Excluding inventories	300	355L	363	364	363	365H	361	—	363
Excluding unemployment	300	351L	358	360	360	360	364H	—	361
Only ASA-NBER variables	300	343L	350	352H	352H	351	345	351	350

L = low   H = high

1. NF1 is a naive model that "predicts" no change from the latest known level.
2. The *fair model* is an econometric model of the U.S. economy, but incorporates no judgmental input. It can be used as a sophisticated NF2 model.
3. BEA is an econometric model of the U.S. economy used in the Bureau of Economic Analysis, Department of Commerce. Its forecasts are not available to the public.
4. Chase Econometrics, Bala Cynwyd, Pa. (a subsidiary of Chase Manhattan Bank), is an econometric model of the U.S. economy.
5. DRI is an econometric model sold by Data Resources, Inc., Lexington, Mass.
6. GE is the forecasting service sold by the General Electric Co. and is a mixed econometric/judgmental model. (It is not simultaneously solved.)
7. Wharton is the econometric model of Wharton Econometric Forecasting Associates, Wharton EFA, a subsidiary of the University of Pennsylvania.
8. ASA-NBER is the median forecast of about 50–60 forecasters surveyed by the American Statistical Assn. and the National Bureau of Economic Research. It is the only "consensus" forecast in this group.
9. The batting averages in column 9 represent the mean of the four commercial services shown in columns 4 through 7.

Source: R. L. McLaughlin, "The Real Record of the Econometric Forecasters," Business Economics, vol. 10, no. 3 (1975), p. 32. Reprinted by permission.

examined by Kirby were compared. Levine concluded that although there was an advantage of simplicity with the moving average method, exponential smoothing offered the best potential accuracy for short-term forecasting. Other studies reported by Gross and Ray (1965), Rayne (1971), and Krampf (1972) have arrived at conclusions similar to those of Levine and Kirby. Essentially, these researchers have found that exponential smoothing models are generally superior in short-term forecasting situations, although among these researchers there was not much agreement as to the specific exponential smoothing model that was best.

Unfortunately, comparisons among alternative decomposition methods and other techniques of forecasting have not been reported in the literature. However, studies have been published that compare exponential smoothing with Box-Jenkins models. Both Reid (1971) and Newbold and Granger (1974) conclude that the Box-Jenkins approach of ARMA models gives more accurate results than exponential smoothing or step-wise regression methods. When the comparison was made for a single-period time horizon, the Box-Jenkins results were found to be the most accurate of the three in 73% of the cases. When the lead time for the forecast was increased to six periods, Box-Jenkins models still gave the best results of the three, but in only 57% of the examples. These results are summarized in Table 16-10.

The conclusion that exponential smoothing can give results as accurate as autoregressive models and sometimes compete with ARMA methods in terms of accuracy may indeed be surprising to many forecasters. However, this conclusion

TABLE 16-10 COMPARISON OF FORECASTING METHODS: PERCENTAGE OF TIME FIRST METHOD OUTPERFORMS SECOND FOR VARIOUS LEAD TIMES

Methods Compared*	Lead Times							
	1	2	3	4	5	6	7	8
B-J : H-W	73	64	60	58	58	57	58	58
B-J : S-A	68	70	67	62	62	61	63	63
H-W : S-A	48	50	58	57	55	56	58	59

* B-J is Box-Jenkins; H-W is Holt-Winters; S-A is step-by-step autoregressive.

Source: P. Newbold and C. W. J. Granger, "Experience with Forecasting Univariate Time Series and the Combinations of Forecasts," Journal of the Royal Statistical Society, Series A, vol. 137, pt. 2 (1974), p. 138. Reprinted by permission.

is further supported by Groff (1973), who concluded that the Box-Jenkins methodology gave results that were approximately equal in accuracy or slightly worse than those achieved using exponential smoothing. That same conclusion was also reached by Geurts and Ibrahim (1975). This latter study is somewhat limited, however, because it relates to only a single time-series application.

The differences in the conclusions reached by researchers examining various time-series methods of forecasting deserve some further consideration. That is particularly true when one recognizes that exponential smoothing models are simply a special case of the general ARMA methods. The best explanation can be found in recognizing that the accuracy of a forecasting method depends upon several factors and that those factors cannot be completely summarized in a single measure of accuracy. Reid (1971) and Newbold and Granger (1974) discuss several of these factors including the number of observations in the series, seasonality of the data, the number of periods in the time horizon to be forecast, the extent of randomness in the series, and others. As reported by Adam (1973), these factors have a substantial impact on the accuracy and performance of individual forecasting models.

A logical explanation for the differences in the results reported in some of these studies is simply that different factors played different roles in the specific situations examined and thus biased the results in terms of accuracy in different ways. Recent research has investigated ways to express the accuracy of a forecasting method as a function of the various factors that affect accuracy (Makridakis and Vandenburgh 1974). A regression equation of the following form was developed:

$$MAPE_m = f(X_1, X_2, \ldots X_9), \qquad (16\text{-}9)$$

where $MAPE_m$ is the MAPE for a forecasting time horizon of m periods,

X_1 is the MAPE of the OF (i.e., the random component of the series),

X_2 is the MAPE of the NF2 (i.e., the seasonally adjusted series),

X_3 is the MAPE in the trend-cycle,

X_4 is the MAPE in the trend,

X_5 is the coefficient of variation,

X_6 is the square root of the number of data points,

X_7 is the autocorrelation of one time lag,

X_8 is the autocorrelation of two time lags,

and X_9 is the autocorrelation of twelve time lags.

The preliminary results of examining the estimation of equation (16-9) using historical data on a number of different series indicates that in fact a linear relationship does exist. However, the R squared obtained is rather small (less than .3) suggesting that additional factors may need to be incorporated or perhaps transformations made on some of those already included.

Eventually, additional research will need to be done on the determinants of accuracy and on developing procedures that can be used by the forecaster in estimating the relative accuracy of different methods. That information can then be used to apply the criterion of accuracy more effectively in comparing and selecting a forecasting method.

16/2 Pattern of the Data and Its Effects on Individual Forecasting Methods

A major consideration in the selection of a forecasting method for a specific situation is the type of patterns in the data. These patterns may represent characteristics that repeat themselves with time or they may represent turning points that are not periodic in nature. As has been pointed out previously, a data series can be described as consisting of two elements—the underlying pattern and randomness. The objective of forecasting is to distinguish between those two elements using the forecasting method that can most appropriately do so. It has also been suggested in describing some of the methods such as decomposition and time-series analysis that the pattern itself can be thought of as consisting of subpatterns or components, each of which can be considered separately. The three components most frequently used in describing elements of the pattern are trend, seasonality, and cycle.

Knowledge of the types of subpatterns included in a data series can be very useful in selecting the most appropriate forecasting method, since different methods vary in their ability to cope with different kinds of patterns. The mean and the simple smoothing techniques can deal only with stationary (horizontal) subpatterns in the data, while linear or higher forms of smoothing (quadratic, cubic, etc.) can deal with linear or higher forms of subpatterns in the data. As was shown previously, a method like Winters' exponential smoothing can deal with both trend and seasonal elements of a pattern.

Regression methods can deal with almost any subpattern that can be transformed into a linear relationship. However, regression is not appropriate when the subpattern is horizontal, since regression techniques measure variation from the horizontal values as part of their mathematical basis. In regression, the ability to handle different subpatterns depends largely on the user's ability to specify the most appropriate regression model.

The decomposition and control methods of forecasting can deal with a wide variety of horizontal, trend, seasonal, and/or cyclical subpatterns. However, like the bulk of the quantitative forecasting techniques, these methods have much more difficulty dealing with cyclical subpatterns and predicting turning points than they do in dealing with seasonal, trend, and horizontal subpatterns. As long as seasonal subpatterns and cyclical subpatterns move together in some stable relationship, ARMA methods will perform well. However the methods are not particularly good at distinguishing the two patterns and decomposing them so that they can be dealt with as separate subpatterns.

Decomposition methods are clearly the strongest available for dealing with cyclical components and providing information that can be used in predicting cyclical turning points. Census II and the Foran systems in particular have been designed specifically to aid in predicting the cyclical component. Multiple regression and econometric models can deal well with both seasonal and cyclical subpatterns as long as they can be isolated in the form of a causal relationship. In some instances, the burden simply shifts from selecting a method that can handle such subpatterns to specifying the appropriate model within that method.

As pointed out in Chapter 12, the forecasting of a change in pattern and particularly of turning points in the cycle is an extremely difficult task. However, if not done adequately it can have a substantial negative impact on the organization and its performance. Researchers have investigated some methods that can more appropriately handle such turning points. These include several of the variations in basic forecasting methods that have been described previously—adaptive exponential smoothing, paired indices, and catastrophe theory. This area of forecasting clearly requires additional study and development of new tools before it can offer the same assistance to users that is now available for handling more stable subpatterns such as trends and seasonal components.

16/3 Time Horizon Effects on Forecasting Methods

In the previous chapter, the interaction between forecasting and planning was discussed in some detail. There the planning task was divided into four time horizons:

immediate term—less than one month
short term—one to three months
medium term—three months to two years
long term—over two years

One of the reasons the time horizon is particularly important in selecting a forecasting method in a given situation is that the relative importance of different subpatterns changes as the time horizon of planning changes. In the very immediate term, the randomness is usually the most important element. As the time horizon lengthens to two or three months, the seasonal subpattern generally becomes dominant. Then in the medium term, the cyclical component becomes more important, and finally in the long term, the trend element dominates. Graphically, the changing importance of each of these subpatterns with a lengthening time horizon can be presented as shown in Figure 16-2. Because the relative importance of various subpatterns changes with the time horizon, the most appropriate method varies for different time horizons. Some methods should be used more frequently in immediate- or short-term situations, and other methods will be more appropriate for medium- or long-term forecasting requirements.

In general, qualitative or technological methods are most appropriate for long-term forecasting requirements. Quantitative methods, however, can be applied for all types of time horizons. Smoothing methods are usually best for immediate or short term and decomposition and ARMA methods are usually better for short to medium term. Regression techniques tend to be best suited for medium- to long-term usage. It should be remembered, however, that the suitability of an individual method will depend not only on the time horizon but on the costs, accuracy, and other factors that are most heavily weighted in that particular situation.

Closely related to the time horizon of planning and its impact on the selection of a forecasting methodology is the number of periods that are to be forecast. The authors have done some research on the impact of the lengthening time horizon on the suitability of aternative forecasting methods. Based on an analysis of a single time series, five forecasting methods were compared for different time horizons and the results shown in Table 16-11 were obtained. As indicated in this table, the mean absolute percentage error for the first month is much lower in all instances than the mean absolute percentage error obtained for two- and three-month periods. These results may be of particular interest, since they refer to a large part of the 1974–75 recession. As cited in the previous chapter, other researchers have obtained similar results when looking at longer time horizons.

Since there generally is greater uncertainty as the time horizon lengthens, the forecaster is often challenged to find better ways of defining the problem in order to minimize that uncertainty. One such way that has not been studied extensively in the literature but that deserves further consideration is forecasting cumulative units rather than units per time period. Part of the difficulty in using cumulative units is that most quantitative methods assume time periods of equal length. However, it is certainly possible to forecast cumulative demand for the next twelve months and to do so on a month-to-month basis rather than simply forecasting demand in each month and adding them together to get a cumulative forecast. Although not yet published, some work has been done in using cumulative units as the basis for forecasting rather than units of a shorter time period. This work indicates that more accurate results can frequently be obtained by making such cumulative forecasts. In situations such as production planning where cumulative forecasts are often what is needed for aggregate planning purposes, this may indeed be a very valuable approach that will be further developed in the future.

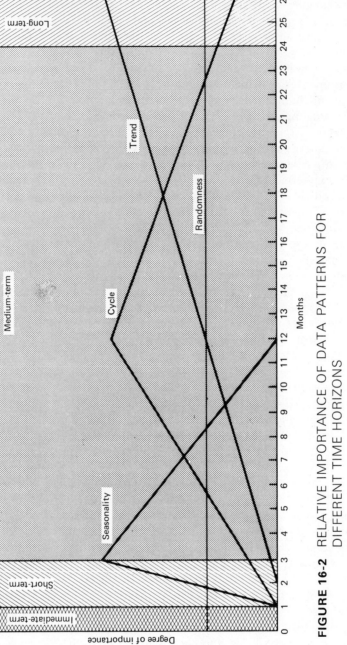

FIGURE 16-2   RELATIVE IMPORTANCE OF DATA PATTERNS FOR DIFFERENT TIME HORIZONS

TABLE 16-11 MEAN ABSOLUTE PERCENTAGE ERRORS OF VARIOUS METHODS FOR ONE-, TWO-, AND THREE-MONTH FORECASTS

Period	% Change in Trend-Cycle	Box-Jenkins			G.A.F.			Census II			Winters'			Harrison's		
		1	2	3	1	2	3	1	2	3	1	2	3	1	2	3
1974																
Jan.	-3.3	5.50	13.01	14.15	5.88	.84	4.32	1.58	10.98	12.56	12.47	34.93	34.96	13.01	13.26	12.69
Feb.	-4.4	8.05	10.74	16.13	2.41	.13	.91	4.77	.91	11.23	32.21	43.06	1.98	2.82	4.14	6.22
Mar.	-2.7	14.17	18.2	20.35	23.63	24.56	24.49	20.32	8.18	15.77	17.64	26.76	41.66	22.38	24.24	26.23
Apr.	-1.2	2.22	10.27	13.61	1.99	7.76	7.78	3.83	16.43	4.27	14.95	39.09	21.49	13.75	15.12	17.41
May	-4.1	4.77	8.44	15.31	11.63	10.06	10.05	2.04	5.80	21.6	35.83	23.94	4.79	15.36	17.74	21.14
June	-3.6	6.09	5.25	2.24	1.1	4.36	3.06	3.87	2.91	1.18	86.67	9.95	35.32	14.59	9.3	12.9
July	-4.3	17.29	14.03	15.43	27.63	27.4	28.2	14.73	12.42	14.02	10.53	133.69	25.04	47.04	45.79	39.66
Aug.	-8.1	3.82	19.38	14.29	16.52	46.97	46.56	11.99	16.99	15.41	2.25	12.99	180.56	6.94	3.95	3.63
Sept.	-10.0	13.91	18.6	32.52	9.65	27.09	38.54	9.83	7.80	23.08	2.98	.33	20.79	42.16	42.44	42.65
Oct.	-7.0	59.35	67.18	66.17	79.33	80.57	90.64	41.76	33.65	51.35	9.7	14.53	9.17	86.79	87.67	88.15
Nov.	-2.3	21.31	60.58	70.34	34.76	91.4	87.02	24.94	39.62	31.44	35.19	24.95	19.89	92.89	92.79	93.63
Dec.	-1.8	9.08	21.64	50.7	3.53	28.3	61.78	7.49	23.61	39.81	3.9	47.85	32.89	79.86	83.32	84.73
1975																
Jan.	4.8	32.33	27.1	19.44	7.21	3.23	13.91	24.07	20.06	4.6	36.67	33.13	80.03	43.29	45.53	46.65
Feb.	8.6	12.49	30.65	27.43	6.72	.19	3.81	12.59	25.69	21.36	32.59	63.69	60.7	24.29	26.55	29.52
Mar.	5.1	4.09	11.97	25.41	1.04	2.3	3.57	4.39	9.38	24.15	9.32	31.55	70.42	34.32	37.28	40.18
Average for all months		14.30	22.47	26.90	15.53	23.68	28.31	12.55	15.63	19.46	22.85	35.97	42.64	35.99	36.6	37.68
Average without Oct., Nov., Dec. 1974, and Jan. 1975		8.40	14.59	17.90	9.84	13.79	15.57	8.18	10.68	14.97	23.4	38.1	45.24	21.5	21.79	22.92
Average of Oct., Nov., Dec. 1974, and Jan. 1975		30.52	44.13	51.66	31.21	50.86	63.34	24.56	29.24	31.8	21.37	30.12	35.50	75.71	77.33	78.29

The components (characteristics) of the series are: Average percentage change in original data. Naive 1 = 33.23.
Average percentage change in seasonally adjusted data. Naive 2 = 23.30. Average percentage change in randomness.
Optimal Forecast = 9.81. Average percentage change in the trend-cycle = 1.45.

16/4 The Costs of Forecasting Methods

There are three main elements of cost in using a forecasting method: development costs, data storage costs, and the costs of repeated applications. The importance of these various costs depends both on the method and the situation. For most qualitative or technological methods of forecasting, a separate cost estimate must be made for each situation. This cost estimate will need to consider human resource inputs and outside data acquisition requirements as a major part of the total costs of forecasting. Generally, these costs are incurred again whenever a new forecast is prepared for that specific situation. In the case of quantitative methods, however, many of the costs are fairly independent of the particular management situation. This section will concentrate on this latter type of costs, since they are the ones about which some generalizations can be made.

Most quantitative methods applied in organizations today use the computer as an integral part of their application. In fact, even in 1966, Reichard found in a survey of business use of forecasting that 68% of the companies surveyed were at that time using the computer in this manner. That percentage is undoubtedly even higher today. Thus in this discussion of cost, it will be assumed that the computer is being used as an integral part of quantitative forecasting applications.

The development cost, D_1, includes the cost of writing and modifying a computer program to apply a given forecasting method. It also covers the human resources required (mainly programming time) for the development of such programs and the computer time cost for establishing them in working order.

Once a computerized version of a forecasting method exists, an appropriate model for the given situation must be developed. This second stage in development can require anywhere from a few minutes, such as would be the case in a simple exponential smoothing model, to several months as would be the case with an econometric model. These development costs can be denoted by D_2 and will include both human resources and computer time expenditures. One of the differences between the costs for these two development stages is that in the first stage a substantial portion of the costs may be in computer time, whereas in the second stage the largest proportion tends to be for human resource expenditures.

In order to use the computerized version of a quantitative forecasting method, the appropriate computer program must be working on the computer system and the data must be stored in a memory device on that system. The data storage itself implies additional costs. These storage costs can be broken into two portions. The first, S_1, can represent the amount of storage required for the computer program of the forecasting method itself. The second, S_2, can represent the amount of storage space required for the data. The measure generally used for such storage is in terms of thousands of words of computer space required.

A third element of the costs for forecasting is the expense incurred when readjustments or modifications are made in the working model for a given forecasting situation. These changes will generally be made when new data become available, when basic changes in the pattern occur, or when additional runs of the model are required. These costs can be denoted by M; they are actually a sub-part of the cost of repeated applications. If no modification or readjustment is needed, this element of cost will be zero.

The final portion of the cost of repeated applications is that for each run of the computerized forecasting method needed to obtain a new forecast. This cost can be denoted by R. Most of this cost is for the computer time usage (CPU—central processing unit time) required to run the program and some small amount of human resources required to supervise that run.

One way of further categorizing these costs is in terms of fixed, semifixed, and variable components. Using this scheme, the elements can be combined as follows:

$$\text{fixed costs} = D_1 + S_1,$$
$$\text{semifixed costs} = D_2 + S_2,$$
$$\text{variable costs} = R + M + S_2.$$

The total cost for a new situation can then be written as

$$\text{total cost} = \frac{D_1 + S_1}{I} + \frac{D_2}{J} + S_2 + (R + M), \qquad (16\text{-}10)$$

where I is the number of items to be forecast using the same computer program,

and J is the number of items that uses the same working model.

These elements of cost have been studied by the authors for several different forecasting methods. Table 16-12 summarizes the results obtained when those methods were applied to a wide range of data series. Although each situation will involve somewhat different costs, this table can serve as a benchmark for comparing different methods and the major elements of cost that each involves.

The authors have gone one step further and tried to forecast the costs of various forecasting methodologies by using regression analysis and a single independent variable—the number of data points involved. In nonseasonal time-series forecasting methods, the results shown in Table 16-13 were obtained. These cost functions are for the amount of computer time required to achieve the optimal model. For example, in a single exponential smoothing model the data must be run for different values of α until the optimal α is found. Thus, this expense is only one element of the total costs described above. As indicated in Table 16-13, the results of trying to forecast this portion of forecasting costs were very good. Over 98% of the variation for different series using each model can be explained by just the simple relationship involving the number of data points.

TABLE 16-12   COSTS OF QUANTITATIVE FORECASTING METHODS

Methods	Number of Trials to Achieve Acceptable Working Model	Overall Development Costs	Program Storage Requirements (1000s of words)	Minimum Data Storage Requirements[a]	Frequency of Program Reruns	Cost per Run[b]
Mean	1	$300	1.8	30	Rarely needed	$.15
Simple moving average	2	300	1.8	7.5	Every time	.03
Simple exponential smoothing	2	150	1.6	2	Every time	.025
Linear moving average	2	250	2.6	15	Every time	.035
Linear exponential smoothing	2	300	2.4	3	Every time	.025
Classical decomposition	2	1200	3.8	60	Every few times	1.00
Census II	1	1800	12.0	72	Every few times	3.25
Foran system	1	1500	10.0	24	Every few times	1.00
Adaptive filtering	4	1200	5.6	60	Every few times	1.50
Box-Jenkins	3	2400	18.0	72	Every few times	4.40
Generalized adaptive filtering	5	1500	7.0	72	Every few times	3.50
Simple regression	1	900	3.4	30	Rarely needed	.50

TABLE 16-12 *Continued*

Methods	Number of Trials to Achieve Acceptable Working Model	Overall Development Costs	Program Storage Requirements (1000s of words)	Minimum Data Storage Requirements[a]	Frequency of Program Reruns	Cost per Run[b]
Multiple regression	6	1800	6.8	30	Rarely needed	1.00
Econometric models	10–20	2400	.6	300	Rarely needed	3.50

[a] Based on a 32 bit, single precision word of an IBM 370.
[b] Based on a cost of $300 an hour of CPU time.

TABLE 16-13 COSTS OF FORECASTING METHODS (OPTIMAL MODEL)

Method	Constant Term	Coefficient of Independent Variable: Number of Data Points	R^2
Single exponential smoothing	.11	.133	.99
Trigg and Leach's adaptive-response-rate exponential smoothing	.10	.78	.99
Single moving average	.10	.335	.98
Brown's one-parameter linear exponential smoothing	.11	.18	.99
Linear moving average	.11	.5	.98
Brown's one-parameter quadratic exponential smoothing	.12	.22	.99
Trend analysis	.10	.25	.99
Holt's two-parameter linear exponential smoothing	.09	.3	.99
Naive method	.11	.008	.99

16/5 The Ease of Application of Forecasting Methods

There are several factors that can be summarized under the heading *ease of application*. These include such things as the basic complexity of the method, its timeliness is providing forecasts when they are needed, the level of expertise required to apply those different methods, and the conceptual appeal that the methods have to the ultimate user. All of these elements are important, since in the end they determine whether or not the forecasts will have an impact on management action.

In a study conducted by Wheelwright and Clarke (1976), it was found that because of the relative complexity of various methods, organizations tend to go through evolutionary stages in their adoption of different forecasting techniques. As would be expected, they usually start with the more simple techniques, such as subjective executive estimates or simple smoothing methods, then gradually move to more complex methods. The reason often given for this evolutionary approach is the need for the increased accuracy that more complex methods seem to provide, but it was also found by Wheelwright and Clarke that the organization required certain expertise before it could effectively apply more complex methods. In the case of one methodology, Box-Jenkins, many organizations that had tried the method no longer used it simply because it was too complex. It was too difficult for the ultimate users of the forecasts to understand the conceptual basis for the method and to feel confident that it was being applied correctly.

In order to really base decisions and plans on forecasts obtained from quantitative methods, the ultimate user must either understand the conceptual basis of the method and feel comfortable that it represents a "correct" approach or put blind trust in the method feeling that it will perform uniformly well over time. Since the latter is seldom in fact the case, both individual users and the organization as a whole need to understand the basics of the methods that are going to be applied rather than applying the methods the forecasting staff may think are most sophisticated in that situation.

16/6 An Interactive Procedure for Selecting, Running, and Comparing Alternative Forecasting Methods

Forecasting methods are useless if they are only described but cannot be applied because of lack of computational means, or for any other reasons. To facilitate the application of quantitative forecasting methods, the authors have developed a set of interactive computer programs that include the great majority of the methods described in Chapters 3 through 11. A description of this interactive system, known as SIBYL/RUNNER, can be found in Makridakis et al. (1974), and there is a detailed explanation of all programs included and the information needed to run them in Makridakis and Wheelwright (1977).

SIBYL/RUNNER has been used extensively for teaching and actual day-to-day forecasting since it was first introduced in 1973. In addition to allowing the usage of all major forecasting methods, SIBYL/RUNNER permits analysis of the data, suggests available forecasting methods, compares results, and provides several accuracy measures in such a way that it is easier for the user to select an appropriate method and forecast needed data under different economic conditions.

Another major advantage of SIBYL/RUNNER is its motivational impact on the user. Since learning to use a forecasting method takes time and effort, this package has been particularly well received because it makes effective use of the user's time and provides rapid feedback as to progress being made in that forecasting situation. In essence, one can start with very little knowledge and a set of real data, then gradually learn about different methods and their characteristics while working on that particular forecasting problem.

In other words SIBYL/RUNNER is a set of programs designed to bring the learning and application of forecasting within the realm of a person who is not an expert in statistics or in use of the computer.

REFERENCES AND SELECTED BIBLIOGRAPHY

Adam, E. E. 1973. "Individual Item Forecasting Model Evaluation." *Decision Sciences*, Vol. 4, October, pp. 458–70.

Christ, C. F. 1951. "A Test of an Econometric Model of the United States, 1921–1974." In *Conference on Business Cycles*. New York: National Bureau of Economic Research.

Cooper, R. L. 1972. "The Predictive Performance of Quarterly Econometric Models of the United States." In *Econometric Models of Cyclical Behavior*, ed. B. C. Hickman. New York: National Bureau of Economic Research.

Cragg, J., and B. Malkiel. 1968. "The Consensus and Accuracy of Some Predictions of the Growth in Corporate Earnings." *Journal of Finance*, March, pp. 67–84.

Dalrymple, D. J. 1975. "Sales Forecasting Methods and Accuracy." *Business Horizons*, December, pp. 69–73.

Elton, E. J., and M. J. Gruber. 1972. "Earnings Estimates and the Accuracy of Expectational Data." *Management Science*, April, pp. B409–B424.

Fromm, G., and L. R. Klein. 1973. "A Comparison of Eleven Econometric Models of the United States." *American Economic Association*, May, pp. 385–401.

Geurts, M. D., and I. B. Ibrahim. 1975. "Comparing the Box-Jenkins Approach with the Exponentially Smoothed Forecasting Model Application to Hawaii Tourists." *Journal of Marketing Research*, Vol. 12, May, pp. 182–88.

Green, D., and J. Segall. 1967. "The Predictive Power of First-Quarter Earnings Reports." *Journal of Business*, Vol. 40, January, pp. 44–55.

Groff, G. K. 1973. "Empirical Comparison of Models for Short-Range Forecasting." *Management Science*, Vol. 20, No. 1, September, pp. 22–31.

Gross, D., and J. L. Ray. 1965. "A General Purpose Forecasting Simulator." *Management Science*, Vol. 11, No. 6, April, pp. B119–B135.

Johnson, T. E., and T. G. Schmitt. 1974. "Effectiveness of Earnings per Share Forecasts." *Financial Management*, Summer, pp. 64–72.

Kiernan, J. D. 1970. "A Survey and Assessment of Air Travel Forecasting." *Urban Mass Transportation Project*. Arlington, Va., April.

Kirby, R. M. 1966. "A Comparison of Short and Medium Range Statistical Forecasting Methods." *Management Science*, No. 4, pp. B202–B210.

Krampf, R. F. 1972. *The Turning Point Problem in Smoothing Models*. Unpublished Ph.D. dissertation, University of Cincinnati.

Levine, A. H. 1967. "Forecasting Techniques." *Management Accounting*, January.

McLaughlin, R. L. 1975. "The Real Record of the Econometric Forecasters." *Business Economics*, Vol. 10, No. 3, pp. 28–36.

McNees, S. K. 1974. "How Accurate Are Economic Forecasts?" *New England Economic Review*, Federal Reserve Bank of Boston, Nov.–Dec., pp. 2–19.

Mabert, V. A. 1975. "Statistical Versus Sales Force-Executive Opinion Short Range Forecasts: A Time Series Analysis Case Study." Krannert Graduate School, Purdue University (working paper).

Makridakis, S., A. Hodgsdon, and S. Wheelwright. 1974. "An Interactive Forecasting System." *American Statistician*, November.

Makridakis, S., and H. M. Vandenburgh. 1974. "The Accuracy and Cost of Non-Seasonal Time Series Forecasting Methods." *INSEAD Research Papers*, Series No. 143, December.

Makridakis, S., and S. C. Wheelwright. 1978. *Interactive Forecasting: Univariate and Multivariate Methods,* 2nd ed. San Francisco: Holden-Day.

Naylor, T. H., T. G. Seaks, and D. W. Wichern. 1972. "Box-Jenkins Methods: An Alternative to Econometric Forecasting." *International Statistical Review*, Vol. 40, No. 2, pp. 123–37.

Nelson, C. 1972. "The Prediction Performance of the FRB-MIT-PENN Model of the U.S. Economy." *The American Economic Review*, Vol. 62, No. 5, December, pp. 902–17.

Newbold, P., and C. W. J. Granger. 1974. "Experience with Forecasting Univariate Time Series and the Combination of Forecasts." *Journal of The Royal Statistical Society*, Series A., Vol. 137, Pt 2, pp. 131–65.

Niederhoffer, V., and D. Regan. 1972. Summarized in *Barron's* magazine, December 18, p. 9.

Raine, J. E. 1971. "Self-Adaptive Forecasting Considered." *Decision Sciences*, April.

Richard, R. S. 1966. *Practical Techniques of Sales Forecasting.* New York: McGraw-Hill.

Reid, D. J. 1971. "Forecasting in Action: A Comparison of Forecasting Techniques in Economic Time Series." Presented at the Joint Conference of Operations Research Society's Group in Long-Range Planning and Forecasting.

Rippe, R. D., and M. Wilkinson. 1974. "Forecasting Accuracy of the McGraw-Hill Anticipatory Data." *Journal of the American Statistical Association*, Vol. 69, No. 348, December, pp. 849–58.

Steckler, H. O. 1968. "Forecasting with Econometric Models: An Evaluation." *Econometrica*, Vol. 34, July–October, pp. 437–63.

Theil, H. 1966. *Applied Economic Forecasting.* Amsterdam: North Holland Publishing Co., pp. 26–32.

Wheelwright, S. C., and D. G. Clarke. 1976. "Corporate Forecasting: Promise and Reality." *Harvard Business Review*, November–December.

Zeeman, E. C. 1976. "Catastrophe Theory." *Scientific American*, April.

17 DATA PROCUREMENT, PREPARATION AND HANDLING

DATA ARE A prerequisite for any forecasting application. Their role is of critical importance in determining the accuracy and value of predictions based on both quantitative and technological methods of forecasting. The form of data required for quantitative techniques clearly differs from that required for technological approaches. In the case of the former specific numbers are needed, while the latter may simply need a description of some event or process. In much of the material covered in this chapter, the focus will be on data for quantitative approaches, since such data are much more restricted in form than data and information used for technological forecasting.

The purpose of data in forecasting is to provide information on those factors relevant to decision making and planning. Such a factor would be a nation's wealth, which can be expressed as the quantity of goods and services produced over a given time period such as one year. This variable, known as GNP (gross national product), will take on different values for different periods of time, and a series of observations represents a time series of values for that variable. Profit is another variable often of interest that can be quantified by specifying the earnings of a business (as one measure of financial performance) for time periods of a specified length. In both of these examples, quantification of the data requires the adoption of a common scale against which the event can be measured.

A major question in the quantification of events in the real world is how well the summarization necessary for such quantification represents reality. Biderman (1966) has focused considerable attention on this topic and has raised a number of points as to the ability of statistical data to represent real events. These points include distortions, hidden information, errors in reporting, and the process of quantification itself. Biderman (1966, p. 136) states: "It is characteristic of statistical work that we are willing to disregard much of what we know about the object of our measurements so as to concentrate on what we can measure accurately and economically." He goes on to propose different forms of social indicators that can be used to measure less quantifiable but equally important aspects of reality.

In a similar fashion, Boulding et al. (1971) talk about the quantity and quality of data and point out that a mere increase in the quantity does not necessarily improve the accuracy with which the data describe reality. For example, Boulding says, "For a baby, growth in weight is evidently desirable. For the adult, it simply means that he is becoming fat. For the poor, growth in income is entirely desirable. For the rich, it may simply mean corruption and luxury" (1971, p. 33). Boulding goes on to say that economic data do not always indicate the true state of affairs of a nation, since they fail to take into account many unmeasurable or hard-to-quantify factors. Because quantitative data do not necessarily give a complete representation of the phenomena they are intended to describe, their limitations are generally of interest to the forecaster. These will be discussed in more detail later in this chapter.

The data required for technological forecasting methods do not necessarily have to be limited to quantitative variables. Although less precise in some regards, these forecasting methods can give results that may be more accurate than those of quantitative methods simply because a more complete set of input data can be used. One method for developing such a set of data is to create from descriptive data various scenarios as to what has happened in the past and what will happen in the future. These scenarios then come to represent a fairly complete set of information for describing an actual event. Thus a scenario becomes comparable in many cases to data on a quantitative variable used in a more traditional form of forecasting.

The purpose of this chapter is to examine several of the major issues and tasks required in data procurement, preparation, and handling. First the question of what to forecast and the issues to be considered in making that decision will be discussed. The chapter will then examine the questions of data sources and their use for various forecasting methods. Next, questions of data preparation ranging from problems in collecting data to the need for possible adjustments once the data have been collected will be dealt with. The final section discusses issues of data management such as data banks and the manipulation of them, the presentation of data to managers and planners, and the need for continual updating of data. In addition Appendix III cites for both Europe and the United States several commonly used data sources.

17/1 Definition and Specification of Variables in Forecasting

Most work on forecasting tends to assume that the variable to be forecast is known and well defined. While that may be the case for ongoing situations in which a forecasting method has been applied in the past, in new situations it is not necessarily true. Thus a first step in forecasting is to decide just what to forecast and how best to define that variable.

The decision as to the appropriate variable to be forecast depends largely on the needs of the manager or planner and the availability of historical information. One useful way to focus on this question is to consider the purpose of the forecast. At the most general level, forecasts either supply information for planning, information for control, or general information for decision making. In terms of data requirements, one of the main differences between forecasts for these first two purposes is that information for planning generally involves activities and events both internal and external to the firm. Thus it is usually the case that a wide range of variables needs to be forecast to help in this planning function.

Information for control, on the other hand, is generally of an internal nature, and frequently the required data is much more readily available as part of the existing accounting system. In addition, information for control often needs to fit the performance evaluation system of the organization and be consistent with other measures commonly included in the control system, rather than being designed solely for the use of the forecaster.

In addition to this general distinction as to the purpose of a forecast, it is useful to define in some detail just how the proposed forecast will help management in order to most appropriately define the variable to be forecast. The contribution that the forecast will make to the manager or planner will determine the time span that should be covered by each value of the variable, the level of detail required, the frequency with which it is required, the most appropriate unit of measurement, the required level of accuracy, the appropriate segmentation of the variable, and the value of the forecast. Because of the importance of each of these aspects to the definition of appropriate variables for forecasting, each will be discussed briefly.

The time period covered by each data value

For practical purposes, most of the factors involved in a business situation can be viewed as taking place in a fairly continuous manner. For example, for a large company sales can be considered to take place continuously rather than taking place at some instant of time each day or each month. However, for accounting purposes it is necessary to define some period of time and to summarize the value of each variable for that time period. Thus the company's sales are talked about in terms of sales per week, sales per month, or sales per year rather than in terms of much smaller units of time. In defining the time period to be covered by each observation of a variable, it is necessary to consider the specific application of the forecast. Forecasts that generally contribute to longer-range decision making usually can be based on observed data values covering fairly long periods of time, such as quarters or complete years. However, forecasts aimed at controlling day-to-day operations need to be based on data values that cover a time period of one day or perhaps even one shift or one hour.

In some instances, the variable to be forecast relates not to a time period but rather to the magnitude of a single observed value. For example, in the production control area one may want to forecast the number of rejects in batches of product coming off a certain machine. In such a case, the batch serves the same function as the time period in defining the span to which the variable refers. In other instances, the span covered by the variable may be defined by batch size, the occurrence of some specific event, or some other factor. However, for quantitative methods there must be some means for specifying the span of reality to which the data refer.

Level of detail required

The time span covered by each value of a variable is one aspect of the level of detail required for a specific application of a forecast. Another aspect is the amount of aggregation involved for that variable. For example, for one situation it may be satisfactory to forecast sales units for the company as a whole. However in another situation, sales by product group or even by product group in each geographical region may be required. During the definition phase of forecasting, determining just what level of detail will be required can save substantial costs later on if management decides that its initial forecasts are too aggregated and that data will have to be recollected at a more detailed level. It is generally best to collect data at the most detailed level possible, then aggregate them as a part of the data preparation phase for forecasting, rather than aggregating them initially.

The frequency of data use

The frequency with which new data are collected generally is related closely to the time period covered by each value of the variable. However, it can differ in some situations. For example, a company may wish to forecast monthly sales for the next year, but it may do so only once each year. Knowledge of the frequency with which the data will be used is important in designing an efficient procurement phase. If data are only used annually, there may be little need to collect them within one or two days of their occurrence. However, if they are to be used for daily internal control, they must be collected much more rapidly as well as more frequently.

The unit of measurement

Historically, accounting systems have been oriented toward reporting in terms of value, such as dollars. Data collection in many accounting systems converts whatever units may naturally exist to some common monetary unit before actually storing the data. This conversion represents a loss of information and can impede the application of effective forecasting. An important step in the design and definition of forecasting situations is determining the appropriate measurement units to be used. As a rule of thumb, those units that would naturally be associated with the variable should be used for purpose of procuring and storing the raw data. Subsequent conversion to more common denominators such as monetary units can then be made as desired.

Level of accuracy required

Different applications of forecasting require different levels of accuracy. The factors that determine the most suitable level of accuracy are the importance of the management situation and the role of the forecast in affecting that situation. In some cases, the forecast prepared for a very important management situation may be peripheral to that situation, and thus the level of accuracy would not be great, even though the situation is of major importance. On the other hand, a management situation of only minimum importance could use as the basis for decision making the forecast for a single variable. In this situation, a high degree of accuracy in the forecast would be desired. Since increased accuracy almost always comes only with increased expense, each new forecasting situation requires that appropriate trade-offs be made in selecting the most desirable level of accuracy. (Some of the problems of attaining desired accuracy will be discussed later in this chapter.)

Segmentation of the variable to be forecast

In many instances it is possible to segment the item to be forecast and/or to use surrogate variables for that item that will greatly improve the accuracy and performance of the forecast. Frequently, spending some time identifying alternative segmentation plans can give much better results than spending that same amount of time simply collecting better data on the wrong variable. The item to be forecast often can be segmented along several different dimensions, and it is best to consider each of those dimensions as well as other possibilities that may occur in specific situations.

One basis for dividing the variable to be forecast is to separate those portions that contain major uncertainties from those that are more stable and easier to forecast. For example, if a company is preparing a sales forecast, it may be best to segment the forecast into two parts, one representing those items that are stable and rather straightforward as a forecasting problem and the other representing new products and items that are much more difficult to forecast. In such an instance, a quantitative approach might be applied to the more stable segment of the company's sales and a more subjective or judgment-based approach to the other segment. The two forecasts could then be combined for a final forecast of company sales.

One of the reasons for segmenting the item to be forecast is that managers making judgmental assessments may overcompensate for the uncertainties in one part of the item being forecast and do less well than they would have done had the more stable items been separated from the more variable items. The authors are aware of such instances. Such errors occur particularly when the pattern for the stable items differs from that for the more variable items. For example when new products are being introduced there may be exponential growth or perhaps an S-curve pattern, while the remainder of the company's products may follow a linear growth trend. Segmentations that take account of these differences in patterns will generally result in better accuracy for forecasting than simply trying to aggregate everything.

Another segmentation scheme that is often used is forecasting cumulatively, such as for a one-year time horizon, then breaking that forecast down by percentages into monthly estimates. This scheme is particularly useful in production planning systems where the aggregate planning tasks looks at a one-year time horizon. In the case of one heavy equipment manufacturer, this approach substantially reduced the errors in their forecasts and gave them the guidance they needed to continually update their aggregate, twelve-month production plans.

Some additional examples of how companies have segmented their forecasting problem may help to illustrate the wide range of possibilities that are available. In one instance, a winery wanted to forecast its corporate sales. However, its market share had been changing in recent years and it did not have good data on its own sales. This company chose to forecast industry sales (there was an industry association that had excellent industry-wide data), and then to apply its own more subjective estimates of its market share to those industry estimates. In this way it was able to move more quickly to a quantitative forecasting method, since it did not have to wait several months for the collection of its own data.

In another example, a printing company was essentially serving two markets. One was the high school yearbook market and the other was the commercial market involving sales through advertising agencies. This company found that prediction of its yearbook sales for production planning purposes was fairly straightforward because those items were handled on one- to three-year contracts. Thus the forecasting was really aimed at the commercial segment. The yearbook sales, based on contract specifications, were then added to the sales forecast for the commercial segment.

Still another firm involved in light manufacturing chose to prepare its sales forecasts by making separate estimates for each geographical region. One reason for doing so was that the seasonal pattern was slightly different from region to region. Another more important reason was that the company was growing rapidly and felt that it would be much easier to incorporate the judgmental assessments of its sales force if it had that sales force react to quantitative sales estimates made for each geographical region rather than for the company as a whole. This segmentation scheme also made it easier to use these forecasts as a standard against which performance could be measured later.

Finally, an organization that the authors are familiar with chose to divide its forecasting problem into several segments: one for contract business and one for each new business by product line. This type of split enabled those managers most informed on each product line to contribute their own inputs to the forecasting process, and also accommodated the need for different patterns to be used with different product lines. The contract base was in fact quite stable and easier to predict. Thus, it could be separated out at the outset, then recombined once individual forecasts were prepared for each product line.

Determining the value of the forecast

A final step in the definition and specification of the variables to be forecast is determining the value of that forecast. Clearly, this value is related to the required level of accuracy and the importance of the management situation. It also depends on the opportunity for improvement in that situation. At this initial phase of data definition, some rough estimate of the value of the forecast is needed so that the cost of alternative data collection procedures can be kept within the upper bound set by the value of the data.

17/2 Data Procurement

The two key items in data procurement are understanding available data sources and their characteristics and use, and understanding the data requirements of various forecasting methods. This section will examine both questions in some detail. In addition, Appendix III presents data sources on national economic variables available in the United States and Europe.

17/2/1 Data Sources

Data can be collected from primary sources or from secondary sources, such as accounting records and published materials. Primary sources include all forms of original collection of data. Data from such sources are more expensive to obtain, but the source generally can be designed to fit a particular forecasting requirement better, since they are selected after the forecasting situation has been defined. Some of the alternative ways for collecting primary data include sampling procedures, continuous surveys, or a complete census covering the items of interest. Technological methods in particular often require primary data sources because of their very nature. For example, the initial stages of the Delphi approach can be thought of as the collection of primary source data. Quantitative methods of forecasting can also use primary data as in the case of a survey aimed at discovering customer inventory levels. However, their use is limited to a few cases because the costs involved are generally higher than costs for data from secondary sources.

Secondary data sources are generally used extensively in the application of quantitative forecasting methods. Existing accounting records are by far the easiest source of data to deal with and usually the cheapest. In addition, their accuracy is more easily assessed. Their major drawback is that they are geared toward legal and reporting purposes and thus may not be directly suited for the forecasting situation. For example, accounting records report sales, but forecasting situations often require information on demand as well as actual sales. The demand may have been higher or lower than indicated by actual sales, and it may have been following a somewhat different pattern at the final level of consumption than the company's shipping records would indicate. Other distortions may also be incorporated in accounting data. For example, advertising may have been used during a certain period, but its effects may not have been observed until several periods later. Thus the accounting figures may not accurately show the effect of advertising on sales because of this time lag. (Clearly if the time lag is constant, it can be accounted for. But in many instances, the effect of one advertising program will have a different time lag from that of another program.)

In many forecasting applications, it becomes necessary to modify or further process accounting data so that it will better meet forecasting requirements. It might also be necessary to add additional account categories to the financial system so that data can be collected in more detail or in a form more suitable for forecasting. In some instances, it may be easiest to use the existing accounting system as a source of most of the data, then establish a parallel collection procedure to supplement that data.

Data collection is generally much more difficult in the initial stages of forecasting than it is later on. Once a continuous effort and pattern of collection have been established, it does not take long before the required data become routinely available. Special care is needed in designing data requirements and data collection procedures, since they usually are left in place for a considerable length of time and thus an efficient design can produce real economies to the organization.

The method by which data are collected depends in large part on the type of organization. A retailing firm can obtain many of its data requirements through billing invoices. Such invoices generally contain information as to the location of the customer, the number of units sold, price, discounts, description of the product, etc. These can be conveniently filed in a computerized data bank and retrieved as needed. Unfortunately in many manufacturing companies and other firms, billing invoices simply indicate movement of goods from one warehouse to another and do not provide the same level of information as they might in a retail firm. In such cases, alternative data sources are often needed. One that is commonly used in manufacturing companies is that of the warranty card. However, since many buyers fail to complete these cards and return them to the manufacturer, the information may be incomplete or biased.

Another method of data collection that can be used in conjunction with a warranty card or on its own is sampling surveys that estimate the inventories of retailers. These surveys can be carried out at regular intervals and consist of selecting a sample of retailers whose inventories of particular items are recorded. This inventory information enables estimation of the sample's retail sales and extrapolation to estimate the retail sales of the entire market. Oftentimes firms such as A. C. Nielson are used to provide this kind of data.

A somewhat less ambitious approach to estimating retailer inventory levels is to use published statistics for large classes of retailers and to extrapolate those statistics to one's own situation. The assumption is that inventories of the product to be forecast move in a fashion similar to more general levels of inventory in the economy. Unfortunately none of these methods of inventory estimation will reveal unfilled demand. Thus in all cases, there is the problem of estimating demand using only a surrogate measure such as actual sales.

In recent years, there has been a tremendous increase in the number of published data sources available to forecasters. This increase is due in part to the realization of government and business managers that more and better information increases the effectiveness of planning and decision making. It is also due in part to the introduction of high-speed computers that substantially reduce the costs of processing and storing such data. Government sources, nonprofit institutions, and international organizations issue a host of statistical data that can be used as relevant information for forecasting. Some o the most important economic data currently available are summarized in Table 17-1. This table summarizes the type and frequency of income and expenditure measures that are reported in the United States, France, United Kingdom, and Germany. These include not only federal government sources but also other sources such as Organization for Economic Cooperation and Development (OECD), International Monetary Fund (IMF), and the United Nations. The table includes the names and addresses of the issuing agencies from which these statistics can be obtained.

Because of the importance such national economic variables can have in an organization's forecasting function, it may be useful to describe what is represented by some of these major accounts. The national income and product accounts generally include the gross national product (GNP) and its expenditure components—personal consumption expenditures, gross private domestic investment, net exports of goods and services, inventories, and government purchases of goods and services. Such GNP figures are usually presented both in terms of constant dollar value and current dollar value. The national income and product accounts are the most comprehensive of all of the general economic data available and governments expend great effort in compiling them. In many causal models, they can be used as independent variables to indicate the level and influence of cyclical factors or to indicate the general environment and its impact on the item to be forecast.

TABLE 17-1 AVAILABLE DATA ON NATIONAL ECONOMIC INDICATORS

Type of Data	France		United Kingdom		Germany	United States			OECD*		IMF†		United Nations	
	Yr.	Mo.	Yr.	Mo.	Yr.	Yr.	Qtr.	Mo.	6 Mo.	Irregular	Yr.	Mo.	Yr.	Mo.
GNP	X	X	X	X	X	X	X	X	X			X	X	X
Personal income and outlays	X	X	X	X	X	X	X	X	X				X	X
Government receipts and expenses	X	X	X	X	X	X	X	X	X		X	X	X	X
Foreign transactions	X	X	X	X	X	X	X	X	X		X	X	X	X
Savings and investment	X	X	X	X	X	X	X							
Income and employment	X	X	X	X	X	X	X	X	X				X	X
Miscellaneous tables	X	X	X	X	X	X	X	X	X				X	X
Price deflators	X	X	X	X	X	X	X							
Index of industrial products	X	X	X	X	X			X		X			X	X
Index of general economic activity	X	X	X	X	X			X			X	X		

Data can be obtained from:
France—Institut National de la Statistique et des Etudes Economiques (INSEE), 29, Quai Branly, 75—Paris 7e.
United Kingdom—Central Statistical Office, Great George St., London SWIP 3Ad; Her Majesty's Stationery Office, P.P. Box 569, London SE7 9NH.
United States—Survey of Current Business, Supt. of Documents, U.S. Govt. Printing Office, Washington D.C., 20402.
OECD—OECD Publications, 2, Rue André Pascal, 75—Paris 16e; OECD Publications Center, Suite 1207, 1750 Pennsylvania Ave. NW, Washington D.C. 20006.
IMF—The Secretary, I.M.F., 19th & H St. NW, Washington D.C. 20431.
United Nations—Publishing Service, United Nations, New York, NY 10017.

* Organization for Economic Cooperation and Development.
† International Monetary Fund.

Most national data sources also provide price deflators for their GNP figures on both an annual and a quarterly (seasonally adjusted) basis. These can be used to remove the effects of inflation on the data and may also be used as deflator indices with other data series. For example, a company may choose to deflate its own corporate sales using such an index.

In addition to the national income and product accounts, many other forms of economic data are published at varying intervals by government institutions and private groups. Some of the most important of these series cover financial and industrial data. Many such data series are available from the Federal Reserve Board in the United States and the national banks in France, the United Kingdom, and Germany. While the majority of these data are gathered and reported on a national basis, some series are also available at regional levels and can be used in regional forecasting.

One source of data that is particularly useful to organizations doing long-range planning in the United States is the National Bureau of Economic Research. This bureau (and corresponding institutions in other countries) provide data on several different business cycle indicators. These include leading, lagging, and co-incidental series that can be used as the basis for predicting turning points or changes in the business cycle.

A third source of government data that has been increasing in importance for forecasting during recent years is the census. In the United States, each census provides detailed information by geographical area on many demographic characteristics. For those companies concerned with forecasting series that depend on such demographic characteristics, the census data can be extremely valuable.

For those organizations involed in international trade or import/export activities, the foreign transaction accounts can be very useful. These present data on both a quarterly and annual basis for the various account groups that make up these transactions.

Finally, the savings and investment accounts can be particularly useful in certain industries. These accounts show the sources and uses of savings in both current and constant dollars and indicate private purchases of producers durable equipment, by type. These accounts also supply a complete breakdown of annual changes in business inventories and in personal savings. They can be used in estimating interest rates, assessing fiscal policy changes, and estimating general levels of economic activity.

In addition to government sources of data, numerous industry associations can provide useful information for forecasting. Frequently trade journals and inter-industry reports from associations contain such data. The most useful source of guidance in locating such data is the published list of industry associations, which includes a list of association publications. Once forecasters have identified the industries that may collect data relevant to forecasting requirements in their organizations, those associations can be contacted directly for more information.

There are a number of public companies that specialize in data collection and sale of information. These companies generally start by using their own primary data sources and then organize them in the way best suited to their customers. For example, the J. Walter Thompson Company maintains a consumer panel of selected families to serve as the basis for estimating consumption patterns for various products. The A. C. Nielson Company collects detailed information on consumer purchase patterns by monitoring sales activity and inventory levels in retail stores. The University of Chicago gathers information on brand switching among consumers, and many other groups gather more narrowly focused data series. These private firms can often supply an organization with the data it needs for its forecasting, either on a one-time or ongoing basis. In many cases, such firms can spread the cost of primary data collection and thus provide very reliable data at much lower cost than could the individual organization.

17/2/2 Data Requirements for Various Forecasting Methods

Data are central to the operation and application of forecasting methodologies. There are two main uses of data in forecasting. First, data are used to determine the pattern of behavior of some variable based on historical observations. The various time-series approaches to forecasting are methodologies for using data in this fashion. Table 17-2 indicates the suggested minimum amount of data required by each of the major quantitative techniques described in this text. Increasing the amount of data will generally increase the accuracy of forecasts, but not necessarily in a manner directly proportional to the amount of data. One of the problems in the quantity of data used is that frequently the pattern changes with time and thus using a longer time span (more data) may in fact give less accurate results than using only the minimum amount of data necessary and using that most recently available.

The second use of data in forecasting is to provide future values of independent variables included in a causal model. This usage requires that those independent variables be forecast before they can be used as part of the input to such a causal model. As pointed out in the chapter on regression analysis, it is often necessary to examine several alternative independent variables and to include only those that give suitable results and that can be most easily predicted in the future.

The above discussion of data relates mainly to quantitative methods of forecasting. For technological or qualitative forecasting methods, data uses and sources are somewhat different. The information or data required by technological forecasting is specialized and generally of a primary nature. Data bases and regular information updates are not so valuable for these methods. Rather data for such methods consist largely of scientific reports, intelligence data, or general information gathered from newspapers, magazines, or other publications. The

TABLE 17-2 MINIMUM DATA REQUIREMENTS OF QUANTITATIVE FORECASTING METHODS

Method	Nonseasonal Data (no. of data points)	Seasonal Data	Yearly (12 mo.) Seasonal Pattern (no. of data points)
Naive	1	—	—
Mean	30	—	—
Simple moving average	2–10	—	—
Simple exponential smoothing	2	—	—
Linear moving average	4–20	—	—
Linear exponential smoothing	3	—	—
Classical decomposition	—	5 times the length of the seasonal pattern	60
Census II	—	6 times the length of the seasonal pattern	72
Foran system	24	—	—
Adaptive filtering	30	5 times the length of the seasonal pattern	60
Box-Jenkins methodology	30	6 times the length of the seasonal pattern	72
Generalized adaptive filtering	30	6 times the length of the seasonal pattern	72
Simple regression	30	—	—
Multiple regression	More than 30, depending upon the number of independent variables	5–6 times the length of the seasonal pattern; or 5–6 times the number of independent variables	60–72
Econometric models	A few hundred	—	—
Life-cycle analysis	30	—	—
Input-output analysis	A few thousand	—	—
Multivariate ARMA models	50	8–9 times the length of seasonal pattern	96–108

data themselves are not of uniform importance in such situations. Rather it is the way the data is processed to form future alternatives that is critical. Technological forecasting involves evaluating these alternative formulations and assessing their chances of realization.

The problem of how best to collect data for technological methods is a difficult one. The collection process requires a constant surveillance of the relevant environment. One approach has been suggested by Aguilar (1967) in his book, *Scanning the Business Environment.* He distinguishes four modes for scanning the business environment and gathering relevant information from it:

> undirected viewing (general exposure to information)
> conditional viewing (directed exposure)
> informal search (limited and unstructured search but with something specific in mind)
> formal search (systematic search for information) [Aguilar 1967, p. 19].

Based on his own research using a survey involving several organizations and managers, Aguilar found that the type of information that managers obtain is mainly in the marketing (58%) and the technological (18%) areas. The remaining classifications accounted for very little of the total information scanned by managers. Regarding information sources, Aguilar (1967, p. 64) found that the following sources were particularly important: customers, suppliers, business and professional associates, bankers, merger brokers, consultants, friends and acquaintances, trade shows, publications, general news media, and personal observations. One of the important classes of information about competitors that Aguilar identified consisted of published sources such as annual reports, news media announcements, and releases to security analysts.

During recent years the importance of environmental and technological information has become better understood by publishers (and managers), and several documents are now aimed at providing information of this kind for organizations. The D.M.S. market intelligence reports compiled by D.M.S., Inc., are an example. In the foreword, the purpose of these reports is described as follows:

> The market intelligence reports serve a much more important function than pure historical reference for you as a subscriber. The emphasis throughout has been placed on highlighting the market opportunities available on each program from development through production and retrofit. Each program is monitored continuously by D.M.S.'s nationwide information gathering network and as new situations develop within a program and its status changes, these developments are immediately reported. . . . All of the information contained herein has been gathered by D.M.S.'s professional intelligence network. All authoritative sources ranging from a personal contact with officials at key government and industrial centers to the monitoring and recording of major publications are utilized

in preparing each report. All of the information contained herein has been verified and is known to be factual and reliable. All rumors, speculation, and hearsay have been carefully culled out of the basic reports. Wherever a departure has been made from factual, objective reporting, it is clearly labeled as a projection or estimate made by D.M.S. on the basis of its knowledge of the particular program involved. Further it has been established as corporate policy that no classified or company proprietary information is knowingly reported. [*D.M.S. Marketing Intelligence Report* 1972, p. 1]

It is this type of information that is often needed to predict the future environment and other long-range planning factors. Such information can be extremely useful as inputs to qualitative or technological methods of forecasting as well as to more subjective and judgmental assessments made by managers.

17/3 Data Preparation

In addition to identifying sources of data that meet forecasting requirements, there are a number of issues related to data preparation that affect the accuracy of the data and their ability to meet the specific requirements of individual forecasts. These issues can be divided into two main parts. First are those related to the collection and use of data, and second are those related to data adjustments. These latter items might be thought of as preprocessing of the data after its collection but before its use in a quantitative forecasting methodology. Both aspects of data preparation will be dealt with in turn.

17/3/1 Problems with Data Collection

In a very extensive and far-reaching study, Morgenstern (1963) considered many of the major aspects of data collection and deficiencies in the resulting data. He not only considered the conceptual problem, but also examined in some detail many of the more commonly used published data sources in the United States. The results of his study are indeed revealing. For example, he concluded that the widely used statistics of GNP and private expenditures in the United States can include errors that range in magnitude from plus or minus 10% to 15%. This means that in addition to the forecasting error resulting from the application of the methodology itself, one must consider additional errors of 20% to 30% that can be built into the results simply because of the source of data being used. Morgenstern found it particularly disconcerting that those preparing such published reports have made no attempt to estimate the magnitude of the errors in their data. He then concluded that one of the reasons that social science has yet to match the achievements of the natural and physical sciences is the softness and inaccuracies in the data that are collected and used for analysis.

There are numerous sources of error in data that influence its accuracy. Morgenstern has classified these sources as follows:

sampling methods
measurement errors
hidden information
poorly designed questionnaires
data aggregates
classification and definition
time factors
miscellaneous errors

These errors not only are important to the government or institution that gathers data for general publication, but also affect primary data collected for specific forecasting situations. Each of these sources of error deserves considered by the forecaster in preparing data for a specific situation

Sampling methods

In many situations, data must be estimated from sample surveys. Sampling theory and its application are fairly well developed in statistics, but there are several problems that frequently arise because of human error or sampling bias. When the rules of sampling theory are followed explicitly, many of these errors can in fact be avoided. The problem arises in not adequately following the rules that ensure the validity and accuracy of the sample.

Measurement errors

Errors that occur in the actual collection and processing of data are usually called measurement errors. They may be the result of deficient measures, or they may involve reporting and processing errors. They range from collecting the wrong information to keypunching errors at the computer end. Once incorrect information is included in the basic set of data, it is often hard to identify and eliminate it. General experience seems to suggest that the more automated the measurement, collection, and storage of data, the smaller the chances of measurement error.

Hidden information

Often information is deliberately hidden or falsified by firms, households, or other responders for fear that the information will be used for tax purposes. Human nature often can be the cause of such falsifications. For example, exaggeration of items related to prestige is not uncommon in surveys and research studies. One must also be aware that although there are general guidelines for the accounting profession, there is still tremendous flexibility as to the exact reporting of items and the way in which expenses are classified. Accounting rules for such things as profit and loss statements must be studied carefully and data adjusted to reflect accounting practices before being used as input for forecasting.

Poorly designed questionnaires

Often the data used in forecasting is collected from respondents who fill in questionnaires. For example, the anticipatory surveys of plant and equipment expenditures and those of consumer expenditures are based on data collected through questionnaires. A questionnaire should be carefully designed to communicate clearly and elicit the needed information. Errors in questionnaire responses can arise for a variety of reasons. These range from the inability of the respondent to understand exactly what is wanted to the respondent's desire to avoid the appearance of ignorance by leaving questions blank.

Data aggregates

When aggregated data is collected from large populations, errors frequently occur as a result either of omitting part of the population or of double counting some parts. Sometimes even the time periods used in reporting in various published sources will overlap, and thus the task of fitting the data together in a meaningful time series is difficult. This problem is particularly significant in the area of financial statistics when different government agencies are involved. It is generally impossible for a corporation using these series to sort out how time periods are defined and how adjustments can be made to compensate for possible differences.

Classification and definition

Proper classification of the items to be measured and the quantifiable variables to be used in the measurement are important aspects of data collection. This can become a particularly difficult problem in the multi-product firm where it is often impossible to allocate costs and profits to the various product lines in an exact way. Since the trend in corporations is toward larger companies of a diversified nature, it is likely that the difficulty of isolating and classifying the factors for individual products will become more difficult in the future. Also, intercompany transactions make it hard to assess and allocate overhead and other charges to various parts of the organization.

Time factors

Data must be collected at discrete intervals, which can create problems with respect to timing. For example, organizations that use cash rather than accrual accounting methods will report financial data for a time period that does not necessarily reflect accurately their economic activity during that period. Even with an accrual accounting method, problems can arise when a physical transaction is reported in a different time period from the corresponding financial transaction. At the corporate level, these time problems can often be minimized by attempting to make all data series consistent with the accounting system. However, in using external published sources it is frequently impossible to maintain such consistency.

Miscellaneous errors

Another source of error in the use of data for forecasting is that the characteristics of a sample or population may change over time. As a result, the observations reported for different time periods may actually represent slightly different samples or populations. All of the forecasting methods discussed thus far are based on the notion that the historical data used by a given method comes from a homogeneous population. This assumption implies that when there are significant changes, substantial error may occur in the forecast.

One other factor that often causes inaccuracy in data is what Morgenstern identifies as functionally false data. A good example of this phenomenon might be the construction of price indices. These are generally based on published prices, but because of rebates, discounts, etc., transactions rarely occur at published prices. In addition, the weights used to calculate price indices may change significantly over short periods of time, which again would cause functionally false data. A solution to this problem is to be certain that the variable for which the data are collected is appropriately defined initially, and that steps are taken to verify that the actual collected data represent that variable.

17/3/2 Preprocessing Data for Forecasting

In many forecasting situations, some preprocessing or adjusting of the data is necessary after they have been collected but before they are used in a quantitative forecasting method. A number of the most common types of adjustments will be described here. It should be stressed that judgment must be exercised in determining when such preprocessing will improve the forecasting results and when it will not. The real problem is that most adjustments involve transformations of the data or additions to the data base that in and of themselves eliminate part of the information contained in the raw data. In many instances, these adjustments make it easier to apply standardized forecasting methodologies and thus the adjustments are worthwhile. However, in other instances such transformations may cause a sufficient loss of information that the results of using the transformed data will not be nearly as reliable as those obtained from using the raw data.

Missing data values

Frequently in collecting data for forecasting, data will not be available for some small fraction of the observations that are desired. This lack may be due to lost records or simply the failure to collect data that are sufficiently accurate to use as part of a time series. In such instances, some estimate of those data values is almost always necessary to make application of a quantitative technique viable. For example, a time series covering 30 monthly periods that is missing an occasional data value could not be used with several forecasting methods that rely on individual values for a continuous sequence of time periods. The most common approach to overcoming this problem is simply to use a moving average estimate in place of the missing values. It will be recalled that this approach was described in Chapter 4 when decomposition methods were discussed and the twelve-month moving averages were computed as an intermediate stage of forecasting. Rather than leaving six values at each end of the series simply as unavailable, shorter moving averages were taken to fill in all but one or two values at each end of the series.

A similar procedure can be used when data values are missing at the outset. For example, if it is a seasonal data pattern and there is no value for a particular January, it may be attractive to assume a value that is simply the average of the previous three January values. That allows a time series method of forecasting to be applied in a very straightforward manner. Similarly, in using a technique such as multiple regression, observed values for all of the independent variables may not be available in every single time period. In such cases, either certain observations must be dropped completely or some estimate must be made of the missing values so that complete observation can be included. Usually, if the number of missing values is small, it is better to use some kind of moving average or exponential smoothing estimate of the missing value and include the observation than it is to drop it. However, if there are several missing values, it may be better to eliminate one or more of the independent variables or several of the observations in order to achieve more accurate results.

Working day adjustments

One of the problems commonly faced in business forecasting is variation in the actual number of business days included in each time period. Some companies have gone to accounting periods of four weeks in length with thirteen periods per year in order to partially overcome this problem. However, in companies where twelve monthly periods are used for reporting purposes, or even in many instances where thirteen four-week periods are used, some kind of working day adjustment is required. This adjustment is often referred to as a *trading day* adjustment.

The first step for making a trading day adjustment is to collect data on the number of working days or business days occurring in each month for the several years covered by the time series. These data can then be used to adjust the actual monthly data so that each month will reflect what the results would have been had that month contained the average number of working days. This adjustment is made by finding the average number of working days for each of the twelve months and adjusting the raw data by the appropriate percentage to reflect what actual values would have been if the month had contained the average number of working days. Thus if the average number of days for a given month over the past several years had been 20 working days and if that month in a particular year actually contained 22 working days, then the raw data would be reduced by 10% (2/20) so that the month would be comparable to a 20-day month. The resulting adjusted series can then be used as the input to forecasting.

Another type of adjustment is often needed when daily data are being used and special events affect the value of the variable on a given day. For example, in the restaurant business there may be individual days that are not representative of that day normally during the week because of local activities or specials offered by the restaurant. In such instances, there may be insufficient data to average out this kind of special fluctuation in the values. When that is the case, one might choose to replace those special values with a more typical value for that day. That can be done simply using a moving average or some other smooth estimate for that day of the week. One must be very cautious in this kind of data adjustment, since it really eliminates fluctuations from the historical data which may in fact recur in the future.

Standardizing the data

When applying many time-series methods, it is often useful to standardize the data so that the parameters resulting from that forecasting method can be compared for different time series. The need for this standardization was described in some detail in dealing with adaptive filtering in Chapter 9. There it was shown that standardizing the data not only improved the performance of that quantitative method, but also made it possible to use parameter values (for example, for the learning constant, k) that were uniform across very different time series. There are, of course, a wide range of standardization procedures that can be followed and those described in Chapter 9 are only a few of them.

Eliminating trend from the data series

As emphasized in Chapter 8, it is often useful to achieve stationarity in the data (eliminate trend) before one uses a specific quantitative forecasting method. The reason for this is that many methods perform much better when handling only a single type of pattern in the data than when handling multiple patterns. The elimination of trend thus minimizes the confusion the method might have in separating the trend from other possible patterns. As described in detail in Chapter 8, this elimination of trend can be achieved using the method of first differences.

Deseasonalizing the data

Just as trend can often be eliminated in order to improve forecasting performance for a particular methodology, similar adjustments can be made to eliminate seasonality. Since many time-series methods cannot deal with seasonality, removing it allows such methods to be used in a much wider range of situations. The process for deseasonalizing a data series is the same as that described in Chapter 4 in connection with decomposition methods. Once the seasonality has been removed, the series can be used as the basic input for a wide range of forecasting methodologies.

One should be cautious in both deseasonalizing data and removing the trend because when these steps are taken, they sometimes eliminate other information contained in the raw data. One approach for minimizing this information loss is that described in Chapter 4 for the Census II method. Essentially, it amounts to an iterative procedure of first eliminating seasonality, then looking at other parts of the pattern, then returning to seasonality to see if all of it has been eliminated and if it might be better eliminated with a slightly different set of seasonal adjustment factors.

Constant versus current price data

In many instances, accounting data are recorded in terms of current prices and thus reflect both inflation and real growth or decline in that item. Such series can be transformed into constant prices using a deflator index such as the GNP deflator. While this transformation allows forecasting to deal with a series that is not biased by inflation, the deflator index itself may further distort the original data. For example, a company selling a single product in a specific industry may have trouble identifying a deflator index that adequately represents that single product. When a more general index relating to the industry as a whole is used, it may over-adjust for some time periods and underadjust for others simply because the inflation pattern for the company's products differs from the industry average.

Raw versus revised data

For many national and regional economic indicators, data are often first collected in a raw form on a sample basis. These raw data are then used to estimate the actual values of the series before the time when those actual values become available. These estimates allow forecasting to respond more quickly to changes in the short-term situation than would be the case if only the final published data were used several months later. For the forecaster, the important concern is whether or not the raw estimates adequately represent the final reported values. In many instances it has been found that these raw estimates may vary by 10% or more from the actual values. Thus a trade-off must be made between more current, and possibly less accurate, information and older, more accurate information.

17/4 Data Management

There are several important aspects of effective data management for purposes of forecasting. These can be grouped into four categories—data base systems, data manipulation, data presentation, and revisions and updates. Each of these will be discussed in turn.

17/4/1 Data Base Systems

During the past few years, interest in establishing data bases has increased. This interest deserves special consideration in connection with forecasting. A data base is a collection of data on a number of different variables that is stored in some easily accessible manner (such as a computerized data processing system) so that the data will be available when needed. There are generally three types of data that can be included in a data base designed to support forecasting: (1) data that are needed for existing requirements, (2) data that are currently available but are not currently required as part of forecasting, and (3) data that may be required in the future but are not currently available.

A data base that focuses only on handling existing data requirements is generally the most straightforward and least expensive system to develop. With small incremental cost, such a base can often be expanded to include the collection of available data that are not currently required but may be useful in the future. Finally, with the use of some planning and management judgment, the data base can often be expanded further to include data that may be required in the future but are not currently available. The attractiveness of a data base that includes all three types of data is that most forecasting applications require historical observations before a technique can actually be applied. Thus if the data base includes a collection of several different items, it is much more likely that the required historical data will be readily available when new forecasts are desired.

The trade-off involved in developing such a general data base to support forecasting is the cost of its development and maintenance. Generally, however, if a flexible data base is developed, the incremental costs of collecting data on an additional variable are quite low. Key aspects in determining the value and flexibility of a proposed data base system are the level of detail involved and the structure of the data actually stored there.

For maximum value, transactions and events should be expressed in their most basic form in the data base rather than being summarized in terms of a single dimension such as dollars. As mentioned earlier, aggregation causes the loss of information. For example, when the daily shipments of a factory are aggregated into a total sales figure for the week, information on the daily pattern of shipments that may be valuable for inventory planning purposes is lost. Similarly, if the sales of a product sold during a special low-priced promotion are aggregated with the sales of that product at a regular price, information concerning the price-quantity relationship is lost. In predicting product volumes, such loss of information may severely limit the forecasting ability of even the most sophisticated methodologies.

One of the basic reasons for aggregation in most accounting data bases is related to their people orientation. Most such systems have been designed to be used by people who are processing data collected by people, to produce information to be filed by people, and to provide reports for other people. Thus the convenience of having a single unit of measure and a single system of accounts provided by summarizing transactions has historically been desirable and necessary. However, for forecasting purposes and with the current level of computerization available in many companies, such summaries are no longer necessary, nor are they attractive.

In today's businesses, machines, not people, do much of the gathering, processing, filing, and reporting of data. The capabilities and deficiencies of such computer systems are very different from those of people. Whereas people have difficulty keeping track of and working with large quantities of data, computer systems have only minimal problems in that area. One of the important considerations in designing a data base system for forecasting is to adequately utilize the capabilities of the computer in storing data in the form that will make it most usable for forecasting purposes.

It is useful to consider how such a basic data system might in fact be organized. Instead of summarizing the data in terms of a common measure or on aggregated transaction levels, it would be much more useful to store the raw data for individual transactions and in the smallest collection units possible, then let each forecasting application determine whether or not additional aggregation is needed before forecasting. Thus rather than posting events to accounts and summarizing the accounts, such a system might create a "trail of pointers" to the data. This trail would provide the computer with the information it needs to find the appropriate data and construct any kind of summary that might be requested. Such a system would have the potential to construct any information based on that data, but would actually construct only those information summaries requested by the forecaster or planner.

A data base system with this type of design would be able to exploit the capabilities of the computer in order to solve two difficulties that have traditionally been associated with more standard accounting systems—inflexibility and loss of information through aggregation. Although this system is being suggested merely to illustrate how a data base for forecasting might be made much more attractive than many existing accounting data bases, it might be interesting to pursue the subject a little further here.

Implemented on today's computers, this data base system might work as follows:

> As relevant events occur in the enterprise and its environment, data describing these events would be transmitted directly to the computer from automatic data gathering devices or by people "phoning in." These relevant events would include those that normally make up accounting transactions as well as other events that are thought to affect the performance or the activities of the enterprise. As each of these event descriptors enters the computer system, it would automatically be assigned an event number and stored in a direct access storage device. These event descriptors, which form the data base for the system, would be filed by their event numbers. Thus one could direct the computer to retrieve any event descriptor from storage simply by giving it the appropriate event number.

The following example might help to clarify how such a data base would be constructed. Suppose there are four kinds of relevant events for a retail enterprise—advertising expenditures, sales, product price, and product cost. Each would come into the system from its own source. The sales event, for example, might come into the system directly from the cash register, whereas the advertising manager might phone in his media and expenditure decisions. If the sampling interval is one week (events are only reported once a week as totals for the week), the system might receive the event descriptors shown in Table 17-3 during weeks 13 through 15.

Three important features should be recognized in the event descriptors recorded in Table 17-3:

1. Each consists of one measurable quantity (for example, quantity sold or price charged) and a series of tags or classifications to which that quantity is associated (for example, product A and week 15).
2. The quantity and tags of an event description are expressed in whatever terms describe them most naturally.
3. The events include those that are controllable (management decisions) as well as so-called uncontrollable events.

The basis for locating and manipulating the appropriate event descriptors for any requested summary is a system of data categories. These categories, which correspond roughly to the accounts of a traditional accounting system, are lists of the event numbers corresponding to the event descriptors containing the data items that pertain to that category. For example, a typical data category might be

TABLE 17-3 ILLUSTRATION OF EVENT DESCRIPTORS ENTERING A FORECASTING DATA BASE

Advertising Expenditures

Event No.	Expenditure	Advertising Media	Week
5	$400	Newspaper	13
12	200	Newspaper	14
13	200	Circular	14
14	400	Newspaper	15

Sales

Event No.	Quantity	Product	Week
1	40	A	13
2	60	B	13
8	50	A	14
9	80	B	14
15	80	A	15
16	60	B	15

Product Prices

Event No.	Price	Product	Week
3	$10	A	13
4	5	B	13
10	10	A	14
11	5	B	14
17	8	A	15
18	3	B	15

Product Costs

Event No.	Cost	Product	Weeks
6	$4	A	13–15
7	1	B	13–15

product A. That category would contain the numbers of all of the event descriptors pertaining to product *A*. Another data category might be *quantity sold*. That category would contain the numbers of all event descriptors having to do with sales quantities regardless of product or time period, etc. In other words, a data category, rather than storing the data (or aggregated data) that logically belongs to the category, would instead consist of a list of pointers that indicate where to get that data, when and if it is needed. In this example, the data categories and the list of pointers relating to each one would be as shown in Table 17-4.

TABLE 17-4 DATA CATEGORIES AND THEIR POINTERS FOR A FORECASTING DATA BASE

Category	Pointers (event numbers)
Sales	1, 2, 8, 9, 15, 16
Product price	3, 4, 10, 11, 17, 18
Product cost	6, 7
Advertising	5, 12, 13, 14
Product A	1, 3, 6, 8, 10, 15, 17
Product B	2, 4, 7, 9, 11, 16, 18
Newspaper	5, 12, 14
Circular	13
Week 13	1, 2, 3, 4, 5, 6, 7
Week 14	6, 7, 8, 9, 10, 11, 12, 13
Week 15	6, 7, 14, 15, 16, 17, 18

It should be noted that the first four data categories shown in Table 17-4 refer to the quantities in the event descriptors, whereas the remaining categories refer to tags that classify the quantities. Of course once the data categories are updated for a new event description, only the quantity portion of the event description needs to be stored. The information contained in the tags is contained in the data categories themselves.

With the data categories defined, it is possible for the computer to construct any summary of the data by expressing that summary in terms of the data categories. For example, if one wanted to know the total quantity of product *A* that was sold during weeks 14 and 15, the computer would scan the list of event numbers in the sales, product *A*, and week 14 categories and would access from storage all event descriptors whose numbers are in all three categories. (Notice that this scanning and matching process could be done relatively efficiently, since the pointers in the data categories are in order of increasing event number.) The computer would then add together the quantities in those event descriptions (in this case there is only one, number 8, for which the quantity is 50), and add that sum to the sum of the quantities in the event descriptors listed in the sales, product A, and week 15 categories. Since the only event description listed in all three categories is number 15 with a quantity of 80, the desired information for this example would be "130 units of product A were sold in weeks 14 and 15."

From this example, it is possible to see how any summary requested could be constructed from the data base as a function of the data categories. For any commonly used summaries (for example, total weekly sales and profit), the defining functions are stored in the computer system for immediate use. In a sense, these summarization functions are pointers to data categories, which in turn are pointers to the event descriptors. Thus while the data base remains intact, the system creates a network of pointers that enables a computer to construct desired summaries upon request.

To use the system for information retrieval and analysis either for forecasting purposes or for other management tasks, the user would simply specify what summaries were desired [for example, profit (week 15)]. Using the summarization functions, the computer would translate that description into an expression in terms of the data categories and, scanning and matching those lists of pointers, would retrieve the necessary event descriptors from the data base. The computer would then perform the required computation on the data and display the results or print a hard copy report for the user.

For purposes of forecasting, such a data base containing the most basic form of transactions or events would be most useful. It would allow maximum flexibility to the forecaster in deciding what variables to forecast for each specific management situation. It would also maximize the usefulness of the information contained in that data base.

17/4/2   Data Manipulation

As indicated in the previous section, once the data base has been established there are a number of summarizations or other forms of data manipulation that the forecaster might want to undertake before actually applying a specific forecasting methodology. Many different systems have been suggested in the literature for handling these tasks of data manipulation. One such data management system is that of ADDATA.*

The ADDATA programs are designed to manage data on n-dimensional direct access data files through the use of a flexible user-oriented command language. In response to the *what next* prompt question, the user may retrieve and display, perform arithmetic calculations on retrieved data, and restore the data to the file. Commands are English words entered in free format. Data

---

*ADDATA is a proprietary product of Applied Decision Systems, Wellesley Hills, Massachusetts, and is publicly available on a nationwide time-sharing service.

descriptors are user-defined labels. Thus the expert user can abbreviate entries at the terminal and gain several responses on the command line for faster processing. The novice user is automatically prompted for any missing specifications.

An illustration of the use of the ADDATA data management programs in retrieving from data files and displaying data at the terminal is shown in Figure 17-1. The sample data consist of annual observations on the gross national product (GNP) from 1947 through 1974. These data are shown in both current dollars and constant (1972) dollars. As the figure indicates, the user has trans-

```
EXE ADDATA                          WHAT NEXT?RETAIN
16K
VERSION A750801                     WHAT NEXT?GET 48-74
1213   04/07/76                        54 ITEMS

DATABASE NAME?VULCAN                 WHAT NEXT?SUBTRACT 47-73
                                       54 ITEMS
WHAT NEXT?GET CURR CONS GNP 47-74
   56 ITEMS                          WHAT NEXT?DIVIDE 47-73
                                       54 ITEMS
WHAT NEXT?DECIMAL 1
                                     WHAT NEXT?MULTIPLY 100.
WHAT NEXT?PRINT FACT YEAR
                                     WHAT NEXT?PRINT
1214   04/07/76
GNP                                  1216   04/07/76
                                     GNP
```

	CONSTANT	CURRENT			CONSTANT	CURRENT
47	468.3	232.8		47	4.1	11.3
48	487.7	259.1		48	.6	-.4
49	490.7	258.0		49	8.7	10.9
50	533.5	286.2		50	8.1	15.4
51	576.5	330.2		51	3.8	5.1
52	598.5	347.2		52	3.9	5.4
53	621.8	366.1		53	-1.3	.1
54	613.7	366.3		54	6.7	9.0
55	654.8	399.3		55	2.1	5.4
56	668.8	420.7		56	1.8	5.3
57	680.9	442.8		57	-.2	1.4
58	679.5	448.9		58	6.0	8.4
59	720.4	486.5		59	2.3	4.0
60	736.8	506.0		60	2.5	3.4
61	755.3	523.3		61	5.8	7.7
62	799.1	563.8		62	4.0	5.5
63	830.7	594.7		63	5.3	6.9
64	874.7	635.7		64	5.9	8.2
65	925.9	688.1		65	6.0	9.4
66	981.0	753.0		66	2.7	5.8
67	1007.7	796.3		67	4.4	9.1
68	1051.8	868.5		68	2.6	7.7
69	1078.8	935.5		69	-.3	5.0
70	1075.3	982.4		70	3.0	8.2
71	1107.5	1063.4		71	5.7	10.1
72	1171.1	1171.1		72	5.3	11.5
73	1233.4	1306.3		73	-1.8	7.7
74	1210.7	1406.9				

FIGURE 17-1 ILLUSTRATION OF ADDATA, A SPECIFIC DATA MANIPULATION PACKAGE

formed the entire matrix of data with some straightforward mathematical commands to obtain period-to-period percentage changes in the data. (Commands typed in at the terminal are underlined in this figure for clarity.)

Applications of data management packages such as ADDATA include four-dimension marketing bases for the consumer goods industry, five-dimension distribution networks for transportation/logistics planning industries, and numerous two- and three-dimension data bases for more straightforward analysis and forecasting applications. The developers of the ADDATA package have linked it directly to a package of multiple regression programs as well as to the interactive forecasting programs developed by Makridakis and Wheelwright for direct use by forecasters in companies. Thus this package, and several others as well, can serve as an integral part of a company's computerized forecasting system.

17/4/3 Data Presentation

Depending on the specific organization setting, the requirements and characteristics desired in a data management system may vary tremendously. In the ADDATA system, the emphasis is on preparing data that are going to be examined by the forecaster in some detail. Thus much of the emphasis is on preliminary analysis and data manipulation so that the substantial amount of time spent on selecting the appropriate forecasting method and applying it to the data can be used most effectively.

In some corporate settings, the emphasis is not so much on the application of sophisticated forecasting methodologies as on meeting the number of diverse requirements for forecasts in a satisfactory manner. When the aim of the data management system is more closely related to the presentation of data for a number of different managers and administrators in a wide range of situations, the system must possess characteristics appropriate to meet those needs. One such system is that developed by Mr. T. W. Hibson, manager of forecasting for the Optical Products Division of American Optical Corporation.

The American Optical system uses a very straightforward approach to forecasting and focuses much more on the manipulation of data and its presentation for management purposes. The actual forecasting routines most commonly used by the system are simply to deseasonalize a time series of data, to apply a trend extrapolation routine to that deseasonalized data, and finally to reincorporate the seasonal factors in coming up with a final forecast. Although this is fairly straightforward as a forecasting application, the volume of different items to be forecast and the number of managers involved places special requirements on the complete system. It must be particularly flexible in presenting a wide range of forecasts and yet must present them in a consistent manner so that different managers can readily compare their own forecasts and those prepared by others.

The sequence of steps involved in forecasting and planning for the variety of product lines and geographical areas handled by American Optical starts with a tracking of actual values and a rather straightforward forecast of future values on either a monthly or annual basis. The next step seeks agreement from those managers involved as to the most appropriate final forecast for the situation and, ultimately, a tracking of performance of that agreed upon forecast against actual values. This system allows management to measure its performance against those forecasts that have been previously agreed upon. Since several managers and a variety of products and geographical areas are handled with the same system, a very structured system and yet a very flexible approach was necessary. This system includes definition of the following elements:

1. *Data Structures*. A consistent set of definitions has been developed for those who use this sytem. Thus data bases can be prepared for each situation in a form that will be suitable to the individual situation and yet will use a consistent structure so that the same types of processing steps can be applied to any such data structure.

2. *Significant Work Files*. A number of intermediate work files are created in the system as part of the data entry and data analysis steps. These work files can be combined easily, depending on the type of reports that are to be generated and the level of detail that is to be included.

3. *Initializing Steps*. These steps provide guidelines for the user in creating work files and in initiating a data base that is subsequently to be used in forecasting and in measuring actual performance.

4. *Tracking Steps*. In order to compare actual with forecast values, steps have been defined for tracking actual performance through the entry of historical data and the comparison of that data with forecasts for those same time periods. The tracking steps also include a mechanism for indicating when forecasts have been approved so that those forecasts can be used as a basis for comparison.

5. *Using Summarized Data Sets*. In order to facilitate management control and evaluation at various levels in the organization, a set of steps has been defined that allows summaries to be compiled for any level of detail. As a result, a group product manager can not only look at the actual versus forecast performance for individual products and individual regional areas, but can also use the same basic report format to summarize those results for several products and/or several regional areas. Thus the product manager can more easily evaluate the performance of individual managers and of the entire group.

In essence, the American Optical system described above has a complete flexible set of operations that facilitate preparation of forecasts using a trend extrapolation and a seasonality index for each of a wide range of products and responsibility centers. Reports are prepared in a manner that is consistent from area to area, thus facilitating management's comparison of performance in different areas. In addition, plotting routines are available that help to graphically illustrate actual versus forecast performance.

17/4/4   Updating and Internal Audits

Once a data base has been created, procedures must be designed and implemented for collecting new data as they are generated and adding them to the data base. As a part of such a procedure, it is important to include a method for determining when additional data are needed and when changes might be necessary in the forecasting methods to accommodate basic changes in pattern. Such a procedure might be thought of as an early warning signal to identify potential changes in data series. One type of signal was described in Chapter 3 in connection with smoothing methods. There, a tracking signal that measures cumulative error was used to identify when the parameter values of the smoothing model should be updated so that they could more quickly accommodate changes in the basic pattern. When a forecasting system is being designed for several different items, some procedures, either formal or informal, are needed to perform the same function as a tracking signal and facilitate the periodic evaluation of the data base and the forecasting methodologies being applied.

Perhaps just as important as regularly validating the forecasting methodologies is establishing ongoing procedures for identifying possible errors and verifying accuracy of the data as they are collected. As stated previously, there are a number of sources of errors in data collection and their occurrence needs to be minimized through periodic checking.

The most standard mechanism for running such checks is simply a regular audit. Such an audit should cover four main areas. First, it should review the procedure underlying the data collection process in order to identify possible improvements. Second, it should make a detailed observation of actual data collection to ensure that the process as originally designed is being followed. Verifying adherence to stated procedures is an important factor in determining the level of confidence that can be placed in the data. Third, the accuracy of the data and their suitability for the variable being forecast must be checked. As management's needs change, the specific forecasting requirements will also change. Thus it is important to periodically review the management tasks for which forecasting is being provided to determine whether different variables would be more appropriate or whether existing forecasting applications are still useful. The fourth and final auditing area involves examining the costs of data collection and determining whether those costs are under control and whether the value of the data still exceeds the costs. The costs of data collection must be allocated, at least in some rough form, in order to make such an evaluation. This is simply a standard cost/benefit analysis where the goal is to make sure that the handling costs are kept lower than the value of additional accuracy provided by the data.

REFERENCES AND SELECTED BIBLIOGRAPHY

Aguilar, F. J. 1967. *Scanning the Business Environment*. New York: Macmillan.

Biderman, A. D. 1966. "Social Indicators and Goals." In *Social Indicators*, ed. R. A. Baner. Cambridge, Mass.: MIT Press, pp. 68–153.

Boulding, K. E., E. J. Starr, S. Fabricant, and M. R. Gainsbrugh. 1971. *Economics of Pollution*. New York: New York University Press.

Butler, W. F., and R. A. Kavesh. 1966. *How Business Economists Forecast*. Englewood Cliffs, N. J.: Prentice-Hall.

Dunn, D. M., W. H. Williams, and T. L. DeChaine. 1975. "Aggregate versus Subaggregate Models in Local Area Forecasting." *Journal of the American Statistical Association*, Vol. 71, No. 353, March, pp. 68–71.

D.M.S. Market Intelligence Report. 1972. Greenwich, Conn.: D.M.S., Inc.

Grether, D. M., and M. Nerlove. 1970. "Some Properties of 'Optimal' Seasonal Adjustment." *Econometrica*, Vol. 38, September, pp. 682–703.

Ijiri, Y. 1967. *The Foundation of Accounting Measurement*. Englewood Cliffs, N.J.: Prentice-Hall.

McRae, T. W. 1964. *The Impact of Computers on Accounting*. London: John Wiley & Sons.

Morgenstern, O. 1963. *On the Accuracy of Economic Observations*. Princeton, N.J.: Princeton University Press.

Porter, W. T., Jr. 1966. *Auditing Electronic Systems*. Belmont, Calif.: Wadsworth.

Sims, C. A. 1974. "Seasonality in Regression." *Journal of the American Statistical Association*, Vol. 69, No. 347, September, pp. 618–26.

Stekler, H. O., and F. W. Burch. 1968. "Selected Economic Data: Accuracy vs. Reporting Speed." *Journal of American Statistical Association*, June, pp. 436–44.

Wheelwright, S. C., and D. G. Clarke. 1976. "Corporate Forecasting: Promise and Reality." *Harvard Business Review*, November–December.

Zschau, E. V. W., 1968. "The Impact of Computers and Information Sciences on Accounting." Presented at the Annual Meeting of the American Accounting Association, San Diego, Calif., August.

18 ORGANIZATIONAL AND BEHAVIORAL ASPECTS OF FORECASTING

THE PAST TWO decades have seen a substantial increase in the range of forecasting methods available and in the number of statisticians, operations researchers, and management scientists trained to apply them. The increases in these two factors provide the building blocks for substantial growth in the systematic and effective use of forecasting methods in the coming decade. The failure of the predicted rapid expansion of management science to materialize in the mid-sixties has demonstrated the importance of developing an effective interface between the management scientist and the user, and of developing supporting organizational efforts. Both are equally necessary to the effective growth and utilization of quantitatively based techniques.

There are two key areas in organizing and implementing the forecasting function in an organization. The first deals with establishing a forecasting function within the firm. That involves determining the necessary resources, gathering them together in a single subunit of the organization, and providing the support and direction necessary to work on forecasting problems effectively. The second area is effectively applying forecasting methods and resources to individual situations. This area includes developing those specific steps for a new forecasting application that will ensure its success. Both of these areas will be discussed in some detail in this chapter. First, however, it is useful to review and assess the current status of forecasting. An understanding of that status can serve as a basis for planning both organizational efforts in forecasting and individual applications of forecasting methods.

Although the major focus in this chapter will be on business organizations, it should be stressed that most of the prescriptive guidelines presented apply equally well to government and nonprofit institutions. However, it is the authors' experience that in many instances such organizations are not as far along in their application of existing forecasting methodologies. A first step in applying the framework and guidelines developed in this chapter is to assess the specific organization's status and base for forecasting development.

18/1 Status of Forecasting in Business Firms

During 1975 Dalrymple (1975a and b) and Wheelwright and Clarke (1976) made two important studies of the status and success of forecasting in business organizations. As a basis for demonstrating dimensions that can be used to assess the status of forecasting in organizations and also to serve as an overview of forecasting in the mid-seventies, these two studies will be referred to repeatedly in this and the following section.

In his study, Dalrymple sent a mailed questionnaire to 500 businessmen in the midwestern United States. Responses were obtained from 35% of them. The

TABLE 18-1 RESOURCE COMMITMENT TO FORECASTING (DALRYMPLE STUDY)

No. of People Preparing Forecasts	Percentage of Firms
1	3
2–4	43
5–10	25
10 or more	25
No answer	4

Time Schedule of Forecasting Activities	Percentage of Firms Preparing	Percentage of Firms Revising
Weekly	7	3
Biweekly	—	1
Monthly	27	28
Quarterly	30	29
Semiannually	13	18
Annually	40	18
1–3 years	7	3
3–5 years	11	3
5 years	1	1

Source: D. J. Dalrymple, "Sales Forecasting Methods and Accuracy," Business Horizons (December 1975), pp. 69–73, copyright 1975 by the Foundation for the School of Business at Indiana University. Reprinted by permission.

composition of the respondents in terms of their firms' size, age, and type appeared to be representative of general business organizations in the United States. While Dalrymple did not report complete information on the level of resources being committed to forecasting, his work did include information on the number of people involved in preparing sales forecasts and the frequency with which the firms revised their sales forecasts. These two measures of resource commitment are summarized in Table 18-1.

In the Wheelwright and Clarke study, a detailed questionnaire was also mailed to about 500 companies. These represented a fairly broad cross section of U.S. firms. Table 18-2 summarizes the profile of the responding companies. The response rate for this study was just over 25%. A major feature of the Wheelwright and Clarke study was that two questionnaires were sent to each firm. One was to be completed by a *preparer* of forecasts and the other by a *user* of forecasts. Approximately 15% of the surveyed companies returned responses from both user and preparer. As will be seen later on, this dual questionnaire provided valuable information on the differences in status and success as perceived by preparers and users of forecast.

The Wheelwright and Clarke study assessed the commitment to forecasting and its status along several dimensions. Three of the most important of these are

---

TABLE 18-2   PROFILE OF RESPONDING COMPANIES
(WHEELWRIGHT AND CLARKE STUDY)

Type of Company
44.4% industrial products
26.2% consumer products
29.4% other (mainly utility and service firms)
Scope of Answers
48.4% entire corporation
37.5% single division
14.1% other corporate subunit
Size of Company (annual sales)
38.4% less than $100 million
30.4% $100 million to $500 million
31.2% more than $500 million

Source: Steven C. Wheelwright and Darral G. Clarke, "Corporate Forecasting: Promise and Reality," Harvard Business Review (November–December 1976), copyright © 1976 by the President and Fellows of Harvard College, all rights reserved. Reprinted by permission.

described in Table 18-3. On the first dimension of organization, about 70% of the companies with sales less than $20 million had chosen to centralize their forecasting organization. That percentage declined until it was just less than 50% for those firms whose sales exceeded $500 million. The level of commitment to forecasting in virtually all of the responding companies was significant. An annual budget of between $10,000 and $50,000 and a forecasting staff of from one to five people was the most common for companies with sales up to $500 million. For 34% of the companies with sales in excess of that level, the forecasting staff was more than ten people, and the budget was over $100,000 for almost 60% of the firms in that sales category.

These studies used different approaches in trying to determine the importance of forecasting in the responding organizations and the progress being

TABLE 18-3 STATUS OF FORECASTING IN SURVEYED COMPANIES (WHEELWRIGHT AND CLARKE STUDY)

	Percentage of Companies with Annual Sales of: (millions)			
	Under $20	$20–$99.9	$100–$499.9	Over $500
Mode of organization				
Centralized	70.5	58.6	51.3	48.8
Decentralized	23.0	41.4	37.8	39.5
Other	6.5	0.0	10.8	11.6
Annual budget				
0	37.5	7.2	5.5	0.0
$1,000–$9,999	12.5	21.4	16.6	5.4
$10,000–$49,999	43.8	60.7	47.3	18.9
$50,000–$99,999	6.2	7.2	16.6	16.2
Over $100,000	0.0	3.5	14.0	59.5
Staff (FTE's)				
Less than 1	33.3	6.9	8.1	5.2
1.0–4.9	66.7	89.6	83.8	44.8
5.0–10.0	0.0	3.5	2.7	15.8
Over 10	0.0	0.0	5.4	34.2

Source: Steven C. Wheelwright and Darral G. Clarke, "Corporate Forecasting: Promise and Reality," Harvard Business Review (November–December 1976), copyright © 1976 by the President and Fellows of Harvard College, all rights reserved. Reprinted by permission.

made in it. In the Dalrymple study, firms were asked directly how important sales forecasting was to the success of their firm. They were also asked to indicate the departments making use of sales forecasts throughout the company. On this

TABLE 18-4   COMPANY'S USE OF FORECASTING
(DALRYMPLE STUDY)

Importance of Sales Forecasting to Success of Firm	Percentage of Firms
Very important	64
Important but not critical	28
Some value	6
Limited value	2

Department	Percentage of Firms with Department Using Sales Forecasts	
	Current Survey	1967 Survey[a]
Finance	80	32
Executive, general or admin. mgt.	78	10
Budgeting	63	3
Manufacturing	61	60
Inventory control	55	2
Purchasing	53	19
Planning	52	3
Accounting	44	14
Advertising	34	10
Personnel	23	8
Merchandising	22	2
Research and development	22	8
Transportation	19	6

[a] From "Sales Forecasting: Is 5% Error Good Enough?" *Sales Management,* vol. 99 (December 15, 1967), pp. 41–48. Reprinted by permission of Sales and Marketing Management. Copyright 1967.

Source: D. J. Dalrymple, "Sales Forecasting Methods and Accuracy," Business Horizons (December 1975), pp. 69–73, copyright 1975 by the Foundation for the School of Business at Indiana University. Reprinted by permission.

latter measure, Dalrymple was able to compare the results obtained in his 1975 study with those obtained in a similar study conducted in 1967. The results on both these measures are shown in Table 18-4.

In the Wheelwright and Clarke study, the responding firms were asked to compare their status in forecasting with the status of other firms in their industry. As shown in Table 18-5, the majority of the respondents viewed themselves as being ahead of their industry in terms of the methods applied, the management use of forecasts, and the accuracy of those forecasts.

TABLE 18-5 COMPANY'S CURRENT STATUS IN FORECASTING (WHEELWRIGHT AND CLARKE STUDY)

	Behind Industry	Average	Ahead of Industry
Forecasting methods applied			
All respondents	19.1%	34.2%	46.7%
Preparers only	17.1	32.5	50.4
Users only	22.4	36.8	40.8
Management use of forecasts			
All respondents	18.2	39.4	42.4
Preparers only	18.1	38.5	43.4
Users only	18.4	40.8	40.8
Accuracy of forecasts			
All respondents	15.8	41.3	42.9
Preparers only	11.6	39.7	48.8
Users only	22.7	44.0	33.3

This study pursued the question of the company's status in forecasting by examining the acceptance and use of alternative forecasting methods in the respondent companies. Eight forecasting methodologies were examined to determine their level of familiarity and usage. As shown in Table 18-6, the *jury of executive opinion* technique was the most widely used by those familiar with it and was used on an ongoing basis by 89% of those firms who had tried it. Regression analysis was almost as broadly used. Of those firms that had tried

TABLE 18-6 ACCEPTANCE AND USE OF ALTERNATIVE FORECASTING
METHODS—PREPARERS' RESPONSES
(WHEELWRIGHT AND CLARKE STUDY)

Method	Use of the Method by Those Familiar with It	Ongoing Use of the Method by Those Who Have Tried It	Unfamiliar with the Method
Jury of executive opinion	82%	89%	6%
Regression analysis	76	91	8
Time-series smoothing	75	84	13
Sales force composite	74	82	10
Index numbers	67	85	33
Econometric models	65	88	12
Customer expectations	57	78	15
Box-Jenkins	40	71	39

Source: Steven C. Wheelwright and Darral G. Clarke, "Corporate Forecasting: Promise and Reality," Harvard Business Review *(November–December 1976), copyright © 1976 by the President and Fellows of Harvard College, all rights reserved. Reprinted by permission.*

regression for forecasting, 91% were still using it. Of those familiar with it, 76% were actually using it.

As can be seen from Table 18-6, most of the remaining six techniques surveyed were also commonly known to the respondent companies. The two exceptions were index numbers (probably known to preparers but not necessarily used for forecasting purposes) and the Box-Jenkins approach. One surprise in the use of the methods was the strong showing of the econometric models. The survey indicated that almost two-thirds of the firms made some use of such models (not necessarily an in-house model) and that of those who had tried such models, 88% were still using them.

Of those companies who had tried one or more of the eight methods summarized in Table 18-6, the major reason for no longer using a method was inadequate accuracy. The one exception was the Box-Jenkins technique for which complexity was most frequently cited as the reason for dropping it.

Wheelwright and Clarke also investigated the developmental stages a company passes through in becoming a more sophisticated user of forecasting. As indicated in Table 18-7, the most commonly used techniques by those who felt they were behind their industry were nonmathematical—jury of executive opinion and sales force composite. For those companies who viewed themselves as being average, the most commonly used techniques were jury of executive opinion, time-series smoothing, and regression analysis. Thus, the average company in 1975 had adopted some mathematical techniques but was still using some of the nonmathematical ones fairly extensively. Finally, for the company that viewed itself as being ahead of its industry in 1975, regression analysis was most frequently used, and several other mathematical techniques were used extensively.

TABLE 18-7 DEPENDENCE OF USE OF METHODS ON FORECASTING STATUS (WHEELWRIGHT AND CLARKE STUDY)

Method	Percentage of Preparers Using Method		
	Behind Industry Category	Average Category	Ahead of Industry Category
Time-series smoothing	32.1	70.6	65.9
Box-Jenkins	10.7	17.6	31.7
Regression analysis	39.3	70.6	75.6
Index numbers	35.7	41.2	41.5
Econometric models	25.0	52.9	63.4
Jury of executive opinion	67.9	84.3	70.7
Sales force composite	50.0	64.7	70.7
Customer expectations	28.6	47.1	51.2
Other	17.9	23.5	31.7

Source: Steven C. Wheelwright and Darral G. Clarke, "Corporate Forecasting: Promise and Reality," Harvard Business Review *(November–December 1976), copyright © 1976 by the President and Fellows of Harvard College, all rights reserved. Reprinted by permission.*

It is interesting to note that use of time-series smoothing and the jury of executive opinion was less for companies placing themselves in this advanced category than for those in the average or behind industry categories. The reason most commonly given for dropping the use of these techniques was lack of accuracy. It appeared that as companies progressed in their use of forecasting, they replaced these less sophisticated techniques with ones that tended to be more accurate. They also appeared to use a wider range of techniques as they became more advanced in their forecasting practices. That is natural, since different situations require different properties in a forecasting method, and one of the best ways to improve accuracy is to have a better match between the situation and the methodology.

In the Dalrymple study, the relative use of a variety of methods was also examined. Table 18-8 summarizes the results, which seem to be fairly consistent with those reported by Wheelwright and Clarke with the exception that the percentage of respondents never having tried some of the methods is somewhat

TABLE 18-8   FORECASTING TECHNIQUES USED AND ERRORS REPORTED (DALRYMPLE STUDY)

Method	Usage				Usage for Forecast Period:		Forecasting Errors Reported by Firms Using Different Techniques	
	Use Regularly	Use Occasion-ally	No Longer Use	Never Tried	Short Term (year or less)	Long Term (1 to 5 years)	Percentage Errors of Firms Who Report Regular Use	Percentage Errors of Firms Who Never Tried
Jury of executive opinion	52%	16%	1%	5%	27%	16%	7.0	5.4
Sales force composite	48	15	3	9	37	6	6.8	5.9
Trend projections	28	16	1	12	13	13	6.2	7.5
Moving average	24	15	2	15	18	7	6.2	7.9
Industry survey	22	20	2	16	17	8	6.7	6.0
Regression	17	13	1	24	8	9	6.4	6.8
Intention to buy survey	15	17	2	23	15	3	8.5	6.2
Exponential smoothing	13	13	3	26	13	7	7.3	7.1
Leading index	12	16	1	24	12	5	5.4	6.9
Life-cycle analysis	8	11	1	28	2	11	4.5	7.2
Diffusion index	8	11	—	30	9	6	8.1	6.7
Simulation models	8	8	1	35	5	5	6.5	6.8
Input/output model	6	8	1	34	6	3	6.2	6.6

Source: D. J. Dalrymple, "Sales Forecasting Methods and Accuracy," Business Horizons (December 1975), pp. 69–73, copyright 1975 by the Foundation for the School of Business at Indiana University. Reprinted by permission.

higher in the Dalrymple study. This suggests that somewhat smaller firms may have been included in that study as compared with the work reported by Wheelwright and Clarke.

In both of the studies, the researchers sought to determine those criteria used in selecting a specific forecasting method in a given situation. The Dalrymple study divided the important factors used in preparing such forecasts into three categories—past sales of the firm, projections of key variables, and leading indicators. These factors and their relative importance are summarized in Table 18-9. In the Wheelwright and Clarke study, the technique of factor analysis was used to identify three key factors in selecting a forecasting method—user environment, cost, and problem-specific characteristics. The detailed components of these three factors are summarized in Table 18-10.

TABLE 18-9 IMPORTANCE OF FORECASTING VARIABLES (DALRYMPLE STUDY)

Variables	Percentage of Firms Reporting			
	Very Important	Important But Not Critical	Some Value	Limited Value
Past sales of firm	40	11	6	—
Projections of:				
Industry sales	45	20	14	6
Customer attitudes	41	19	15	7
Retail sales	20	14	16	22
Income	17	10	18	26
GNP	13	16	18	29
Population	12	14	22	21
Scrappage rate of your product	9	7	10	34
Leading indicators				
Changes in inventories	26	19	12	15
Interest rates	24	18	17	17
Housing starts	21	19	14	23
New orders durables	17	13	17	26
Changes installment debt	9	12	18	30
Stock market	5	11	14	37

Source: D. J. Dalrymple, "Sales Forecasting Methods and Accuracy," Business Horizons (December 1975), pp. 69–73, copyright 1975 by the Foundation for the School of Business at Indiana University. Reprinted by permission.

TABLE 18-10 CRITERIA FOR SELECTING A FORECASTING METHOD (WHEELWRIGHT AND CLARKE STUDY)

Factor 1—User Environment
    User's level of forecasting sophistication
    User's understanding of the method
    Relationship between user and preparer
    Company experience in forecasting
    User's formal training in forecasting

Factor 2—Cost
    User's time
    Preparer's time
    Computer time
    Data collection

Factor 3—Problem-Specific Characteristics
    Time horizon to be forecast
    Length of each time period
    Accuracy
    Degree of top management support

Source: Steven C. Wheelwright and Darral G. Clarke, "Corporate Forecasting: Promise and Reality," Harvard Business Review *(November–December 1976), copyright © 1976 by the President and Fellows of Harvard College, all rights reserved. Reprinted by permission.*

It should be clear from both of these studies, that by the mid-1970s business firms had made substantial progress in the application of forecasting methods. In addition, the Wheelwright and Clarke study sought to determine future plans regarding forecasting, and these results will be summarized in the next section.

18/2 Reasons for the Organizational Status of Forecasting in the Mid-1970s

One of the major purposes of the Wheelwright and Clarke study was to identify problems hindering the further development and application of forecasting in business organizations. Through asking a number of specific questions and contrasting the responses given by users and preparers of forecasts, a number of important shortcomings and areas for possible improvement were identified.

One of the most important areas identified for improvement was the major differences in the perceptions held by users and preparers. Some of these difficulties regarding the company's current status in forecasting are indicated in Table 18-5. Although both preparers and users gave similar responses as to the status of management use of forecasts, significantly more preparers than users viewed their companies as ahead of their industry on the other two factors—forecasting methods applied and the accuracy of those forecasts. These differences are important because both users and preparers are faced with the same facts, particularly regarding forecasting accuracy. The difference is due to the perceived adequacy of forecast accuracy as it applies to the usefulness of the forecasts.

To better understand the differences in user and preparer perceptions of forecasting performance, the Wheelwright and Clarke survey questioned both users and preparers about characteristics basic to understanding forecasting performance. Based on the responses given for 19 such characteristics (9 relating to preparers and 10 relating to users), four major groupings were identified:

1. preparer's ability
2. user's technical ability
3. user/preparer interaction
4. user's management skill

The first of these four characteristics related to the preparer's ability in forecasting and included such things as the preparer's understanding of the methods and ability to provide forecasts that met the user's needs and requirements. A much larger percentage of the preparers rated themselves good or excellent in these characteristics than did the users, as can be seen in Table 18-11. Specifically, preparers rated themselves better than users did at identifying the best technique for a given situation and providing forecasts in new situations. Also, preparers rated themselves higher than users did on providing forecasting results in the management time frame required and on preparing cost effective forecasts. The one area in which users and preparers agreed on the ability of the preparer was the preparer's understanding of sophisticated mathematical forecasting methods. These differences in perceptions regarding the preparer's ability are particularly interesting because although technical competence (or even excellence) is attributed to the preparers by the users, the confidence of the users in the ability of the preparers to choose the best techniques or to provide cost-effective forecasts is relatively low.

Under the heading of user's technical ability were included such characteristics as the user's understanding of forecasting methods, the user's ability to evaluate them, and the user's skill in using forecasts. While most users tended to think that they were better able to understand forecasting methods than preparers thought they were (even though the users rated themselves appallingly low), both groups seemed to agree on how well (be it very low) users could identify new applications for forecasting and how well they could effectively use

TABLE 18-11 DIFFERENCES IN PERCEPTIONS OF USERS AND PREPARERS OF FORECASTS

	Rating (%)
Preparer's Ability	
Understand sophisticated mathematical forecasting techniques	1
Understand management problems	−25*
Provide forecasts in new situations	−42
Provide forecasts in ongoing situations	−13
Identify important issues in a forecasting situation	−30
Identify the best technique for a given situation	−56
Provide cost-effective forecasts	−33
Provide results in the time frame required	−38
User's Technical Ability	
Understand the essentials of forecasting techniques	+27
Understand sophisticated mathematical forecasting techniques	+12
Identify new applications for forecasting	+5
Effectively use formal forecasts	−6
Evaluate the appropriateness of a forecasting technique	+24
User/Preparer Interaction Skills	
Understand management problems (preparers)	−25
Work within the organization (preparers)	−10
Understand management problems (users)	−5
Communicate with preparers of forecasts (users)	−1
Work within the organization in getting forecasts (users)	+2
User's Management Abilities	
Make the decisions required in their jobs	−3
Effectively use formal forecasts	−6
Describe important issues in forecasting situations	−8
Work within the organization in getting forecasts	+2

* 25% more preparers rated themselves good or excellent than did users.

$$\text{Rating} = 100 \times \frac{\text{percentage of users rating good or excellent} - \text{percentage of preparers rating good or excellent}}{\text{percentage of preparers rating good or excellent}}$$

Source: Steven C. Wheelwright and Darral G. Clarke, *"Corporate Forecasting: Promise and Reality,"* Harvard Business Review *(November–December 1976), copyright © 1976 by the President and Fellows of Harvard College, all rights reserved. Reprinted by permission.*

formal forecasts. Thus the range of differences in perceptions concerning the user's ability were much smaller than they were for the preparer's ability.

The third category in Table 18-11 relates to user/preparer interactive skills. While preparers rated themselves more highly than users did on such dimensions as understanding management problems and working within the organization, both groups agreed on the user's ability to understand management problems, communicate with the preparers of forecasts, and work within the organization in obtaining those forecasts.

The final category of perceived abilities examined by Wheelwright and Clarke was that of the user's management abilities. Characteristics in this group ranged from the user's ability to make the decisions required by the job to describing issues in new forecasting situations and actually using forecasts. As was the case in evaluating the company's current status in its management use of forecasts, both users and preparers were in agreement as to management's abilities to do such things.

A number of important implications can be drawn from the results shown in Table 18-11. It is not surprising that the technical ability of the forecast preparer is seen as a key element of forecasting choice. Nor should it be surprising that preparers of forecasts are more favorably impressed with their efforts and abilities than are the users of their services (for whom the forecast is but a single, if important, input to their jobs). What is perhaps most important in this analysis is the existence of a major gap between users and preparers of forecasts. This gap is reflected in the technical emphasis of the preparers and the managerial emphasis of the users. If the managers do not understand enough of the details of the forecasting methods to visualize new applications of them or to make reasonable demands for modifications that will lead to greater useful-ness, and if the preparers do not understand the applications well enough to require situational integrity of their forecasting methods—what hope is there for progress in the effective use of forecasts?

The need expressed by both users and preparers for improved communica-tion in the definition of forecasting problems is really symptomatic of the problem. However, there is a serious question as to whether excellent communication alone can possibly be sufficient. The basic problem is probably insufficient knowledge on the part of both preparers and users of the problems and abilities of the other. It may well be that each will have to expand his knowledge of the other's field of interest.

Wheelwright and Clarke also examined different perceptions as to which forecasting activities needed improvement. As might be expected, there were some substantial differences between the preparers as a group and the users as a group. The six areas most commonly cited by users as requiring substantial improvement included five of the six areas similarly cited by preparers. These areas were data processing support, development and maintenance of internal data bases, and user communication to preparers in identifying and defining requirements for forecasting applications. These results are summarized in Table 18-12.

Among users, the next four activities given a high level of importance for future improvement included preparer-to-user communication in defining forecasting requirements and identifying applications, and top management support for forecasting. It is interesting that the users felt that almost as important as their communication to preparers about specific situations and their needs, was their desire to have preparers help them in these definition and identification steps.

TABLE 18-12   FORECASTING ACTIVITIES MOST COMMONLY SIGHTED AS NEEDING IMPROVEMENT

Area of Forecasting Activity	Rank of Importance According to :[a]	
	Users	Preparers
EDP support—report generation	1	6
EDP support—software development	2	1
Development of internal data sources	3	—
EDP data base management	4	3
$U \rightarrow P$[b] communication—identifying applications	5	4
$U \rightarrow P$ communication—defining requirements	6	2
$P \rightarrow U$[c] communication—defining requirements	7	—
$P \rightarrow U$ communication—identifying applications	8	—
Top management support for forecasting staff	9	—
Top management support through organizational influence	10	—
$P \rightarrow U$ communication—establishing routine usage	—	5
$U \rightarrow P$ communication—establishing routine usage	—	7
$U \rightarrow P$ communication—presentation of the forecast	—	8
$P \rightarrow U$ communication—selecting method	—	9
$P \rightarrow U$ communication—preparing the forecast	—	10

[a] The percentage of users listing each of their top ten areas was between 36.1% and 50%.
The percentage of preparers listing each of their top ten areas was between 40.7% and 53.3%.
[b] User to preparer.
[c] Preparer to user.

Source: Steven C. Wheelwright and Darral G. Clarke, "Corporate Forecasting: Promise and Reality," Harvard Business Review (November–December 1976), copyright © 1976 by the President and Fellows of Harvard College, all rights reserved. Reprinted by permission.

Unfortunately, while the users felt these were important needs, the preparers did not agree on their importance.

The activities on which the preparers had the highest level of agreement as to need for future improvement (following the five shared with users) were communication in establishing routine use of forecasts, communication from the user to the preparer in the presentation of the forecast, and communication from preparers to users in regard to the technical aspects of forecasting.

Perhaps the most interesting and important difference in the collection of activities given top priority by the two groups was the infrequent perception by the preparers of the user's desire for help in identifying and defining management forecasting requirements. The preparers focused on their technical responsibility and the users focused on the performance of the functional tasks. This disparity has led to the neglect of the important task of fitting the forecast to the function required of it.

Another important difference was that the preparers seemed to feel that the activities most urgently needed to improve forecasting were things that should be done by people other than themselves—for example, by data processing and the users. The users, on the other hand, seemed to feel that although some activities from people other than themselves—for example, preparers, top managers, and data processing—were needed, they also felt that they had an important role to play in furthering the effectiveness of forecasting.

The fact that preparers mentioned establishment of routine usage as being an important area for emphasis and users did not was also an interesting difference. One explanation for this difference was that what the preparers viewed as routine, the users did not. If the preparers did the same kind of forecasting tasks once a month, they would clearly view that as being routine and see a need for establishing an ongoing procedure for handling it. However, if the user did not make the same use of that forecast every month, or if the decisions for which that forecast were used were not made on a periodic basis, then the user would tend not to see that as a routine use of forecasting. This interpretation was supported by the fact that preparers felt their forecasts were much more timely than did users.

Probably the most prominent feature of the areas needing improvement shown in Table 18-12 is the dominance of communication problems: nine of the fifteen. Both users and preparers agreed on the need for improvement. However, the preparers were more adamant about it than were the users; seven of their top ten problem areas were communication related.

Evidence from this survey suggested that the communication problem, although indeed real, was merely a symptom of the deeper problem for many companies. The problem inherent in a number of the responding firms centered around the definition of responsibilities and skills required by users and preparers. It appeared that both groups had abdicated some tasks and skills to their counterparts with the result that some basic skills and responsibilities were not being covered. This situation can be seen from Figure 18-1. No amount of effort at improved communication could compensate for such missing elements. The impression gained from the Wheelwright and Clarke survey was that both users and preparers would view communication improvement as bringing their own roles together at a point of tangency. In fact, as Figure 18-1 shows, they would still be separated by a gap resulting from their different rule perceptions.

For many companies improved communication would still leave key tasks uncovered. Table 18-13 lists four major functions central to forecasting and the percentage of companies responding to the survey in which neither user nor preparer was considered better than adequate at performing these functions. It is clear from this table that for a sizable number of companies, better communication between two people lacking in these skills would still result in a shortfall and an unfortunate situation for achieving the full potential of forecasting.

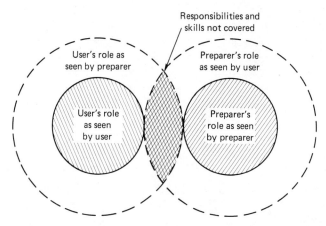

FIGURE 18-1 ROLE PERCEPTIONS OF PREPARERS AND USERS OF FORECASTS

Source: Steven C. Wheelwright and Darral G. Clarke, "Corporate Forecasting: Promise and Reality," Harvard Business Review *(November–December 1976), copyright © 1976 by the President and Fellows of Harvard College, all rights reserved. Reprinted by permission.*

Wheelwright and Clarke concluded from their survey results that communication about a complex application and a sophisticated methodology is not possible with the less than tangential contact between users and preparers (shown in Figure 18-1). It was apparent from their survey findings that preparers needed to become much more of an integral part of the management process that their methodologies were called upon to serve. It was also concluded that communication between two people without a common vocabulary would be tedious at best and impossible at worst. Thus users would seem to have the obligation to learn the basic vocabulary and concepts of the forecasters. These two areas seem to be

TABLE 18-13   FIRMS LACKING BASIC SKILLS FOR EFFECTIVE FORECASTING

Ability to:	Percentage of Companies in which both User and Preparer Perform Skill Only Adequately or Less than Adequately
Understand the management problem	15
Identify the important issues in a forecasting situation	29.2
Identify the best forecasting technique	55.4
Identify new forecasting situations	52.3

Source: Steven C. Wheelwright and Darral G. Clarke, "Corporate Forecasting: Promise and Reality," Harvard Business Review *(November–December 1976), copyright © 1976 by the President and Fellows of Harvard College, all rights reserved. Reprinted by permission.*

the minimal overlap that must exist for effective utilization of forecasting resources. If adding such dimensions to the roles of users and preparers seems to require too much for each party, then serious consideration should be given to the acquisition of a third party who could serve as an interpreter or an interface between preparers and users.

Based on the conclusions of Wheelwright and Clarke, a number of needs for improving forecasting in business organizations can be identified. Some of these simply involve organizational changes and new definitions of the responsibilities and roles of users and preparers. Others are more substantial. The remaining sections of this chapter will seek to pursue some of the specific actions that a firm can take in order to more fully develop its forecasting capabilities and to realize their full potential.

18/3 Organizational Steps for Improved Forecasting

As the previous discussion of forecasting in business firms shows, there are a number of steps that can be taken to improve the effective use of forecasting and to provide organizations with its full benefits. The activities that will lead to successful forecasting can be divided into two parts. This section will deal with activities that relate to the forecasting support staff and organization in the company, and the next section will deal with the individual steps involved in specific forecasting projects.

In smaller organizations forecasting will generally be performed by the manager. In such instances the main task required for more effective forecasting is teaching managers the basic values of forecasting and the mechanics for getting started. In larger organizations, people in staff positions usually prepare the forecasts for others who use them. In this section considerations important to establishing and directing the forecasting staff function within an organization will be examined. As a starting point the elements of an ongoing forecasting procedure will be described in order to identify the skills and resources that a firm needs to successfully carry out forecasting. Next, the question of forecasting organization and its sponsorship within the company will be examined. The last topic discussed will be the tasks of integrating forecasting with the existing planning procedures and actually changing the behavior of individual managers so that the full potential of forecasting can be realized.

18/3/1   Elements of an Ongoing Forecasting Procedure

A number of elements are important to the design and execution of any specific forecasting applications. Certain resources and capabilities must be available if the application is to be carried out effectively. In some instances the firm may need to acquire resources and skills, while in others it may need to use outside experts or conduct some additional training for existing personnel. The best combination of these approaches will depend on the company, the opportunities it has for better forecasting, and its general management policies in such areas.

Identification of management's forecasting requirements

A starting point for assessing and planning an organization's forecasting commitment is identification of management's forecasting requirements. Because of the nature of forecasting and its supportive role in decision making, the forecasting group will often identify what it thinks is needed in the way of forecasts. The group then asks management about these needs and management will confirm them and/or offer additional suggestions. Since supplying a forecast to a manager does not necessarily require any change in the manager's behavior, the tendency is to say *yes* when asked if a specific forecast would be of value. However, such a procedure for determining forecasting requirements and opportunities can be detrimental to the forecasting function in the long run. When the forecasting staff identifies the potential needs, the number of forecasts supplied to management will probably increase rapidly with time, but management's ability to prepare a better plan and make better decisions, will not necessarily increase at the same pace.

What is required is a procedure that involves the manager in determining those forecasts that would be most useful in a specific situation. Although it is more difficult to involve a busy manager in the identification process, firms that have done so have found that it is much more profitable in the long run. One approach that has been successful is to have the forecasting staff initiate interest in forecasting by holding discussion sessions with small groups of managers. These sessions introduce managers to some of the advantages of forecasting and the ease with which initial forecasts can be prepared. This step is generally followed by discussing a procedure that enables the managers to identify situations that seem to be appropriate for forecasting applications. A staff person can then meet on a one-to-one basis with the manager to discuss the possible applications and to identify those that appear to be most promising and should be pursued first.

Bell (1968) describes an interesting application of successful forecasting for planning that includes a number of different ways that managers can be encouraged to become involved in the planning and forecasting process. He also discusses the topic of feedback in forecasting and the motivation necessary to make such feedback effective.

Component staff support

In medium to large companies, it is generally attractive to have a specific staff group of one or more people available to support the development and application of forecasting. The main tasks of such a group are to support each of the steps required for individual forecasting applications and to act as a catalyst in getting management involved in this area. It is imperative that the members of such a group be competent in their understanding of the available forecasting methods, and in discussing management problems in general and the planning needs of the particular organization. In most cases, the training of such a staff will have been on the technical side, but they must have had sufficient exposure to management that they can discuss the manager's problems and situation on a one-to-one basis. This ability will allow the forecasting staff to take an active role in identifying opportunities for appropriate forecasting methods to be applied.

The problems most often encountered in developing a forecasting staff are similar to those that accompany the development of an operations research staff or any other technical group that serves in a support role to line management. Generally there is a trade-off to be made between technical competence on the part of individual staff members and their ability to understand management problems. Ideally, one would like to identify people who are experts both in the technical aspects of management science and forecasting and who are capable of applying mathematical concepts to organization problems. However, as pointed out earlier in this chapter, members of such a forecasting staff often emphasize the technical requirements of their job to the exclusion of the managerial and marketing aspects.

Many companies who have considerable experience with technical staff groups have moved toward use of intermediates who can serve as communicators between the technical specialists and practicing managers. Some of the research in systems theory has also looked in depth at this problem and at the need for management to be able to communicate and trust the judgment of the person who serves in such a role (see Makridakis 1971 for example). Other firms have found that it is most sensible to use some of their resources committed to forecasting in training their staff specialists in some of the basic areas of management and decision making, and in giving them experience closely related to managerial tasks. This training may involve rotation schemes for those serving in such a specialist group and may also mean that instead of a single centralized forecasting staff, individual technicians will be dispersed throughout the company, so that they are more closely related to the ongoing managerial function that they support. That allows them to develop a better rapport with those managers whom they serve and to gain a better appreciation of the decision-making situations surounding the forecasting applications with which they deal.

Data collection

An important consideration in developing successful forecasting applications is providing the manager with concrete results at an early stage. Although sometimes it requires months or even years to obtain forecast results, it is best to start with projects that can show an early return. Oftentimes this requires that the task of data collection be given high priority in order to acquire published sources of information and to make data bases maintained by independent companies accessible.

The actual collection of data is generally done under the direction of the forecasting staff and may either be performed by them or by someone in the accounting or data processing group. Once the procedure has been established for collecting the data, the data must be put into a form that can be used to apply forecast methods. That generally involves getting the data stored on some memory device of a computer system and making those transformations that are necessary. Again, the forecasting staff must be intimately familiar with the computer system to be used and must take responsibility for seeing that the necessary data are obtained quickly and accurately.

Applying forecasting methods to the data

Once forecasting inputs necessary for a specific situation have been determined and the data collected, the forecasting staff must apply appropriate methods to forecasting that situation. If quantitative methods are employed, their utilization on a large scale often presents certain technical problems. Frequently the forecasting staff may choose to maintain an extensive set of computer programs, each representing individual forecasting methods that can be readily applied in a given situation. It is also often useful for the manager to become involved in this step, since a basic understanding of the method can strengthen the manager's confidence in the technique and the usefulness of its results. This involvement may require training the manager in the fundamental concepts behind various methods and their strengths and weaknesses, or it may go so far as to provide an interactive computer system where the manager can actually try different methods.*

As an integral part of supporting the forecasting effort, the organization must supply the computer time needed to efficiently code the data and apply various methods. This support generally requires programmer time to develop different methods and time for data entry people to keypunch and record the information in the format needed. In larger organizations, it is often attractive to have forecasting people work with data processing people in this area of computerization, rather than do their own computer programming. When these activities are separated, the forecasting experts usually have more time to become better acquainted with management's forecasting requirements. Thus, the organization is best advised to have its forecasting staff concentrate on forecasting and the management uses of forecasting, rather than have them expand into more technical areas.

Communicating the forecast to the manager

For a forecast to be of maximum usefulness, the manager must receive it at the time required and in a form suitable for the manager's needs. The forecasting staff must be fully aware of the time limits within which the manager operates in a given situation, and must have sufficient communication with the manager to know when alterations in those limits are possible and necessary. So far as format is concerned, it is always useful to supply the manager not only with the forecast, but also with an indication of the assumptions inherent in the data and in the method used in preparing the forecast. Thus if there were special problems in obtaining data for that forecast, or if the staff had specific doubts about the accuracy of it, the manager should be informed of it.

---

*The authors have developed an extensive set of interactive forecasting programs covering a wide range of forecasting methods. These are described in detail in Makridakis and Wheelwright (1978).

It is also important not to overload the manager with information. For example, the manager does not need to know all of the data used in preparing the forecast or all of the assumptions imbedded in the results. Rather, one should highlight those factors of major importance and those that may be different from what the manager would otherwise assume. The best form for presenting the results of forecasting is to give a range of values as well as a most likely value. Such a range can then be explained in terms of the assumptions made and the inherent accuracy of the method applied.

Feedback and comparison of actual results to forecasts

In order to measure the effectiveness of a forecasting application, the actual results must be compared with those predicted. Generally this comparison is made through periodic reviews. For such reviews, the forecasting staff should analyze the errors in the forecasts and identify any bias or pattern that they may contain. At the same time, a comparison between naive and formal methods can be made. It should be a staff responsibility to perform this type of analysis and to inform the manager as to any systematic errors in the forecasts and any need for revising existing forecasting procedures.

In some instances, the presence of systematic errors does not necessarily imply that a forecasting application should be dropped or improved. For example, optimistic forecasts from salespeople may be accepted as such with the idea that high quotas will motivate salespeople and therefore lead to increased sales. Also, it may be easier to correct bias after the forecast has been prepared than to eliminate it from the forecast itself. However, whatever the form of systematic error, it should be recognized as such so that the manager can effectively deal with it.

18/3/2   Forecasting Organization and Sponsorship

As a starting point in developing a forecasting function, the organization's forecasting needs and readiness for forecasting should be analyzed. Clearly some organizations are in a much better position to initiate a forecasting operation than others. The three factors that seem to be most important in determining an organization's degree of readiness are management's attitudes towards forecasting, the commitment of resources to the task of forecasting, and competence among the forecasting staff. If these conditions are not favorable, it is often better to plan a gradual buildup through additional training rather than to embark on developing a major forecasting function.

Unfortunately, forecasting can be viewed as one of the many fads that have appeared in management circles in the past. Management's attitude toward forecasting is indeed crucial, and the reasons for wanting to develop a forecasting function should be clearly understood so that continuation and long-term development will be possible. It is often useful at the outset to ask very specific questions as to what management hopes to gain from forecasting, how those benefits will be measured, and what will constitute success.

When a competent forecasting staff is not available in the organization, the introductory steps for establishing forecasting are substantial. The organization can hire persons with previous training and experience in forecasting or retrain existing specialists in the organization. The former approach has generally been found to be most successful, particularly with the recent increase in the teaching of quantitative methods at graduate schools of business. Although the specialists still must be trained as to the practical problems of the management use of forecasts, hiring trained forecasters allows an organization to move much more quickly toward its goal of effective forecasting.

In setting up the forecasting organization, a number of problems often arise. With satisfactory planning these can be minimized or avoided. The following problems are among the most common:

1. Mistakes are made in recording data, and these errors cause poor forecasts. As a result, managers may lose confidence in the forecasting staff's ability or the appropriateness of various forecasting techniques.
2. The decision maker may find that forecasting results are not ready when needed, but only become available after the decision has already been made.
3. The manager may not be committed to using the forecasts simply because he does not adequately understand them.
4. Many of the individuals whose contributions are required to make forecasting successful may not feel any need for changing their own procedures and behavior in a way that will adequately support forecasting applications.
5. Because of a lack of complete understanding about the management situation, the forecasting staff may apply an inappropriate methodology and obtain poor forecasts.
6. Accuracy may be overemphasized, and as a result the forecasts may be much more expensive than the situation justifies or than management had anticipated.

There are four general areas in which careful planning and support can eliminate problems such as those listed above. These involve the allocation of responsibility, determining who will make decisions, specifying who is to pay for forecasting applications, and determining who will do the work.

Assigning responsibility

A major mistake organizations often make in establishing a forecasting function is not clearly defining the responsibility and leadership for the overall forecasting effort. Assigning responsibility is particularly important because of the interdisciplinary nature of forecasting applications. Often top management may simply hope that this responsibility will naturally develop and be assumed with time. Such an approach can lead to misunderstandings and friction and cause the forecasting function to get off to a slow start.

The responsibility for developing forecasting applications or some form of forecasting system should be placed under a member of the top management group. This person may be in charge of accounting/control or of some other staff activity within the firm. There is no set rule as to what area is most appropriate. The assignment of responsibilities should fit the organization's past experience and current design. For example, if a company has done well with special projects when a staff individual has been put in charge, then this same pattern of organization will probably work well in the forecasting area. However, if the company as a general rule puts staff specialist responsibility under an operating manager, that pattern will probably work better. The key in assigning responsibility is to be certain that one person has both the responsibility for the success of the forecasting function and the authority to implement the actions necessary to success.

Assigning decision-making authority

There are two kinds of decisions that need to be made in operating a system for forecasting within the organization. The first kind is made by the person responsible for forecasting. That person must make policy decisions as to the role and support that forecasting will give to different managers. The other type of decision is made by persons working on specific projects and applications. The difficulty in these decisions is determining which will be under the control of the forecasting staff and which will be the direct responsibility of the managers or users of the forecasts.

It is clear that many of the smaller technical decisions should be made by the forecasting staff. However, major technical decisions should at least be reviewed by the manager or planner who will use the forecast. It is often appropriate to involve the manager in the final decision as to which forecasting method is to be used. Some of the other areas in which the manager should be involved include determining the need for forecasts, the requirements in each situation, and the frequency with which forecasts will be prepared. As a general rule, organizations must divide decision-making responsibility for forecasting in such a way that the staff can act as a catalyst in getting decisions made and in taking joint responsibility with the users for identifying and implementing new applications. Even in ongoing situations it is important that the forecasting authority be agreed upon by both the staff and operating people. It is only through mutual agreement and understanding that the efficient development of specific applications can be achieved.

Assigning charges for forecasting projects

In answer to the question of who pays for forecasting, it is possible to simply say that the organization itself pays. However, more detailed assignment is needed and can often play an important role in determining the success of specific applications. There will generally be overhead costs for maintenance of the forecasting staff, although the bulk of the forecasting cost should be assignable to individual projects. Past experience has shown that it is often best to assign these costs whenever possible to the organization unit making use of the services. The advantage of this procedure is that the operating manager will be much more inclined to evaluate the benefits of specific forecasts in relationship to their costs than would otherwise be the case. When the organization unit does not have to pay for such forecasts, it may tend to accept and justify any additional information without clearly understanding its use or value.

The process of cost allocation includes developing a budget for each forecasting application. This budget should be part of the initial analysis, and the manager involved should agree to cover the cost of that budget. The forecasting staff can then evaluate the budget limitations and reaffirm its ability to accomplish the agreed-upon objectives within that budget. Also, the user of the forecast will have a clear idea as to costs and benefits and the standards to be used in evaluating specific projects.

When a forecast is being supplied to several subunits in the organization—for example, at the start of a long-range planning cycle—it is often best to assign the forecasting cost in a manner consistent with other similar projects in the company. Thus, if the cost of long-range planning is allocated to general corporate overhead, then the forecasts supplied in connection with that planning should be allocated in the same manner. On the other hand, if such costs are generally assigned to individual divisions, forecasting costs should be so assigned.

Assigning tasks

Determining who will perform each of the work tasks is an important step in a forecasting application. In most large organizations there are three groups (or persons) involved in each forecasting application: the forecasting staff who identifies and carries out the application of forecasting methods, the management user who applies that forecast in decision making and planning, and the computer group who actually makes the computer runs of the forecasting methods required. To coordinate the efforts of these different groups, one person must have responsibility for seeing that the project is completed on schedule and that coordinating procedures are established. Generally, the individual placed in charge of the project should be a member of the forecasting staff. The role of coordinator will vary, depending on the type of forecasting system in operation and the developmental stage of the organization in terms of forecasting expertise.

One of the most common problems in the allocation of the work is scheduling computer support time. Since the computer group is also generally a staff support function, the forecasting people often find it difficult to get the response from the computer staff they feel is necessary. One solution to this problem is to have both staff groups reporting to the same individual. An alternative solution is to establish procedures and priorities for projects and make the computer group responsible for following them.

Developing project teams can be an effective approach in forecasting. While many forecasting situations are small and require the support of only a few people, in other situations the forecasts are used by several organization units and the project may involve considerable complexity. In such cases, team assignments to provide the resources necessary for success of the project may be most helpful. The project team can serve as a communication link to report the progress being made and to ensure that the application will incorporate the needs and requirements of the users. Using project teams also expands the number of people in the organization who understand forecasting and its value.

18/3/3 Integrating Forecasting with Existing Procedures

As indicated previously, an important consideration in organizing the forecasting function is making it consistent with the rest of the organization structure. In addition, forecasting procedures need to be consistent with other planning and operating procedures in the organization. The two areas that are frequently most closely related to forecasting are formal budgeting and planning. Although many organizations have established budgeting and planning systems that do not explicitly include forecasting, these systems usually can get substantial benefits from forecasting. It is useful to examine how the forecasting procedure can be integrated with at least these two functions before attempting to use forecasting in fields such as scheduling, purchasing, inventory control, etc.

In the budgeting process followed in most organizations, an annual cycle is set up that usually includes preparing a budget for the coming year and for each of the subsequent two to four years. Forecasting can play at least two important roles in most budgeting processes. The major one is to actually prepare a budget forecast for each item by using historical relationships. Base forecasts can then be reviewed and modified by management to incorporate new developments and the impact of new decisions. In this role, forecasting can save considerable time in the budgeting process, particularly in areas that are not usually considered as being accurately budgeted. The second function of forecasting in budgeting is to serve as a backup to management's own estimate. In this role the forecast can identify harsh discrepancies that need to be justified.

One of the major differences between these two roles of forecasting in budgeting is the identity of the user. In the first case, the manager responsible for preparing the budget uses the forecasts. In the second, the accounting department responsible for checking the appropriateness of budgets uses them.

An important step in establishing a budgeting procedure that effectively uses forecasting is to assign responsibility for it to the appropriate user. Clearly the accuracy desired by the manager would be different from that required by the accounting department. Thus, the ultimate user must be identified and involved in establishing the forecasting procedure and specifying its performance characteristics.

Timing is also an important consideration. Since budgeting procedures generally follow a very tight time schedule, forecasts must meet the demands of that schedule. In the long run it may be most efficient for the firm to actually adjust its timing to the budgeting cycle so that forecasting can fit the cycle more effectively. Initially, however, that is not practical. Instead, the forecasting application must be designed to fit the existing budgeting procedure.

The potential application of forecasting to formal corporate planning procedures can take on at least three different roles. Two of these are similar to the roles identified for forecasting in the budgeting process. They involve either using forecasts to verify the feasibility and soundness of plans or using them as part of the plan itself. In the first instance the forecast is used by the corporate planning group and in the second, by the manager responsible for preparing the plan. A third role of forecasting in formal planning systems, and one in which it is often most useful, is to establish a basic set of assumptions to be used at the outset of the planning process.

An organization may prepare a set of forecasts for the economy and the industry within which the company operates and distribute them at the outset of the planning cycle. Also, information about competitors, government policies, and technological possibilities can be provided. These details can serve as a basis for the operating managers in developing their individual plans. In this role, forecasting supplies the manager with general information about the environment for the next year or several years. One task of the forecasting staff must be to recognize the differences in strategic and tactical planning needs and to disseminate selected background and forecast information to the appropriate level of management accordingly.

Establishing a forecasting procedure that will serve as a basis for environmental information for planning can in one respect be one of the most difficult types of forecasting applications. The problem is that the forecasts are being prepared for both the corporate planning group and a number of different management users. That makes it much more difficult to determine exactly what forecasts would be most useful and what form they should take. In such a situation the project team approach described earlier is often the most effective. A project team consisting of someone from the forecasting staff, a member of the corporate planning staff, a member of each management group using the forecasts, and possibly a member of the R&D group can work effectively in defining those items that would be most useful. In this situation, however, a single individual must still be given responsibility for seeing that the forecasts are prepared and distributed on time. Many organizations have found that a member of the planning staff is the most appropriate person to have this overall responsibility. This planner can assure that the forecasting procedures are consistent with the planning cycle and can obtain feedback from operating managers as to the appropriateness and usefulness of the forecasts.

In any application of forecasting it is important to take an evolutionary approach. This approach implies that the initial application, far from being perfect in every respect, should be satisfactory and useful and should serve as a starting point from which improvements can be made. Stated another way, it means that the initial application should be at the appropriate level for the user group, rather than be the most sophisticated application the forecasting specialists can devise. Trying to second guess all of the possible problems and possible considerations in a new forecasting situation is impractical if not impossible. It is much more useful to start with something satisfactory and feasible that can be understood by management and then, as more information is obtained through feedback on forecasting performance, to revise and improve the process. Through this iterative procedure an efficient forecasting system can be developed that will fill management's needs in providing accurate and timely forecasts.

18/3/4 Behavioral Changes Required by Implementation

In the final analysis, the behavior of individuals within the company will determine the success or failure of any attempt to establish an effective forecasting function. Individuals involved with forecasting will have to alter their behavior in order to perform the tasks required and take full advantage of the results obtained. It is probably fair to say that the resulting forecasts will have value only if behavioral changes occur. If the decisions made after forecasting is instituted are no different from those made before its adoption, the forecasting procedure is of little or no value.

Considerable work has been done in the past few decades on the problems involved in changing individual behavior. Edward Schein's contributions to research in this area of forecasting are particularly helpful. Schein's model of behavioral change provides some very useful guidelines to the manager considering the changes necessary to apply formal forecasting procedures successfully. A psychologist himself, Schein made an extensive study of brainwashing techniques, from which he developed his model. This model involves a three-step process.

1. *Unfreezing.* First, the person whose behavior is to be changed must perceive a need for making that change. This need can arise either

because the individual feels some aspect of his or her behavior is inadequate, or because the individual identifies the opportunity for improving that behavior.

2. *Change.* The second step in Schein's model is the change itself. Here the person must see the change as his or her own and must incorporate that change into individual behavior patterns. This step requires that the person be fully involved in developing and implementing the change.

3. *Refreezing.* The final step is that of refreezing. The change that has been made in the second step must be personally incorporated into the individual's everyday pattern of behavior. Effective refreezing ensures that the individual will not easily go back to former behavioral patterns.

Some examples of how unfreezing, change, and refreezing have been used will help to illustrate their relevance in forecasting situations. The first example comes from a course in speed reading called *Reading Dynamics*. This course advertises that readers can triple their reading speed within a very short period of time. To unfreeze the individual, the Reading Dynamics Institute offers free introductory sessions to demonstrate how easy it is to improve reading speed and to convince the individual of the need for making such an improvement. The institute then offers teaching sessions on speed reading techniques in which the individual makes the behavioral changes required for faster reading. Finally, for refreezing, the institute offers "whip" sessions or refresher sessions that aim at reenforcing the individual's use of the technique and ensuring that old reading habits do not return.

This three-step process of unfreezing, change, and refreezing can be used by people who wish to change their own behavior or the behavior of others who are involved in making the forecasting procedure successful. Many of the problems outlined earlier in this chapter can actually be traced to a failure at one of these three stages of behavioral change. For example, the failure of the manager to use the forecast in making decisions could well be the result of a weak refreezing following the change in behavior. The manager may be well aware of the need for forecasting and may feel that the forecasting procedure is appropriate, but perhaps the manager has not followed the procedure for a sufficient length of time to ensure appropriate refreezing. As a result, the forecast may not be used effectively.

Again, the data may not be available on time because the person collecting the data feels no urgency to have it prepared according to the time schedule specified by the forecasting group. This problem typically occurs when those implementing the forecasting system fail to make the person who is collecting the data feel that the need to get the data on time is of personal importance. If the clerk or accountant who gathers the data does not personally feel that the required change in procedures is worth the trouble perhaps because it was proposed by someone else and is not fully understood, the change is unlikely to be carried out effectively.

Before the manager can expect behavioral change to occur in a manner that effectively supports forecasting, the steps required to successfully use a given forecasting procedure must be clear to the manager. It is usually best to put them in writing so that each person's responsibility can be checked from time to time and any failures in the application of the forecasting system can be easily analyzed and corrected. In this sense, establishing a forecasting system can be extremely useful, since it outlines the steps needed to apply forecasting.

By way of summary, it is useful to consider some of the characteristics researchers have identified as contributing to successful forecasting applications. As one would anticipate, success in applying formalized forecasting methods is closely related to the type of manager who is using the forecasts. Three characteristics seem to contribute to successful managerial use of forecasts.

First, the manager understands the situation for which the forecast is to be prepared and knows what is required for successful decision making in that area. This knowledge ensures that forecasts are prepared for appropriate situations and their integration into decision making can be handled effectively.

Second, the manager must be interested in real improvements in decision making. A manager who simply implements a forecasting procedure because the boss thought it was a good idea will never be as successful as a manager who adopts forecasting because of a real desire to improve personal decision making and planning ability.

Third, the manager must understand the forecasting technique and its value. Even in a large firm where adequate staff support is available, only when the manager takes time to become familiar with the fundamental concepts of the forecasting technique and its strengths and weaknesses is the forecast likely to have significant value.

Another aspect of successful forecasting application is the environment in a company. Elements of this aspect include communicating successful application to others, training managers in regard to general procedures for application of forecasting techniques, obtaining top management support to such applications, training forecasters as to the management tasks important to the company and introducing them to the managers performing those tasks, and providing the resources necessary for those involved in forecasting.

Finally, the situation itself is important in ensuring forecasting success. Situations must be chosen in which the opportunity for reducing uncertainty and improving decision making are substantial. Although it may be easy to use forecasting on well-established problems where substantial historical data is available, the firm's decision-making procedures in many such areas are also well developed. Thus, there is little room for improvement, even with formal forecasting. Instead, what is needed are situations in which there are opportunities for substantial improvements and in which the managers are interested in improving their own personal decision making.

18/4 Organizing for Individual Forecasting Projects

There are a number of ways in which the task of successfully directing and implementing a specific forecasting application can be described. The most common way in the literature is to describe the technical tasks that must be performed by the forecasting specialist in order to complete the application and obtain a forecast. Since those technical aspects have repeatedly been the focus of attention in previous chapters, that is not the approach that will be taken here. Rather, the focus will be on what might be called a marketing procedure for handling forecasting applications. It has been the authors' observation that those people who are generally most successful at forecasting not only possess the necessary skills and abilities to perform the technical tasks required, but also understand and utilize some very fundamental marketing concepts in managing the project.

The focus in this section will be on an approach that effectively utilizes basic marketing concepts. The interaction between the approach itself and some of the technical requirements involved in forecasting will also be discussed. Clearly there will be many possible variations in handling individual forecasting projects. The intent here is simply to provide one complete framework so that the reader can vary that or build upon it in accordance with individual needs.

A good starting point for describing the essential procedural tasks in a specific forecasting application is to examine the basic steps involved in any marketing situation. These might be summarized as the *elements* of marketing, shown in Table 18-4.

Using Table 18-14 as a guide, one can discuss the individual steps as they relate to specific applications of forecasting. The first step, that of market research, involves determining what is wanted so that it can subsequently be coordinated with what it is possible to deliver. This step involves dealing directly with the manager and those who work with the manager (user group) in order to understand their operations and the way they interact with the balance of the organization. Some of the assessments that must be made at this stage are determining what can be done with forecasting technology and assessing the ability of the user group to absorb the technology. This amounts to determining the stage of development of that user group (as opposed to relying on the stage of development of the forecasting group). The effective determination of wants and needs is a critical element to all of the subsequent steps in the process. The literature is replete with applications of technical problem-solving techniques in which either the wrong problem was solved or a problem was solved that was of little or no value to the potential user. These difficulties can be avoided through adequate market research.

TABLE 18-14 BASIC ELEMENTS OF MARKETING

Market Research—Determining what the customer wants.
1. The customer's goal is *not* to keep the forecaster in business.
2. The customer doesn't always know what he or she wants. The customer who does know, may be unwilling to tell the forecaster what it is.
3. What the customer says is wanted and what is actually wanted may be two different things.
4. What the customer wants may not be what the customer needs.

Product Design—Developing a product that will satisfy the customer's wants. In addition to the product itself, product design includes:
1. Price
2. Delivery
3. Convenience
4. Style

Selling—Convincing the customer that the product will satisfy his or her wants at acceptable cost. The important steps in selling include:
1. Qualifying the prospective customer.
2. Establishing the forecaster's credibility.
3. Knowing the customer.
4. Knowing the product.
5. Selling benefits not features. (It should be noted that features usually increase cost, while benefits increase value.)
6. Taking the order. (One of the most prevalent failings of salespersons is not asking for the order.)

Product Creation
1. Develop the product as agreed upon.
2. Get customer input on major options identified during product development.
3. Continue to market the product actually being developed.

Delivery—Delivering a product that meets the customer's wants:
1. As specified and as expected
2. On time
3. At quoted cost

Service—Ensuring that the product continues to meet the customer's wants.
1. Maintenance
2. Postaudit of costs and benefits
3. Identification of new wants and opportunities arising from use of the product (Repeat the entire cycle.)

Source: G. M. Hoffman, "Selling Operations Research to Management," presented at TIMS/ORSA '75, Chicago, April 30–May 2, 1975. Reprinted by permission.

The second step is that of product design—developing a product that will meet the customer's wants. Central to this stage is reaching agreement between the forecaster and the user as to the product to be delivered, its specifications, and the performance standards that will be used to evaluate it. An integral part of this step is also avoiding what might be termed technological overkill. Woolsey (1975, p. 169) has hypothesized the following law in this regard: "A manager would rather live with a problem that he cannot tolerate than use a solution he cannot understand." A final important aspect of this step is considering the manager-machine problems that may be inherent in the product to be delivered. These include such things as data input requirements, report content and format, and ease and convenience of use. At this stage the designer must be aware of the need for eventual behavioral change if the application is to realize its full potential and must design the product so that the behavioral change can most easily be made.

The third step is that of selling—convincing the customer than the product will in fact satisfy the customer's wants. Expanding on some of the elements in Table 18-14 can provide a useful overview of some of the tasks the forecaster must bear in mind at this stage. In order to qualify the prospect, the forecaster must determine whether the customer has the authority to buy the product and whether the customer has the inclination to buy. If the latter requirement is not met, it may not be worth the effort to try to change the customer's mind. It may be better to seek initial applications elsewhere. To establish credibility, the forecaster must rely on past successes, establish a history of fulfilling promises, and acknowledge incidents of failure in the past.

Further aspects of selling involve knowing the customer and the customer's operations. This knowledge includes understanding the customer's ability and willingness to cope with technology and with change. The forecaster must also know the product. This knowledge is necessary along practical dimensions as well as along technical dimensions. Important considerations in designing the product are determining what data can be obtained (and what it will cost), what turnaround can actually be achieved, and how useful (partially reflected by accuracy) the resulting forecast will be. Many times such questions regarding the product and its delivery are the most challenging to the expert forecaster.

Perhaps one of the most important aspects of selling the product is selling benefits and not features. Features include such things as the sophistication and intricacies of the model to be used in forecasting. The benefits (the manager's real concern), include the impact of the forecast in that particular decision-making situation, the kinds of risks that improved forecasting will be able to reduce, and the time that accurate forecasts may be able to save the decision maker.

The final stage of selling, and one that is usually done badly by all sales-people, particularly forecasters, is taking the order—that is, getting the specifications down in writing. The forecaster must know when to stop selling (rather than forcing the manager to listen to the complete presentation) and when to take no for an answer.

Another important aspect of selling is that although listed as the third step, it actually goes on continuously throughout the project, particularly as the fourth step is entered.

The fourth step is developing the product to be delivered. In many management science applications, the product development is fairly removed from the management user. The management scientist follows the first three steps in Table 18-14 and then goes off to do step four and does not return to the manager until step five. However, in most forecasting situations that is not practical. As additional information is received on the forecasting situation and as preliminary results are obtained, the manager should be involved in assessing them and determining what refinements are necessary before the procedure is agreed upon. During the process of development, the product and its benefits should not be completely changed from their initial definition, since that would reduce the manager's confidence in the forecasting staff's ability to deliver. However, the manager should know what is happening during development so that when the product is completed it will be usable and will incorporate those essential features that will make it most successful. In these stages of interaction, continued selling as well as solving the technical problems should be the guideline for the forecaster.

The fifth step is that of delivering the product. Essentially, it involves being certain that the product has been adequately tested and validated before it is delivered and turned over to the manager and that the manager knows how it works. Clearly, as with any product being sold, the forecasting application must be delivered on time and within budget if the manager is to be fully satisfied.

The final step in the individual application is that of ongoing service. This step involves maintaining (including debugging and making minor modifications) and performing postaudits of the application's costs and benefits. Such postaudits might be performed at the time it is installed, after six months, and again after a year, if it continues to be used. Two important aspects of this step are that the user must have solid reinforcement to support the refreezing phase of behavioral change, and the forecasting group must recognize the additional opportunities and needs that exist, once the first few forecasting applications have been made. This final step of service, in fact, often becomes the first step of market research for the next forecasting application.

REFERENCES AND SELECTED BIBLIOGRAPHY

Armstrong, J. S., and M. C. Grohman. 1972. "A Comparative Study of Methods for Long-Range Market Forecasting." *Management Science*, Vol. 19, No. 2, October, pp. 211–21.

Bell, E. C. 1968. "Practical Long-Range Planning." *Business Horizons*, December, pp. 45–49.

Dalrymple, D. J. 1975a. "Sales Forecasting Methods and Accuracy." *Business Horizons*, December, pp. 69–73.

———. 1975b. "Sales Forecasting Methods and Accuracy." Working paper, Marketing Department, School of Business, Indiana University, Bloomington, Ind., September.

Elton, E. J., and M. J. Gruber. 1972. "Earnings Estimates and the Accuracy of Expectational Data." *Management Science*, Vol. 18, No. 8, April, pp. 409–24.

Hoffman, G. M. 1975. "Selling Operations Research to Management." Presented at TIMS/ORSA, 1975, Chicago, April 30–May 2.

McLaughlin, R. L., and J. J. Boyle. 1968. *Short-Term Forecasting*. New York: American Marketing Association.

Makridakis, S. 1971. "The Whys and Wherefores of the Systems Approach." *European Business*, No. 30, Summer, pp. 64–70.

Makridakis, S., and S. C. Wheelwright. 1978. *Interactive Forecasting*, 2nd ed. San Francisco: Holden-Day.

Schein, E. H. 1961. "Management Development as a Process of Influence." *Industrial Management Review*, Vol. 2, No. 2, May.

Wheelwright, S. C., and Darral G. Clarke. 1976. "Corporate Forecasting: Promise and Reality." *Harvard Business Review*, Vol. 54, No. 6, November–December, pp. 40 ff.

Wheelwright, S. C., and S. Makridakis. 1977. *Forecasting Methods for Management*, 2nd ed. New York: John Wiley & Sons.

Woolsey, R. E. D., and H. F. Swanson. 1975. *Operations Research for Immediate Application: A Quick and Dirty Manual*. New York: Harper & Row.

APPENDIX I
STATISTICAL TABLES

TABLE A AREAS UNDER THE NORMAL CURVE

An entry in the table is the proportion under the entire curve that is between $z = 0$ and a positive value of z. Areas for negative values of z are obtained by symmetry.

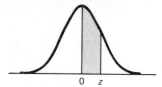

Second decimal place of z

z	.00	.01	.02	.03	.04	.05	.06	.07	.08	.09
0.0	.0000	.0040	.0080	.0120	.0160	.0199	.0239	.0279	.0319	.0359
0.1	.0398	.0438	.0478	.0517	.0557	.0596	.0636	.0675	.0714	.0753
0.2	.0793	.0832	.0871	.0910	.0948	.0987	.1026	.0164	.1103	.1141
0.3	.1179	.1217	.1255	.1293	.1331	.1368	.1406	.1443	.1480	.1517
0.4	.1554	.1591	.1628	.1664	.1700	.1736	.1772	.1808	.1844	.1879
0.5	.1915	.1950	.1985	.2019	.2054	.2088	.2123	.2157	.2190	.2224
0.6	.2257	.2291	.2324	.2357	.2389	.2422	.2454	.2486	.2517	.2549
0.7	.2580	.2611	.2642	.2673	.2703	.2734	.2764	.2794	.2823	.2852
0.8	.2881	.2910	.2939	.2967	.2995	.3023	.3051	.3078	.3106	.3133
0.9	.3159	.3186	.3212	.3238	.3264	.3289	.3315	.3340	.3365	.3389
1.0	.3413	.3438	.3461	.3485	.3508	.3531	.3554	.3577	.3599	.3621
1.1	.3643	.3665	.3686	.3708	.3729	.3749	.3770	.3790	.3810	.3830
1.2	.3849	.3869	.3888	.3907	.3925	.3944	.3962	.3980	.3997	.4015
1.3	.4032	.4049	.4066	.4082	.4099	.4115	.4131	.4147	.4162	.4177
1.4	.4192	.4207	.4222	.4236	.4251	.4265	.4279	.4292	.4306	.4319
1.5	.4332	.4345	.4357	.4370	.4382	.4394	.4406	.4418	.4429	.4441
1.6	.4452	.4463	.4474	.4484	.4495	.4505	.4515	.4525	.4535	.4545
1.7	.4554	.4564	.4573	.4582	.4591	.4599	.4608	.4616	.4625	.4633
1.8	.4641	.4649	.4656	.4664	.4671	.4678	.4686	.4693	.4699	.4706
1.9	.4713	.4719	.4726	.4732	.4738	.4744	.4750	.4756	.4761	.4767
2.0	.4772	.4778	.4783	.4788	.4793	.4798	.4803	.4808	.4812	.4817
2.1	.4821	.4826	.4830	.4834	.4838	.4842	.4846	.4850	.4854	.4857
2.2	.4861	.4864	.4868	.4871	.4875	.4878	.4881	.4884	.4887	.4890
2.3	.4893	.4896	.4898	.4901	.4904	.4906	.4909	.4911	.4913	.4916
2.4	.4918	.4920	.4922	.4925	.4927	.4929	.4931	.4932	.4934	.4936
2.5	.4938	.4940	.4941	.4943	.4945	.4946	.4948	.4949	.4951	.4952
2.6	.4953	.4955	.4956	.4957	.4959	.4960	.4961	.4962	.4963	.4964
2.7	.4965	.4966	.4967	.4968	.4969	.4970	.4971	.4972	.4973	.4974
2.8	.4974	.4975	.4976	.4977	.4977	.4978	.4979	.4979	.4980	.4981
2.9	.4981	.4982	.4982	.4983	.4984	.4984	.4985	.4985	.4986	.4986
3.0	.4987	.4987	.4987	.4988	.4988	.4989	.4989	.4989	.4990	.4990

Source: Donald J. Koosis, Business Statistics *(New York: John Wiley & Sons, 1972). Reprinted by permission.*

TABLE B   STUDENT t DISTRIBUTION

The first column lists the number of degrees of freedom (k). The headings of the other columns give probabilities (P) for t to exceed the entry value. Use symmetry for negative t values.

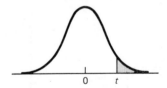

df \ P	.10	.05	.025	.01	.005
1	3.078	6.314	12.706	31.821	63.657
2	1.886	2.920	4.303	6.965	9.925
3	1.638	2.353	3.182	4.541	5.841
4	1.533	2.132	2.776	3.747	4.604
5	1.476	2.015	2.571	3.365	4.032
6	1.440	1.943	2.447	3.143	3.707
7	1.415	1.895	2.365	2.998	3.499
8	1.397	1.860	2.306	2.896	3.355
9	1.383	1.833	2.262	2.821	3.250
10	1.372	1.812	2.228	2.764	3.169
11	1.363	1.796	2.201	2.718	3.106
12	1.356	1.782	2.179	2.681	3.055
13	1.350	1.771	2.160	2.650	3.012
14	1.345	1.761	2.145	2.624	2.977
15	1.341	1.753	2.131	2.602	2.947
16	1.337	1.746	2.120	2.583	2.921
17	1.333	1.740	2.110	2.567	2.898
18	1.330	1.734	2.101	2.552	2.878
19	1.328	1.729	2.093	2.539	2.861
20	1.325	1.725	2.086	2.528	2.845
21	1.323	1.721	2.080	2.518	2.831
22	1.321	1.717	2.074	2.508	2.819
23	1.319	1.714	2.069	2.500	2.807
24	1.318	1.711	2.064	2.492	2.797
25	1.316	1.708	2.060	2.485	2.787
26	1.315	1.706	2.056	2.479	2.779
27	1.314	1.703	2.052	2.473	2.771
28	1.313	1.701	2.048	2.467	2.763
29	1.311	1.699	2.045	2.462	2.756
30	1.310	1.697	2.042	2.457	2.750
40	1.303	1.684	2.021	2.423	2.704
60	1.296	1.671	2.000	2.390	2.660
120	1.289	1.658	1.980	2.358	2.617
∞	1.282	1.645	1.960	2.326	2.576

Source: Donald J. Koosis, Business Statistics (New York: John Wiley & Sons, 1972). Reprinted by permission.

TABLE C   VALUES OF THE *F*-TEST

Degrees of Freedom for Numerator (df_1)

Degrees of Freedom for Denominator (df_2)	1	2	3	4	5	6	7	8	9	10	11	12	14	16	20	24	30	40	50	75	100	200	500	∞
1	161 *4052*	200 *4999*	216 *5403*	225 *5625*	230 *5764*	234 *5859*	237 *5928*	239 *5981*	241 *6022*	242 *6056*	243 *6082*	244 *6106*	245 *6142*	246 *6169*	248 *6208*	249 *6234*	250 *6258*	251 *6286*	252 *6302*	253 *6323*	253 *6334*	254 *6352*	254 *6361*	254 *6366*
2	18.51 *98.49*	19.00 *99.01*	19.16 *99.17*	19.25 *99.25*	19.30 *99.30*	19.33 *99.33*	19.36 *99.34*	19.37 *99.36*	19.38 *99.38*	19.39 *99.40*	19.40 *99.41*	19.41 *99.42*	19.42 *99.43*	19.43 *99.44*	19.44 *99.45*	19.45 *99.46*	19.46 *99.47*	19.47 *99.48*	19.47 *99.48*	19.48 *99.49*	19.49 *99.49*	19.49 *99.49*	19.50 *99.50*	19.50 *99.50*
3	10.13 *34.12*	9.55 *30.81*	9.28 *29.46*	9.12 *28.71*	9.01 *28.24*	8.94 *27.91*	8.88 *27.67*	8.84 *27.49*	8.81 *27.34*	8.78 *27.23*	8.76 *27.13*	8.74 *27.05*	8.71 *26.92*	8.69 *26.83*	8.66 *26.69*	8.64 *26.60*	8.62 *26.50*	8.60 *26.41*	8.58 *26.30*	8.57 *26.27*	8.56 *26.23*	8.54 *26.18*	8.54 *26.14*	8.53 *26.12*
4	7.71 *21.20*	6.94 *18.00*	6.59 *16.69*	6.39 *15.98*	6.26 *15.52*	6.16 *15.21*	6.09 *14.98*	6.04 *14.80*	6.00 *14.66*	5.96 *14.54*	5.93 *14.45*	5.91 *14.37*	5.87 *14.24*	5.84 *14.15*	5.80 *14.02*	5.77 *13.93*	5.74 *13.83*	5.71 *13.74*	5.70 *13.69*	5.68 *13.61*	5.66 *13.57*	5.65 *13.52*	5.64 *13.48*	5.63 *13.46*
5	6.61 *16.26*	5.79 *13.27*	5.41 *12.06*	5.19 *11.39*	5.05 *10.97*	4.95 *10.67*	4.88 *10.45*	4.82 *10.27*	4.78 *10.15*	4.74 *10.05*	4.70 *9.96*	4.68 *9.89*	4.64 *9.77*	4.60 *9.68*	4.56 *9.55*	4.53 *9.47*	4.50 *9.38*	4.46 *9.29*	4.44 *9.24*	4.42 *9.17*	4.40 *9.13*	4.38 *9.07*	4.37 *9.04*	4.36 *9.02*
6	5.99 *13.74*	5.14 *10.92*	4.76 *9.78*	4.53 *9.15*	4.39 *8.75*	4.28 *8.47*	4.21 *8.26*	4.15 *8.10*	4.10 *7.98*	4.06 *7.87*	4.03 *7.79*	4.00 *7.72*	3.96 *7.60*	3.92 *7.52*	3.87 *7.39*	3.84 *7.31*	3.81 *7.23*	3.77 *7.14*	3.75 *7.09*	3.72 *7.02*	3.71 *6.99*	3.69 *6.94*	3.68 *6.90*	3.67 *6.88*
7	5.59 *12.25*	4.74 *9.55*	4.35 *8.45*	4.12 *7.85*	3.97 *7.46*	3.87 *7.19*	3.79 *7.00*	3.73 *6.84*	3.68 *6.71*	3.63 *6.62*	3.60 *6.54*	3.57 *6.47*	3.52 *6.35*	3.49 *6.27*	3.44 *6.15*	3.41 *6.07*	3.38 *5.98*	3.34 *5.90*	3.32 *5.85*	3.29 *5.78*	3.28 *5.75*	3.25 *5.70*	3.24 *5.67*	3.23 *5.65*
8	5.32 *11.26*	4.46 *8.65*	4.07 *7.59*	3.84 *7.01*	3.69 *6.63*	3.58 *6.37*	3.50 *6.19*	3.44 *6.03*	3.39 *5.91*	3.34 *5.82*	3.31 *5.74*	3.28 *5.67*	3.23 *5.56*	3.20 *5.48*	3.15 *5.36*	3.12 *5.28*	3.08 *5.20*	3.05 *5.11*	3.03 *5.06*	3.00 *5.00*	2.98 *4.96*	2.96 *4.91*	2.94 *4.88*	2.93 *4.86*
9	5.12 *10.56*	4.26 *8.02*	3.86 *6.99*	3.63 *6.42*	3.48 *6.06*	3.37 *5.80*	3.29 *5.62*	3.23 *5.47*	3.18 *5.35*	3.13 *5.26*	3.10 *5.18*	3.07 *5.11*	3.02 *5.00*	2.98 *4.92*	2.93 *4.80*	2.90 *4.73*	2.86 *4.64*	2.82 *4.56*	2.80 *4.51*	2.77 *4.45*	2.76 *4.41*	2.73 *4.36*	2.72 *4.33*	2.71 *4.31*
10	4.96 *10.04*	4.10 *7.56*	3.71 *6.55*	3.48 *5.99*	3.33 *5.64*	3.22 *5.39*	3.14 *5.21*	3.07 *5.06*	3.02 *4.95*	2.97 *4.85*	2.94 *4.78*	2.91 *4.71*	2.86 *4.60*	2.82 *4.52*	2.77 *4.41*	2.74 *4.33*	2.70 *4.25*	2.67 *4.17*	2.64 *4.12*	2.61 *4.05*	2.59 *4.01*	2.56 *3.96*	2.55 *3.93*	2.54 *3.91*

Note: 5% points for the distribution of *F* are presented in roman type; 1% points are in italic type.
Source: Donald J. Koosis. Business Statistics (New York: John Wiley & Sons, 1972). Reprinted by permission.

TABLE C   Continued

Degrees of Freedom for Numerator (df_1)

Degrees of Freedom for Denominator (df_2)	1	2	3	4	5	6	7	8	9	10	11	12	14	16	20	24	30	40	50	75	100	200	500	∞
11	4.84 / 9.65	3.98 / 7.20	3.59 / 6.22	3.36 / 5.67	3.20 / 5.32	3.09 / 5.07	3.01 / 4.88	2.95 / 4.74	2.90 / 4.63	2.86 / 4.54	2.82 / 4.46	2.79 / 4.40	2.74 / 4.29	2.70 / 4.21	2.65 / 4.10	2.61 / 4.02	2.57 / 3.94	2.53 / 3.86	2.50 / 3.80	2.47 / 3.74	2.45 / 3.70	2.42 / 3.66	2.41 / 3.62	2.40 / 3.60
12	4.75 / 9.33	3.88 / 6.93	3.49 / 5.95	3.26 / 5.41	3.11 / 5.06	3.00 / 4.82	2.92 / 4.65	2.85 / 4.50	2.80 / 4.39	2.76 / 4.30	2.72 / 4.22	2.69 / 4.16	2.64 / 4.05	2.60 / 3.98	2.54 / 3.86	2.50 / 3.78	2.46 / 3.70	2.42 / 3.61	2.40 / 3.56	2.36 / 3.49	2.35 / 3.46	2.32 / 3.41	2.31 / 3.38	2.30 / 3.36
13	4.67 / 9.07	3.80 / 6.70	3.41 / 5.74	3.18 / 5.20	3.02 / 4.86	2.92 / 4.62	2.84 / 4.44	2.77 / 4.30	2.72 / 4.19	2.67 / 4.10	2.63 / 4.02	2.60 / 3.96	2.55 / 3.85	2.51 / 3.78	2.46 / 3.67	2.42 / 3.59	2.38 / 3.51	2.34 / 3.42	2.32 / 3.37	2.28 / 3.30	2.26 / 3.37	2.24 / 3.21	2.22 / 3.18	2.21 / 3.16
14	4.60 / 8.86	3.74 / 6.51	3.34 / 5.56	3.11 / 5.03	2.96 / 4.69	2.85 / 4.46	2.77 / 4.28	2.70 / 4.14	2.65 / 4.03	2.60 / 3.94	2.56 / 3.86	2.53 / 3.80	2.48 / 3.70	2.44 / 3.62	2.39 / 3.51	2.35 / 3.43	2.31 / 3.34	2.27 / 3.26	2.24 / 3.21	2.21 / 3.14	2.19 / 3.11	2.16 / 3.06	2.14 / 3.02	2.13 / 3.00
15	4.54 / 8.68	3.68 / 6.36	3.29 / 5.42	3.06 / 4.89	2.90 / 4.56	2.79 / 4.32	2.70 / 4.14	2.64 / 4.00	2.59 / 3.89	2.55 / 3.80	2.51 / 3.73	2.48 / 3.67	2.43 / 3.56	2.39 / 3.48	2.33 / 3.36	2.29 / 3.29	2.25 / 3.20	2.21 / 3.12	2.18 / 3.07	2.15 / 3.00	2.12 / 2.97	2.10 / 2.92	2.08 / 2.89	2.07 / 2.87
16	4.49 / 8.53	3.63 / 6.23	3.24 / 5.29	3.01 / 4.77	2.85 / 4.44	2.74 / 4.20	2.66 / 4.03	2.59 / 3.89	2.54 / 3.78	2.49 / 3.69	2.45 / 3.61	2.42 / 3.55	2.37 / 3.45	2.33 / 3.37	2.28 / 3.25	2.24 / 3.18	2.20 / 3.10	2.16 / 3.01	2.13 / 2.96	2.09 / 2.89	2.07 / 2.86	2.04 / 2.80	2.02 / 2.77	2.01 / 2.75
17	4.45 / 8.40	3.59 / 6.11	3.20 / 5.18	2.96 / 4.67	2.81 / 4.34	2.70 / 4.10	2.62 / 3.93	2.55 / 3.79	2.50 / 3.68	2.45 / 3.59	2.41 / 3.52	2.38 / 3.45	2.33 / 3.35	2.29 / 3.27	2.23 / 3.16	2.19 / 3.08	2.15 / 3.00	2.11 / 2.92	2.08 / 2.86	2.04 / 2.79	2.02 / 2.76	1.99 / 2.70	1.97 / 2.67	1.96 / 2.65
18	4.41 / 8.28	3.55 / 6.01	3.16 / 5.09	2.93 / 4.58	2.77 / 4.25	2.66 / 4.01	2.58 / 3.85	2.51 / 3.71	2.46 / 3.60	2.41 / 3.51	2.37 / 3.44	2.34 / 3.37	2.29 / 3.27	2.25 / 3.19	2.19 / 3.07	2.15 / 3.00	2.11 / 2.91	2.07 / 2.83	2.04 / 2.78	2.00 / 2.71	1.98 / 2.68	1.95 / 2.62	1.93 / 2.59	1.92 / 2.57
19	4.38 / 8.18	3.52 / 5.93	3.13 / 5.01	2.90 / 4.50	2.74 / 4.17	2.63 / 3.94	2.55 / 3.77	2.48 / 3.63	2.43 / 3.52	2.38 / 3.43	2.34 / 3.36	2.31 / 3.30	2.26 / 3.19	2.21 / 3.12	2.15 / 3.00	2.11 / 2.92	2.07 / 2.84	2.02 / 2.76	2.00 / 2.70	1.96 / 2.63	1.94 / 2.60	1.91 / 2.54	1.90 / 2.51	1.88 / 2.49
20	4.35 / 8.10	3.49 / 5.85	3.10 / 4.94	2.87 / 4.43	2.71 / 4.10	2.60 / 3.87	2.52 / 3.71	2.45 / 3.56	2.40 / 3.45	2.35 / 3.37	2.31 / 3.30	2.28 / 3.23	2.23 / 3.13	2.18 / 3.05	2.12 / 2.94	2.08 / 2.86	2.04 / 2.77	1.99 / 2.69	1.96 / 2.63	1.92 / 2.56	1.90 / 2.53	1.87 / 2.47	1.85 / 2.44	1.84 / 2.42
21	4.32 / 8.02	3.47 / 5.78	3.07 / 4.87	2.84 / 4.37	2.68 / 4.04	2.57 / 3.81	2.49 / 3.65	2.42 / 3.51	2.37 / 3.40	2.32 / 3.31	2.28 / 3.24	2.25 / 3.17	2.20 / 3.07	2.15 / 2.99	2.09 / 2.88	2.05 / 2.80	2.00 / 2.72	1.96 / 2.63	1.93 / 2.58	1.89 / 2.51	1.87 / 2.47	1.84 / 2.42	1.82 / 2.38	1.81 / 2.36
22	4.30 / 7.94	3.44 / 5.72	3.05 / 4.82	2.82 / 4.31	2.66 / 3.99	2.55 / 3.76	2.47 / 3.59	2.40 / 3.45	2.35 / 3.35	2.30 / 3.26	2.26 / 3.18	2.23 / 3.12	2.18 / 3.02	2.13 / 2.94	2.07 / 2.83	2.03 / 2.75	1.98 / 2.67	1.93 / 2.58	1.91 / 2.53	1.87 / 2.46	1.84 / 2.42	1.81 / 2.37	1.80 / 2.33	1.78 / 2.31
23	4.28 / 7.88	3.42 / 5.66	3.03 / 4.76	2.80 / 4.26	2.64 / 3.94	2.53 / 3.71	2.45 / 3.54	2.38 / 3.41	2.32 / 3.30	2.28 / 3.21	2.24 / 3.14	2.20 / 3.07	2.14 / 2.97	2.10 / 2.89	2.04 / 2.78	2.00 / 2.70	1.96 / 2.62	1.91 / 2.53	1.88 / 2.48	1.84 / 2.41	1.82 / 2.37	1.79 / 2.32	1.77 / 2.28	1.76 / 2.26
24	4.26 / 7.82	3.40 / 5.61	3.01 / 4.72	2.78 / 4.22	2.62 / 3.90	2.51 / 3.67	2.43 / 3.50	2.36 / 3.36	2.30 / 3.25	2.26 / 3.17	2.22 / 3.09	2.18 / 3.03	2.13 / 2.93	2.09 / 2.85	2.02 / 2.74	1.98 / 2.66	1.94 / 2.58	1.89 / 2.49	1.86 / 2.44	1.82 / 2.36	1.80 / 2.33	1.76 / 2.27	1.74 / 2.23	1.73 / 2.21

TABLE C *Continued*

Degrees of Freedom for Numerator (df_1)

df_2	1	2	3	4	5	6	7	8	9	10	11	12	14	16	20	24	30	40	50	75	100	200	500	∞
25	4.24 / 7.77	3.38 / 5.57	2.99 / 4.68	2.76 / 4.18	2.60 / 3.86	2.49 / 3.63	2.41 / 3.46	2.34 / 3.32	2.28 / 3.21	2.24 / 3.13	2.20 / 3.05	2.16 / 2.99	2.11 / 2.89	2.06 / 2.81	2.00 / 2.70	1.96 / 2.62	1.92 / 2.54	1.87 / 2.45	1.84 / 2.40	1.80 / 2.32	1.77 / 2.29	1.74 / 2.23	1.72 / 2.19	1.71 / 2.17
26	4.22 / 7.72	3.37 / 5.53	2.89 / 4.64	2.74 / 4.14	2.59 / 3.82	2.47 / 3.59	2.39 / 3.42	2.32 / 3.29	2.27 / 3.17	2.22 / 3.09	2.18 / 3.02	2.15 / 2.96	2.10 / 2.86	2.05 / 2.77	1.99 / 2.66	1.95 / 2.58	1.90 / 2.50	1.85 / 2.41	1.82 / 2.36	1.78 / 2.28	1.76 / 2.25	1.72 / 2.19	1.70 / 2.15	1.69 / 2.13
27	4.21 / 7.68	3.35 / 5.49	2.96 / 4.60	2.73 / 4.11	2.57 / 3.79	2.46 / 3.56	2.37 / 3.39	2.30 / 3.26	2.25 / 3.14	2.20 / 3.06	2.16 / 2.98	2.13 / 2.93	2.08 / 2.83	2.03 / 2.74	1.97 / 2.63	1.93 / 2.55	1.88 / 2.47	1.84 / 2.38	1.80 / 2.33	1.76 / 2.25	1.74 / 2.21	1.71 / 2.16	1.68 / 2.12	1.67 / 2.10
28	4.20 / 7.64	3.34 / 5.45	2.95 / 4.57	2.71 / 4.07	2.56 / 3.76	2.44 / 3.53	2.36 / 3.36	2.29 / 3.23	2.24 / 3.11	2.19 / 3.03	2.15 / 2.95	2.12 / 2.90	2.06 / 2.80	2.02 / 2.71	1.96 / 2.60	1.91 / 2.52	1.87 / 2.44	1.81 / 2.35	1.78 / 2.30	1.75 / 2.22	1.72 / 2.18	1.69 / 2.13	1.67 / 2.09	1.65 / 2.06
29	4.18 / 7.60	3.33 / 5.52	2.93 / 4.54	2.70 / 4.04	2.54 / 3.73	2.43 / 3.50	2.35 / 3.33	2.28 / 3.20	2.22 / 3.08	2.18 / 3.00	2.14 / 2.92	2.10 / 2.87	2.05 / 2.77	2.00 / 2.68	1.94 / 2.57	1.90 / 2.49	1.85 / 2.41	1.80 / 2.32	1.77 / 2.27	1.73 / 2.19	1.71 / 2.15	1.68 / 2.10	1.65 / 2.06	1.64 / 2.03
30	4.17 / 7.56	3.32 / 5.39	2.92 / 4.51	2.69 / 4.02	2.53 / 3.70	2.42 / 3.47	2.34 / 3.30	2.27 / 3.17	2.21 / 3.06	2.16 / 2.98	2.12 / 2.90	2.09 / 2.84	2.04 / 2.74	1.99 / 2.66	1.93 / 2.55	1.89 / 2.47	1.84 / 2.38	1.79 / 2.29	1.76 / 2.24	1.72 / 2.16	1.69 / 2.13	1.66 / 2.07	1.64 / 2.03	1.62 / 2.01
32	4.15 / 7.50	3.30 / 5.34	2.90 / 4.46	2.67 / 3.97	2.51 / 3.66	2.40 / 3.42	2.32 / 3.25	2.25 / 3.12	2.19 / 3.01	2.14 / 2.94	2.10 / 2.86	2.07 / 2.80	2.02 / 2.70	1.97 / 2.62	1.91 / 2.51	1.86 / 2.42	1.82 / 2.34	1.76 / 2.25	1.74 / 2.20	1.69 / 2.12	1.67 / 2.08	1.64 / 2.02	1.61 / 1.98	1.59 / 1.96
34	4.13 / 7.44	3.28 / 5.29	2.88 / 4.42	2.65 / 3.93	2.49 / 3.61	2.38 / 3.38	2.30 / 3.21	2.23 / 3.08	2.17 / 2.97	2.12 / 2.89	2.08 / 2.82	2.05 / 2.76	2.00 / 2.66	1.95 / 2.58	1.89 / 2.47	1.84 / 2.38	1.80 / 2.30	1.74 / 2.21	1.71 / 2.15	1.67 / 2.08	1.64 / 2.04	1.61 / 1.98	1.59 / 1.94	1.57 / 1.91
36	4.11 / 7.39	3.26 / 5.25	2.86 / 4.38	2.63 / 3.89	2.48 / 3.58	2.36 / 3.35	2.28 / 3.18	2.21 / 3.04	2.15 / 2.94	2.10 / 2.86	2.06 / 2.78	2.03 / 2.72	1.98 / 2.62	1.93 / 2.54	1.87 / 2.43	1.82 / 2.35	1.78 / 2.26	1.72 / 2.17	1.69 / 2.12	1.65 / 2.04	1.62 / 2.00	1.59 / 1.94	1.56 / 1.90	1.55 / 1.87
38	4.10 / 7.35	3.25 / 5.21	2.85 / 4.34	2.62 / 3.86	2.46 / 3.54	2.35 / 3.32	2.26 / 3.15	2.19 / 3.02	2.14 / 2.91	2.09 / 2.82	2.05 / 2.75	2.02 / 2.69	1.96 / 2.59	1.92 / 2.51	1.85 / 2.40	1.80 / 2.32	1.76 / 2.22	1.71 / 2.14	1.67 / 2.08	1.63 / 2.00	1.60 / 1.97	1.57 / 1.90	1.54 / 1.86	1.53 / 1.84
40	4.08 / 7.31	3.23 / 5.18	2.84 / 4.31	2.61 / 3.83	2.45 / 3.51	2.34 / 3.29	2.25 / 3.12	2.18 / 2.99	2.12 / 2.88	2.07 / 2.80	2.04 / 2.73	2.00 / 2.66	1.95 / 2.56	1.90 / 2.49	1.84 / 2.37	1.79 / 2.29	1.74 / 2.20	1.69 / 2.11	1.66 / 2.05	1.61 / 1.97	1.59 / 1.94	1.55 / 1.88	1.53 / 1.84	1.51 / 1.81
42	4.07 / 7.27	3.22 / 5.15	2.83 / 4.29	2.59 / 3.80	2.44 / 3.49	2.32 / 3.26	2.24 / 3.10	2.17 / 2.96	2.11 / 2.86	2.06 / 2.77	2.02 / 2.70	1.99 / 2.64	1.94 / 2.54	1.89 / 2.46	1.82 / 2.35	1.78 / 2.26	1.73 / 2.17	1.68 / 2.08	1.64 / 2.02	1.60 / 1.94	1.57 / 1.91	1.54 / 1.85	1.51 / 1.80	1.49 / 1.78
44	4.06 / 7.24	3.21 / 5.12	2.82 / 4.26	2.58 / 3.78	2.43 / 3.46	2.31 / 3.24	2.23 / 3.07	2.16 / 2.94	2.10 / 2.84	2.05 / 2.75	2.01 / 2.68	1.98 / 2.62	1.92 / 2.52	1.88 / 2.44	1.81 / 2.32	1.76 / 2.24	1.72 / 2.15	1.66 / 2.06	1.63 / 2.00	1.58 / 1.92	1.56 / 1.88	1.52 / 1.82	1.50 / 1.78	1.48 / 1.75
46	4.05 / 7.21	3.20 / 5.10	2.81 / 4.24	2.57 / 3.76	2.42 / 3.44	2.30 / 3.22	2.22 / 3.05	2.14 / 2.92	2.09 / 2.82	2.04 / 2.73	2.00 / 2.66	1.97 / 2.60	1.91 / 2.50	1.87 / 2.42	1.80 / 2.30	1.75 / 2.22	1.71 / 2.13	1.65 / 2.04	1.62 / 1.98	1.57 / 1.90	1.54 / 1.86	1.51 / 1.80	1.48 / 1.76	1.46 / 1.72

Degrees of Freedom for Denominator (df_2)

TABLE C Continued

Each cell shows two values: the upper (roman) and lower (italic) critical value.

df₂												Degrees of Freedom for Numerator (df₁)												
	1	2	3	4	5	6	7	8	9	10	11	12	14	16	20	24	30	40	50	75	100	200	500	∞
48	4.04 / 7.19	3.19 / 5.08	2.80 / 4.22	2.56 / 3.74	2.41 / 3.42	2.30 / 3.20	2.21 / 3.04	2.14 / 2.90	2.08 / 2.80	2.03 / 2.71	1.99 / 2.64	1.96 / 2.58	1.90 / 2.48	1.86 / 2.40	1.79 / 2.28	1.74 / 2.20	1.70 / 2.11	1.64 / 2.02	1.61 / 1.96	1.56 / 1.88	1.53 / 1.84	1.50 / 1.78	1.47 / 1.73	1.45 / 1.70
50	4.03 / 7.17	3.18 / 5.06	2.79 / 4.20	2.56 / 3.72	2.40 / 3.41	2.29 / 3.18	2.20 / 3.02	2.13 / 2.88	2.07 / 2.78	2.02 / 2.70	1.98 / 2.62	1.95 / 2.56	1.90 / 2.46	1.85 / 2.39	1.78 / 2.26	1.74 / 2.18	1.69 / 2.10	1.63 / 2.00	1.60 / 1.94	1.55 / 1.86	1.52 / 1.82	1.48 / 1.76	1.46 / 1.71	1.44 / 1.68
55	4.02 / 7.12	3.17 / 5.01	2.78 / 4.16	2.54 / 3.68	2.38 / 3.37	2.27 / 3.15	2.18 / 2.98	2.11 / 2.85	2.05 / 2.75	2.00 / 2.66	1.97 / 2.59	1.93 / 2.53	1.88 / 2.43	1.83 / 2.35	1.76 / 2.23	1.72 / 2.15	1.67 / 2.06	1.61 / 1.96	1.58 / 1.90	1.52 / 1.82	1.50 / 1.78	1.46 / 1.71	1.43 / 1.66	1.41 / 1.64
60	4.00 / 7.08	3.15 / 4.98	2.76 / 4.13	2.52 / 3.65	2.37 / 3.34	2.25 / 3.12	2.17 / 2.95	2.10 / 2.82	2.04 / 2.72	1.99 / 2.63	1.95 / 2.56	1.92 / 2.50	1.86 / 2.40	1.81 / 2.32	1.75 / 2.20	1.70 / 2.12	1.65 / 2.03	1.59 / 1.93	1.56 / 1.87	1.50 / 1.79	1.48 / 1.74	1.44 / 1.68	1.41 / 1.63	1.39 / 1.60
65	3.99 / 7.04	3.14 / 4.95	2.75 / 4.10	2.51 / 3.62	2.36 / 3.31	2.24 / 3.09	2.15 / 2.93	2.08 / 2.79	2.02 / 2.70	1.98 / 2.61	1.94 / 2.54	1.90 / 2.47	1.85 / 2.37	1.80 / 2.30	1.73 / 2.18	1.68 / 2.09	1.63 / 2.00	1.57 / 1.90	1.54 / 1.84	1.49 / 1.76	1.46 / 1.71	1.42 / 1.64	1.39 / 1.60	1.37 / 1.56
70	3.98 / 7.01	3.13 / 4.92	2.74 / 4.08	2.50 / 3.60	2.35 / 3.29	2.23 / 3.07	2.14 / 2.91	2.07 / 2.77	2.01 / 2.67	1.97 / 2.59	1.93 / 2.51	1.89 / 2.45	1.84 / 2.35	1.79 / 2.28	1.72 / 2.15	1.67 / 2.07	1.62 / 1.98	1.56 / 1.88	1.53 / 1.82	1.47 / 1.74	1.45 / 1.69	1.40 / 1.63	1.37 / 1.56	1.35 / 1.53
80	3.96 / 6.96	3.11 / 4.88	2.72 / 4.04	2.48 / 3.56	2.33 / 3.25	2.21 / 3.04	2.12 / 2.87	2.05 / 2.74	1.99 / 2.64	1.95 / 2.55	1.91 / 2.48	1.88 / 2.41	1.82 / 2.32	1.77 / 2.24	1.70 / 2.11	1.65 / 2.03	1.60 / 1.94	1.54 / 1.84	1.51 / 1.78	1.45 / 1.70	1.42 / 1.65	1.38 / 1.57	1.35 / 1.52	1.32 / 1.49
100	3.94 / 6.90	3.09 / 4.82	2.70 / 3.98	2.46 / 3.51	2.30 / 3.20	2.19 / 2.99	2.10 / 2.82	2.03 / 2.69	1.97 / 2.59	1.92 / 2.51	1.88 / 2.43	1.85 / 2.36	1.79 / 2.26	1.75 / 2.19	1.68 / 2.06	1.63 / 1.98	1.57 / 1.89	1.51 / 1.79	1.48 / 1.73	1.42 / 1.64	1.39 / 1.59	1.34 / 1.51	1.30 / 1.46	1.28 / 1.43
125	3.92 / 6.84	3.07 / 4.78	2.68 / 3.94	2.44 / 3.47	2.29 / 3.17	2.17 / 2.95	2.08 / 2.79	2.01 / 2.65	1.95 / 2.56	1.90 / 2.47	1.86 / 2.40	1.83 / 2.33	1.77 / 2.23	1.72 / 2.15	1.65 / 2.03	1.60 / 1.94	1.55 / 1.85	1.49 / 1.75	1.45 / 1.68	1.39 / 1.59	1.36 / 1.54	1.31 / 1.46	1.27 / 1.40	1.25 / 1.37
150	3.91 / 6.81	3.06 / 4.75	2.67 / 3.91	2.43 / 3.44	2.27 / 3.13	2.16 / 2.92	2.07 / 2.76	2.00 / 2.62	1.94 / 2.53	1.89 / 2.44	1.85 / 2.37	1.82 / 2.30	1.76 / 2.20	1.71 / 2.12	1.64 / 2.00	1.59 / 1.91	1.54 / 1.83	1.47 / 1.72	1.44 / 1.66	1.37 / 1.56	1.34 / 1.51	1.29 / 1.43	1.25 / 1.37	1.22 / 1.33
200	3.89 / 6.76	3.04 / 4.71	2.65 / 3.88	2.41 / 3.41	2.26 / 3.11	2.14 / 2.90	2.05 / 2.73	1.98 / 2.60	1.92 / 2.50	1.87 / 2.41	1.83 / 2.34	1.80 / 2.28	1.74 / 2.17	1.69 / 2.09	1.62 / 1.97	1.57 / 1.88	1.52 / 1.79	1.45 / 1.69	1.42 / 1.62	1.35 / 1.53	1.32 / 1.48	1.26 / 1.39	1.22 / 1.33	1.19 / 1.28
400	3.86 / 6.70	3.02 / 4.66	2.62 / 3.83	2.39 / 3.36	2.23 / 3.06	2.12 / 2.85	2.03 / 2.69	1.96 / 2.55	1.90 / 2.46	1.85 / 2.37	1.81 / 2.29	1.78 / 2.23	1.72 / 2.12	1.67 / 2.04	1.60 / 1.92	1.54 / 1.84	1.49 / 1.74	1.42 / 1.64	1.38 / 1.57	1.32 / 1.47	1.28 / 1.42	1.22 / 1.32	1.16 / 1.24	1.13 / 1.19
1000	3.85 / 6.66	3.00 / 4.62	2.61 / 3.80	2.38 / 3.34	2.22 / 3.04	2.10 / 2.82	2.02 / 2.66	1.95 / 2.53	1.89 / 2.43	1.84 / 2.34	1.80 / 2.26	1.76 / 2.20	1.70 / 2.09	1.65 / 2.01	1.58 / 1.89	1.53 / 1.81	1.47 / 1.71	1.41 / 1.61	1.36 / 1.54	1.30 / 1.44	1.26 / 1.38	1.19 / 1.28	1.13 / 1.19	1.08 / 1.11
∞	3.84 / 6.64	2.99 / 4.60	2.60 / 3.78	2.37 / 3.32	2.21 / 3.02	2.09 / 2.80	2.01 / 2.64	1.94 / 2.51	1.88 / 2.41	1.83 / 2.32	1.79 / 2.24	1.75 / 2.18	1.69 / 2.07	1.64 / 1.99	1.57 / 1.87	1.52 / 1.79	1.46 / 1.69	1.40 / 1.59	1.35 / 1.52	1.28 / 1.41	1.24 / 1.36	1.17 / 1.25	1.11 / 1.15	1.00 / 1.00

Degrees of Freedom for Denominator (df₂)

TABLE D VALUES OF THE DURBIN-WATSON STATISTIC

5 Percent Significance Points of d_l and d_u

	$k=1$		$k=2$		$k=3$		$k=4$		$k=5$	
n	d_l	d_u	d_l	d_u	d_l	d_u	d_l	d_u	d_l	d_u
15	.95	1.23	.83	1.40	.71	1.61	.59	1.84	.48	2.09
16	.98	1.24	.86	1.40	.75	1.59	.64	1.80	.53	2.03
17	1.01	1.25	.90	1.40	.79	1.58	.68	1.77	.57	1.98
18	1.03	1.26	.93	1.40	.82	1.56	.72	1.74	.62	1.93
19	1.06	1.28	.96	1.41	.86	1.55	.76	1.73	.66	1.90
20	1.08	1.28	.99	1.41	.89	1.55	.79	1.72	.70	1.87
21	1.10	1.30	1.01	1.41	.92	1.54	.83	1.69	.73	1.84
22	1.12	1.31	1.04	1.42	.95	1.54	.86	1.68	.77	1.82
23	1.14	1.32	1.06	1.42	.97	1.54	.89	1.67	.80	1.80
24	1.16	1.33	1.08	1.43	1.00	1.54	.91	1.66	.83	1.79
25	1.18	1.34	1.10	1.43	1.02	1.54	.94	1.65	.86	1.77
26	1.19	1.35	1.12	1.44	1.04	1.54	.96	1.65	.88	1.76
27	1.21	1.36	1.13	1.44	1.06	1.54	.99	1.64	.91	1.75
28	1.22	1.37	1.15	1.45	1.08	1.54	1.01	1.64	.93	1.74
29	1.24	1.38	1.17	1.45	1.10	1.54	1.03	1.63	.96	1.73
30	1.25	1.38	1.18	1.46	1.12	1.54	1.05	1.63	.98	1.73
31	1.26	1.39	1.20	1.47	1.13	1.55	1.07	1.63	1.00	1.72
32	1.27	1.40	1.21	1.47	1.15	1.55	1.08	1.63	1.02	1.71
33	1.28	1.41	1.22	1.48	1.16	1.55	1.10	1.63	1.04	1.71
34	1.29	1.41	1.24	1.48	1.17	1.55	1.12	1.63	1.06	1.70
35	1.30	1.42	1.25	1.48	1.19	1.55	1.13	1.63	1.07	1.70
36	1.31	1.43	1.26	1.49	1.20	1.56	1.15	1.63	1.09	1.70
37	1.32	1.43	1.27	1.49	1.21	1.56	1.16	1.62	1.10	1.70
38	1.33	1.44	1.28	1.50	1.23	1.56	1.17	1.62	1.12	1.70
39	1.34	1.44	1.29	1.50	1.24	1.56	1.19	1.63	1.13	1.69
40	1.35	1.45	1.30	1.51	1.25	1.57	1.20	1.63	1.15	1.69
45	1.39	1.48	1.34	1.53	1.30	1.58	1.25	1.63	1.21	1.69
50	1.42	1.50	1.38	1.54	1.34	1.59	1:30	1.64	1.26	1.69
55	1.45	1.52	1.41	1.56	1.37	1.60	1.33	1.64	1.30	1.69
60	1.47	1.54	1.44	1.57	1.40	1.61	1.37	1.65	1.33	1.69
65	1.49	1.55	1.46	1.59	1.43	1.63	1.40	1.66	1.36	1.69
70	1.51	1.57	1.48	1.60	1.45	1.63	1.42	1.66	1.39	1.70
75	1.53	1.58	1.50	1.61	1.47	1.64	1.45	1.67	1.42	1.70
80	1.54	1.59	1.52	1.63	1.49	1.65	1.47	1.67	1.44	1.70
85	1.56	1.60	1.53	1.63	1.51	1.66	1.49	1.68	1.46	1.71
90	1.57	1.61	1.55	1.64	1.53	1.66	1.50	1.69	1.48	1.71
95	1.58	1.62	1.56	1.65	1.54	1.67	1.52	1.69	1.50	1.71
100	1.59	1.63	1.57	1.65	1.55	1.67	1.53	1.70	1.51	1.72

Source: J. Durbin and G. S. Watson, "Testing for Serial Correlation in Least Squares Regression," Biometrika, vol. 38 (1951), pp. 159–77. Reprinted by permission.

TABLE E CRITICAL POINTS OF THE CHI-SQUARED (χ^2) STATISTIC

The first column lists the number of degrees of freedom.
The headings of the other columns give probabilities (P)
for χ^2 to exceed the entry value.

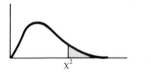

P df	.050	.025	.010	.005
1	3.84146	5.02389	6.63490	7.87944
2	5.99147	7.37776	9.21034	10.5966
3	7.81473	9.34840	11.3449	12.8381
4	9.48773	11.1433	13.2767	14.8602
5	11.0705	12.8325	15.0863	16.7496
6	12.5916	14.4494	16.8119	18.5476
7	14.0671	16.0128	18.4753	20.2777
8	15.5073	17.5346	20.0902	21.9550
9	16.9190	19.0228	21.6660	23.5893
10	18.3070	20.4831	23.2093	25.1882
11	19.6751	21.9200	24.7250	26.7569
12	21.0261	23.3367	26.2170	28.2995
13	22.3621	24.7356	27.6883	29.8194
14	23.6848	26.1190	29.1413	31.3193
15	24.9958	27.4884	30.5779	32.8013
16	26.2962	28.8454	31.9999	34.2672
17	27.5871	30.1910	33.4087	35.7185
18	28.8693	31.5264	34.8053	37.1564
19	30.1435	32.8523	36.1908	38.5822
20	31.4104	34.1696	37.5662	39.9968
21	32.6705	35.4789	38.9321	41.4010
22	33.9244	36.7807	40.2894	42.7956
23	35.1725	38.0757	41.6384	44.1813
24	36.4151	39.3641	42.9798	45.5585
25	37.6525	40.6465	44.3141	46.9278
26	38.8852	41.9232	45.6417	48.2899
27	40.1133	43.1944	46.9630	49.6449
28	41.3372	44.4607	48.2782	50.9933
29	42.5569	45.7222	49.5879	52.3356
30	43.7729	46.9792	50.8922	53.6720
40	55.7585	59.3417	63.6907	66.7659
50	67.5048	71.4202	76.1539	79.4900
60	79.0819	83.2976	88.3794	91.9517
70	90.5312	95.0231	100.425	104.215
80	101.879	106.629	112.329	116.321
90	113.145	118.136	124.116	128.299
100	124.342	129.561	135.807	140.169

Source: Donald J. Koosis, Business Statistics *(New York: John Wiley & Sons, 1972).
Reprinted by permission.*

GLOSSARY OF FORECASTING TERMS

Accuracy

The most commonly used criterion for evaluating the performance of alternative forecasting methods and models is accuracy. It refers to the correctness of the forecast as measured against actual events. Accuracy can be measured using such dimensions as mean squared error (MSE); mean absolute percentage error (MAPE); or mean percentage error or bias (MPE).

Adaptive filtering

This method of time-series forecasting determines the optimal set of parameters (weights) to be applied to a time series in such a way that the square of the errors will be minimized. It is a time-series method belonging to the group of autoregressive/moving average techniques.

Adaptive response rate

In many time-series forecasting methods a trade-off must be made between smoothing randomness and reacting quickly to changes in the basic pattern. Adaptive-response-rate forecasting involves using a decision rule that instructs the forecasting methodology (such as exponential smoothing) to adapt more quickly when it appears that a change in pattern has occurred and to do more smoothing of randomness when it appears that no such change has occurred.

Algorithm

A systematic set of rules for solving a particular problem. The sets of rules used in applying many of the quantitative methods of forecasting are algorithms.

Alpha (α)

Alpha is a constant (whose value is between 0 and 1) that is used in the equation for computing exponentially smoothed values of a time series. A small value for alpha indicates minimal smoothing and greater reaction to changes in the pattern, while a large value of alpha maximizes the amount of smoothing and minimizes responses to changes of pattern.

Applicability

Recently, applicability has gained recognition as an important criterion in selecting a forecasting method. Applicability refers to the ease with which a method can be applied to a given situation with a specific user of forecasting. Increased complexity of sophisticated forecasting methods often reduces applicability.

Autocorrelated residual

When the residual or error terms remaining after application of a forecasting method are autocorrelated it indicates that the forecasting method has not removed all of the pattern from the data. When the autocorrelation of the residuals are random it suggests that in fact the forecasting method has effectively identified all of the pattern contained in the data. See also *autocorrelation*.

Autocorrelation

This term is used to describe the association or mutual dependence between values of the same time series at different time periods. It is similar to correlation, but relates the series for different time lags. Thus there would be an autocorrelation for a time lag of 1, another autocorrelation for a time lag of 2, etc. The pattern of autocorrelation coefficients is frequently used to identify whether or not seasonality is present in a given time series (and the length of that seasonality), to identify appropriate time-series models for specific situations, and to determine the presence of stationarity in the data.

Autoregressive (AR)

Autoregression is a form of regression, but instead of the dependent variable (the item to be forecast) being related to independent variables, it is related to past values of itself at varying time lags. Thus an autoregressive model would express the forecast as a function of previous values of that time series.

Autoregressive/moving average (ARMA) scheme

This type of time-series forecasting model can be autoregressive (AR) in form, moving average (MA) in form, or a combination of the two (ARMA). In an ARMA model, the series to be forecast is expressed as a function of both previous values of the series (auto-regressive terms) and previous error values from forecasting (the moving average terms).

Back forecasting

In applying quantitative forecasting techniques based on past errors, starting values are required so certain recursive calculations can be made. One way to obtain these is to apply the forecasting method to the series starting from the end and going to the beginning of the data. This procedure is called back forecasting and provides a set of starting values for the errors that can then be used for applying that forecasting method to the standard sequence of starting from the data and forecasting through the end.

Beta (β)

Beta is a smoothing constant used in both Winters' and Holt's exponential smoothing methods. Its value varies between 0 and 1 and is specified in a manner similar to that described for the parameter alpha. It smooths the trend in the data.

Biased estimator

An estimator is a value that must be estimated in order to forecast. Biased estimators occur when there are distortions in the values of the estimate as a result of the sampling procedure or the method of forecasting. This bias can lead to substantial errors in forecasting.

Box-Jenkins methodology

George E. Box and G. M. Jenkins have popularized the application of autoregressive/moving average schemes to time-series forecasting problems. While this approach was originally developed in the 1930s, it did not become widely known until Box and Jenkins published a detailed description of it in book form in 1970.* The general methodology suggested by Box and Jenkins for applying ARMA models to time-series analysis, forecasting, and control has come to be known as the Box-Jenkins methodology for time-series forecasting.

Brown

Robert G. Brown made important contributions to the literature on forecasting during the 1960s. His work was aimed particularly at the use of exponential smoothing models for handling inventory forecasting problems. Some of the higher orders of exponential smoothing carry his name, such as Brown's linear exponential smoothing and Brown's quadratic exponential smoothing.

Business cycle

Periods of prosperity generally followed by periods of depression make up what is called the business cycle. Such cycles tend to vary in length and magnitude and are often dealt with as a separate subcomponent of the basic pattern contained in a time series.

Causal or explanatory model

This type of forecasting model assumes that the factor to be forecast exhibits a cause/effect relationship with one or more other factors. Regression models and multivariate time-series models are the most common forecasting approaches of this type.

Census II

The Census II method of forecasting is a refinement of the classical decomposition method. It attempts to decompose a time series into seasonal, trend, cycle, and random components that can be analyzed separately, then recombined for predictive purposes. This method has been developed by using the empirical results obtained from its application at the U.S. Bureau of Census and elsewhere.

Central limit theorem

This theorem of statistical theory states that the sampling distribution of a mean approaches a normal distribution when the sample size is sufficiently large (generally greater than 30).

Chi-squared test (χ^2)

The chi-squared test is a statistical test used to determine whether the mean value of the autocorrelation (or any other statistic of interest) is significantly different from 0. If the com-

---

*G. E. Box and G. M. Jenkins, *Time Series Analysis* (San Francisco: Holden-Day, 1976).

puted value of the chi-squared test is smaller than the corresponding value from a table of chi-squared values, then the data are concluded to be random.

Classical decomposition method

This approach to forecasting seeks to decompose the underlying pattern of a time series into cyclical, seasonal, trend, and random subpatterns. These subpatterns are then analyzed individually, extrapolated into the future, and recombined to obtain forecasts of the original series.

Coefficient of autocorrelation

See *autocorrelation*.

Coefficient of determination

See R^2.

Coefficient of multiple correlation

The degree of association between a dependent variable and two or more independent variables can be measured by the coefficient of multiple correlation. This coefficient is expressed as R. The square of R (R^2) is a measure of fit indicating the percentage of variation in the dependent variable explained by variations in the independent variables.

Coefficient of regression

For simple regression, the coefficient of regression is the slope of the regression line. It is the average number of units of either increase or decrease in the dependent variable that are associated with a one-unit increase in the independent variable. A similar interpretation of the coefficients of multiple regression also applies.

Coefficient of variation

This statistic is a measure of the relative dispersion of a data series. Its value varies between 0 and 1, and it is useful in time-series analysis as an aid to determining whether or not the data are stationary.

Confidence limits

Based on statistical theory and probability distributions, a confidence interval, or set of confidence limits, can be established for future forecasts. These limits are based on the extent of variation of the data and the time horizon of forecasting.

Correlation coefficient

Often two variables or two time series are related, but it is inappropriate to say that one depends on the other. The degree of relationship between two such variables can be measured using the coefficient of correlation often denoted as r. The value of this coefficient varies between -1 and $+1$, indicating correlation ranging from strongly negative, to 0, to strongly positive.

Correlation matrix

Most computer programs designed to perform multiple regression analysis include the computation of the simple correlation coefficients between each pair of variables. The set of these correlation coefficients is often presented in the form of a matrix, referred to as the simple correlation matrix.

Cost

Cost is often a significant criterion in determining which method is best for a given situation. The most important elements of forecasting costs include development costs, storage costs, and running costs.

Covariance

This statistic is a measure of the joint variation between two variables, such as X and Y. Covariance is similar to correlation in concept, except that it is not standardized. Thus, the values of the covariance can range from minus infinity to plus infinity.

Cross autocorrelation

These values perform the same function in multivariate time-series analysis as autocorrelation performs for univariate time-series analysis. The cross autocorrelations (or cross autos, as they are frequently called) are standardized measures (they vary between -1 and $+1$) of the association between the present values of a given variable and past, present, and future values of another time-series variable.

Cross autocovariance

This statistic provides a measure of the association between present values of a given variable with past, present, and future values of another time-series variable. It is similar in concept to the cross autocorrelation, except that it is not standardized.

Cross-impact matrix

In technological forecasting, several future events often interact with one another in affecting the likelihood that any single event will occur. The cross-impact matrix is a technological method of forecasting that seeks to determine the net effect of the probabilities of occurrence of several interrelated items on the probability that a specific item will occur.

Cumulative forecasting

Instead of forecasting values for sequential time periods of equal length, users of forecasting often prefer to forecast the cumulative level of a variable over several periods. For example, one might forecast cumulative sales for the next twelve months, rather than forecast an individual value for each of those twelve months.

Curve fitting

One approach to forecasting is simply to fit some form of curve, perhaps a polynomial, to the historical time-series data. Use of a linear trend is, in fact, a curve fitting method. Higher forms of curve fitting are also possible, and they frequently provide better results.

Cyclical data

See *business cycle*.

Cyclical index

A cyclical index is a number, usually standardized around 100, that indicates the cyclical pattern of a given set of time-series data.

Decomposition

See *classical decomposition method*.

Degrees of freedom

This statistical term indicates the number of variables or data points (minus some adjustments) used for different statistical tests. The greater the degrees of freedom, all other things being equal, the greater the confidence that can be placed in the statistical significance of the results.

Delay

See *lag* and *multivariate ARMA models*.

Delphi method

This qualitative or technological approach seeks to use the judgment of experts systematically in arriving at a forecast of what future events will be or when they may occur. The approach uses a series of questionnaires to elicit responses from a panel of experts.

Demand

The quantity of goods that buyers are ready to purchase at a specific price, in a particular market, at a given period of time is referred to as demand.

Dependent variable

A variable that is determined by some other factor or factors is referred to as a dependent variable. In regression analysis the variable being predicted is the dependent variable.

Depression

This term is used to describe that portion of the business cycle in which production and prices are at their lowest point, unemployment is highest, and general economic activity is low.

Deseasonalized data

Removal of the seasonal pattern in a data series results in deseasonalized data. Deseasonalizing facilitates the comparison of month-to-month changes. It is used in dealing with such data as unemployment statistics, economic indicators, or product sales.

Difference

The method of differencing converts a nonstationary time series into a stationary one. It consists of subtracting successive values of a time series from the adjacent value, and using that difference as a new series. Taking the first difference gives a stationary series if a linear trend was originally present. Higher orders of differencing (that is, differencing the different series) are required for higher order trends.

Double moving average

When a moving average is taken of a series of data that already represents the result of a moving average, it is referred to as a double moving average. It results in additional smoothing or the removal of more randomness than an equal-length single moving average.

Dummy variable

Often referred to as a binary variable whose value is either 0 or 1, a dummy variable is frequently used to quantify qualitative events. For example, a strike/nonstrike situation could be represented by a dummy variable. Similarly, the month of December/not the month of December could be represented by a dummy variable. These variables are most commonly used in the application of multiple regression analysis.

Durbin-Watson test (D-W test)

The Durbin-Watson statistic, named after its creators, tests the hypothesis that there is no autocorrelation of one time lag present in the residuals obtained from forecasting. By comparing the computed value of the Durbin-Watson test with the appropriate values from the table of values of the D-W statistic (Table D of Appendix I), the significance can be determined.

Econometric forecasting

This methodology is conceptually an extension of regression analysis. It allows for mutual dependence among all the variables included in the forecasting equations used in the model. Thus it often expresses a more accurate relationship by developing a system of simultaneous equations.

Economic indicator

An economic indicator is a time series that has a reasonably stable relation (it lags, leads, or is coincident) to the average of the whole economy, or to some other time series of particular interest. Leading indicators are frequently used to identify turning points in the level of general economic activity.

Elasticity

This term is used to describe the amount of change in supply or demand when there is a change in price. For a highly elastic product there would be a substantial change in quantity with any change in price. The opposite is true for an inelastic product.

Endogenous variable

An endogenous variable is one whose value is determined within the system. For example, in an econometric model the market price of a product may be determined within the model, thus making that an endogenous variable.

Error

See *residual.*

Estimating systems of simultaneous equations

There are many alternative methods for estimating the parameters for systems of simultaneous equations. These vary in terms of complexity, cost, and statistical completeness. The most common method is probably that of two-stage least squares.

Estimation

Estimation consists of finding appropriate values for the parameters of an equation in such a way that some criterion will be optimized. The most commonly used criterion is that of mean squared error. Oftentimes, an iterative procedure is needed in order to determine those parameter values that minimize this criterion.

Exogenous variable

An exogenous variable is one whose value is determined outside of the model or system. For example, in an econometric model the gross national product might be an exogenous variable. In a multiple regression equation, the independent variables would be exogenous variables.

Exploratory forecasting

The general class of technological forecasting methods that seek to predict long-run outcomes are known as exploratory approaches. These contrast with the normative approaches that seek to determine how best to achieve certain long-term results.

Exponential curve

Patterns that exhibit a form characteristic of an exponential curve, such as compounded growth, are generally said to be exponential in nature. Various forms of exponential curves can be fit to such patterns.

Exponential smoothing, linear (Brown's)

Single exponential smoothing cannot deal with nonstationary data. Linear exponential smoothing seeks to overcome this problem by taking the difference between the single smoothed value and the second application of smoothing to those single smoothed values, in order to adjust the results of exponential smoothing for the trend. This approach is referred to as double or linear exponential smoothing.

Exponential smoothing, linear (Holt's two-parameter method)

This approach to handling nonstationary series with exponential smoothing is similar to that of Brown's method. However, Holt's approach uses two parameters, one of which is used to add a trend adjustment to the single smoothed value.

Exponential smoothing, quadratic (Brown's one-parameter method)

This approach is an extension of linear exponential smoothing that is aimed at dealing with trends that are of higher order than linear. The method uses a triple exponential smoothing form. Although frequently referred to as quadratic exponential smoothing, it is not limited to quadratic functions only, but can be used for nonstationary series of higher than first degree.

Exponential smoothing, seasonal (Winters' three-parameter method)

Winters has extended Holt's two-parameter exponential smoothing by including an extra equation that is used to adjust the smoothed forecast to reflect seasonality. This form of exponential smoothing can thus account for data series that include both trend and seasonal elements, as well as randomness.

Exponential smoothing, single

This is the most basic form of exponential smoothing. It uses the parameter alpha to smooth past values of the data and errors in forecast. It is most commonly used in inventory control systems where many items are to be forecast and low cost is a primary concern.

File

A file is a collection of data arranged in some order for future reference. When stored on a computer, files may represent actual computer programs for performing certain forecasting methods or simply historical data to be used by those computer programs.

Filter

The purpose of a filter, as developed in engineering, is to eliminate random variations (high or low frequencies) so that only the true pattern remains. As applied to time-series forecasting, filters generally involve one or more parameters that are used to weight historical values of the series, or of the residuals of the series, in some optimal way that eliminates randomness.

First difference

See *difference*.

FORAN system

This approach to forecasting is based on the fundamental concepts of time-series decomposition. It is similar to the Census II approach, except that it tends to be more oriented to corporate forecasting problems than to government forecasting. It incorporates the notion of economic indicators as an integral part of forecasting.

Forecasting

Forecasting is the prediction of future values of a variable based on known or past values of that variable or other related variables. Alternatively, forecasts may be based on expert judgments, which in turn are based on historical data and experience.

Forecasting horizon

The forecasting horizon is the length of time into the future for which forecasts are to be prepared. These generally vary from short-term forecasting horizons (less than three months) to long-term horizons (more than two years).

F-test

This statistical test indicates whether a regression line fits a particular set of data. It is used to measure the existence of an overall relationship between the dependent variable and the independent variable(s).

Function

A function is a statement of a relationship between one or more variables. Virtually all of the quantitative forecasting methods involve a functional relationship between the item to be forecast and either previous values of that item, previous error values, or other independent variables.

Gamma (γ)

Gamma is a smoothing parameter used in Winters' seasonal exponential smoothing method. It varies in value between 0 and 1, and is specified in a manner similar to that used for alpha. It smooths the seasonality in the series.

Generalized adaptive filtering

This time-series method of forecasting is an extension of adaptive filtering. It facilitates the repeated application of the basic concept to both the original data series and the resulting series of residuals.

Gross national product (GNP)

The most comprehensive measure of a nation's income is the gross national product. It includes the total output of goods and services for a specific economy over a specific period of time (usually one year).

Harmonic smoothing (Harrison's method)

This approach to smoothing time series is based on the use of sine and cosine functions. Harmonic analysis is aimed at fitting some combination of sine and cosine terms to the historical values of a time series, and then extrapolating that to prepare forecasts for the future.

Heteroscedasticity

This condition exists when the errors do not have a constant variance across an entire range of values. For example, if the residuals from a time series have increasing variance with increasing time, they would be said to exhibit heteroscedasticity.

Heuristic

A heuristic is a set of steps or procedures that uses a trial and error approach to achieve some desired objective. The word comes from Greek, meaning *to discover or find*.

Homoscedasticity

This condition exists when the variance of a series is constant over the entire range of values of that series. It is the opposite of heteroscedasticity. When a series of residuals exhibits constant variance over the entire range of time periods it is said to exhibit homoscedasticity.

Horizontal or stationary data

See *type of data*.

Hypothesis testing

An approach commonly used in classical statistics is to formulate a hypothesis and test the statistical significance of a set of sample data in order to determine whether or not that hypothesis holds true. For example, a hypothesis might be that the residuals from applying a time-series method of forecasting are random. The statistical test would then be set up to determine whether or not those residuals behave in a pattern that makes them significantly different (statistically) from 0.

Identification

Identification is used to describe the process required to find an appropriate forecasting model. In econometrics it is used to denote methods of distinguishing the demand and supply equations.

Impulse response parameter

The series of weights that appear in a multivariate ARMA model relating an input (independent) series and an output (dependent) series is referred to as the impulse response function. The parameters are simply the individual weights included in such a function. See *multivariate Box-Jenkins methodology.*

Independent variable

An independent variable is one whose values are determined outside of the system being modeled. An independent variable is used in a causal relationship to predict values of a dependent variable.

Index numbers

These numbers are frequently used as summary indicators of the level of economic activity and/or corporate performance. For example, the Federal Reserve Board Index of Industrial Production summarizes a number of factors that indicate the overall level of industrial production activity. Similar index numbers can be prepared for economic variables, as well as for corporate variables.

Input lag

See *prewhitening.*

Input-output analysis

This approach to planning an analysis deals with the modeling of a total system in terms of the relationship among several variables. Some of the best known work in this area is that by Leontief.* His models indicate the interrelationship between the outputs of one segment of the economy and the inputs to another segment.

Input variable

See *multivariate ARMA model.*

Interactive forecasting

This term has been used to describe forecasting packages that are run on a time-shared computer. They allow the user to interact directly with the data and with the results of alternative forecasting methods. SIBYL/RUNNER, a set of programs developed by Makridakis and Wheelwright, is one such interactive forecasting package.

---

* Leontief, *The Structure of American Economy, 1913–1931* (New York: Oxford University Press, 1951), and *Input-Output Economics* (New York: Oxford University Press, 1966).

Intercept (*A*)

In simple regression the constant term is referred to as the intercept of the regression equation with the *Y*-axis. If the independent variable (*X*) is 0, then the value of the dependent variable will be the intercept value.

Interdependence

If two or more factors are interdependent or mutually dependent, it indicates that their values move together in some specific manner. Thus a change in the value of one of the variables would correlate with a change in the value of the other variable.

Intervention analysis

This approach to forecasting is an extension of multivariate ARMA models. It facilitates determining the effects of unusual changes in the independent variables on the dependent variable. The most important characteristic of intervention analysis is that transient effects caused by such changes can be measured and their influence on the dependent variable can be predicted.

Kalman filter

This engineering approach to estimating the parameters of a function or filter is the most general approach to estimation in time-series forecasting. Although extremely powerful and computationally quite straightforward, Kalman filters have not yet found widespread use in forecasting applications.

Lag

It is frequently useful in time-series forecasting to relate the variable to be forecast to lagged values of itself or other variables. The lag is the number of time periods by which the lagged variable is offset from the variable being forecast.

Leading indicator

When a stable relationship exists between some variable and the series to be forecast, the leading indicator can be used to identify changes in the cycle and other elements in the pattern of the variable to be forecast. See also *economic indicator*.

Lead time

This term refers to the time interval between two events, when one must precede the other. In many inventory and order entry systems, the lead time is the interval between the time when an order is placed and the time when it is actually delivered.

Learning constant, *K*

This parameter is of importance in the adaptive filtering method. It determines the speed with which the weights in the forecasting equation are adapted to fit the historical data. Its "normal" value is $1/p$, where p is the number of parameters used.

Least squares estimation

This approach to estimating the parameter values in an equation minimizes the squares of the deviations that result from fitting that particular model. For example, if a trend line is being estimated to fit a data series, the method of least squares estimation could be used to minimize the mean squared error. This would give a line whose estimated values would minimize the sum of the squares of the actual deviations from that line for the historical data.

Linear exponential smoothing

See *exponential smoothing, linear*.

Logistic curve

This curve has the typical S shape often associated with the product life cycle. It is frequently used in connection with long-term curve fitting as a technological method.

Long difference

In order to achieve stationarity before applying the Box-Jenkins methodology to time-series forecasting, the first or second differences of the data must often be taken. A long (or seasonal) difference refers to a difference that is taken between seasonal values that are separated by one complete season. Thus, if monthly data are used with an annual seasonal pattern, a long difference would simply compute the difference for values separated by twelve months rather than using the first difference, which is for values adjacent to one another in a series.

Macrodata

This type of data describes the behavior of macroeconomic factors such as GNP, inflation, the index of industrial production, etc. Macroeconomics deals with the study of economics in terms of whole systems, usually at national or regional levels.

Marginal analysis

This type of analysis is incremental in nature. It seeks to determine the marginal change in one variable for a marginal change in a related variable.

Marquardt's nonlinear estimation

See *nonlinear estimation*.

Matrix

In mathematical terminology a matrix is a rectangular array of elements arranged in rows and columns. There may be one or more rows or one or more columns in such a matrix.

Mean

This statistic is often used as a measure of the most likely value for a set of data. It can also be used as a forecasting method when the data is stationary. It is frequently referred to as the arithmetic average for a set of data.

Mean absolute percentage error (MAPE)

The mean absolute percentage error is the mean or average of the sum of all of the percentage errors for a given data set taken without regard to sign. (That is, their absolute values are summed and the average computed.) It is one measure of accuracy commonly used in quantitative methods of forecasting.

Mean percentage error (MPE)

The mean percentage error is the average of all of the percentage errors for a given data set. This average allows positive and negative percentage errors to cancel one another. Because of this, it is sometimes used as a measure of bias in the application of a forecasting method.

Mean squared error (MSE)

The mean squared error is a measure of accuracy computed by squaring the individual error for each item in a data set and then finding the average or mean value of the sum of those squares. The mean squared error gives greater weight to large errors than to small errors because the errors are squared before being summed.

Medial average

The middle number of a data set is the median. It can be found by arranging the items in the data set in ascending order and identifying the middle item. The medial average includes only those items grouped around the median value. For example, the highest and lowest value may be excluded from a medial average.

Microdata

Micro comes from the Greek word meaning small. Microdata refers generally to data collected at the level of an individual organization or a company. Microeconomics refers to the study of such data as contrasted with macroeconomics, which deals generally with a regional or national level.

Mixed process

In time-series analysis a process or model that combines moving average forms with autoregressive forms is frequently referred to as a mixed process.

Model

A model is the symbolic representation of reality. In quantitative forecasting methods a specific model is used to represent the basic pattern contained in the data. This may be a regression model, which is causal in nature, or a time-series model.

Months for cyclical dominance (MCD)

The months for cyclical dominance is computed as the ratio of the average percentage change in the random component of a series to the average percentage change in the trend-cycle component. It indicates the number of months that it takes for the trend-cycle element to dominate the random component.

Morphological research

This approach to technological forecasting seeks to enumerate the major classes of activity that will affect the successful development of a certain outcome. Those major classes can then be subdivided and used to examine different combinations of variables and the possibilities that they provide for achieving some specified technological goal.

Moving average, single

The single moving average is obtained by finding the average for a set of values, then using that average as a forecast for the coming period. It is often used as a basis for eliminating seasonality in data. The term *moving* or *rolling* is used because as each new observation becomes available a new average is computed that excludes the oldest value previously included and adds the most recently observed value.

Multicollinearity

Multicollinearity exists when two or more variables are highly interrelated. Its presence is identified by high correlation coefficients. Multicollinearity can create computational problems for the technique of regression analysis and make the results erroneous and therefore meaningless.

Multiple correlation

See *correlation coefficient* and R^2.

Multiple regression

The technique of multiple regression is an extension of simple regression. It allows for more than one independent variable to be included in predicting the value of a dependent variable. For forecasting purposes a multiple regression equation is often referred to as a causal or explanatory model.

Multivariate autoregressive/moving average (ARMA) model

Multivariate ARMA models express future values of a time series (the output variable) as a function of both past values and/or past errors of that series and past, present, or future values of related series (the input variables). Such approaches to time-series analysis provide an alternative to regression techniques for those wishing to develop a causal model.

Multivariate Box-Jenkins methodology

This form of multivariate ARMA modeling extends the basic Box-Jenkins concept of univariate ARMA models to include more than one variable. The multivariate Box-Jenkins methodology involves identification of an appropriate model, estimation of the parameters of that model, and diagnostic checking of it.

Multivariate generalized adaptive filtering

This approach to adaptive filtering extends the univariate concept of generalized adaptive filtering to include more than one time-series variable. It is similar to the multivariate Box-Jenkins methodology except that the parameters are estimated using the method of steepest descent as opposed to the nonlinear estimation procedures used by Box-Jenkins.

n

A small n is used frequently to represent the number of observations examined in estimating a given model. In statistical terms, n is often the sample size or the total number of observations included in the data set.

N

The number of periods used in the calculation of a moving average is generally represented by capital N. When so used, N is always a positive number greater than zero. It is also used in statistics to represent the total size of a population.

Naive forecast

Forecasts obtained with a minimal amount of effort and data manipulation and based solely on the most recent information available are frequently referred to as naive forecasts. One such naive method would be to use the most recent datum available as the future forecast. A slightly more sophisticated naive method would be to adjust that most recent datum for seasonality.

Noise

The randomness often found in data series is frequently referred to as noise. This term comes from the field of engineering where a filter is used to eliminate noise so that the true pattern can be identified.

Nonlinear estimation

Nonlinear estimation procedures determine the parameter values of a given function in a nonlinear fashion. As with linear estimation this procedure generally involves determining those parameter values that minimize the mean squared error.

Nonstationary

A time series that contains some trend is frequently referred to as being non-stationary.

Observation

An observation is the value of a specific event as expressed on some measurement scale by a single data value. In most forecasting applications a set of observations is used to provide the data to which the selected model is fit.

Optimal parameter or weight value

The optimal, final parameters or weights are those values that give the best performance for a given model applied to a specific set of data. It is those optimal parameters that are then used in forecasting.

Outlier

An outlier is a data value that is unusually large or small. Such outliers are sometimes removed from the data set before fitting a forecasting model so that unusually large deviations from the pattern will not affect the fitting of the model.

Output lag

See *prewhitening.*

Output variable

See *multivariate ARMA model.*

Parsimony

The concept of parsimony holds that as few parameters as possible should be used in fitting a model to a set of data. This concept is a basic premise of the Box-Jenkins approach to time-series analysis.

Partial autocorrelation

This measure of correlation is used to identify the extent of relationship between current values of a variable with earlier values of that same variable (values for various time lags) while holding the effects of all other time lags constant. Thus, it is completely analogous to partial correlation but refers to a single variable.

Partial correlation

This statistic provides a measure of the association between a dependent variable and one or more independent variables when the effect of the relationship with other independent variables is held constant.

Pattern

The basic set of relationships and the underlying process over time is referred to as the pattern in the data.

Period

Virtually all approaches to time-series forecasting deal with the value of some variable for a defined period of time. In contrast, a technique such as spectral analysis deals with the frequency with which an event occurs as opposed to the quantity of that event in a specific time period.

Polynomial

A polynomial is an algebraic expression (a function) that contains two or more terms. Quantitative forecasting models are polynomials.

Polynomial fitting

It is possible to fit a polynomial of any number of terms to a set of data. If the number of terms (the order) equals the number of data observations, the fit can be made perfectly.

Prewhitened series

See *prewhitening*.

Prewhitening

In multivariate ARMA models it is important to know the type of model to be fitted to the data. The process of finding an appropriate model (identification) is aimed at determining the number of terms of past values of the dependent variable to be included in the model, the number of terms of past values of the independent variable to be included, and the noise parameters to be used. Prewhitening of both the dependent variable and each of the independent variables involves fitting the appropriate univariate ARMA model to the independent variable, then using the residuals as the prewhitened model. This process eliminates the within-series variation and allows the between-series variation to be more easily identified in fitting the appropriate multivariate ARMA model. The dependent variable is also prewhitened by applying the univariate ARMA model used for the independent variable to the dependent variable, then using the resulting residuals as the prewhitened dependent variable.

Probability

The language of probability is a symbolic system for describing uncertainty and explicitly accounting for the likelihood of various outcomes. Frequently, the probability of occurrence of a given event is based on the frequency with which that event has occurred in the past.

Product life cycle

The concept of the product life cycle is particularly useful in forecasting and analyzing historical data. It presumes that demand for a product follows an S-shaped curve—growing slowly in the early stages, achieving rapid and sustained growth in the middle stages, and slowing again in the mature stage.

Quadratic exponential smoothing

See *exponential smoothing, quadratic.*

Qualitative or technological forecasting

Qualitative or technological methods of forecasting are appropriate when the assumption of constancy is invalid (the pattern contained in past data can not be assumed to continue into the future), when information about the past can not be obtained, or when the forecast is about unlikely or unexpected events in the future.

Quantitative forecasting

Quantitative forecasting methods can be applied when information about the past is available if that information can be quantified and if the pattern included in past information can be assumed to continue into the future.

Randomness

The noise or random fluctuations in a data series are frequently described as the randomness of that data series.

Random sampling

This statistical sampling method involves taking a sample selected from a statistical population in such a way that every unit or every combination of units within that population has the same probability of being selected as any other unit.

Rate of adaptation

See *learning constant, K.*

Regression equation

A regression equation is the mathematical representation of a regression model. It states that one or more independent variables and a constant term are related to the dependent variable in an additive fashion.

Regression line

A regression line describes the average relationship between a dependent variable and one or more independent variables. The coefficients of such a regression line are usually estimated by fitting the line to a set of sample observations using the method of least squares.

Relevance tree

This normative approach to technological forecasting specifies top-level goals and objectives, then subdivides them to lower-level goals until the current level of technology is reached. Probabilities can then be assigned to determine the likelihood of various goals and objectives being reached and to identify those areas where major resources will need to be expended in order to accomplish certain goals.

Residual

This term is synonymous with error. It is calculated by subtracting the forecast value from the actual value. This is often referred to as the A − F value.

R Squared (R^2) or coefficient of determination

The square of the correlation coefficient is R squared and is the ratio of the explained variation to the total variation. As such it indicates how good a fit is provided by a particular regression model.

Sample

A sample is a finite or limited number of observations or data values selected from a universe or population of such data values.

Sampling error

The sampling error is an indication of the magnitude of difference between the true values of a population parameter and the estimated value of that parameter based on a sample.

S-Curve

An S-curve is most frequently used to represent the product life cycle. Several different mathematical forms, such as the logistics curve, can be used to fit an S-curve to actual observed data.

Seasonal data

See *type of data.*

Seasonal exponential smoothing

See *exponential smoothing, seasonal.*

Seasonal index

A seasonal index is a number that indicates the seasonality for a given time period. For example, a seasonal index for observed values in July would indicate the way in which that July value is affected by the seasonal pattern in the data. Seasonal indices are used to obtain deseasonalized data.

Seasonal variation

The change that seasonal factors cause in a data series is frequently called seasonal variation.

Serial correlation

See *autocorrelation.*

Short (regular or nonseasonal) difference

A short difference is aimed at removing nonstationarity that is caused by period-to-period trends, i.e., $(X_t - X_{t-1})$. It is often used in conjunction with long differences.

Significance

See *hypothesis testing*.

Simple regression

Simple regression is a special case of multiple regression involving a single independent variable. As with multiple regression it assumes a linear relationship between the independent variable and the dependent variable. That relationship is estimated using the method of least squares and a set of observed values.

Slope

The slope of a curve at a given point indicates the amount of change in the dependent variable for a one-unit change in the independent variable. In simple regression the coefficient of the independent variable indicates the slope of the regression line.

Smoothing

This term refers to the smoothing or averaging of a data series in order to eliminate fluctuations that are caused by randomness.

Smoothing constant

See *Alpha*, *Beta*, and *Gamma*.

Spectral analysis

This approach to data analysis analyzes the frequency with which certain outcomes are observed, rather than measuring the magnitude of an outcome as summarized for a specified period of time.

Spencer's weighted moving average

The Spencer's weighted moving average is an approach to computing a moving average that will compensate for a cubic trend in the data. It consists of two averages, one for 15 periods and the other for 21 periods. Both have been used widely in many decomposition methods.

Standard deviation

Denoted by the small Greek letter, sigma (σ), the standard deviation is the square root of the variance. It provides a statistical measure of the dispersion of a set of values around the mean.

Standard error

The term standard error is applied to various statistical measures (such as the mean) and gives the distribution within which that measure will fall when samples are obtained from any population or distribution.

Stationary

A stationary (horizontal) time series is one that oscillates around a constant mean. Thus it contains no trend. Stationarity can be achieved by using the method of differencing.

Statistic

Any summary measure that is used to describe a set of data or a population of values is referred to as a statistic. The mean, standard deviation, and variance are the most commonly used statistics.

Supply

Supply is the amount of an item that will be offered at a given price at a given period of time.

Technological forecasting

See *qualitative or technological forecasting*.

Time-series model

A time-series model is a function that relates the values of a time series to previous values of that time series, its errors, or other related time series.

Tracking signal

Since quantitative methods of forecasting assume the continuation of some historical pattern into the future, it is often useful to develop some measure that can be used to determine when the basic pattern has changed. A tracking signal is the most common such measure. One frequently used tracking signal involves computing the cumulative error over time and setting limits so that when the cumulative error goes outside those limits, the forecaster can be notified and a new model can be considered.

Trading day

A trading day is an active business day. In many business time series the number of business days in a month or some other specified period of time may vary. Frequently trading-day adjustments must be made to reflect the fact that every January (or similar period) may not include the same number of trading days.

Transfer function

See *multivariate ARMA model*.

Transformation

Transformation involves changing the scale of measurement in variable(s). For example, data can be transformed from a linear to a logarithmic scale, or from a linear to a square root scale. Transformations play two roles: (1) in time series they are used to achieve stationarity in variance and (2) in regression they are used to make the relationship linear or to improve the fit of the model.

Trend analysis

Trend analysis is a special form of simple regression in which time is the independent variable. It consists of fitting a linear relationship to a past series of values, with time as the independent variable.

t-test

The *t*-test is a statistical test used extensively in regression analysis to test the hypothesis that the individual coefficients are significantly different from 0. It is computed as the ratio of the coefficient to the standard error of that coefficient.

Turning point

Any time a data pattern changes direction it can be described as having reached a turning point. For seasonal patterns these turning points are usually very predictable and can be handled by many different forecasting methods because the length of a complete season remains constant. In many cyclical data patterns the length of the cycle varies as does its magnitude. Here the identication of turning points is a particular difficult and important task.

Type of data

In many forecasting methods, such as decomposition, data is classified as having one or more subpatterns. These include a seasonal pattern, a trend pattern, and a cyclical pattern. Frequently, when forecasters refer to the type of data they mean the specific forms of sub-patterns that are included in that data.

Variance

The variance is a statistical measure of the amount of variation that a set of data has from its mean value. The standard deviation is the square root of the variance.

Weight

The term weight, when used in the statistical sense, indicates the relative importance given to an individual item included in forecasting. In the method of moving averages all of those past values included in the moving average are given equal weight. In more sophisticated methods of time-series analysis, the problem of model identification involves determining the most appropriate values of those weights.

White noise

When there is no pattern whatsoever in the data series, it is said to represent white noise. Thus, it is analogous to a series that is completely random.

Winters' exponential smoothing

See *exponential smoothing, seasonal.*

DATA SOURCES

SOURCES OF INTERNATIONAL DATA

United Nations

U.N. Statistical Yearbook. Published annually (since 1948) by Statistical Office of the United Nations, Department of Economic and Social Affairs, New York, NY.

Monthly Bulletin of Statistics. Inquiries should be directed to Publishing Service, United Nations, New York, NY.
Includes GNP per country, total and per capita national income, national accounts, finance per country and international capital flow, output and employment by industry and country, and industrial production:

> world summary
> population
> manpower
> land, agriculture, forestry, fishing, energy
> international trade, external trade
> transport, communications
> health, housing, education, culture

Other U.N. statistical publications:

Yearbook of National Accounts Statistics (since 1957)
Yearbook of International Trade Statistics (since 1950)
Economic Studies of the World (since 1947)
Economic Study of Europe (since 1947)

Organization for Economic Cooperation and Development

OECD Economic Outlook (since 1967). Published twice a year (July and December). Includes study of general current economic situations, followed by results and forecasts on production, demand, costs, prices, and foreign trade.

Financial Statistics. Published twice a year in three parts:

> Data by country on capital operations and financial transactions, interest rates, and the market for long-term securities

Market for international security issues

Comparative tables

Main Economic Indicators (since 1960). Published monthly with supplements (business outlook and economic indicators of member countries).

OCDE. *Études Economiques* (since 1964).

A series of separate economic studies published annually on each of the member OECD countries.

Separate publications giving statistics for various branches of industry over a given period, e.g. *The Chemical Industry*, 1969–1970.

Labor Force Statistics (1956–1967)

Statistics of Energy (1952–1966, 1955–1969)

Statistics of Foreign Trade (since 1960). Published by:

> Bureau des Publications de l'OCDE
> 2, Rue André Pascal
> 75—Paris 16ᵉ

> OECD Publications Center, Suite 1207
> 1750 Pennsylvania Avenue NW
> Washington, D.C. 20006

International Monetary Fund

International Financial Statistics (since 1948). Issued monthly, includes monetary and banking statistics, both international and national. Published by:

> The Secretary, International Monetary Fund
> 19th and H Streets NW
> Washington, D.C. 20431

I.M.F. Annual Report (since 1946). Includes balance of payments statements for separate countries.

European Economic Communities

General Statistical Bulletin. Published monthly (11 issues a year).

National Accounts. Published annually (since 1966).

Energy Statistics. Published annually (since 1963).

Statistical Studies and Surveys. Published quarterly.

Basic Statistics of the Community. Published annually (since 1958).

Industrial Statistics. Published annually (since 1963).

All these EEC publications provide general statistical information for each of the six common market countries. Published by:

Statistical Office of the European Communities
Office Statistique des Communautés Européenes (OSCE)
170, Rue de la Loi
Bruxelles 4
Belgique

Service de Vente en France des
Publications des Communautés Européennes
26, Rue Desaix
75—Paris 15e

SOURCES OF DATA IN FRANCE

Ministère de l'Economie et des Finances
Service de l'Information
41, Quai Branly
75—Paris 7e

Statistiques et Études Financières. Published monthly and quarterly by Ministère de l'Economie et des Finances (since 1949). Contains statistical studies and reports.

Institut National de la Statistique et des Études Economiques (INSEE)
29, Quai Branly
75—Paris 7e

Bulletin Mensuel de Statistique. Published monthly by INSEE (since 1950). Contains information (weekly, monthly, and quarterly) on demography, labor, industry, trade, foreign trade, wages, and prices, finance and stock exchange operations, etc.

Annuaire Statistique de la France (since 1878). Contains the annual statistics for the above information.

Les Collections de l'INSEE: Série C—Comptes et Planification (since 1969) before *Études et Conjoncture.* Contains annual reports published on national accounts and information on gross national product, industrial production, and consumption.

Census. Published by INSEE. Data includes breakdown of total population by department, district, municipality, commune, households, housing, urban zones, industrial, agricultural, structure of total population (sex, age, marital status, nationality, etc.).

SOURCES OF DATA IN GREAT BRITAIN

Central Statistical Office publications available from:
Central Statistical Office
Great George Street
London SWIP 3Ad

Economic Trends. Published monthly. Contains tables and graphs of employment. output, consumption, prices, balance of payments, trade and finance.

National Income and Expenditure. Published annually. Contains information on British economy as a whole, including gross national product, national expenditure, personal income and expenditure, taxation, capital formation, etc.

Financial Statistics. Published monthly (since 1946). Contains information on financial accounts, public sector, central government, banking sector, money stock, and domestic credit expansion, etc.

Monthly Digest of Statistics. Published monthly (since 1946). Contains information on national income and expenditure, population and vital statistics, production, output and costs, various branches of trade and industry, external trade, home and overseas finance, wages and prices, etc.

Annual Abstract of Statistics. (1840–1953). The *Monthly Digest of Statistics,* covering the series of tables for which monthly or quarterly figures are available.

British Government publications available from:
Her Majesty's Stationery Office (H.M.S.O.)
P.O. Box 569
London S.E.1 9NH

Census. Information published by the Office of Population Censuses and Surveys, available from H.M.S.O. Data includes age, marital status, general tables, industry tables, occupation tables, socioeconomic group tables, housing tables, household composition tables, etc.

Registrar General's Statistical Review of England and Wales. Published annually by H.M.S.O. Contains data on mortality, births, marriages, population estimates, etc.

SOURCES OF DATA IN GERMANY

Issued by Statistisches Bundesamt, Wiesbaden.
Printed by W. Kohlhammer Gmbh, Stuttgart and Mainz.

Statistisches Jahrbuch für die Bundesrepublik Deutschland. Complete collection of German statistics, including economic, financial and demographic, published retrospectively.

Wirtschaft und Statistik
Monthly publication of economic statistics

English version: *Studies on Statistics*

Abridged form, published irregularly

Wirtschaftskalender. Quarterly and annual publication of main economic dates.

Das Arbeitsgebiet der Bundesstatistik
Work of the Federal Statistics Office, published irregularly

English version: *Survey of German Federal Statistics*, abridged, annual

Census. Information available from Statistisches Bundesamt. Data includes marriages, births, deaths, divorces, age, sex, migrations, etc.

SOURCES OF DATA IN THE UNITED STATES

U.S. Department of Commerce
Social and Economic Statistics Administration
Bureau of Economic Analysis
Washington D.C., 20230

Survey of Current Business. Published monthly; available from:

Superintendent of Documents
U.S. Government Printing Office
Washington D.C., 20402

Census. Information available from Bureau of the Census. Its "Catalog of U.S. Census Publications" lists all U.S. census publications. Data includes sex, age, and marital status of the population; education; racial characteristics; occupations; etc.; but many characteristics are collected in sample only. Special censuses are sometimes taken and the results published in series P28 of *Current Population Reports.* For more information about U.S. statistics see Chapter 17, Section 17.2.

INDEX